EXPERIENCING MIS

EXPERIENCING MIS

FIFTH CANADIAN EDITION

David M. **Kroenke**
University of Washington

Randall J. **Boyle**
Weber State University

Andrew **Gemino**
Simon Fraser University

Peter **Tingling**
Simon Fraser University

 Pearson

VICE PRESIDENT, EDITORIAL: Anne Williams
ACQUISITIONS EDITOR: Karen Townsend
MARKETING MANAGER: Spencer Snell
CONTENT MANAGER: Kamilah Reid-Burrell
PROJECT MANAGER: Sarah Gallagher
CONTENT DEVELOPER: Suzanne Simpson Millar
MEDIA CONTENT DEVELOPER: Leona Burlew
MEDIA DEVELOPER: Kelli Cadet

PRODUCTION SERVICES: Cenveo® Publisher Services
PERMISSIONS PROJECT MANAGER: Joanne Tang
PHOTO PERMISSIONS RESEARCH: Integra Publishing Services
TEXT PERMISSIONS RESEARCH: Integra Publishing Services
INTERIOR DESIGNER: Anthony Leung
COVER DESIGNER: Alex Li
COVER IMAGE: Preechar Bowonkitwanchai/Shutterstock
VICE-PRESIDENT, DIGITAL STUDIO: Gary Bennett

Pearson Canada Inc., 26 Prince Andrew Place, North York, Ontario M3C 2H4.

9780134711669

2 18

Library and Archives Canada Cataloguing in Publication
Kroenke, David M., 1948-, author
    Experiencing MIS / David M. Kroenke, Andrew Gemino, Peter Tingling.
— Fifth Canadian edition.

Includes index.
ISBN 978-0-13-471166-9 (softcover)

    1. Management information systems—Textbooks. 2. Business—Data processing—Textbooks. 3. Textbooks. I. Gemino, Andrew C. (Andrew Carlo), 1962-, author II. Tingling, Peter M. (Peter Maxwell), 1960-, author III. Title.

T58.6.K767 2018   658.4'038011   C2017-907507-1

To C.J., Carter, and Charlotte
—David Kroenke

To Courtney, Noah, Fiona, and Layla
—Randy Boyle

This book is dedicated to my wife Kathy, my children
Christina and Matthew, and all of the students, teachers,
reviewers, and colleagues who helped make this a better book.
—Andrew Gemino

This book is dedicated to those who continue to teach me
great things. I am the fortunate recipient of knowledge from my partner Susanne, our children,
my parents, my colleagues, and, of course, my students, who never fail to
astound and inspire me.
—Peter Tingling

About the Authors

David Kroenke

David Kroenke has many years of teaching experience at Colorado State University, Seattle University, and the University of Washington. He has led dozens of seminars for college professors on the teaching of information systems and technology. In 1991, the International Association of Information Systems named him Computer Educator of the Year. In 2009, David was named Educator of the Year by the Association of Information Technology Professionals-Education Special Interest Group (AITP-EDSIG).

David worked for the U.S. Air Force and Boeing Computer Services. He was a key contributor in the startup of three companies, serving as the vice president of product marketing and development for the Microrim Corporation and as chief of database technologies for Wall Data, Inc. He is the father of the semantic object data model. David's consulting clients have included IBM, Microsoft, and Computer Sciences Corporation, as well as numerous smaller companies. Recently, David has focused on using information systems for teaching collaboration and teamwork.

His text *Database Processing* was first published in 1977 and is now in its 14th edition. He has authored and coauthored many other textbooks, including *Database Concepts*, 7th ed. (2015), *Using MIS*, 9th ed. (2017), *SharePoint for Students* (2012), *Office 365 in Business* (2012), and *Processes, Systems, and Information: An Introduction to MIS*, 2nd ed. (2015).

Randall J. Boyle

Randall J. Boyle received his Ph.D. in Management Information Systems from Florida State University in 2003. He also has a master's degree in Public Administration and a B.S. in Finance. He has received university teaching awards at Longwood University, the University of Utah, and the University of Alabama in Huntsville. He has taught a wide variety of classes, including Introduction to MIS, Cyber Security, Networking & Servers, System Analysis and Design, Telecommunications, Advanced Cyber Security, Decision Support Systems, and Web Servers.

His research areas include deception detection in computer-mediated environments, secure information systems, the effects of IT on cognitive biases, the effects of IT on knowledge workers, and e-commerce. He has published in several academic journals and has authored additional textbooks, including *Using MIS*, 7th ed., *Corporate Computer and Network Security*, 4th ed., *Applied Information Security*, 2nd ed., and *Applied Networking Labs*, 2nd ed.

Andrew Gemino

Andrew Gemino has taught at the Beedie School of Business at Simon Fraser University (SFU) for 20 years. He is an accomplished teacher who received the SFU Teaching Excellence Award, the TD Canada Trust Distinguished Teaching Award with the Beedie School of Business, and the MBA Teaching Excellence Award at the University of British Columbia.

Andrew is the Associate Dean of Graduate Programs at the Segal Graduate School in the Beedie School of Business. He is a past President of the Special Interest Group on Systems Analysis and Design in the Association of Information Systems and founding director of the Charles Chang Institute for Entrepreneurship at Simon Fraser University. He teaches and consults in IT project management. He co-founded a software company that specialized in professional sports scouting and scheduling/payroll systems for sports and entertainment companies.

Andrew's research has been funded through grants from the National Sciences and Engineering Research Council (NSERC) and the Social Sciences and Humanities Research Council (SSHRC). His work has been published in *Communications of the ACM, Journal of MIS, European Journal of IS, Data and Knowledge Engineering, Requirements Engineering,* and *Data Mining and Knowledge Discovery.* He lives in Coquitlam, B.C., with his wife and two children.

Peter Tingling

Peter Tingling has worked in information-intensive industries for more than 30 years. He has held senior line and staff positions at a variety of top-tier firms, and has provided consultations to government, startup, and Fortune 500 companies across North America.

Peter's research interests include decision process and analysis. He has worked with clients and organizations from banks and financial institutions to professional sports associations and small businesses. Peter's research has been published in academic and practitioner journals and has often been referenced in the public media.

Joining academia because he was interested in "why," Peter considers himself an eclectic reader, although he prefers biographies. His favourite authors are Feynman, Halberstam, Lewis, and Ferguson. Peter is the Associate Dean of Undergraduate Programs at the Beedie School of Business at Simon Fraser University and the founder and chief executive officer of Octothorpe Software Corporation, a Decision Sciences Company. He lives in Vancouver with his partner of 30 years.

Brief Contents

Contents

5 Database and Content Management, p. 130

Part 3   Using IS for Competitive Advantage, p. 232
7   Organizations and Information Systems, p. 234

8   Decision Making and Business Intelligence, p. 258

9 Social Networking, Ecommerce, and the Web, p. 282

12 Managing Information Security and Privacy, p. 384

Preface

We undertook the development of the fifth Canadian edition of *Experiencing MIS* because we believe that the skills inherent in the study of information systems are important to the innovation and productivity of every Canadian industry. We are not alone in this belief. The Canadian Coalition for Tomorrow's ICT Skills (www.ccict.ca), a collection of companies and educational institutions, has recognized the growing innovation gap and the challenge of developing the skills for tomorrow's workplace in students today. The foundations for these skills are firmly rooted in studies of both information technology and business. We view this course as a gateway to these topics for many students. Our hope in developing this edition is to interest students in furthering their knowledge in the combined study of business and technology.

In the coming years, technologies will radically change how people relate to one another. Organizations will become more virtual, and people will work with clients and colleagues they may never meet face to face. Many jobs that are here today will be eliminated, and new jobs will take their place. Change will be driven by people who are familiar with business and technology. So, start your MIS experience today!

KEY UPDATES TO THIS EDITION

The fifth Canadian edition is updated to closely align to the new CPA Canada IT Knowledge Supplement.

We have revised this edition of *Experiencing MIS* to include the latest innovations in the field of information systems. We have also added unique new features and application information to help students interact with and apply the material. Key updates to the fifth Canadian edition include the following:

- New and updated material on Database Design
- New thorough coverage on how to use Microsoft Access 2016
- New useful information covering an Introduction to Microsoft Excel 2016 including Pivot Tables and sensitivity analysis
- New discussion regarding *Big Data* and the controversies about this new term
- Expanded coverage of ereaders and tablets and their influence on information sharing
- Expanded and up-to-date discussion on cloud computing

In addition, for those instructors looking for a more detailed discussion of enterprise systems, we have coordinated the material in this fifth Canadian edition to fit neatly with Chapters 7 and 8 from the book *Processes, Systems and Information: An Introduction to MIS*. These additional resources focus on procurement (Chapter 7) and sales (Chapter 8) as detailed in SAP enterprise application. These chapters are available on the MyLab platform.

The features in this book are designed to encourage students to take an active role in developing their own understanding of MIS and how it relates to their business careers. We believe that when we experience MIS from our own personal perspective, we realize the important role that information systems play in our lives now and in our future careers.

FEATURES

Experiencing MIS is the theme of this book and student engagement is the ultimate objective. We have designed the book to engage students through a variety of features and to provide opportunities for students to ground their knowledge in practical exercises and real-life examples.

Running Cases

The book has four parts with each part containing three chapters. It begins with a running case introduction to help introduce students to Part 1. Following this running case introduction, Chapter 1 opens with an additional running case. Chapter 2 and Chapter 3 also begin with a running case. The remaining parts and chapters have a similar format. The running cases in the text include rich examples and thought provoking insights. These cases can be used in class as a platform for relatable discussions.

Chapter Study Questions

We made a choice to organize all of our content around questions. Each chapter typically focuses on approximately five to eight questions that guide students through the content. Using questions helps engage students in a search for relevant knowledge and challenges students to think about the material rather than memorize sections and lists.

Active Review

The chapter study questions are supported by Active Review questions near the end of each chapter. These questions are more detailed and offer an opportunity for students to see how much they have learned. If students are unable to answer the Active Review questions, they can turn back and review the appropriate section earlier in the chapter. This reinforces learning and provides feedback to students so they can better target their study.

MIS in Use and Case Studies

Each chapter includes an MIS in Use mini-case that provides a real-life example of the questions discussed in the chapter. Each MIS in Use mini-case also comes with a set of questions that can be used in the lecture or as assignments. The mini-cases and their questions provide an additional opportunity to highlight important issues and create student engagement with the material. A Case Study at the end of most chapters provide additional real-world examples. We have worked to provide a wide range of case studies so that students are aware of the differences in MIS across organizations.

Using Your Knowledge

At the end of each chapter, we have included a number of Using Your Knowledge questions. These questions provide opportunities for written assignments or discussions that often integrate the various issues raised in the chapter. The Using Your Knowledge questions provide another mechanism for engaging students in developing their own ideas about what MIS means to them.

What Do You Think?

These exercises are a unique feature of *Experiencing MIS* because they are designed to encourage students to develop their personal perspectives about issues in MIS. Several of the exercises (Chapters 3, 8, 9, and 10) focus on ethical issues. In addition, a variety of interesting topics and conundrums are introduced. These exercises can be used in class for discussion or outside the classroom as personal assignments. The answers to these exercises are not hard and fast—they require students to develop their own opinions. This forging of opinions creates further engagement with the material. We encourage instructors to find ways to incorporate these exercises in their classes so that students can experience MIS in a personal way.

Collaborative Exercises

Students often comment that they learn from group experiences. The Collaborative Exercises at the end of each chapter provide opportunities for students to interact and discuss topics related to chapter content. These assignments allow students to engage with the material in a group format designed to stimulate discussion and feedback that supports individual learning.

Application-specific Knowledge Extensions

We have included five Knowledge Extensions that focus on practical introductory skills for MS Visio, MS Excel, Database Design, MS Access, and MS Project. The Knowledge Extensions on MS Excel and MS Project reflect the personal productivity skills that are now expected of graduating students in any business career.

Additional Chapters on SAP Enterprise Systems

Through Pearson Canada, we have the unique opportunity to coordinate the material in this fifth Canadian edition to fit neatly with Chapters 7 and 8 from the book *Processes, Systems, and Information: An Introduction to MIS* by Kroenke and McKinney. Instructors who would like to provide students with more in-depth knowledge of how SAP treats the procurement and sales processes are encouraged to consider these additional resources. We have adjusted Chapters 1 through 7 in the Canadian edition so that the definitions and business process approach provide a seamless transition to these additional resources. These additional chapters are available on MyLab.

We believe that the key to creating an effective experience for students in this course is to provide opportunities for them to engage with the material and to develop their own personal perspective on MIS. The features provided in this book are designed to support this development, while providing a stimulating introduction to the world of MIS. We believe this book effectively presents information that students will need to be successful in their careers. We trust that this book demonstrates that the field of MIS remains as important today as it was in the past and that our success in developing students with knowledge of MIS will play a critical role in our future economic development.

SUPPLEMENTS

The fifth Canadian edition of *Experiencing MIS* is accompanied by a range of supplementary material available to both instructors and students.

These instructor supplements are available for download from a password-protected section of Pearson Canada's online catalogue (www.pearsoncanada.ca/highered). Navigate to your book's catalogue page to view a list of available supplements. Speak to your local Pearson sales representative for details and access.

Instructor's Manual

This valuable resource features numerous teaching tools to help instructors make the most of the textbook in the classroom. Chapter objectives, chapter outlines, and answers to questions posed in the text are provided for each chapter.

PowerPoint® Presentations

These presentations combine lecture notes with images from the textbook. The lecture presentations for each chapter can be viewed electronically in the classroom or printed as black-and-white transparency masters.

Image Library

This library contains .gif or .jpg versions of figures from the textbook.

Computerized Test Bank

Pearson's computerized test banks allow instructors to filter and select questions to create quizzes, tests, or homework. Instructors can revise questions or add their own, and may be able to choose print or online options. These questions are also available in Microsoft Word format.

Learning Solutions Managers

Pearson's Learning Solutions Managers work with faculty and campus course designers to ensure that Pearson technology products, assessment tools, and online course materials are tailored to meet your specific needs. This highly qualified team is dedicated to helping schools take full advantage of a wide range of educational resources, by assisting in the integration of a variety of instructional materials and media formats. Your local Pearson Canada sales representative can provide you with more details on this service program.

MyLab

MyLab MIS

MyLab MIS for Kroenke/Boyle/Gemino/Tingling's *Experiencing MIS*, Fifth Canadian Edition, is a state-of-the-art learning management system complete with diagnostic tests, customized study plans, student remediation, and media resources such as simulations, videos, and an eText. MyLab is the most effective way to manage and deliver your course and help your students master the material.

MyLab delivers proven results in helping individual students succeed. It provides engaging experiences that personalize, stimulate, and measure learning for each student. And, it comes from a trusted partner with educational expertise and an eye on the future. MyLab can be used independently or linked to other types of management learning systems. To learn more about how MyLab combines proven learning applications with powerful assessment, visit www.pearson.com/mylab.

Acknowledgments

We have many people to thank for their help in developing this textbook. Our first thanks go to David Kroenke, who sold us on his teaching approach when he visited Vancouver and gave us the material from which to develop this text. We would also like to acknowledge our colleagues at Simon Fraser University, JM Goh and in particular Kamal Masri, for helping us develop our introductory MIS course. We would like to thank Zorana Svedic for her teaching and Canvas design and support. Of course, we recognize the input from the many students we have had the pleasure of teaching in our introductory courses. Their feedback played a significant role in how the Canadian edition was developed and has evolved.

We would like to acknowledge the input from colleagues from other Canadian schools, who provided their comments and ideas while the book was being developed. These include Anita Beecroft, Ed Bosman, John Bryant, Richard Crothers, Nelson Eng, Debbie Gorval, David Horspool, Jai-Yeol Son, Peter Thesiger, Robert Wood, and Jock Wylie.

We express our appreciation to the following reviewers of the previous edition, whose comments on various chapters and aspects of the entire project helped us understand the needs of both instructors and students and improve the book.

Victor Bilodeau, MacEwan University
Malcolm Ferrier, British Columbia Institute of Technology
Glen Greencorn, Saint Mary's University

John Laugesen, Sheridan College
Louis (Max) Magguilli, Western University
Shauna Roch, Fanshawe College
Stephen Thomson, Conestoga College Institute of Technology and Advanced Learning
Ozgur Turetken, Ryerson University

Thanks to all of the talented and patient people at Pearson Canada who guided us through the process of revising this book. Our thanks go to Karen Townsend, Acquisitions Editor; Kamilah Reid-Burrell, Program Manager; Suzanne Simpson Millar, Developmental Editor at Simpson Editorial Services; and Spencer Snell, Marketing Manager.

Most importantly, we would like to thank our families for providing us with the love, patience, and time necessary to create this fifth Canadian edition.

Andrew Gemino
Peter Tingling

Letter to Students

Dear Student:

Regardless of whether or not you have chosen to concentrate in management information systems (MIS) or are reading this book because it is the required text for a mandatory course, there is no denying the impact that information systems have and will have on you as an individual and on society in general.

Much of the popular discussion about information technology is centred on a few companies (Apple, Facebook, Amazon.com, Netflix, and Google) and a handful of contemporary technologists, entrepreneurs, and scientists (Gates, Jobs, Zuckerberg, Paige, Brin, Bezos, and Berners-Lee). The reality is that information systems have a much wider range than this narrow media focus provides. It is a complex ecosystem where the only certainty is continuous change. Ignoring the importance of information systems invites ignorance about important technological disruptions that change the way people live and work around the globe. As a student, you must realize that your attitude towards technology and how it is used will have an impact on organizations you work in. We encourage you to invest in increasing your knowledge about information systems.

The overall purpose of this book is to help you understand and adapt to the rapid and disruptive changes that technology brings and to help you prepare for management success. While you could argue that technical disruption is nothing new (your grandparents adapted to the introduction of both automobiles and flight), we think that this time is different. Unlike manufacturing which tends, historically at least, to require physically unmovable assets and require a large number of co-located employees, information based systems are location and distance independent. In many ways, it makes little difference where Netflix or Amazon.com's data centres are located. Accordingly, in today's business environment, success will most likely come through your resilience, flexibility, and ability to innovate with technology. Canadian businesses face increasing pressure to improve the effectiveness and efficiency with which products and services are delivered to global customers. This innovation will require a workforce with new skills and an improved understanding of the role of information systems in business. In writing the book, we kept in mind three goals:

1. To explain the impact of information systems on organizational issues and how you can apply it to address problems and make better decisions in business
2. To show you how to increase your unique value (and marketability) in business by applying knowledge of information systems

3. To describe, in the context of management information systems (MIS), how you can become a better business professional

Note that the emphasis is on you. It is up to you to prepare yourself. No particular book, no course, no professor, and no teaching assistant can do it for you. However, many people have worked hard to structure this book, so you can maximize the benefit from your study time.

To help you achieve your goals, we have updated the content to ensure that it is as current as possible. Beyond the new sections added to the fifth edition (User Generated Content, Crowdsourcing Social Media, etc.), we have updated specific technologies such as cloud computing, social trends including showrooming, and the accelerating business environment.

We have completely changed the running cases in the book. In addition, each chapter includes questions to promote analysis of the running case and collaborative questions that can be used to solidify your understanding of the running case and the material presented in each chapter.

We have retained and updated the five Application-specific Knowledge Extensions, one for database design and one each on MS Excel, MS Access, MS Visio, and MS Project. We believe that these knowledge extensions provide some basic skills for personal productivity software that will be important for future business professionals. The introduction that each of these knowledge extensions provides is intended to make you aware of the capabilities of each application and enable you to explore the further power these applications offer.

In addition to content changes, the book contains four unique features that provide interesting opportunities for learning. First, we have organized the material in every chapter around a set of questions. Use these questions to manage your study time. Read until you can answer the questions.

Second, Collaborative Exercises have been included at the end of every chapter. These new assignments are designed to be accomplished in groups and are meant to help strengthen your teamwork skills and provide an opportunity for developing your interpersonal communication skills. These skills are critical for business professionals.

Third, short MIS in Use cases are included in each chapter, and we have added a number of new cases to this edition. These cases provide real-life examples of how organizations deal with information systems issues. You will also find a Case Study near the end of each chapter for additional insight.

Finally, the "What Do You Think?" feature found at the end of each chapter provides stimulating ideas for class discussion and individual thinking. The exercises often include ethical issues and ask you to develop opinions about important concerns related to information systems. If possible, discuss these questions with other people. Such discussions will give you a chance to develop your own opinions about important topics in information systems.

Like all worthwhile endeavours, this course takes work. That is just the way it is. A sustainable competitive advantage and success in business is rarely achieved without focus, determination, desire, effort, and hard work. It will not always be easy, and it will not always be fun. However, you will learn concepts, skills, and behaviours that will serve you well throughout your business career.

We wish you, as an emerging business professional, the very best success!

Sincerely,

David Kroenke
Randy Boyle
Andrew Gemino
Peter Tingling

PART 1

Why MIS?

MIS in Action

Falcon Security is a 5-year-old, privately owned company that uses aerial drones to provide surveillance and inspection services for customers. Its customers are large industrial companies that want to reduce their physical security labor costs or need periodic inspection services for industrial sites. Falcon has contracts with several large oil refineries in Alberta to provide real-time video surveillance of their sizable industrial facilities. It also does occasional safety inspections on critical infrastructure components (e.g., flare stacks), which would be difficult and dangerous to do in person.

Falcon Security's CEO and cofounder is Mateo Thomas. In the early part of his career, Mateo was a captain in the Canadian Armed forces in charge of physical security at a military base in the Middle East. After retiring from the military, Mateo went to work as the director of security at a large Calgary-based industrial manufacturer. While serving on a security policy steering committee with business unit managers, he met the young and ambitious Joni Campbell. He told Joni that the company was paying way too much for physical security. He thought the company could buy a few drones to do the work of several physical security guards at a fraction of the cost. From his time in the military, he had seen how drones could be used successfully to improve security with much less time and effort than regular pilot operated helicopters. The problem was that he didn't know much about actually operating the drones. Neither did Joni.

A week later, Joni was at a friend's wedding and saw a wedding video that included amazing aerial shots of the bride and groom on the beach, driving, and walking in the park. Curious, she approached the photographer, Camillia (Cam) Forset, and asked her how she produced those stunning videos. Turns out that Cam did weddings part-time during the summer months. Her day job, which she didn't especially like, was as a regional sales representative for a drone manufacturer. She experimented with drones at a few photo shoots and the results were spectacular. Everyone who saw the aerial footage wanted it. She was the only photographer in the metro area who could produce aerial video, and her business thrived. However, weddings were mostly seasonal or sporadic, and she still needed her day job to pay the bills. Joni knew she had found the drone expert she needed and invited Cam to have lunch with her and Mateo the following Saturday.

After hearing Cam talk about all the things commercial drones could do, Mateo and Joni realized that using drones for corporate security was a much bigger opportunity than they had initially imagined. Mateo and Joni founded Falcon Security and subsequently hired Cam. Five years later, Falcon Security has 15 large industrial clients that pay for daily security surveillance and dozens of industrial clients that contract for aerial safety inspections. It also recently contracted with a few clients requesting one-time aerial land survey, videography (commercials, real estate, etc.), and agricultural monitoring.

Falcon Security has revenues of about $14M a year, most of which comes from providing physical security to its large industrial clients. Mateo wants to grow Falcon Security nationally. He knows there are plenty of industrial clients outside of Alberta that would pay for Falcon's services, and envisions a possible lucrative contract with the federal government. Joni is worried that Falcon is not ready. It has been a bumpy ride. Buying fleets of drones (planes and helicopters) has been expensive and, at times, frustrating. People have to be trained to operate the drones, the drones seem to break frequently, and newer models are always coming out. Then there is the hugely expensive systems development project that is currently underway to automate the collection, storage, and analysis of the data from the drones.

Mateo has also been exploring 3D printing as a way to reduce the costs of the drones. Cam's team was able to rapidly create an innovative prototype of a new passive recharging platform using a 3D printer. Now Falcon's drones can land, charge, and take off again without any human intervention. This has saved countless hours managing the drones and has increased the overall effective range of the drones. Fleets of autonomous drones can now be deployed across long distances by stopping every 10 to 15 miles at a recharging station.

Mateo hopes the company can have the same success in making its own drones. However, he is not sure he wants to manufacture drones. How many new employees will he need to hire and train? How much will it cost to buy additional equipment and information systems to support the manufacturing process? Will these new drones be compatible with their existing data collection and processing system? Mateo asks Joni and Cam to figure out if manufacturing drones is the right move for Falcon Security.

The Importance of MIS

STUDY QUESTIONS

Q1-1   WHAT IS AN INFORMATION SYSTEM?

Q1-2   WHAT IS MIS?

Q1-3   HOW DOES AN IS DIFFER FROM IT?

Q1-4   HOW IMPORTANT ARE INFORMATION SYSTEMS TO OUR ECONOMY?

Q1-5   HOW DO SUCCESSFUL BUSINESS PROFESSIONALS USE INFORMATION SYSTEMS?

Q1-6   WHAT IS THE SHAPE OF THINGS TO COME?

Q1-7   WHAT IS THIS COURSE ABOUT?

MIS in Action

"Fired? You're firing me?"

"Well, *fired* is a harsh word, but…well, Falcon Security has no further need for your services."

"But, Joni, I don't get it. I really don't. I worked hard, and I did everything you told me to do."

"Jennifer, that's just it. You did everything *I* told you to do."

"I put in so many hours. How could you fire me?"

"Your job was to find ways to reduce our fleet costs using 3D printing."

"Right! And I did that."

"No, you didn't. You followed up on ideas *that I gave you*. But we don't need someone who can follow up on my plans. We need someone who can figure out what we need to do, create her own plans, and bring them back to me…. and others."

"How could you expect me to do that? I've only been here six months!"

"It's called initiative and teamwork. Sure, you're just learning our business, but I made sure all of our senior staff would be available to you…"

"I didn't want to bother them."

Chapter 1 optional knowledge extension is

Knowledge Extension 1: Collaboration Information Systems for Decision Making, Problem Solving, and Project Management available in the MyLab MIS

"Well, you succeeded. I asked Cam what she thought of the plans you're working on. 'Who's Jennifer?' she asked."

"But doesn't she work down at the hangar?"

"Right. She's the operations manager … and it would probably be worthwhile talking to her."

"I'll go do that!"

"Jennifer, do you see what just happened? I gave you an idea and you said you'd do it. That's not what I need. I need you to find solutions on your own."

"I worked really hard. I put in a lot of hours. I've got all these reports written."

"Has anyone seen them?"

"I talked to you about some of them. But I was waiting until I was satisfied with them."

"Right. That's not how we do things here. We develop ideas and then kick them around with each other. Nobody has all the smarts. Our plans get better when we comment and rework them…I think I told you that."

"Maybe you did. But I'm just not comfortable with that."

"Well, it's a key skill here."

"I know I can do this job."

"Jennifer, you've been here almost six months; you have a degree in business. Several weeks ago, I asked you for your first idea for a process that would identify potential drones, or drone parts, that could be 3D-printed. Do you remember what you said?"

"Yes, I wasn't sure how to proceed. I didn't want to just throw something out that might not work."

"But how would you find out if it would work?"

"I don't want to waste money…"

"No, you don't. So, when you didn't get very far with that task, I backed up and asked you to send me a list of parts that could be printed based on our existing drones, a list of replacement repair parts we buy on a regular basis, the specifications for future drones that we might buy, and a description of how existing 3D-printed drones are made. Not details, just an overview."

"Yes, I sent you those part lists and specifications."

"Jennifer, they made no sense. Your lists included parts that can't be 3D-printed, and your list of potential future drones included models that can't even carry cameras."

"I know which parts can be printed, I just wasn't sure which ones to include. But I'll try again!"

"Well, I appreciate that attitude, but we're a small company, really still a startup in many ways. Everyone needs to pull more than their own weight here. Maybe if we were a bigger company, I'd be able to find a spot for you, see if we could bring you along. But we can't afford to do that now."

"What about my references?"

"I'll be happy to tell anyone that you're reliable, that you work 40 to 45 hours a week, and that you're honest and have integrity."

"Those are important!"

"Yes, they are. But today, they're not enough."

For many, the concept of an information system can be difficult to define and understand. Despite the fact that information systems underlie some of the most popular services available (such as Facebook, Amazon, Netflix, and Google (four companies often referred to as the "Fang economy") or Twitter, Uber, Instagram, and Snapchat), for most people the overwhelming majority of our interactions with such systems involve only the "front end" or "user interface" with little thought to what is actually occurring on the "back end" or behind the scenes. In much the same way that it is possible to cook with a microwave oven while knowing only how to set the power level and time controls rather than understanding how a magnetron functions or the physics of microwaves, information systems often operate like an invisible but powerful magic box.

The effect of information systems however has been far from invisible. In fact the effects of information systems have been so large and so widespread that it is difficult to imagine an industry or organization that has not been affected. Whether we consider the largest for-profit corporations, the smallest sole proprietorship business, any level of government, or nonprofit agencies, the accelerating rate of technology adoption has enabled changes that are difficult to believe. Entire industries, such as publishing and distribution, photography, music, and news, have either fallen or been radically restructured, and newer organizations, such as Google, Airbnb, Uber, Pinterest, and Facebook, have displaced giants in relatively short time periods.

With this in mind, we can say with some certainty that having a foundational understanding of management information systems (MIS) and the key concepts of information technology is essential not only for a career in business but also to be an informed and knowledgeable member of society. Regardless of whether you plan to be involved in accounting, finance, marketing, human resources, or international business, and irrespective of whether your personal goal is to create significant wealth or make a positive impact on society (or perhaps both), the purpose of Part 1 of this textbook is to demonstrate why a basic understanding of MIS and technology are important to every professional today.

Q1-1   WHAT IS AN INFORMATION SYSTEM?

A *system* is a group of components that interact to achieve some purpose. As you might guess, an **information system (IS)** is a group of components that interact to produce information. However, while true, this definition raises two questions: Do all information systems involve technology, and what are the interacting components? As it turns out, these seemingly simple questions remain uncomplicated if we only have common or conversational definitions for *information* and *technology*. For now, if we consider that most people think of technology as involving computers (at least when thinking about information systems and information technology) and consider information as something that reduces uncertainty, then we can confidently say that not all information systems require computerization. For example, a public library organized with the Dewey Decimal System or a calendar posted outside a conference room that is used to organize bookings can both be considered information systems, even though they may not be computerized.

Later we will provide much clearer definitions for *information* and a structure in which to discuss technology. But for now, if we accept the common definitions, we can then describe a computerized information system (which we will now simply call an *Information System*, since that is the focus of this course) as illustrated in Figure 1-1. In this figure,

Figure 1-1 Five Components of an Information System

we show that all information systems, from the simple (someone using a smartphone to find out when the next bus arrives) through to the most complicated (a high-technology Customer Relationship Management (CRM) system that uses algorithms and databases to predict customer behaviours), comprise a **five-component framework** of **computer hardware**, **software**, **data**, **procedures**, and **people**.

These five components are often linked through networks that leverage the power of connectivity to tie software, hardware, and data together to make information more accessible and powerful. Social networks, such as Facebook and LinkedIn, and systems, such as Alibaba and Uber, use the Internet to eliminate the effects of distance and to allow people to remain connected and interact in new ways.

You may already be familiar with the term *hardware*. Hardware has sometimes been used erroneously to refer to all the tangible or physical aspects of a computer system. More correctly, hardware refers to the electronic components and associated gadgetry that constitute a computer system. CDs, for example, do not technically qualify as hardware. *Software*, which has occasionally been used to refer to all the intangible or non-hardware components of a system, is nowadays more correctly used to refer only to programs (or **applications**) that run, or operate, on computer systems. The correct use of these terms is maintained throughout this book. *Data* are the basic building blocks of information, such as facts and observations. *Procedures* are the instructions or processes that you follow to achieve your desired objective; these can be formal and documented policies that are extensive and written down or less detailed, informal instructions. *People* are the actors who want to achieve a particular outcome by interacting with the system.

Let us look at what is hopefully a familiar example—the support system that your university or college uses to provide active learning (perhaps even in this course), such as Moodle, Canvas, or Desire2Learn. Like all systems, it has all five components illustrated in Figure 1-1, and, like many, it makes extensive use of networking technology. The *hardware* of the system includes the electronic devices used to access the system, such as tablets, computers, or smartphones. It is important to note that although most modern computer systems are designed to be used by multiple types of devices, there are still cases where specific types of hardware are required. The *software* of the system includes the stored set of instructions that run on your device, as well as the specific program that your university or college has licensed to provide the service. *Data* for the system may be stored on specialized computers called *servers*, which, through the power of networking, can be located almost anywhere in the world. Data for this system include such things as student identification numbers, enrollment dates, and answers to test questions. The system *procedures* are the steps that you follow to achieve your goal and include how you log on to, or access, the system and how you save or submit your work. You are one of the *people* in this system, but so are the IS professionals who built and maintain the site. Information systems are not just computers and data. An important point to learn in this course is that people are often the most critical part of an information system. Although we have not yet covered the communications aspects of modern information systems, in many cases, not only must systems be available to thousands, if not millions, of people at all hours of the day, but also they may use varying devices and be located in different places. Tying them all together is a network infrastructure.

Q1-2 WHAT IS MIS?

Management information systems (MIS) comprise the development and use of information systems that help organizations achieve their goals and objectives. The definition of MIS has three key elements: *development and use, information systems,* and *goals and objectives*. We have just discussed information systems. Now, let us consider development and use, followed by goals and objectives.

Development and Use of Information Systems

Information systems do not magically appear. Instead, they are designed and created by business analysts and systems designers at the request of senior managers or entrepreneurs in order to solve a particular problem or meet a perceived need. With this in mind, you might be thinking, "Wait a minute. I am a finance (or accounting, or marketing) major, not an information systems major. I do not need to know how to put together information systems" or (as we have been told by students in our classes), "I know what I want, I can get my staff to do it."

This could be a sign that you are headed for trouble. Consider, for example, that you are driving to work and you hear a strange noise from your car or you remember that it is due for some maintenance work. Imagine how an unscrupulous or perhaps mistaken person could talk you into a major engine repair, even if all you needed was air in your tires or to replace an inexpensive part. Think about how knowing even just a little about the basic operation of the car would enable you to have a much more insightful discussion with your mechanic, get better performance, and avoid being overcharged. A lack of easily obtainable knowledge could be quite detrimental to your wallet. Throughout your career, in whatever field you choose, you will need new information systems. To have an information system that meets your requirements, you should take an *active role* in that system's development. Without active involvement on your part, only good luck can enable the new system to meet your needs.

Throughout this book we will discuss your role in acquiring information systems (Chapter 10 is specifically focused on this important topic). As you read this book (perhaps electronically) and think about information systems, you will learn how to ask critical questions, such as "Where did that information come from?" "What new information or opportunities are enabled by technology?" "How was that system constructed?" and "What roles did the actual people who will use it play in its development?" Important consequences could depend on your answers so, if you start thinking about these questions now, you will be better prepared to address them later.

In addition to helping choose and implement information systems, you will have important roles to play in the *use* of information systems. Of course, you will need to learn how to employ the system to accomplish your goals. But you will also have other important functions. For example, when using corporate information systems, you may be responsible for protecting the security of the system and its data. When managing your own computer and system usage, you may need to back up data to protect yourself from losing important information. If the system fails (and most do at some point), you may have tasks to perform while the system is down to help restore the system quickly and correctly.

Achieving Business Goals and Objectives

The last part of the definition of MIS is that information systems exist to help organizations achieve their *goals* and *objectives*. This statement has many important implications. First, because all businesses are organizations but not all organizations are businesses, information systems are found in almost every type of enterprise, social, and nonprofit organization, as well as all levels of government. Indeed, we believe it is easier to find an organization without a marketing system than to find one without an information system. (Consider, for example, the justice system. Although prisons do not generally run advertising campaigns, they still have computerized systems for keeping track of prisoners.) More importantly, you are probably aware that organizations at a conceptual level do not really *do* anything. Although corporations are legally considered to have many of the characteristics of humans, they are not truly living beings and, thus, need people to think and act on their behalf. It is the people within an organization or business who sell, buy, design, produce, finance, market, account, and manage. Information systems exist to help organizational actors achieve the goals and objectives of that organization.

Social media connect people, and when people connect, they talk, share, and let others know what they think about the world. When instant messaging (IM), web logs (blogs), wikis, video logs, podcasts, and an additional assortment of **social networking (SN)** sites first became popular, many business organizations responded by simply ignoring them. From a pure financial perspective, many SN sites did not, and may never, make positive cash flows; as a result, it seemed that there were few good business reasons to consider using social media. Some organizations, therefore, allowed only limited access to IM and SN sites because they did not want their employees wasting time on these sites while at work. Some organizations even created policies that restrained employees from responding to blogs about the company.

Companies rapidly learned that ignoring social media could be bad for business. For example, video recording of passenger David Dao being physically removed from an overbooked United Airlines flight was shared millions of times and resulted in a 4% drop (more than a billion dollars) in the United stock price. United Airlines, of course, is not alone (and this was not their first negative experience with social media). Governments, large organizations, and even individuals have had to learn to deal with the influence that connectedness can bring to bear on social issues (including the Arab Spring and HeforShe, movements that advocate for government change and to reduce gender inequality).

Some Examples of Using Social Media

As social media mature, organizations are formulating strategies that incorporate blogs, wikis, and SN sites into their business practices. For example, SCENE cards offered by Scotiabank and Cineplex have been used by Facebook (www.facebook.com/SCENE) to provide special offers and events that support the use of the cards. Another example is Deloitte Pixel (https://www2.deloitte.com/us/en/pages/operations/solutions/enterprise-crowdsourcing-solution-pixel.html), which provides a platform to organizations to crowdsource various aspects of idea generation, selection or execution using best practices rather than individually building their own mechanisms. Combining machine learning and adapted for multiple devices (including mobile) this website showcases various approaches and use cases. Similarly, the Big Wild (www.thebigwild.org) was founded by the Canadian Parks and Wilderness Society (CPAWS) and Mountain Equipment Co-op to allow people to share pictures and videos of wild spaces and to connect with others who are interested in preserving these areas.

What About Small Business?

The examples above are all large organizations, but perhaps the most exciting thing about social media has been its impact on small businesses. Mabel's Labels, a company based in Hamilton, Ontario, is a great example of how a small company can effectively use social media. Mabel's Labels has a blog called The Mabelhood (www.blog.mabel.ca), a podcast series on parenting, a Facebook fan page, a Twitter account (twitter.com/mabelhood), a photostream on Flickr, and a YouTube account. All these social media channels help Mabel's Labels connect with customers and increase the size of the network familiar with their products. Social media are changing the way small businesses connect with their customers, and this is a message that entrepreneurs everywhere are listening to.

QUESTIONS

1. Are the social media sites that Mabel's Labels uses information systems?

2. What are the benefits and costs of Mabel's Labels' participation in various social media sites?

3. Can larger companies do the same social media marketing and promotion that Mabel's Labels does? Do small businesses have an advantage in social media over larger organizations? Justify your answers.

4. What risks does Mabel's Labels face in its social networking strategy? That is, what are the downsides of using social media for small businesses?

5. Not all social media sites make money or make a direct and measurable financial contribution to organizations' bottom lines. Will this always be the case, and how will this fact affect management in planning social media initiatives?

In most cases, information systems are not developed for the sheer joy of exploring technology. They are not created to make the company more modern or so the company can claim to be part of the "new-economy." They are not created because the information systems department thinks they need to be created or because an executive thinks the company is "falling behind the technology curve."

This may seem so obvious that you wonder why we mention it, but every day organizations acquire and develop information systems for the wrong reasons. Right now, somewhere in the world, a company is probably creating a website simply because they think "every other business has one" or "their competitor might put up a site," rather than asking important questions such as "What is the purpose of the website?" "What is it going to do for us?" or "Are the costs of the website sufficiently offset by the benefits?"

Even more seriously, somewhere right now, a business manager has likely been convinced by a technology vendor's sales team or by an article in a business magazine that his or her company must upgrade to the latest, greatest high-tech gadget or application. In turn, this manager then attempts to convince his or her senior team member(s) that this expensive upgrade is a good idea. We hope that someone, somewhere, in the company (perhaps you) is asking questions, such as "What business goal or objective will be served by the investment in the gadget? Do we really need it, and does it add value for our customers?"

Throughout this book, we will consider many different information system types and underlying technologies. We will show the benefits of these systems and technologies, and we will illustrate successful implementations of each. The "MIS in Use" cases provided throughout the book discuss information systems in real-world organizations. As a future business professional and as a member of society, you need to learn to include your assessment of information systems and technologies through the lens of *organizational need*. Learn to ask, "All this technology may be great in and of itself, but what will it do for us? What will it do for our business and our particular goals? Is it worth the investment?"

Again, MIS is the development and use of information systems that help organizations achieve their goals and objectives. Already you should be realizing that there is much more to this course than buying a tablet, writing a program, downloading an application for your smartphone, or working with a spreadsheet.

Q1-3 HOW DOES AN IS DIFFER FROM IT?

Information technology and *information system* are two closely related terms, and although they are often used interchangeably, they are different. **Information technology (IT)** refers to methods, inventions, standards, and products. As the term implies, IT refers to raw technology, and it concerns only the hardware, software, and data components of an information system and how they are networked together. In contrast, information system (IS) refers to a system of hardware, software, data, procedures, and people who produce information.

IT, by itself, will not help an organization achieve its goals and objectives. It is only when IT is embedded into an IS—that is, only when the technology within the hardware, software, and data is combined with the people and procedure components—that IT becomes useful.

Think about this from the standpoint of your college or university's IS. Do you care that the university network uses the latest, greatest technology to send messages or that the website uses the latest, fastest hardware to show you available classes? Perhaps somewhat. However, it is likely when you and others are trying to use the procedures to do something— to enroll in a class, for example—that IS becomes increasingly relevant.

Consider Falcon Security and their overall objectives. Although IT is used extensively, it is not the primary interest. Instead the goal is to combine the hardware, software, data, and procedures with people to grow the business and maintain and expand profitability. The people who will use these resources—customers, employees, and suppliers—are the most important part of the system.

So, the real difference between IT and IS is that IS includes people. It turns out that if you include people and the way they work in how you think about IS, it makes a *big* difference in how you design and implement systems. Successful business people understand this crucial difference between IT and IS, and they take advantage of it, as we show in this chapter.

Q1-4 HOW IMPORTANT ARE INFORMATION SYSTEMS TO OUR ECONOMY?

Information systems are an increasingly important part of the Canadian economy. Industry Canada[1] is the federal government agency responsible for categorizing sectors and collecting information about them. The sector most closely related to the use of information systems in Canada is the **Information and Communications Technology (ICT) sector**.[2] This sector is special because it provides products and services that other industries, such as retail, manufacturing, insurance, and banking, rely on to get their work done. For many people, the ICT sector is a "hidden" industry. Would it surprise you to know that in 2016 the ICT sector accounted for 4.4 percent of national GDP and generated $181 billion in revenue? The ICT sector includes companies involved in software and computer services, cable and other program distributors, telecommunication services, ICT manufacturing, and ICT wholesaling. Figure 1-2 shows the companies by ICT subsector and employee size.

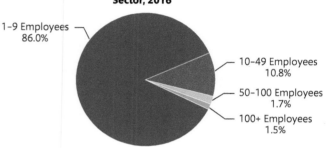

Figure 1-2 Canada's ICT Sector, 2016

Source: Reproduced with the permission of the Minister of Industry, 2017

In 2016, the Canadian ICT sector included over 39 000 companies. Most of these companies—more than 98 percent—had fewer than 100 employees. In 2016, only 100 companies in the ICT sector had more than 500 employees.[3]

In 2016, the ICT sector added $73 billion to the Canadian GDP, up 2.3% from 2015 and growth has been almost double that of the rest of the Canadian economy (at 1.2 percent). ICT industries are also the largest performer of research and development (R&D) in Canada, accounting for 30.8 percent of all private R&D in 2016.

So, what should all these numbers mean to you? In a word, *jobs*. The total number of workers in the ICT sector in 2016 was 594 871. So, where are the jobs? Most of the employment gains have occurred in the software and computer-services industries. These service industries include software publishers, business-communications services, data processing, computer system design, and related services. While ICT manufacturing jobs, reflecting overall structural change, was flat at 6.0 percent in 2016, ICT sector employment as a whole grew at 1.7%, much faster than that of the overall economy which grew at 0.7%.

What we learn from these employment numbers is that there will likely be more jobs in the future in what are termed "service" industries. These are industries that supply services that improve business processes, rather than those that mainly produce products. These service

---

[1] www.ic.gc.ca

[2] http://strategis.ic.gc.ca/epic/site/ict-tic.nsf/en/Home

[3] The facts and graphs provided in this section come from the Canadian ICT Sector Profile, updated 2017 and located at http: https://www.ic.gc.ca/eic/site/ict-tic.nsf/vwapj/ICT_Sector_Profile_2016_EN.pdf/$file/ICT_Sector_Profile_2016_EN.pdf

companies help other businesses more effectively use information systems across almost every industry in Canada. Even companies that make software are realizing that much of their revenue is based on services. In a recent study, Cushman (2008) noted that many large software development companies (such as Oracle and Seibel) derive more than half of their revenues from the services they provide and not from the software products they produce.[4]

These numbers indicate that understanding how to choose IT and implement it effectively is an increasingly important skill to have. You might be asking yourself, "Who are these people getting jobs in this industry, and what do they earn?" Employment in the ICT sector is usually characterized by a high level of education (typically post-secondary). In 2015, more than half of all ICT workers had a university degree; the Canadian workforce average is 28.8 percent.

Figure 1-3 shows that employees in the ICT sector are relatively well paid. According to Industry Canada, workers in ICT industries earned, on average, $75 960 in 2016, 52.7 percent above the economy-wide average of $49 738. ICT wholesaling were the most highly paid at $80 860 followed by employees in the software and computer services industries with average earnings of $80 074.

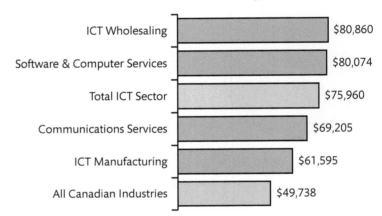

Average Annual Earnings by Major ICT Industry, 2016

ICT Wholesaling — $80,860
Software & Computer Services — $80,074
Total ICT Sector — $75,960
Communications Services — $69,205
ICT Manufacturing — $61,595
All Canadian Industries — $49,738

Figure 1-3 Average Annual Earnings by Major ICT Industry, 2016

Source: Reproduced with the permission of the Minister of Industry, 2017

So, what does all this mean to you? The information presented in this section should help you understand that information systems are an increasingly important part of our economy. In particular, the delivery of services (where people serve other businesses) is a growing area of employment. This employment can be financially rewarding, with higher-than-average salaries, but it is a very knowledge-intensive industry, where more than half of all workers possess a university degree. Students in the Canadian economy who are working toward becoming business professionals cannot ignore the importance of understanding and working with information systems.

Q1-5 HOW DO SUCCESSFUL BUSINESS PROFESSIONALS USE INFORMATION SYSTEMS?

In a world where nearly everyone has a connected smartphone used to gather information during a meeting or to verify the status of a particular order, it can be easy to forget that Facebook was not started until 2004 and that the ten-year anniversary edition of the iPhone (the X) was only launched in November of 2017. However, in the years since customers have continued to be accustomed to yearly advances where devices are either

[4] M. A. Cusumano, "The Changing Software Business: Moving from Products to Services," *Computer* 41, no. 1 (January 2008): 20–27.

smaller or more powerful (or both), services are faster and more reliable, and costs are either lower or services are greater for the same cost. In essence, capitalism, consumerism, and the global economy have resulted in a situation where organizations have to meet expectations of services and goods that are "free, perfect, and now". "Free" in that they are either literally free or at least delivered at no visible cost to the consumer. For example, Twitter, Instagram, Facebook, and Google provide free access while typically earning their revenue in other ways such as advertising. If not free, then goods and services are usually supplied at a cost that is as low as it can be and price increases are minimized (inexpensive prices are often offset by high volume and low overhead (such as Netflix)). "Perfect" since they are expected not to contain any errors or mistakes and are competitive with or superior to alternatives. "Now" in that goods are delivered almost immediately and are usable and available 7 days a week 24 hours a day with zero wait or downtime.

While much of the focus of this book (and perhaps your classes) will be on commerce and business, information systems underlie the structure of many more organizations than those charged with simply earning a profit (the excess of revenue over expenses). Indeed, information systems and the information that they create are so essential and embedded in the structure that they are frequently taken for granted and it is difficult to identify any organization that does not have some reliance on or an information system in its core and at the individual level it is hard to find anyone who does not use or interact with a variety of information systems every day. In the industrialized world, almost everyone is able to use email, access webpages, use word processors and spreadsheets, create presentations, and use instant messaging and location-based services on their smartphones. Although the ability to use such basic information systems is essential, this level of knowledge and use does not give anyone a competitive advantage in the workplace. To be effective in today's economy, you have to know how to do more than the basics. Business professionals need to expand their knowledge of mobile devices and applications that include project management software (e.g., Microsoft Project, OpenProject), business graphics (e.g., MS Visio, SmartDraw), and collaborative systems, such as Google Docs (http://docs.google.com).

Knowing how to use mobile devices and applications is a necessary first step. However, one of the most important tasks is to understand the technologies and businesses well enough to identify opportunities for innovation through technology and assess the potential risks. It is useful to have a wide range of skills in any industry. Notwithstanding, the fast changing pace of the global technological environment makes diversity a necessity. Business majors with specializations in information systems, marketing, accounting, human resources, international business, and finance are developing core skills that will continue to be in high demand in Canada and internationally. However, more can be done to establish a competitive edge.

This fact is demonstrated in reports produced by the Information and Communications Technology Council (ICTC) of Canada (www.ictc-ctic.ca). In its 2017 report "The Next Talent Wave: Navigating the Digital Shift – Outlook 2021," the ICTC lays out the challenge ahead for Canadian employers in this high-tech sector.[5] The report identifies five key transformative technologies, Virtual and Augmented reality, 5G Mobile, 3D Printing, Blockchain, and Artificial Intelligence that join social media, mobile computing, applications, analytics, and cloud technology as major shapers of things to come. According to the ICTC, there will be a rather dramatic need for individuals with a core set of skills, including the following:

- Technical skills
- Specific technology and industry experience
- Satisfactory communication and other business skills

[5] https://www.ictc-ctic.ca/wp-content/uploads/2017/04/ICTC_Outlook-2021.pdf.

While the list of skills does begin with technological ones, do not underestimate how important communication and business skills are. Even in a high-tech sector, such as ICT, business skills are at the core of establishing and maintaining a competitive advantage. The report also outlines the difference between ICT industries and ICT *user* industries. ICT user industries comprise companies, organizations, and public sector bodies that use ICT in their operations—in other words, all the industries other than those companies in the ICT sector.

For business majors, this is an important fact to keep in mind because it means that adding just a little bit of technical knowledge to your skills portfolio will increase your ability to work across a wide spectrum of industries.

You might ask, "What jobs will these skilled individuals do?" The report lists five occupations that the ICTC believes will have above-average growth rates:

- Computer and information systems managers
- Computer engineers (except software engineers and designers)
- Database analysts and database administrators
- Computer programmers and interactive media developers
- Graphic arts technicians

Many of these appear to be business jobs and they are. Successful business professionals recognize that they can gain a competitive advantage and widen their opportunities by adding some technical knowledge to their business skills. The line between business and technology is rapidly blurring. Business professionals need to consider IT and IS when they think about the problems and opportunities that confront a department or organization.

To remain productive, organizations in the Canadian economy will have to innovate. Much of this innovation will be driven by IT. To take advantage of this trend and be a part of the changes that are coming, you do not have to be a software programmer, data administrator, or network guru. Rather, you need to develop your business skills and then learn to think creatively about the challenges and opportunities in your business and organization and how you can apply new technology and knowledge of information systems to address these business needs.

Q1-6 WHAT IS THE SHAPE OF THINGS TO COME?

Predictions of any kind can be difficult because innovation and human ingenuity are rarely linear. The five key technologies identified by ICTC are expected to have a large, ongoing influence on IT. In addition, a few general underlying ideas seem to continue to affect IT. Having knowledge of these ideas is useful for understanding how we got where we are and where we may be headed. Some concepts are obvious. Technology keeps getting easier to use. Think of how intuitive tablets have become. Most smartphone systems now offer some form of artificial intelligence speech recognition, and Global Positioning System (GPS) receivers talk to us using text-to-speech technology while we are driving.

Much of the rise in ICT can be explained by a relatively short (four-page) article that Gordon Moore, co-founder of Intel, published in a 1965 edition of the magazine *Electronics*:[6]

> The complexity for minimum component costs has increased at a rate of roughly a factor of two per year. . . . Certainly over the short term this rate can be expected to continue, if not to increase. . . . That means by 1975, the number of components per integrated circuit for minimum cost will be 65 000. I believe that such a large circuit can be built on a single wafer.

[6] G. E. Moore, Cramming more components onto integrated circuits in Electronics Vol. 38, Issue 08, pp. 114–117, 1965

This observation, which later became known as **Moore's Law**, noted that the density of circuits on an integrated chip was doubling approximately every two years or so. Although this is not a real or natural law (like gravity), the prediction has proven to be surprisingly robust and generally accurate for almost five decades. The practical implication of this observation has been that the power of computers (as measured in transistor counts) has increased exponentially over the past 50 years. This trend has shown little sign of slowing suggesting that computing power will continue to increase at this rate. Indeed, just knowing that computer power is going to continue to increase has allowed entrepreneurs to plan new products and services that in the past would have been impractical from either a cost or size perspective.

A second major characteristic of IT has been what economists call network effects and lock-in of certain technologies, where an increase in the number of participants results in a significant rise in the value of the good or service. In simpler terms "the more the merrier." Imagine, for example, how hard it would have been to sell the first fax machine. (In fact, the first sale probably was at least a pair of machines.) However, once a core group have fax machines, it is so much easier to get subsequent adoption because the number of people you can connect to is considerably higher. A similar situation exists with networks involving user generated content (UGC) such as Facebook or Instagram, where the most recent people to join have access to more connections compared with the first ones. Of course, an additional characteristic of this effect is that, once established, network effects and lock-in make it harder to switch. One of the most famous examples of this is the QWERTY keyboard. Although there is some ongoing debate about the quality of the research, what is unarguable and true is that this keyboard layout was largely designed to slow down the rate of typing and by doing so reduce the mechanical sticking of keys. This, of course, has not been a problem for electronic devices for many years, and alternatives that speed up typing have been proposed. However, the sheer number of existing devices and the large investment required (what accountants and economists call *sunk costs*) tend to prohibit adoption.

The final factors affecting information systems today are the general shrinking of device size (which, of course, is tied to Moore's Law); the tendency for ubiquity, that is, existence everywhere (many people take their cellphones everywhere with them, for example); and the adoption of location-based services facilitated by GPS technology and mobile use.

So, why is the future of IT so difficult to predict? The primary reason is that IT is all about innovation, and this brings unexpected results. Few people, for example, would have predicted the popularity of the Apple iPad before it was introduced or that MP3 players would destroy the compact disc (CD) market (which had demolished the cassette tape market earlier). Indeed, the ICT sector has enabled a considerable amount of what famed economist Joseph Schumpeter termed creative destruction—the overturning of established industries, such as video stores, by new industries, such as video on demand (or the replacement of film-based cameras by digital cameras). The future is not always obvious. Before the smartphone was perfected, the Apple Newton and the Palm Pilot were both once prominent challengers that struggled initially. The history of the IT industry is full of "can't-miss" ideas that somehow found a way to miss and "best" technologies, even the first in a niche, that are not always successful.

Although IT certainly has a colourful history, in this book, we are more interested in the business of IT and IS. The question we pose is, "How will the changes in IT and IS affect the way we live and work?" Hal Varian, chief economist at Google, provides some perspective on this question.[7] He suggests that business is changing because of advances in IS and IT and that business people need a better understanding of how IT can be used to support innovation. For example, Varian suggests that mobile devices will change what it means to go to work. The work will come to you, wherever you are, and you will deal with

[7] The full Hal Varian interview (on how the Web challenges managers) can be found at www.mckinseyquarterly.com/Strategy/Innovation/Hal_Varian_on_how_the_Web_challenges_managers_2286.

your work at any time and in any place using the networks that have become so readily available. He notes that for business people, the ability to handle—that is, find, process, understand, visualize, and then communicate—data is going to be an important skill for decades to come. Varian also notes that industries are undergoing significant changes because of shifts in technology. For example, the traditional marketing industry (print, newspaper, television, and radio) has to come to grips with the prevalence and potential of the Internet. This technological change affects how and where advertisers will spend their dollars. Traditional industries have to adapt to the changes at a pace that is faster than these industries are usually accustomed to. A 2015 book, Rise of the Robots: Technology and the Threat of a Jobless Future by Martin Ford and a popular YouTube video "Humans Need Not Apply" describe a future where artificial intelligence robots such as IBM's Watson result in widespread job losses and increased inequality. Although it is far from clear the outcome will be quite that dystopian these topics are obviously important for business students, and we will cover them in more detail throughout the book.

MIS in Use | Google Knows Best

Every day, millions of people worldwide log in to Gmail, Google's free Web-based mail service. Launched 14 years ago, Gmail is supported entirely by advertising and can be considered a success by almost any standard. When email is sent or received, a fresh column of ads appears on the right-hand side of the screen. Type in the title of a book, and ads for online bookstores pop up. Mention a camping trip, and you will see ads for canoe rentals in the area. The ads are chosen to be relevant to the content of the email.

The ability to scan email, understand its content, and provide contextual advertising is what distinguishes Gmail from other Web-based email providers. Yahoo! tracks what people view online and uses these data to customize ads, while Hotmail displays banner ads based on demographic information provided when users register, and the geographical decoding of their IP (Internet Protocol) addresses. But only Gmail attempts to understand what you are writing—the company calls it content extraction—to sell the data to advertisers. Google is tight lipped about the details, but content extraction involves sophisticated algorithms that examine all the information in a message, including the recipient's location, and links to webpages and attachments.

Privacy experts say that unlike the postal service, which does not read your letters, and telephone companies, which do not eavesdrop on your calls, Gmail is changing the role of the communication carrier and violating democratic principles. Commenting on this example in *Macleans*, Marc Rotenberg, executive director of the Electronic Privacy Information Center (EPIC) in Washington, said that "Gmail has broken a fundamental trust." Other commentators go even further, suggesting that Google does not have a great track record with regard to privacy. When you visit a Google site, your IP address is recorded,

and all your searches are tracked. Because Google can track users across its various products, it has the potential to create complex profiles, combining search terms and email information.

Sarah Elton, a Toronto journalist, discovered recently just how relevant the ads were when she wrote an email (using Gmail) to a friend. Her message mentioned a pregnant woman whose husband had had an affair. The Google ads did not push baby gear and parenting books. Rather, Gmail understood that "pregnant" in this case was not a good thing because it was coupled with the word "affair." So, it offered the services of a private investigator and a marriage therapist.

QUESTIONS

1. **Do people who use free email systems understand the implications of the trade-offs that they have made? (*Hint:* Do you?)**

2. **Is email different from the postal or telephone services? Is it more like a postcard, where privacy should not be assumed?**

3. **How complete a profile can Google assemble of a typical user? (*Hint:* What Google services—Calendar, Google Maps, etc.—do you use?)**

4. **Is there a way you could use free email systems and still protect your messages from being contextually scanned?**

5. **Should these forms of communication service be regulated? If so, how, and by whom?**

6. **Is there a difference between what Google is doing and how spam filters work?**

7. **What are your privacy rights and expectations while using the Internet?**

Source: Courtesy of Sarah Elton.

A view of the future is also provided by David Ticoll in his report "ICTS Jobs 2.0," which was presented to the ICTC of Canada.[8] Ticoll suggests that within the next decade, unlimited storage will be almost free, that analytical software will reveal hidden information, and that the real world and the virtual world will collide as wide-area networks (WANs) become cheap, reliable, and widely available. He notes that these technology trends will enable deep, powerful, performance-enhancing innovations that will be felt in almost every industry.

So, what does all this talk about the future of IT mean to you? It means that our Canadian economy is undergoing some fundamental changes, but that shifts have occurred before and will occur again. When the world is shifting, the most important skill to develop is the ability to innovate and to adapt to the changes. So, rather than focusing on the learning of specific technical skills that may fade in importance over time, this book will focus on providing you with broad knowledge that will enable you to quickly understand and adapt to technological changes as they occur. Understanding the implications of technological changes will allow you to be a more effective business professional as well as a more flexible individual.

In many cases, the adaptations do not have to be dramatic. A sample innovation is shown in Case Study 1 at the end of this chapter. In this case, a small retail store, The Running Room, which sells jogging and walking equipment, uses the Web to expand its business and increase its reach to customers. What this case demonstrates may not be rocket science, but it shows how organizations can adopt technology to make better products and services for their customers and employees.

The effects of innovation can be difficult to predict and can lead to unintended consequences that are both good and bad. For example, the MIS in Use case "Google Knows Best" described how Google ties advertising to email content. Although the idea is the result of significant innovation, the change has implications for privacy and security that our society has yet to fully understand.

Q1-7 WHAT IS THIS COURSE ABOUT?

Many students enter this course with an erroneous idea of what they will be studying. Often, students think of it as a computer class—or at least a class that has something to do with computers and business. Other students think that this course is about learning how to use Excel, Access, or some Web development tool. Figure 1-4 lists a number of reasons

---

- "I already know how to use Excel and Word. I can build a website with FrontPage. Okay, it's a simple website, but I can do it. And when I need to learn more, I can. So, let me out of this course!"

- "We're going to learn how to work with information systems? That's like practising having the stomach flu. If and when the time comes, I'll know how to do it."

- "I'm terrified of computers. I'm a people person, and I don't do well with engineering-like things. I've put this course off until the last quarter of my final year. I hope it's not as bad as I fear; I just wish they didn't make me take it."

- "There's really no content in this course. I mean, I've been programming since high school, I can write in C++, though PERL is my favourite language. I know computer technology. This course is just a bunch of management babble mixed up with some computer terms. At least it's an easy class, though."

- "Well, I'm sure there is some merit to this course, but consider the opportunity cost. I really need to be taking more microeconomics and international business. The time I spend on this course could be better spent on those subjects."

- "The only thing I need to know is how to surf the Web and how to use email. I know how to do those, so I just don't need this course."

- "What, you mean this course is not about learning Excel and FrontPage? That's what I thought we were going to learn. That's what I need to know. Why all this information systems stuff? How do I make a website? That's what I need to know."

Figure 1-4 Student Thoughts About "Why I Don't Need This Course"

[8] The report can be found at http://ccict.ca/reports/jobs-2-0.

students have given us when explaining why they do not need to take this course. As you can see, opinions vary on what the class is about.

By now, you should have an idea that this course is about much more than learning how to use applications such as Excel or Access. You may, in fact, use those programs in this course, but the focus will not be on learning what keys to push to make the program work. Instead, the focus will be on *learning to use those tools to accomplish organizational goals*.

Consider again the definition of MIS: the development and use of information systems that help organizations (and the people who work in them) achieve their goals and objectives. Thus, to understand MIS, you need to understand both business (that is the concept of delivering a good or service at a reasonable cost) and technology, and you need to be able to relate one to the other.

This book's table of contents will give you an idea of how we will proceed. In the next two chapters, we discuss the relationship of business processes and information systems, and we show how information systems can be used to gain competitive advantages. Then, in Chapters 4 to 6, you will learn about hardware, software, content, and databases, along with network and communications technology. In Chapters 7 to 9, we will illustrate how and with that foundation, technology can be used to gain a competitive advantage. Finally, in Chapters 10 to 12, you will learn how IT departments work, how the IT architecture is managed, about IS ethics and green IT, and about personal privacy and security. The exercise "Duller Than Dirt?" at the end of this chapter on pages 21–22 shares our opinion about why these chapters—and this book—matter to you.

How Does the Knowledge in This Chapter Help You?

It's too late for Jennifer, at least at Falcon Security. However, it's not too late for you, and it might not be too late for Jennifer at her next job. So, what are the takeaways from this chapter?

First, realize that the future belongs to businesspeople with the ability to creatively envision new applications of information systems and technology. For example, according to a September 4, 2017 CBC article,[9] the smaller size and low cost of aerial drones enables them to go places and get footage in areas most helicopter film pilots cannot safely navigate. This reduces the jobs available for traditional pilots but opens up lots of other opportunities. You do not have to be an IS major (though it is a very good major with excellent job prospects), but you should be able to innovate the use of MIS into the discipline in which you do specialize. How can management, marketing, accounting, production, and so on, take advantage of the benefits of Moore's Law and Metcalfe's Law?

Second, learn four key skills: abstract thinking, systems thinking, experimentation, and collaboration. And practice, practice, practice them. This class will help you establish and reinforce these skills. As you study and perform assignments, ask yourself how your activity relates to these four abilities and endeavor to improve your proficiency at them.

Next, learn the components of an IS and understand that every business professional needs to take an active role in new information systems development. Such systems are created for your needs and require your involvement. Know the difference between IT, IS, and MIS. Finally, learn how to create a strong password and begin using such passwords and proper password etiquette.

We're just getting started; there's lots more to come that can benefit Jennifer (in her next job) and you!

---

[9] http://www.cbc.ca/news/entertainment/helicopter-drone-film-1.4265519.

Use this Active Review to verify that you have understood the material in the chapter. You can read the entire chapter and then perform the tasks in this review, or you can read the material for just one question and perform the tasks for that question before moving on to the next one.

Q1-1   WHAT IS AN INFORMATION SYSTEM?

List the components of an information system. Explain how knowledge of these components guide Mateo Thomas and Joni Campbell at Falcon Security.

Q1-2   WHAT IS MIS?

List the three elements of MIS. Why does a nontechnical business professional need to understand all three? Why are information systems developed? Why is part of the definition of MIS misleading?

Q1-3   HOW DOES AN IS DIFFER FROM IT?

Define *IS* and *IT*. Does IT include IS, or does IS include IT? Why does technology, by itself, not constitute an information system?

Q1-4   HOW IMPORTANT ARE INFORMATION SYSTEMS TO OUR ECONOMY?

What does ICT stand for? How important is ICT to the economy? Is the ICT sector growing faster than the Canadian economy? Why are services of growing importance? How knowledge intensive is the ICT sector? What can an employee in the ICT sector expect to earn?

Q1-5   HOW DO SUCCESSFUL BUSINESS PROFESSIONALS USE INFORMATION SYSTEMS?

What new applications should a business professional be familiar with? What combination of skills is of growing importance in the economy? Can a business student work in the ICT sector?

Q1-6   WHAT IS THE SHAPE OF THINGS TO COME?

Describe Moore's Law and the fundamental change that technology can bring to an economy, an organization, and you.

Q1-7   WHAT IS THIS COURSE ABOUT?

In your own words, state what this course is about. Look at this book's table of contents. What major themes does it address? How will those themes relate to you as a business professional? If you were (or are) employed and you had to justify the expense of this course to your boss, how would you do it?

MyLab MIS

MyLab MIS is an online learning and testing environment that features the perfect study tools to help you master the concepts covered in this chapter. Log in to MyLab to test your knowledge of key chapter concepts and explore additional practice tools, including videos, flashcards, and more!

KEY TERMS AND CONCEPTS

Applications 7
Computer hardware 7
Data 7
Five-component
    framework 7

Information and
    Communications
    Technology (ICT)
    sector 11
Information system (IS) 6

Information technology
    (IT) 10
Management information
    systems (MIS) 7
Moore's Law 15

People 7
Procedures 7
Social networking (SN) 9
Software 7

USING YOUR KNOWLEDGE

1-1. "Outlook on Human Resources in the ICT Labour Market: 2008–2015" suggests that ICT workers need to have several core skills.

    a. What are these key skills?

    b. Identify ways that you can best obtain these skills.

    c. Do you believe a business student can work effectively in the ICT sector? Would a business student have a competitive advantage over a computer science student? Why, or why not?

1-2. The interview with Hal Varian, chief economist at Google, focuses on six themes:

(i) flexible corporations, (ii) corporations and work, (iii) free goods and value, (iv) workers and managers, (v) computer monitoring and risks, and (vi) changes in industries. Choose one of these themes and discuss in more detail the implications of the change for you personally. Provide specific examples where possible. You can find the article at www.mckinseyquarterly.com/Strategy/Innovation/Hal_Varian_on_how_the_Web_challenges_managers_2286.

1-3. Consider the costs of a system in light of these five components:

(i) the costs to buy and maintain the hardware; (ii) the costs to develop or acquire licences to the software programs and to maintain them; (iii) the costs to design databases and fill them with data; (iv) the costs to develop procedures and keep them current; and (v) finally, the human costs, both to develop and use the system.

    a. Over the lifetime of a system, many experts believe that the single most expensive component is people. Does this belief seem logical to you? Explain why you agree or disagree.

    b. Consider a poorly developed system that does not meet its defined requirements. The needs of the business do not go away, but they do not conform to the characteristics of the poorly built system. Therefore, something has got to give. Which component picks up the slack when hardware and software programs do not work correctly? What does this say about the cost of a poorly designed system? Consider both direct money costs as well as intangible personnel costs.

    c. What implications do you, as a future business manager, recognize after answering questions (a) and (b)? What does this say about the need for your involvement in requirements and other aspects of systems development? Who will eventually pay the costs of a poorly developed system? Against which budget will those costs accrue?

COLLABORATIVE EXERCISES

1-1. Watch the video "Humans need not apply" available at https://www.youtube.com/watch?v=7Pq-S557XQU. Discuss this video with your group, and identify three specific impacts that you think the information in this video will have on your business career. Be as specific as possible, and link the ideas to your intended major, interests, and career aspirations.

1-2. Watch the video "A Vision of Students Today" (www.youtube.com/watch?v=dGCJ46vyR9o). Discuss this video with your group, and identify three ways that courses could be designed to improve student engagement. Be as specific as possible, and be prepared to share your ideas with the class.

CASE STUDY 1

RUNNING AT THE SPEED OF THE WEB: THE RUNNING ROOM

The Running Room (www.runningroom.com) is North America's largest specialty retailer of sporting goods, apparel, and footwear for runners and walkers. The company operates over 90 corporately owned stores in Canada and the United States. The Running Room website was created in early 2000.

Questions

1. Do you think The Running Room would be as successful as it is if it did not have a website? In other words, is the company's website a critical component for success or simply a nice extra for its customers?

2. Could The Running Room provide the same customer experience without using its website? For example, could the company use more mailings and telephone calls to stay in touch with its customers?

3. Do you think The Running Room's website creates a barrier to entry for its potential competitors? Explain your answer.

4. Check out the goals that the company highlights in the About Us section of the Running Room's website. Does the website help the company meet these goals? Discuss why or why not.

WHAT DO YOU THINK?

DULLER THAN DIRT?

Yes, you read that title correctly: This subject can seem duller than dirt. Take the phrase *development and use of IS in organizations*.

Read just that phrase and you start to yawn, wondering, "How am I going to absorb almost 400 pages of this stuff?" Do not worry. You are not alone. Take a few minutes and look at this video: "A Vision of Students Today." (www.youtube.com/watch?v=dGCJ46vyR9o).

Now stop and think: Why are you reading this book? Right now in the Sea of Cortez, Mexico, the water is clear and warm, and the swimming and diving are wonderful. You could be kayaking to Isla San Francisco this very minute. So, why are you here reading this book? Why are you not there?

Suppose you take an hour tonight to read your assigned chapter in this book. For a typical person, that is 4320 heartbeats (72 beats times 60 minutes) you have used to read this book—heartbeats you will never have again. For some reason, you chose to major in business.

For some reason, you are taking this course. And, for some reason, you have been instructed to read this textbook.

Now, given that you made a good decision to major in business, the question becomes, "How can you maximize the return on the 4320 heartbeats you are investing each hour?" The secret is to personalize the material. At every page, ask yourself, "How does this pertain to me? How can I use this to further my goals?"

MIS is all-encompassing. To us, that is one of its beauties. Consider the components: hardware, software, data, procedures, and people. Do you want to be an engineer? Then, work the hardware component. Do you want to be a programmer? Write software. Do you like people? Become an IS trainer or a computer systems salesperson. Do you like business systems and sociology? Learn how to design effective organizational procedures. Do you enjoy management? Learn how to bring all those disparate elements together. We have worked in this industry for many years. The breadth of MIS and the rapid change of technology have kept us fascinated for every one of those years.

So, wake up. Why are you reading this? How can you make it relevant? Jump onto Google, and search for a career as a business analyst or in project management, or use some other phrase from this chapter as key search words and see what you get. Challenge yourself to find something that is important to you personally in every chapter.

You just invested 780 heartbeats in reading this editorial. Was it worth it? Keep asking!

Discussion Questions

1. Are you awake to your life? How do you know? What can you do once a week to ensure that you are awake?

2. What are your professional goals? Are they yours, or are they someone else's? How do you know?

3. How is this course relevant to your professional goals?

4. How are you going to make the material in this course interesting?

STUDY QUESTIONS

Q2-1	**"HOW DID THIS STUFF GET HERE?"**
Q2-2	**WHAT IS A BUSINESS PROCESS?**
Q2-3	**WHAT ARE THE COMPONENTS OF A BUSINESS PROCESS?**
Q2-4	**WHAT IS INFORMATION?**
Q2-5	**WHAT IS THE ROLE OF INFORMATION IN BUSINESS PROCESSES?**
Q2-6	**HOW DO INFORMATION SYSTEMS SUPPORT BUSINESS PROCESSES?**
Q2-7	**HOW DO INFORMATION SYSTEMS SUPPORT DECISION MAKING?**
Q2-8	**WHAT IS YOUR ROLE?**

MIS in Action

"No, Felix! Not again! Over, and over, and over! We decide something one meeting and then go over it again the next meeting and again the next. What a waste!"

"What do you mean, Cam?" asks Felix, Falcon Security's customer service manager. "I think it's important we get this right."

"Well, Felix, if that's the case, why don't you come to the meetings?"

"I just missed a couple."

"Right. Last week we met here for, oh, 2, maybe 3 hours, and we decided to print and assemble a new prototype quadcopter using as many 3D-printed parts as possible."

"But Cam, 3D printing a stationary recharging platform is a lot different than 3D printing a complex machine like a drone. What difference does it make if we print a drone that can't fly?"

 Chapter 2 optional knowledge extensions are

Knowledge Extension 2: Business Process Modelling, page 44

Knowledge Extension 3: Collaborative Information Systems for Student Projects available in the MyLab MIS

Felix! We discussed that last week. We found some existing drone plans that we can use for free. They've already been tested and they do work. We're going to see if we can use existing internal components from an existing quadcopter in the new 3D-printed quadcopter. It might even be possible to use generic parts to reduce costs even more."

"Look, Cam, Joni just wants something reasonable to tell Mateo. If we tell her these new 3D-printed quadcopters can't fly, which they probably won't, Mateo will cancel this project and we can get back to work . . . flying high-quality drones manufactured by those who know what they're doing!"

"Felix, you're driving me nuts. We discussed this *ad nauseam* last week. Let's make some progress. Why don't some of you other guys help me? Alexis, what do you think?"

"Felix, Cam is right," Alexis, Falcon Security's head of sales, chimes in. "We did have a long discussion on how to go about this—and we did agree to focus first on building a functional drone that might reduce our costs. This could save us a lot of money and give us a more customizable drone platform."

"Well, Alexis, I think it's a mistake. Why didn't anyone tell me? I put in a lot of time looking into flight performance of these 3D-printed drones."

"Did you read the email?" Alexis asks tentatively.

"What email?"

"The meeting summary email that I send out each week," Alexis says with a sigh.

Q2-1 "HOW DID THIS STUFF GET HERE?"

Imagine you have graduated and, with a few years of hard work, you have achieved exactly the position you wanted. One April day, you find yourself in Toronto for a meeting at First Canadian Place. Like any responsible business professional, you arrived a bit early, so you decide to have a latte and a breakfast sandwich at the Tim Hortons in the PATH underground walkway beneath First Canadian Place.

Sitting down with your latte and breakfast sandwich, your mind begins to wander. As you look around, you wonder, "How did this stuff get here—the milk, the coffee, the sandwich? How did it all get here?"

You realize that some how, some way, somebody delivered the latte and sandwich ingredients, to this particular location. Who decided how much to ship to this Tim Hortons that morning? What company delivered the stuff? How many other Tim Hortons locations did they deliver to?

For that matter, how did the coffee for your latte get here? Perhaps the coffee beans were grown in Kenya, shipped to the United States, roasted in Rochester, New York, distributed through the head office in Oakville, Ontario, and delivered to the store. Who organized that? And the breakfast sandwich—who decided how many breakfast sandwiches were going to be made today and who was going to make them? Who is coordinating all of these decisions?

The more you think about it, the more you begin to realize that a seemingly simple thing, like getting your latte and breakfast sandwich, is a near-miracle in product and service coordination. Hundreds—if not thousands—of different processes successfully interacted just to bring together a breakfast sandwich, coffee, milk and you. It is truly amazing.

And here's the kicker. All those processes had to do more than just barely work. They had to work in such a way that all the companies and people who worked with those processes covered their costs and earned a profit. How did that occur? Who set the prices? Who determined how much nonfat milk had to be shipped to Toronto the night before? How does all this come about? The more you think about the processes, the more amazing it becomes.

The reality is that all this activity comes through the interaction of business processes. Tim Hortons has processes for ordering, receiving, storing, and paying for ingredients such as milk and coffee. The coffee roaster has a process for assessing demand, ordering its raw materials, and making deliveries. All the other businesses have processes for conducting their affairs as well. Organizations make use of these processes to deliver goods and services to customers. So, business processes are central to what every organization does. That is why understanding business processes is critical to understanding how business works.

Q2-2   WHAT IS A BUSINESS PROCESS?

A **business process** is a series of activities, tasks, or steps designed to produce a product or service. A business process is best thought of as a system and is sometimes also referred to as a **business system**. In this book, we will use the term *business process*. In Chapter 7, we will introduce enterprise resource planning (ERP) systems that are used by many organizations to support their business processes.

We can start by considering an example. Examples of business processes include inventory management processes, manufacturing processes, sales processes, and customer support processes. Figure 2-1 shows a model of a sales and inventory-management business process

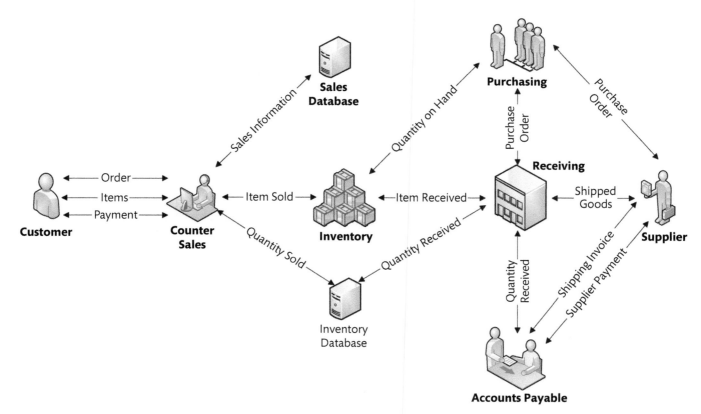

Figure 2-1   Model of an Inventory Management Business Process

that might be used at a Tim Hortons restaurant. These sales and inventory elements are often considered to be part of a "supply chain" for an organization. We will discuss the supply chain in more detail in Chapter 3 and also cover supply chain management systems later in Chapter 7.

Inventory for a Tim Hortons restaurant includes all the goods (coffee, donuts, muffins, milk, etc.) that a Tim Hortons restaurant sells. Managing this inventory is a business process. The goal of this process is to ensure that there is enough inventory to fulfill customers' requests while making sure that there is not too much inventory (otherwise the goods might spoil or profitability could suffer).

The inventory management process works to balance the demands of customers with the inventory purchased from suppliers. Purchasing, therefore, is an important activity in the inventory management process. But how can a manager at a Tim Hortons restaurant know how much coffee to purchase?

This is where an inventory management system comes in. An inventory management system supports the inventory process by collecting information. An inventory database might keep track of what the customers have ordered (*quantity ordered*) and what is currently in inventory (*quantity on hand*). As customers make purchases, stock moves out of inventory. At some point, stock in inventory hits a critical point, often called the *reorder point*. When a good in stock hits this point, the inventory management system advises the manager that it is time to order new supplies. Since goods are bought and sold at different rates, each good can have its own reorder point.

To order new inventory, the manager creates a *purchase order (PO)*, which lists the items ordered and the quantity desired. This *purchase order* is sent to the supplier. The supplier receives the *purchase order* and then ships the appropriate goods along with the *shipping invoice* to the restaurant. The *shipped goods* are first checked to make sure the restaurant received what was ordered. The newly received goods are then placed in inventory and the inventory database is updated with the *quantity received*. The supplier is then paid for the goods the supplier has shipped.

The diagram in Figure 2-1 is a snapshot of the system. The diagram does not show the logic behind the process; that is, it does not show what causes what. The diagram is just a picture of the elements of the business process and how they interact. There are many different ways of representing a business process. Understanding, modelling, and redesigning business processes are a big part of what business analysts do. In information systems, these modelling and design activities are called *systems analysis and design*. The goal is to develop an understanding of how an organization works. If you are interested in this type of work, you can learn more about business process analysis in a systems analysis and design course.

Q2-3 WHAT ARE THE COMPONENTS OF A BUSINESS PROCESS?

A business process consists of activities, resources, facilities, and information. Activities transform resources and information of one type into resources and information of another type. The payment activity transforms quantity received and shipping invoice information into a supplier payment (resource). The payment activity has rules and procedures that it follows for doing this.

Activities can consist of purely manual actions (people following procedures), automated or controlled procedures used by computers (hardware directed by software), or, as is often the case, a combination of manual and automated procedures.

Resources are items of value. A case of milk is a resource, a person working is a resource, and the customer's cash is a resource. In Figure 2-1, both suppliers and customers are considered resources because they have value in this process. They are not considered activities because they are external and, therefore, not under the restaurant's direction and control.

Facilities are structures used within the business process. Resources can be stored within facilities. Examples of facilities include factories, pieces of equipment, trucks, filing cabinets, and the like. In the case of digital resources, facilities might include inventories and databases (as in Figure 2-1).

Information is the fourth element of a business process. Activities use information to determine how to transform the inputs received into the outputs produced. Because this book is about information systems, and understanding the nature of information and ways of defining it are crucial, information created in processes will be our focus.

We have defined a business process in terms of activities, resources, facilities, and information. It should be noted that many other definitions are used by other authors, industry analysts, and software products. Other business modelling software products use other definitions and terms.

Accordingly, a software industry standards organization called the *Object Management Group (OMG)* created a standard set of terms and graphical notations for documenting business processes. The standard, called **Business Process Modelling Notation (BPMN)**, is documented at www.bpmn.org. BPMN provides four graphical elements that can be used to document a process. A complete description of BPMN is beyond the scope of this text, but we have included a brief introduction in the Business Process Modelling Knowledge Extension at the end of this chapter. The basic symbols for BPMN are relatively easy to understand, and they work naturally with our definition of business process in terms of activities, resources, facilities, and information.

Q2-4 WHAT IS INFORMATION?

Information is one of those fundamental terms that we use every day but it turns out to be surprisingly difficult to define.

Definitions Vary

In this text, we will try to avoid the technical issues of defining information and will use common, intuitive definitions instead. Probably the most common definition is that information is knowledge derived from data, whereas *data* is defined as recorded facts or figures. Thus, the facts that employee Maddie Milsip earns $70.00 per hour and that Nima Sarhangpour earns $50.00 per hour are *data*. The statement that the average hourly wage of all the graphic designers is $60.00 per hour is *information*. Average wage is knowledge derived from the data of individual wages.

Another common definition is that *information is data presented in a meaningful context*. The fact that Maycko Macapugas earns $30.00 per hour is data.[1] The statement that Maycko Macapugas earns half the average hourly wage of the graphic designers, however, is information. It is data presented in a meaningful context.

Another definition of information that you will hear is that *information is processed data* or, sometimes, *information is data processed by summing, ordering, averaging, grouping, comparing, or other similar operations*. The fundamental idea of this definition is that we do something to data to produce information.

---

[1] Actually, the word *data* is plural; to be correct, we should use the singular form *datum* and say, "The fact that Maycko Macapugas earns $30.00 per hour is a datum." The word *datum*, however, sounds pedantic and fussy, and we will avoid it in this text.

There is yet a fourth definition of information, which was set out by the great research psychologist Gregory Bateson. He defined information as a *difference that makes a difference.* For example, if you get new information and it does not make a difference to your decision, is what you received really information?

For the purposes of this text, any of these definitions of information will do. Choose the definition that makes sense to you for the purpose you have at hand. The important point is that you discriminate between data and information. You also may find that different definitions work better in different situations.

Where Is Information?

Suppose you create a graph of Amazon.com's stock price and net income over its history, like that shown in Figure 2-2. Does the graph contain information? Well, if it presents data in a meaningful context or if it shows a difference that makes a difference, then it fits two of the definitions of information, and it's tempting to say that the graph contains information.

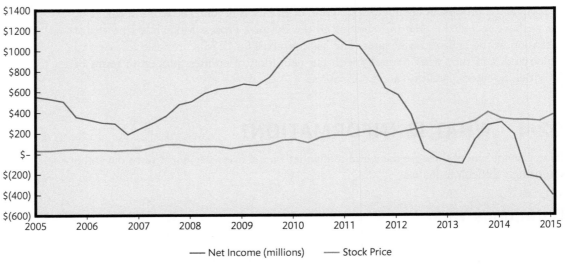

Figure 2-2   Amazon.com Stock Price and Net Income

However, show the graph to your family dog. Does your dog find information in the graph? Well, probably nothing about Amazon.com, anyway. At best the dog might learn what you had for lunch, instead of obtaining information about Amazon.com's stock price over time.

Reflect on this experiment and you will realize that the graph is not, itself, information. The graph is data that you and other humans *perceive,* and from that perception you *conceive* information. In short, if it's on a piece of paper or on a digital screen, it's data. If it's in the mind of a human, it's information.

Why, you're asking yourself, do I care? Well, for one, it explains why you, as a human, are the most important part of any information system you use. The quality of your thinking, of your ability to conceive information from data, is determined by your cognitive skills. *The data is just the data; the information you conceive from it is the value you add to the information system.*

Characteristics of Good Information

All information is not equal: Some information is better than other information. Figure 2-3 lists the characteristics of good information.

Figure 2-3 Characteristics of Good Information

Accurate   Good information is **accurate information**. Good information is based on correct and complete data that have been processed correctly and as expected. Accuracy is crucial; managers must be able to rely on the results of their information systems. The **information system (IS)** function can develop a bad reputation in the organization if the system is known to produce inaccurate information. In such a case, the IS becomes a waste of time and money as users develop workarounds to avoid the inaccurate data.

A corollary to this discussion is that you, a future user of information systems, ought not to rely on information just because it appears on a webpage, in a seemingly well-formatted report, or as part of a fancy query. It is sometimes hard to be skeptical about information that is delivered with beautiful, active graphics. Do not be misled. When you begin to use an IS, be skeptical. Cross-check the information you are receiving. When you are certain that it is accurate, you may be able to relax a little. Begin, however, with skepticism, and keep in mind that, over time, information may lose its level of accuracy. In fact, because this can often occur gradually, it can sometimes create serious problems.

Timely   Good information is **timely information**—produced in time for its intended use. A monthly report that arrives six weeks late is most likely useless. An IS that tells you not to extend credit to a customer after you have shipped the goods is unhelpful and frustrating. Note that timeliness can be measured against a calendar (six weeks late) or against events (before we ship).

When you participate in the development of an IS, timeliness will be part of the requirements you will request. You need to give appropriate and realistic timeliness needs. In some cases, developing systems that provide information in near real-time is much more difficult and expensive than producing information a few hours later. If you can get by with information that is a few hours old, it is important to say so during the requirements specification phase.

Consider this example. Suppose you work in marketing and you need to be able to assess the effectiveness of new online ad programs. You want an IS that will not only deliver ads over the Web but also enable you to determine how frequently customers click on those ads. Determining click ratios in near real-time can be very expensive; saving the data and processing them some hours later may be much easier, cheaper, and sufficient for your needs.

Relevant   Information should be **relevant** both to the context and to the subject. A chief executive officer (CEO) needs information that is summarized to an appropriate level for her position. A list of the hourly wage of every employee in the company is unlikely to be useful to a CEO. More likely, she will expect the average wage information by department or division. A list of all employee wages is irrelevant in the CEO's context.

Information should also be relevant to the subject at hand. If you want information about short-term interest rates for a possible line of credit, then a report that details 15-year mortgage interest rates is irrelevant. Similarly, a report that buries the information you need in pages and pages of results is also irrelevant to your purposes.

Just Barely Sufficient   Information needs to be **sufficient** for the purpose for which it is generated, but **just barely so**. We live in an information age; a critical decision that each of us must make is what information to ignore. The higher you rise in management, the more information you will be given and the more information you will need to ignore. So, information should be sufficient, but just barely so. Knowing what information to ignore is, of course, difficult. Studying, for example, would be so much easier and more efficient if your professors told you exactly which questions were going to be on their exams. But their input might not help you to learn or prepare you for your career.

Worth Its Cost   Information is not free. There are costs associated with an IS—the costs of developing, operating, and maintaining the system, and the costs of your time and salary for reading and processing the information the system produces. For information to be **worth its cost**, there must be an appropriate relationship between the cost of information and its value.

You need to ask, "What is the value of the information?" or "What is the cost?" or "Is there an appropriate relationship between value and cost?" For example, spending $10 to find out how to save $8 is not particularly useful. Information and information systems should be subject to the same financial analyses to which other assets are subjected.

Q2-5   WHAT IS THE ROLE OF INFORMATION IN BUSINESS PROCESSES?

This discussion about information may seem overly theoretical. What does information have to do with real business processes that move actual goods and provide services to real people?

The first thing to realize is that any time a good is moved or a service is provided, data and information are always created. Moving something from one place to another place creates new information about the location of that thing. During the move, the thing may change ownership (data) or may itself be modified (data). Any time there is a physical flow, there is the potential to capture a flow of information. We do not always collect the information, but we have the potential to do so if we need to. The same is true of a service. Flows of a service are always accompanied by a potential flow of data and information.

Look again at the inventory management process in Figure 2-1. Consider the payment process, which compares the *quantity received* (from receiving and stocking) to the *shipping invoice* (from the supplier). If the goods received match the goods billed, then payment generates a *supplier payment.*

Now, let us apply some of the definitions from the last section. Is *quantity received* an example of data, or is it information? By itself, it is just data, a recorded fact or figure: "We received these items from that supplier on this date." Similarly, the *shipping invoice* could also be considered to be just data: "We, Supplier X, delivered these items on this date."

When we bring these two items together, however, we generate information. As noted earlier, Gregory Bateson's definition of information suggested, "Information is a difference that makes a difference." If the *quantity received* indicates we received five cases of milk, but the *shipping invoice* is billing us for eight cases, we have a difference that makes a difference. By comparing records of the amount we received to records of the amount we were billed, we are presenting data in a meaningful context, which is a definition of information. Thus, a business process generates information by bringing together important items of data in a context.

The information generated by a business process is important for several reasons. For example, it lets us know when we need to make payments for goods or services received. Information also helps us keep track of what we have delivered and what has not been delivered; it keeps our inventory up to date. But information can take us beyond just collecting facts. Information becomes even more useful when we start using information to manage business processes.

Business Process Management

George Box, a pioneer in quality control, noted that a byproduct of every business process is information about how the process can be improved. For example, we could use the information produced by the process in Figure 2-1 over a period of a few months to determine the cheapest, the fastest, or the most reliable suppliers. We could use the information in the inventory database to assess our inventory ordering strategy. We could also use the information to estimate how much the organization might be losing from waste and theft. This type of work is called **business process management (BPM)**.

BPM is a field of management that promotes the development of effective and efficient processes through continuous improvement and innovation. Often, innovations in business processes are developed by integrating information technology into a business process. There are many methods that organizations have developed to support their improvements in business processes, including **total quality management (TQM)**, **six sigma**, and **lean production**. If you are interested in finding out more about these methods, two collaborative exercises at the end of this chapter ask you to explore these methods and use business process simulation to better understand how to manage business processes.[2]

We will not go into detail about the different methods of BPM, but what is important for you to remember is that information about the process provides the ability to better manage the process itself. Well-run organizations constantly seek better ways of providing goods and services to their customers. These organizations use various tools, including lean value map streaming, and process mapping tools, such as MS Visio, to support their work on business processes. Information about the business process is always the starting point for understanding what can and should be changed. So, whether you work in marketing, human resources, finance, or accounting, remember that as a manager, you will need to understand how to collect and use the information that is generated by business processes within your organization. The more you are able to understand business processes, the better you will be able to successfully manage the process. Information is, therefore, an important part of effective management.

Q2-6 HOW DO INFORMATION SYSTEMS SUPPORT BUSINESS PROCESSES?

Information systems are used by the activities in a business process, but the particular relationship varies among the processes. In some processes, several activities use one information system. In other processes, each activity has its own information system; in still other processes, some activities use several different information systems.

During systems analysis and design, the analysts and designers determine the relationship of activities to information systems. You will learn more about this topic in Chapter 10 and 11 and can read more about how information systems support business process in "MIS in Use" (pages 37–38). The case describes how an information system, Edoc, was used in the tugboat industry to support several manual business processes.

What Does It Mean to Automate a Process Activity?

We will consider the role of information systems for several of the activities depicted in Figure 2-1, but before we do that, think about the five components of an IS that we introduced in Chapter 1. Note the symmetry of components in Figure 2-4. The outermost components, hardware and people, are both actors; they can take actions. The software and procedure components are both sets of instructions: Software is instructions for hardware, and procedures are instructions for people. Finally, data form the bridge between the computer side on the left and the human side on the right.

An activity in a business process being handled by an **automated system** means that work formerly done by people who followed procedures has been changed so that computers

---

[2] IBM created an interactive game called INNOV8 that supports learning about business process management using business process simulation. You can access the game at www-01.ibm.com/software/solutions/soa/innov8/index.html.

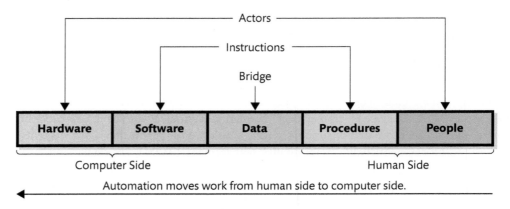

Figure 2-4 Characteristics of the Five Components of an information system

now do that work by following instructions in software. Thus, the automation of a process activity consists of moving work from the right side of Figure 2-4 to the left side.

An Information System to Support Counter Sales

According to Figure 2-1, the counter sales activity at a Tim Hortons restaurant interacts with the customer. This activity receives the customer's order, takes the items from inventory, and receives the customer's payment. This is the familiar process of ordering a latte and a breakfast sandwich at a restaurant.

Counter sales uses the IS shown in Figure 2-5. This system is, however, automated, and the cashiers may not even know they are using an IS. Each cash register contains a computer that communicates with another computer that hosts the inventory database. Programs in the cash register record sales and make appropriate changes to the inventory database whenever the cashier rings in a sale. The cashiers need to be trained only in how to use the cash register; they never need to work directly with the sales-recording programs on the computer.

Hardware	Software	Data	Procedures	People
- Cash register computer - Database host computer	- Sales-recording program on cash register	- Sales data - Inventory database	- Operate cash register	- Cashier

Mostly an automated system.
Almost all work is done by computers and software.

Figure 2-5 Sales Recording Information System Used by Counter Sales in Figure 2-1

The designers of this IS decided to fully automate the counter sales process because the cashier's job is seen as a low-skill-level position with high turnover. (Turnover refers to the rate at which new employees arrive and existing ones depart. Different jobs have different rates of turnover.) The designers wanted to reduce the amount of training time required for cashiers before they could productively use the cash registers.

An Information System to Support Payment

Now consider the payment activity in Figure 2-1. Payment receives the *quantity received* and the *shipping invoice*, and it produces the *supplier payment*. (In reality, payment does not generate a cheque to the supplier. Because of accounting controls, no single person should approve a payment and generate a cheque.) Instead, payment generates an authorization, which is sent to someone else who produces the cheque. These details are omitted here for simplicity—they are important, however!

As you can see in Figure 2-6, the IS that supports the payment activity is mostly a **manual system**. The accounts payable clerk receives both the *quantity received* and the *Shipping Invoice* as Adobe Acrobat PDF files (the same sort of PDF files you receive over the Internet). He or she then reads those documents, compares the quantities, and issues the payment authorization, as appropriate. If there is a discrepancy, the accounts payable clerk investigates and takes action, as appropriate.

Hardware	Software	Data	Procedures	People
- Personal computer	- Adobe Acrobat Reader - Email	- Quantity Received - Shipping Invoice	- Reconcile receipt document with invoice. - Issue payment authorization, if appropriate. - Process exceptions	- Accounts payable

Mostly a manual system.
Little work is done by computers and software.
Most work is done by Accounts Payable clerk.

Figure 2-6 Payment System Used by Payment Activity in Figure 2-1

The designers of this system chose to leave it as a manual system because processing exceptions is complicated: There are many different exceptions, and each requires a different response. The designers thought that programming all those exceptions would be expensive and probably not very effective, so they decided it would be better to let humans deal with the various situations. This means, by the way, that the accounts payable clerks will need much more training than the cashiers.

An Information System to Support Purchasing

Now consider the information system that supports the purchasing activity depicted in Figure 2-1. This system, shown in Figure 2-7, balances the work between automation and manual activity. The person doing the purchasing has a personal computer that is connected to the computer that hosts the database. Her computer runs an inventory application program that queries the database and identifies items that are low in stock and need to be ordered. That application produces a report that she reads periodically.

The purchasing clerk then decides which items to order and from which suppliers. In making this decision, she is guided by the inventory management practices. When she decides to order, she uses the purchasing program on her computer. It is that program that generates the *purchase order* shown in Figure 2-1.

Hardware	Software	Data	Procedures	People
– Personal computer – Database host computer	– Inventory application program – Purchasing program	– Inventory database	– Issue Purchase Order according to inventory management practices and guidelines	– Purchasing clerk

Balance between computer and human work.

Figure 2-7   Purchasing Information System Used by Purchasing Activity in Figure 2-1

The designers of this IS decided to balance the work between the computer and the human. Searching the inventory database for items that are low in stock is a perfect application for a computer. It is a repetitive process that humans find tedious. However, selecting which supplier to use is a process that requires human judgment. The clerk needs to balance a number of factors: the quality of the supplier, recent supplier experience, the need to have a variety of suppliers, and so forth. Such complicated balancing is better done by a human. Again, this means that the purchasing clerks will need much more training than the cashiers.

The three different information systems at the restaurant support the needs of users in the company's various business processes—counter sales, payments, and purchasing.

Before we leave this discussion, it is important to understand how *you* will relate to information systems. One of the most important tasks a business manager has is making decisions, and information is often a critical part of any decision making process. Therefore, we consider how information systems support business decisions next.

Q2-7   HOW DO INFORMATION SYSTEMS SUPPORT DECISION MAKING?

Making decisions is central to managing organizations. We found earlier in this chapter that data are an important part of any IS and that data can be transformed into information. Information is an important starting point for decision making in most organizations. So, the first point we can make is that information systems support decision making by providing the information—the raw material—for many decisions.

Decision making in organizations is varied and complex, and before discussing the role of information systems in supporting decision making, we need to investigate the characteristics and dimensions of decision making itself.

- Decision level
  - Operational
  - Managerial
  - Strategic
- Decision process
  - Structured
  - Unstructured

Figure 2-8   Decision Making Dimensions

Decisions Vary by Level

As shown in Figure 2-8, decisions occur at three levels in organizations: operational, managerial, and strategic. The types of decisions vary, depending on the level. **Operational decisions** concern day-to-day activities. Typical operational decisions include the following, for example: How many widgets should we order from vendor A? Should we extend credit to vendor B? Which invoices should we pay today? Information systems that support operational decision making are called **transaction processing systems (TPS)**.

Managerial decisions concern the allocation and utilization of resources. Examples of typical managerial decisions include the following: How much should we budget for computer hardware and programs for department A next year? How many engineers should we assign to project B? How many square metres of warehouse space do we need for the coming year? Information systems that support managerial decision making are called **management information systems (MIS)**. (Note that the term can be used in two ways: broadly, to mean the subjects in this entire book, and narrowly, to mean information systems that support managerial-level decision making. The context will make the meaning of the term clear.)

Strategic decisions concern broader organizational issues. Examples of typical decisions at the strategic level include the following: Should we start a new product line? Should we open a centralized warehouse in Calgary? Should we acquire company A?

Note that, in general, the decision time frame increases as we move from operational to managerial to strategic decisions. Operational decisions normally involve actions in the short term: What should we do today or this week? Managerial decisions involve longer time frames: What is an appropriate goal for the next quarter or year? Strategic decisions involve the long term; their consequences may not be realized for years.

Decisions Vary by Structure

Figure 2-9 shows levels of information systems with two decision processes: *structured* and *unstructured*. These terms refer to the method by which the decision is to be made, not to the nature of the underlying problem. A **structured decision** is one for which there is an understood and accepted method for making the decision. A formula for computing the reorder quantity of an item in inventory is an example of a structured decision process. A standard method for allocating furniture and equipment to employees is another structured decision process.

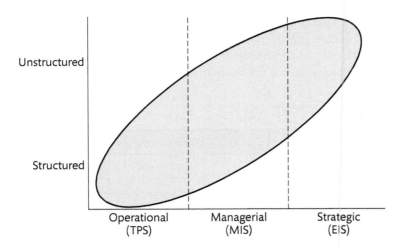

Figure 2-9 Relationship of Decision Level and Decision Making Process

An **unstructured decision** process is one for which there is no agreed-upon decision making method. Predicting the future direction of the economy or the stock market is a common example. The prediction method varies from person to person; it is neither standardized nor broadly accepted. (As one pundit put it, "If you laid all the economists in the world end to end, they still would not reach a conclusion.") Another example of an unstructured decision making process is assessing how well suited an employee is for performing a particular job. Managers vary in the manner in which they make such assessments.

Again, keep in mind that the terms *structured* and *unstructured* refer to the decision making process, not to the underlying subject. Weather forecasting is a structured decision because the process used to make the decision is standardized among forecasters. Weather itself, however, is an unstructured phenomenon, as tornadoes and hurricanes demonstrate every year.

Supporting Decision Making

The decision type and decision making process are loosely related. As shown by the oval in Figure 2-9, decisions at the operational level tend to be structured and decisions at the strategic level tend to be unstructured. Managerial decisions tend to be both structured and unstructured.

We say "tend to be" because there are exceptions to the relationship illustrated in Figure 2-9. Some operational decisions are unstructured (e.g., "How many taxicab drivers do we need on the night before the homecoming game?"), and some strategic decisions can be structured (e.g., "How should we assign sales quotas for a new product?"). In general, however, the relationship shown in Figure 2-9 holds.

Another way to examine the relationship between information systems and decision making is to consider how an IS is used during the steps of the decision making process. The first two columns of Figure 2-10 show the typical steps in the decision making process: intelligence gathering, formulation of alternatives, choice, implementation, and review. During **intelligence gathering**, the decision makers determine what is to be decided, what the criteria for the decision will be, and what data are available. **Alternatives formulation** is the stage in which decision makers lay out various alternatives. They analyze the alternatives and select one during the **choice** step, and then they implement the decision in the **implementation** step. Finally, the organization reviews the results of the decision. The **review** step may lead to another decision—and another iteration through the decision process.

As summarized in the right column of Figure 2-10, each of these decision making steps needs a different type of IS. During intelligence gathering, email and videoconferencing facilitate communication among the decision makers. As well, during the first phase, decision makers use query and reporting systems as well as other types of data analysis applications to obtain relevant data. They use email and videoconferencing systems for communication during the alternatives formulation step. During the choice step,

Decision Step	Description	Examples of Possible Information Systems
Intelligence gathering	• What is to be decided? • What are the decision criteria? • Obtain relevant data.	• Communications applications (email, video-conferencing, word processing, presentation) • Query and reporting systems • Data analysis applications
Alternatives formulation	• What are the choices?	• Communications applications
Choice	• Analyze choices against criteria using data. • Select alternative.	• Spreadsheets • Financial modelling • Other modelling
Implementation	• Make it so!	• Communications applications
Review	• Evaluate results of decision; if necessary, repeat process to correct and adapt.	• Communications applications • Query and reporting Systems • Spreadsheets and other analysis

Figure 2-10 Decision Making Steps

analysis applications, such as spreadsheets, and financial and other modelling applications, help the decision makers to analyze alternatives. The implementation stage again involves the use of communications applications, and all types of information systems can be used during review.

Q2-8 WHAT IS YOUR ROLE?

You are part of every IS you use. When you look at the five components of an IS, you can see that the last component—people—includes you. Your mind and your thinking are not merely components of the information systems you use, they are the most important components.

Consider this example. Suppose you have the perfect IS, one that can predict the future. (No such IS exists, but, for this example, assume that it does.) Now, suppose that on December 14, 1966, your perfect IS tells you that the next day Walt Disney, the founder of Disney empire, will die. Say you have $50 000 to invest; you can either buy Disney stock or you can "short" it (an investment technique that will net you a positive return if the stock value decreases). Given that your IS is perfect, how would you invest?

Before you read on, think carefully about this question. If Walt Disney is going to die the next day, will Disney stock go up or down? Most students assume that the stock will go down, so they short it, on the basis of the theory that the loss of a company's founder will mean a dramatic drop in the share price.

In fact, the day after Walt Disney died, the value of Disney stock increased substantially. Why? There are several possible reasons, but one that many analysts agree on is that the market saw Walt Disney as an artist; once he died, it would no longer be possible for more art to be created. Thus, the value of the existing art would increase because of scarcity, and the value of the corporation that owned that art would increase as well (another possible reason was that Disney would now be run by more professional management).

MIS in Use | Helm: Software Making Waves

Tugboats might seem like the last place to look for innovative information technology. But Edoc Systems Group (www.helmoperations.com), a company with headquarters in Victoria, B.C., recognized the potential of information technology to automate business processes in this industry.

Tugboat companies are often family businesses that have been running for more than 100 years using paper-based systems. Things do not change quickly in this industry. For example, a Helm employee visiting an Oregon company found that the dispatch log sheet the company was currently using had been in use in the same format since 1952! How can information technology help this industry?

The first step is to understand the challenges the tugboat companies face. Each company has a fleet of vessels, a set of crews that run the vessels, and a list of jobs from various customers that need to be done. The dispatcher is the person at the centre of the business process that matches jobs with crews and vessels. It is a complicated process in which new jobs come in daily, vessels and crews have different capabilities, and customers have different priorities. Tugboats are also expensive (a tugboat can cost upward of $5 million and require thousands of dollars per day to run). Dispatchers require years of experience before they are ready to balance these factors and make efficient scheduling decisions.

Paper-based systems worked for decades, but they were relatively inefficient and prone to error. Why? To understand this, you need a more detailed view of the process: It began with a customer order (usually via phone or fax). An employee at the tug company wrote down the work that needed to be done; that description would then be rewritten and handed to tug captains as

Continued ➜

a job to do; dispatchers would copy it again onto the dispatch log sheet. When the job was completed, the captains handed their log sheets back to the dispatchers. Dispatchers reviewed the sheets and sent a delivery notice to their customer. The log sheets would then get passed to accounting staff, who rewrote (or retyped) the entire job into an invoice and sent it out. Finally, the accountant would have to re-enter all the invoicing details into the accounting system.

Each job, therefore, was handwritten seven different times by at least four different people. Each written entry not only took a good deal of time but was also prone to copying errors.

Several years of work with tugboat companies resulted in developing HELM Marine Operations software. HELM supports the dispatch process first by equipping each vessel with a computer that runs HELM software. The software is used to keep track of the jobs assigned to the tugboat, details about each job, and information about when the job is completed. This information from each of the boats is linked, through a computer network, with a central computer at the company's main office. This electronic linkage reduces the reliance on dispatch sheets and automates the job-completion notices that dispatchers need to send to their customers. The software also automatically produces invoices and links with the accounting system, thereby reducing even more data entry. HELM, therefore, provides more accurate and timely information. The hardware and software are used to save time for the dispatchers, captains, and accounting staff. HELM software has eliminated up to 60 percent of the steps involved in the invoicing process and saved companies tens of thousands of dollars each year by reducing errors. Reporting times have also been decreased by up to 90 percent—from 7 hours to 30 minutes in some cases. Helm now has customers around the world.

QUESTIONS

1. What are the primary benefits realized by the use of HELM software?

2. Could HELM also result in increased revenue? Explain your answer.

3. Can you think of other benefits that might arise from the use of the software? For example, it is hard to find experienced dispatchers in the industry. Could the system help meet this challenge?

How Does the Knowledge in This Chapter Help You?

Mateo and the others at Falcon Security know they need to assess business processes if they are going to start 3D printing their own drones. They do not know, however, how to go about making this assessment. With the knowledge contained in this chapter, they should be able to document Falcon's business processes and explain in a professional way how they think 3D printing might affect Falcon. In doing so, they would demonstrate, using the terms from Chapter 1, their ability to engage in systems thinking, abstraction, collaboration, and experimentation. Hence, this knowledge would not only help Falcon; it would help the career prospects of the team members as well.

If Falcon Security were to move forward with 3D drone printing, the next steps would likely involve hiring new employees to print the drones and work with IS professionals—either in-house or as outside contractors to ensure the new drones would be compatible with their existing systems. The knowledge gained in this chapter would help prepare Mateo, Joni, Cam, and the others to communicate effectively with those professionals and their counterparts. Such communication not only results in better solutions; it also enables the IS professionals to have a clearer understanding of business needs, which would allow them to respond more quickly to predicaments and opportunities. Falcon's costs could also be potentially reduced by adopted efficiencies. Think about how Falcon's experience can help you, as you will likely encounter similar issues in your career.

ACTIVE REVIEW

Use this Active Review to verify that you have understood the material in the chapter. You can read the entire chapter and then perform the tasks in this review, or you can read the material for just one question and perform the tasks for that question before moving on to the next one.

Q2-1 "HOW DID THIS STUFF GET HERE?"

Imagine yourself at a hockey or football game, or at a concert. What business processes are involved in producing that event? How did you buy a ticket? What processes were involved in that activity? What processes are needed to print the ticket? Who cleaned the stadium? What processes are involved in hiring, managing, and paying the cleaning staff?

Q2-2 WHAT IS A BUSINESS PROCESS?

What is the definition of a business process? Consider one of the processes in your answer to Q2-1, and make a diagram similar to the one in Figure 2-1.

Q2-3 WHAT ARE THE COMPONENTS OF A BUSINESS PROCESS?

List the components of a business process. Define each component. Identify each type of component on your diagram from your answer to Q2-2.

Q2-4 WHAT IS INFORMATION?

Give four definitions of *information*. Rank those definitions in the order of usefulness in business. Justify your ranking.

Q2-5 WHAT IS THE ROLE OF INFORMATION IN BUSINESS PROCESSES?

Explain how information is created in the payment activity in Figure 2-1. Describe three different types of information that could be produced from the data in the inventory database. Describe business process management and how it is related to information in business processes.

Q2-6 HOW DO INFORMATION SYSTEMS SUPPORT BUSINESS PROCESSES?

Explain the meaning of each cell in Figures 2-5, 2-6, and 2-7. Explain the differences in the balance between automated and manual systems in these three information systems. Summarize the justification that the systems' designers used for constructing systems with the balance shown.

Q2-7 HOW DO INFORMATION SYSTEMS SUPPORT DECISION MAKING?

Describe the differences among operational, managerial, and strategic decision making. What are the steps in a decision making process? Explain how information systems can support these steps.

Q2-8 WHAT IS YOUR ROLE?

Explain why the quality of your thinking has a lot to do with the quality of the information system.

MyLab MIS

MyLab MIS is an online learning and testing environment that features the perfect study tools to help you master the concepts covered in this chapter. Log in to MyLab to test your knowledge of key chapter concepts and explore additional practice tools, including videos, flashcards, and more!

KEY TERMS AND CONCEPTS

USING YOUR KNOWLEDGE

2-1. Consider the four definitions of information presented in this chapter. The problem with the first definition, "knowledge derived from data," is that it merely substitutes one word we don't know the meaning of (information) for a second word we don't know the meaning of (knowledge). The problem with the second definition, "data presented in a meaningful context," is that it is too subjective. Whose context? What makes a context meaningful? The third definition, "data processed by summing, ordering, averaging, etc.," is too mechanical. It tells us what to do, but it doesn't tell us what information is. The fourth definition, "a difference that makes a difference," is vague and unhelpful.

Also, none of these definitions helps us to quantify the amount of information we receive. What is the information content of the statement that every human being has a navel? Zero—you already know that. However, the statement that someone has just deposited $50,000 into your checking account is chock-full of information. So, good information has an element of surprise.

Considering these points, answer the following questions:

a. What is information made of?

b. If you have more information, do you weigh more? Why or why not?

c. If you give a copy of your transcript to a prospective employer, is that information? If you show that same transcript to your dog, is it still information? Where is the information?

d. Give your own best definition of information.

e. Explain how you think it is possible that we have an industry called the *information technology industry*, but we have great difficulty defining the word information.

2-2. Suppose you work at a large regional health care provider. The CIO of the company has asked you to gather data about the organization's operations. More specifically, the CIO wants to more carefully track supplies and equipment at hospitals and clinics within the organization. The problem is, few of the health care workers are interested in giving you that information. They don't want management interfering with their patient care. They worry that management will start reducing their supplies if they think they have an overabundance of certain items. Then, when they need these items the most, they'll run short of essential supplies!

a. Describe why it's important in this case to gather accurate information.

b. Describe why it's important in this case to gather timely information.

c. Describe why it's important in this case to gather relevant information.

d. Describe why it's important in this case to gather information worth its cost.

2-3. Reread the "MIS in Use" case to refresh your memory of the HELM system.

a. Using Figure 2-1 as a guide, draw the paper-based process described in the case.

b. Now draw the process after HELM was introduced.

c. What are the major differences between the two processes?

d. What are the improvements that have been made through the introduction of HELM? (*Hint*: Consider tangible and intangible benefits.)

2-4. The text states that information should be worth its cost. Both cost and value can be broken into tangible and intangible factors. Tangible factors can be directly measured; intangible ones arise indirectly and are difficult to measure. For example, a tangible cost is the cost of a computer monitor, while an intangible cost is the lost productivity related to a poorly trained employee.

Give five important tangible and five important intangible costs of an IS. If it helps to focus your thinking, use the class scheduling system at your university or some other university IS to come up with your answer. When determining whether an IS is worth its cost, how do you think the tangible and intangible factors should be considered?

2-5. Singing Valley Resort is a top-end (rooms cost from $400 to $2500 per night), 50-unit resort located high in the Alberta Rockies. Singing Valley prides itself on its beautiful location, its relaxing setting, and its superb service. The resort's restaurant is highly rated and has an extensive list of exceptional wines. The affluent clients are accustomed to the highest levels of service.

a. Give an example of three different operational decisions that Singing Valley personnel might make each day. Describe an IS that could be used to facilitate those decisions.

b. Give an example of three different managerial decisions that Singing Valley managers might make each week. Describe an IS that could be used to facilitate those decisions.

c. Give an example of three different strategic decisions that Singing Valley's owners might make in a year. Describe an IS for each.

d. Which of the decisions in your answers to questions (a) through (c) are structured? Which, if any, are unstructured?

COLLABORATIVE EXERCISES

2-1. This chapter introduced the concept of business process management (BPM). In the discussion, three methods for improving business processes were listed: total quality management (TQM), six sigma, and lean production. Do the following with your team:

a. Choose one of the methods listed above. Create a definition of the method, elaborate on how it works, and indicate where and when it was developed. Discuss how this method differs from other BPM methods.

b. Using the Internet, find an example of at least one company that has used this method.

c. Combine what you have discovered in parts (a) and (b), and create a two-page (maximum) description of the method, aimed at an audience that has never heard of BPM or your method. Focus on what a manager should know about this method, and provide a list of useful web resources where more information is available. Be prepared to present your findings to the class.

CASE STUDY 2
HIGH TOUCH, HIGH TECH

Founded in 1945, Vancity (www.vancity.ca) is Canada's largest credit union, with more than $13 billion in assets and 350 000 customers. The company is different from many other financial institutions because it is owned by its member customers rather than shareholders. Vancity's 2500 employees pride themselves on providing outstanding service that is personal and professional, while at the same time demonstrating innovation and social responsibility.

Like most financial institutions, Vancity offers its customers traditional banking products, such as savings and chequing accounts, loans, and credit cards, as well as a growing number of mutual funds and other investment and financial planning services. However, this increase in the number of products and services is not without its challenges, particularly when coupled with increased customer access. The days when customers could transact business only while in a branch are long gone. Although a branch visit is still a cornerstone of banking, modern customers are just as likely to connect and do business with Vancity over the telephone or via the Internet. Banking now happens anywhere and anytime, and customers are supported by sophisticated computer systems that are safe and secure. However, it is not just high technology for its own sake. Instead, as Tony Fernandes, former vice-president of Technology Strategy, puts it, "High tech is used to create high touch."

Although many people still visit their local branch and have developed a relationship with the customer service representatives (CSRs), this is not always possible and is increasingly becoming the least frequent way that customers do business. Staff changes, growth in the number of customers, and the fact that people are increasingly mobile mean that the in-branch staff are less likely to recognize their customers, and even if they do recognize them, staff may simply not be aware of the complete relationship the customer has with Vancity.

To address this problem, Vancity has implemented Customer Information File (CIF) technology to keep track of all the various types of business a customer has. Now, when customers visit the branch and present their customer card to the CSR, the CIF searches all the system records, identifies the services used, and develops a profile of the complete consolidated relationship between the client and Vancity. As a result, each customer receives the same high level of personal service even if it is his or her first time inside a particular branch, and Vancity is able to tailor or customize the experience specifically for that customer. For example, rather than ask all customers if they would like information on one of the new credit cards that Vancity offers, the system can advise the customer service representative as to whether the customer already has the card or should be offered something else. Alternatively, if a CSR member sees that a customer has an investment plan already set up, the CSR could be prompted to ask the customer about a new retirement product being launched by Vancity's mutual fund department.

Source: Data From Vancity. Published by Vancity Group.

Questions

1. What challenges are created when providing anywhere, anytime services? (*Hint:* How and when did you conduct your last banking transaction?)

2. What business and technology issues would be faced by an organization that wants to have a complete view of its customers? (*Hint:* What are the benefits and costs of cooperation, and are there any privacy issues?)

3. Can you think of any examples where a lack of information or failure to consider the information could affect the profitability of a business?

4. If a customer has more than one account at a particular organization, should he or she receive separate mailings or should all the documentation be included in the same envelope?

5. Does being a credit union rather than a share corporation affect Vancity's structure?

WHAT DO YOU THINK?

YOUR PERSONAL COMPETITIVE ADVANTAGE

Consider the elements of competitive advantage as they apply to you personally. What are the skills that set you apart from the competition? Create a list of these skills. As an employee, the skills and abilities you offer are your personal product. Examine the first three items on the list, and ask yourself, "How can I use my time in school—and in this MIS class, in particular—to create new skills, to enhance those I already have, and to differentiate my skills from the competition?" (By the way, you will enter a national market and an international market. Your competition is not just the students in your class—it is also students attending classes in New York, China, Florida, Finland, and everywhere else MIS is taught today.)

Suppose you are interested in a sales job. What skills can you learn from your MIS class that will make you more competitive as a future salesperson? Get on the Internet, and find examples of the use of information systems in the industry you are interested in. What about buyers and suppliers? How can you interpret those elements in terms of your own personal competitive advantage?

To get a job, you first need to have a working relationship. Do you have a co-op position or an internship? If not, can you get one? And once you have that co-op job or internship, how can you use your knowledge of MIS to lock in your job so that you get a job offer?

Human resources personnel say that networking is one of the most effective ways of finding a job. How can you use this class to establish alliances with other students? Does your class have a website? Is there an email list server for the students in your class? How can you use those facilities to develop job-seeking alliances with other students? Who in your class already has a job or an internship? Can any of those people provide suggestions or opportunities for finding a job?

Do not restrict your job search to your local area. Are there regions of Canada where jobs that interest you are more plentiful? How can you find out about student organizations in those regions? Search the Web for MIS classes in other cities, and make contact with students there. Find out what opportunities there are in other places.

Finally, as you study MIS, think about how the knowledge you gain can help you save money for your employer. Even more, see if you can build a case that an employer would actually save money by hiring you. The line of reasoning might be that because of your knowledge of IS, you will be able to facilitate cost savings that more than compensate for your salary.

In truth, few of the ideas you generate for a potential employer will be feasible or pragmatic. The fact that you are thinking creatively, however, will indicate to a potential employer that you have initiative and are grappling with the problems that real businesses have. Keep thinking about competitive advantage and strive to understand how the topics you study can help you accomplish, personally, one or more of the objectives you have set out for yourself.

Discussion Questions

1. Summarize the efforts you have taken thus far to build an employment record that will lead to job offers after graduation.

2. Describe one way in which you have a competitive advantage over your classmates. If you do not have such a competitive advantage, describe actions you can take to obtain one.

3. To build your network, you can use your status as a student to approach business professionals. That is, you can contact them for help with an assignment or for career guidance. For example, suppose you want to work in banking, and you know that your local bank has a customer information system. You could call the bank manager and ask him or her how that system creates a competitive advantage for the bank. Also, you could ask to interview other employees. Describe two specific ways in which you can use your status as a student to build your network in this way.

4. Describe two ways you can use student alliances to obtain a job. How can you use information systems to build, maintain, and operate such alliances?

KNOWLEDGE EXTENSION 2

Chapter 2 provides the background for this extension.

Business Process Modelling

STUDY QUESTIONS

KE2-1 HOW CAN BUSINESS PROCESS MODELLING HELP ORGANIZATIONS?

KE2-2 HOW CAN INFORMATION SYSTEMS IMPROVE PROCESS QUALITY?

KE2-1 HOW CAN BUSINESS PROCESS MODELLING HELP ORGANIZATIONS?

In this question, we will look at the business model of a hypothetical online bicycle part retailer named Best Bikes. We will show how to create an abstraction of Best Bikes' basic business processes and then how these processes could be modified if the company decided to 3D-print its own parts rather than buy them from its parts suppliers.

How Best Bikes Works

Best Bikes negotiates with vendors to supply parts at given prices and under certain terms. Once it has a commitment from a vendor to provide parts, it places the parts' descriptions, photos, prices, and related sales data on its website. Best Bikes then orders an initial quantity of parts, receives them from the vendor, and places them in inventory. When customers order parts, operations personnel remove items from inventory and ship them to the customers. From time to time, parts need to be ordered to restock inventory, but we will not consider the reorder process in this example. Of course, Best Bikes must keep records of all these activities in order to pay vendors, bill customers, check inventory levels, pay taxes, and so forth.

Best Bikes' business activities are typical of a small online retailer with a relatively simple inventory. Even so, you will see there are ways for Best Bikes to improve what it is doing, even if it does not pursue 3D printing.

The Existing Best Bikes Process

A **business process** is a network of activities for accomplishing a business function. Figure KE2-1 shows a diagram of the existing Best Bikes process. This diagram, which is a model, or an abstraction, of Best Bikes' activities, is constructed using the symbols of **Business Process Modelling Notation (BPMN)**. This notation is an international standard for creating business process diagrams.[1] A key to these symbols is shown in Figure KE2-2.

Figure KE2-1 is organized in what is called **swimlane format**, which is a graphical arrangement in which all of the activities for a given role (job type) are shown in a single

---

[1] These symbols are included with Microsoft's Visio 2013 Professional edition. If your college or university is a member of Microsoft DreamSpark, you can obtain a licence-free copy of Visio and use it to make your own BPMN diagrams.

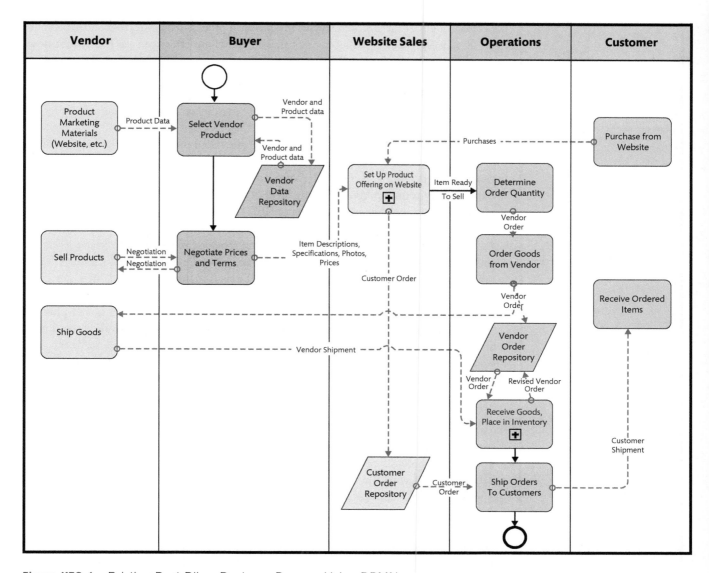

Figure KE2-1   Existing Best Bikes Business Process Using BPMN

vertical lane. Each swimlane has **activities**, which are specific tasks that need to be accomplished as part of the process. A **role** is a subset of the activities in a business process that is performed by an **actor**, which is a person, a group, a department, an organization, or an information system. Figure KE2-1 shows the roles of Vendor, Buyer, Website Sales, Operations, and Customer.

Notice that we do not write people's names at the top of a swimlane, but rather we write the name of the role. This is because a given role may be fulfilled by many people and because a given employee may have many roles. Furthermore, over time, the organization may change the people who are assigned given roles. In some cases, a role can be fulfilled by an information system.

According to the BPMN standard, the start of a business process is symbolized by a circle having a narrow border. The end of a business process is symbolized by a circle having a thick border. So, in Figure KE2-1, the process starts with the Buyer role, or we can also say that a Buyer starts the process.

Activities within a business process are shown in rectangles with rounded corners. The first activity for the Buyer role is *Select Vendor Product.* According to Figure KE2-1, buyers obtain vendor and product data from the Vendor Data Repository. A **repository** is a

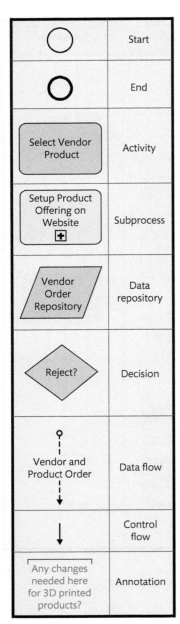

○	Start
◯	End
Select Vendor Product	Activity
Setup Product Offering on Website ⊞	Subprocess
Vendor Order Repository	Data repository
Reject?	Decision
Vendor and Product Order	Data flow
↓	Control flow
Any changes needed here for 3D printed products?	Annotation

Figure KE2-2 Process Symbols (BPMN Standard)

collection of data that is stored within the business process. Repositories can be computer databases, or they can be collections of files in the cloud (think *on the Internet* for now), or they can be printed records stored in a file cabinet or a shoebox. For the purpose of documenting a business process, the particular medium in which repository data is stored is unimportant. The Vendor Data Repository contains not only data from prior purchases but also the results of vendor sales calls, vendor mailings, prior Buyer searches of vendor and product data on the Internet, and so forth.

The labelled dashed lines in Figure KE2-1 are called **data flows**. They represent the movement of data from one activity to another. The data can be delivered via email or text message, over the phone, by fax, or by some other means. In a BPMN diagram, the medium of data delivery is unimportant. For the level of our discussion, the format of the data item is also not important. According to Figure KE2-1, Buyers both read and write Vendor and Product data from and to the Vendor Data Repository.

The solid line between the activities *Select Vendor Product* and *Negotiate Prices and Terms* means that after a Buyer finishes the *Select Vendor Product* activity, the Buyer's next action is to perform the *Negotiate Prices and Terms* activity. Such solid lines are called **sequence flows**.

Another BPMN symbol used in Figure KE2-1 is an activity with a boxed plus sign inside it. This notation indicates a subprocess and is used when the work to be done is sufficiently complex as to require a process diagram of its own. In Figure KE2-1, the *Setup Product Offering on Website* activity involves many activities and several different roles. In the complete set of process documentation, it would have a BPMN diagram of its own. Here we will not be concerned with those details.

With the understanding of these symbols, you can interpret the rest of Figure KE2-1 on your own. One point to note concerns the *Receive Goods, Place in Inventory* subprocess performed by the Operations Role. When Best Bikes receives a Vendor Shipment, it compares the goods received to those ordered on the original Vendor Order. It will notate that order with the items received and place the Revised Vendor Order back into the Vendor Order Repository. It will also note the items that were missing or received in damaged condition.

To summarize, a business process is a network of activities. Each activity is performed by a role. Roles are actioned by people, groups, departments, organizations, and sometimes information systems. Repositories are collections of data. Data flows between activities; when one activity follows directly after another, the flow is shown with a sequence flow. Complex activities are represented by a separate subprocess diagram and denoted by a boxed plus sign in the activity.

How Best Bikes Processes Must Change To Support 3D Printing

Best Bikes was considering 3D printing its own parts in an effort to reduce costs and carry a larger selection of parts. The process diagram in Figure KE2-3 shows the existing process, but with a new role for 3D printing. The diamond in this diagram represents a decision. For example, when stocking a part, operations will need to decide whether the part is manufactured in-house using 3D printing. Figure KE2-3 also includes annotations, which are just comments that Best Bikes' operations manager had about the diagram.

The diagram in Figure KE2-3 provides a basis for discussions with others. Best Bikes' operations manager can use it to document where the existing processes need to be altered and to demonstrate the need for additional personnel. If Best Bikes proceeds with 3D printing, it will need to further define the subprocesses *Make the Product* and *Check Product Quality*. From this example, though, you can see how process diagrams provide a means to communicate with others about process structure and possible changes.

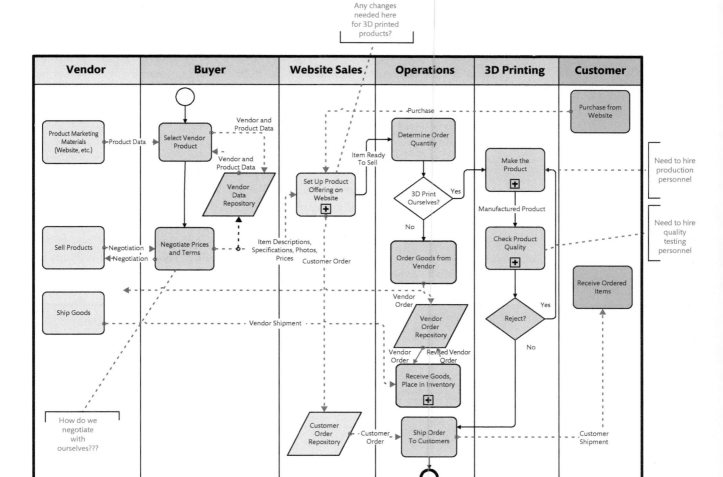

Figure KE2-3   Revised Best Bikes Process Using BPMN

KE2-2 HOW CAN INFORMATION SYSTEMS IMPROVE PROCESS QUALITY?

Information systems benefit business processes in many ways. For our purposes, the most succinct summary is to say that *information systems improve process quality.* To understand why that is so, you first need to understand process quality.

What Is Process Quality?

Process quality can be measured in two dimensions: process *effectiveness* and process *efficiency.* An **effective business process** is one that enables the organization to accomplish its strategy. One element of Best Bikes' strategy is to have the largest selection of parts in the industry. It is investigating whether 3D printing will help accomplish that strategy. If so, its current processes are ineffective because they do not support 3D printing. It will need to implement processes like those called for in Figure KE2-3 instead.

The second dimension of process quality is efficiency. **Efficiency** is the ratio of benefits to costs. Consider two versions of a business process for accomplishing some function. If both versions create the same benefit, but one costs more than the other, then the higher-cost version is less efficient than the lower-cost version. Or if both versions cost the same, but one generates less benefit than the other, then the lower-benefit one is less efficient.

Examine Figure KE2-1 closely and you will see that there are two different repositories of vendor data. One is used by Buyers to select vendors, and another is used by Operations to store order data. Such separated data may be appropriate, but more likely it is creating process inefficiencies. For example, what happens when a vendor moves? The vendor's address needs to be updated in two places; duplicate updating is not difficult, but it is unnecessary. Further, consider the confusion if the vendor address is changed in one place but not the other.

Figure KE2-4 shows an alteration of Figure KE2-1 in which vendor data is stored in a single repository. Most likely this second process will be less costly, generate fewer errors, and still be as effective as the first version. Hence, the quality of the process in Figure KE2-4 is improved because the process will be more efficient.

If you look at the business processes in Figures KE2-1, KE2-3, and KE2-4, you will not see any costs—at least not directly. So, where are they? One major source of cost is the labour of the employees who perform the process activities. If it takes someone 10 hours to perform the *Select Vendor Product* activity, then the cost of that activity is the cost of those

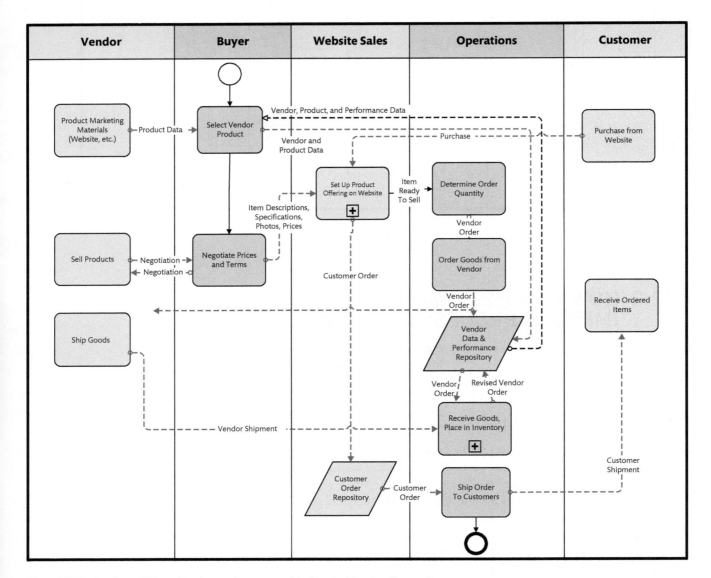

Figure KE2-4   Best Bikes Business Process with Single Vendor Repository

10 labour hours. Behind the scenes, there are also infrastructure costs. Data does not just flow automatically from one activity to another. Some type of computer network, email, or other system needs to exist to support those data flows. The cost of that infrastructure is part of the costs of the business process.

Using Information Systems to Improve Process Quality

To understand how information systems improve process quality, consider Figure KE2-5, which shows the five components of an information system. Notice the symmetry of these components; the outermost components, hardware and people, are both actors—they take action. The software and procedure components are both sets of instructions. Software is instructions for hardware, and procedures are instructions for people. Finally, data is the bridge between the computer side on the left and the human side on the right.

When an activity in a business process is automated, activities formerly done by people following procedures are moved to computers that perform the work by following instructions in software. Thus, the automation of a process activity consists of moving work from the right-hand side of Figure KE2-5 to the left.

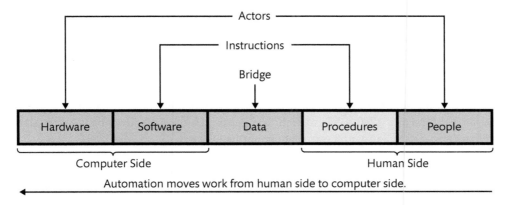

Figure KE2-5 Characteristics of the Five Components

Use an Information System to Store Vendor Data

To understand this, consider the *Select Vendor Product* activity in Figure KE2-1. That process could be entirely manual. The buyer could use the Internet (for this example, ignore the fact that she is using a computer system to access the Internet), gather data about vendors and products, make analyses of costs and margins by hand, and store the results of those analyses on paper in a file folder in her desk. When she wants to access past records for a particular vendor, she would manually search through her desk to find those records.

One way to use information systems in this process would be for buyers to store the results of vendor analyses in an Excel file. If this were done, the buyer would have a faster and more reliable means of finding relevant data. The time required to perform the analysis and locate past analyses would be reduced, the cost of the process would decrease, the process would be more efficient, and hence process quality would increase.

Store Vendor Product and Performance Data in a Database

Consider another example. Suppose Best Bikes implements the improved process shown in Figure KE2-4 and stores the Vendor Data Repository in a computer database that combines both product specifications as well as vendor performance data. Now buyers can not

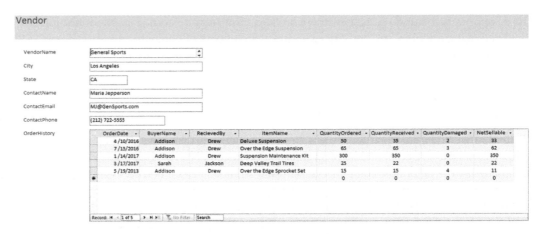

Figure KE2-6 Best Bikes Data on General Sports

only use their own data about vendors and products, but they can also view past vendor performance data to choose among vendors when parts are available from several vendors. Figure KE2-6 shows an example display of such performance data.

A process that uses this new information system saves buyer labour and, on the surface, is more efficient. But the new information system will cost something to develop and operate. Those costs must also be considered before the organization can decide if making such a change makes the process more efficient. You can see from this simple example why it is vital that business professionals be involved in the development of information systems. If systems development is left solely to technical personnel, they may develop a system that is technically elegant but with costs that cannot be justified.

In addition to improving process efficiency, information systems can also improve process effectiveness. If the buyers, for example, share vendor data, they may be able to identify new parts for Best Bikes to carry. By doing so, they are helping achieve the goal of having the largest availability of bicycle parts in the industry.

Furthermore, consider the performance data in Figure KE2-6. General Sports frequently ships fewer items (Quantity Received) than were requested (Quantity Ordered), and in one case, it shipped too many parts. In addition, Best Bikes received many items in damaged condition. If Best Bikes can find another vendor to supply these or equivalent parts, its parts availability will increase and it will better achieve its strategy. Therefore, the information system that produces the display in Figure KE2-6 makes Best Bikes' buying process more effective.

Of course, we are assuming that the data in Figure KE2-6 is correct. But is it? Before we close this chapter, you need to understand the factors that lead to quality information. Accordingly, you first need to understand the difference between information and data. We discuss that topic next.

ACTIVE REVIEW

KE2-1 HOW CAN BUSINESS PROCESS MODELLING HELP ORGANIZATIONS?

Summarize Best Bike's business operations. Define *business process* and give three examples. Define *BPMN, swimlane format, activity, role, actor, repository, data flow, sequence flow*, and *subprocess*. Describe the BPMN symbols used for each. Review Figure KE2-1 and ensure you can explain how this business process works. Explain differences between the processes in Figures KE2-1 and KE2-3 and relate those differences to the 3D printing opportunity.

KE2-2 HOW CAN INFORMATION SYSTEMS IMPROVE PROCESS QUALITY?

Define two dimensions of process quality. Explain how information systems can improve both of these dimensions. Summarize the ways that information systems can improve the process quality of the processes in Figures KE2-1 and KE2-4. Explain how automation relates to the five components in Figure KE2-5. Describe uses that buyers can make of the data in Figure KE2-6.

MyLab MIS

MyLab MIS is an online learning and testing environment that features the perfect study tools to help you master the concepts covered in this chapter. Log in to MyLab to test your knowledge of key chapter concepts and explore additional practice tools, including videos, flashcards, and more!

KEY TERMS AND CONCEPTS

Activities 45	Business Process Modelling	Effective business process 47	Role 45
Actor 45	Notation (BPMN) 44	Efficiency 47	Sequence flows 46
Business process 44	Data flows 46	Repository 45	Swimlane format 44

CHAPTER 3
Productivity, Innovation, and Strategy

STUDY QUESTIONS

Q3-1   WHY SHOULD I CARE ABOUT PRODUCTIVITY AND INNOVATION?

Q3-2   WHAT IS BUSINESS TECHNOLOGY MANAGEMENT (BTM), AND HOW IS IT RELATED TO PRODUCTIVITY AND INNOVATION?

Q3-3   HOW DO INFORMATION SYSTEMS IMPROVE PRODUCTIVITY?

Q3-4   HOW ARE ORGANIZATIONAL STRATEGY AND INDUSTRY STRUCTURE RELATED?

Q3-5   WHAT IS THE RELATIONSHIP BETWEEN INNOVATION AND INFORMATION TECHNOLOGY?

Q3-6   HOW DO INFORMATION SYSTEMS PROVIDE COMPETITIVE ADVANTAGE?

Q3-7   CAN COMPETITIVE ADVANTAGE THROUGH INFORMATION SYSTEMS BE SUSTAINED?

MIS in Action

"Hey Cam, let's get some lunch. I need to hear more about the new LiDAR imaging we're going to start offering," says a well-dressed Alexis as she pops into the development lab where Cam is closely watching an employee testing a large quadcopter.

"Yeah, sure, I could use the break."

"What's that? Are you testing a new quad?"

"Um, well… yes. Mateo wanted to see if we could 3D-print our own drones. We're testing a new prototype we just finished building. It might be a lot cheaper than buying them. But I've never *built* a drone before."

"Wow. So, we've decided to get into the drone-making business?"

Cam motions to Alexis to move out into the hall so they can talk privately.

"Honestly, I hope not. But we'll see how this turns out. We're still trying to figure out if it will save us enough money to make it worth our while."

"Well, better you than me. They've got the right woman for the job!" Alexis smiles and tries to keep the conversation light.

 KE   Chapter 3 optional knowledge extension is
Knowledge Extension 4 Introduction to Microsoft Excel, page 75

"Yeah, well, this project is the least of my worries." Cam rolls her eyes and looks sincerely frustrated.

"What do you mean?"

"Who are we?"

"What do you mean?" Alexis is a little taken aback.

"Well, as a company, who are we? We've always been known as a company that provides security monitoring and we've got some big contracts. I get that. But... there's a lot of money we could be making in agricultural survey, industrial inspection, real estate videos, and wedding videos. I think we're really missing out."

"Have you talked with Mateo about this?"

"Yes, he agreed that these are all good ideas, but he wants to stay focused on big security contracts. He's even talking about contracting with law enforcement agencies, search and rescue, and the federal government."

"And . . . what's the downside?" Alexis asks. "It sounds like if I could close a few big sales we'd be sittin' pretty. From the sales side I'd be doing less work for more money."

"Yeah, but that's a big 'if.' What if we can't sign them? What if the funding dries up? What if the public doesn't like the idea of the Canadian government using drones to video its citizens?"

"I don't know. If the money's as good as Mateo thinks it is, it might be worth a shot."

"Yes, but we could be spending our time and money developing accounts that we already know are profitable and will be for a long time. People are always getting married. It just seems like a no-brainer to think of Falcon Security as more than just a 'security' company. There's so much money on the table." Cam is clearly frustrated and shakes her head.

"Cam, I completely agree. The side projects we've done have been profitable. There's no arguing that."

"Well?"

"Well, it comes down to focus. We can't be everything to everybody. Providing long-term security monitoring for a chemical company is very different from doing a weekend wedding photo shoot."

"But what about all the money we could be making right now? If we don't earn it, somebody else will."

Alexis starts to smile and says, "Hey, let's grab Joni on the way out to lunch. She's the one who really needs to hear this. You two can talk strategy while I get some of those tasty fish tacos!"

Q3-1 WHY SHOULD I CARE ABOUT PRODUCTIVITY AND INNOVATION?

Productivity, or, more precisely, labour productivity, is the ratio of the gross domestic product (GDP) of a country divided by the total paid hours worked by people in the country. Productivity is an important issue that we need to think about. The Conference Board of Canada has suggested that labour productivity is the primary indicator of our per capita income[1] and that increasing labour productivity is the best measure of Canada's future growth. Unfortunately, by all measures, Canada has not been doing well in increasing its labour productivity. Labour productivity in Canada measures the value that Canadian workers generate per hour, which, for the latest data available, was about $50 per hour (compared with $67 for the U.S. and $75 for Norway[2]).

It has not always been this way. Historically, Canada had a strong 4 percent average annual labour productivity growth from 1950 to 1975. This was followed by a weaker period of growth with an average of 1.6 percent from 1975 to 2000 and an even weaker period of growth since 2000. In 2012, Canada's relative productivity ranking improved to a ranking of fifth among a grouping of its 16 peers. However, since the mid 1980's Canada's productivity compared to the United States has declined from a high of 91% to 80%.[3]

Increasing productivity is not necessarily about working harder or spending more hours working. The fact is that even if Canadian employees worked more intensely, Canada would still not have addressed its productivity issues. Increasing productivity in our current global economy is all about working smarter. What will determine a country's level of productivity in the future is its ability to innovate and adapt to changing economic conditions.[4]

Canada has been trying to increase its productivity and innovative capacity for many years. Most experts agree that to enhance productivity, Canada must foster a culture of innovation, open its industries to more competition, and increase the amount of machinery and equipment (M&E) in the economy (particularly in the **Information and Communications Technology (ICT)** sector). Raising the economy's ICT capital intensity means increasing the amount of technology that supports people working. You may find it difficult to argue that computers do not have any impact on the productivity of our economy. But in 1989, that is precisely what economist Stephen Roach reported.[5]

Roach said that his analysis found no evidence of an increase in labour productivity associated with the massive increase in investment in information technology (IT). This result, along with those of other similar studies, led the Nobel Prize-winning economist Robert Solow to make the now-famous statement, "We see computers everywhere except in the productivity statistics." Thus, the **productivity paradox** was born. Although this issue is more than 30 years old, the question of how IT adds to **productivity**—that is, how IT can be used to create **business value**—remains important. Perhaps the most interesting fact about the productivity paradox is that it was never really viewed as a paradox by most organizations. Despite the widespread publicizing of the paradox, organizations continued to pour investment dollars into information technology. The majority of businesses seemed able to justify large investments in IT.

Over time, it has been recognized that measurement error may be a critical reason for the observed lack of productivity increase from IT investments;[6] this measurement difficulty may be more evident due to our increasingly service-based rather than manufacturing or goods-based economy. The mismeasurement is also, in part, due to the often invisible or intangible benefits associated with IT. (For example, suppose you completed your latest essay assignment using only online sources rather than physically visiting your library but still used the same amount of time. Did the use of computer technology make you more productive and by how much did it improve your performance?)

[1] See discussion on "Economy" at www.conferenceboard.ca/hcp/Details/Economy.aspx.

[2] Data accessed May 24, 2014, and quoted from http://en.wikipedia.org/wiki/List_of_countries_by_GDP_%28PPP%29_per_hour_worked.

[3] There are many sources for these data, but an excellent one can be found at http://www.conferenceboard.ca/hcp/details/economy/measuring-productivity-canada.aspx.

[4] See discussion on "Innovation" at www.conferenceboard.ca/hcp/Details/Innovation.aspx.

[5] S. S. Roach, "America's White-Collar Productivity Dilemma," *Manufacturing Engineering* (August 1989): 104.

[6] See E. Brynjolfsson, "The Productivity Paradox of Information Technology: Review and Assessment," *Communications of the ACM* 36, no. 12 (December 1993): 67–77; and J. L. King, "IT Responsible for Most Productivity Gains," *Computing Research News* 15, no. 4 (September 2003): 1–6, http://archive.cra.org/CRN/articles/sept03/king.html.

One response to the productivity paradox is a careful consideration of the value that can be derived from IT investment.[7] Researchers have suggested three different ways in which the value of IT can be realized. The first is through productivity. IT allows a company to create more and/or better output from the same inputs and create them faster than before the technology was in place. For example, if you had a small accounting firm, investing in IT might allow you to add more customers, automate basic tasks (e.g., completing tax forms), and provide more up-to-date information for clients. This investment makes the firm more efficient and potentially more effective.

The second way to realize the investment value of IT is through the structure of competition. IT can alter the way corporations compete. For example, if one accounting firm invests in IT, then rival firms will often follow suit to stay current. The competitive structure changes because of IT to include the software accounting firms offer and the technical support they can provide. Another example is in the video rental industry. When IT enabled people to stream and watch movies at home (usually through Netflix), it eliminated the need to patronize the local video rental store. It also put an end to desired movies being unavailable, late fees, damaged merchandise, and other hardcopy related customer grievances. The industry changed irrevocably because technological advancement altered the structure of competition.

The final way that IT investment value is realized through benefits to the end customer. IT helps make processes more efficient and changes the nature of competition. With increased competition, the reduction of costs associated with new processes is often passed on to the final consumer. The consumer may, therefore, see cheaper and better goods and services as a result of IT. For example, Netflix can offer predictive analytics to recommend additional movies based upon your viewing history (to say nothing of the convenience of streaming). Thus, the consumer, rather than the provider, often reaps the benefits of higher investment in IT.

Some controversy remains with regard to how productive IT investments are. In today's world, although it is important to "keep up" so that you are not at a competitive disadvantage (for example, if you are the only student in this class that does not have a computer or access to this textbook), organizations cannot afford to invest in IT simply because "everybody else is doing it" and hope for the best. We call that strategy "technology for technology's sake," and it simply does not work. Successful organizations need to understand specifically what business value, what they are seeking, and how IT can help secure that value. Doing this consistently and successfully requires knowledge of both IT and business. It is for this reason that organizations value people who are able to understand both technology and business, leading to our next topic: Business Technology Management.

Q3-2 WHAT IS BUSINESS TECHNOLOGY MANAGEMENT (BTM), AND HOW IS IT RELATED TO PRODUCTIVITY AND INNOVATION?

One of the responses to the challenge of low productivity has been to look more closely at the ICT industry sector in Canada. The ICT industry sector is considered an important industry for productivity and **innovation** because it includes technologies that can enhance individual and organizational productivity across many industries. It has sometimes been referred to as the "invisible" industry sector because it does not produce as much direct output as other industries, such as forestry, mining, or auto manufacturing. Instead, the ICT industry sector indirectly supports activities in other industries with tools that make these industries more productive. Canadian policymakers, therefore, look to the ICT industry as

---

[7] L. Hitt and E. Brynjolfsson, "Productivity, Profit and Consumer Welfare: Three Different Measures of Information Technology's Value," *MIS Quarterly* 20, no. 2 (June 1996): 121–42.

a primary driver of innovation and increased productivity among all Canadian industries. In Canada, the ICT sector accounts for 3.3% of national employment or 548 850 jobs and employment in ICT increased at a rate of 4.2% in 2015, far greater than the rate of growth in the overall economy (0.8%).

The focus on innovation in ICT has influenced the set of skills that workers in this industry are expected to have to be successful. In previous decades, success in the ICT industry was often directly related to a person's level of technical skill. The more highly technical the skills, the higher the salary, and the better the prospects in the job market. In the past 10 years, the types of skills demanded in the ICT industry have broadened. Businesses are increasingly looking for people who can drive technological innovation within their organizations. These new skills combine both technology and more traditional business skills.[8]

The 2017 Canadian federal budget noted that the economy is in a state of tremendous change and that Canada's agenda was to be a world-leading centre for innovation. Although the specifics of this are still to be worked out the future path seems clear. Jobs that combine business and technology will be in high demand in the future.

This requirement has increased the need for educational programs that incorporate technology and business training. In 2009, a working group designed a set of learning outcomes for a new program named **Business Technology Management (BTM)**. These learning outcomes drew on skills frameworks, such as the **Skills Framework for the Information Age (SFIA)** and developed CareerMash (www.careermash.ca) to provide more specific information on jobs within the ICT industry. Many people are surprised to learn that the ICT sector has a wide variety of jobs and that not all jobs are highly technical in nature.

Now that these learning outcomes have been defined, universities across Canada are developing programs for BTM. They include a variety of course topics, such as business and technical training, financial accounting, system analysis and design, project management, IT infrastructure, marketing, international business management, writing and business communication, organizational behaviour, and teamwork skills. BTM programs are designed for students who are inspired to use technology to innovate and improve productivity.[9]

Q3-3 HOW DO INFORMATION SYSTEMS IMPROVE PRODUCTIVITY?

We saw in Chapter 2 that companies organize work through business processes. Business processes use resources, facilities, and information to accomplish activities. Business processes are, therefore, an important consideration in productivity. Productivity for organizations can be increased either through increased efficiency or more effective business processes.

Increasing **efficiency** means that business processes can be accomplished either more quickly or with fewer resources and facilities (or both). Efficiency is usually relatively easy to measure once you have decided which contributors are important. When organizations focus on efficiency, they are working toward "doing things right." Doing things right often means using just the right amount of resources, facilities, and information to complete the job satisfactorily.

When companies focus on increasing **effectiveness** rather than efficiency, they are interested in "doing the right things." Increased effectiveness means that the company considers offering either new or improved goods or services that the customer values. Doing the right things often requires companies to consider changing their business processes to deliver something new and improved.

Sometimes, "doing the right things" and "doing things right" can be in conflict. For example, an organization specializing in movie rentals could be so focused on increasing

[8] A discussion of these skills can be found in a report titled "Jobs 2.0: How Canada Can Win in the 21st Century Global Marketplace for Information and Communications Technologies and Services (ICTS)," http://ccict.ca/reports/jobs-2-0.
[9] For more information please visit https://www.btm-forum.org/

efficiency that it misses the fact that the market has changed and no longer values the service being offered. The organization might be doing things right, but it is not doing the right things.

In another example, a different organization (perhaps one that delivers online videos) may have a service that customers really value, but the organization is so focused on adjusting the service parameters to perfectly suit its customers that it does not spend enough time thinking about how efficient its processes are. This organization might be doing the right things, but it is not doing things right. It operates relatively inefficiently and would be at a cost disadvantage relative to other organizations that are more efficient.

There are often situations where it may be unclear which is more important "doing things right" or "doing the right things." Peter Drucker, a famous management theorist (he is credited with introducing, in 1957, the term "knowledge worker") said that "It is fundamentally the confusion between effectiveness and efficiency that stands between doing the right things and doing things right. There is surely nothing quite so useless as doing with great efficiency what should not be done at all." For most organizations operating in a global capitalistic environment, success requires that organizations do both.

Business Processes and Value Chains

Business processes are closely related to the concept of a value chain. A **value chain** is a network of activities that improve the effectiveness (or value) of a good or service. A value chain is, therefore, made up of at least one and often many business processes.

Let us look at a specific example. A customer in Canada does not see much value in a large blob of natural rubber harvested at a rubber farm in Vietnam. What would you pay for something like this? Likely not much. But when a tire manufacturing company ships that blob of rubber to a factory, has engineers design a high-performance, all-season radial tire, and then sends the blob of rubber through the various processes required to make the tire, the blob of rubber has gained some value. How much would you pay for the rubber now? Even more value is gained when the tire is shipped to a tire store close to the customer, and more still is created when a mechanic at the store installs the tire. Each of these steps in the chain—each of these business processes—adds some value, as shown in Figure 3-1. This is why we refer to this chain of events as a value chain.

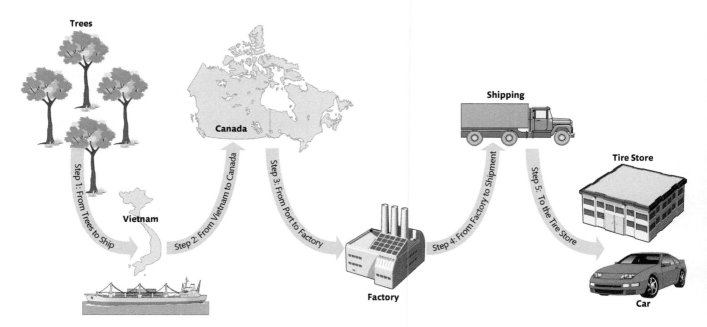

Figure 3-1   Business Process

Value chains have directions—upstream and downstream. Organizations that expand into activities related to the basic raw materials of a process—such as a tire company that decides to manufacture its own rubber or a coffee store that decides to grow its own coffee—are said to be undertaking backward integration or to be moving upstream in the value chain. Those that move closer to end customers—for example, a mining company that begins to cut and finish its own diamonds rather than sell raw stones wholesale—would be undertaking forward integration, or moving downstream in the value chain.

In general, the more value a company adds to a good or service in its value chain, the higher the price the company can charge for the final product. The difference between the price the customer is willing to pay and the cost the company incurs in moving the good (or service) through the value chain is defined as the **margin**. Raw diamonds, for example, are sold at a much lower margin than finished diamonds. The greater the margin, the higher the profit (per unit) the company receives.

The concept of a value chain was formalized by Michael Porter, a professor at Harvard University. He identified two types of activities that support value chains. **Primary activities** are activities in which value is added directly to the product. In our example above, shipping raw materials, designing the tires, manufacturing the tires, shipping the finished tires, and installing the tires are all primary activities. Each of these primary activities adds value for the customer.

But there is a whole range of activities in companies that do not add value directly to the product. For instance, who pays the workers in the factory? Who bought the machines at the factory that makes the tires? Who maintains the machines inside the factory and keeps the lights on and the heat working? Who schedules the shipping of the finished tires? Who keeps track of the mechanics' hours? These activities, and many more, are referred to as **support activities**, because they support the primary activities.

Support activities add value only indirectly. For example, nobody buys a tire because a company has a great payroll system. But a company could not run a factory without the ability to pay its workers. The benefit of the payroll system may not directly add to the value as seen by the customer, but these support activities are critical to the success of the organization. Figure 3-2 summarizes the concepts we have just discussed. The questions accompanying the "Winterbourne Bicycle Institute" in "MIS in Use" at the end of this chapter can be used to further explore the concept and ideas of the value chain.

Primary Activity	Description
Inbound logistics	Receiving and storing inventory
Operations	Using inputs to create or generate the final product
Outbound logistics	Retrieving and distributing the product or service to the customers
Marketing and sales	Convincing the customer and enabling purchase of the good or service
Service	Supporting the customers use of the product or service

Figure 3-2 Task Descriptions for Primary Activities of the Value Chain

Source: M. E. Porter, Competitive Advantage: Creating and Sustaining Superior Performance (Simon & Schuster, Inc., 1985)

Understanding the concept of the value chain helps us understand how information systems can increase productivity. One way is by enabling the development of more efficient or more effective supporting activities. These systems include such applications as financial accounting systems, human resources systems, production systems, and customer relationship management systems. Increasing the efficiency and effectiveness of these support systems increases the profit margin enjoyed by the company.

Information systems also increase productivity by offering new and improved services, primarily activities that would not be available without IT. These might include customer shopping through the Web, 24-hour customer support through online discussion boards and frequently asked questions, online package tracking for the courier business, and online airline ticket and hotel reservations. Providing these new or improved services adds value for the customer and can contribute to the company's margin and its ability to compete.

Q3-4 HOW ARE ORGANIZATIONAL STRATEGY AND INDUSTRY STRUCTURE RELATED?

An organization's strategy reflects its goals and objectives. A company's strategy is influenced by the competitive structure of the company's industry. Generally speaking, a company's information systems strategy should support, or be aligned with, the overall company strategy. In the real world, it is possible for the organizational strategy and information systems strategy to be somewhat out of alignment. We will address this alignment in Chapter 7.

Organizational strategy begins with an assessment of the fundamental characteristics and structure of an industry. One model commonly used to assess an industry structure is Porter's **five forces model**.[10] According to this model, five competitive forces determine industry profitability: (1) bargaining power of customers, (2) threat of substitutions, (3) bargaining power of suppliers, (4) threat of new entrants, and (5) rivalry among existing firms. The intensity of each of the five forces determines the characteristics of the industry, how profitable the industry is, and how sustainable profitability will be.

To understand this model, consider a particular industry—the soft drink industry. Let us look at each of the forces, beginning with the bargaining power of the customers. Customers can switch pretty easily between competing soft drinks. So, the companies within the industry have to be ready to please customers because their tastes and desires are important forces. The threat of customers turning to substitutes, such as water (bottled or not), juice, or caffeine-laden energy drinks is ever present, so the soft drink companies must constantly respond to it, partly by expanding their product offerings to include these other choices.

Companies within this industry also have significant amounts of power over their suppliers because a contract with Coca-Cola or PepsiCo can often be very lucrative. Thus, soft drink companies get highly competitive prices for their ingredients. New entrants to the soft drink industry have a hard time because they are unable to obtain the same kinds of terms from their suppliers, so their costs are higher, placing them at a disadvantage. As well, the large firms that dominate the industry have made huge investments in the distribution network, so a new small firm will have a hard time gaining access to the stores and restaurants that sell established brands. This is a real uphill battle—many companies that want to compete choose not to because of these challenges. Finally, competition within the industry can be very intense—you may recall the Pepsi Challenge (a direct taste test). What is interesting is that the firms very rarely compete on price. Instead, they spend massive amounts of money on marketing their brand.

So, what does all of this mean? To make a profit in the soft drink industry, it helps if you are a large company that has access to the lowest-priced ingredients, an established network of distributors, and expertise in brand development and responding to changing consumer desires. The nature of the competitive forces in the soft drink industry suggests a certain competitive structure. Other industries will have different structures because competitive forces are different in each industry.

---

[10] M. Porter, *Competitive Strategy: Techniques for Analyzing Industries and Competitors* (New York: Free Press, 1980).

Winterbourne Bicycle Institute (www.winterbornebikes.com) was founded in 2001 in picturesque Guelph, Ontario by Jason Filer (see photo on the Right side). Winterbourne is a small company whose typical customer is a cycling enthusiast—a serious rider who knows a considerable amount about bicycles and is ready to move up to a high-quality, custom-designed, hand-built bicycle.

The main parts of a custom bike are the frame and wheels, and the company offers a number of choices for each type, style, and price range. Extensive bike-fitting sessions are part of the design process. The customer can also specify the paint finish and component set that completes the bike build.

In conjunction with a local college, Winterborne has also begun to offer intensive bicycle-maintenance and training courses so that customers and current and aspiring bicycle mechanics can gain practical knowledge and experience with regard to all major bicycle components, including frames, bearings, wheels, drive trains, brakes, and shifting systems, on a variety of bicycle styles and vintages.

Many customers come to the shop looking to purchase a custom bike or wheels or to upgrade pieces for their current bike, such as forks, suspension, handlebars, pedals, gearing, shifting, brakes, saddles, and seatposts. The company offers a number of brands in a wide range of styles and sizes.

Filer and his business partner, retired information systems executive Alan Medcalf, both consider Winterborne more of a vocation than a business, and they help customers make the best possible choices for their cycling wants and needs. Both Filer and Medcalf are well-trained technicians, who set up each bike and offer such services as customization and bike repairs. Customers also rely on them for recommendations on a wide range of biking

Image Source/Alamy Stock Photo

accessories, such as helmets, riding gear, lighting, gloves, and shoes.

The company's website provides customers with information about products and promotes events, such as weekend maintenance clinics, the advanced maintenance course, group rides and clubs, trail-maintenance days, and educational seminars.

QUESTIONS

1. Identify the value chain involved in obtaining a new bicycle from Winterborne Bicycle Institute. Can you identify the primary activities that create value for the customer when purchasing a new bike?

2. What information systems do you think could be used to support these primary activities?

3. Check out the company's website (www.winterbornebikes.com). Does the site fill the role of a primary activity, or is it more appropriately considered a support activity? Justify your answer.

To be successful, organizations examine the five forces mentioned above and determine how they intend to respond to them. An organization responds to the structure of its industry by choosing a **competitive strategy**. Porter followed his five forces model with a model of four competitive strategies, as shown in Figure 3-3.[11] According to Porter, a firm can engage in any one of these four fundamental competitive strategies. An organization can focus on being the cost leader, or it can focus on differentiating its products from those of the competition. Further, the organization can employ the cost or differentiation strategy across an industry, or it can focus its strategy on a particular industry segment.

Consider the car rental industry, for example. According to the first column of Figure 3-3, a car rental company can strive to provide the lowest-cost car rentals across the industry, or it can seek to provide the lowest-cost car rentals to an industry segment—say, domestic business travellers.

[11] M. Porter, *Competitive Strategy* (New York: Free Press, 1985).

	Cost	**Differentiation**
Industry-wide	Lowest cost across the industry	Better product/service across the industry
Focus	Lowest cost within an industry segment	Better product/service within an industry segment

Figure 3-3 Porter's Four Competitive Strategies

Source: Based on The Free Press, a Division of Simon & Schuster Adult Publishing Group, from Competitive Advantage: Creating and Sustaining Superior Performance by Michael E. Porter. 1985, 1998.

As indicated in the second column, a car rental company can seek to differentiate its products from the competition. It can do so in various ways—for example, by providing a wide range of high-quality cars, by providing the best reservations system, by having the cleanest cars or the fastest check-in, or even by bringing the cars to its customers' homes.

According to Porter, to be effective, the organization's goals, objectives, culture, and activities must be consistent with the organization's strategy. To those in the MIS field, this means that all information systems in the organization must facilitate and be aligned with the organization's competitive strategy. We will discuss the concept of alignment further in Chapter 11.

Q3-5 WHAT IS THE RELATIONSHIP BETWEEN INNOVATION AND INFORMATION TECHNOLOGY?

Changes to industry structure often occur through innovation. Over the last hundred years, technology has enabled much of the innovation we have seen in our economy. This technological innovation is all around us today. One hundred years ago, there was little electrical power. There were few telephones. Automobiles were just beginning to be produced. The world had just witnessed the first powered flight. Radio was still being developed, and television was just a dream. Now we take these innovations for granted and wonder how people ever lived without them.

When considering technological innovation, professors Bower and Christensen[12] described two general types of technological innovations. **Sustaining technologies** are changes in technology that maintain the rate of improvement in customer value. For example, the vulcanization of rubber allowed tire manufacturers to produce tires that facilitated faster and more comfortable rides. This innovation improved the experience of driving a car and helped sustain the original innovation.

In contrast, **disruptive technologies** introduce a very new package of attributes to accepted mainstream products. In the music industry, for example, the advent of the MP3 file format was a disruptive technology because it offered the ability to store and play music through digital devices. In less than a decade, people moved from buying CDs and tapes for their Sony Walkmans to downloading MP3s and listening to music through their Apple iPods and over the next decade perhaps moving to streaming services such as Spotify or Pandora.

IT has been an important part of technological innovations since the 1950s. From the first electronic computer in 1939 to the first personal computer in 1980 and the commercialization of the Internet in the early 1990s, the rate of innovation in IT has been staggering. In some instances, IT acts as a sustaining technology. Improved size and speed

[12] J. Bower and C. Christensen, "Disruptive Technologies: Catching the Wave," *Harvard Business Review* 73, no. 1 (January/February 1995): 43–53.

of electronic memory help us store and retrieve data more quickly. Faster processors help us accomplish more with our computers in less time. Sustaining technologies help make processes more efficient (and often more effective) and thus create value for organizations.

In other cases, IT acts as a disruptive technology. For example, when the Royal Bank of Canada (RBC) first offered a national automated banking machine (ABM) network in Canada in 1980,[13] it presented customers with new choices. The other banks in Canada quickly responded with machines of their own. Similarly, when the Waterloo, Ontario based company Blackberry (at that time called *Research In Motion or RIM*), launched the first BlackBerry in 1999, it provided worldwide customers with new communication options. Wireless companies around the globe had to respond to these new sets of choices. In some cases businesses have built upon and surpassed the original innovation (Apple for example with their iPhone and other banks by introducing the ability to deposit cheques by taking a picture or electronically transfer funds).

Both RBC and RIM gained competitive advantage by employing IT. When a company gains competitive advantage using a disruptive technology, the potential to alter the structure of an industry is created. Competing companies must react to the new conditions or risk losing their profit margins and customers. Both large and small companies within the industry must react to these changes. You can learn more about how small companies react to a disruptive technology by reading Case Study 3, about Amazom.com, at the end of this chapter.

In some cases, the competitive advantage is so large that it leads to a new industry. Such was the case for the microcomputer. Its advent led to the development of the microcomputer industry and the creation of new companies, such as Microsoft, Intel, Apple, Oracle, and Dell. Amazon, eBay, and Google were born out of the commercialization of the Internet. Wireless network technology innovation led to the development of such Canadian companies as RIM (www.rim.com) and Sierra Wireless (www.sierrawireless.com). More recently, innovations in networking services have created new industries in social networking and messaging, such as Facebook, Tumblr, Groupon, Foursquare, and Twitter.

One of the more important considerations when thinking about innovation is how quickly the innovation catches on or diffuses through society. The theory of the **diffusion of innovation** was defined by Everett Rogers as "the process by which an innovation is communicated through certain channels over time among the members of a social system."[14] In his 1964 book, Rogers identified five stages through which the diffusion of an innovation occurs. The stages, or steps in the process, are, as shown in Figure 3-4, (1) knowledge, (2) persuasion,

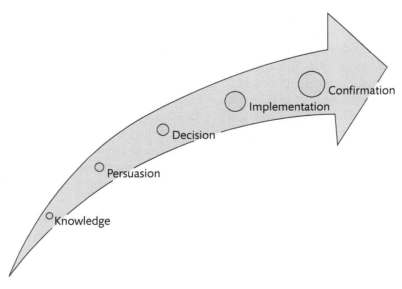

Confirmation

Implementation

Decision

Persuasion

Knowledge

Figure 3-4 Roger's Theory of Diffusion of Innovation

---

[13] See www.rbc.com/history/anytimeanywhere/self_service-detail.html#2.

[14] E. M. Rogers, *Diffusion of Innovations* (Glencoe, IL: Free Press, 1964), p. 79.

(3) decision, (4) implementation, and (5) confirmation. Since many innovations are not adopted, an individual or organization thinking about adoption does not necessarily have to go through all of these steps. It can drop the process at any point.

In Rogers's theory of diffusion of innovation, the *knowledge* stage occurs when you first hear about an innovation but lack specific information about it. For example, you may have heard about a particular phone application such as Slack, but you may not know much about it. The next stage is *persuasion*, when you become interested in the innovation and find out more about it. Once you have collected enough information, you move into the *decision* stage. Here, you consider the pros and cons of adopting the innovation, and make a decision to adopt or reject it. If you decide to pursue the innovation, you have reached the *implementation* stage. In this stage, you use the innovation and figure out whether to continue using it or look for an even better way. If you are happy, then you reach the peaceful state of *confirmation*, where you use the innovation to its full potential.

The theory of diffusion of innovation provides us with a way of thinking about the process of adoption of new technology. In Chapter 11, we will return to the concept of diffusion of innovation when we discuss why organizations invest in IT and what characteristics of the innovation are important to decision makers.

Q3-6 HOW DO INFORMATION SYSTEMS PROVIDE COMPETITIVE ADVANTAGE?

If you take a business strategy class, you will study the Porter models in greater detail than we have discussed here. When you do so, you will learn numerous ways that organizations respond to the five competitive forces. For our purposes, we can summarize those ways in the list of principles shown in Figure 3-5. Keep in mind that we are applying these principles in the context of an organization's competitive strategy. (You can also apply these principles to a personal competitive advantage, as discussed in the exercise "The Digital Divide" at the end of this chapter on pages 73–74.)

Some of these competitive strategies are created via products and services, and others are enabled via the development of business processes. Each of these strategies is considered below.

Competitive Advantage via Products and Services

The first three principles in Figure 3-5 relate to products and services. Organizations gain a competitive advantage by creating new products or services, by enhancing existing products or services, and by differentiating their products and services from those of their competitors. As you think about these three principles, realize that an information system can be part of a product or service or it can provide support for a product or service. The MIS in Use box on page 60 discusses how a company that builds bikes and offers bike-maintenance courses uses the Internet to provide additional services to its customers. The company's use of the Internet adds value to customer interactions with the company.

Consider a car sharing service such as evo or Car2Go. An information system keeps track of where cars are and provides the particulars to customers who may wish to rent them. The location and type of car is part of the car rental package and, thus, is part of the product itself. In contrast, an information system that schedules car maintenance is not part of the product but, instead, supports the product. Either way, information systems can achieve the first three principles listed in Figure 3-5.

The remaining five principles listed in Figure 3-5 are about competitive advantage created by the implementation of business processes.

Product Implementations
1. Create a new product or service
2. Enhance products or services
3. Differentiate products or services

System Implementations
4. Lock in customers and buyers
5. Lock in suppliers
6. Raise barriers to market entry
7. Establish alliances
8. Reduce costs

Figure 3-5 Principles of Competitive Advantage

Competitive Advantage via Business Processes

Organizations can retain customers by making it difficult or expensive for them to switch to another product. This business strategy is sometimes referred to as adding **switching costs**. Organizations can also lock in suppliers by making it difficult for them to switch to another organization or, in a positive sense, by making it easy for them to connect to and work with the organization. Finally, competitive advantage can be gained by creating entry barriers that make it difficult and expensive for new competition to enter the market.

Another way to gain competitive advantage is to establish alliances with other organizations. Such alliances create standards, promote product awareness and needs, develop market size, reduce purchasing costs, and provide other benefits. Finally, organizations can gain competitive advantage by reducing costs. Such reductions enable the organization to decrease prices and/or increase profitability. Increased profitability means not just greater shareholder value but also more cash, which can fund further infrastructure development for even greater competitive advantage.

Q3-7 CAN COMPETITIVE ADVANTAGE THROUGH INFORMATION SYSTEMS BE SUSTAINED?

We have noted that IT can provide a competitive advantage for companies. But can these advantages be sustained? After all competitors often react to innovations by replicating the technology and as we have seen there are many examples of new or existing companies such Apple overtaking incumbent leaders such as Blackberry. Since the effects of IT can often be readily seen, it may be hard to hide the innovation. Technology and software can be purchased or developed. It is, therefore, almost impossible to keep competitors from developing competing technology.

The credit unions that adopted the first bank machines were quickly copied by competitors. Although patents can provide some initial protection for technologies (such as the BlackBerry), patents are difficult and expensive to enforce, and they are not permanent. Does this mean that all IT innovations are doomed to offer only temporary advantage?

In his *Harvard Business Review* article "IT Doesn't Matter,"[15] Nicholas Carr suggested that the evolution of IT in business follows a pattern similar to earlier disruptive technologies, such as railway and electricity. As disruptive technologies are being developed, they open opportunities for companies to gain strong competitive advantages. But as the availability of the technologies increases and their cost decreases, these technologies become more like commodities. From a strategic standpoint, the technologies become invisible and no longer provide advantages. In other words, the more ubiquitous (i.e., existing everywhere) IT becomes, the less competitive advantage IT provides.

We have noted above that this is true to a certain degree. But it is important to understand clearly what we are talking about. If we are considering IT (hardware, software, and networks), then what Carr has said is largely true. Hardware and software have become readily accessible to almost all companies and, although not entirely a commodity, they have largely become commoditized. These investments are not a source of long-term competitive advantage.

However, if we consider information systems (which also include procedures and people along with hardware and software), then what Carr has stated is less convincing. The same IT installed in different organizations might result in very different outcomes. The machines and the software may be commodities, but organizational procedures and the people in the organizations are not standardized. Some companies (and some people)

---

[15] N. Car, "IT Doesn't Matter," *Harvard Business Review* 81, no. 5 (May 2003): 41–49.

might be able to quickly adapt to new technology. Other companies (or people) may be less willing or able to do so.

It is important to recognize that long-term competitive advantage lies not with the technology but rather in how a company and its people adopt the technology. The most important thing you can learn from this chapter is that when it comes to IT, people make all the difference. So, while the IT itself may not provide a sustainable competitive advantage, the effective integration of people, procedures, and technology can certainly provide an organization with the potential for long-term advantages.

So, what is **sustained competitive advantage**? It requires companies to find a distinctive way to compete. This way of competing will change over time. The emphasis should be placed on developing increasingly sophisticated integration of IT and the people and procedures in the organization. Companies with sustainable competitive advantage work to integrate many activities: marketing, customer service, product design, and product delivery. When a company successfully integrates many technology systems with its people and procedures, competitors have to match the whole system. Although competitors might be able to purchase the technology component, it takes time for their people to gain the necessary experience and skill to really make the technology work for those organizations. Matching the entire set of information systems can be a steep hill to climb for companies that have less experience and success in integrating people and technology. So, sustained competitive advantage comes from developing people and procedures that are well supported by the underlying technology.

So What? | Your Personal Competitive Advantage

Consider the following possibility: After working hard to earn your degree in business, you graduate, only to discover that you cannot find a job in your area of study. You look for 6 weeks or so, but then you run out of money. In desperation, you take a job waiting tables at a local restaurant. Two years go by, the economy picks up, and the jobs you had been looking for become available. Unfortunately, your degree is now 2 years old; you are competing with students who have just graduated with recent degrees (and fresh knowledge). Two years of waiting tables, good as you are at it, does not appear to be appropriate experience for the job you want. You're stuck in a nightmare that will be hard to get out of—and one that you cannot allow to happen.

Examine Figure 3-5 again, but this time consider those elements of competitive advantage as they apply to you personally. As an employee, the skills and abilities you offer are your personal product. Examine the first three items in the list and ask yourself, "How can I use my time in school—and in this MIS class, in particular—to create new skills, to enhance those I already have, and to differentiate my skills from the competition?" (By the way, you will enter a national/international market. Your competition is not just the students in your class; it is also students in classes in Ohio, California, British Columbia, Singapore, Sydney, and everywhere else they are teaching MIS today.)

Suppose you are interested in a sales job. Perhaps you want to be involved in the pharmaceutical industry. What skills can you learn from your MIS class that will make you more competitive as a future salesperson? Ask yourself, "How does the pharmaceutical industry use MIS to gain competitive advantage?" Use the Internet to find examples of the use of information systems in the pharmaceutical industry. How does Pfizer, for example, use a customer information system to sell to doctors? How can your knowledge of such systems differentiate you from your competition for a job there? How does Pfizer use a knowledge management system? How does the firm keep track of drugs that have an adverse effect on each other?

The fourth and fifth items in Figure 3-5 concern locking in customers, buyers, and suppliers. How can you interpret those elements in terms of your personal competitive advantage? Well, to lock in a relationship, you first need to have one. So do you have an internship? If not, can you get one? And once you have an internship, how can you use your knowledge of MIS to lock in your job so that you get a job offer? Does the company you are interning for have an information system for managing customers (or any other information system that is important to the company)? If users are happy with the system, what characteristics make it worthwhile? Can you lock in a job by becoming an expert user of this system? Becoming an expert user not only locks you into your job, but it also

Continued ➔

→ Continued

raises barriers to entry for others who might be competing for the job. Also, can you suggest ways to improve the system, thus using your knowledge of the company and the system to lock in an extension of your job?

Human resources personnel say that networking is one of the most effective ways of finding a job. How can you use this class to establish alliances with other students? Does your class have a website? Is there an email list server for the students in your class? How about a Facebook group? How can you use these to develop job-seeking alliances with other students? Who in your class already has a job or an internship? Can any of those people provide hints or opportunities for finding a job?

Do not restrict your job search to your local area. Are there regions of your country where jobs are more plentiful? How can you find out about student organizations in those regions? Search the Web for MIS classes in other cities, and make contact with students there. Find out what the hot opportunities are in other cities.

Finally, as you study MIS, think about how the knowledge you gain can help you save costs for your employers. Even more, see if you can build a case that an employer would actually save money by hiring you. The line of reasoning might be that because of your knowledge of IS, you will be able to facilitate cost savings that more than compensate for your salary.

In truth, few of the ideas that you generate for a potential employer will be feasible or pragmatically useful. The fact that you are thinking creatively, however, will indicate to a potential employer that you have initiative and are grappling with the problems that real businesses face. As this course progresses, keep thinking about competitive advantage, and strive to understand how the topics you study can help you to accomplish, personally, one or more of the principles in Figure 3-5.

QUESTIONS

1. **Summarize the efforts you have taken thus far to build an employment record that will lead to job offers after graduation.**

2. **Considering the first three principles in Figure 3-5, describe one way in which you have a competitive advantage over your classmates. If you do not have such a competitive advantage, describe actions you can take to obtain one.**

3. **In order to build your network, you can use your status as a student to approach business professionals. Namely, you can contact them for help with an assignment or for career guidance. For example, suppose you want to work in banking and you know that your local bank has a customer information system. You could call the manager of that bank and ask him or her how that system creates a competitive advantage for the bank. You also could ask to interview other employees and go armed with the list in Figure 3-5. Describe two specific ways in which you can use your status as a student and the list in Figure 3-5 to build your network in this way.**

4. **Describe two ways that you can use student alliances to obtain a job. How can you use information systems to build, maintain, and operate such alliances?**

How Does the Knowledge in This Chapter Help You?

You now know the relationship between productivity and innovation and how these affect competition and strategies. This chapter's opening vignette illustrates how Falcon's dependence on a few large accounts puts them at risk and how Cam's suggestion to diversify the markets they serve and the types of work they do might be a good strategic response to reduce risk while increasing revenue. You may have recently heard about how drones have been used by a search and rescue team to locate swimmers in difficulty and drop lifesaving equipment.[16] This is not only faster and therefore more likely to save lives than the traditional lifeguard swimming, it is also safer, since it does not put the lifeguard at risk. Being aware of the changes in an organization's technological environment and identifying ways to apply innovation and reduce costs and risks are very important for companies in today's markets.

---

[16] D Etherington, "Drone comes to the rescue of two swimmers in Australia," *Tech Crunch*, January 18, 2018. https://techcrunch.com/2018/01/18/drone-comes-to-the-rescue-of-two-swimmers-in-australia/

Use this Active Review to verify that you have understood the material in the chapter. You can read the entire chapter and then perform the tasks in this review, or you can read the material for just one question and perform the tasks for that question before moving on to the next one.

Q3-1 WHY SHOULD I CARE ABOUT PRODUCTIVITY AND INNOVATION?

What is labour productivity? How does Canada compare globally with regard to labour productivity and innovation? Explain what is meant by the productivity paradox. Can you explain how using a computer makes you more productive than using a typewriter? List three ways in which information systems can create value.

Q3-2 WHAT IS BUSINESS TECHNOLOGY MANAGEMENT (BTM), AND HOW IS IT RELATED TO PRODUCTIVITY AND INNOVATION?

Why is the ICT industry important to innovation in Canada? How are ICT skills changing? Is BTM a worthwhile certification and will it add to your own personal competitive advantage?

Q3-3 HOW DO INFORMATION SYSTEMS IMPROVE PRODUCTIVITY?

Explain the relationship between business processes and value chains. What are the differences between primary and support activities? How does IT affect value chains?

Q3-4 HOW ARE ORGANIZATIONAL STRATEGY AND INDUSTRY STRUCTURE RELATED?

Briefly describe Porter's five forces model. Can you analyze an industry based on the strengths of the different forces? What are the four main types of competitive strategy identified by Porter?

Q3-5 WHAT IS THE RELATIONSHIP BETWEEN INNOVATION AND INFORMATION TECHNOLOGY?

Explain the differences between sustaining and disruptive technologies. Provide examples in which IT is a sustaining technology and those in which IT is a disruptive technology. What is meant by diffusion of innovation? Describe the steps in the process of diffusion of innovation.

Q3-6 HOW DO INFORMATION SYSTEMS PROVIDE COMPETITIVE ADVANTAGE?

List and briefly describe eight principles of competitive advantage. Consider the bookstore at your school. List one application of IT that takes advantage of each of these principles for the bookstore.

Q3-7 CAN COMPETITIVE ADVANTAGE THROUGH INFORMATION SYSTEMS BE SUSTAINED?

Describe what is meant by sustained competitive advantage. Explain why IT does not generally provide sustained competitive advantage. Explain why information systems can provide sustained competitive advantage.

MyLab MIS

MyLab MIS is an online learning and testing environment that features the perfect study tools to help you master the concepts covered in this chapter. Log in to MyLab to test your knowledge of key chapter concepts and explore additional practice tools, including videos, flashcards, and more!

KEY TERMS AND CONCEPTS

Business Technology
    Management
    (BTM) 56
Business value 54
Competitive strategy 60
Diffusion of innovation 62
Disruptive technologies 61

Effectiveness 56
Efficiency 56
Five forces model 59
Information and
    Communications
    Technology (ICT) 54
Innovation 55

Margin 58
Primary activities 58
Productivity 54
Productivity paradox 54
Skills Framework for the
    Information Age
    (SFIA) 56

Support activities 58
Sustained competitive
    advantage 65
Sustaining technologies 61
Switching costs 64
Value chain 57

USING YOUR KNOWLEDGE

3-1. Apply the value chain model to a video game developer, such as Electronic Arts (www.EA.com). What is its competitive strategy? Describe the tasks Electronic Arts must accomplish for each of the primary value chain activities. How does EA's competitive strategy and the nature of its business influence the general characteristics of EA's information systems?

3-2. Apply the value chain model to a video game retail company, such as EB Games (www.EBGames.com). What is its competitive strategy? Describe the tasks EB Games must accomplish for each of the primary value chain activities. How does EB Games' competitive strategy and the nature of its business influence the general characteristics of its information systems?

3-3. Suppose you decide to start a business that recruits students for summer jobs. You will match available students with available jobs. You need to learn what jobs are available and who is available to fill those positions. In starting your business, you know you will be competing with local newspapers, craigslist (www.craigslist.org), and your college or university. You will probably have other local competitors as well.

a. Analyze the structure of this industry according to Porter's five forces model.

b. Given your analysis in (a), recommend a competitive strategy.

c. Describe the primary value chain activities as they apply to this business.

d. Describe a business process for recruiting students.

e. Describe information systems that could be used to support the business process in (d).

f. Explain how the process you describe in (d) and the system you describe in (e) reflect your competitive strategy.

3-4. Samantha Green owns and operates Twigs Tree Trimming Service. Samantha graduated from the forestry program of a nearby university and worked for a large landscape design firm, doing tree trimming and removal. After several years at the company, she bought a truck, a stump grinder, and other equipment and opened her own business in Winnipeg.

Although many of her contracts are one-time operations (e.g., removing a tree or a stump), others are recurring ones (e.g., trimming a tree or group of trees every year or every other year). When business is slow, she calls former clients to remind them of her services and of the need to trim their trees on a regular basis.

Samantha has never heard of Michael Porter or his theories. She operates her business using intuition.

a. Explain how an analysis of the five competitive forces could help Samantha.

b. Do you think Samantha has a competitive strategy? What competitive strategy would seem to make sense for her?

c. How would knowledge of her competitive strategy help her sales and marketing efforts?

d. Describe, in general terms, the kind of information system Samantha needs to support sales and marketing efforts.

3-5. FiredUp Inc. is a small business owned by Curt and Julie Robards. Based in Brisbane, Australia, FiredUp manufactures and sells a lightweight camping stove called *FiredNow*. Curt, who previously worked as an aerospace engineer, invented and patented a burning nozzle that enables the stove to stay lit in very high winds—up to 140 kilometres per hour. Julie, an industrial designer by training, developed an elegant folding design that is small, lightweight, easy to set up, and very stable. Curt and Julie manufacture the stove in their garage, and they sell it directly to their customers over the Internet and on the phone.

a. Explain how an analysis of the five competitive forces could help FiredUp.

b. What does FiredUp's competitive strategy seem to be?

c. Briefly summarize how the primary value chain activities pertain to FiredUp. How should the company design these value chains to conform to its competitive strategy?

d. Describe business processes that FiredUp needs to implement its marketing and sales and also its service value chain activities.

e. Describe, in general terms, information systems to support your answer to question (d).

COLLABORATIVE EXERCISES

The High-Value Bike Rental Company rents bikes to business executives at conference resorts. A well-dressed rental agent greets each potential customer and has a discussion to determine his or her biking needs. When the customer is ready to rent a bike, the agent enters his or her information into the customer database and checks to see if a bike is available in the bike inventory database. When the customer returns the bike, he or she pays for the rental by providing the hotel room number. The bike is then cleaned and put back into the bike inventory database. This triggers an update to the database, which then bills the customer for the rental. A charge is sent from the database to the hotel billing system. Figure 3-6 shows the rental process and related information systems for the High-Value Bike Rental Company. Using this information, collaborate with your team to answer the following questions:

3-1. Explain the relationship of value and cost according to Porter's value chain model. When does it make sense to add cost to a business process?

3-2. Suppose you are told that the business process in Figure 3-6 has a negative margin. Explain what that means. Suppose the margin of some business process is negative $1 million. If costs are reduced by $1.2 million, will the margin necessarily be positive? Explain why or why not.

3-3. Consider alternatives for replacing the rental agent from the business process in Figure 3-6.

a. Describe changes that will need to be made to the process documented in Figure 3-6.

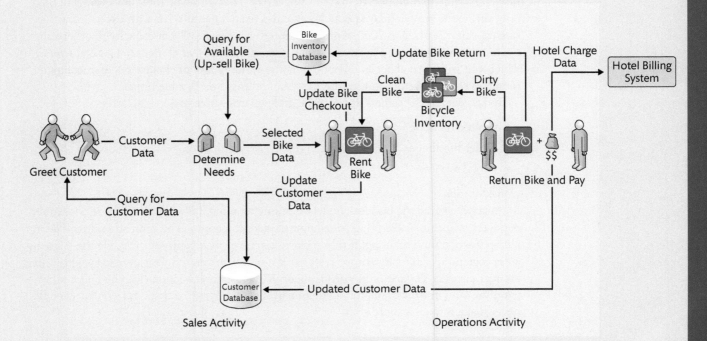

Figure 3-6 Rental Process for High-Value Bike Rental

    b. Would eliminating the rental agent change the competitive strategy of this company? Is it possible to be a high-value company with no rental personnel? Explain why or why not.

    c. Would eliminating the rental agent necessarily reduce costs? What costs would increase as a result of this change?

3-4. Consider the alternative of increasing the value delivered by the existing rental agent—for example, renting more kinds of equipment or selling items of use to guests who are renting bicycles. Consider other options as well.

    a. Describe four ways that you think the existing personnel could increase the value of this business process.

    b. For the four options you developed in part (a), name and describe criteria for selecting among them.

    c. Using the criteria developed in part (b), evaluate the options you identified in part (a) and select the best one. Explain your selection.

    d. Redraw Figure 3-6 using the option you selected in part (c).

CASE STUDY 3
THE AMAZON OF INNOVATION

On Cyber Monday, December 1, 2014, Amazon.com customers ordered more than 18 toys per *second*. And almost 60 percent of Amazon's holiday shoppers bought gifts using a mobile device. This contributed to a 20 percent increase in Amazon's total annual sales of $89B. Amazon's last order for the holiday season was placed on December 24 at 10:24 PM and was delivered at 11:06 PM just in time for Christmas.

You may think of Amazon as simply an online retailer, and that is indeed where the company has achieved most of its success. To do this, Amazon had to build an enormous supporting infrastructure—just imagine the information systems and fulfillment facilities needed to ship 36.8 million items on a single day. That infrastructure, however, is needed only during the busy holiday season. Most of the year, Amazon is left with excess infrastructure capacity. Starting in 2000, Amazon began to lease some of that capacity to other companies. In the process, it played a key role in the creation of what are termed *cloud services*, which you will learn about in Chapter 6. For now, just think of cloud services as computer resources somewhere out in the Internet that are leased on flexible terms.

Today, Amazon's business lines can be grouped into three major categories:

- Online retailing
- Order fulfillment
- Cloud services

Consider each.

Amazon created the business model for online retailing. It began as an online bookstore, but every year since 1998 it has added new product categories. The company is involved in all aspects of online retailing. It sells its own inventory. It incentivizes you, via the Associates program, to sell its inventory as well. Or it will help you sell your inventory within its product pages or via one of its consignment venues. Online auctions are the major aspect of online sales in which Amazon does not participate. It tried auctions in 1999, but it could never make inroads against eBay.[17]

---

[17] For a fascinating glimpse of this story from someone inside the company, see "Early Amazon: Auctions" at http://glinden.blogspot.com/2006/04/early-amazon-auctions.html, accessed August 2012.

Today, it is hard to remember how much of what we take for granted was pioneered by Amazon. "Customers who bought this, also bought that"; online customer reviews; customer ranking of customer reviews; books lists; Look Inside the Book; automatic free shipping for certain orders or frequent customers; and Kindle books and devices were all novel concepts when Amazon introduced them (Figure 3-7).

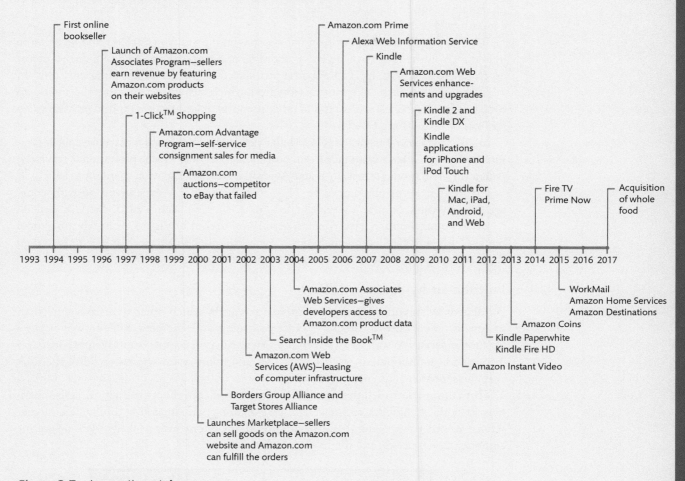

Figure 3-7 Innovation at Amazon

Source: Data from Amazon.com, http://phx.corporateir.net/phoenix.zhtml?c=176060&p=irolcorporate *Timeline* (accessed July 2013).

Amazon's retailing business operates on very thin margins. Products are usually sold at a discount from the stated retail price, and 2-day shipping is free for Amazon Prime members (who pay an annual fee of $99). How does it do it? For one, Amazon drives its employees incredibly hard. Former employees claim the hours are long, the pressure is severe, and the workload is heavy. But what else? It comes down to Moore's Law and the innovative use of nearly free data processing, storage, and communication.

In addition to online retailing, Amazon also sells order fulfillment services. You can ship your inventory to an Amazon warehouse and access Amazon's information systems just as if they were yours. Using technology known as *Web Services*, your order processing information systems can directly integrate, over the Web, with Amazon's inventory, fulfillment, and shipping applications. Your customers need not know that Amazon played any role at all. You can also sell that same inventory using Amazon's retail sales applications.

Amazon Web Services (AWS) allow organizations to lease time on computer equipment in very flexible ways. Amazon's Elastic Cloud 2 (EC2) enables organizations to expand and contract the computer resources they need within minutes. Amazon has a variety of payment plans, and it is possible to buy computer time for less than a penny an hour. Key to this capability is the ability for the leasing organization's computer programs to interface with Amazon's to automatically scale up and scale down the resources leased. For example, if a news site publishes a story that causes a rapid ramp-up of traffic, that news site can, programmatically, request, configure, and use more computing resources for an hour, a day, a month, whatever.

With its Kindle devices, Amazon has become both a vendor of tablets and, even more importantly in the long term, a vendor of online music and video. And to induce customers to buy Kindle apps, in 2013 Amazon introduced its own currency, Amazon Coins. In 2014, Amazon opened a 3D printing store from which customers can customize their own toys, jewelry, dog bones, and dozens of other products. It also made a push to provide video services by introducing Fire TV.[18]

In 2015, Amazon introduced WorkMail, a potential cloud-based replacement for Microsoft Exchange. It also introduced Amazon Home Services (local professional services), Amazon Destinations (travel site), and Amazon Dash (a one-button reordering device).[19]

Finally, Jeff Bezos announced in 2014 that Amazon was experimenting with package delivery using drones, a service called *Prime Air*.[20] In March 2015, the U.S. Federal Aviation Administration gave Amazon permission to start testing its drones in the United States.[21] It seems likely drone delivery is something that will happen in the future given the services Amazon.com is currently offering.

Fulfillment by Amazon (FBA)

Fulfillment by Amazon (FBA) is an Amazon service by which other sellers can ship goods to Amazon warehouses for stocking, order packaging, and shipment. FBA customers pay a fee for the service as well as for inventory space. Amazon uses its own inventory management and order fulfillment business processes and information systems to fulfill the FBA customers' orders.

FBA customers can sell their goods on Amazon.com, sell them via their own sales channels, or both. If the FBA customer sells on Amazon.com, Amazon will provide customer service for order processing (handling returns, fixing erroneously packed orders, answering customer order queries, and the like).

	FBA Costs*
Order handling (per order)	$1.00
Pick & pack (per item)	$1.04
Weight handling (per pound)	Between $0.50 for less than 1 pound, and $1.59 plus $0.39 per pound for items over 2 pounds
Storage (cubic foot per month)	$0.51 between January and September and $0.68 from October to December

* Fulfillment by Amazon Fee Changes 2015," Amazon.com, accessed April 30, 2015, www.amazon.com/gp/help/customer/display.html/?nodeId=201119410.

[18] www.amazon.com/b?ie=UTF8&node=8323871011.

[19] Andy Meek, "Amazon's Roadmap for 2015: Move Fast, Launch as Much as Possible," *BGR Media*, April 24, 2015, accessed May 16, 2015, https://bgr.com/2015/04/24/amazon-earnings-q1-2015-analysis-roadmap.

[20] Marcus Wholes, "Jeff Bezos Says Amazon Is Seriously Serious About Drone Deliveries," *Wired*, accessed May 22, 2014, www.wired.com/2014/04/amazon-delivery-drones.

[21] Bart Jansen, "FAA Approves Amazon Drone Research Again," *USA Today*, accessed April 30, 2015, www.usatoday.com/story/money/2015/04/09/faa-amazon-drone-approval-prime-air/25534485.

The costs for Fulfillment by Amazon depend on the type and size of the goods to be processed. The FBA fees for standard-size products as of February 2015 are shown in the above table.

If goods are sold via Amazon.com, Amazon uses its own information systems to drive the order fulfillment process. However, if the goods are sold via an FBA customer's sales channel, then the FBA customer must connect its own information systems with those at Amazon. Amazon provides a standardized interface by which this is done called *Amazon Marketplace Web Service (MWS)*. Using Web-standard technology (see Chapter 6), FBA customers' order and payment data are directly linked to Amazon's information systems.

FBA enables companies to outsource order fulfillment to Amazon, thus avoiding the cost of developing their own processes, facilities, and information systems for this purpose.

Questions

1. Based on the facts presented in this case, what do you think is Amazon.com's competitive strategy? Justify your answer.

2. Jeff Bezos, CEO of Amazon.com, has stated that the best customer support is none. What does that mean?

3. Suppose you work for Amazon or a company that takes innovation as seriously as Amazon does. What do you suppose is the likely reaction to an employee who says to his or her boss, "But, I don't know how to do that!"?

4. Using your own words and your own experience, what skills and abilities do you think you need to have to thrive at an organization like Amazon?

5. What should UPS and FedEx be doing in response to Amazon.com's interest in drone delivery?

6. Summarize the advantages and disadvantages for brick-and-mortar retailers to sell items via Amazon.com. Would you recommend that they do so?

7. If a brick-and-mortar retailer were to use FBA, what business processes would it not need to develop? What costs would it save?

8. If a brick-and-mortar retailer were to use FBA, what information systems would it not need to develop? What costs would it save?

9. If a brick-and-mortar retailer were to use FBA, how would it integrate its information systems with Amazon's? (To add depth to your answer, Google the term *Amazon MWS*.)

WHAT DO YOU THINK?

THE DIGITAL DIVIDE

An adage of investing is that it is easier for the rich to get richer. Someone who has $10 million invested at 5 percent earns $500 000 per year. Another investor with $10 000 invested at that same 5 percent earns $500 per year. Every year, the disparity increases as the first investor pulls further and further ahead of the second.

This same principle can also apply to intellectual wealth. It is easier for those with considerable knowledge and expertise to gain even more knowledge and expertise. Someone who knows how to search the Internet can gather information more readily than someone who does not. And every year, the person with greater knowledge pulls further and further ahead. Intellectual capital can grow in a way similar to financial capital.

Searching the Internet is not just a matter of knowledge, however—it is also a matter of access. The increasing reliance on the Web for information and commerce has created a digital divide between those who have Internet access and those who do not. This divide continues to deepen as those who are connected pull further ahead of those who are not.

Various groups have addressed this problem by making Internet access available in public places, such as libraries, community centres, and retirement homes. But not everyone can be served this way. Also, there is a big convenience difference between venturing out to the library (where you may experience line ups, time limits, and "hours of operation") and walking across your bedroom or reaching into your bag for your phone to access the Internet.

The advantages accrue to everyone with access, every day. Do you want directions to your friend's house? Need to know what movie is playing at a local theatre? Want to buy music, books, or tools? Need convenient access to your chequing account? Want help to decide whether to refinance your condo? Want to know what TCP/IP means? Use the Internet.

All of this intellectual capital resides on the Internet because businesses benefit by putting it there. It is much cheaper to provide product support information over the Internet than in printed documents. The savings include not only the costs of printing but also the costs of warehousing and mailing. As well, when product specifications change, an organization just needs to update its website. There is no obsolete material to dispose of and there are no costs for printing and distributing the revised material. Those who have Internet access gain current information faster than those who do not.

If you are taking MIS, you are already connected; you are already one of the haves, and you are already pulling ahead of the have-nots. The more you learn about information systems and their use in commerce, the faster you will pull ahead. And so the digital divide increases.

What happens to those who do not have Internet access? They fall further and further behind. The digital divide segregates the haves from the have-nots, creating new class structures. Such segregation is subtle, but it is segregation, nonetheless.

Do organizations have a responsibility to address this matter? If 98 percent of our market segment has Internet access, do we have a responsibility to provide non-Internet materials to that other 2 percent? On what assumptions is that responsibility based? Does a government agency have the responsibility to provide equal information to those who have Internet access and those who do not? When those who are connected can obtain information nearly instantaneously, 24/7, is it even possible to provide equal information to the connected and the unconnected?

This is a worldwide problem. Connected societies and countries continue to outpace regions that have less available technological resources. How can any economy that relies on traditional mail compete with an Internet-based economy?

Discussion Questions

1. Do you see evidence of a digital divide on your campus? in your hometown? among your relatives? Describe personal experiences you have had with regard to the digital divide.

2. Do organizations have a legal responsibility to provide the same information for unconnected customers as they do for connected customers? If not, should laws be passed requiring organizations to do so?

3. Because it may be impossible to provide equal information, another approach for reducing the digital divide is for the government to enable unconnected citizens to acquire Internet access via subsidies and tax incentives. Do you favour such a program? Why, or why not?

4. Suppose that nothing is done to reduce the digital divide and that it is allowed to grow wider and wider. What are the consequences? How will society change?

KNOWLEDGE EXTENSION 4

Chapter 4 provides the background for this extension.

Introduction to Microsoft Excel 2016

This Knowledge Extension teaches basic skills with Microsoft Excel, a product for creating and processing spreadsheets. If you already know how to use Excel, use this Knowledge Extension for review. Otherwise, use this Knowledge Extension to gain essential knowledge that every businessperson needs.

KE4-1 WHAT IS A SPREADSHEET?

A **spreadsheet** is a table of data having rows and columns. Long before the advent of the computer, accountants and financial planners used paper spreadsheets to make financial calculations. Today, the term *spreadsheet* almost always refers to an *electronic* spreadsheet, and most frequently to a spreadsheet that is processed by Microsoft Excel. Electronic spreadsheets provide incredible labour savings over paper spreadsheets and were a major factor in the early adoption of personal computers.

As shown in Figure KE4-1, Excel spreadsheets have rows and columns. The rows are identified by numbers, and the columns are identified by letters. Because there are only 26 letters in the alphabet, the following scheme is used to label columns: The letters A through Z identify the first 26 columns; the letters AA through AZ identify the next 26; BA through BZ the next 26; and so forth.

In Excel, the term **worksheet** refers to a spreadsheet. One or more worksheets are combined to form a **workbook**.

In the lower left-hand corner of Figure KE4-1, notice the tab called Sheet 1. Excel creates just one worksheet when you create a new workbook, but you can create more worksheets if needed.

Figure KE4-1 Excel
Spreadsheet Showing Rows
and Columns

Source: Microsoft Excel 2016

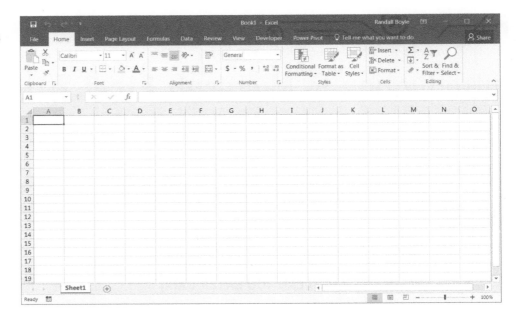

Figure KE4-1 shows a spreadsheet processed by Excel 2016, the current version of Excel. You can process spreadsheets in earlier versions of Excel, but the structure of commands and menu items will be different from the instructions described here. If you are just starting to learn Excel, learn Excel 2016 rather than an earlier version.

The intersection of a row and a column is called a **cell**. Each cell is identified by the name of its row and column. In Figure KE4-1, the cell named A1 is highlighted. The cell K5 is the cell in the K column, row number 5. The cell AB1207 (not visible in Figure KE4-1) is the cell located in column AB and row 1207.

You may be asking, "Row 1207? How many rows and columns can I have?" Do not bother asking…you can have more than you will ever need or want. And if you should ever run out of rows and columns, you are using the wrong tool. In that case, you probably should be using Microsoft Access or another DBMS (see Chapter 5) instead.

KE4-2 HOW DO YOU GET STARTED WITH EXCEL?

When you first start Excel 2016, it will create a workbook exactly like the one shown in Figure KE4-1. Even though you have not done anything yet, your first task should be to save your workbook under an appropriate name. Life is uncertain; you never know when a computer might fail or power might be cut off or some other unplanned event might occur. Get in the habit of saving your work initially and then frequently after that.

To save your workbook, click *File* with your left mouse button (in the following text, unless otherwise specified, the term *click* means to click with the left mouse button), and click *Save As* as shown in Figure KE4-2. The choices available to you will depend on the licence you have and your working environment. In this example, Excel displays a Share-Point site named *David Kroenke*, a Microsoft OneDrive location, Computer, and *Add a Place* where you can define new locations for saving documents. For now, click Computer, then Browse as shown in Figure KE4-2. Navigate to the location on your computer where you want to save your workbook. The display in Figure KE4-3 will appear. In the lower centre, find the label *File name:* and to the right of that label enter a name for this file. In Figure KE4-3, I have entered the file name *Learning_Excel_1*. Your instructor may have given you instructions for creating file names; if so, follow them. Otherwise, follow this

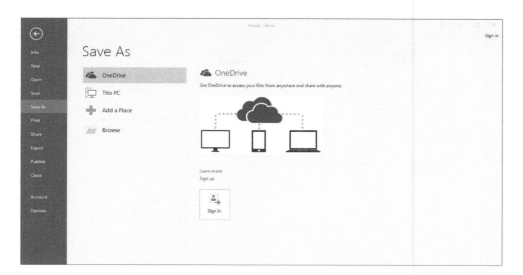

Figure KE4-2 Saving Your Workbook in Excel
Source: Microsoft Excel 2016

example or use some other scheme. Click the *Save* button to save your workbook. Once you have saved your workbook, you can perform subsequent saves by clicking the small disk icon located next to the Excel icon at the top left.

Figure KE4-4 shows the workbook. A sequence of tabs appears in a horizontal line, just below the Excel icon. These tabs control the contents of the **ribbon,** which is the wide bar of tools and selections that appears just under the tabs. In Figure KE4-4, the *HOME* tab has been selected, and the contents of the ribbon concern fonts, alignment, and so forth. Figure KE4-5 shows the appearance of the ribbon when the *PAGE LAYOUT* tab is selected.

In general, you choose a tab depending on the task at hand. For general work, the tools and selection under the *HOME* tab are most useful. If you are inserting pictures, graphs, hyperlinks, or other items into your spreadsheet, click the *INSERT* tab. You would use *PAGE LAYOUT* to format your page, often for printing. The *FORMULAS* tab is used for creating more complex formulas, the *DATA* tab for filtering and sorting data in your spreadsheet, the *REVIEW* tab for tracking changes and making comments, and the *VIEW* tab for configuring the appearance of Excel.

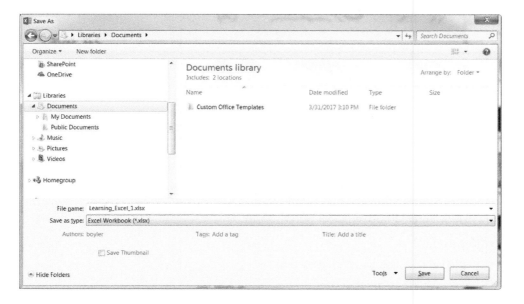

Figure KE4-3 Entering a File Name in Excel
Source: Microsoft Excel 2016

Figure KE4-4 Excel Menu Tabs and Ribbon Bar

Source: Microsoft Excel 2016

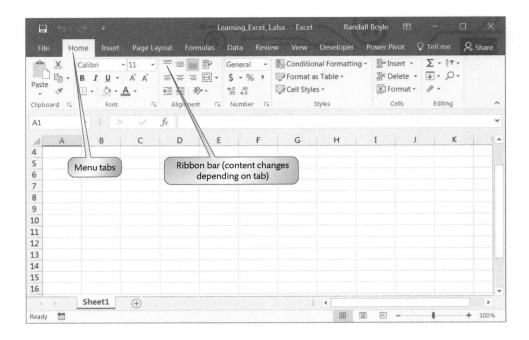

At this point, do not worry about which tab to choose; just click around to see the tools and selections available. If in doubt, click on the *Home* tab because it holds the most frequently used tools and selections.

Figure KE4-5 Ribbon with Page Layout Tab Selected

Source: Microsoft Excel 2016

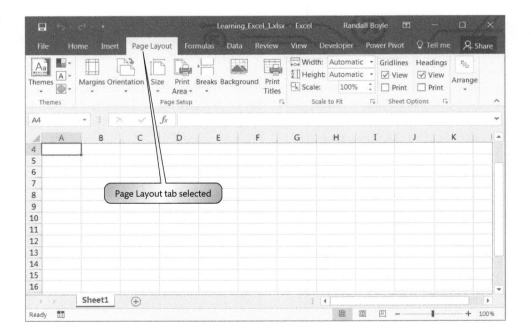

KE4-3 HOW CAN YOU ENTER DATA?

Data can be entered into an Excel worksheet in three ways:

- Key in the data.
- Let Excel add data based on a pattern.
- Import data from another program.

Here we will illustrate the first two options. Knowledge Extension 8 discusses how to import data from Microsoft Access into Excel.

Key in the Data

Nothing very sophisticated is needed to key the data. Just click in the cell in which you want to add data, type the data, and press *Enter* when you are done. In Figure KE4-6 the user has keyed names of cities into column E and is in the process of adding *Miami*. After typing the second *i*, she can press *Enter*. The value will be entered into the cell, and the focus will stay on cell E6. You can tell the focus is on E6 because Excel highlights column E and row 6.

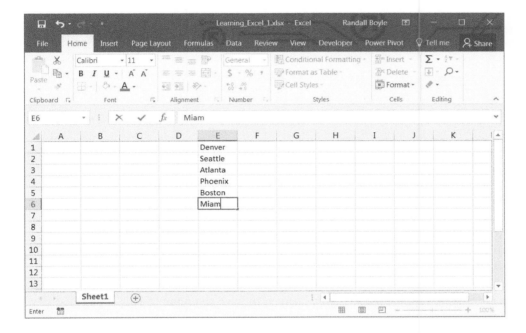

Figure KE4-6 Entering City Names in Column E

Source: Microsoft Excel 2016

If the user enters the second *i* and presses the down arrow, the value will be added to cell E6, and Excel will move the focus down to cell E7. The latter is useful if you are adding a vertical sequence of names like this. Also, you can press a left arrow to add the data and move the focus left or a right or an up arrow to move right or up.

In Figure KE4-6, notice the row just above the spreadsheet, immediately above the names of the columns. In that row, the value E6 indicates that cell E6 has the focus and further to the right the letters *Miam* indicate the current value of that cell.

Figure KE4-7 shows a sequence of seven city names. But notice that the user never entered the second *i* in Miami. To correct this, she can go back to that cell and retype the entire word *Miami* or she can go to the cell and press the <F2> function key. In the latter case, she can just add the missing *i* to the word and press Enter (or down or up, etc.). Using the F2 key is recommended when you have a long value in a cell and you just want to fix a letter or two without retyping the whole entry. (If nothing happens when you press F2, press the F Lock key on your keyboard. Then press F2 again.)

Let Excel Add the Data Using a Pattern

Suppose that for some reason for each of the cities we want to have the number 100 in column G of the spreadsheet in Figure KE4-7. Another way of saying this is that we want

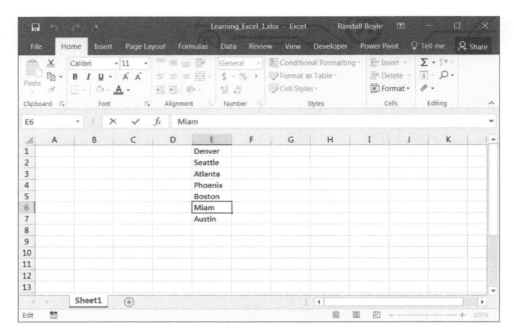

the value 100 to be entered into cells G1 through G7. One way of proceeding is to type the
value 100 in each of the seven rows. There is a better way, however.

If our user types the value 100 into cell G1, presses Enter, and then clicks cell G1, a
rectangle will be drawn around the cell with a little black box in the lower right-hand corner,
as shown in Figure KE4-8. Now if the user drags (left-click and hold the mouse button down
as you move the mouse) that little black box down to cell G7, Excel will fill in the value
100 into all of those cells. Figure KE4-9 shows the user dragging the cells, and Figure KE4-10
shows the result.

But it gets much better! Suppose we want the numbers in column G to identify
the cities. Say we want the first city, Denver, to have the number 100, the second city,

Figure KE4-8 Entering
Identical Data in Multiple
Cells, Step 1

Source: Microsoft Excel 2016

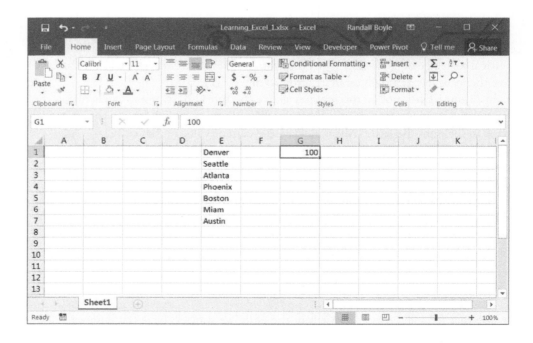

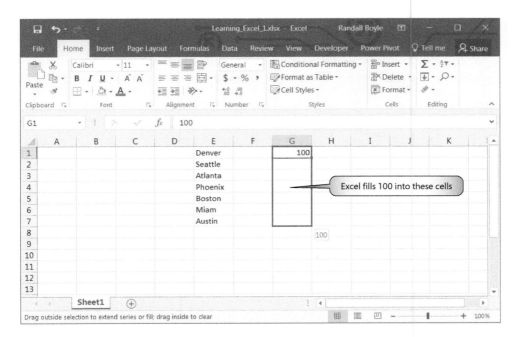

Figure KE4-9 Entering Identical Data in Multiple Cells, Step 2

Source: Microsoft Excel 2016

Seattle, to have the number 200, the third city, Atlanta, to have the number 300, and so forth.

Excel will fill in the values we want if we give it an indication of the pattern to follow. So, if our user types 100 in cell G1, 200 in cell G2, and then *selects both cells G1 and G2*, Excel will draw a rectangle around the two cells and again show the small black box, as shown in Figure KE4-11. If the user drags the small black box, Excel will fill in the numbers in a sequence, as shown in Figure KE4-12.

Excel is sophisticated in its interpretation of the patterns. If you key *January* and *February* into cells C1 and C2 and then select both cells and drag down, Excel will fill in with March, April, May, and so on. Or, if in column A you key in the sequence *Q1*,

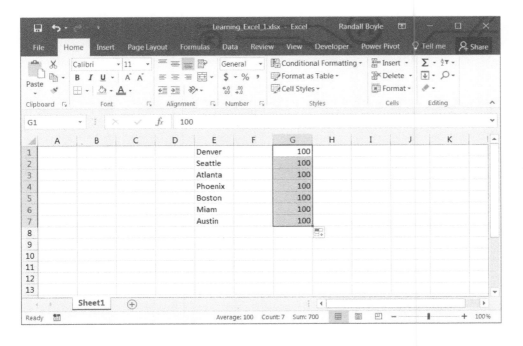

Figure KE4-10 Identical Data Entered in Multiple Cells

Source: Microsoft Excel 2016

Figure KE4-11 Entering Patterned Data in Multiple Cells

Source: Microsoft Excel 2016

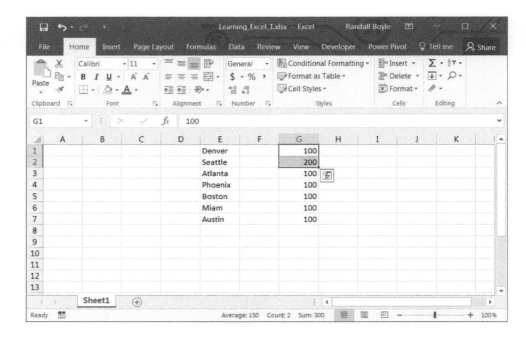

Q2, *Q3*, and *Q4* and then select all four values and drag the small black box, Excel will repeat the sequence Q1 through Q4. Figure KE4-13 shows the results of these last two operations.

Excel will also find patterns within text values. In Figure KE4-14, the user entered Figure 1-1 into cell J1 and 1-2 into cell J2. Selecting and dragging cells J1 and J2 produced the sequence shown in Figure KE4-14.

Figure KE4-12 Patterned Data Entered in Multiple Cells

Source: Microsoft Excel 2016

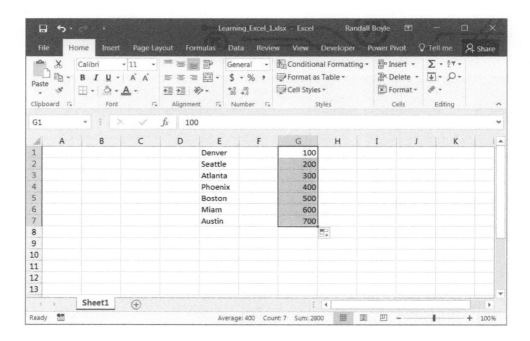

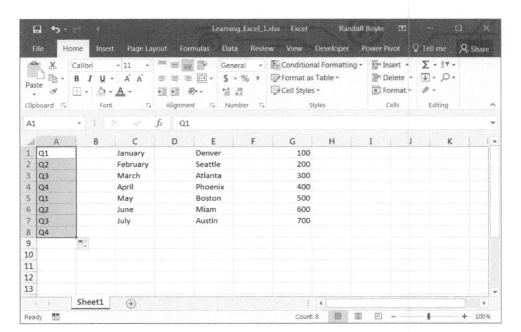

Figure KE4-13 Sophisticated Entry of Patterned Data in Multiple Cells

Source: Microsoft Excel 2016

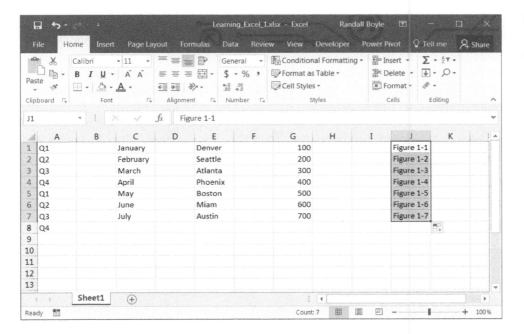

Figure KE4-14 Patterned Data Within Text Values

Source: Microsoft Excel 2016

KE4-4 HOW CAN YOU INSERT AND DELETE ROWS AND COLUMNS AND CHANGE THEIR SIZE?

Suppose you are the manager of a sales team and you are recording this month's sales into the spreadsheet in Figure KE4-15. You enter the data shown but then realize that you have forgotten to add column headings. You would like column A to have the heading *Sales Rep* and column B to have the heading *Sales*. You do not want to retype all of the data; instead, you want to insert two new rows so that you can add the labels as well as a blank line.

To insert new rows, click the number of the row above which you want new rows, and select as many rows as you want to insert. In Figure KE4-16, the user has clicked row 1 and selected two rows. Now, using the right mouse button, click the selection. The menu shown

Figure KE4-15
Spreadsheet to Which User
Wants to Add New Rows for
Column Headings

Source: Microsoft Excel 2016

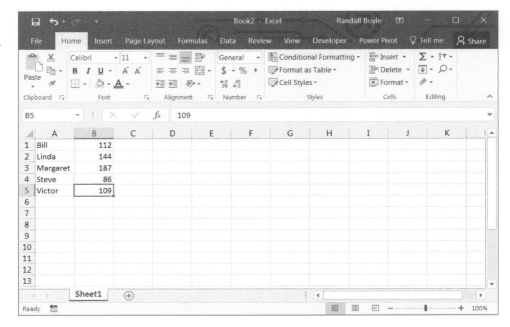

in Figure KE4-16 will appear. Using your mouse, left-click the word *Insert* and two rows will be inserted, as shown in Figure KE4-17. If you had selected only one row, then only one row would be added. If you had selected five rows, then five rows would be added.

Notice that when you click the name of a row (or column) you are selecting the *entire* row (or column). Thus, when you click the 1 of row 1, you are selecting the entire row, even if it has 1000 or more columns.

You can use a similar approach to delete rows. Click the name of the row (or rows) you want to delete and then right-click. Then left-click the word *Delete*. Those rows will be deleted and any remaining rows moved up.

Adding and deleting columns are similar. To add a column, click the name of the column before which you want to insert columns, select as many columns to the right of that as you want to add, right-click, and then select *Insert*. To delete, click the name of the columns you want to delete, right-click, and then select *Delete*.

Figure KE4-16 Menu for
Adding Inserts Such as
New Rows

Source: Microsoft Excel 2016

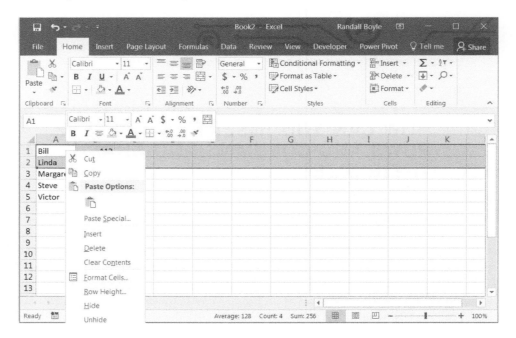

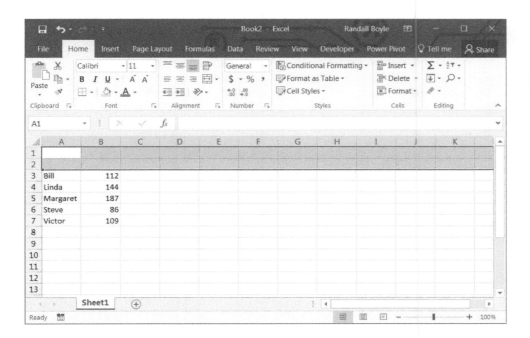

Figure KE4-17
Spreadsheet to Which User Has Added New Rows for Column Headings

Source: Microsoft Excel 2016

Changing the width of a column or the height of a row is easy. Suppose in Figure KE4-17 that you want to include both first and last names in column A. At present, column A is not large enough to show both names. To make it larger, in the column headings click the line between the A and the B. Your cursor changes to a vertical bar with an arrow on each side, as shown in Figure KE4-18. Move the cursor to the right to increase the size of the column and to the left to decrease it. Similarly, to increase or decrease the height of a row, click the line between the line numbers and drag up to decrease the row height and down to increase it.

Figure KE4-19 shows the spreadsheet after column A has been made wider and row 1 has been increased in height. *Sales Rep* has been entered as the heading for column A, and *Sales* has been entered as the name for column B.

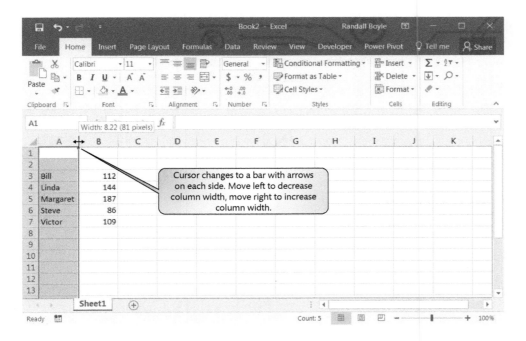

Figure KE4-18 Changing Cursor to a Vertical Bar to Change Column Widths

Source: Microsoft Excel 2016

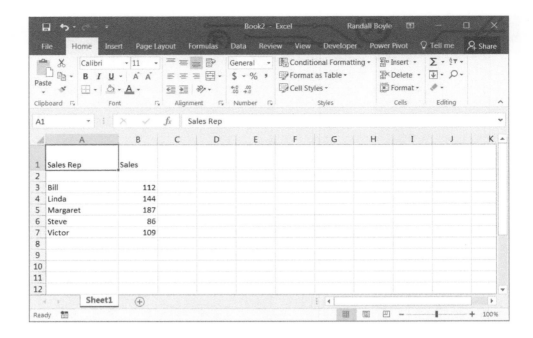

KE4-5 HOW CAN YOU FORMAT DATA?

Excel has a powerful and complicated set of tools for formatting spreadsheets. Here we will just scratch the surface with a few of the hundreds of possibilities.

The spreadsheet in Figure KE4-19 is boring and misleading. It would be better if the headings were centred over the columns and if they looked like headings. Also, are the sales in dollars or some other currency? If in dollars, they should have a dollar sign and maybe two decimal places.

To make the headings more interesting, highlight cells A1 and B1 (to do this, click A1 and hold the mouse button down as you move the mouse pointer to B1) and in the *Font* section of the ribbon select 16 rather than 11. This action increases the font size of the

Figure KE4-20 Centring
Labels in Cells

Source: Microsoft Excel 2016

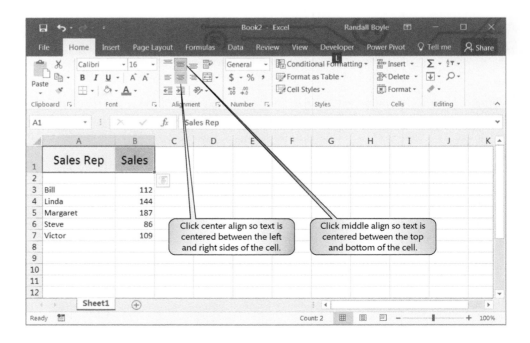

Click center align so text is
centered between the left
and right sides of the cell.

Click middle align so text is
centered between the top
and bottom of the cell.

labels. In the same *Font* section of the ribbon, with A1 and B1 selected, click the bucket of paint. Select a medium blue. Now, still with cells A1 and B1 selected, in the *Alignment* section of the ribbon click the centre icons, as shown in Figure KE4-20. Your labels will appear centred both horizontally and vertically in the cell.

The sales figures are actually in dollars, but they are formatted incorrectly. To place dollar signs in front of them, select cells B3 to B7 and in the *Number* section of the ribbon click the down arrow next to the dollar sign. Select $ English (United States), and your spreadsheet will be formatted as shown in Figure KE4-21.

As stated, Excel provides hundreds of options for formatting your spreadsheet. You can add lines and borders, you can change the font color, and you can even add conditional formatting so that large sales numbers appear in bold, red type. There is insufficient room in this short introduction to explain such capabilities, but explore on your own using Excel Help (the question mark in the upper right-hand corner).

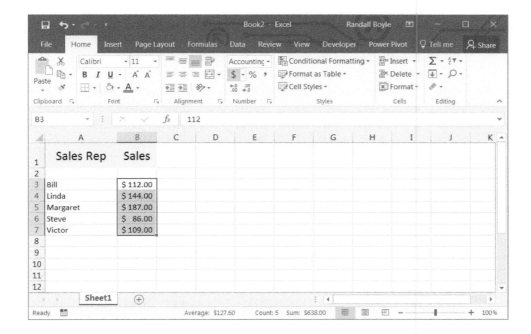

Figure KE4-21 Adding Dollar Signs in Cells

Source: Microsoft Excel 2016

KE4-6 HOW CAN YOU CREATE A (SIMPLE) FORMULA?

In spite of how it might appear to you at this point, the power of Excel is not the ease by which you can enter data or change the form of the spreadsheet, nor is it in the flexible ways you can format your data. The real power of Excel lies in its amazing computational capability. In this section, we will introduce a few simple formulas.

Consider the spreadsheet in Figure KE4-22. Suppose that we want to add Bill's sales numbers together to obtain his total sales for the months of March, April, and May. Those sales are located in cells C3, D3, and E3, respectively. A logical way to add the three together is with the following formula: *C3 + D3 + E3*.

To enter this formula in Excel, first choose the cell into which you want to place the total. For the spreadsheet in Figure KE4-22, suppose that is cell G3. Click that cell and enter the expression = C3 + D3 + E3 and then press *Enter*. The result will appear as shown in Figure KE4-23. (Be sure to start with an equal sign. If you omit the equal sign, Excel will think you are attempting to enter a label or text value and will just show the letters C3 + D3 + E3 in the cell.)

Figure KE4-22 Selecting Cells to Be Summed

Source: Microsoft Excel 2016

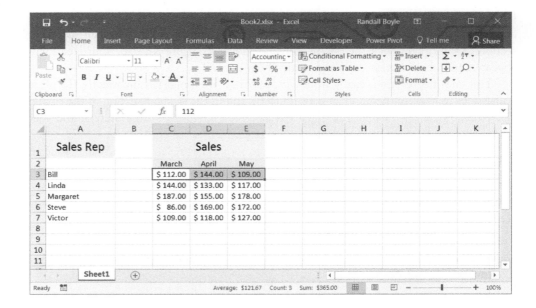

Before you go on, select cell G3 and press the F2 function key, as shown in Figure KE4-24. Notice the colour coding that Excel presents. The term *C3* is shown in blue text, and the C3 cell is outlined in blue; *D3* and *E3* are shown in other colours. Whenever you have a problem with a calculation, press F2 to have Excel highlight the cells involved in that calculation.

The next operation is actually quite amazing. Suppose that you want to add the 3 months' sales data for all of the salespeople. To do that, right-click cell G3 and select *Copy*. Next, highlight cells G4 through G7, right-click, and select *Paste*. The formula will be copied into each of the cells. The correct totals will appear in each row.

Here is the amazing part: When Excel copied the formula, it did not do so blindly. Instead, it adjusted the terms of the formula so that each would refer to cells in the row to which it was copied. To verify this, highlight cell G5, for example, and press F2, as shown in Figure KE4-25. Notice that the formula in this cell is = *C5 + D5 + E5*. The formula you copied was = *C3 + D3 + E3*. Excel adjusted the row numbers when it copied the formula!

Suppose now we want to total the sales for each month. To obtain the total for March, for example, we want to total cells C3 + C4 + C5 + C6 + C7. To do so, we could go to

Figure KE4-23 The Result of Applying a Formula that Summed Cells C3, D3, and E3

Source: Microsoft Excel 2016

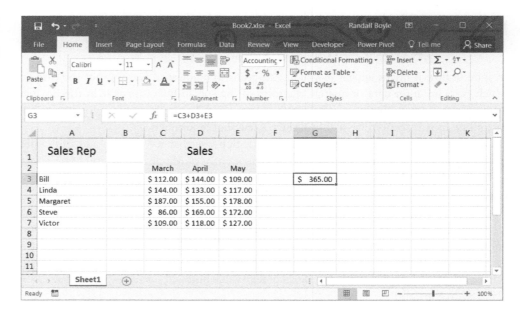

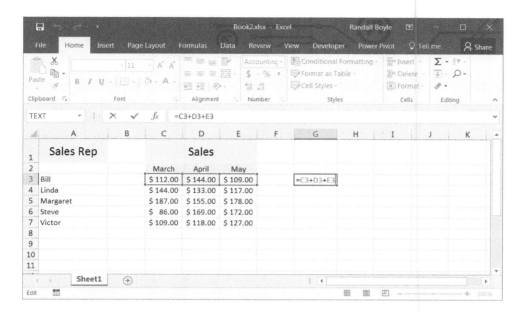

Figure KE4-24 Using the F2 Function Key to Show Colour Coding of Cells Involved in a Calculation

Source: Microsoft Excel 2016

an appropriate cell, say, C9, and enter the formula = C3 + C4 + C5 + C6 + C7. This will work, but there is an easier way to proceed.

Highlight cell C9 and then select the *Formulas* tab at the top of the ribbon. At the top of the tab, click *Auto Sum*, as shown in Figure KE4-33. Press *Enter*, and Excel will total the values in the column. If you click cell C9 and press F2, you will see that Excel entered the formula = *SUM(C3:C8)*. This is a shorthand way of summing the values in those cells using a built-in function called **SUM**. To finish this spreadsheet, copy the formula from cell C9 to cells D9, E9, and G9. The spreadsheet will appear as in Figure KE4-34. Now all that remains to do is to add labels to the *total* row and *total* column.

You can use an Excel formula to create just about any algebraic expression. However, when you create a formula, remember the rules of high school algebra. For example, = *(B2 + B3)/7* will add the contents of cell B2 to those of B3 and divide the sum by 7. In contrast, = *B2 + B3/7* will first divide B3 by 7 and then add the result to the contents of B2. When in doubt, just key in a formula you think might work and experiment until you get the results you want.

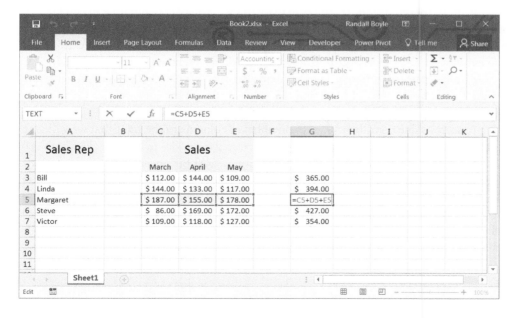

Figure KE4-25 Using the F2 Function Key to Confirm That a Formula Was Correctly Copied into Multiple Cells

Source: Microsoft Excel 2016

KE4-7 HOW DO I USE VLOOKUP?

As you may imagine an Excel spreadsheet can quickly contain a large amount of data. Information can be placed both in rows (numbered sequentially) and columns (the first 26 are labelled A – Z, the 27th and 28th are labelled AA and AB, and so on). Not only can such large sheets exceed the viewing area of a computer screen but it can take a long time to scroll through them even when you freeze the title headings[1] (sheets with 10 000 cells or more are not uncommon). One way to address this is by using what is essentially a search and lookup command or Vlookup. Vlookup works like a traditional paper based telephone list search where you start with something that you know, for example a person's name, and you look up what you need to know, for example their number or address.

Consider the spreadsheet in Figure KE4-26 (imagine that it is considerably larger). Suppose that we want to know sales in the month of May for a particular sales representative. This is easy if the sheet is small and there are only a few names, but this could be much more difficult if we have thousands of sales representatives identified by employee numbers. Vlookup makes this a much easier task.

Figure KE4-26 Sample Sales Data for Vlookup

Source: Microsoft Excel 2016

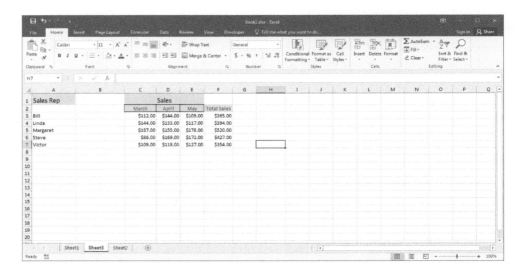

First choose a cell where you would like to enter the sales representative that you are looking for. In this case we enter the title (easy to use) Sales Representative in cell H2 and keep cell I2 as the place where we will enter the name that we wish to search. Underneath, in cell H3 we similarly put the title Quarterly Sales so that we know what we are interested in. Then in cell I2 enter = vlookup(I2, A3:F7,6,FALSE) as shown in Figure KE4-27.

Let's take apart this formula. The first item after the "Vlookup" expression indicates we will use the contents of cell I I2 to find the value that we want to search for (in this case Steve). The item after the comma tells Excel (A3:F7) where to look for the data we are trying to search. The next item "6" is the number of columns to the right that we will grab the result from. In this case, the data we are interested in resides in column (F) which is 6 columns to the right of column A. Finally, the item " FALSE" means that we are looking for an exact match (if you are looking for an approximate match you specify TRUE rather than FALSE). Now if you enter Steve in cell I2 you will have his sales ($427.00) returned in cell I3. Of course we can use Vlookup for any type of cell data (numeric and alphabetic) and because we can manage very complex sheets this can be extremely useful, especially when coupled with more complex formulas and even more advanced tools (such as Solver).

---

[1] This is called "Freeze Panes" and is done by choosing the appropriate row or column that has the headings or titles that you want to retain and selecting Freeze Panes from the view tab or ribbon.

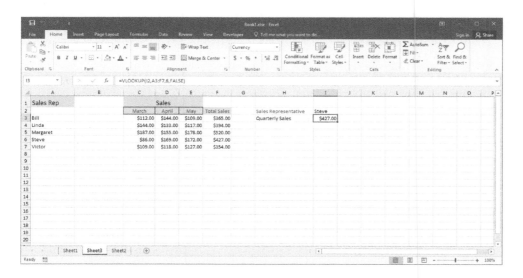

KE4-8 HOW DO I USE ADVANCED FUNCTIONS SUCH AS SOLVER?

Sometimes in Excel rather than work forwards and calculate a number from a series of data we instead want to work backwards to determine what we would have to do in order to arrive at a particular goal or target.[2] For example, consider a fast food restaurant (such as McDonalds) where there are a variety of menu items (drinks, fries, hamburgers, and desserts), which have different prices and costs. A manager might be interested in knowing what the sales mix would have to be in order to achieve a particular revenue number (for example, $20 000 in a day) or what the optimal mix might be to achieve a particular net profit (revenue minus costs).

Of course you could do this manually or by trial and error. You could construct a spreadsheet that listed each item, that is drinks (small, medium, large, and extra large), fries (small, medium, large, and supersized), hamburgers (cheeseburgers, Big Mac, etc.), and desserts, and the costs and prices of each in a formula that calculates profit. However, this could get very complicated very quickly. Some combinations cost more than others and the margins can also vary (generally the highest profit margins are made on drinks and fries). Furthermore, there are limits and considerations that you may need to take into account. Not everyone likes hamburgers for breakfast and coffee might be more popular at different times. In addition, some items are sold in combinations and you might have a limited capacity for certain things (you can learn more about the logistics of these considerations in a supply chain or operations course).

An alternative to trial and error, trying different numbers until you get a value that that you like, is to use **Solver**. Solver is a type of "what if" tool that lets you identify an optimal (high or low) value for a formula in a particular cell (usually called the *target* or *objective cell*). Solver automatically alters a variety of values in other cells (typically called *decision variables* or *constraint cells* (or, in early versions of Excel changing or adjustable cells)).

The step-by-step method to use Solver is as follows:

(1) Open the Data tab and select Solver.

(2) In the set objective box enter a cell reference or name for the objective cell. This must contain a formula (for example, Net Profit (=revenue-cost) or Total Revenue (all sales)).

---

[2] This is actually a very common activity for an analyst and there are many ways (such as Goal Seek and Scenarios) to do this. These can be quite advanced (though easy once you get used to it). All require an Excel add-in to be activated or installed. This can be accessed from the File menu, select Options, and Add-Ins and choose the modules that you like. Once enabled they appear on the Data ribbon.

(3) Choose Max (if you want the value to be as high as possible), Min (if you want the value to be as low as possible), or if you are trying to achieve a particular number (such as $20 000) choose that exact value.

(4) In the By Changing Variable box enter a name or reference call that relates directly or indirectly to the objective function. There can be up to 200 of these variable cells.

(5) In the subject to the constraints box enter any constraints (such as maximum value for any variable cell) and specify the type of constraining (less than, equal to, greater than, etc.).

(6) Select Solve and either keep the Solver results or restore the original values.

Once this problem has been entered and saved using the options parameter you can alter how solutions are computed by selecting Generalized Reduced Gradient (GRG) Nonlinear for nonlinear problems, LP simplex for linear problems, and Evolutionary for non-smooth problems.

This may sound complicated but in fact the Excel part is relatively easy. The most difficult part is setting up the overall model and building the calculations and formulas. Once this is done and you understand the basic constraints and relationships between the variables the Excel part is straightforward.

Figure KE4-28   Using Solver

Source: Microsoft Excel 2016

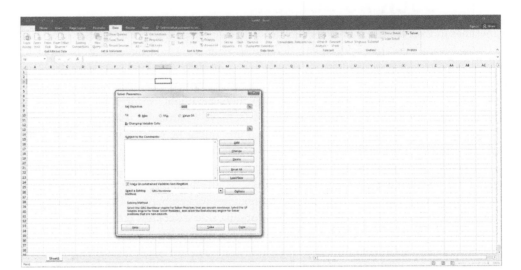

KE4-9 WHAT ARE PIVOT TABLES AND HOW DO I USE THEM?

Next to Solver, **Pivot Tables** are also fairly common, potentially very sophisticated, and relatively simple to use. As a data analysis tool Pivot Tables are quickly becoming "table stakes" or an entry-level tool for business analysts. To the uninitiated Pivot Tables may seem intimidating but just like riding a bicycle once you get the hang of it you are likely to employ them constantly. They can greatly simplify analysis and turn what would otherwise take the creation of numerous formulas into a few simple drag and drop selections.

Imagine a simple spreadsheet from a bicycle shop containing Order numbers, SKU (Stock Keeping Units), Brand, Class, Description, Price, Cost, and Markup.

Notice first that we have added filters to each of the columns (on the data tab choose filter when you have selected the label cell). These allow us to easily sort the entire table simply by selecting the drop down tab and choosing the type and method of sort (small to large, A to Z or Z to A, etc.). By adding the appropriate formulas we can use this data to determine things such as total dollar value of sales or the number of units sold.

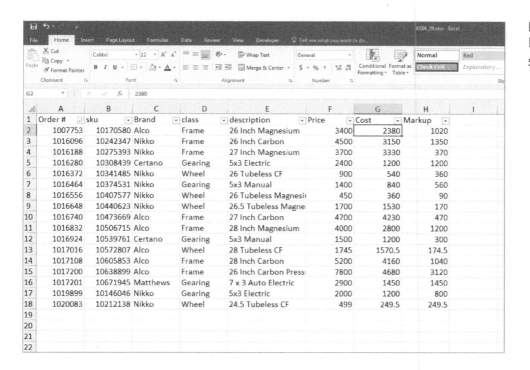

Figure KE4-29 Sample Data for Pivot Tables

Source: Microsoft Excel 2016

However, rather than using formulas it is very easy to use a Pivot Table. Simply choose Pivot Table from the insert table and enter the data range. (It is likely prefilled since Excel makes fairly good assumptions about your data.) Until you become very skilled at Pivot Tables it is usually best to choose New Worksheet for the location of where you want the Pivot Table to be.

Once you have selected OK a new sheet will open and if you select Brand and Price you will have a report that shows total sales for each of the brands.

Not only is this quick and accurate but it is easily customizable by adjusting the filters. For example, if you select Sum of Price from the Values box you can change the Value Field Settings from Sum (which is the total) to Count and the number reported will now be the number of sales.

Pivot Tables, which literally "pivot" or turn the data, are highly useful tools for quickly working with data rather than building potentially complicated individual speadsheets where you have to create formulas that either sum (total) or count (using the count or

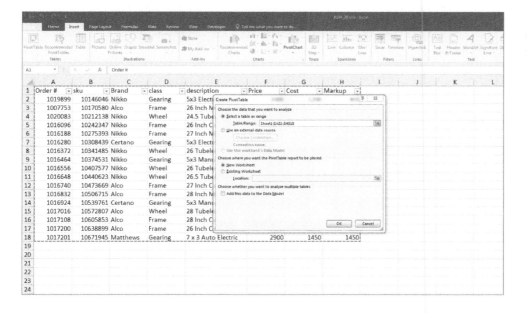

Figure KE4-30 Creating a Pivot Table

Source: Microsoft Excel 2016

Figure KE4-31 Pivot Table

Source: Microsoft Excel 2016

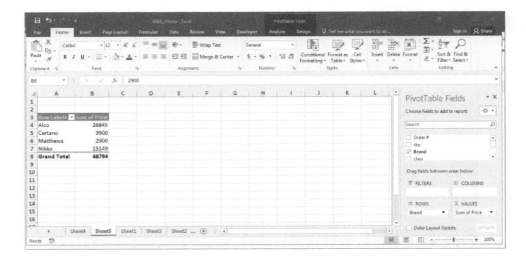

Figure KE4-32
Changing Value Field Settings and Ending Table

Source: Microsoft Excel 2016

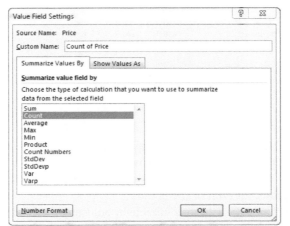

Figure KE4-33 Auto Sum Function

Source: Microsoft Excel 2016

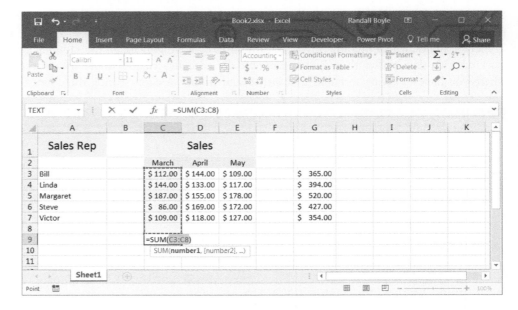

countif commands) columns. One caution with using Pivot Tables is that they are very powerful and so it is important that you are extremely comfortable with your data and what it means. For example, counting the number of sales orders might be useful and needed but knowing the average number of a Stock Keeping Unit is usually meaningless. Excel does not know anything about the context of your data. That is the responsibility of the analyst.

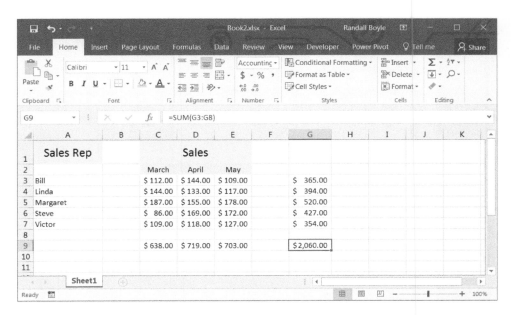

Figure KE4-34 Summing Sales by Month

Source: Microsoft Excel 2016

KE4-10 HOW CAN YOU PRINT RESULTS?

Excel provides a wide variety of tools and settings for printing worksheets. Here we will illustrate several features that will give you an idea of the possibilities. After you have read this section, you can experiment on your own.

Before you start printing, you can save paper and ink if you make use of Excel's Print Preview feature. To do so, click *FILE* and then *Print*. The result is shown in Figure KE4-35. Before you click the large *Print* button (next to Copies), examine the *Print Preview* thumbnail of your printout to see if you approve. If you do, press *Print*, and Excel will print your document. For now, however, select the *PAGE LAYOUT* tab in the Excel ribbon.

The tools and selections in the PAGE LAYOUT ribbon determine how the document will be arranged as a printed document. In this ribbon, the next to last group is *Sheet Options*; in that group, notice that you have the option of viewing and printing gridlines as well as column and row headings.

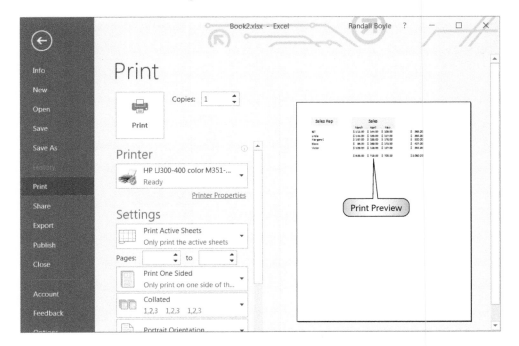

Figure KE4-35 The Print Preview Screen in Excel

Source: Microsoft Excel 2016

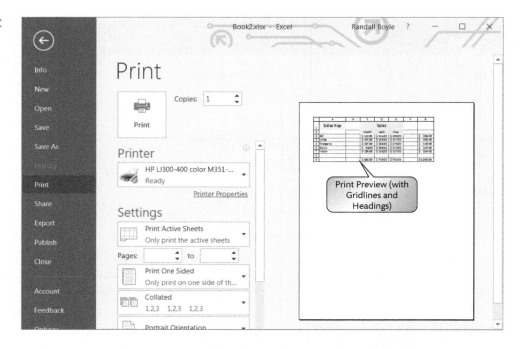

If you now select *Print* under *Gridlines* and *Headings* and then select *Print Preview*, you can see that your worksheet will be printed with gridlines and headings, as shown in Figure KE4-36. Most people prefer to see gridlines and headings in the screen display but not see them, or at least not see the headings, in the printed display. Click *Close Print Preview* to return to the spreadsheet view. For now, check *View* and *Print Gridlines*, but under *Headings* check only *View*.

As you can see, you have many other options in the PAGE LAYOUT ribbon. Use *Margins* to set the size of the page margins. *Orientation* refers to whether the worksheet is printed normally (upright) on the page (called *Portrait*) or sideways on the page (called *Landscape*). Try each and preview your print to see the impact each has.

You can use print area to specify the portion of the spreadsheet that you want to print. If for some reason you want to list only the name of the sales reps, you can highlight cells

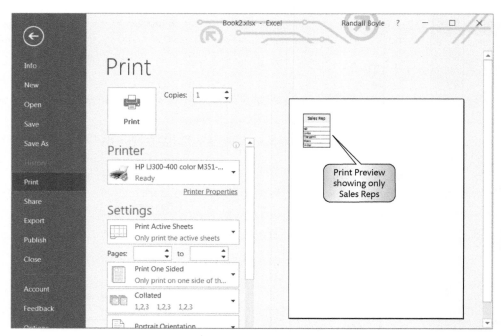

A1 through A7 and then click *Print Area* and then click *Set Print Area*. If you do this, your print preview will appear as in Figure KE4-37.

These commands should be enough for you to print basic assignments. Of course, Excel offers many more options for you to explore. Experiment with them!

ACTIVE REVIEW

Use this Active Review to verify that you understand the ideas and concepts that answer this Knowledge Extension's study questions.

KE4-1 WHAT IS A SPREADSHEET?

Explain how the following terms are related: *spreadsheet, electronic spreadsheet, Microsoft Excel, worksheet,* and *workbook*. Explain how spreadsheet cells are addressed. Where would you find cell Q54?

KE4-2 HOW DO YOU GET STARTED WITH EXCEL?

Describe the first task you should do when creating a spreadsheet. Open a new workbook and give it the name *My_Sample_WB*. Explain the relationship of tabs and tools and selections. Which tab is the most likely one to have the tools and selections you need?

KE4-3 HOW CAN YOU ENTER DATA?

List three ways of entering data into Excel. Describe the advantage of using the F2 key to edit data. Explain two ways that Excel uses a pattern to enter data.

KE4-4 HOW CAN YOU INSERT AND DELETE ROWS AND COLUMNS AND CHANGE THEIR SIZE?

Describe how to insert and delete rows. Describe a circumstance in which you would need to insert rows. Describe how to make a row taller or shorter. Describe how to change the width of a column.

KE4-5 HOW CAN YOU FORMAT DATA?

Open Excel and explain the purpose of each of the icons in the *Font* section of the *Home* tab of the ribbon. Explain the purpose of the *Alignment* and *Number* sections.

KE4-6 HOW CAN YOU CREATE A (SIMPLE) FORMULA?

Write the expression you would need to add the content of cell B2 to the content of cell B7. Write the expression to multiply the content of cell C4 by 7.3. Write the expression to find the average of the values in cells D7, D8, and D9. Use a built-in formula to total the values in cells E2, E3, E4, E5, E6, and E7.

KE4-7 HOW DO I USE VLOOKUP?

Explain why Vlookup is better than using the standard "Find" command in a spreadsheet. Write the expression to search for (or lookup) a sales representative's sales for a particular month using the sample sales data table in the text.

KE4-8 HOW DO I USE ADVANCED FUNCTIONS SUCH AS SOLVER?

What is solver? How would it help an analyst in their position or how could it be used in a meeting? What are constraints and why are they important? Assuming you were an analyst at McDonalds Corporation, provide an example of a constraint used in a solution that maximizes revenue during breakfast hours.

KE4-9 WHAT ARE PIVOT TABLES AND HOW DO I USE THEM?

Describe the advantages of Pivot Tables over embedded formulas in spreadsheets. Explain why it is important to fully know your data before using Pivot Tables.

KE4-10 HOW CAN YOU PRINT RESULTS?

Explain the purpose and use of *Print Preview*. Open Excel, go to the *PAGE LAYOUT* tab, and explain the purpose of the *Margins, Orientation*, and *Print Area* tools in the *Page Setup* section. Also, explain the function of the *View* and *Print* checkboxes in the *Gridlines* and *Headings* portion of the *Sheet Options* section.

MyLab MIS

MyLab MIS is an online learning and testing environment that features the perfect study tools to help you master the concepts covered in this chapter. Log into MyLab to test your knowledge of key chapter concepts and explore additional practice tools, including videos, flashcards, and more!

KEY TERMS AND CONCEPTS

Cell 76	Spreadsheet 75	Workbook 75	solver 91
Ribbon 77	SUM 89	Worksheet 75	pivot tables 92

USING YOUR KNOWLEDGE

KE4-1. Open Excel and duplicate each of the actions in this Knowledge Extension.

KE4-2. Create a new workbook and take the following actions:

a. Name and save your workbook using a name of your own choosing.

b. Enter the value *This is the content of cell C7* into cell C7.

c. Use F2 to change the value in cell C7 to *This is part of the content of cell C7*.

d. Add the value *January* to cells B2 through B14. Key the data just once.

e. Add the value *January* to cell C2 and the value *February* to cell C3. Highlight both cells C2 and C3 and drag the small black box down to cell C14. Explain what happens.

f. Create a list of odd numbers from 1 to 11 in cells C3 through C8. Key only the values 1 and 3.

g. Enter the value *MIS-1* in cell D2 and the value *MIS-2* in cell D3. Highlight cells D2 and D3 and drag the small black box down to cell D14. Explain what happens.

KE4-3. Click the tab named *Sheet2* in the workbook you used for question 2.

a. Place the labels *Part Description*, *Quantity on Hand*, *Cost*, and *Total Value* in cells B2, C2, D2, and E2, respectively. Centre each label in its cell and make the labels bold. (Do this by highlighting the labels and clicking the bold B in the *Font* section of the *Home* tab.) Make each column large enough to show the entire label after formatting.

b. In cells B3, B4, B5, B6, and B7, respectively, enter the following values:

- This is where one would type the description of Part 1
- This is where one would type the description of Part 2
- This is where one would type the description of Part 3
- This is where one would type the description of Part 4
- This is where one would type the description of Part 5

Enter these values using the fewest possible keystrokes.

c. Enter the quantity-on-hand values *100*, *150*, *100*, *175*, and *200* in cells C3 through C7, respectively. Enter these values using the fewest possible keystrokes.

d. Enter the values *$100*, *$178*, *$87*, *$195*, and *$117* in cells D3 through D7, respectively. Do not enter the dollar signs. Instead, enter only the numbers and then reformat the cells so that Excel will place them.

e. In cell E3, enter a formula that will multiply the quantity on hand (C3) by the cost (D3).

f. Create the same formula in cells E4 through E7. Use select and copy operations.

g. Explain what is magic about the operation in part f.

h. Print the result of your activities in parts a–f. Print your document in landscape mode, showing cell boundaries and row and column names.

KE4-4. Create a spreadsheet containing the sales data.

a. Label cell G2 "Average Sales".

b. In cells G3 to G7 calculate the mean average monthly sales by either averaging the cells C, D, and E or dividing cell F by three.

c. Label cell H2 "Sales Representative" and cell H3 as "Average Monthly Sales".

d. In cell I3 enter a formula that will use the value in cell I2 to lookup the average sales.

e. Explain why this is better than using the find (cntl F) command.

KE4-5. Create a spreadsheet containing the Sample Data for Pivot Tables. This will be used to Pivot the sample data to show the minimum and maximum price (in dollars) for each type of SKU (frame, wheels, and gearing).

a. Select the cells containing data (A1 – H18).

b. Create a Pivot Table from the Insert Ribbon (select New Worksheet as the destination).

c. Drag Class and Description fields into ROWS box.

d. Drag Price into VALUES box.

e. Select Sum of Price drop down icon and select Value Field Settings.

f. Choose Maximum to identify the highest price for each type of item.

g. Repeat step f but change the value to Minimum to identify the lowest price for each item type.

h. Experiment with other types of tables including calculating the average SKU number.

Explain why Pivot Tables can be powerful but can also be dangerous if you do not understand the types and format of your variables and fields.

MyLab MIS

Go to the Assignments section of your MyLab to complete these writing exercises.

KE4-1 Explain why spreadsheets are so widely used in business. Why are they so useful to so many different types of business workers? How does their relative ease of use compared to databases affect their use by workers?

KE4-2 Explain why knowing how to use spreadsheets effectively could impact your future employment opportunities. How might the ability to create more complex spreadsheets increase your earnings potential? Why is it important to know how to use spreadsheets effectively regardless of the industry you are working in?

PART 2

Using Information Technology

MIS in Action

Using Information Technology

The next three chapters address the technology that underlies information systems. You may think that such technology is unimportant to you as a business professional. However, as you will see, today's managers and business professionals work with information technology constantly, as consumers, if not in more involved ways.

Chapter 4 discusses hardware, software, and open source alternatives and defines basic terms and fundamental computing concepts. It briefly touches on new developments in self-driving cars, 3D printing, and the Internet of Things.

Chapter 5 addresses the data component of information systems by describing database processing. You will learn essential database terminology and be introduced to techniques for processing databases. We will also introduce data modelling because you may be required to evaluate data models for databases that others develop for you.

Chapter 6 continues the discussion of computing devices begun in Chapter 4 and describes data communications, Internet technologies, and the cloud. It also addresses potential security problems that may come from using the cloud.

The purpose of these three chapters is to teach you technology sufficient for you to be an effective IT consumer, like Mateo, Joni, Cam, and Alexis at Falcon Security. You will learn basic terms, fundamental concepts, and useful frameworks so that you will have the knowledge to ask insightful questions and make appropriate requests of the information systems professionals who will work with you.

It is difficult to stay up to date with the latest technology advancements because things are changing so quickly. Every year a slew of new innovations come out. Some of them may represent real threats to your organization's strategy. Others may represent potential new opportunities for growth. It is important to be able to understand the strategic implications these new technologies represent. You need to be able to ask the right questions.

The concepts and frameworks presented in these chapters will be far more useful to you than learning the latest technology trends. Trends come and go. The technology you are using now will probably be outdated in 10 years, if not sooner. Understanding how to assess the business implications behind any new technological innovation will be a benefit to you throughout your career.

Hardware and Software

STUDY QUESTIONS

Q4-1   **WHAT DO BUSINESS PROFESSIONALS NEED TO KNOW ABOUT COMPUTER HARDWARE?**

Q4-2   **HOW CAN NEW HARDWARE AFFECT COMPETITIVE STRATEGIES?**

Q4-3   **WHAT DO BUSINESS PROFESSIONALS NEED TO KNOW ABOUT SOFTWARE?**

Q4-4   **IS OPEN SOURCE SOFTWARE A VIABLE ALTERNATIVE?**

MIS in Action

Cam Forset, the operations manager of Falcon Security, asked Mateo Thomas, CEO, Joni Campbell, CFO, and Alexis Moore, head of sales, to come down to the small hangar bay to see how the testing of the new 3D-printed drone is coming along. Mateo asked Cam to investigate the possibility of using 3D-printed parts to make drones in-house rather than buy them from vendors. This could be a tremendous cost-savings opportunity and give the company greater flexibility in updating its current fleet of drones.

Cam waves to Mateo and Joni to come over and look at the screen that she and Alexis are looking at. The screen is showing a live video feed from the new drone as it flies around the perimeter of the building.

"Well, it works—sort of." Cam says to Mateo and Joni with a forced smile. "It's *pretty* stable, and we can get streaming video. I just wish it hadn't taken 2 weeks to get it running." Cam's voice has an undeniably displeased tone.

"That's OK. What was the total cost to make it?" Mateo asks.

"Well, this specific quad cost nearly nothing. We harvested all of the internals from a couple broken quads we had lying around. Everything else we printed." Cam points to a rack of dismantled quadcopters. "We found some free designs on the Web, but we had to make some changes so they would work with our internals."

"Well that's good news, isn't it?" Mateo asks.

"Well, not really," Cam says with a skeptical tone. "If we wanted to build more drones, we'd need to harvest more parts from existing drones or buy generic parts and try to see if they'll work together."

 KE   **Chapter 4 optional knowledge extension is**
Knowledge Extension 5 Mobile Systems available in the MyLab MIS

Joni and Mateo both look confused. Mateo shakes his head and asks, "Well, why didn't you build it with generic parts in the first place?"

"Well, honestly, we weren't sure we could make it work even if we used existing internal components. I've never *made* a quadcopter before," Cam says flatly. "We ended up printing about 20 parts, but we still needed motors, a speed controller, a flight control board, a radio transmitter and receiver, propellers, batteries, and a charger."

"We also needed to make sure it could integrate with our internal systems. We didn't want to start experimenting with generic components until we knew we could actually make a quad that could fly," she adds.

"So your next step is to take out the existing internal components and replace them with generic parts to see if they will work, right?" Mateo asks.

"Well…" Cam starts to say.

Joni interrupts, "It probably won't matter if the generic components work or not. Essentially we've just replaced the frame, skids, and a few other parts to hold the camera. We still have to buy the other nonprintable component parts. Those won't be cheap. Add in the additional labor costs to assemble and test each quad…" she trails off.

"Plus the time and labor to integrate them with our internal systems," Alexis picks up her train of thought. "That won't be easy or cheap."

"Exactly," Cam says. "3D printing our own drones isn't going to save us enough money. There aren't enough parts that can be replaced. Yes, the passive recharging platform we developed using 3D-printed parts was a huge success. It has allowed us to automate the recharging process and extend the reach of our drones. But I just don't think 3D printing our own drones is going reduce our hardware costs enough to justify us becoming a drone manufacturer."

Mateo looks disappointed. "Well, maybe you're right. I really wish there was some way to make it work. It just seems like we keep burning through cash buying dozens of drones that become obsolete in a few years. It's really frustrating being on the cutting edge."

"You mean the bleeding edge…right?" Joni says with a smirk.

Q4-1 WHAT DO BUSINESS PROFESSIONALS NEED TO KNOW ABOUT COMPUTER HARDWARE?

Our discussion begins by recognizing three important themes that have emerged from information technology adoption over the past four decades:

1. *Price and performance advances:* IT is continuously evolving. According to Moore's Law[1] in 18 months the price of a given integrated circuit (IC) will be halved or, for the same amount of money, you will be able to buy a new IC with twice as much functionality.

---

[1] For more information, see www.intel.com/content/www/us/en/silicon-innovations/moores-law-technology.html.

However, it is not just the price of processing power that has decreased. Data storage and network capacity have also improved dramatically, so inexpensive access to high-bandwidth resources, such as YouTube and Netflix, have quickly become a reality.

2. *Smaller is better:* The history of IT can be summarized as an ongoing effort to make IT smaller and more powerful, with the capability to be used almost anywhere. This trend is not likely to stop, as proven by the advancement of nanotechnology.[2] The three main components of a modern computer—the processor, the memory, and the storage—have all been getting smaller and costing less, and current technology is both small enough and powerful enough to be useful almost everywhere.

3. *The network is the thing:* The value of IT can be measured not only in the power of the processor but also in the power of the network that can be accessed through the machine. All computing machines have inevitably moved toward networks for communication and collaboration, and the bandwidth—the rate at which computers can communicate—has increased significantly. The pervasiveness of IT will continue to increase as networks become cheaper and easier to join. The interesting question to ponder is, after microcomputers, the Internet, and social networking, what is next? As we will see in Chapters 6 and 9, the answer may be as close to you as your phone.

Most people think of computer hardware as a laptop, a desktop, a server, or maybe even a tablet. As time passes, however, the way we envision computer hardware is changing. Take phones as an example. Twenty-five years ago, phones were strictly used for voice communication. No one would have considered a phone as a piece of computer hardware, let alone the primary computing device for many individuals.

Smartphones have substantial processing power, the ability to connect to networks, internal memory, and virtual keyboards and can interconnect with other devices. Now a "phone" is a powerful piece of computing hardware. Computing hardware is also being integrated into other devices, such as watches, glasses, TVs, cars, and even toothbrushes.

Computer hardware consists of electronic components and related gadgetry that input, process, output, and store data according to instructions encoded in computer programs or software. All hardware today has more or less the same components, at least to the level that is important to us. We will begin with a look at those components, and then we will quickly survey basic types of hardware and the capacity of these devices.

Hardware Components

Every computer has a **central processing unit (CPU)**, which is sometimes called "*the brain*" of the computer. Although the design of the CPU has nothing in common with the anatomy of animal brains, this description is helpful because the CPU does have the "smarts" of the machine. The CPU selects instructions, processes them, performs arithmetic and logical comparisons, and stores results of operations in memory. Some computers have two or more CPUs. A computer with two CPUs is called a **dual-processor** computer. **Quad-processor** computers have four CPUs. Some high-end computers have 16 or more CPUs.

CPUs vary in speed, function, and cost. Hardware vendors such as Intel, Advanced Micro Devices, and National Semiconductor continually improve CPU speed and capabilities while reducing CPU costs (as discussed in Moore's Law earlier in the chapter). Whether you or your department needs the latest, greatest CPU depends on the nature of your work.

The CPU works in conjunction with **main memory**. The CPU reads data and instructions from memory and then stores the results of computations in main memory. Main memory is sometimes called **RAM**, for random access memory.

---

[2] Learn more about nanotechnology at http://science.howstuffworks.com/nanotechnology.htm.

In addition to RAM and one or more CPUs, all computers also include **storage hardware**, which is used to save data and programs. Magnetic disks (also called *hard disks*) are the most common storage device. Solid-state storage (also known as an *SSD drive*) is much faster than a hard drive and gaining in popularity, but is several times more expensive. USB flash drives are small, portable solid-state storage devices that can be used to back up data and transfer it from one computer to another. Optical disks such as CDs and DVDs are also popular portable storage media.

Types of Hardware

Figure 4-1 lists the basic types of hardware. **Personal computers (PCs)** are classic computing devices which in the past were the primary computer type used by individuals and businesses. Changing consumer preferences and more compact technology has resulted in PCs gradually being supplanted by tablets and other mobile devices (though many PC users still exist). The Mac Pro is an example of a modern PC. Apple brought **tablets** to prominence with the iPad in 2010. In 2012, Microsoft announced Surface and Google announced the Nexus series, all tablets. Tablets continue to evolve.

Hardware Type	Example(s)
Personal computer (PC) *Including desktops and laptops*	Apple Mac Pro
Tablet *Including e-book readers*	iPad, Microsoft Surface, Google Nexus, Kindle Fire
Phablet	Samsung Galaxy Note, iPhone 6 Plus
Smartphone	Samsung Galaxy, iPhone
Server	Dell PowerEdge 12G server
Server farm	Racks of servers (Figure 4-2)

Figure 4-1 Basic Types of Hardware

Moving down the list of hardware, a mobile device called a *phablet* combines the functionality of a smartphone with the larger screen of a tablet. Devices like Samsung's Galaxy Note or Apple's iPhone Plus would fall into this crossover category. Smartphones are cell phones with processing capability; the Samsung Galaxy S8, Google Pixel 2, or iPhone 8 are good examples. Since it is hard to find a cell phone that is not "smart," people often just call them phones.

A **server** is a computer that is designed to support processing requests from many remote computers and users. A server is essentially a PC on steroids, and it differs from a PC principally because of what it does. The relationship between PCs and servers is similar to the relationship between clients and servers at a typical restaurant: In short, servers take requests from clients and then bring them things. In restaurants, these things are food, drinks, and cutlery. Similarly, in computing environments, servers can send webpages, email, files, or data to PCs or other devices. PCs, tablets, and smartphones that access servers are called **clients**. As of 2015, one good example of a server is the Dell PowerEdge server.

Finally, a **server farm** is a collection of, typically, thousands of servers. (See Figure 4-2.) Server farms are often placed in large truck trailers that hold 5,000 servers or more. Typically a trailer has two large cables coming out of it; one is for power, and the other is for data communications. The operator of the farm backs a trailer into a pre-prepared slab (in a warehouse or sometimes out in the open air), plugs in the power and communications cables, and, voilà, thousands of servers are up and running!

Figure 4-2 Server Farm

Source: Andrew Twort/Alamy

Increasingly, server infrastructure is delivered as a service via the Internet, which is often referred to as *the cloud*. We will discuss cloud computing in Chapter 6, after you have some knowledge of data communications.

The capacities of each type of computer hardware are specified according to data units, as you will see in the section that follows.

Computer Data

Computers represent data using **binary digits**, also called **bits**. A bit is either a zero or a one. Bits are used for computer data because they are easy to represent physically, as illustrated in Figure 4-3. A switch can be either closed or open. A computer can be designed so that an open switch represents zero and a closed switch represents one. Or the orientation of a magnetic field can represent a bit: magnetism in one direction represents a zero, while magnetism in the opposite direction represents a one. Alternatively, with optical media, small pits are burned onto the surface of the disk so that they will reflect light. In a given spot, a reflection indicates a one, whereas no reflection indicates a zero.

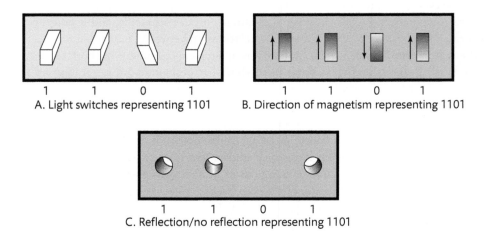

Figure 4-3 Bits Are Easy to Represent Physically

Computer Data Sizes

All forms of computer data are represented by bits. The data can be numbers, characters, currency amounts, photos, recordings, or whatever—all are simply a string of bits. For reasons that interest many but are probably irrelevant for future managers, bits are grouped into 8-bit chunks called **bytes**. For character data, such as the letters in a person's name, one character will fit into one byte. Thus, when you read a specification stating that a computing device has 100 million bytes of memory, you know that the device can hold up to 100 million characters.

Bytes are used to measure sizes of non-character data as well. Someone might say, for example, that a given picture is 100 000 bytes in size. This statement means the length of the bit string that represents the picture is 100 000 bytes or 800 000 bits (because there are 8 bits per byte).

The specifications for the data storage capacity of main memory, disks, and other computer devices are expressed in bytes. Figure 4-4 shows the set of abbreviations that are used to represent data storage capacity. A **kilobyte,** abbreviated **KB**, is a collection of 1024 bytes. A **megabyte,** or **MB**, consists of 1024 kilobytes. A **gigabyte,** or **GB**, is 1024 megabytes; a **terabyte,** or **TB**, is 1024 gigabytes; a **petabyte,** or **PB**, is 1024 terabytes; an **exabyte,** or **EB**, is 1024 petabytes; and a **zettabyte,** or **ZB**, is 1024 exabytes. Sometimes you will see these definitions simplified to say that 1KB equals 1000 bytes, 1MB equals 1000KB, and so on. Such simplifications are incorrect, but they do ease the math.

Term	Definition	Abbreviation
Byte	Number of bits to represent one character	
Kilobyte	1024 bytes	KB
Megabyte	1024 K = 1 048 576 bytes	MB
Gigabyte	1024 MB = 1 073 741 824 bytes	GB
Terabyte	1024 GB = 1 099 511 627 776 bytes	TB
Petabyte	1024 TB = 1 125 899 906 842 624 bytes	PB
Exabyte	1024 PB = 1 152 921 504 606 846 976 bytes	EB
Zettabyte	1024 EB = 1 180 591 620 717 411 303 424 bytes	ZB

Figure 4-4 Important Storage-Capacity Terminology

To put these sizes in perspective consider that Cisco estimates that annual global Internet traffic volume in 2021 will be 7.7 Exabytes per day, which is equivalent to 707 billion DVDs per year, 59 billion DVDs per month, or 81 million DVDs per hour.[3]

Specifying Hardware with Computer Data Sizes and Processing Speeds

Computer disk capacities are specified according to the amount of data they can contain. Thus, a 500GB disk can contain up to 500GB of data and programs. There is some overhead, so the actual available storage capacity is not quite 500GB, but it's close enough.

Storage capacity is not the only thing to consider when selecting a device; you can also purchase computers with CPUs of different speeds. CPU speed is expressed in cycles

---

[3] Cisco Systems, Inc., "VNI Forecast Highlights," Cisco.com, accessed July 15, 2017, www.cisco.com/web/solutions/sp/vni/vni_forecast_highlights/index.html.

called **hertz**. In 2017, a slow personal computer had a speed of 3.0 Gigahertz, whereas a fast personal computer had a speed of 4.0+ Gigahertz, with multiple processors. As predicted by Moore's Law, CPU speeds continually increase.

An employee who does only simple tasks such as word processing does not need a fast CPU; a 2.0 Gigahertz CPU will be fine. However, an employee who processes large, complicated spreadsheets; manipulates large database files; or edits large picture, sound, or video files needs a fast computer like a dual processor with 4.0 Gigahertz or more. Similarly, when it comes to data storage, employees whose work requires them to use many large applications at the same time need 16 GB or more of RAM. Others can manage sufficiently with less.

One last comment: A device's cache and main memory are **volatile**, meaning their contents are lost when the power is off. In contrast, magnetic and optical disks are **nonvolatile**, meaning their contents survive when the power is off. Thus, if you suddenly lose power, the contents of unsaved memory—say, documents that have been altered—will be lost. To better protect your data, get into the habit of frequently (every few minutes or so) saving documents or files that you are changing. Save your documents before your roommate trips over your power cord!

Q4-2 HOW CAN NEW HARDWARE AFFECT COMPETITIVE STRATEGIES?

Organizations are interested in new hardware because they represent potential opportunities, or threats, to their ability to generate revenue. It is important to keep an eye on new tech hardware for the same reason you watch the weather forecast: You care about how the future will affect you. In the following sections, we will look at three new hardware developments that have the potential to disrupt existing organizations: the Internet of Things, self-driving cars, and 3D printing.

The Internet of Things

The first disruptive force that has the power to change business is the **Internet of Things (IoT)**. This is the idea that objects are becoming connected to the Internet so that they can interact with other devices, applications, or services. In other words, everyday objects are increasingly being embedded with hardware capable of sensing, processing, and transmitting data. These objects can then connect to a network and share data with other applications, services, or devices.

Take your mobile phone, for example. It is probably a smartphone, but it wasn't always "smart." It started out as a simple device that just handled voice calls. Over time it became a **smart device** by adding more processing power, more memory, Internet access, Wi-Fi connectivity, and the ability to interconnect with other devices and applications (Figure 4-5). People began to use their mobile phones much differently than before. This shift also changed the way businesses operate. Increasingly, people are using their mobile phones as their primary computing device and organizations are racing to find ways to incorporate mobile purchasing.

What do you think will happen when other devices become smart? How would your life change if you had access to a smart car, smart home appliances, or an entire smart building? Within a few short decades, it is possible that you may be able to interact with nearly every object around you from your smartphone. In fact, your devices may be able to talk to other devices, anticipate your actions, make unsolicited changes, and autonomously configure themselves.

This shift away from "dumb" machines to interconnected smart devices is not lost on businesses. Consumers like smart electronics and are willing to pay more for them.

Figure 4-5 The first generation iPhone

Source: Cristo95/Shutterstock

Accordingly, businesses want to improve the existing devices they manufacture into smart devices and then sell them for considerably more. If they don't, their competition will.

The iPhone, for example, was introduced by Apple Inc. in 2007 when Apple was thought of as a computer hardware and software company. When the iPhone was first released, the mobile phone market was already mature and to some extent saturated. Industry leaders could have created a smartphone, but they didn't. Apple's success with the iPhone was probably unanticipated by other phone manufacturers. The iPhone fundamentally altered the way people used their mobile phones and changed consumer perception of wanted (*needed*) devices. Just as the iPhone revolutionized the mobile phone industry, a wave of other smart devices will likely revolutionize other industries as well.

Impact of the Internet of Things

In the years to come, the impact of IoT will be felt by many different high-tech industries. Smart devices need microprocessors, memory, wireless network connections, power sources, and new software. These devices will also need new protocols, more bandwidth, and tighter security, and they will consume more energy.

One of the most attractive targets for smart devices is in consumer homes. The Canadian home is increasingly connected though one of the main barriers to adoption is simply a lack of awareness of connected technologies. According to Nielsen's Connected Home Report, 46% of Canadian consumers will either own or say they plan to purchase connected home technologies by 2018.[4]

A good example of the long term push toward smart devices used in industry is exemplified by General Electric's (GE) Industrial Internet.[5] The Industrial Internet is a broad program focused on creating smart devices, analyzing data from these devices, and then making changes that increase efficiencies, reduce waste, and improve decision making. There is considerable potential for smart devices in hospitals, power grids, manufacturing plants, and transportation. For instance, GE estimates that an average airline using smart devices

[4] See Neilsen Connected Home Report, accessed July 15, 2017, www.nielsen.com/ca/en/insights/news/2016/the-increasingly-connected-canadian-home.html.

[5] Peter C. Evans and Marco Annunziata, "Industrial Internet: Pushing the Boundaries of Minds and Machines," General Electric, November 26, 2012, accessed July 15, 2017, www.ge.com/docs/chapters/Industrial_Internet.pdf.

in its jet aircraft could save an average of 2 percent in fuel consumption. The resulting fuel and carbon dioxide savings would be the equivalent of removing 10 000 cars from the road.[6]

Microsoft has also made significant gains using smart buildings. The company has created a network of 125 smart buildings spread over 500 acres in their home campus in Redmond, Washington (Figure 4-6).[7] This campus's operations center processes 500 million data transactions every day from 30 000 devices, including heaters, air conditioners, lights, fans, and doors. Thanks to this network, Microsoft engineers were able to reduce energy costs by 6 percent to 10 percent a year by identifying problems like wasteful lighting, competing heating and cooling systems, and rogue fans. For Microsoft, that's millions of dollars in savings.

Figure 4-6 Microsoft's Redmond, WA, Campus

Source: Ian Dagnall/Alamy Stock Photo

What if every corporate building were a smart building? When you consider that 40 percent of the world's energy is consumed in corporate buildings, you can start to get an idea of the potentially immense cost savings.

Self-driving Cars

The second disruptive force that could change the way businesses operate is self-driving cars. A **self-driving car** (also known as a *driverless car* or *autonomous vehicle*) will use a variety of sensors to navigate like a traditional car but without human intervention. It will be full of advanced hardware and integrated software, and it will be the epitome of a mobile system. In fact, it will be so mobile that it will be able to move without anyone being inside.

Whether you approve or disapprove, self-driving cars are in your very near future. The Ontario government recently launched an automated vehicle pilot project (January 2016),

---

[6] Ibid.

[7] Jennifer Warnick, "88 Acres: How Microsoft Quietly Built the City of the Future," Microsoft Corp., April 15, 2013, accessed Jul 15, 2017, www.microsoft.com/en-us/news/stories/88acres/88-acres-how-microsoft-quietly-built-the-city-of-the-future-chapter-1.aspx.

the first in Canada.[8] The project allows researchers to test self-driving technology on public roads once they obtain a permit. As a precaution, a licensed driver needs to be in the driver's seat ready to take over if something goes wrong.

Google started its self-driving vehicle program in 2009. The program continued to grow and Google eventually created Waymo in 2016 as a technology company focused on driverless cars. As of 2017, Google's prototype cars have logged more than 3 million miles.[9] The following sections illustrate how self-driving cars could make things easier, cheaper, and safer. They may also disrupt many well-established industries including much of the trucking industry (automated trucks) and other industries where automated transport is an emerging reality.

Self-driving Cars Will Make Things Easier

Imagine how a self-driving car could change the life of a typical family. For example, a self-driving car could allow Dad to review sales reports while "driving" to work. As a result, he would probably be less stressed—and much more productive—during his commute than he was with his old car. The self-driving car could then drop the kids off at school—without Dad in the car—and return home to take Mom to work.

After work, the family could go shopping and be dropped off curbside at the store. No need to park anymore. Getting around town would be safer, too. While shopping, Dad might get a message from his college-aged daughter saying that she needs him to send the car to pick her up at the airport. Dad will certainly be glad he doesn't have to drive all the way out there himself!

As Dad thinks fondly about his new car, he might remember the days when he had to drive himself. It was a long and tedious process. Now, the car plans the route for him, fills itself up with gas, communicates with intersections so he never gets a red light, and reroutes itself if there is an accident or traffic. Most importantly, Dad no longer gets annoyed at other drivers. Travelling is just easier now.

Later, the family plans a vacation to a distant locale. Taking the self-driving car is the way to go. No airport security lines; family members no longer need to be frisked by overzealous TSA agents; they get comfortable seats that face each other and they can sleep while "driving"; there are no baggage fees; and renting a car once they reach to their destination is unnecessary. Plus, they can leave anytime they'd like. Driving isn't so bad when you don't actually drive!

Self-driving Cars Will Make Things Cheaper

You have seen how a self-driving car can make life easier. But what about cost? Will a self-driving car be more or less expensive than the car you have now?

Self-driving cars will probably be much less expensive over time than your current car—particularly once other related costs are considered. Early adopters will pay a premium when self-driving cars first hit the market, but that is true of most new products. As time passes, however, cost savings will show up in several ways.

In the preceding scenario, for example, you may have noticed that the family had only one car. This reflects the likelihood that self-driving cars will be used more effectively than cars are used now. Today, most cars sit dormant for 22 hours a day. Sharing a self-driving car could eliminate the need for multiple cars.

Self-driving cars will probably have superior driving skills, which may result in additional savings. You could also save on fuel because your car will drive more efficiently (less braking, engine revving, and street racing!). Costly traffic tickets and parking tickets could be avoided, and your car insurance might drop dramatically. Imagine a world where automobile accidents become a thing of the past.

[8] CBC news report, Nov. 28, 2016, accessed July 15, 2017, www.cbc.ca/news/business/automated-vehicles-1.3870605.
[9] See https://waymo.com/ontheroad/, accessed July 15, 2017.

Self-driving Cars Will Make Things Safer

Yes, you read that right—safer. Currently, 90 percent of motor vehicle crashes are caused by human error.[10] Motor vehicle crashes are the leading cause of death for people ages 3 to 33. In fact, driving may be your most dangerous daily activity.

In the future, however, your car will be able to better assess road conditions, react more quickly than you, and have better information about your driving environment. It will be able to communicate with other surrounding cars, dynamically analyze traffic patterns, avoid construction sites, and contact emergency services if needed.

Self-driving cars should result in safer driving, fewer accidents, fewer drunk drivers, fewer road-rage incidents, and fewer auto–pedestrian accidents. Cars should be able to go faster with fewer crashes. In the future, "manual" driving may be a risky and expensive hobby.

Self-driving Cars Will Disrupt Businesses

As the preceding discussion suggests, self-driving cars have the potential to disrupt several well-established industries. Self-driving cars may mean fewer cars on the road. Fewer cars on the road may mean fewer cars sold (affecting the transportation industry), fewer auto loans written (affecting the finance industry), fewer automobile insurance policies under-written (affecting the insurance industry), fewer auto parts sold due to fewer accidents (manufacturing), and fewer parking lots (affecting the real estate industry). Also, if driving is a more attractive alternative, consumers might take more trips by car than by plane or train (again affecting the transportation industry).

On the other side of the coin, the production of self-driving cars will mean more jobs for engineers, programmers, and systems designers. There will be more computer hardware, sensors, and cameras in these vehicles.

Corporations may not completely appreciate the far-reaching effects of self-driving cars on existing industries—but what about you? How might self-driving cars disrupt your lifestyle? Suppose you get married in a few years and have a child. Will your child ever drive a car? Will driving a "manual" car be too costly? Your potential offspring may never learn how to drive a car, but that may not be so strange. Do you know how to ride a horse? Your ancestors did.

3D Printing

The third disruptive force that has the power to change businesses is 3D printing. As you learned in Chapter 3, 3D printing alters the competitive landscape. Moreover, it may change the nature of businesses themselves. Think back to the Falcon Security case at the start of this chapter. The Falcon Security team chose to not make its own drones because doing so wasn't going to save the company enough money. It didn't want to use 3D printing to become a drone manufacturer.

While manufacturing wasn't right for Falcon, it is a viable option for some companies. Consider how Nike has used 3D printing to improve the way it designs and creates shoes. It used a 3D printer to create the world's first 3D-printed cleat plate for a shoe called the *Nike Vapor Laser Talon*.[11] Nike chose to use a 3D printer to produce the cleat because it could create the optimal geometric shape for optimal traction. Thus, Nike was able to design and produce a lighter, stronger cleat much more quickly than before.

3D printers have the potential to affect a broad array of industries. You can get an idea of the scope of change when you realize that 3D printers can print in more than just plastics

---

[10] Network of Employers for Traffic Safety, "10 Facts Employers Must Know," accessed July 15, 2017, http://trafficsafety.org/safety/fleet-safety/10-facts-employers-must-know.

[11] Liz Stinson, "For Super Bowl, Nike Uses 3-D Printing to Create a Faster Football Cleat," *Wired*, January 10, 2014, accessed July 15, 2017, www.wired.com/2014/01/nike-designed-fastest-cleat-history.

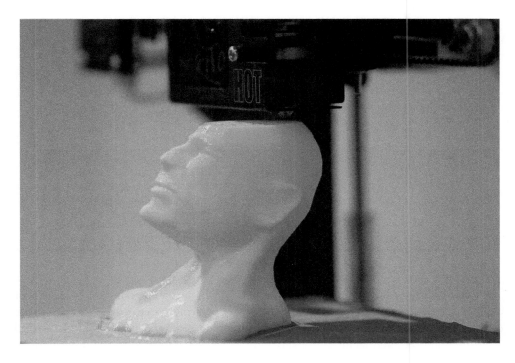

Figure 4-7 3D Printer

Source: Justin Sullivan/Staff/ Getty Images

(Figure 4-7). The printing capabilities of 3D printers also include metals, ceramics, foods, and biological materials.

New advances will provide the ability to 3D-print in an even wider variety of materials. This printing can be considered across many industries including aerospace, defense, automotive, entertainment, and healthcare. What happens when it becomes feasible to 3D-print extra-large objects like cars, planes, boats, houses, and drones?

Below are three examples of nontraditional 3D printing (i.e., they do not use plastics). Consider how disruptive each one would be to its respective industry:

- 3D Systems ChefJet[tm] Pro can print complex sugary structures in flavours like chocolate, vanilla, mint, cherry, sour apple, and watermelon.[12] With a ChefJet, even a culinary novice could produce intricate, beautiful, and fully customized deserts.

- Researchers at the Harvard School of Engineering and Applied Sciences were able to print a 3D biological structure with blood vessels that could deliver nutrients and remove waste.[13] This development means doctors may someday be able to print fully functional replacements for damaged tissues by simply pressing print. Not only could this save lives, but it could also lower insurance premiums and the overall cost of health care.

- The San Francisco APIS Cor 3D printed a 400 sq.ft. structure in 24 hours.[14] The 3D printer used a large, mobile crane-like piece of equipment to continuously pour layers of cement in one continuous process, building both the internal and external structure simultaneously. Building this way costs much less than traditional fabrication.

[12] Venessa Wong, "A Guide to All the Food That's Fit to 3D Print (So Far)," *BusinessWeek,* January 28, 2014, accessed July 15, 2017, www.businessweek.com/articles/2014-01-28/all-the-food-thats-fit-to-3d-print-from-chocolates-to-pizza.

[13] Dan Ferber, "An Essential Step Toward Printing Living Tissues," Harvard School of Engineering and Applied Sciences, February 19, 2014, accessed July 15, 2017, www.seas.harvard.edu/news/2014/02/essential-step-toward-printing-living-tissues.

[14] "This San Francisco start-up will 3D print your house in 24 hours and it will only cost US$10K," *National Post,* March 7, 2017, accessed July 15, 2017, http://nationalpost.com/news/world/this-san-francisco-start-up-will-3d-print-your-house-in-24-hours-and-it-will-only-cost-10k-u-s/.

Q4-3 WHAT DO BUSINESS PROFESSIONALS NEED TO KNOW ABOUT SOFTWARE?

As a future manager or business professional, you need to know the essential terminology and software concepts that will enable you to be an intelligent software consumer. To begin, consider the basic categories of software shown in Figure 4-8.

Figure 4-8 Categories of Computer Software

	Operating Systems	Application Programs
Client	Programs that control the client computer's resources	Applications that are processed on client computers
Server	Programs that control the server computer's resources	Applications that are processed on server computers

Every computer has an **operating system (OS)**, which is a program that controls that computer's resources. Some of the functions of an operating system are to read and write data, allocate main memory, perform memory swapping, start and stop programs, respond to error conditions, and facilitate backup and recovery. In addition, the operating system creates and manages the user interface, including the display, keyboard, mouse, and other devices.

Although the operating system makes the computer usable, it does little application-specific work. If you want to check the weather or access a database, for example, you need application programs, such as an iPad weather application or Oracle's customer relationship management (CRM) software.

Both client and server computers need an operating system, though they need not be the same. Further, both clients and servers can process application programs. The application's design determines whether the client, the server, or both process it.

To be an educated computer consumer, you also need to understand two important software-related constraints. First, remember that particular versions of an operating system are written for particular types of hardware. For example, Microsoft Windows works only on processors from Intel and from companies that make processors that conform to the Intel instruction set (i.e., the commands that a CPU can process). With other operating systems, such as Linux, many versions exist for many different instruction sets.

Second, be aware that two types of application programs exist: native and Web. **Native applications** are programs that are written to use a particular operating system. Microsoft Access, for example, will only run on the Windows operating system. Some applications come in multiple versions; for example, there are Windows and Macintosh versions of Microsoft Word. But unless you are informed otherwise, assume that a native application runs on just one operating system. Native applications are sometimes called **thick-client applications**.

A Web application (also known as a **thin-client application**) is designed to run within a computer browser such as Firefox, Chrome, Opera, or Edge (formerly Internet Explorer). Web applications run within the browser and can therefore run on any type of computer. Ideally, a Web application can also run within any browser, although this is not always true (as you will learn).

What Are the Major Operating Systems?

Every business professional needs to know the three major types of operating systems listed in Figure 4-9. Each is also discussed in more detail in the sections that follow.

Category	Operating System	Used for	Remarks
Nonmobile Clients	Windows	Personal computer clients	Most widely used operating system in business. Current version is Windows 10. Includes a touch interface.
	Mac OS	Macintosh clients	First used by graphic artists and others in arts community; now used more widely. First desktop OS to provide a touch interface. Current version is the Mac OS X El Capitan.
	Unix	Workstation clients	Popular on powerful client computers used in engineering, computer-assisted design, architecture. Difficult for the nontechnical user. Almost never used by business clients.
	Linux	Just about anything	Open-source variant of Unix. Adapted to almost every type of computing device. On a PC, used with LibreOffice application software. Rarely used by business clients.
Mobile Clients	Symbian	Nokia, Samsung, and other phones	Popular worldwide, but less so in North America.
	BlackBerry OS	Research in Motion Blackberries	Device and OS developed for use by business. Very popular in beginning, but losing market share to iOS and Android.
	iOS	iPhone, iPod Touch, iPad	Rapidly increasing installed base with success of the iPhone and iPad. Based on Mac OS X.
	Android	Samsung, Google, HTC, and Sony smartphones and tablets	Linux-based phone/tablet operating system from Google. Rapidly increasing market share.
	Windows 10	Nokia and Microsoft Surface	Windows 10 tailored specifically for mobile devices. Full Windows 10 on Surface Pro.
Servers	Windows Server	Servers	Used by businesses with a strong commitment to Microsoft.
	Unix	Servers	Fading from use. Replaced by Linux.
	Linux	Servers	Very popular. Aggressively pushed by IBM.

Figure 4-9   Major Operating Systems

Nonmobile Client Operating Systems

Nonmobile client operating systems are used on personal computers. The most popular is **Microsoft Windows**. Some version of Windows resides on more than 85 percent of the world's desktops, and, if we consider just business users, the figure is more than 95 percent. As of the time of this writing, the most recent version of Windows is Windows 10. Net Applications estimates that overall market share of Windows as of 2017 is Windows 10 at 26.8 percent, Windows 8.1 at 6.4 percent, Windows 8 at 1.8 percent, Windows 7 at 49 percent, and Windows XP at 7.0 percent.[15]

For more on modern-style interfaces, see Knowledge Extension 5, Mobile Systems.

Windows 8 was a major rewrite of prior versions of the Windows operating system. Windows 8 was distinguished by its ability to run what Microsoft calls **modern-style applications**.[16] These applications, now carried over into Windows 10, are touch-screen oriented and provide context-sensitive, pop-up menus. They can also be used with a mouse and keyboard. Microsoft claims that modern-style applications work just as well on portable, mobile devices, such as tablet computers, as they do on desktop computers. One key feature of modern-style applications is the minimization of menu bars, status lines, and other visual overhead. Figure 4-10 shows an example of a modern-style version of searching for images in Windows Explorer.

[15] Net Market Share, June 2017, accessed July 15, 2017, https://www.netmarketshare.com/operating-system-market-share.aspx.
[16] Previously called metro-style. Name change by Microsoft, reputedly because of a trademark lawsuit from Europe.

Figure 4-10   Example of the Modern-Style Interface

Source: Microsoft Corporation

Not all computers use Windows, however. For example, Apple Computer, Inc., developed its own operating system for the Macintosh, **macOS**. The current version is macOS 10.13 High Sierra. In the past, macOS was used primarily by graphic artists and workers in the arts community. But for many reasons, primarily the strength of the MacBook products and integration with the iPhone, macOS has made headway into the traditional Windows market. According to Net Applications, as of 2017, the desktop operating system market share was divided between versions of Windows (91 percent), macOS X (6 percent), and Linux (2 percent).[17]

The two other nonmobile client operating systems mentioned in Figure 4-9 are Unix and Linux. **Unix** is an operating system that was developed at Bell Labs in the 1970s. It has been the workhorse of the scientific and engineering communities since then. Unix is seldom used in business.

Linux is a version of Unix that was developed by the open source community. This community is a loosely coupled group of programmers who mostly volunteer their time to contribute code to develop and maintain Linux. The open source community owns Linux, and there is no fee to use it. Linux can run on client computers, but usually only when budget is of paramount concern. By far, Linux is most popular as a server OS.

Mobile Client Operating Systems

Figure 4-9 also lists the five principal mobile operating systems in use in 2017. **Symbian** is popular on phones in Europe and the Far East, but less so in North America. **Android** and **iOS** are the most popular mobile operating systems.

Android is a mobile operating system licensed by Google. Android devices have a very loyal following, especially among technical users. Net Applications estimates Android's market share to be nearly 64 percent in 2017.[18]

iOS is the operating system used on the iPhone, iPod Touch, and iPad. When first released, it broke new ground with its ease of use and compelling display. According to Net Applications, as of 2017, iOS is used on 33 percent of mobile devices. The current version of iOS is iOS 8.

---

[17] "Net Applications," June 2017, 2014, accessed July 15, 2017, www.netapplications.com.
[18] Ibid.

Most industry observers would agree that Apple has led the way, both with the macOS and the iOS, in creating easy-to-use interfaces. Certainly, many innovative ideas have first appeared in a Macintosh or iSomething and then later were added, in one form or another, to the Android and Windows operating systems.

Users who want Windows 10 on mobile devices will get either **Windows 10 (mobile)** on smartphones or a full version of Windows 10 on Surface Pro devices. Windows garners about 1 percent of the mobile OS market share in 2017.

The smartphone market has always been huge, but recently, e-book readers and tablets have substantially increased the market for mobile client operating systems. In addition, migration toward wireless services continues. For example, more Canadian households subscribed *exclusively* to mobile wireless services (23.7%) than to exclusively wireline (i.e. landline) telephone services (13.6%). Similarly, more Canadian households in 2016 also reported subscribing to mobile telephone services (85.6%) than to landline telephone services (75.5%).[19]

Server Operating Systems

The last three rows of Figure 4-9 show the three most popular server operating systems. Windows Server is a version of Windows that has been specially designed and configured for server use. It has much more stringent and restrictive security features than other versions of Windows and is popular on servers in organizations that have made a strong commitment to Microsoft.

Unix can also be used on servers, but it is gradually being replaced by Linux.

Linux is frequently used on servers by organizations that want, for whatever reason, to avoid a server commitment to Microsoft. IBM is the primary proponent of Linux and in the past has used it as a means to better compete against Microsoft. Although IBM does not own Linux, IBM has developed many business systems solutions that employ Linux. By using Linux, neither IBM nor its customers have to pay a licensing fee to Microsoft.

Virtualization

Virtualization is the process by which one physical computer hosts many different virtual (not literal) computers within it. One operating system, called the **host operating system**, runs one or more operating systems as applications. Those hosted operating systems are called **virtual machines (vm)**. Each virtual machine has disk space and other resources allocated to it. The host operating system controls the activities of the virtual machines it hosts to prevent them from interfering with one another. With virtualization, each vm is able to operate exactly the same as it would if it were operating in a stand-alone, nonvirtual environment.

Three types of virtualization exist:

- PC virtualization
- Server virtualization
- Desktop virtualization

With **PC virtualization**, a personal computer, such as a desktop or laptop, hosts several different operating systems. Say a user needs to have both Linux and Windows 10 running on a computer for training or a development project. In that circumstance, the user can load software like Oracle VirtualBox or VMWare Workstation on the host operating system in order to create Linux and Windows 10 virtual machines. The user can run both systems on the same hardware at the same time if the host operating system has sufficient resources (i.e., memory and CPU power), as shown in Figure 4-11.

---

[19] Canadian Radio-television and Telecommunications Commission, accessed July 15, 2017, http://www.crtc.gc.ca/eng/publications/reports/policymonitoring/2016/cmr2.htm.

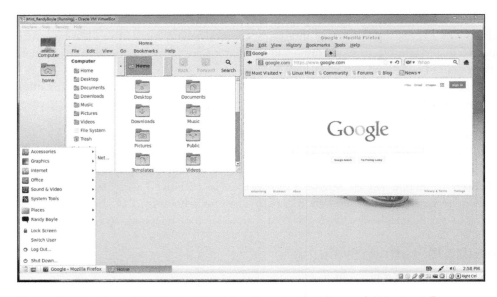

Figure 4-11   Linux Mint Virtual Machine Running in Microsoft Windows 7 Professional

Source: Microsoft Corporation

With **server virtualization**, a server computer hosts one or more other server computers. In Figure 4-12, for instance, a Windows Server computer is hosting two virtual machines. Users can log on to either of those virtual machines, and they will appear as normal servers. Figure 4-13 shows how virtual machine VM3 appears to a user of that server. Notice that a user of VM3 is running a browser that is accessing SharePoint. In fact, this virtual machine was used to generate many of the SharePoint figures in Chapter 2. Server virtualization plays a key role for cloud vendors, as you will learn in Chapter 6.

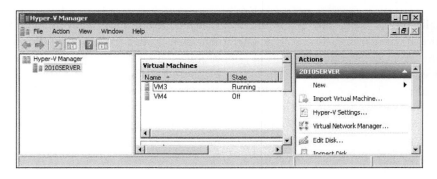

Figure 4-12   Windows Server Computer Hosting Two Virtual Machines

Source: Microsoft Corporation

PC virtualization is interesting as well as quite useful, as described in Chapter 6. Desktop virtualization, on the other hand, has the potential to be revolutionary. With **desktop virtualization**, a server hosts many versions of desktop operating systems. Each of those desktops has a complete user environment and appears to the user to be just another PC. However, the desktop can be accessed from any computer to which the user has access. Thus, you could be at an airport and go to a terminal computer from which you can access your virtualized desktop. To you, it would appear as if that airport computer is your own personal computer. Using a virtual desktop also means that you won't have to worry about losing a corporate laptop or confidential internal data. In addition, it means that many different users could access their own "personal" computers using only a single terminal, like the one in the airport example. IBM offers PC virtualization for as low as $12 a month per PC.

Desktop virtualization is in its infancy, but it might have a major impact during the early years of your career.

Figure 4-13 Virtual Machine Example

Source: Microsoft Corporation

Owning Versus Licensing

Note that when you buy a computer program, you are not actually buying that program. Instead, you are buying a **license** to use that program. For example, when you buy a macOS license, Apple is selling you the right to use macOS; Apple itself continues to own the macOS program. Unlike individuals, large organizations do not buy a license for each computer user. Instead, they negotiate a **site license**, which is a flat fee that authorizes the organization to install the product (operating system or application) on all of that organization's computers or on all of its computers at a specific site.

In the case of Linux, no company can sell you a license to use it. That's because Linux is owned by the open source community, which states that Linux has no licensing fee (with certain reasonable restrictions). Large companies such as IBM and smaller companies such as RedHat can make money by *supporting* Linux, but no company makes money selling Linux licenses.

What Types of Applications Exist, and How Do Organizations Obtain Them?

As previously mentioned, **application software** performs a service or function. Some application programs are general purpose, such as Microsoft Excel or Word. Other application programs provide specific functions. QuickBooks, for example, is an application program that provides general ledger and other accounting functions. In the following sections, we begin by describing categories of application programs and then describe sources for them.

> **To learn more about Microsoft Excel, see Knowledge Extension 4.**

Horizontal Applications

Horizontal-market application software provides capabilities common across all organizations and industries. Word processors, graphics programs, spreadsheets, and presentation programs are all horizontal-market application software.

Some well-known examples of horizontal applications are Microsoft Word, Excel, and PowerPoint. Examples from other vendors include Adobe's Acrobat, Photoshop, and Page-Maker and Jasc Corporation's Paint Shop Pro. These applications are used in a wide variety of businesses across all industries. They are purchased off the shelf, and little customization of features is necessary (or even possible). These applications are the automobile equivalent of a sedan: Everybody buys them and then uses them for different purposes.

Vertical Applications

Vertical-market application software serves the needs of a specific industry. Examples of such programs include those used by dental offices to schedule appointments and bill patients, those used by auto mechanics to keep track of customer data and repairs, and those used by parts warehouses to track inventory, purchases, and sales. If horizontal-market applications are sedans, then vertical-market applications would be construction vehicles, like an excavator, because they are specialized for use in a particular field.

Vertical applications usually can be altered or customized. Typically, the company that sold the application software will provide such services or offer referrals to qualified consultants who can provide these services.

One-of-a-Kind Applications

One-of-a-kind application software is developed for a specific, unique need. The U.S. Department of Defense develops such software, for example, because it has needs that no other organization has.

You can think of one-of-a-kind application software as the automotive equivalent of a military tank. Tanks are developed for a very specific and unique need. Tanks cost more to manufacture than sedans, and cost overruns are common. They take longer to make and require unique hardware components. However, tanks are highly customizable and fit the requirements of a heavy-duty battle vehicle very well.

Selecting an Application Type

If you are headed into battle, you would not want to be driving a four-door sedan. Sometimes paying for a custom vehicle, while expensive, is warranted. It all depends on what you are doing. Militaries, for example, purchase sedans, construction vehicles, and tanks. Each vehicle fills its own need. Similarly, you can buy computer software to suit your needs: as **off-the-shelf software**, as **off-the-shelf with alterations software**, or as **custom-developed software**.

Organizations usually develop custom application software themselves or hire a development vendor. Like buying a tank, such development is done in situations where the needs of the organization are so unique that no horizontal or vertical applications are available. By developing custom software, the organization can tailor its application to fit its requirements.

Custom development is difficult and risky. Staffing and managing teams of software developers is challenging. Managing software projects can be daunting. Many organizations have embarked on application development projects only to find that the projects take twice as long—or longer—to finish than planned. Cost overruns of 200 percent and 300 percent are not uncommon. We will discuss such risks further in Chapter 12.

In addition, every application program needs to be adapted to changing needs and changing technologies. The adaptation costs of horizontal and vertical software are amortized over all the users of that software, perhaps thousands or millions of customers. For custom-developed software, however, the using organization must pay all of the adaptation costs itself. Over time, this cost burden is usually heavy.

Software Source

Software Type	Off-the-shelf	Off-the-shelf and then customized	Custom-developed
Horizontal applications	▓		
Vertical applications	▓	▓	
One-of-a-kind applications			▓

Figure 4-14 Software Sources and Types

Because of the risk and expense, custom development is the last-choice alternative, used only when there is no other option. Figure 4-14 summarizes software sources and types.

What Is Firmware?

Firmware is a computer software that is installed into devices such as printers, print servers, and various types of communication devices. This software is coded just like other software, but it is installed into special, read-only memory in the printer or other device. In this way, the program becomes part of the device's memory; it is as if the program's logic is designed into the device's circuitry. Therefore, users do not need to load firmware into the device's memory. Firmware can be changed or upgraded, but this is normally a task for IS professionals.

Q4-4 IS OPEN SOURCE SOFTWARE A VIABLE ALTERNATIVE?

Business leaders frequently ask whether open source software is a reasonable, cost-effective alternative to more expensive, commercially sold or custom designed software. To answer this question, you first need to know something about the open source movement and process. Most computer historians would agree that Richard Matthew Stallman is the father of the movement. In 1983, he developed a set of tools called **GNU** (a self-referential acronym meaning *GNU Not Unix*) for creating a free Unix-like operating system. Stallman made many other contributions to open source, including the **GNU general public license (GPL) agreement**, one of the standard license agreements for open source software. Stallman was unable to attract enough developers to finish the free Unix system, but he continued making other contributions to the open source movement.

In 1991, Linus Torvalds, working in Helsinki, began work on another version of Unix, using some of Stallman's tools. That version eventually became Linux, the high-quality and very popular operating system discussed previously.

The Internet proved to be a great enabler for the open source movement and the software it created. **Open source** software is typically free and modifiable, and its source code is publicly available. **Source code** is a computer code as written by humans and understandable by humans. Many open source projects became successful, including:

- LibreOffice (the default office suite in Linux distributions)
- Firefox (a browser)
- MySQL (a DBMS, see Chapter 5)
- Apache (a Web server, see Chapter 6)
- Ubuntu (a Windows-like desktop operating system)

- Android (a mobile-device operating system, described earlier)
- Cassandra (a NoSQL DBMS, see Chapter 5)
- Hadoop (a BigData processing system, see Chapter 9)

Why Do Programmers Volunteer Their Services?

To a person who has never enjoyed writing computer programs, it is difficult to understand why anyone would donate his or her time and skills to contribute to open source projects. Programming is, however, an intense combination of art and logic, and designing and writing a complicated computer program can be exceedingly pleasurable (and addictive). Many programmers joyfully write computer programs—day after day. If you have an artistic and logical mind, you ought to try it.

Thus, the first reason why people contribute to open source projects is that it is great fun! Also, some people contribute to open source because it gives them the freedom to choose the projects they work on. They may have a programming day job that is not terribly interesting—say, writing a program to manage a computer printer. Their job pays the bills, but it may not be fulfilling, so they turn to another outlet.

To better understand the allure of open source projects, consider the following example. In the 1950s, Hollywood studio musicians suffered as they recorded the same style of music over and over for a long string of uninteresting movies. To keep their sanity, those musicians would gather on Sundays to play jazz, and a number of high-quality jazz clubs resulted. That's what open source is to programmers: a place where they can exercise their creativity while working on projects they find interesting and fulfilling.

Another reason for contributing to open source is to exhibit one's skill, both for pride and to find a job or consulting employment. A final reason is to start a business selling services that support an open source product.

How Does Open Source Work?

Source code is compiled into **machine code** that is processed by a computer. Figure 4-15, for instance, shows a portion of the computer code written for the PRIDE project (see the start of Chapter 7). Machine code is, in general, not understandable by humans and cannot be modified.

For example, when a user accesses a website, the machine code version of the program runs on the user's computer. We do not show machine code in a figure because it would look like this:

1101001010010111111100111011111001000111000001111111011101111100111 …

In a **closed source** project, say, Microsoft Office, the source code is highly protected and only available to trusted employees and carefully vetted contractors. The source code is protected like gold in a vault. Only trusted programmers can make changes to a closed source project.

With open source, however, anyone can obtain the source code from the open source project's website. Programmers can then alter or add to this code depending on their interests and goals. In most cases, programmers incorporate code they find into their own projects. Later, they may be able to resell those projects depending on the type of license agreement the project uses.

Open source succeeds because of collaboration. A programmer examines the source code and identifies a need or project that seems interesting. He or she then creates a new feature, redesigns or reprograms an existing feature, or fixes a known problem. That code is then sent to others in the open source project. They evaluate the quality and merits of the work and add it to the product, if appropriate.

```
/// <summary>
/// Allows the page to draw itself.
/// </summary>
private void OnDraw(object sender, GameTimerEventArgs e)
{
    SharedGraphicsDeviceManager.Current.GraphicsDevice.Clear(Color.CornflowerBlue);

    SharedGraphicsDeviceManager.Current.GraphicsDevice.Clear(Color.Black);

    // Render the Silverlight controls using the UIElementRenderer.
    elementRenderer.Render();

    // Draw the sprite
    spriteBatch.Begin();

    // Draw the rectangle in its new position
    for (int i = 0; i < 3; i++)
    {
        spriteBatch.Draw(texture[i], bikeSpritePosition[i], Color.White);
    }

    // Using the texture from the UIElementRenderer,
```

Figure 4-15 Source Code Sample

Typically, there is a lot of give and take within the open source community. Or, as described in Chapter 2, there are many cycles of iteration and feedback. Because of this iteration, a well-managed project with strong peer reviews can result in very high quality code, like that in Linux.

So, Is Open Source Viable?

The answer to this question depends on to whom and for what. Open source has certainly become legitimate. According to *The Economist*, "It is now generally accepted that the future will involve a blend of both proprietary and open-source software."[20] During your career, open source will likely take a more amplified role in software. However, whether open source works for a particular situation depends on the requirements and constraints of that situation. You will learn more about matching requirements and programs in Chapter 12.

In some cases, companies choose open source software simply because it is "free." It turns out that this advantage may be less important than you might think, because in many cases, the support and operational costs related to an open source application swamp the initial licensing fee for an existing proprietary application that meets a company's needs.

How Does the Knowledge in This Chapter Help You?

Being involved with the use of technology in business is becoming a mandatory requirement. You can be a passive participant or actively involved. The information given in this chapter will help you choose the latter. From it, you know enough about hardware and software to ask insightful questions and to avoid embarrassing gaffes. You also now know sources of application software and the reasons for choosing one source over another. Finally, you know that open source is not just a "bunch of amateurs" but a movement that has created numerous quality software products and is a viable alternative for many situations. However, this knowledge is perishable, just like tomatoes at the farmers' market. You will need to continually update your expertise and refresh your skills.

[20] "Unlocking the Cloud," *The Economist*, May 28, 2009, accessed August 9, 2014, www.economist.com/node/13740181.

ACTIVE REVIEW

Use this Active Review to verify that you understand the ideas and concepts that answer the chapter's study questions.

Q4-1 WHAT DO BUSINESS PROFESSIONALS NEED TO KNOW ABOUT COMPUTER HARDWARE?

List categories of hardware and explain the purpose of each. Define *bit* and *byte*. Explain why bits are used to represent computer data. Define the units of bytes used to size memory.

Q4-2 HOW CAN NEW HARDWARE AFFECT COMPETITIVE STRATEGIES?

Define *IoT* and describe a smart device. Explain why smart devices are desirable. Give two examples of how businesses could benefit from smart devices. Describe how self-driving cars could be safer and cheaper and make life easier. Explain how 3D printing works and how it could affect new product design, manufacturing, distribution, and consumer purchasing.

Q4-3 WHAT DO BUSINESS PROFESSIONALS NEED TO KNOW ABOUT SOFTWARE?

Review Figure 4-9 and explain the meaning of each cell in this table. Describe three kinds of virtualization and explain the use of each. Explain the difference between software ownership and software licenses. Explain the differences among horizontal-market, vertical-market, and one-of-a-kind applications. Describe the three ways that organizations can acquire software.

Q4-4 IS OPEN SOURCE SOFTWARE A VIABLE ALTERNATIVE?

Define *GNU* and *GPL*. Name three successful open source projects. Describe four reasons programmers contribute to open source projects. Define *open source, closed source, source code,* and *machine code.* In your own words, explain why open source is a legitimate alternative but may or may not be appropriate for a given application.

MyLab MIS

MyLab MIS is an online learning and testing environment that features the perfect study tools to help you master the concepts covered in this chapter. Log in to MyLab to test your knowledge of key chapter concepts and explore additional practice tools, including videos, flashcards, and more!

KEY TERMS AND CONCEPTS

Android 116
Application software 119
Binary digits 106
Bits 106
Bytes 107
Central processing unit (CPU) 104
Client 105
Closed source 122
Computer hardware 104
Custom-developed software 120
Desktop virtualization 118

Dual processor 104
Exabyte (EB) 107
Firmware 121
Gigabyte (GB) 107
GNU 121
GNU general public license (GPL) agreement 121
Hertz 108
Horizontal-market application 119
Host operating system 117
Internet of Things (IoT) 108

iOS 116
Kilobyte (KB) 107
License 119
Linux 116
macOS 116
Machine code 122
Main memory 104
Megabyte (MB) 107
Microsoft Windows 115
Modern-style applications 115
Native application 114
Nonvolatile 108

Off-the-shelf software 120
Off-the-shelf with alterations software 120
One-of-a-kind application 120
Open source 121
Operating system (OS) 114
PC virtualization 117
Personal computers (PCs) 105
Petabyte (PB) 107
PixelSense 126

USING YOUR KNOWLEDGE

4-1. Suppose your roommate, a political science major, asks you to help her purchase a new laptop computer. She wants to use the computer for email, Internet access, and note taking in class. She wants to spend less than $1000.

    a. What CPU, memory, and disk specifications would you recommend?

    b. What software does she need?

    c. Compare prices using www.dell.com, www.hp.com, and www.lenovo.com.

    d. Which computer would you recommend, and why?

4-2. Microsoft offers free licenses of certain software products to students at colleges and universities that participate in its DreamSpark program (formerly known as the *Microsoft Developer Network [MSDN] Academic Alliance [AA]*). If your college or university participates in this program, you have the opportunity to obtain hundreds of dollars of software for free. Here is a partial list of the software you can obtain:

- Microsoft Access 2013
- OneNote 2013
- Windows 2012 Server
- Microsoft Project 2013
- Visual Studio Developer
- SQL Server 2014
- Visio 2013

    a. Search www.microsoft.com, www.google.com, or www.bing.com and determine the function of each of these software products.

    b. Which of these software products are operating systems, and which are application programs?

    c. Which of these programs are DBMS products (the subject of the next chapter)?

    d. Which of these programs should you download and install tonight?

    e. Either (1) download and install the programs in your answer to part d or (2) explain why you would choose not to do so.

    f. Does DreamSpark provide an unfair advantage to Microsoft? Why or why not?

4-3. Visit the Open Source Initiative's website at www.opensource.org. Summarize the mission of this foundation. Find the definition of *open source* on this site, and summarize that definition in your own words. Explain this foundation's role with regard to open source licenses. Summarize the process for having a license approved by the foundation. Describe the advantage of having the foundation's approval.

COLLABORATION EXERCISES

Read Knowledge Extensions 1 and 3 if you have not already done so. Meet with your team and build a collaboration IS that uses tools like Google Docs, SharePoint, or other collaboration tools. Do not forget the need for procedures and team training. Now, using that IS, answer the questions below.

In the past few years, Microsoft has been researching **PixelSense**, a hardware–software product that enables people to interact with data on the top of a table. PixelSense began as the technology behind the Windows Surface computer. PixelSense now initiates a new product category.

PixelSense paints the top of the 30-inch table with invisible, near-infrared light to detect the presence of objects. It can respond to as many as 52 different touches at the same time. According to Microsoft, this means that four people sitting around the PixelSense table could use all 10 of their fingers to manipulate up to 12 objects, simultaneously.

PixelSense uses wireless and other communications technologies to connect to devices that are placed on it, such as cameras or cell phones. When a camera is placed on PixelSense, pictures "spill" out of it, and users can manipulate those pictures with their hands. Products can be placed on PixelSense, and their product specifications are displayed. Credit cards can be placed on PixelSense, and items to be purchased can be dragged or dropped onto the credit card. Currently, Microsoft PixelSense is marketed and sold to large-scale commercial organizations in the financial services, healthcare, hospitality, retail, and public service business sectors.

One of the first implementers of PixelSense was the iBar lounge at Harrah's Rio All-Suite Hotel and Casino in Las Vegas, Nevada. The subtitle for the press release announcing iBar's system read, "Harrah's Reinvents Flirting and Offers New Uninhibited Fun and Play to iBar Patrons."[21]

The potential uses for PixelSense are staggering. Maps can display local events, and consumers can purchase tickets to those events by just using their fingers. PixelSense can also be used for new computer games and gambling devices. Children can paint on PixelSense with virtual paintbrushes. Numerous other applications are possible. Microsoft envisions PixelSense as a ubiquitous billion dollar technology that will find its way to tabletops, countertops, and mirrors.[22]

As you can see on the PixelSense website, this product can be used for many different purposes in multiple places, such as restaurants, retail kiosks, and eventually at home. Probably most of the eventual applications for PixelSense have not yet been envisioned. One clear application, however, is in the gambling and gaming industry. Imagine placing your credit card on a PixelSense gambling device and playing the night away. Every time you lose, a charge is made against your credit card. Soon, before you know it, you've run up $15 000 in debt, which you learn when PixelSense tells you you've reached the maximum credit limit on your card.

Recall the RAND study cited in Chapter 1 that stated there will be increased worldwide demand for workers who can apply new technology and products to solve business problems in innovative ways. The PixelSense interface is an example of a breakthrough technology that will be applied innovatively.

4-1. Consider uses for PixelSense at your college or university. How might PixelSense be used in architecture, chemistry, law, medicine, business, geography, political science, art, music, or any other discipline in which your team has interest? Describe one potential application for PixelSense for five different disciplines.

4-2. List specific features and benefits for each of the five applications you selected in question 4-1.

4-3. Describe, in general terms, the work that needs to be accomplished to create the applications you identified in question 4-1.

[21] Microsoft envisions PixelSense as a ubiquitous billion dollar technology that will find its way to tabletops, countertops, and mirrors in the future.

[22] Microsoft press release, May 29, 2007, accessed August 9, 2014, www.microsoft.com/en-us/news/press/2007/may07/05-29mssurfacepr.aspx.

4-4. Until June 2012, PixelSense was called *Surface*. At that time, Microsoft repurposed the name to use on its tablet devices. Surface was changed to PixelSense. What conclusions do you draw from these naming decisions?

4-5. You will sometimes hear the expression "Emerging technology is constantly levelling the playing field," meaning that technology eliminates competitive advantages of existing companies and enables opportunities for new companies. How does this statement pertain to PixelSense, Surface, Windows 10, Apple, and Google?

CASE STUDY 4
NETWORK EFFECTS, INCREASING RETURNS, AND LOCK-IN

How do the choices made by others affect your own options, and how should you evaluate new software? Those are two of the questions facing Brent North, managing partner of Stantec's Vancouver office, as he considered using a new three-dimensional drafting tool.

Founded in 1954, Stantec is an architecture and engineering firm that evolved from a single-person consultancy into a publicly traded corporation with more than 100 offices worldwide and 6500 employees through a combination of acquisitions and natural growth. The Vancouver office, which has recently been acquired by Stantec, has approximately 125 professional staff and is largely focused on architecture.

Architecture has changed a great deal in 60 years. While grounded in creativity and design, architects today are far more proficient in computer technology. Although some of Stantec's senior architects still look fondly upon the slide rules and Mylar plastic that was used to create designs in the past, modern-day architects are far more likely to turn to their computers and use Computer-Assisted Design (CAD), and engineering tools such as Computer Aided Manufacturing (CAM) and Computer Aided Engineering (CAE). There has been a large and growing market for these products, and numerous suppliers delivered a variety of tools. However, as in other software markets, one or two suppliers dominated and acquired the majority of the market share, and the other software products occupied niches that lacked widespread adoption. An example of a niche product is CATIA (Computer Aided Three-Dimensional Interactive Application), from Dassault Systems, widely used in manufacturing at Chrysler, General Electric, and Airbus (and had been used by Frank Gehry to design the Guggenheim Museum in Bilbao, Spain).

Several years ago, Stantec adopted AutoCAD by Autodesk. The de facto standard program, at that time AutoCAD had approximately 80 percent adoption among architectural firms. Virtually all new architects had been taught how to use it while in university and, provided they were using the same version, cooperating firms working on large projects could share and transfer files knowing that they were compatible and interchangeable.

Although Brent is generally satisfied with Stantec's existing software tools, he has recently become aware of a product with features and capabilities that he thinks can change the way Stantec competes. What concerns Brent, however, is the level of training required to make the change and the advantages of remaining with the industry standard. Not only will the new product require education and adjustment among the architects, but it is also incompatible with AutoCAD. While the new program can open files created by AutoCAD, files created by the new program cannot be used by AutoCAD. This means that if Brent brought the new product in for a trial, he would no longer be able to easily cooperate with other firms on joint projects and, perhaps more importantly, it could reduce the level of cooperation and sharing within the firm. At the same time, he knows that, if pushed to the limit, this kind of conservative thinking will hold Stantec hostage and prevent positive change. Is it worth considering a new and incompatible product—and if he brings it in for a trial, how should he proceed?

Questions

1. How do the challenges faced by Stantec differ from those faced by other industries? (*Hint:* Think about sharing files among students for group projects.)

2. What are the implications of this case for companies that develop new software tools? How could adoption barriers be reduced? (*Hint:* Think of disruptive technologies.)

3. Are there any examples of inferior technologies that have achieved lock-in and would therefore be hard to improve? (*Hint:* You probably have used one already today.)

4. How do the ideas of switching costs and of networks effects relate to high technology? Do they exist in other industries? (*Hint:* Consider the railway industry, for example.)

5. How should new software be evaluated? How important is market share? Are these factors more or less important to smaller firms?

MyLab MIS

Go to the Assignments section of your MyLab to complete these writing exercises.

4-1 Suppose your first job after graduating from college or university is working at a large insurance company. Your boss asks you to analyze the impact self-driving cars will have on revenues from car insurance policies. List four ways self-driving cars could affect the insurance industry. Justify your answers.

4-2 Visit *www.distrowatch.com*. Click on one of the top five listed Linux distributions (like Mint, Ubuntu, Debian, Fedora, or OpenSUSE). Click on the Screenshots link for that distribution. List some similarities between this operating system and your current operating system. Summarize the advantages and disadvantages of switching from your current operating system to a Linux distribution.

WHAT DO YOU THINK?

KEEPING UP TO SPEED

Have you ever seen a hamster running on a hamster wheel in its cage? That hamster wheel can remind us of technology. Like the hamster wheel, technology just moves along, and all of us jump on the technology hamster wheel, running hard trying to keep up. We hope to keep pace with the relentless change of technology through an entire career but it sometimes feels that the faster you run, the harder it becomes to keep up.

Technological change is a fact, and the most appropriate response is deciding, "What am I going to do about it?" One strategy is to bury your head in the sand: "Look, I'm not a technology person. I'll leave it to the pros. As long as I can send email and use the Internet, I'm happy. If I have a problem, I'll call someone to fix it."

A strategy that depends on the expertise of someone else ("the pros") is fine, but it will not give you a competitive advantage over anyone—in fact, it will give someone else a competitive advantage over you. If you develop your competitive advantage elsewhere, then you might be okay—provided your competitive advantage remains relevant.

Is this strategy consistent with being a team player in your department? If an IS expert says, "Every computer needs an 8 TB disk," are you going to nod your head and say, "Great. Sell 'em to me!" Or will you know enough to realize that it is a big disk (by 2017 standards, anyway) and ask the expert why everyone needs such a large amount of storage? Maybe you will be told, "Well, it's only another $75 per machine compared with the 2 TB disk." At that point, can you consider a selection using your own decision making skills, and not rely solely on the expert recommendation? The prudent business professional in the twenty-first century has a number of reasons not to bury his or her head in the sand as far as technology is concerned.

At the other end of the spectrum are those who love technology. You will find them everywhere—whether accountants, marketing professionals, or production-line supervisors, who not only are knowledgeable about their own field but also enjoy information technology. Maybe they were IS majors or had double majors that combined IS with another area of expertise (e.g., accounting). These people read *CNET News* and *ZDNet* most days, and they can provide the latest updates on IPv6 addresses. Technology lovers are sprinting along and keeping abreast of technology. They will use their knowledge of IT to gain a competitive advantage throughout their careers.

Many business professionals are in-between these extremes. They do not want to shun technology, but they have no desire or interest in becoming technophiles (lovers of technology) either. So, what should you do? There are a few useful strategies. First, do not allow yourself to ignore technology. When you see a technology article in the newspaper or online, read it. Also read the technology ads. Many vendors invest heavily in ads that subtly instruct their potential customers. Another option is to participate in seminars or attend professional events that combine your specialized field with technology. For example, when you go to the bankers' convention, attend a session or two on technology trends for bankers. You might also develop important connections with similar minded individuals and/or companies.

Probably the best option, if you have the time, is to get involved as a user representative in technology committees within your organization. If your company is doing a review of its CRM (customer relationship management) system, for instance, see if you can get on the review committee. When there is a request for a representative from your department to discuss operational needs related to technology, sign up. Or, later in your career, become a member of the business practice technology committee, or whatever they call it at your organization.

Just working with such groups will add to your knowledge of technology. Presentations made to these groups, discussions about uses of technology, and ideas about using IT for competitive advantage will all add to your IT knowledge. You will gain important contacts and exposure to leaders in your organization as well.

Remember: You choose how you relate to technology, now and throughout your career. Assess your ambitions and choose wisely.

Discussion Questions

1. Do you agree that the pace of technology is relentless? What do you think that means to most business professionals? To most organizations?

2. Think about the three stances with regard to technology presented here. Which camp will you join? Why?

3. Write a two-paragraph memo to yourself justifying your choice in Question 2. If you chose to ignore technology, explain how you will compensate for the loss of competitive advantage. If you are going to join one of the other two groups, explain why, and describe how you are going to accomplish your goal.

4. Given your answer to Question 2, assume that you are in a job interview and the interviewer asks about your knowledge of technology. Write a three-sentence response to the interviewer's question.

Database and Content Management

STUDY QUESTIONS

Q5-1 WHY DO YOU NEED TO KNOW ABOUT DATABASES AND WHAT IS THEIR PURPOSE?

Q5-2 WHAT IS CONTENT AND HOW IS IT ORGANIZED?

Q5-3 WHAT DOES A DATABASE CONTAIN?

Q5-4 WHAT IS A DBMS, AND WHAT DOES IT DO?

Q5-5 WHAT IS A DATABASE APPLICATION?

Q5-6 WHAT IS THE DIFFERENCE BETWEEN DATABASES AND WHERE ARE WE HEADED?

MIS in Action

It's Friday night, and Camillia (Cam) Forset is on her way to an art show opening. She gets an urgent call from Jess Denkar, the head of security at PetroAlta. PetroAlta is a large oil refinery based in Alberta and one of Falcon Security's biggest industrial clients. Jess is looking for information that could help him find out who stole almost $75 000 worth of custom piping and copper wiring.

Cam made sure Jess had her personal cell phone number and told him to call her anytime—day or night. She knows it's important to show Jess that the money PetroAlta spends on Falcon's services is worth it. She immediately calls Toshio Sato, director of IT Services, and tells him to come back into the office. She also sends a text message to CEO Mateo Thomas and CFO Joni Campbell.

"Have you found anything yet?" Joni asks. She quickly sets down her purse at a nearby workstation and begins hovering behind Toshio.

KE **Chapter 5 optional knowledge extensions are**

Knowledge Extension 6 Database Design page 157

Knowledge Extension 7 Using Microsoft Access 2016 page 172

Knowledge Extension 8 Using Excel and Access Together available in the MyLab MIS

"Not yet—we're working as fast as we can," Cam replies tersely. Cam wants to focus on helping Toshio find the correct security footage, not discuss the importance of the PetroAlta account to Falcon Security.

"Is there anything I can do to help?" Joni wonders.

"No, we're just trying to find the right footage. There's a lot of it to review," Cam sighs.

"What's the problem? Why do we have to look through so much footage?"

Toshio is tempted to tell Joni that "we" aren't looking through anything. He's the one doing the searching. But he holds his tongue. "Well, the problem is we have footage of dozens of different buildings at PetroAlta, from several different drones, over about a 2-week period. Tracking down the footage of exactly when the equipment was stolen means we have to search through hundreds of different video files. This could take all night," he answers matter-of-factly.

"There's got to be a faster way to do this. Can't we just search for the footage somehow?" Joni says.

"No," Toshio says calmly. "We don't have a way to track the data about the videos. The video files are sequentially numbered and stored in directories for a specific company. We can also see the date and time the video file was created, but there are several different drones. It's just …"

Cam interrupts Toshio to try to keep him from getting distracted. "Toshio and I have talked about creating a database to track all of our video files. We've just been busy trying to automate the data collection and storage process."

"Well, how long would it take to make it? How much would it cost?" Joni asks.

"We're not sure. We don't even know which database management system we'd use. Toshio and I have both used Microsoft Access, but Toshio mentioned something called MongoDB that might be better for tracking video files."

Toshio pauses the video he's reviewing and starts pointing at a listing of video files in a directory. "Instead of searching through all of these manually, I could just specify characteristics about each video like company name, building name, date, time, and elevation. It would return the URLs for videos matching those characteristics. We'd know right where they are on our file server."

"Sounds good to me. Anything to keep us from spending our Friday nights looking through video footage. Let's do it," Joni quips.

Cam tries to get things back on track. "OK, great, we'll put it on our list. There's no doubt that a database will keep us from having to search through all this footage. For now, though, we should probably focus on finding the footage for Jess. We've got a lot to go through tonight."

Q5-1 WHY DO YOU NEED TO KNOW ABOUT DATABASES AND WHAT IS THEIR PURPOSE?

This chapter and its related Knowledge Extensions introduce you to database technology. This knowledge is important to you as a future business professional. For one, databases are everywhere. Although you may not realize it, you access dozens, if not hundreds, of databases every day. Every time you make a cell phone call, log on to the Internet, or buy something online using a credit card, applications behind the scenes are processing numerous databases. Use Snapchat, Facebook, Twitter, or LinkedIn, and again applications are processing databases on your behalf. Google something, and yet again dozens of databases are processed to obtain the search results.

Reasons for Learning Database Technology

As a user, you need know nothing about the underlying technology. From your perspective, "it just works," to quote the late Steve Jobs. However, as a business professional in the 21st century, it's a different story. You need the knowledge from this chapter and the related Knowledge Extensions for four principal reasons:

1. When you participate in the development of any new business initiative, you need to know if database technology can facilitate your project goals. If so, you need sufficient knowledge to assess whether building that database is akin to building a small shed or is closer to building a skyscraper. Joni, in the opening vignette of this chapter, needs to have some knowledge to assess how hard (and thus how expensive) building that new database will be.

2. Because databases are ubiquitous in commerce, billions of bytes of data are stored every day. You need to know how to turn that data into a format from which you can construct useful information. To that end, you might use one of many different graphical tools to query that data. Or, to become truly proficient, you might learn SQL, an international standard language for querying databases, something that many business professionals have done.

3. Business is dynamic, and information systems must adapt. Often, such adaptation means that the structure of the database needs to be changed. Sometimes, it means that entirely new databases must be created. As you will learn in this chapter, only the users, such as yourself, know what and how details should be stored. You may be asked to evaluate a data model like those described in Knowledge Extension 6.

4. Finally, you might someday find yourself or your department in a material mess. Maybe you are unsure who has a sought after piece of equipment, or where certain tools are located, or what is really in your supply closet. In that case, you might choose to build your own database. Unless an IS professional is available, that database will probably be small and relatively simple, but it can still be very useful to you and your colleagues.

What Is the Purpose of a Database?

A database keeps track of things. When most people become aware of this, they wonder why technology is needed for such a simple task. Why not just use a list? And if the list is long, can it just be put in a spreadsheet?

Many professionals do keep track of things using spreadsheets. If the structure of the list is simple enough, there is no need to use database technology. The list of student grades in Figure 5-1, for example, works perfectly well in a spreadsheet.

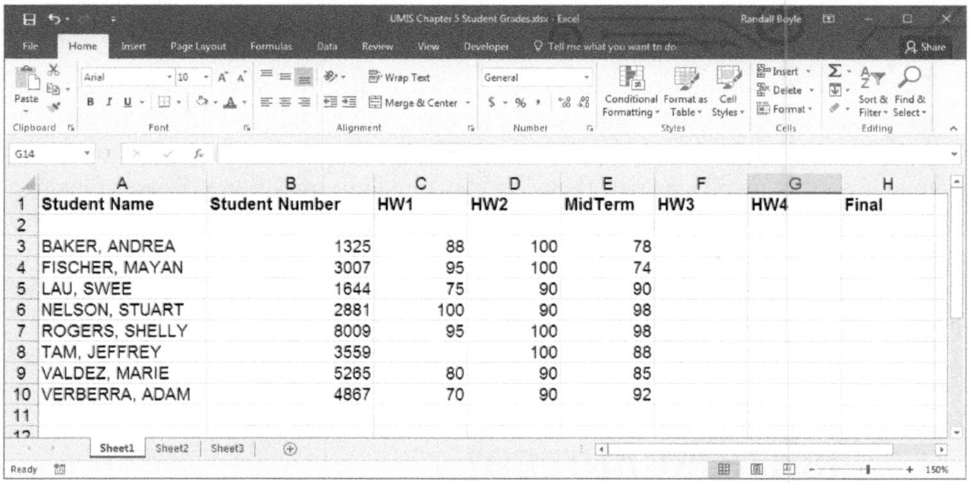

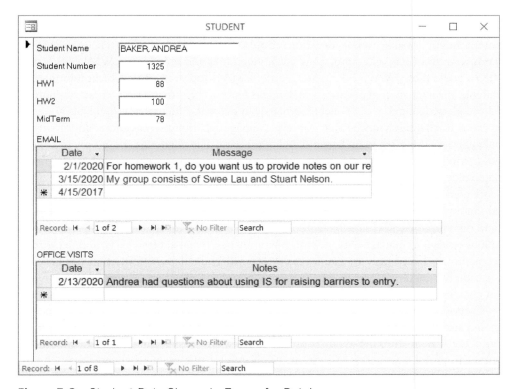

Figure 5-1 A List of Student Grades

Source: Microsoft Excel

Suppose, however, that the professor wants to track more than just grades. He or she may want to record email messages as well. Or, perhaps, the professor wants to record both email messages and office visits. There is no designated place in the spreadsheet shown in Figure 5-1 to record the extra information. Of course, the professor could set up a separate spreadsheet for email messages and another for office visits, but that awkward solution would be difficult to implement because it does not provide all the data in one place.

Instead, the professor may want a form similar to the one shown in Figure 5-2. With it, he or she can record student grades, emails, and office visits all in one place. Technically it

Figure 5-2 Student Data Shown in Form of a Database

Source: Microsoft Excel

might be possible to create a similar form like this in a spreadsheet, but with a database, it is much easier to develop and maintain.

The key distinction between Figures 5-1 and 5-2 is that the list in Figure 5-1 is about a single theme or concept—student grades. The list in Figure 5-2 has multiple themes—it shows student grades, emails, and office visits. We can create a general rule from these examples: Lists that involve a single theme can be stored in a spreadsheet; lists that involve multiple themes require a database. We will learn more about this general rule later in this chapter.

To summarize, the purpose of a database is to keep track of things that involve more than one theme.

Q5-2 WHAT IS CONTENT AND HOW IS IT ORGANIZED?

Content can be difficult to define. In the broadest sense, content is something of value and can be considered an asset just like other items of property. It is often closely related to **intellectual property**, which, in Canada, is defined as a form of creative endeavour that can be protected through a trademark, patent, copyright, industrial design, or integrated circuit topography.[1] Content varies by industry. In the advertising industry, content refers to the pictures, commercials, and text used to promote ideas about products and services. In the publishing industry, content refers to words. In the banking industry, content is account information.

Before the advent of computers, content was mostly available on physical assets such as paper, photographs, or film. But computers create digital content that can be stored, and networks, such as the Internet, can distribute this content. Organizations have databases that store large amounts of data related to customers, employees, orders, and so on. Organizations also store various other types of content. Word-processing documents (.doc, .txt, and .pdf), spreadsheets (.xls), and presentations (.ppt) are a part of everyday work. Other content might include webpages (.htm, .html), text from blogs, Twitter, or discussion boards, graphics (.jpg, .gif, .bmp, .png, etc.), video files and video logs (.WMV, .AVI, and .MPG), audio files (.WAV, .MP3, .ACC, and .WMA), and even geographical information available through such applications as Google Earth. The expanding volume of content and the growing number of available formats can make it difficult for individuals and corporations to effectively utilize that content. Managing content is, therefore, an important challenge for businesses to understand and appreciate. The challenge is not only to collect and distribute content but also to present it appropriately for various stakeholders inside and outside of organizations.

A company's website has become an important source of content for both customers and employees. Students who concentrate in marketing recognize that websites help to brand organizations. Websites have also become a critical part of customer support. It was arduous enough to manage data and information when it was exclusively contained within a company and used only by employees. More widely available information has become increasingly difficult to manage due in part to the increased volume, format, and presentation choices for content accessible to individuals and corporations.

Content management involves indexing or cataloguing the right information, processing and storing it, and then getting it to the right person in the right format at the right time. One way of thinking about content management is to separate the *management* of content from the *presentation* of content. We learned in the previous chapter that all data in computing systems are represented by bytes. Content management focuses on how to

[1] You can read more about intellectual property at www.cipo.ic.gc.ca.

efficiently and effectively store and process these bytes. Content presentation focuses on how best to present data to the person using the system.

The management of many types of content has traditionally been handled through organizational database management systems (DBMSs). DBMSs are central to the management of content data, and we will learn more about them later in the chapter. The presentation of content has gone through changes as company websites have matured. In the early days of the Web, employees might have been able to post content directly to a company's website. This practice did not provide a consistent look and feel and left the company at risk if incorrect data or inappropriate posts were included on the website. As organizational websites became more complex, employees could not be expected to keep up with all of the changes. Instead, the presentation of content in organizations is increasingly handled through a series of steps supported by software. **Content management systems (CMSs)** have been developed to help companies organize this process.

When an employee wants to place some content on the organization's website, he or she will access the Web CMS. The Web CMS of a company is usually located on its website server. The employee typically loads the raw content into the Web CMS. A copyeditor then reviews the document and makes any needed changes. He or she then passes the content on to layout artists, who prepare the content for presentation. The content and presentation are stored with the help of a DBMS. The manager in charge of the website will then review the content and presentation and publish the work to the public website. The Web CMS helps manage each step of this process and enables a company to standardize the look and feel of a website and control the information available to customers and employees.

CMSs have also evolved. They have grown beyond their original role of simply organizing documents for corporate websites. These systems now actively seek out documents located across an organization and automatically manage access to this content. Media files, word-processing documents, html pages, and many other documents can all be categorized and searched by CMSs. This capability allows for the increased organization of a wider range of a corporation's data assets. Current CMSs also handle document archiving and the increased use of electronic files for document management. OpenText (see box below), a Canadian company located in Waterloo, Ontario (www.opentext.com) is an example of a CMS.

Opentext: From Spinoff to Market Leader

How does a small spinoff company from the University of Waterloo grow to become Canada's largest software company and the world leader in enterprise content management systems? It all started with a project to bring the *Oxford English Dictionary (OED)* into the computer age. The *OED* had become so large that it was unwieldy to update. Researchers at the University of Waterloo, with funding help from the Canadian government, worked to build full-text indexing and string-search technology for the *OED*. The project resulted in a product that was close to a Web-based search engine—in 1989, years before Web search engines were well known. OpenText was started in 1991. The company continued to develop increased functionality in the search engine through 1995. When management believed that the market for search engines no longer looked promising, the company turned to document management systems. (Astute students may note that Google, the current leader among Internet search engines, was founded in 1998 and has a value 55 times greater than that of OpenText. In business, as in many areas, timing is everything.) Web-based document management systems proved to be a lucrative market. OpenText grew from a company of 20 employees in 1995 to a company of more than 14,000 employees with over $2.3 billion in sales supporting 100 million users in 120 countries by 2017. The company has continued its rapid growth and is recognized as the market leader in enterprise content management. OpenText is used by 90% of the world's Fortune 500 companies.

Source: You can find out more about the history of OpenText at www.opentext.com/corporate/our_history.html.

Q5-3 WHAT DOES A DATABASE CONTAIN?

Database design is a specialized skill that everyone in the field of management information systems (MIS) should understand and any business student who plans to work with corporate data should be familiar with. You will learn the basics in this chapter. In addition, two extensions to this chapter, "Database Design" and "Using Microsoft Access," contain more in-depth information on this topic.

A **database** is a self-describing collection of integrated records. To understand this definition, you first need to understand the terms illustrated in Figure 5-3. As you learned in Chapter 4, a **byte** is a character of data. Bytes are grouped into **columns**, such as *Student Number* and *Student Name*. Columns are also called **fields**. Columns or fields, in turn, are grouped into **rows**, which are also called **records**. In Figure 5-3, the collection of data for all columns (*Student Number, Student Name, HW1, HW2,* and *MidTerm*) is called a *row* or a *record*. Finally, a group of similar rows or records is called a **table** or a **file**. From these definitions, you can see that there is a hierarchy of data elements, as shown in Figure 5-4.

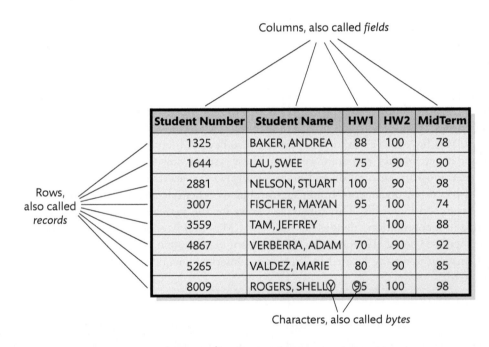

Columns, also called *fields*

Student Number	Student Name	HW1	HW2	MidTerm
1325	BAKER, ANDREA	88	100	78
1644	LAU, SWEE	75	90	90
2881	NELSON, STUART	100	90	98
3007	FISCHER, MAYAN	95	100	74
3559	TAM, JEFFREY		100	88
4867	VERBERRA, ADAM	70	90	92
5265	VALDEZ, MARIE	80	90	85
8009	ROGERS, SHELLY	95	100	98

Rows, also called *records*

Characters, also called *bytes*

Figure 5-3 Student Table (also called a *file*)

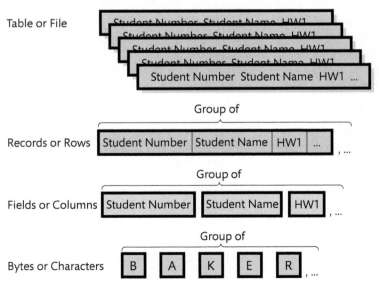

Table or File

Student Number Student Name HW1
Student Number Student Name HW1
Student Number Student Name HW1
Student Number Student Name HW1
Student Number Student Name HW1 ...

Group of

Records or Rows

| Student Number | Student Name | HW1 | ... | , ... |

Group of

Fields or Columns

| Student Number | | Student Name | | HW1 | , ... |

Group of

Bytes or Characters B A K E R , ...

Figure 5-4 Hierarchy of Data Elements

It is tempting to continue this grouping process by saying that a database is a group of tables or files. This statement, although true, does not go far enough, however. As shown in Figure 5-5, a database is a collection of tables *plus* relationships among the rows in those tables, *plus* special data, called *metadata*, that describe the structure of the database. Note that the cylindrical symbol represents a computer disk drive. It is used in diagrams, such as in Figure 5-5, because databases were originally stored on direct access storage devices such as magnetic disks.

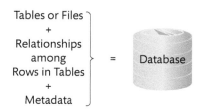

Figure 5-5 Components of a Database

Relationships Among Records

Consider the terms on the left side of Figure 5-5. You know what *tables* are. To understand what is meant by *relationships among rows in tables*, examine Figure 5-6. It shows sample data from the three tables *Email*, *Student*, and *Office_Visit*. Note the column named *Student Number* in the *Email* table. That column indicates the row in the *Student* table to which a row of *the Email* table is connected. In the first row of the *Email* table, the *Student Number* value is 1325. This indicates that this particular email was received from the student whose *Student Number* is 1325. If you examine the *Student* table, you will see that the row for Andrea Baker contains this value. Thus, the first row of the *Email* table is related to Andrea Baker.

Email Table

EmailNum	Date	Message	Student Number
1	2/1/2007	For homework 1, do you want us to provide notes on our references?	1325
2	3/15/2007	My group consists of Swee Lau and Stuart Nelson.	1325
3	3/15/2007	Could you please assign me to a group?	1644

Student Table

Student Number	Student Name	HW1	HW2	MidTerm
1325	BAKER, ANDREA	88	100	78
1644	LAU, SWEE	75	90	90
2881	NELSON, STUART	100	90	98
3007	FISCHER, MAYAN	95	100	74
3559	TAM, JEFFREY		100	88
4867	VERBERRA, ADAM	70	90	92
5265	VALDEZ, MARIE	80	90	85
8009	ROGERS, SHELLY	95	100	98

Office_Visit Table

VisitID	Date	Notes	Student Number
2	2/13/2007	Andrea had questions about using IS for raising barriers to entry.	1325
3	2/17/2007	Jeffrey is considering an IS major. Wanted to talk about career opportunities.	3559
4	2/17/2007	Will miss class Friday due to job conflict.	4867

Figure 5-6 Example of Relationships among Rows

Now consider the last row of the *Office_Visit* table at the bottom of the figure. The value of *Student Number* in that row is 4867. This value indicates that the last row in *Office_Visit* belongs to Adam Verberra.

From these examples, you can see that values in one table relate rows of that table to rows in a second table. Several special terms are used to express these ideas. A **key** is a column or group of columns that identifies a unique row in a table. *Student Number* is the key of the *Student* table. Given a value of *Student Number*, you can determine one and only one row in *the Student table*. Only one student has the number 1325, for example.

Every table must have a key. The key of the *Email* table is *EmailNum*, and the key of the *Office_Visit* table is *VisitID*. Sometimes more than one column is needed to form a unique identifier. In a table called *City*, for example, the key would consist of the combination of columns (*City, Province*) because a given city name can appear in more than one province.

Student Number is not the key of the *Email* or the *Office_Visit* tables. We know that about *the Email table* because there are two rows in *Email* that have the *Student Number* value 1325. The value 1325 does not identify a unique row; therefore, *Student Number* is not the key of the *Email* table.

Nor is *Student Number* a key of the *Office_Visit* table, although you cannot tell that from the data in Figure 5-6. If you think about it, however, there is nothing to prevent a student from visiting a professor more than once. If that were to happen, there would be two rows in the *Office_Visit* table with the same value of *Student Number*. It just happens that no student has visited twice in the limited data in Figure 5-6.

Columns that fulfill a role like that of *Student Number* in the *Email* and *Office_Visit* tables are called **foreign keys**. This term is used because such columns are keys, but they are keys of a different (foreign) table from the one in which they reside.

Before we go on, note that databases that carry their data in the form of tables and that represent relationships using foreign keys are called **relational databases**. (The term *relational* is used because another, more formal name for a table is **relation**.) In the past, databases existed that were not relational in format, but such databases have nearly disappeared. Chances are you will never encounter one, and we will not consider them further.[2]

Metadata

Recall the definition of *database*—a self-describing collection of integrated records. The records are integrated because, as you have just learned, relationships among rows are represented in the database. But what does *self-describing* mean?

It means that a database contains, within itself, a description of its contents. Think of a library. A library is a self-describing collection of books and other materials. It is self-describing because the library contains a catalogue that describes its contents. The same idea also holds true for a database. They are self-describing because they contain not only data but also data about the data in the database.

Metadata are data that describe data. Figure 5-7 shows metadata for the *Email* table. The format of metadata depends on the software product that is processing the database. Figure 5-7 shows the metadata as they appear in Microsoft Access. Each row of the top part of this form describes a column of the *Email* table. The columns of these descriptions are *Field Name, Data Type*, and *Description. Field Name* contains the name of the column, *Data Type* shows the type of data the column may hold, and *Description* contains notes that explain the source or use of the column. Clearly, there is one row of metadata for each of the four columns of the *Email* table: *EmailNum, Date, Message*, and *Student Number*.

The bottom part of this form provides more metadata, which Access calls *Field Properties*, for each column. In Figure 5-7, the focus is on the *Date* column. Because the focus is on *Date* in the top pane, the details in the bottom pane pertain to the *Date* column. The *Field*

---

[2] Another type of database, the object-relational database, is rarely used in commercial applications. Later in the chapter we will touch upon other types of databases although due to the importance of databases and the need for them to be so responsive the subject can quickly become very complex and technical.

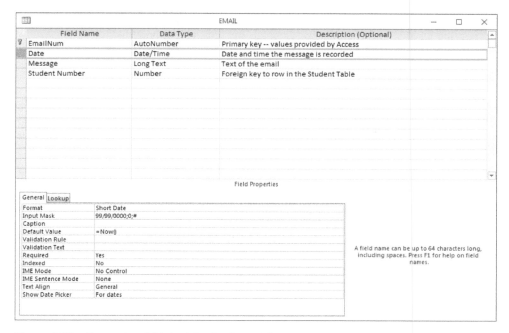

Figure 5-7 Example of Metadata (in Access)

Source: Microsoft Access

Properties describe formats, a default value for Access to supply when a new row is created, and the constraint that a value is required for this column. It is not important for you to remember these details. Instead, just understand that metadata are data about data and that such metadata are always a part of a database.

The presence of metadata makes databases much more useful than spreadsheets or data in other lists. Because of metadata, no one needs to guess, remember, or even record what is in the database. To find out what a database contains, we just look at the metadata inside the database. Metadata make databases easy to use—for both authorized and unauthorized purposes, as described in the exercise "Nobody Said I Shouldn't" at the end of this chapter on page 156.

Q5-4 WHAT IS A DBMS, AND WHAT DOES IT DO?

A database, all by itself, is not very useful. The tables in Figure 5-6 have all the data the professor wants, but the format is unwieldy. The professor wants to see the data in a form like that in Figure 5-2 and also as a formatted report. Pure database data are correct but in raw form, and they are probably not pertinent or useful.

Figure 5-8 shows the components of a **database application system**. Such applications make database data more accessible and useful. Users employ a *database application* that consists of forms (such as the form in Figure 5-2), formatted reports, queries, and application

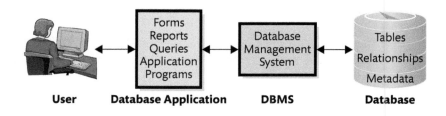

Figure 5-8 Components of a Database Application System

programs. Each of these, in turn, calls on the DBMS to process the database tables. We will first describe DBMSs and then discuss database application components.

The Database Management System

A **DBMS** is a program used to create, process, and administer a database. As is the case with operating systems, almost no organization develops its own DBMS. Instead, companies license DBMS products from vendors, such as IBM, Microsoft, and Oracle. Popular DBMS products are **DB2** from IBM, **Access** and **SQL Server** from Microsoft, and **Oracle** from Oracle Corporation. Another popular DBMS is **MySQL**, an open source DBMS product that is free for most applications. Other DBMS products are available, but the five listed above account for the vast majority of databases used by small and mid-sized enterprises.

Note that a DBMS and a database are two different things, even though many in the trade press, and even some books, confuse the two. A DBMS is a software program; a database is a collection of tables, relationships, and metadata. The two concepts are very different.

Creating the Database and Its Structures

Database developers use the DBMS to create tables, relationships, and other structures in the database. The form in Figure 5-7 can be used to define a new table or to modify an existing one. To create a new table, the developer just fills out a new form, such as the one in Figure 5-7.

To modify an existing table—for example, to add a new column—the developer opens the metadata form for that table and adds a new row of metadata. For example, in Figure 5-9, the developer has added a new column called *Response?* The developer created this new column by adding the label "Response?" under the Field Name column. This new column has the Data Type *Yes/No*, which means that the column can contain only one of the values—yes or no. A professor will use this column to indicate whether he or she has responded to the student's email. Other database structures are defined in similar ways.

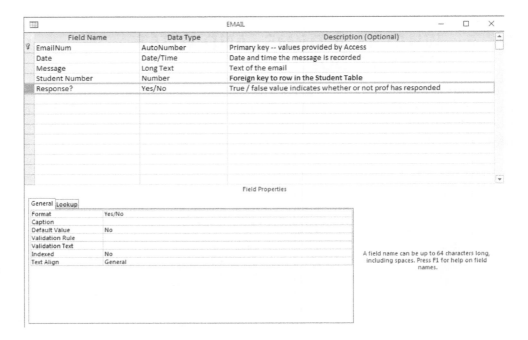

Figure 5-9 Adding a New Column to a Table (in Access)

Source: Microsoft Access 2010

Processing the Database

The second function of the DBMS is to process the database. Applications use the DBMS for four operations: *read*, *insert*, *modify*, or *delete* data. The applications call upon the DBMS in different ways. For example, when the user enters new data or changes data on a form, a computer program processes the data provided on the form and then calls the DBMS to make the necessary database changes. At other times, an application program can call directly on the DBMS to make the change. No matter which way the database is called, there is only one language that relational databases use when communicating data from a database: **Structured Query Language (SQL)**, which is an international standard language for processing a database. A query can be thought of as a question. SQL (pronounced "see-quell") can then be thought of as a formal way of putting a question to a database. The answer to that query will be the data that is specified. All five of the DBMS products mentioned earlier accept and process SQL statements. As an example, the following SQL statement inserts a new row into the *Student* table:

> INSERT INTO Student ([Student Number], [Student Name], HW1, HW2, MidTerm)
> VALUES (1000, 'Franklin, Benjamin', 90, 95, 100)

Such statements are issued behind the scenes by programs that process forms. Alternatively, they can also be issued directly to the DBMS by an application program.

You do not need to understand or remember SQL language syntax. Instead, just be aware that SQL is an international standard for processing a database. As well, SQL can be used to create databases and database structures. You will learn more about SQL if you take a database management course.

Administering the Database

A third DBMS function is to provide tools to assist in the administration of the database. Database administration involves a wide variety of activities. For example, the DBMS can be used to set up a security system involving user accounts, passwords, permissions, and limits for processing the database. To provide database security, a user must sign on using a valid user account before he or she can process the database.

Permissions can be limited in very specific ways. In the *Student* database example, it is possible to limit a particular user to reading only *Student Name* from the *Student* table. A different user could be given permission to read the entire *Student* table, but limited to update only the *HW1*, *HW2*, and *MidTerm* columns. Other users can be given still other permissions.

In addition to security, DBMS administrative functions include backing up database data, adding structures to improve the performance of database applications, removing data that are no longer wanted or needed, and similar tasks. One of these tasks involves setting up a system for dealing with database growth, as discussed in "MIS in Use," on page 142.

Q5-5   WHAT IS A DATABASE APPLICATION?

A **database application** is a collection of forms, reports, queries, and application programs that process a database. A database may have one or more applications, and each application may have one or more users. Figure 5-10 shows three applications; the top two have multiple users. These applications have different purposes, features, and functions, but they all process the same inventory data stored in a common database.

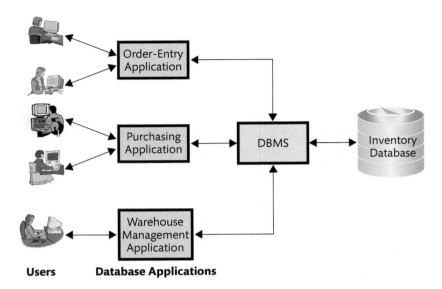

Figure 5-10 Use of Multiple Database Applications

Users   **Database Applications**

Founded in 1945, Vancouver-based Vancity is Canada's largest credit union, with more than $16 billion in assets. By a combination of organic (natural) and inorganic (acquisition) growth, Vancity now has 57 branches in Metro Vancouver, the Fraser Valley, Victoria, and Squamish and 501 000 individual and business customers.

The majority of Vancity's member customers did not have just a single product or service but, rather, a variety of products and services that could include savings and chequing accounts, loans, credit cards, and mutual funds and other investment products. Indeed, further complicating the relationship was that customers not only had multiple products/services but also had multiple instances of individual products/services. That is, a customer could have two savings accounts, multiple credit cards, and a number of mutual funds in a variety of ownerships (such as registered retirement savings programs [RRSPs], registered education savings plans [RESPs], and nonregistered investment plans), and these could be held or have been set up at different branches.

This diversity of products and services—although attractive to both Vancity and its member customers—created a major data-quality headache for Tony Fernandes. As the former vice-president of technology strategy, one of his responsibilities was the overall quality of information. His challenge was to ensure that the data in the customer information file (CIF), the database that held all customer data, were accurate and that the CIF identified customers uniquely and completely. As he put it, "My job is to manage similarities and differences. We need to know if the Jon Doe who lives on Victoria Street and has a savings account is the same Jonathan Doe who has a business account and a residence on Boundary Road."

The challenge was significant. In many cases, names were not unique and were complicated by short forms or by people having a variety of legal, given, and familiar names.

Vancity attempted to resolve many of these problems as customers activated each new product or service, but it was not always feasible. Something as relatively simple as spelling an address could result in duplicate entries that had to be reconciled. For example, the address "35 Westforest Trail" could also be entered as "35 Westforest Tr." At the lowest level, these types of entries caused inefficiencies, such as sending duplicate information. More troubling to Tony, of course, were problems of incomplete customer information or more complicated issues, such as misidentification of financial records.

QUESTIONS

1. How serious a problem is duplicate information to the financial services industry? Is it more serious for some industries than others? (*Hint:* How much of an issue is it for the health industry?)

2. Are there any other costs to Vancity when duplicate information is sent to customers? (*Hint:* What impression would you have if you received duplicate marketing information from various organizations?)

3. What are the various challenges in cleaning and grooming data? (*Hint:* Are there reasons why customers may have separate or changing information?)

4. Would the problem be solved by identifying customers numerically? How would customers perceive this? Are there legal issues?

Forms, Reports, and Queries

Figure 5-2 shows a typical database application data entry **form**, and Figure 5-11 shows a typical **report**. Data entry forms are used to read, insert, modify, and delete data. Reports show data in a structured context.

Some reports, like the one in Figure 5-11, also compute values as they present the data. An example is the computation of *Total weighted points* in Figure 5-11.

Recall from Chapter 2 that one of the definitions of information is "data presented in a meaningful context." The structure of this report creates information because it shows the student data in a context that will be meaningful to the professor.

DBMS programs provide comprehensive and robust features for querying database data. For example, suppose the professor who uses the *Student* database remembers that one of the students referred to the topic *barriers to entry* in an office visit, but he or she cannot remember which student or when. If there are hundreds of students and visits recorded in the database, it will take some effort and time for the professor to search through all the office visit records to find that event. The DBMS, however, can find any such record

---

Student Report with Emails

Student Name	BAKER, ANDREA	HW1	88
		HW2	100
Student Number	1325	MidTerm	78 (53 homeworks)
		Total weighted points:	422

Emails Received

Date	Message
2/1/2007	For homework 1, do you want us to provide notes on our references?
3/15/2007	My group consists of Swee Lau and Stuart Nelson.

Student Name	LAU, SWEE	HW1	75
		HW2	90
Student Number	1644	MidTerm	90 (53 homeworks)
		Total weighted points:	435

Emails Received

Date	Message
3/15/2007	Could you please assign me to a group?

Figure 5-11 Example of a Student Report

quickly. Figure 5-12(a) shows a **query** form in which the professor types in the keyword for which he or she is looking. Figure 5-12(b) shows the results of the query.

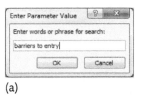

(a)

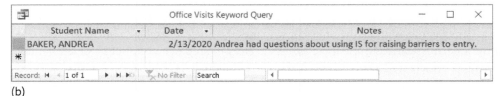

Figure 5-12 Example of a Query

Source: Microsoft Access 2010

(b)

Database Application Programs

Forms, reports, and queries work well for standard functions. However, most applications have unique requirements that a simple form, report, or query cannot meet. For example, in the order entry application in Figure 5-10, what should be done if only a portion of a customer's request can be met? If someone wants 10 widgets and there are only 3 in stock, should a backorder for 7 more be generated automatically? Or should some other action be taken?

Application programs process logic that is specific to a given business need. In the *Student* database, an example application is one that assigns grades at the end of the term. If the professor grades on a curve, the application reads the breakpoints for each grade from a form and then processes each row in the *Student* table, allocating a grade based on the breakpoints and the total number of points earned.

Another important use of application programs is to enable database processing over the Internet. For this use, the application program serves as an intermediary between the Web server and the database. The application program responds to events, such as when a user presses a submit button; it also reads, inserts, modifies, and deletes database data.

Figure 5-13 shows four different database application programs running on a Web server computer. Users with browsers connect to the Web server via the Internet. The Web server directs user requests to the appropriate application program. Each program then processes the database, as necessary.

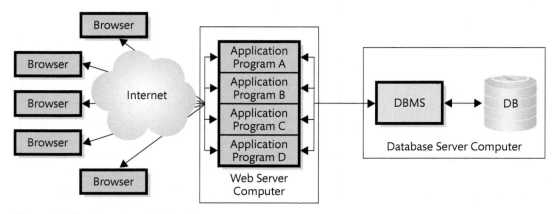

Figure 5-13 Four Application Programs on a Web Server Computer

Multiuser Processing

Figures 5-10 and 5-13 show multiple users processing the database. Such **multiuser processing** is common, but it does pose unique problems that you, as a future manager, need to be aware of. To understand the nature of those problems, consider the following scenario:

> Two users, Andrea and Jeffrey, are using the order entry application in Figure 5-10. Andrea is on the phone with her customer, who wants to purchase 5 widgets. At the same time, Jeffrey is talking with his customer, who wants to purchase 3 widgets. Andrea reads the database to determine how many widgets are in inventory. (She unknowingly invokes the order entry application when she types in her data entry form.) The DBMS returns a row showing 10 widgets in inventory.
>
> Meanwhile, just after Andrea accesses the database, Jeffrey's customer says she wants widgets, and so he also reads the database (via the order entry application program) to determine how many widgets are in inventory. The DBMS returns the same row to him, indicating that 10 widgets are available.
>
> Andrea's customer now says that he will take 5 widgets, and Andrea records this fact in her form. The application rewrites the widget row back to the database, indicating that there are 5 widgets in inventory.
>
> Meanwhile, Jeffrey's customer says that he will take 3 widgets. Jeffrey records this fact in his form, and the application rewrites the widget row back to the database. However, Jeffrey's application knows nothing about Andrea's work and subtracts 3 from the original count of 10, thus storing an incorrect count of 7 widgets in inventory. Clearly, there is a problem. We began with 10 widgets, Andrea took 5 and Jeffrey took 3, but the database says there are 7 widgets in inventory. It should show 2, not 7.

This problem, known as the **lost-update problem**, exemplifies one of the special characteristics of multiuser database processing. To prevent this problem, some type of locking must be used to coordinate the activities of users who are unaware of each other. Locking brings its own complexity and problems that must be addressed, but these are beyond the scope of this chapter and text.

The purpose of this example is to illustrate that making a system usable by more than one person requires much more than simply enabling computer connections. The logic of the underlying application processing needs to be adjusted as well.

Be aware of possible data conflicts when you manage business activities that involve multiuser processing. If you find inaccurate results that seem not to have a cause, you may be experiencing multiuser data conflicts. Contact your MIS department for assistance.

Q5-6 WHAT IS THE DIFFERENCE BETWEEN DATABASES AND WHERE ARE WE HEADED?

DBMS products fall into two broad categories. **Enterprise DBMS** products process large organizational and workgroup databases. These products support many (perhaps thousands of) users and many different database applications. They also support 24/7 operations and can manage databases that span dozens of different magnetic disks with thousands of gigabytes or more of data. IBM's DB2, Microsoft's SQL Server, and Oracle's Oracle are examples of enterprise DBMS products.

Personal DBMS products are designed for smaller, simpler database applications. Such products are used for personal or small workgroup applications that involve fewer than 100 users, and normally fewer than 15. In fact, the great bulk of databases in this category have only a single user. The professor's *Student* database is an example of a database that is processed by a personal DBMS product.

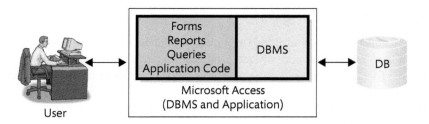

Figure 5-14 Personal Database System

In the past, there were many personal DBMS products—Paradox, dBase, R:BASE, and FoxPro. Microsoft phased out these products when it developed Access and included it in the Microsoft Office suite. Today, the only remaining personal DBMS is Microsoft Access.

To avoid one point of confusion for you in the future, note that the separation of application programs and the DBMS shown in Figure 5-10 is true only for enterprise DBMS products. Microsoft Access includes features and functions for application processing along with the DBMS itself. For example, Access has a form generator and a report generator. Thus, as shown in Figure 5-14, Access is both a DBMS and an application development product.

More broadly however, although the relational model was the single, standard way of processing databases for more than 30 years, recently that has started to change. Part of the reason is that the major principles of the relational model—fixed-sized tables, representing relationships with foreign keys, and the theory of normalization—came about because of limited storage space and limited processing speeds back in the 1960s and early 1970s.[3] At some point, maybe the mid-1990s, these limitations were removed by improved storage and processing technology, and no longer exist. In other words, the relational model is not needed today.

Furthermore, the relational model was never a natural fit with business documents. For example, users want to store sales orders; they do not want to break up sales orders via normalization and store the data in separate tables. It is like taking your car into a parking garage and having the attendant break it up into pieces, store the pieces in separate piles, and then reassemble the pieces when you come back to get your car. And why? For the efficiency and convenience of the parking garage management. Thus, the primary reason for the relational model's existence is gone, and document piece-making via normalization is no longer necessary.

Need to Store New Data Types Differently

There are other reasons for the appearance of new styles of database processing. For one, many organizations, like Falcon Security, want to store new types of data such as images, audio, and videos. Those files are large collections of bits, and they do not fit into relational structures. As you learned in Q5-5, collections of such files still need metadata; we need such data to record when, where, how, and for what purpose the files exist, but we do not need to put them into relational databases just to obtain metadata.

Also, many Internet applications process many, many more transactions against much simpler data than traditional applications do. A tweet has a trivial data structure when compared to the configuration of a Kenworth truck, but there are so many more tweets than truck configurations.

Even more important, traditional relational DBMS products devote considerable code and processing power to support what are termed **ACID** (atomic, consistent, isolated, durable) transactions. In essence, this acronym means that either all of a transaction is

---

[3] For a summary of this early history and an amplification of these ideas, see David Kroenke, "Beyond the Relational Model," *IEEE Computer*, June 2005.

processed or none of it is (atomic), that transactions are processed in the same manner (consistent) whether processed alone or in the presence of millions of other transactions (isolated), and that once a transaction is stored, it never goes away—even in the presence of failure (durable).

ACID transactions are critical to traditional commercial applications. Even in the presence of machine failure, a system must process both the sell and the buy sides of a transaction: It cannot process part of a transaction. Also, what it stores today must be stored tomorrow. But, many new Internet applications do not need ACID. Who cares if, one time out of 1 million, only half of your tweet is stored? Or if it is stored today and disappears tomorrow?

Need for Faster Processing Using Many Servers

Another reason for the development of nonrelational databases is the need to gain faster performance using many servers. A few years ago, Amazon.com determined that relational database technology would not meet its processing needs, and it developed a nonrelational data store called **Dynamo**.[4] Meanwhile, for many of the same reasons, Google developed a nonrelational data store called **Bigtable**.[5] Facebook took concepts from both of these systems and developed a third nonrelational data store called **Cassandra**.[6] In 2008, Facebook turned Cassandra over to the open source community, and now Apache has dubbed it a Top-Level Project (TLP), which is the height of respectability among open source projects.

Nontraditional DBMS Types

These new requirements have led to three new categories of DBMS:

1. **NoSQL DBMS.** This acronym is misleading. It really should be NonRelational DBMS. It refers to new DBMS products that support very high transaction rates processing relatively simple data structures, replicated on many servers in the cloud, without ACID transaction support. MongoDB, Cassandra, Bigtable, and Dynamo are NoSQL products.

2. **NewSQL DBMS.** These DBMS products process very high levels of transactions, like the NoSQL DBMS, but provide ACID support. They may or may not support the relational model. Such products are a hotbed of development with new vendors popping up nearly every day. Leading products are yet unknown.

3. **In-memory DBMS.** This category consists of DBMS products that process databases in main memory. This technique has become possible because newer computer memories can be enormous and can hold an entire database at one time, or at least very large chunks of it. Usually, these products support or extend the relational model. SAP HANA is a computer with an in-memory DBMS that provides high-volume ACID transaction support simultaneously with complex relational query processing. Tableau Software's reporting products are supported by a proprietary in-memory DBMS using an extension to SQL.

---

[4] Werner Vogel, "Amazon's Dynamo," All Things Distributed blog, last modified October 2, 2007, *www.allthingsdistributed. com/2007/10/amazons_dynamo.html.*

[5] Fay Chang, Jeffrey Dean, Sanjay Ghemawat, Wilson C. Hsieh, Deborah A. Wallach, Mike Burrows, Tushar Chandra, Andrew Fikes, and Robert E. Gruber, "Bigtable: A Distributed Storage System for Structured Data," OSDI 2006, Seventh Symposium on Operating System Design and Implementation, Seattle, WA, last modified November 2006, *http://labs. google.com/papers/bigtable.html.*

[6] Jonathan Ellis, "Cassandra: Open Source Bigtable + Dynamo," accessed June 2011, *www.slideshare.net/jbellis/ cassandra-open-source-bigtable-dynamo.*

Will These New Products Replace the Relational Model?

Does the emergence of these new products mean the death knell for relational databases? It seems unlikely because organizations have created thousands of traditional relational databases with millions of lines of application code that process SQL statements against relational data structures. No organization wants to endure the expense and effort of converting those databases and code to something else. There is also a strong social trend among older technologists to hang onto the relational model. However, these new products are loosening the stronghold that relational technology has enjoyed for decades, and in the future it is likely that many NoSQL, NewSQL, and in-memory databases will exist in commerce.

Furthermore, existing DBMS vendors like Oracle, Microsoft, and IBM will not sit still. With substantial cash and highly skilled developers, they will likely incorporate features of these new categories of DBMS into their existing or new products. Acquisitions of some of the NewSQL startups, in particular, are likely.

Using the vocabulary of Chapter 3, for the first time in more than 20 years, the database software market experienced viable new entrants. So, will Microsoft and Oracle and other DBMS vendors lose some of their market to nontraditional products and vendors? Or will they follow IBM's path? Become less of a vendor of software and more a seller of services supporting open source software such as Cassandra? Or will we soon see companies like Oracle, which is rich with cash, purchasing one of these new companies? Indeed, that may have happened by the time you read this.

What Do Nonrelational DBMS Mean for You?

During the early years of your career, many nontraditional databases will be developed, and not just by leading-edge companies like Amazon.com, Google, and Facebook. So, what does that mean to you as a business professional? First, such knowledge is useful; stay abreast of developments in this area. If you were a junior person at Falcon and you went to a meeting today with Toshio and said something like, "Have you thought about using MongoDB for storing our videos?" you would gain his attention and admiration immediately. You would likely find yourself on Falcon's key users' committee (or whatever Falcon calls it), and that would be a great career opportunity for you. Also, watch nonrelational DBMS product developments from an investor's perspective. Not all such products will be open source; even if they are, there will be companies that integrate them into their product or service offerings, and those companies may well be good investment opportunities.

If you are interested in IS as a discipline or as a second major, pay attention to these products. You still need to learn the relational model and the processing of relational databases; they will be the bread-and-butter of the industry for many more years. But exciting new opportunities and career paths will also develop around nonrelational databases. Learn about them as well, and use that knowledge to separate yourself from the competition when it comes to job interviews.

Lots of interesting, promising developments are under way!

How Does the Knowledge in This Chapter Help You?

You now understand the purpose of a database and have an introduction to the ways that databases are processed. You also know about new categories of nontraditional DBMS. This knowledge will enable you to be an effective team member when your organization has needs like those at Falcon Security. You can add substantial value to this knowledge by studying Knowledge Extensions 6, 7, and 8.

ACTIVE REVIEW

Use this Active Review to verify that you have understood the material in the chapter. You can read the entire chapter and then perform the tasks in this review, or you can read the material for just one question and perform the tasks for that question before moving on to the next one.

Q5-1 WHY DO YOU NEED TO KNOW ABOUT DATABASES AND WHAT IS THEIR PURPOSE?

Explain three ways in which you interact with a database each day, even though that database is not directly apparent. Describe the purpose of a database. Explain when you should use a spreadsheet and when you should use a database.

Q5-2 WHAT IS CONTENT AND HOW IS IT ORGANIZED?

Describe what is meant by the term *content*. How has content changed with computers and access to the Internet? What is a Web content management system? How have content management systems evolved over time?

Q5-3 WHAT DOES A DATABASE CONTAIN?

Explain the hierarchy of data from bytes to tables. Show how a database stores the relationships among rows. Define *key* and *foreign key*. Define *metadata*, and explain how metadata makes databases more useful.

Q5-4 WHAT IS A DBMS, AND WHAT DOES IT DO?

Describe a database application system. Define *DBMS*. Name three prominent DBMS products. Describe the difference between a database and a DBMS. Explain the three major functions of a DBMS. What is SQL used for?

Q5-5 WHAT IS A DATABASE APPLICATION?

Name and describe the components of a database application. Describe the circumstances that require a special logic for database applications. Describe the lost-update problem. Explain, in general terms, how this problem is prevented.

Q5-6 WHAT IS THE DIFFERENCE BETWEEN DATABASES AND WHERE ARE WE HEADED?

Explain the function of an enterprise DBMS and describe its characteristics. Explain the function of a personal DBMS and describe its characteristics. Name the only surviving personal DBMS.

MyLab MIS

MyLab MIS is an online learning and testing environment that features the perfect study tools to help you master the concepts covered in this chapter. Log in to MyLab to test your knowledge of key chapter concepts and explore additional practice tools, including videos, flashcards, and more!

KEY TERMS AND CONCEPTS

Access 140
ACID 146
Byte 136
Columns 136
Content management
    systems (CMSs) 135
Database 136
Database application 141
Database application
    system 139

DBMS 140
DB2 140
Enterprise DBMS 145
Fields 136
File 136
Foreign keys 138
Form 143
Intellectual
    property 134
Key 138

Lost-update
    problem 145
Metadata 138
Multiuser
    processing 145
MySQL 140
Oracle 140
Personal DBMS 145
Query 144
Records 136

Relation 138
Relational databases 138
Report 143
Rows 136
SQL Server 140
Structured Query Language
    (SQL) 141
Table 136

USING YOUR KNOWLEDGE

5-1. Suppose you are a marketing assistant for a consumer electronics company and are in charge of setting up your company's booth at trade shows. Weeks before the shows, you meet with the marketing managers and determine what displays and equipment they want to display. Then you identify each of the required components and schedule a shipper to deliver them to the trade show site. You then supervise convention personnel as they set up the booths and equipment. Once the show is over, you supervise the packing of the booth and all equipment as well as schedule its shipment back to your home office. When the equipment arrives, you check it into your warehouse to ensure that all pieces of the booth and all equipment are returned. If there are problems due to shipping damage or loss, you handle those problems. Your job is important; at a typical show, you are responsible for more than a quarter of a million dollars' worth of equipment.

a. You will need to track data about booth components, equipment, shippers, and shipments. List typical fields for each type of data.

b. Could you use a spreadsheet to keep track of this data? What would be the advantages and disadvantages of doing so?

c. Using your answer to part a, give an example of two relationships that you need to track. Show the keys and foreign keys for each.

d. Which of the following components of a database application are you likely to need: data entry forms, reports, queries, or application programs? Explain one use for each that you will need.

e. Will your application be for one user or for multiple users? Will you need a personal DBMS or an enterprise DBMS? If a personal DBMS, which product will you use?

5-2. Samantha Green (the same Samantha we met at the end of Chapter 3, page 68) owns and operates Twigs Tree Trimming Service. Recall that Samantha has a degree from a forestry program and recently opened her business in St. Louis, Missouri. Her business consists of many one-time operations (e.g., removing a tree or stump), as well as recurring services (e.g., trimming customers' trees every year or two). When business is slow, Samantha calls former clients to remind them of her services and of the need to trim their trees on a regular basis.

a. Name and describe tables of data that Samantha will need to run her business. Indicate possible fields for each table.

b. Could Samantha use a spreadsheet to keep track of this data? What would be the advantages and disadvantages of doing so?

c. Using your answer to part a, give an example of two relationships that Samantha needs to track. Show the keys and foreign keys for each.

d. Which of the following components of a database application is Samantha likely to need: data entry forms, reports, queries, or application programs? Explain one use for each that she needs.

e. Will this application be for one user or for multiple users? Will she need a personal DBMS or an enterprise DBMS? If a personal DBMS, which product will she use?

5-3. YourFire Inc. (the same YourFire we met at the end of Chapter 3, page 68) is a small business owned by Curt and Julie Robards. Based in Brisbane, Australia, YourFire manufactures and sells the YourFire, a lightweight camping stove. Recall that Curt used his previous experience as an aerospace engineer to invent a burning nozzle that enables the stove to stay lit in very high winds. Using her industrial design training, Julie designed the stove so that it is small, lightweight, easy to set up, and very stable. Curt and Julie sell the stove directly to their customers over the Internet and via phone. The warranty on the stove covers 5 years of cost-free repair for stoves used for recreational purposes.

YourFire wants to track every stove and the customer who purchased it. They want to know which customers own which stoves in case they need to notify customers of safety problems or need to order a stove recall. Curt and Julie also want to keep track of any repairs they have performed.

a. Name and describe tables of data that YourFire will need. Indicate possible fields for each table.

b. Could YourFire use a spreadsheet to keep track of this data? What would be the advantages and disadvantages of doing so?

c. Using your answer to part a, give an example of two relationships that YourFire needs to track. Show the keys and foreign keys for each.

d. Which of the following components of a database application is YourFire likely to need: data entry forms, reports, queries, or application programs? Explain one use for each needed component.

e. Will this application be for one user or for multiple users? Will YourFire need a personal DBMS or an enterprise DBMS? If a personal DBMS, which product will it use? If an enterprise DBMS, which product can it obtain license-free?

CASE STUDY 5
SEARCHING FOR PIANOS ...

Dean Petrich is a certified piano tuner and technician who has been repairing and restoring pianos since 1973. He also has a career as Deano the Clown, a clown entertainer who performs at children's parties in the Seattle, WA, metro area (see Figure 5-15, *http://deanotheclown.com/*). The schedules of his two businesses balance each other: He is busy as a clown in the late spring, summer, and fall, and during the rest of the year, he repairs and restores pianos.

Over the past 20 years, the demand for pianos has dramatically declined. When Grandma dies, or the kids move out, or some other life change occurs, families have no further use for their piano, and when they find there is no market for it, they call Dean, who picks up the piano for a modest fee. For a number of years, Dean restored these pianos and either resold or rented them. Since the turn of the century, however, the decreasing demand for pianos has affected him as well, and over time, he has accumulated far too many pianos. Even after discarding the worst of them, he still has nearly 100.

Figure 5-15 Deano the Clown

Source: Dean Petrich

Figure 5-16 Pianos in Shed

Source: David Kroenke

As you can imagine, 100 pianos consume a considerable amount of storage. At first, Dean stored them in his workshop. When he ran out of room in his workshop, he built a large metal shed and stored them there (Figure 5-16). When the shed overflowed with pianos, he moved them to plastic tents in a meadow on his property (Figure 5-17). Unfortunately, the plastic tents are prone to rips and tears, and because Dean lives in the Pacific Northwest, many pianos have been ruined by rain, even when he covers them with plastic tarps inside the plastic tents.

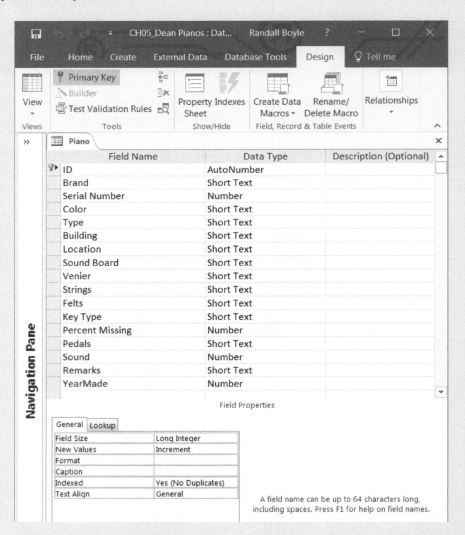

Figure 5-17 Columns in the Piano Table

Source: Microsoft Corporation

Two years ago, sinking in his steadily increasing piano inventory, Dean began to offer pianos for free. Not the very best pianos—those he hopes to sell—but he offers many quality pianos for free. However, Dean has two problems. First, he does not know which pianos are best and where they are located in the shop, shed, or tents. Second, few people are willing to crawl over the tops of the pianos in the large shed and tents (through refuse of squirrels, rats, and mice) looking for their perfect piano.

To resolve this issue, Dean created a Microsoft Access database with only one table: Piano. To fill the database with data, Dean had to first take an inventory of all the pianos and record the data shown in the columns of Figure 5-17.

A one-table database could just as easily have been stored in Excel, but Dean used Access because he wants to query his data in a variety of ways. He wants to know, for example, all of the pianos located in a tent that have a sound quality of 4 or higher. And he wants to know which pianos have a sound quality of 1 or less so he can dispose of them. Further, customers have particular needs. One might, for example, want a Baldwin spinet (a brand and type of piano); without a database he has no idea whether he has one or where. Or, when he needs a replacement key top, he might want to know the location of all the pianos in the workshop that have ivory keys and a sound quality of 2 or less, and so on.

Because of the dynamic nature of his needs, Dean uses the Access query facility. Figure 5-18 shows an example query that returns all of the pianos of a sound quality higher than 4 that are located in a tent, and Figure 5-19 shows the result of that query. Dean also suspects that the quality deteriorates faster in the tents than in the shed or the shop. To determine if this is the case, he created the report shown in Figure 5-20.

Questions

1. Explain why a one-table database could be stored just as readily in Excel as in Access.

2. Justify the decision to use Access to store the piano database.

3. Examine the columns in Figure 5-18. Name three characteristics of pianos that are not represented in this table.

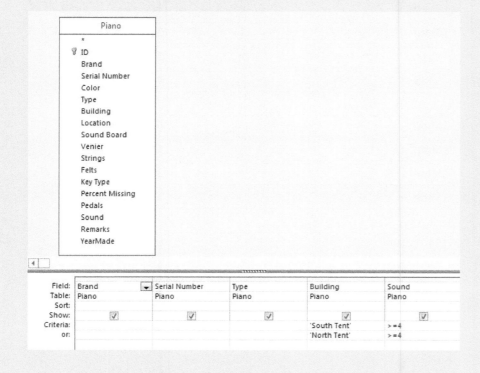

Figure 5-18 Example of Access Query

Source: Microsoft Corporation

Brand	Serial Number	Type	Building	Sound
Baldwin	70452	Spinet	South Tent	4
Esteu	20158	Upright	North Tent	4
H.G. Johnson	10749	Upright	North Tent	4
Winter ???	326493	Spinet	North Tent	4
Baldwin	637957	Spinet	North Tent	4
Briggs	80360	Upright	North Tent	4
Hobart Cable	77182	Upright	North Tent	4
Mehlin	28733	Upright	North Tent	4
Aeolian	182562	Spinet	North Tent	4
Farrand	27631	Upright	South Tent	4
Kurtzman	21398	Upright	South Tent	5
Mathushek	12963	Upright	South Tent	4

Figure 5-19 Results of Query from Figure 5-19

Source: Microsoft Corporation

Piano Sound Quality by Building

Building	Sound Quality	Number Pianos
North Tent	1	1
North Tent	3	3
North Tent	4	8
Shed	0	10
Shed	1	1
Shed	2	7
Shed	3	13
Shed	4	12
Shop	0	2
Shop	1	2
Shop	3	5
Shop	4	2
South Tent	0	6
South Tent	2	3
South Tent	3	2
South Tent	4	3
South Tent	5	1

Figure 5-20 Piano Sound Quality by Building

Source: Microsoft Corporation

a. If you were a consultant advising Dean, what criteria should you recommend he use when deciding whether to include additional data?

b. Is this database a model of an inventory of pianos, or is it a model of Dean's model of an inventory of pianos? Explain the difference.

c. How does your answer to question 5-14b influence your answer to question 5-14a?

4. Suppose, in addition to the data about pianos, Dean wants to store data about the manufacturer such as addresses (or last known address), years of operation, and general related comments.

a. Design a Manufacturer table.

b. Alter the design of the Piano table (Figure 5-17) to represent the relationship between Piano and Manufacturer. State and justify any assumptions.

5. Using the data in Figure 5-20, draw conclusions about the effect of location on piano sound quality. Justify your statements using this data.

6. Explain the statement "A database is an abstraction of some aspect of a business." Using this example, explain the ways that processing an abstraction is more effective than examining pianos. Explain the ways that processing an abstraction is more efficient that examining pianos. Generalize your observation to databases for business in general.

7. This database will soon become useless if it is not kept up to date. List procedures that Dean needs to create and follow to keep his database current.

MyLab MIS

Go to the Assignments section of your MyLab to complete these writing exercises.

5-1 Go to *http://aws.amazon.com* and search for AWS database offerings. Explain the differences among Amazon's RDS, DynamoDB, ElastiCache, and Redshift services. Which of these three would you recommend for storing Falcon Security's data? (Note: Whenever you query the Internet for any AWS product, be sure to include the keyword *AWS* in your search. Otherwise, your search will result in Amazon's lists of books about the item you are searching for.)

5-2 Suppose you have just been hired by a tech startup that focuses on helping small businesses in South America market their handmade products to consumers around the world. They store a large amount of images and video of the products they sell. In addition, videos of the craftsmen making their products and talking about new products are very popular with customers. The CEO has asked you to look at the potential benefits of using a NoSQL DBMS like MongoDB or Cassandra for these images and videos. Describe the benefits of using a NoSQL DBMS to store this type of data. Would a relational database be a good option? Why?

WHAT DO YOU THINK?

NOBODY SAID I SHOULDN'T

"My name is Kelly, and I do systems support for our group. I configure the new computers, set up the network, make sure the servers are operating, and so forth. I also do all the database backups. I've always liked computers. After high school, I worked odd jobs to make some money. I knew I wanted to work with computers as a career. It took awhile, but I got an associate degree in information technology from our local community college."

"Anyway, as I said, I make backup copies of our databases. One weekend, I didn't have much going on, so I copied one of the database backups to a CD and took it home. I had taken a class on database processing as part of my associate degree, and we used a SQL Server (our database management system) in my class. In fact, I suppose that's part of the reason I got the job. Anyway, it was easy to restore the database on my computer at home, and I did."

"Of course, as they'll tell you in your database class, one of the big advantages of database processing is that databases have metadata, or data that describe the content of the database. So, although I didn't know what tables were in our database, I did know how to access the SQL server metadata. I just queried a table called *sysTables* to learn the names of our tables. From there it was easy to find out what columns each table had."

"I found tables with data about orders, customers, salespeople, and so forth, and just to amuse myself and to see how much of the query language SQL I could remember, I started playing around with the data. I was curious to know which order-entry clerk was the best, so I started querying each clerk's order data, the total number of orders, total order amounts, things like that. It was easy to do and fun."

"I know one of the order-entry clerks, Jason, pretty well, so I started looking at the data for his orders. I was just curious, and it was very simple SQL. I was just playing around with the data when I noticed something odd. All his biggest orders were with one company, Valley Appliances; even stranger, every one of its orders had a huge discount. I thought, *Well, maybe that's typical.* Out of curiosity, I started looking at data for the other clerks, and very few of them had an order with Valley Appliances. But when they did, Valley didn't get a big discount. Then I looked at the rest of Jason's orders, and none of them had much in the way of discounts, either."

"The next Friday, a bunch of us went out for beer after work. I happened to see Jason, so I asked him about Valley Appliances and made a joke about the discounts. He asked me what I meant, and then I told him that I'd been looking at the data for fun and that I saw this odd pattern. He laughed, said he 'just did his job,' and then changed the subject."

"Well, to make a long story short, when I got to work on Monday morning, my office was cleaned out. There was nothing there except a note telling me to go see my boss. The bottom line was, I was fired. The company also threatened that if I didn't return all of its data, I'd be in court for the next five years. I was so mad I didn't even tell them about Jason. Now my problem is that I'm out of a job, and I can't exactly use my last company for a reference."

Discussion Questions

1. Where did Kelly go wrong?

2. Do you think it was illegal, unethical, or neither for Kelly to take the database home and query the data?

3. Does the company share culpability with Kelly?

4. What do you think Kelly should have done upon discovering the odd pattern in Jason's orders?

5. What should the company have done before firing Kelly?

6. "Metadata make databases easy to use—for both authorized and unauthorized purposes." Explain what organizations should do in light of this fact.

KNOWLEDGE EXTENSION 6
Chapter 5 provides the background for this extension.
Database Design

STUDY QUESTIONS

KE6-1	**WHO WILL VOLUNTEER?**
KE6-2	**HOW ARE DATABASE APPLICATION SYSTEMS DEVELOPED?**
KE6-3	**WHAT ARE THE COMPONENTS OF THE ENTITY-RELATIONSHIP DATA MODEL?**
KE6-4	**HOW IS A DATA MODEL TRANSFORMED INTO A DATABASE DESIGN?**
KE6-5	**WHAT IS THE USERS' ROLE?**
KE6-6	**WHO WILL VOLUNTEER? (CONTINUED)**

In this Knowledge Extension, you will learn about data modelling and how data models are transformed into database designs. You will also learn the important role that business professionals have in the development of a database application system.

KE6-1 WHO WILL VOLUNTEER?

Suppose you are the manager of fund-raising for a local public television station. Twice a year you conduct fund drives during which the station runs commercials that ask viewers to donate. These drives are important; they provide nearly 40 percent of the station's operating budget.

One of your job functions is to find volunteers to staff the phones during these drives. You need 10 volunteers per night for 6 nights, or 60 people, twice per year. The volunteers' job is exhausting, and normally a volunteer will work only one night during a drive.

Finding volunteers for each drive is a perpetual headache. Two months before a drive begins, you and your staff start calling potential volunteers. You first call volunteers from prior drives, using a roster that your administrative assistant prepares for each drive. Some volunteers have been helping for years; you would like to know that information before you call them so that you can tell them how much you appreciate their ongoing support. Unfortunately, the roster does not have that data.

Additionally, some volunteers are more effective than others. Some have a particular knack for increasing the callers' donations. Although those data are available, the information is not in a format that you can use when calling for volunteers. You think you could better staff the fund-raising drives if you had that missing information.

You know that you can use a computer database to keep better track of prior volunteers' service and performance, but you are not sure how to proceed. By the end of this Knowledge Extension, when we return to this fund-raising situation, you will know what to do.

KE6-2 HOW ARE DATABASE APPLICATION SYSTEMS DEVELOPED?

You learned in Chapter 5 that a database application system consists of a database, a DBMS, and one or more database applications. A database application, in turn, consists of forms, reports, queries, and possibly application programs. The question then becomes: How are such systems developed? And, even more important to you, what is the users' role? We will address these questions in this Knowledge Extension.

Figure KE6-1 summarizes the database application system development process. First, the developers interview users and develop the requirements for the new system. During this process, the developers analyze existing forms, reports, queries, and other user activities. They also determine the need for new forms, reports, and queries. The requirements for the database are then summarized in something called a **data model**, which is a logical representation of the structure of the data. The data model contains a description of both the data and the relationships among the data. It is akin to a blueprint. Just as building architects create a blueprint before they start construction, so, too, database developers create a data model before they start designing the database.

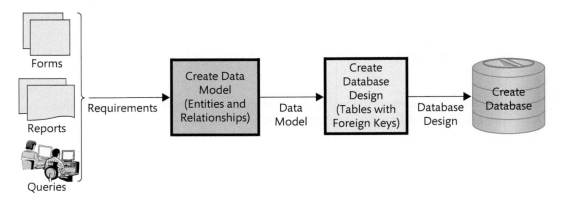

Figure KE6-1 Database Development Process

Once the users have validated and approved the data model, it is transformed into a database design. After that, the design is implemented in a database, and that database is then filled with user data.

You will learn much more about systems development in Chapter 12 and its related extensions. We discuss data modelling here because users have a crucial role in the success of any database development: They must validate and approve the data model. Only the users know what should be in the database.

Consider, for example, a database of students that an adviser uses for his or her advisees. What should be in it? Students? Classes? Records of emails from students? Records of meetings with students? Majors? Student organizations? Even when we know what themes should be in the database, we must ask, how detailed should the records be? Should the database include campus addresses? Home addresses? Billing addresses?

In fact, there are many possibilities, and the database developers do not and cannot know what to include. They do know, however, that a database must include all the data necessary for the users to perform their jobs. Ideally, it contains that amount of data and no more. So during database development, the developers must rely on the users to tell them what they need in the database. They will rely on the users to check the data model and to verify it for correctness, completeness, and appropriate level of detail. That verification will be your job. We begin with a discussion of the entity-relationship data model—the most common tool to use to construct data models.

KE6-3 WHAT ARE THE COMPONENTS OF THE ENTITY-RELATIONSHIP DATA MODEL?

The most popular technique for creating a data model is the **entity-relationship (E-R) data model**. With it, developers describe the content of a database by defining the things (*entities*) that will be stored in the database and the *relationships* among those entities. A second, less popular tool for data modelling is the **Unified Modelling Language (UML)**. We will not describe that tool here. However, if you learn how to interpret E-R models, with a bit of study you will be able to understand UML models as well.

Entities

An **entity** is something that the users want to track. Examples of entities are *Order, Customer, Salesperson,* and *Item*. Some entities represent a physical object, such as *Item* or *Salesperson*; others represent a logical construct or transaction, such as *Order* or *Contract*. For reasons beyond this discussion, entity names are always singular. We use *Order*, not *Orders*; *Salesperson*, not *Salespersons*.

Entities have **attributes** that describe characteristics of the entity. Example attributes of *Order* are *OrderNumber, OrderDate, SubTotal, Tax, Total,* and so forth. Example attributes of *Salesperson* are *SalespersonName, Email, Phone,* and so forth.

Entities have an **identifier,** which is an attribute (or group of attributes) whose value is associated with one and only one entity instance. For example, *OrderNumber* is an identifier of *Order* because only one *Order* instance has a given value of *OrderNumber*. For the same reason, *CustomerNumber* is an identifier of *Customer*. If each member of the sales staff has a unique name, then *SalespersonName* is an identifier of *Salesperson*.

Before we continue, consider that last sentence. Is the salesperson's name unique among the sales staff? Both now and in the future? Who decides the answer to such a question? Only the users know whether this is true; the database developers cannot know. This example underlines why it is important for you to be able to interpret data models because only users like you will know for sure.

Figure KE6-2 shows examples of entities for the Student database. Each entity is shown in a rectangle. The name of the entity is just above the rectangle, and the identifier is shown in a section at the top of the entity. Entity attributes are shown in the remainder of the rectangle. In Figure KE6-2, the *Adviser* entity has an identifier called *AdviserName* and the attributes *Phone, CampusAddress,* and *EmailAddress*.

Observe that the entities *Email* and *Office_Visit* do not have an identifier. Unlike *Student* or *Adviser*, the users do not have an attribute that identifies a particular email. In fact, *Email* and *Office_Visit* are identified, in part, by their relationship to *Student*. For now, we need not worry about that. The data model needs only to show how users view their world. When it comes to database design, the designer will deal with the missing identifiers by

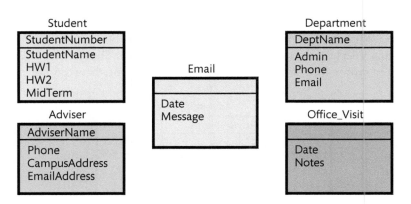

Figure KE6-2 Student Data Model Entities

adding columns, possibly using hidden identifiers, to implement the users' view. You can learn about the modelling and representation of such entities in a database course.

Relationships

Entities have **relationships** to each other. An *Order*, for example, has a relationship to a *Customer* entity and also to a *Salesperson* entity. In the Student database, a *Student* has a relationship to an *Adviser*, and an *Adviser* has a relationship to a *Department*.

Figure KE6-3 shows sample *Department, Adviser,* and *Student* entities and their relationships. For simplicity, this figure shows just the identifier of the entities and not the other attributes. For this sample data, *Accounting* has three professors, Jones, Wu, and Lopez, and *Finance* has two professors, Smith and Greene.

The relationship between *Advisers* and *Students* is a bit more complicated because in this example an adviser is allowed to advise many students and a student is allowed to have many advisers. Perhaps this happens because students can have multiple majors. In any case, note that Professor Jones advises students 100 and 400 and that student 100 is advised by both Professors Jones and Smith.

Figure KE6-3 Example of *Department, Adviser,* and *Student* Entities and Relationships

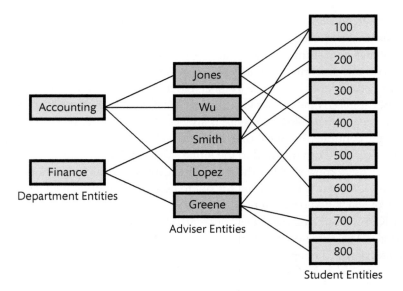

Diagrams like the one in Figure KE6-3 are too cumbersome for use in database design discussions. Instead, database designers use diagrams called **entity-relationship (E-R) diagrams**. Figure KE6-4 shows an E-R diagram for the data in Figure KE6-3. In this figure, all of the entities of one type are represented by a single rectangle. Thus, there are rectangles for the *Department, Adviser,* and *Student* entities. Attributes are shown as before in Figure KE6-2.

Additionally, a line is used to represent a relationship between two entities. Notice the line between *Department* and *Adviser*, for example. The forked lines on the right side of that line signify that a department may have more than one adviser. The angled lines, which are referred to as a **crow's foot**, are shorthand for the multiple lines between *Department* and

Figure KE6-4 Example Relationships—Version 1

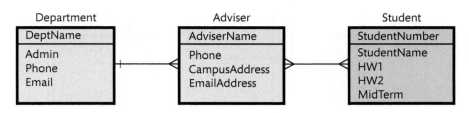

Adviser in Figure KE6-3. The left end of the line has a single vertical bar, indicating that an adviser works in just one department. Relationships like this one are called **one-to-many (1:N) relationships** because one department can have many advisers.

Now examine the line between *Adviser* and *Student*. Here a crow's foot appears at each end of the line. This notation signifies that an adviser can be related to many students and that a student can be related to many advisers, which is the situation in Figure KE6-3. Relationships like this one are called **many-to-many (N:M) relationships** because one adviser can have many students and one student can have many advisers.

Students sometimes find the notation N:M confusing. Interpret the N and M to mean that a variable number, greater than one, is allowed on each side of the relationship. Such a relationship is not written N:N because that notation would imply that there are the same number of entities on each side of the relationship, which is not necessarily true. N:M means that more than one entity is allowed on each side of the relationship and that the number of entities on each side can be different.

Figure KE6-4 is an example of an entity-relationship diagram. Unfortunately, there are several different styles of entity-relationship diagrams. This one is called, not surprisingly, a **crow's-foot diagram** version. You may learn other versions if you take a database management course.

Figure KE6-5 shows the same entities with different assumptions. Here advisers may advise in more than one department, but a student may have only one adviser, representing a policy that students may not have multiple majors.

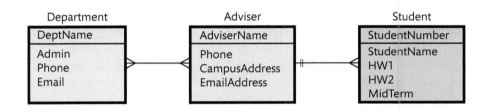

Figure KE6-5 Example Relationships—Version 2

Which, if either of these versions—Figure KE6-4 or Figure KE6-5—is correct? Only the users know. These alternatives illustrate the kinds of questions you will need to answer when a database designer asks you to check a data model for correctness.

The crow's-foot notation shows the maximum number of entities that can be involved in a relationship. Accordingly, they are called the relationship's **maximum cardinality**. Common examples of maximum cardinality are 1:N, N:M, and 1:1 (not shown).

Another important question is, "What is the minimum number of entities required in the relationship?" Must an adviser have a student to advise, and must a student have an adviser? Constraints on minimum requirements are called **minimum cardinalities**.

Figure KE6-6 presents a third version of this E-R diagram that shows both maximum and minimum cardinalities. The second vertical bar on the lines means that at least one entity of that type is required. The small oval means that the entity is optional; the relationship need not have an entity of that type. Using this notation, if there are two vertical bars, both the minimum and maximum cardinality are one. If there is a vertical bar with a crow's foot, then the minimum cardinality is one and the maximum is many.

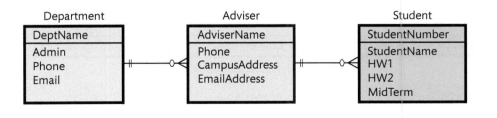

Figure KE6-6 Example of Relationships Showing Both Maximum and Minimum Cardinalities

Thus, in Figure KE6-6, a department is not required to have a relationship to any adviser, but an adviser is required to belong to a department. Similarly, an adviser is not required to have a relationship to a student, but a student is required to have a relationship to an adviser. Note, also, that the maximum cardinalities in Figure KE6-6 have been changed so that both are 1:N.

Is the model in Figure KE6-6 a good one? It depends on the rules of the college or university. Again, only the users know for sure.

KE6-4 HOW IS A DATA MODEL TRANSFORMED INTO A DATABASE DESIGN?

Database design is the process of converting a data model into tables, relationships, and data constraints. The database design team transforms entities into tables and expresses relationships by defining foreign keys. Database design is a complicated subject; as with data modelling, it occupies weeks in a database management course. In this section, however, we will introduce two important database design concepts: normalization and the representation of two kinds of relationships. The first concept is a foundation of database design, and the second will help you understand key considerations made during design.

Normalization

Normalization is the process of converting poorly structured tables into two or more well-structured tables. A table is such a simple construct that you may wonder how one could possibly be poorly structured. In truth, there are many ways that tables can be malformed—so many, in fact, that researchers have published hundreds of papers on this topic alone.

Consider the *Employee* table in Figure KE6-7. It lists employee names, hire dates, email addresses, and the name and number of the department in which the employee works. This table seems innocent enough. But consider what happens when the Accounting department changes its name to Accounting and Finance. Because department names are duplicated in this table, every row that has a value of "Accounting" must be changed to "Accounting and Finance."

Employee

Name	HireDate	Email	DeptNo	DeptName
Jones	Feb 1, 2010	Jones@ourcompany.com	100	Accounting
Smith	Dec 3, 2007	Smith@ourcompany.com	200	Marketing
Chau	March 7, 2007	Chau@ourcompany.com	100	Accounting
Greene	July 17, 2010	Greene@ourcompany.com	100	Accounting

a. Table Before Update

Employee

Name	HireDate	Email	DeptNo	DeptName
Jones	Feb 1, 2010	Jones@ourcompany.com	100	Accounting and Finance
Smith	Dec 3, 2007	Smith@ourcompany.com	200	Marketing
Chau	March 7, 2007	Chau@ourcompany.com	100	Accounting and Finance
Greene	July 17, 2010	Greene@ourcompany.com	100	Accounting

b. Table with Incomplete Update

Figure KE6-7 A Poorly Designed *Employee* Table

Data Integrity Problems   Suppose the Accounting name change is correctly made in two rows, but not in the third. The result is shown in Figure KE6-7b. This table has what is called a **data integrity problem:** Two rows indicate that the name of Department 100 is Accounting and Finance, and another row indicates that the name of Department 100 is Accounting.

This problem is easy to spot in this small table. But consider a table in a large database that has more than 300 000 rows. Once a table that large develops serious data integrity problems, months of labour will be required to remove them.

Data integrity problems are serious. A table that has data integrity problems will produce incorrect and inconsistent information. Users will lose confidence in the information, and the system will develop a poor reputation. Information systems with poor reputations become heavy burdens to the organizations that use them.

Normalizing for Data Integrity   The data integrity problem can occur only if data are duplicated. Because of this, one easy way to eliminate the problem is to eliminate the duplicated data. We can do this by transforming the table design in Figure KE6-7a into two tables, as shown in Figure KE6-8. Here the name of the department is stored just once; therefore, no data inconsistencies can occur.

Employee

Name	HireDate	Email	DeptNo
Jones	Feb 1, 2010	Jones@ourcompany.com	100
Smith	Dec 3, 2011	Smith@ourcompany.com	200
Chau	March 7, 2007	Chau@ourcompany.com	100
Greene	July 17, 2010	Greene@ourcompany.com	100

Department

DeptNo	DeptName
100	Accounting
200	Marketing
300	Information Systems

Figure KE6-8   Two Normalized Tables

Of course, to produce an employee report that includes the department name, the two tables in Figure KE6-8 will need to be joined back together. Because such joining of tables is common, DBMS products have been programmed to perform it efficiently, but it still requires work. From this example, you can see a trade-off in database design: Normalized tables eliminate data duplication, but they can be slower to process. Dealing with such trade-offs is an important consideration in database design.

The general goal of normalization is to construct tables such that every table has a *single* topic or theme. In good writing, every paragraph should have a single theme. This is true of databases as well; every table should have a single theme. The problem with the table design in Figure KE6-7 is that it has two independent themes: employees and departments. The way to correct the problem is to split the table into two tables, each with its own theme. In this case, we create an *Employee* table and a *Department* table, as shown in Figure KE6-8.

As mentioned, there are dozens of ways that tables can be poorly formed. Database practitioners classify tables into various **normal forms** according to the kinds of problems they have. Transforming a table into a normal form to remove duplicated data and other problems is called *normalizing* the table.[1] Thus, when you hear a database designer

[1] See David Kroenke and David Auer, *Database Concepts*, 7th ed. (Upper Saddle River, NJ: Pearson Education, 2015) for more information.

say, "Those tables are not normalized," she does not mean that the tables have irregular, not-normal data. Instead, she means that the tables have a format that could cause data integrity problems.

Summary of Normalization   As a future user of databases, you do not need to know the details of normalization. Instead, understand the general principle that every normalized (well-formed) table has one and only one theme. Further, tables that are not normalized are subject to data integrity problems.

Be aware, too, that normalization is just one criterion for evaluating database designs. Because normalized designs can be slower to process, database designers sometimes choose to accept non-normalized tables. The best design depends on the users' requirements.

Representing Relationships

Figure KE6-9 shows the steps involved in transforming a data model into a relational database design. First, the database designer creates a table for each entity. The identifier of the entity becomes the key of the table. Each attribute of the entity becomes a column of the table. Next, the resulting tables are normalized so that each table has a single theme. Once that has been done, the next step is to represent the relationship among those tables.

Figure KE6-9   Transforming a Data Model into a Database Design

- Represent each entity with a table
  - Entity identifier becomes table key
  - Entity attributes become table columns
- Normalize tables as necessary
- Represent relationships
  - Use foreign keys
  - Add additional tables for N:M relationships

For example, consider the E-R diagram in Figure KE6-10a. The *Adviser* entity has a 1:N relationship to the *Student* entity. To create the database design, we construct a table for *Adviser* and a second table for *Student*, as shown in Figure KE6-10b. The key of the *Adviser* table is *AdviserName*, and the key of the *Student* table is *StudentNumber*.

Further, the *EmailAddress* attribute of the *Adviser* entity becomes the *EmailAddress* column of the *Adviser* table, and the *StudentName* and *MidTerm* attributes of the *Student* entity become the *StudentName* and *MidTerm* columns of the *Student* table.

The next task is to represent the relationship. Because we are using the relational model, we know that we must add a foreign key to one of the two tables. The possibilities are: (1) place the foreign key *StudentNumber* in the *Adviser* table or (2) place the foreign key *AdviserName* in the *Student* table.

The correct choice is to place *AdviserName* in the *Student* table, as shown in Figure KE6-10c. To determine a student's adviser, we just look into the *AdviserName* column of that student's row. To determine the adviser's students, we search the *AdviserName* column in the *Student* table to determine which rows have that adviser's name. If a student changes advisers, we simply change the value in the *AdviserName* column. Changing *Jackson* to *Jones* in the first row, for example, will assign student 100 to Professor Jones.

For this data model, placing *StudentNumber* in *Adviser* would be incorrect. If we were to do that, we could assign only one student to an adviser. There is no place to assign a second adviser.

This strategy for placing foreign keys will not work for N:M relationships, however. Consider the data model in Figure KE6-11a (page 166); here there is an N:M relationship between advisers and students. An adviser may have many students, and a student may

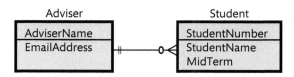

a. 1: N Relationship Between Adviser and Student Entities

Adviser Table—Key Is AdviserName

AdviserName	EmailAddress
Jones	Jones@myuniv.edu
Choi	Choi@myuniv.edu
Jackson	Jackson@myuniv.edu

Student Table—Key Is StudentNumber

StudentNumber	StudentName	MidTerm
100	Lisa	90
200	Jennie	85
300	Jason	82
400	Terry	95

b. Creating a Table for Each Entity

Adviser Table—Key Is AdviserName

AdviserName	EmailAddress
Jones	Jones@myuniv.edu
Choi	Choi@myuniv.edu
Jackson	Jackson@myuniv.edu

Student—Key Is StudentNumber

Foreign Key Column Represents Relationship

StudentNumber	StudentName	MidTerm	AdviserName
100	Lisa	90	Jackson
200	Jennie	85	Jackson
300	Jason	82	Choi
400	Terry	95	Jackson

c. Using the AdviserName Foreign Key to Represent the 1:N Relationship

have multiple advisers (for multiple majors). The strategy we used for the 1:N data model will not work here. To see why, examine Figure KE6-11b. If student 100 has more than one adviser, there is no place to record second or subsequent advisers.

It turns out that to represent an N:M relationship, we need to create a third table, as shown in Figure KE6-11c. The third table has two columns, *AdviserName* and *Student-Number*. Each row of the table means that the given adviser advises the student with the given number.

As you can imagine, there is a great deal more to database design than we have presented here. Still, this section should give you an idea of the tasks that need to be accomplished to create a database. You should also realize that the database design is a direct consequence of decisions made in the data model. If the data model is wrong, the database design will be wrong as well.

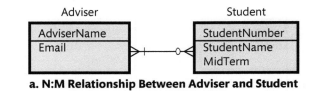

Adviser

AdviserName
Email

Student

StudentNumber
StudentName
MidTerm

a. N:M Relationship Between Adviser and Student

Adviser—Key Is AdviserName

AdviserName	**Email**
Jones	Jones@myuniv.edu
Choi	Choi@myuniv.edu
Jackson	Jackson@myuniv.edu

No room to place second or third AdviserName

Student—Key Is StudentNumber

StudentNumber	**StudentName**	**MidTerm**	**AdviserName**
100	Lisa	90	Jackson
200	Jennie	85	Jackson
300	Jason	82	Choi
400	Terry	95	Jackson

b. Incorrect Representation of N:M Relationship

Adviser—Key Is AdviserName

AdviserName	**Email**
Jones	Jones@myuniv.edu
Choi	Choi@myuniv.edu
Jackson	Jackson@myuniv.edu

Student—Key Is StudentNumber

StudentNumber	**StudentName**	**MidTerm**
100	Lisa	90
200	Jennie	85
300	Jason	82
400	Terry	95

Adviser_Student_Intersection

AdviserName	**StudentNumber**
Jackson	100
Jackson	200
Choi	300
Jackson	400
Choi	100
Jones	100

Student 100 has three advisers.

c. Adviser_Student_Intersection Table Represents the N:M Relationship

Figure KE6-11   Representing an N:M Relationship

KE6-5 WHAT IS THE USERS' ROLE?

As stated, a database is a model of how the users view their business world. This means that the users are the final judges of what data the database should contain and how the records in that database should be related to one another.

The easiest time to change the database structure is during the data modelling stage. Changing a relationship from 1:N to N:M in a data model is simply a matter of changing the 1:N notation to N:M. However, once the database has been constructed, and loaded with data and application forms, reports, queries, and application programs have been created, changing a 1:N relationship to N:M means weeks of work.

You can glean some idea of why this might be true by contrasting Figure KE6-10c with Figure KE6-11c. Suppose that instead of having just a few rows, each table has thousands of rows; in that case, transforming the database from one format to the other involves considerable work. Even worse, however, is that application components will need to be changed as well. For example, if students have at most one adviser, then a single text box can be used to enter *AdviserName*. If students can have multiple advisers, then a multiple-row table will need to be used to enter *AdviserName*, and a program will need to be written to store the values of *AdviserName* into the *Adviser_Student_Intersection* table. There are dozens of other consequences as well, consequences that will translate into wasted labour and wasted expense.

The conclusion from this discussion is that user review of a data model is crucial. When a database is developed for your use, you must carefully review the data model. If you do not understand any aspect of it, you should ask for clarification until you do. The data model must accurately reflect your view of the business. If it does not, the database will be designed incorrectly, and the applications will be difficult to use, if not worthless. Do not proceed unless the data model is accurate.

As a corollary, when asked to review a data model, take that review seriously. Devote the time necessary to perform a thorough review. Any mistakes you miss will come back to haunt you, and by then the cost of correction may be very high with regard to both time and expense. This brief introduction to data modelling shows why databases can be more difficult to develop than spreadsheets.

KE6-6 WHO WILL VOLUNTEER? (CONTINUED)

Knowing what you know now, if you were the manager of fund-raising at the TV station, you would hire a consultant and expect the consultant to interview all of the key users. From those interviews, the consultant would then construct a data model.

You now know that the structure of the database must reflect the way the users think about their activities. If the consultant did not take the time to interview you and your staff or did not construct a data model and ask you to review it, you would know that you are not receiving good service and would take corrective action.

Suppose you found a consultant who interviewed your staff for several hours and then constructed the data model shown in Figure KE6-12. This data model has an entity for

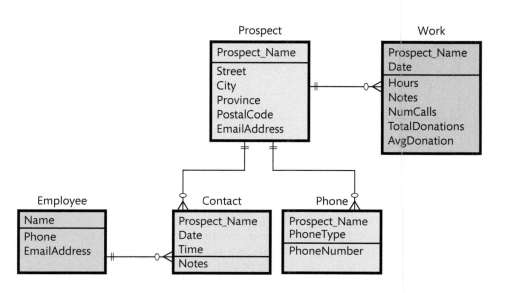

Figure KE6-12 Data Model for Volunteer Database

Prospect, an entity for *Employee*, and three additional entities for *Contact*, *Phone*, and *Work*. The *Contact* entity records contacts that you or other employees have made with the prospective volunteer. This record is necessary so that you know what has been said to whom. The *Phone* entity is used to record multiple phone numbers for each prospective volunteer, and the *Work* entity records work that the prospect has performed for the station.

After you reviewed and approved this data model, the consultant constructed the database design shown in Figure KE6-13. In this design, table keys are underlined, foreign keys are shown in italics, and columns that are both table and foreign keys are underlined and italicized. Observe that the *Name* column is the table key of *Prospect*, and it is both part of the table key and a foreign key in *Phone*, *Contact*, and *Work*.

Figure KE6-13 First Table Design for Volunteer Database

Prospect (<u>Name</u>, Street, City, Province, Postal, EmailAddress)
Phone (<u>*Name*</u>, <u>PhoneType</u>, PhoneNumber)
Contact (<u>*Name*</u>, <u>Date</u>, <u>Time</u>, Notes, *EmployeeName*)
Work (<u>*Name*</u>, <u>Date</u>, Notes, NumCalls, TotalDonations)
Employee (<u>EmployeeName</u>, Phone, EmailAddress)

Note:
Underline means table key.
Italics means foreign key.
Underline and italics mean both table and foreign key.

The consultant did not like having the *Name* column used as a key or as part of a key in so many tables. Based on her interviews, she suspected that prospect names are fluid—and that sometimes the same prospect name is recorded in different ways (e.g., sometimes with a middle initial and sometimes without). If that were to happen, phone, contact, and work data could be misallocated to prospect names. Accordingly, the consultant added a new column, *ProspectID*, to the prospect table and created the design shown in Figure KE6-14. Values of this ID will have no meaning to the users, but the ID will be used to ensure that each prospect obtains a unique record in the Volunteer database. Because this ID has no meaning to the users, the consultant will hide it on forms and reports that users see.

Figure KE6-14 Second Table Design for Volunteer Database

Prospect (<u>*ProspectID*</u>, Name, Street, City, Province, Postal, EmailAddress)
Phone (<u>*ProspectID*</u>, <u>PhoneType</u>, PhoneNumber)
Contact (<u>*ProspectID*</u>, <u>Date</u>, <u>Time</u>, Notes, *EmployeeName*)
Work (<u>*ProspectID*</u>, <u>Date</u>, Notes, NumCalls, TotalDonations)
Employee (<u>EmployeeName</u>, Phone, EmailAddress)

Note:
Underline means table key.
Italics means foreign key.
Underline and italics mean both table and foreign key.

There is one difference between the data model and the table designs. In the data model, the *Work* entity has an attribute, *AvgDonation*, but there is no corresponding *AvgDonation* column in the *Work* table. The consultant decided that there was no need to store this value in the database because it could readily be computed on forms and reports using the values in the *NumCalls* and *TotalDonations* columns.

Once the tables had been designed, the consultant created a Microsoft Access 2016 database. She defined the tables in Access, created relationships among the tables, and constructed forms and reports. Figure KE6-15 shows the primary data entry form used for

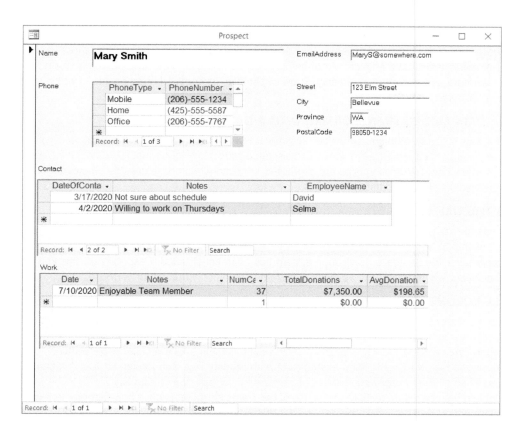

Figure KE6-15 Volunteer Prospect Data Entry Form

Source: Microsoft Access 2016

the Volunteer database. The top portion of the form has contact data, including multiple phone numbers. It is important to know the type of the phone number so that you and your staff know if you are calling someone at work or another setting. The middle and bottom sections of this form have contact and prior work data. Observe that *AvgDonation* has been computed from the *NumCalls* and *TotalDonations* columns.

You were quite pleased with this database application, and you are certain that it helped you to improve the volunteer staffing at the station. Of course, over time, you thought of several new requirements, and you already have changes in mind for next year.

ACTIVE REVIEW

Use this Active Review to verify that you understand the ideas and concepts that answer this Knowledge Extension's study questions.

KE6-1 WHO WILL VOLUNTEER?

Summarize the problem that the fund-raising manager must solve. Explain how a database can help solve this problem. Describe the missing information. In your own words, what data must be available to construct the missing information?

KE6-2 HOW ARE DATABASE APPLICATION SYSTEMS DEVELOPED?

Name and briefly describe the components of a database application system. Explain the difference between a database application system and a database application program. Using Figure KE6-1 as a guide, describe the major steps in the process of developing a database application system. Explain what role is crucial for users and why that role is so important.

KE6-3 WHAT ARE THE COMPONENTS OF THE ENTITY-RELATIONSHIP DATA MODEL?

Define the terms *entity*, *attributes*, and *relationship*. Give an example of two entities (other than those in this book) that have a 1:N relationship. Give an example of two entities that have an N:M relationship. Explain the difference between maximum and minimum cardinality. Show two entities having a 1:N relationship in which one is required and one is optional.

KE6-4 HOW IS A DATA MODEL TRANSFORMED INTO A DATABASE DESIGN?

Give an example of a data integrity problem. Describe, in general terms, the process of normalization. Explain how normalizing data prevents data integrity problems. Explain the disadvantage of normalized data. Using your examples from KE6-3, show how 1:N relationships are expressed in relational database designs. Show how N:M relationships are expressed in relational database designs.

KE6-5 WHAT IS THE USERS' ROLE?

Describe the major role for users in the development of a database application system. Explain what is required to change a 1:N relationship to an N:M relationship during the data modelling stage. Explain what is required to make that same change after the database application system has been constructed. Describe how this knowledge impacts your behaviour when a database application system is being constructed for your use.

KE6-6 WHO WILL VOLUNTEER? (CONTINUED)

Examine Figure KE6-12. Describe the maximum and minimum cardinality for each relationship. Justify these cardinalities. Change the relationship between *Prospect* and *Phone* to N:M, and explain what this means. Change the relationship between *Prospect* and *Work* to 1:1, and explain what this means. Explain how each relationship is represented in the design in Figure KE6-14. Show examples of both primary keys and foreign keys in this figure. In *Contact*, determine whether *EmployeeName* is part of a primary key or part of a foreign key.

Explain what problem the consultant foresaw in the use of the *Name* attribute. Explain how that problem was avoided. The consultant added an attribute to the data model that was not part of the users' world. Explain why that attribute will not add unnecessary complication to the users' work experiences.

MyLab MIS

MyLab MIS is an online learning and testing environment that features the perfect study tools to help you master the concepts covered in this chapter. Log in to MyLab to test your knowledge of key chapter concepts and explore additional practice tools, including videos, flashcards, and more!

KEY TERMS AND CONCEPTS

Attributes 159
Crow's foot 160
Crow's-foot diagram 161
Data integrity
    problem 163
Data model 158

Entity 159
Entity-relationship (E-R)
    data model 159
Entity-relationship (E-R)
    diagrams 160
Identifier 159

Many-to-many (N:M)
    relationship 161
Maximum cardinality 161
Minimum cardinalities 161
Normal forms 163
Normalization 162

One-to-many (1:N)
    relationship 161
Relationships 160
Unified Modelling Language
    (UML) 159

USING YOUR KNOWLEDGE

KE6-1. Explain how you could use a spreadsheet to solve the volunteer problem at the television station. What data would you place in each column and row of your spreadsheet? Name each column and row of your spreadsheet. What advantages does a database have over a spreadsheet for this problem? Compare and contrast your spreadsheet solution to the database solution shown in the text.

KE6-2. Suppose you are asked to build a database application for a sports league. Assume that your application is to keep track of teams and equipment that is checked out to teams. Explain the steps that need to be taken to develop this application. Specify entities and their relationships. Build an E-R diagram. Ensure your diagram shows both minimum and maximum cardinalities. Transform your E-R diagram into a relational design.

KE6-3. Suppose you are asked to build a database application for a bicycle rental shop. Assume your database is to track customers, bicycles, and rentals. Explain the steps that need to be taken to develop this application. Specify entities and their relationships. Build an E-R diagram. Ensure your diagram shows both minimum and maximum cardinalities. Transform your E-R diagram into a relational design.

MyLab MIS

Go to the Assignments section of your MyLab to complete these writing exercises.

KE6-1 Assume you work at the television station and are asked to evaluate the data model shown in KE6-6. Suppose that you want to differentiate between prospects who have worked in the past and those who have never worked but who are prospects for future work. Say that one of the data modellers tells you, "No problem. We'll know that because any *Prospect* entity that has no relationship to a *Work* entity is a prospect who has never worked." Restate the data modeller's response in your own words. Does this seem like a satisfactory solution? What if you want to keep *Prospect* data that pertains only to prospects who have worked? (No such attributes are shown in *Prospect* in the data model shown in KE6-6, but say there is an attribute such as *YearFirstVolunteered* or some other attribute that pertains to prospects who have worked in the past.) Show an alternative E-R diagram that would differentiate between prospects who have worked in the past and those who have not. Compare and contrast your alternative to the one shown in the data model in KE6-6.

KE6-2 Suppose you are the accounts manager at a wholesale auto parts distributor. You use spreadsheets to keep track of just about everything. So do your employees. You have hundreds of different spreadsheets to update, back up, and share. Some of them are getting extremely large and unwieldy. You are worried about losing track of them or, worse, having a malicious employee permanently destroy them. A new hire fresh out of college/university says building a database would solve most of your problems. How would you determine if a database would really solve your problems? If you chose to develop a centralized database, how would you choose the employees to create the database? What criteria would you use to select those employees? How would you justify allocating people and money to developing this database?

KNOWLEDGE EXTENSION 7

Chapter 5 provides the background for this extension.

Using Microsoft Access 2016

STUDY QUESTIONS

KE7-1   HOW DO YOU CREATE TABLES?

KE7-2   HOW DO YOU CREATE RELATIONSHIPS?

KE7-3   HOW DO YOU CREATE A DATA ENTRY FORM?

KE7-4   HOW DO YOU CREATE QUERIES USING THE QUERY DESIGN TOOL?

KE7-5   HOW DO YOU CREATE A REPORT?

In this Knowledge Extension, you will learn fundamental techniques for creating a database and forms, queries, and reports with Microsoft Access.

KE7-1 HOW DO YOU CREATE TABLES?

Before using Access or any other DBMS, you should have created a data model from the users' requirements, and you must transform that data model into a database design. For the purpose of this Knowledge Extension, we will use a portion of the database design created in Knowledge Extension 6. Specifically, we will create a database with the following two tables:

PROSPECT (ProspectID, Name, Street, City, Province, Postal Code Email Address)

and

WORK (*ProspectID*, *Date*, *Hour*, NumCalls, TotalDonations)

As in Knowledge Extension 6, an underlined attribute is the primary key, and an italicized attribute is a foreign key. Thus, ProspectID is the primary key of PROSPECT, and the combination (ProspectID, Date, Hour) is the primary key of WORK. *ProspectID* is also a foreign key in WORK; hence it is shown both underlined and in italics. The data model and database design in Knowledge Extension 6 specified that the key of WORK is the combination (*ProspectID*, Date). Upon review, the users stated that prospects will sometimes work more than one time during the day. For scheduling and other purposes, the users want to record both the date and the hour that someone worked. Accordingly, the database designer added the Hour attribute and made it part of the key of WORK.

The assumption in this design is that each row of WORK represents an hour's work. If a prospect works for consecutive hours, say, from 7 to 9 P.M., then he or she would have two rows, one with an Hour value of 1900 and a second with an Hour value of 2000. Figure KE7-1 further documents the attributes of the design. Sample data for this table are shown in Figure KE7-2 on page 174.

Note the ambiguity in the name *PROSPECT*. Before someone has become a volunteer, he is a prospect, and the term is fine. However, once that person has actually done work, he is no longer merely a prospect. This ambiguity occurs because the database is used both for finding

Table	Attribute (Column)	Remarks	Data Type	Example Value
PROSPECT	ProspectID	An identifying number provided by Access when a row is created. The value has no meaning to the user.	AutoNumber	55
PROSPECT	Name	A prospect's name.	Text (50)	Emily Jones
PROSPECT	Street	Prospect's contact street address.	Text (50)	123 West Elm
PROSPECT	City	Prospect's contact city.	Text (40)	Miami
PROSPECT	State	Prospect's contact state.	Text (2)	FL
PROSPECT	Zip	Prospect's contact ZIP code.	Text (10)	30210-4567 or 30210
PROSPECT	EmailAddress	Prospect's contact email address.	Text (65)	ExamplePerson@somewhere.com
WORK	ProspectID	Foreign key to PROSPECT. Value provided when relationship is created.	Number (Long Integer)	55
WORK	Work Date	The date of work.	Date	9/15/2014
WORK	Hour	The hour at which work is started.	Number (Integer)	0800 or 1900 (7 P.M.)
WORK	NumCalls	The number of calls taken.	Number (Integer)	25
WORK	TotalDonations	The total of donations generated.	Currency	$10 575
WORK	AvgDonations	The average donation.	Currency	To be computed in queries and reports

Figure KE7-1 Attributes of the Database

volunteers and for recording their experiences once they have joined. We could rename PROSPECT as VOLUNTEER, but then we would still have a problem. The person is not a volunteer until he has actually agreed to become one. So, for now, just assume that a PROSPECT who has one or more WORK records is no longer a prospect but has become a volunteer.

Starting Access

Figure KE7-3 shows the opening screen for Microsoft Access 2016. (If you use another version of Access, your screen will appear differently, but the essentials will be the same.) To create a new database, select Blank desktop database in the templates displayed in the centre of the screen, as shown in Figure KE7-4. Then type the name of your new database under *File Name* (here we use *Volunteer*). Access will suggest a directory; change it if you want to use another one, and then click *Create*. You will see the screen shown in Figure KE7-5 on page 175.

Creating Tables

Access opens the new database by creating a default table named Table. We want to modify the design of this table, so in the upper left-hand corner, where you see a pencil and a right angle square, click *View* and select *Design View*. Access will ask you to name your table. Enter *PROSPECT* and click *OK*. Your screen will appear as in Figure KE7-6 on page 175.

The screen shown in Figure KE7-6 has three parts. The left-hand pane lists all of the tables in your database. At this point, you should see only the PROSPECT table in this list.

Example of PROSPECT Data

Prospect ID	Name	Street	City	State	Zip	EmailAddress
1	Carson Wu	123 Elm	Los Angeles	CA	98007	Carson@somewhere.com
2	Emily Jackson	2234 17th	Pasadena	CA	97005	JacksonE@elsewhere.com
3	Peter Lopez	331 Moses Drive	Fullerton	CA	97330	PeterL@ourcompany.com
4	Lynda Dennison	54 Strand	Manhattan Beach	CA	97881	Lynda@somewhere.com
5	Carter Fillmore III	Restricted	Brentwood	CA	98220	Carter@BigBucks.com
6	CJ Greene	77 Sunset Strip	Hollywood	CA	97330	CJ@HollywoodProducers.com
7	Jolisa Jackson	2234 17th	Pasadena	CA	97005	JacksonJ@elsewhere.com

Example of WORK Data

ProspectID	Work Date	Hour	NumCalls	TotalDonations
3	9/15/2014	1600	17	8755
3	9/15/2014	1700	28	11578
5	9/15/2014	1700	25	15588
5	9/20/2014	1800	37	29887
5	9/10/2015	1700	30	21440
5	9/10/2015	1800	39	37050
6	9/15/2014	1700	33	21445
6	9/16/2014	1700	27	17558
6	9/10/2015	1700	31	22550
6	9/10/2015	1800	37	36700

Figure KE7-2
Sample Data

Figure KE7-3 Opening Screen for Microsoft Access 2016

Source: Microsoft Access 2016

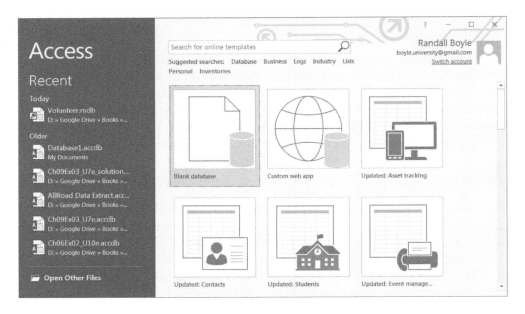

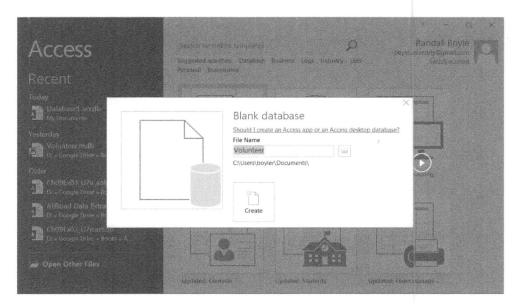

Figure KE7-4 Naming a Desktop Database

Source: Microsoft Access 2016

Figure KE7-5 Access Opens with an Initial Table Definition

Source: Microsoft Access 2016

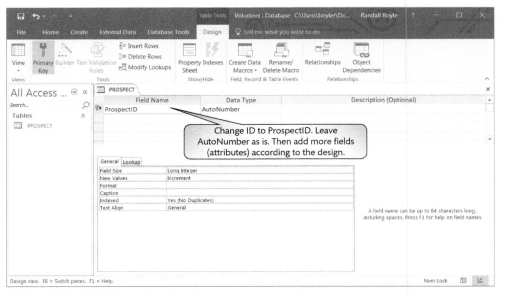

Figure KE7-6 Creating Tables in Access, Step 1

Source: Microsoft Access 2016

Change ID to ProspectID. Leave AutoNumber as is. Then add more fields (attributes) according to the design.

Figure KE7-7 Creating
Tables in Access, Step 2

Source: Microsoft Access 2016

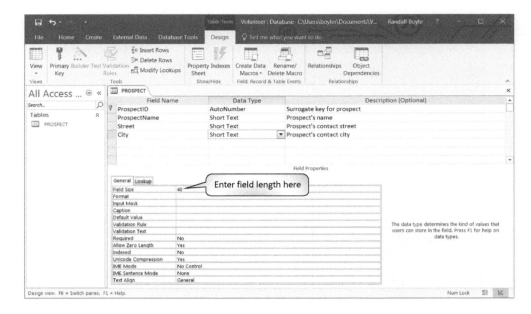

We will use the upper part of the right-hand pane to enter the name of each attribute (which Access calls *Fields*) and its *Data Type*. We can optionally enter a *Description* of that field. The Description is used for documentation; as you will see, Access displays any text you enter as help text on forms. In the bottom part of the screen, we set the properties of each field (or attribute, using our term). To start designing the table, replace the *Field Name* ID with *ProspectID*. Access has already set its type to *AutoNumber*, so you can leave that alone.

To create the rest of the table, enter the *Field Names* and *Data Types* according to our design.[1] Figure KE7-7 shows how to set the length of a Short Text Data Type. In this figure, the user has set City to *Text* and then has moved down into the bottom part of this form and entered 40 under *Field Size*. You will do the same thing to set the length of all of the Short Text Field Names. The complete table is shown in Figure KE7-8.

Figure KE7-8 Complete
Sample PROSPECT Table

Source: Microsoft Access 2016

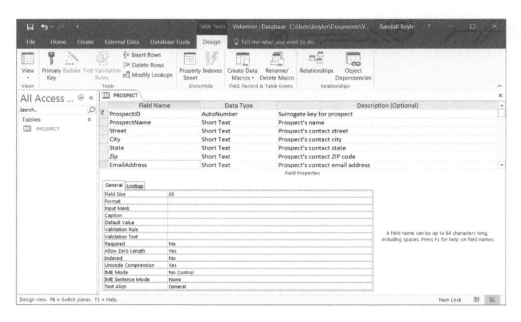

[1] When you enter the Name field, Access will give you an error message. Ignore the message and click OK. The fact that you are using a reserved word for this example will not be a problem. If you want to be safe, you could enter *PName* or *ProspectName* (rather than *Name*) and avoid this issue. Many people believe that Access is poorly designed in this respect. You ought to be able to enter any value for Field Name the way you want. Access should stay out of your way; you should not have to stay out of its way!

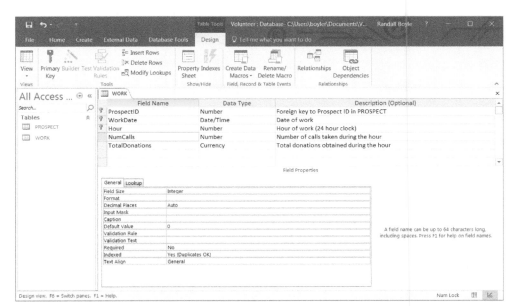

ProspectID is the primary key of this table, and the little key icon next to the Prospec-tID *Field Name* means Access has already made it so. If we wanted to make another field the primary key, we would highlight that field and then click the *Primary Key* icon in the left-hand portion of the *DESIGN* ribbon.

Follow similar steps to create the WORK table. The only difference is that you will need to create a key of the three columns (ProspectID, WorkDate, Hour). To create that key, highlight all three rows by dragging over the three squares to the left of the names of ProspectID, WorkDate, and Hour. Then click the *Key* icon in the *DESIGN* ribbon. Also, change the *Required Field Property* for each of these columns to *Yes*. The finished WORK table is shown in Figure KE7-9. This figure also shows that the user selected *Number* for the *Data Type* of *NumCalls* and then set its *Field Size* (lower pane) to *Integer*. This same technique was used to set the *Data Type* of ProspectID (in WORK) to *Number* (*Field Size* of *Long Integer*) and that of *Hour* to *Number* (*Field Size* of *Integer*).

At this point, close both tables and save your work. You have created your first database!

KE7-2 HOW DO YOU CREATE RELATIONSHIPS?

After you have created the tables, the next step is to define relationships. To do so, click the *DATABASE TOOLS* tab in the ribbon and then click the *Relationships* icon near the left-hand side of that ribbon. The *Relationships* window will open and the *Show Table* dialog box will be displayed, as shown in Figure KE7-10. Double-click both table names and both tables will be added to the *Relationships* window. Close the *Show Table* dialog box.

To create the relationship between these two tables, click on the attribute *ProspectID* in PROSPECT and drag that attribute on top of the *ProspectID* in WORK. (It is important to drag *ProspectID* from PROSPECT to WORK and not the reverse.) When you do this, the screen shown in Figure KE7-11 will appear.

In the dialog box, click *Enforce Referential Integrity*, click *Cascade Update Related Fields*, and then click *Cascade Delete Related Records*. The specifics of these actions are beyond the scope of our discussion. Just understand that clicking these options will cause Access to make sure that ProspectID values in WORK also exist in PROSPECT. The completed relationship is shown in Figure KE7-12. The notation *1 . . . ∞* at the end of the relationship

Figure KE7-10 The Show
Table Dialog Box in Access

Source: Microsoft Access 2016

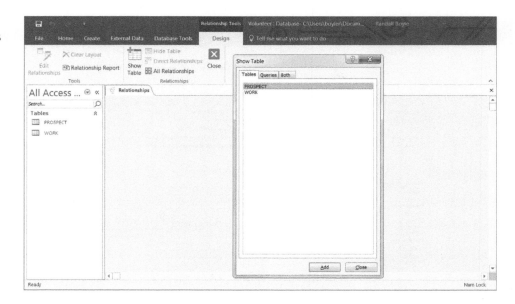

Figure KE7-11 Creating a
Relationship Between Two
Tables

Source: Microsoft Access 2016

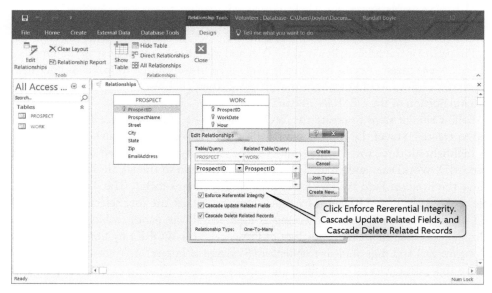

Figure KE7-12 Completed
Relationship Between
PROSPECT and WORK
Tables

Source: Microsoft Access 2016

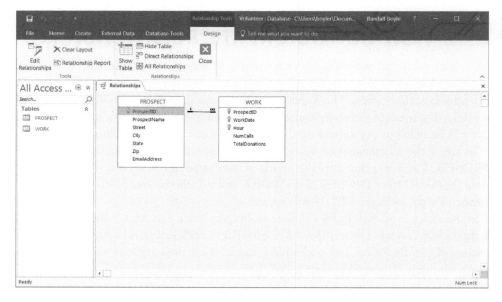

line means that one row of PROSPECT can be related to an unlimited number (*N*) of rows in WORK. Close the *Relationships* window and save the changes when requested to do so. You now have a database with two tables and a relationship.

The next step is to enter data. To enter data, double-click the table name in the *left hand* pane. The table will appear, and you can enter values into each cell. You cannot and need not enter values for the *ProspectID* field. Access will create those values for you.

Enter the data in Figure KE7-2 for both PROSPECT and WORK, and you will see a display like that in Figures KE7-13a and KE7-13b. Examine the lower left-hand corner of Figure KE7-13b. The text *Foreign key to ProspectID in PROSPECT* is the Description that you provided when you defined the ProspectID column when the WORK table was created. (You can see this in the ProspectID column in Figure KE7-9.) Access displays this text because the focus is on the ProspectID column in the active table window (WORK). Move your cursor from field to field and watch this text change.

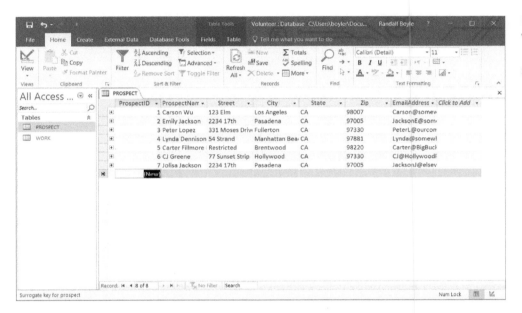

Figure KE7-13a Tables with Data Entered for PROSPECT

Source: Microsoft Access 2016

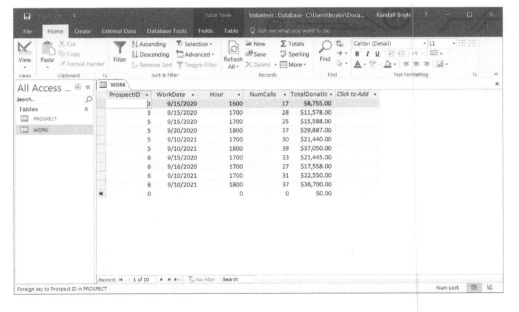

Figure KE7-13b Tables with Data Entered for WORK

Source: Microsoft Access 2016

KE7-3 HOW DO YOU CREATE A DATA ENTRY FORM?

Access provides several alternatives for creating a data entry form. The first is to use the default table display, as you did when you entered the data shown in Figure KE7-13a. In the PROSPECT table, notice the plus sign on the left. If you click those plus signs, you will see the PROSPECT rows with their related WORK rows, as shown in Figure KE7-14. This data entry display, although convenient, is limited in its capability. It also does not provide a very pleasing user interface. For more generality and better design, you can use the Access form generator.

Figure KE7-14 Default Table Display

Source: Microsoft Access 2016

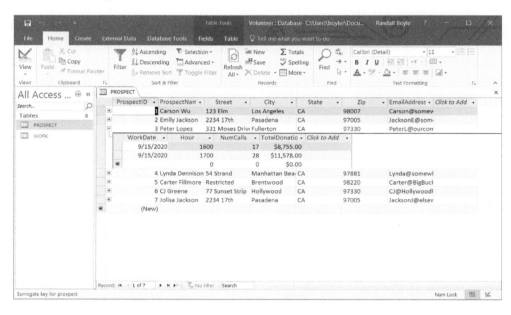

Access can generate a data entry form that is more pleasing to view and easier to use than that in Figure KE7-14. The process is shown in Figure KE7-15. First, click the *CREATE* tab to open the *CREATE* ribbon. Next, click the PROSPECT table (this causes Access to create a form for PROSPECT). Finally, click *Form*. Access uses metadata about the tables and their relationship to create the data entry form in Figure KE7-16.

Figure KE7-15 Starting the Form Generator

Source: Microsoft Access 2016

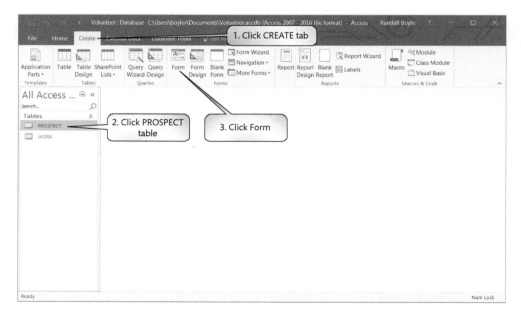

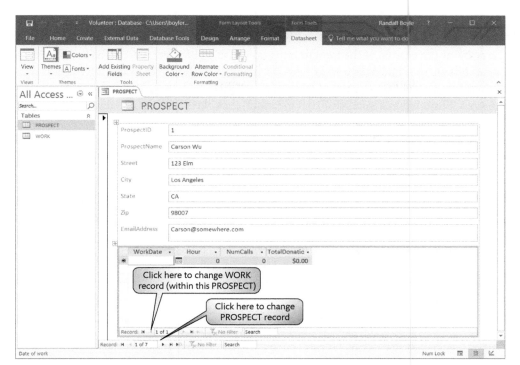

Figure KE7-16 Resulting Data Entry Form

Source: Microsoft Access 2016

You can use this form to modify data; just type over any data that you wish to change. You can also add data. To add work data, just click in the last row of the work grid; in this case that would be the first row of this grid. To delete a record, click the *HOME* tab, and then in the *Records* section click the down arrow next to *Delete* and select *Delete Record*. This action will delete the prospect data and all related work data (not shown in Figure KE7-16).

This form is fine, but we can make it better. For one, ProspectID is a surrogate key and has no meaning to the user. Access uses that key to keep track of each PROSPECT row. Because it has no meaning to the user (in fact, the user cannot change or otherwise modify its value), we should remove it from the form. Also, we might like to reduce the size of the fields as well as reduce the size of the work area and centre it on the form. Figure KE7-17 shows the form after these changes. It is smaller and cleaner, and it will be easier to use.

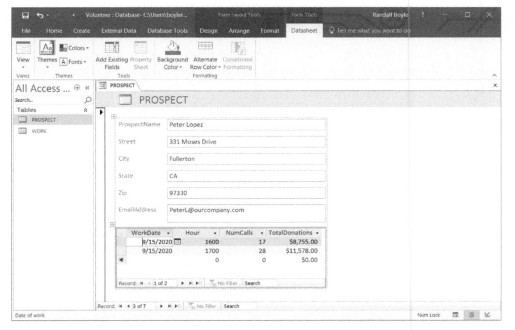

Figure KE7-17 Reformatted Data Entry Form

Source: Microsoft Access 2016

The data about a prospect is shown in the top portion of this form, and data about that person's work sessions is shown in the bottom portion. The user of this form has clicked the arrow at the bottom of the form to bring up the third Prospect record, the one for Peter Lopez. Notice that he has two work sessions. If you click the arrow in the next-to-last row of this form, you will change the focus of the work record. To make the changes shown, see the steps illustrated in Figure KE7-18. First, right-click the PROSPECT tab and then select *Design View*. The form will open in Design mode; click the right edge of the rightmost rectangle and, holding your mouse down, drag to the left. Access will reduce the width of each of these fields as well as the table.

Figure KE7-18 Process for Reformatting Data Entry Form

Source: Microsoft Access 2016

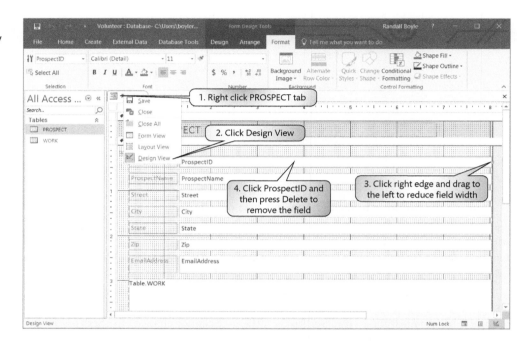

Finally, click *ProspectID*, as shown in step 4. Press the *Delete* key, and the ProspectID field will be removed from the form. Click *View/Form View*, and your form should look like that in Figure KE7-17. You can go back to *Design View* to make more adjustments, if necessary.

To save your form, either close it and Access will give you the chance to save it or click *FILE* and select *Save*. Save with an informative file name, such as PROSPECT Data Entry Form.

There are many options for customizing Access forms. You can learn about them if you take a database processing course after you complete this MIS course.

KE7-4 HOW DO YOU CREATE QUERIES USING THE QUERY DESIGN TOOL?

Like all relational DBMS products, Access can process the SQL query language. Learning that language, however, is beyond the scope of this textbook. However, Access does provide a graphical interface that we can use to create and process queries, and that graphical interface will generate SQL statements for us, behind the scenes.

To begin, first clean up your screen by closing the PROSPECT Data Entry Form. Click the *CREATE* tab in the ribbon, and in the *Queries* section click the *Query Design* button. You should see the display shown in Figure KE7-19. Double-click the names of both the

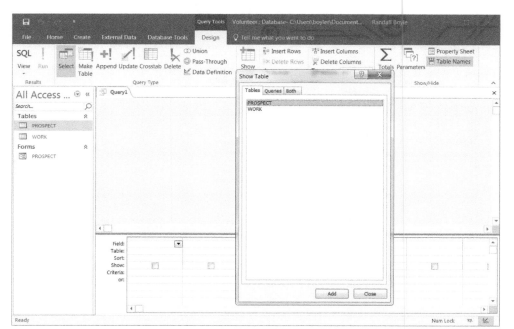

PROSPECT and WORK tables, and close the *Show Table* window. Access will have placed both tables into the query design form, as shown in Figure KE7-20. Notice that Access remembers the relationship between the two tables (shown by the line connecting Prospect-tID in PROSPECT to the same attribute in WORK).

To create a query, drag columns out of the PROSPECT and WORK tables into the grid in the lower part of the query definition form. In Figure KE7-21, the *Name, EmailAddress, NumCalls,* and *TotalDonations* columns have been placed into that grid. Note, too, that the

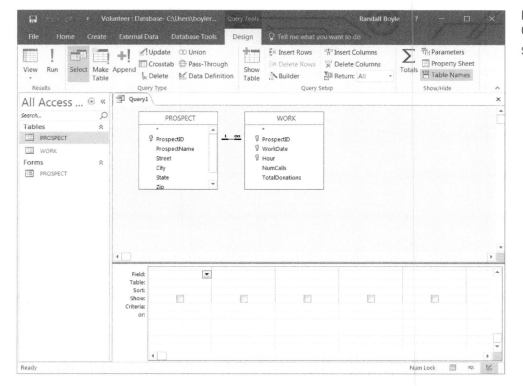

Figure KE7-21 Creating a Query, Step 3

Source: Microsoft Access 2016

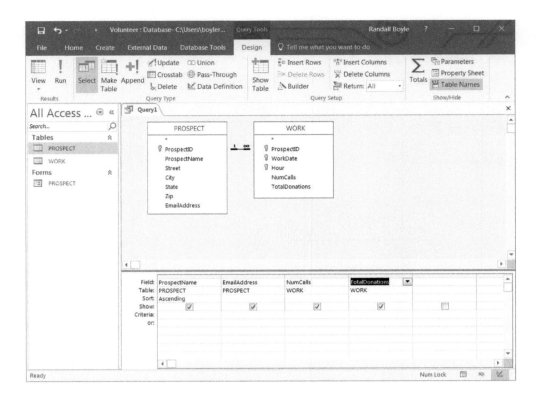

Ascending keyword has been selected for the *Name* column. That selection tells Access to present the data in alphabetical order by name.

If you now click the red exclamation point labelled *Run* in the *Results* section of the ribbon, the result shown in Figure KE7-22 will appear. Notice that only PROSPECT rows that have at least one WORK row are shown. By default, for queries of two or more tables

Figure KE7-22 Results of *TotalDonations Query*

Source: Microsoft Access 2016

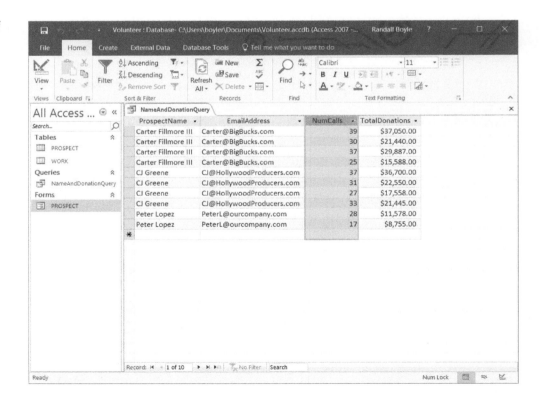

Access (and SQL) shows only those rows that have value matches in both tables. Save the query under the name *NameAndDonationQuery*.

Queries have many useful purposes. For example, suppose we want to see the average dollar value of donations generated per hour of work. This query, which is just slightly beyond the scope of this Knowledge Extension, can readily be created using either the Access graphical tool or SQL. The results of such a query are shown in Figure KE7-23. This query processes the *NameAndDonationQuery* query just created. Again, if you take a database course, you will learn how to create queries like this and others of even greater complexity (and utility).

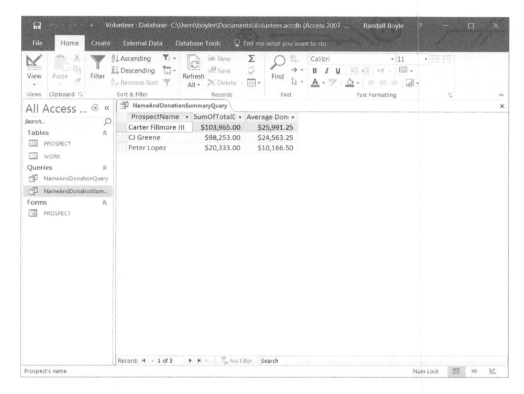

Figure KE7-23 Result of More Advanced Query

Source: Microsoft Access 2016

KE7-5 HOW DO YOU CREATE A REPORT?

You can create a report using a process similar to that for forms, but the report won't include the WORK data. To create a report with data from two or more tables, we must use the Report Wizard. Click the *CREATE* tab, and then in the Reports section click *Report Wizard*.

Now, click *Table: PROSPECT* in the *Table/Queries* combo box, highlight *Name* in the *Available Fields* list, and click the single chevron (>) to add Name to the report. You will see the display shown in Figure KE7-24.

Using a similar process, add *EmailAddress*. Then select *Table: WORK* in the *Table/Queries* combo box and add *WorkDate*, *Hour*, *NumCalls*, and *TotalDonations*. Click *Finish*, and you will see the report shown in Figure KE7-25. (By the way, we are skipping numerous options that Access provides in creating reports.)

We will consider just one of those options now. Suppose we want to show the total donations that a prospect has obtained, for all hours of his or her work. To do that, right-click the *PROSPECT* tab, and then click *Design View*. Your report will appear as shown in Figure KE7-26. (If it does not appear like this, click *View, Design View* in the ribbon.)

Figure KE7-24 Selecting Data to Show in a Report

Source: Microsoft Access 2016

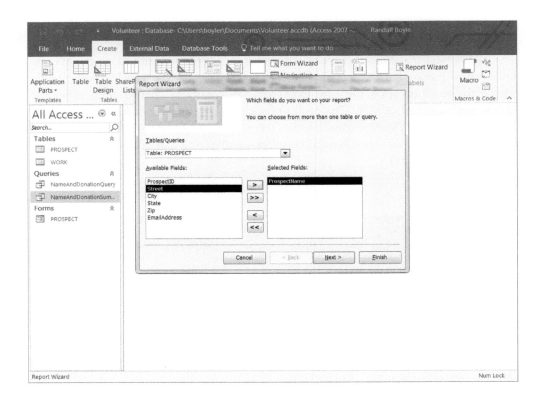

In the ribbon, click *Group & Sort* in the *Grouping & Totals* section. In the bottom of the form, under Group, Sort, and Total click *More*, and then click the down arrow next to the phrase *with no totals*. Next, select *TotalDonations* from the *Total On* box, and then check *Show Grand Total* and *Show subtotal in group footer*, as illustrated in Figure KE7-27.

Figure KE7-25 Report on Donations, by Prospect

Source: Microsoft Access 2016

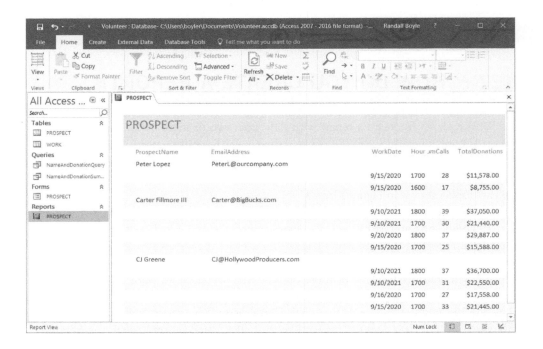

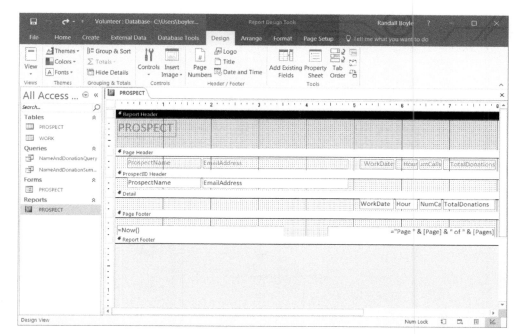

Figure KE7-26 Report Design View

Source: Microsoft Access 2016

Click the *Report* icon in the *View* section of the ribbon, and you will see the report shown in Figure KE7-28. The only remaining problem is that the label NumCalls is cut off. We need to expand the box that contains this value. To do so, select *Layout View* from *View* in the ribbon, click *Date*, and then slide it slightly to the left. Do the same with Hour. Then expand NumCalls until you can see all of the label, as shown in Figure KE7-29. Click *Report View* in *View*, and your report should appear as shown in Figure KE7-30.

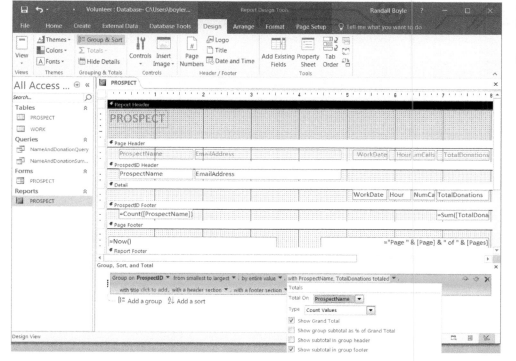

Figure KE7-27 Creating a Sum of *TotalDonations* for Each Prospect

Source: Microsoft Access 2016

Figure KE7-28 Report with Sum of *TotalDonations*

Source: Microsoft Access 2016

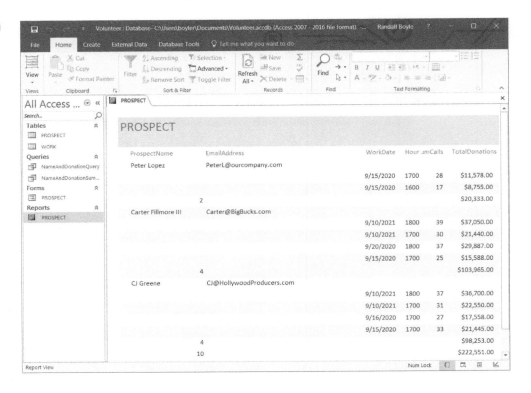

Figure KE7-29 Increasing the Size of the *NumCalls* Field

Source: Microsoft Access 2016

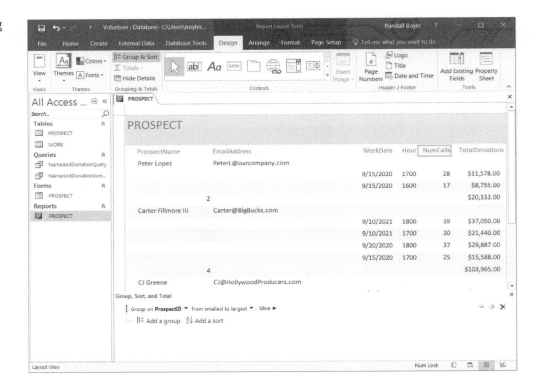

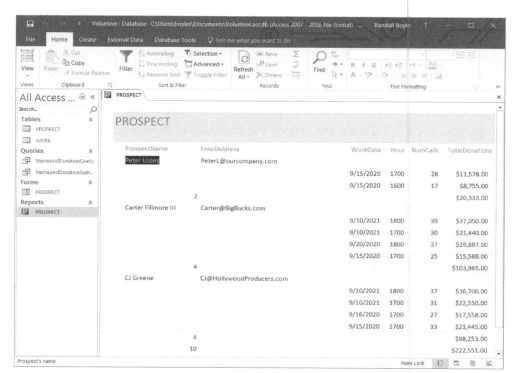

ACTIVE REVIEW

Use this Active Review to verify that you understand the ideas and concepts in this Knowledge Extension's study questions.

For this Active Review, assume that you are creating a database application having the following two tables:

CUSTOMER (<u>CustomerID</u>, Name, Email)

CONTACT (*CustomerID*, Date, Subject)

KE7-1 HOW DO YOU CREATE TABLES?

Open Access and create a new database with a name of your choosing. Create the CUSTOMER and CONTACT tables. Assume the following data types:

Attribute (Field)	Data Type
CustomerID (in CUSTOMER)	AutoNumber
Name	Text (50)
Email	Text (75)
CustomerID (in CONTACT)	Number (long integer)
Date	Date
Subject	Text (200)

Add Description entries to the Field definitions that you think are appropriate.

KE7-2 HOW DO YOU CREATE RELATIONSHIPS?

Open the *Relationships* window and create a relationship from CUSTOMER to CONTACT using the CustomerID attribute. Click all of the check boxes. Enter sample data. Add at least five rows to CUSTOMER and at least seven rows to CONTACT. Ensure that some CUSTOMER rows have no matching CONTACT rows.

KE7-3 HOW DO YOU CREATE A DATA ENTRY FORM?

Open the default data entry form for the CUSTOMER table. Click the CUSTOMER rows to display the related CONTACT data. Now use the *Form* tool to create a data entry form. Navigate through that form to see that the CONTACT rows are correctly connected to the CUSTOMER rows. Adjust spacing as you deem appropriate while removing the CustomerID field from the CUSTOMER section.

KE7-4 HOW DO YOU CREATE QUERIES USING THE QUERY DESIGN TOOL?

Create a query that displays Name, Email, Date, and Subject. Sort the results of Name in alphabetical order.

KE7-5 HOW DO YOU CREATE A REPORT?

Use the Report Wizard to create a report that has Name, Email, Date, and Subject. View that report. Add a group total for each CUSTOMER that counts the number of contacts for each customer. Follow the procedure shown, except instead of selecting Sum for Type choose *Count Records* instead.

MyLab MIS

MyLab MIS is an online learning and testing environment that features the perfect study tools to help you master the concepts covered in this chapter. Log in to MyLab to test your knowledge of key chapter concepts and explore additional practice tools, including videos, flashcards, and more!

USING YOUR KNOWLEDGE

KE7-1. Answer question KE6-2 at the end of Knowledge Extension 6 (page 169). Use Access to implement your database design. Create the tables and add sample data. Create a data entry form that shows teams and the equipment they have checked out. Verify that the form correctly processes new checkouts, changes to checkouts, and equipment returns. Create a report that shows each team, the items they have checked out, and the number of items they have checked out. (Use *Count Records* as explained in Active Review KE7-5.)

KE7-2. Answer question KE6-3 at the end of Knowledge Extension 6 (page 170). Create an Access database for the CUSTOMER and RENTAL tables only. Create the tables and add sample data. Create a data entry form that shows customers and all of their rentals (assume customers rent bicycles more than once). Verify that the form correctly processes new rentals, changes to rentals, and rental returns. Create a report that shows each customer, the rentals they have made, and the total rental fee for all of their rentals.

There are no Assisted-graded writing questions in this knowledge extension.

CHAPTER 6
The Cloud

STUDY QUESTIONS

Q6-1   **WHY SHOULD I CARE ABOUT NETWORKS?**

Q6-2   **WHAT IS A COMPUTER NETWORK?**

Q6-3   **WHY IS THE CLOUD THE FUTURE FOR MOST ORGANIZATIONS?**

Q6-4   **HOW DO ORGANIZATIONS USE THE CLOUD?**

Q6-5   **HOW CAN ORGANIZATIONS USE CLOUD SERVICES SECURELY?**

Q6-6   **WHAT DOES THE CLOUD MEAN FOR YOUR FUTURE?**

Q6-7   **HOW IS MOBILE COMPUTING CHANGING THE WAY WE WORK AND LIVE?**

MIS in Action

"What's your plan, Toshio?"

Mateo Thomas, CEO of Falcon Security, is meeting with Toshio Sato, IT director, and Joni Campbell, CFO, to discuss Falcon Security's data storage costs.

"Right now, Mateo, we're fine. We just got our new NAS online and we've increased our storage capacity by almost 30 percent, but ..." Toshio trails off.

Joni can't stand this. "Well, we're fine until you look at the bills we're running up. The money we've spent on storage has increased 350 percent *in 1 year.*"

"Yes, Joni, it has, but our volume's gone up 400 percent," Toshio replies.

"True enough, but ..."

Mateo has had enough and interrupts. "We've been over this before. No need to rehash it. We all agree that our storage costs are too high. Toshio, I'd asked you to look into alternatives. What have you got?"

"The cloud."

"The *what?*" Joni hopes he's not losing it.

"The cloud," Toshio repeats. "We move all of our video to the cloud."

Mateo is curious. "OK, Toshio, I'll bite. What's the cloud?"

"It's a movement—I'd call it a fad, except I think it's here to stay."

"So how does it help us?" Mateo asks.

"We lease storage capacity from a third party."

 Chapter 6 optional knowledge extension is
Knowledge Extension 9 Network and Cloud Technology page 216

Joni's confused. "You mean we'd lease hard drives rather than buy them?"

"Well, not exactly," Toshio explains. "We wouldn't be installing any more hard drives in our data centre. We can lease online storage on very, very flexible, pay-as-you-go terms. If we get a large new client, we can acquire more storage and scale it to meet our needs."

"You mean each day? We can change the terms of our lease on a daily basis?" Joni thinks that's not possible. "OK, so how much does it cost? This can't be cheap."

"How about $10 per terabyte?"

Mateo's puzzled at that. "What do you mean $10 per terabyte?"

"I mean we can get 1 terabyte of online storage for about $10 per month." Toshio grins as he says this.

"*What?*" Joni's dumbfounded.

"Yeah, that's it. We can get as much storage as we want, and our systems automatically upload all incoming data from our drones. The net difference would be that our average monthly storage costs would be at least 50 percent less than they are now. And that's not counting the power savings, the time saved doing backups, or the fact that we wouldn't have to configure any more new hardware." Toshio isn't quite sure, but he thinks the actual storage costs could be less.

"Toshio, you've got to be kidding. We can save tens of thousands of dollars in storage costs. This is *huge*." As Joni says this, in the back of her mind she's thinking, "If it's true."

"Well, it's good; I don't know about huge. We'd have additional development costs to set up our systems, and that will take some time."

"Toshio, give me a plan. I want a plan." Mateo's thinking what these savings could mean to their next two quarters … and beyond.

"I'll give you something next week," Toshio says.

"I want it by Friday, Toshio."

Q6-1 WHY SHOULD I CARE ABOUT NETWORKS?

Picture this: You have flown in to St. John's, Newfoundland, for a business trip. It is your first time in the city. The night is young, and you find yourself sitting in the Oppidan restaurant in the Sheraton Hotel Newfoundland. You have just finished savouring your Pan Seared Newfoundland Cod with Scrunchions, and you are relaxing and taking in the harbour view. Suddenly, your smartphone rings. You can barely hear your friend's voice over the music in the background. "You've got to get down here," he says. "Drake is onstage with The Barenaked Ladies here at O'Reilly's on George Street. I'll hold you a space." Your cellphone drops the call. You use your credit card to pay the bill at your table and then make your way to your hotel room. You open the door with an electronic key. Along the way you think, "Where is George Street? Is there a cover charge at O'Reilly's?"

Once in your room, you connect your phone to Wi-Fi. There is a slight delay, which seems like forever. You find five updates to your Twitter feed while you were at dinner. They can wait, however. You type "O'Reilly's George Street St. John's" into google maps. A few seconds roll by, and you wonder why the system seems so slow. The search comes back with information about the pub, and you think about using Street View to get a look at the building but think that it will be too slow and that it is only a short walk. In the lobby, you use your debit card to get some cash from the automated banking machine (ABM). You get your current position on your phone using the global positioning system (GPS) and you navigate the short distance to the pub. You get to the pub and take a selfie with Drake in the background and store the photo on the cloud. You send an Instagram to your friends.

Let us think about this scenario. How many networks did you use? There was (1) the public switched telephone network (PSTN), which is tied to the cellphone network so that your friend could reach you; (2) the financial networks used for your ABM and credit card transactions (this could be a chapter in itself); (3) the local area network (LAN), which handles electronic key access in the hotel; (4) the Wi-Fi (wireless_ network (802.11) operating over a LAN (802.3), which provides wireless Internet access in the hotel; (5) the wide area network (WAN), which provides Internet access for email and Web browsing; (6) the cellphone network using short message service (SMS) for the text message and multimedia messaging service (MMS) for the picture; and, finally, (7) the GPS in the automated navigation system, which is a satellite network service. That is a lot of networks!

Our view of technology (Chapter 4) showed that computers become more useful to people when computing devices are connected to networks. You will learn in this chapter that when you are connected to the Internet, you are actually part of a network of networks comprised of millions of computers and other devices. This network allows you to send and receive texts and emails, browse webpages stored across the globe, download audio and video files, and talk with friends using the telephone.

The technology behind computer networks is complex and can be intimidating to those who are unfamiliar with its terminology. And because a large number of electronic networks exist, it can become overwhelming. We will focus on only a few electronic networks that are related to computers. The goal of this chapter is not to turn you into a networking guru but to improve your understanding of the basic terminology of computer networks. Knowing these terms and understanding the basics of how networks work will make you a more informed user of network technology and help you realize the potential and limitations of collaborating through computer networks in business.

Networks and Collaboration

Networks enable collaboration. **Collaboration** occurs when two or more people work together to achieve a common goal, result, or product. When collaboration is effective, the results of the group are greater than what could be produced by any of the individuals working alone. Collaboration involves coordination and communication and often makes use of computer networks.

The effectiveness of a collaborative effort is driven by four critical factors (Figure 6-1):

- Communication skills and culture
- Communication systems
- Content management
- Workflow control

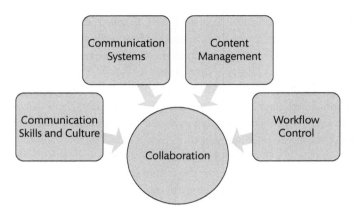

Figure 6-1 Critical Factors in Collaboration

Communication skills and culture are often the key to an effective collaborative effort. The ability to be a part of a group and to give and receive critical feedback is particularly important for employers. Surveys of companies frequently list communication as the most important skill they look for in employees. Most companies believe that the product of any group effort can improve significantly when group members believe they can openly share and contribute ideas. Group members should be able to respectfully and constructively critique each other's work based on an honest assessment of how the overall outcome can be improved. It is important for individuals within the group to give and receive feedback without creating bad feelings and/or resentment. This can be difficult for many people, but it is essential to working well in groups.

The second important element is the availability of effective **communication systems**. Few collaborative meetings are conducted solely in-person. Group members may be travelling, geographically inaccessible, or simply unavailable (a multitude of reasons could suffice). In such cases, the availability of email, virtual private networks, instant messaging, video conferencing, and more sophisticated communications systems is crucial. These communication systems depend on an organization's network technology, which is the focus of this chapter.

Another driver of effective collaboration is content management (the focus of the previous chapter). When multiple users are contributing and changing documents, schedules, task lists, assignments, and so forth, one user's work might interfere with another's, and keeping track of and synchronizing and integrating the various versions is critically important. Users need to manage content so that conflicts do not occur. Databases and content management systems help ensure that conflicts are handled correctly. It is also important to know why the changes were made, when, and by whom. Content management systems track and report these data. Finally, in some collaborations, members have different rights and privileges. Some team members have full permission to create, edit, and delete content, others are restricted to editing that content, and still others are restricted to a read-only status. Information systems and database management systems play a key role in enforcing such restrictions.

Workflow control is the final driver of effective collaboration. A **workflow** is a process or procedure by which content is created, edited, used, and discarded. The concept of a workflow is very close to the concept of a business process, which we discussed in Chapter 2. The difference is that a business process focuses on delivering a good or a service *externally* to a customer, whereas a workflow focuses on the *internal* delivery of a good or a service to other employees in the organization. For a team that supports a website, for example, a workflow design might specify that certain members create webpages, other members review those pages, and still others post the reviewed and approved pages to the site. The workflow specifies a particular ordering of tasks and includes processes for handling rejected changes as well as for dealing with exceptions.

It is important to recognize that effective collaboration requires support for all four of these collaboration drivers, even if all the drivers are not equally important. For one-time, ad hoc workgroups (for example, group projects in this course), it might not be necessary to create and formalize workflows. However, for a team of engineers designing a new model of smartphone, a formally defined workflow is crucial. In this chapter, our focus is on understanding, at a high level, the network technologies that provide the foundation for communication systems. This understanding will allow you to make more effective choices for communication systems in your organizations.

Network Externalities

It is important to understand one fundamental fact about networks: In general, the larger the number of people using a network, the more valuable that network becomes. This phenomenon is called the network effect, or **network externality**. For example, consider YouTube (www.YouTube.com). The first person to join as a member gets almost no benefit—that person can only see the videos that he or she already has. The second user gets a little more benefit. As more and more people are added, the benefits get larger for everyone in the network.

When networks are first started, people often look for the critical mass. This is the point at which the value of being part of the network is larger than the cost of being on it. Once networks hit critical mass, they usually grow at a faster rate. People who start networks usually have a keen interest in the critical mass.

There are limits, of course, to networks and network growth. As a network continues to gain users, congestion can result or the market may become saturated or change (does anyone remember myspace?). When this occurs, the rate of growth diminishes and then either flattens or becomes negative. Astute business users recognize the importance of network life cycles and assess the value and costs rather than only responding to enthusiasm and trends.

What Is the Global Positioning System (GPS)?

The **global positioning system (GPS)** uses a collection of dozens of satellites that orbit Earth and transmit precise microwave signals. A GPS receiver (perhaps you have one in your car) can calculate its position by measuring the distance between itself and several of the satellites. Believe it or not, with microwave signals from at least three satellites (triangulation), you can compute a GPS receiver's position. The GPS can even calculate the direction and speed of a GPS receiver. Sophisticated navigation systems have resulted from combining GPS technology with map databases. These systems typically sell for less than a few hundred dollars. GPS type of functionality has also been incorporated into cellphones and even watches although in many cases cellular towers rather than satellites are used for triangulation.

Neo Edmund/Shutterstock

Q6-2 WHAT IS A COMPUTER NETWORK?

A computer **network** is a collection of computers that transmit and/or receive electronic signals through transmission media. The **transmission media** might be physical media, such as copper cable and **optical fibre** (glass fibre) **cable**, or wireless media transmitting light or

Type	Characteristic
Local area network (LAN)	Computers connected at a single physical site
Wide area network (WAN)	Computers connected between two or more separated sites
The Internet and internets	Networks of networks

Figure 6-2 Major Network Types

radio frequencies (including cellular and satellite systems). As shown in Figure 6-2, the three major types of networks are local area networks, wide area networks, and internets.

The **local area network (LAN)** connects devices within a relatively small, single geographical location. The number of connections can range from two to several hundred. The distinguishing characteristic of a LAN is that it is in *a single location*. **Wide area networks (WANs)** connect devices at different geographical locations.

This distinction between a single site and multiple sites is important. With a LAN, an organization can usually place communications lines wherever it wants because all lines reside on its premises. The same is not true for a WAN. A company with offices in Vancouver and Toronto cannot run fiber to connect the computers in the two cities. Instead, it must contract with a communications vendor that is licensed by the government and already has capacity or the authority to install more connections between the two cities.

An **Internet** is a network of networks. Internets connect LANs, WANs, and other internets. The most famous Internet is **the Internet**, the collection of networks that you use when you send email or access a website. In addition to the Internet, private networks of networks, called *intranets*, also exist.

The networks that comprise an Internet use a large variety of communication methods and conventions, and data must flow seamlessly across them. To provide seamless flow, an elaborate scheme called a *layered protocol* is used. A **protocol** is a set of rules that communicating devices follow. There are many different protocols; some are used for LANs, some are used for WANs, some are used for internets and the Internet, and some are used for all of these. The important point is that for devices to communicate, they must use the same protocol.

Computer networks have evolved quickly over the past decade, too fast for many people to keep track of. When people talk about networks now, they often refer to "the Cloud." The cloud is a general concept that describes sets of distributed and integrated networks that support the storage and transfer of electronic data. Most experts realize that the cloud is the future for network technology. The next section describes why the cloud is so important.

Q6-3 WHY IS THE CLOUD THE FUTURE FOR MOST ORGANIZATIONS?

Until 2010 or so, most organizations constructed and maintained their own computing infrastructure. Organizations purchased or leased hardware, installed it on their premises, and used it to support organizational emails, websites, e-commerce sites, and in-house applications such as accounting and operations systems. As the prices for network storage and data transfer decreased, organizations began to consider moving their computing infrastructure to the cloud. The cloud was viewed as an opportunity for cost savings and increased accessibility. It is likely that in the future all, or nearly all, computing infrastructure will be leased from distributed networks that we refer to as "the cloud." So, just what is the cloud, and why is it the future?

What Is the Cloud?

We define the **cloud** as the *elastic* leasing of *pooled* computer resources *over the Internet*. The term *cloud* is used because most early diagrams of three-tier and other Internet-based systems used a cloud symbol to represent the Internet and organizations came to view their infrastructure as being "somewhere in the cloud."

Elastic   Consider each of the italicized terms in the definition. The term **elastic**, which was first used this way by Amazon.com, means that the computing resources leased can be increased or decreased dynamically, programmatically, in a short span of time and that organizations only pay for the resources they use.

Suppose that a car manufacturer creates an ad to run during the Academy Awards. The manufacturer believes the ad is fantastic and will result in millions of hits on the company website. However, it is unknown ahead of time if there will be a thousand, a million, 10 million, or even more site visits. Further, the ad may appeal more to one nationality or potential customer than another. Will 70 percent of site visits be from the United States and the rest in Europe? Or will there be millions of visits from Japan? Or Australia? Given this uncertainty, how does the car manufacturer prepare its computing infrastructure? The car manufacturer knows that if it cannot provide very short response times (say, a fraction of a second) it may lose the benefit of an incredibly expensive ad. Alternatively, if the ad is a flop, preprovisioning of thousands of servers will add to the accumulation of wasted money.

Figure 6-3 shows an example of this situation, based on a real case supported by Amazon.com's CloudFront. Suppose this figure shows the processing activity on the car manufacturer's website on the day of the Academy Awards. Throughout most of the day, the car manufacturer is delivering less than 10 Gbps of content to users. However, as soon as the ad runs (2 P.M. in the Hawaii-Aleutian time zone where the data was collected), demand increases seven-fold and stays high for half an hour. After the announcement of Best Picture, when the ad runs again, demand again increases to between 30 and 40 Gpbs for an hour and then returns to its base level.

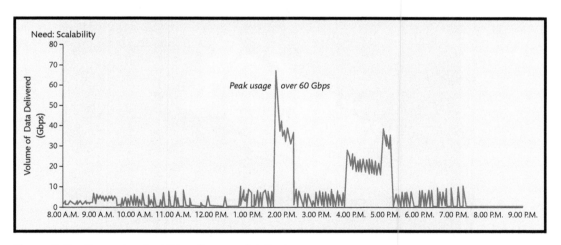

Figure 6-3   Example of a Video Banner Ad Customer

Without an increase in servers, response time will be 3 to 5 seconds or more, which is far too long to maintain the attention of an Academy Awards viewer. However, the car manufacturer has contracted with a cloud vendor to add servers, wherever needed worldwide, to keep response time to less than 0.5 seconds. Using cloud technology, the cloud vendor will programmatically increase its servers to keep response time below the 0.5 second threshold. As demand rises and falls the cloud vendor reallocates servers in response to demand levels (such as after the Best Picture announcement).

In this way, the car manufacturer need not build or contract for infrastructure that supports maximum demand. Had it done so, the vast majority of its servers would have been idle most of the day. And, as you will learn, the cloud vendor can provision servers worldwide using the cloud; if a good portion of the excess demand is in Singapore, for example, it can provision extra servers in Asia and reduce wait time due to global transmission delays.

Pooled   The second key term in the definition of the cloud is *pooled*. Cloud resources are **pooled** because many different organizations use the same physical hardware; they share that hardware through virtualization. Cloud vendors dynamically allocate virtual machines to physical hardware as customer needs increase or decrease. Thus, servers that advertisers need for the Academy Awards can be reallocated to CPA firms that need them earlier in the day, to textbook publishers who need them for an online student activity Monday afternoon, or to the hotel industry that needs them next week.

An easy way to understand the essence of this development is to consider electrical power. In the very earliest days of electric power generation, organizations operated their own generators to create power for their company's needs. Over time, as the power grid expanded, it became possible to centralize power generation so that organizations could purchase just the electricity they needed from an electric utility.

Both cloud vendors and electrical utilities benefit from *economies of scale*. According to this principle, the average cost of production decreases as the size of the operation increases. Major cloud vendors operate enormous Web farms. Figure 6-4 shows the building that contains the computers in the Web farm constructed by Apple in 2011 to support its iCloud offering. This early implementation was a billion-dollar facility and it contains more than 500 000 square feet.[1] Google, for example, chose the Dalles, in Oregon as the location for their data centre because it had the right combination of energy infrastructure (close to a hydroelectric dam), developable land, and available workforce.[2] Amazon.com, IBM, Google, Microsoft, Oracle, and other large companies each operate many similar farms worldwide.

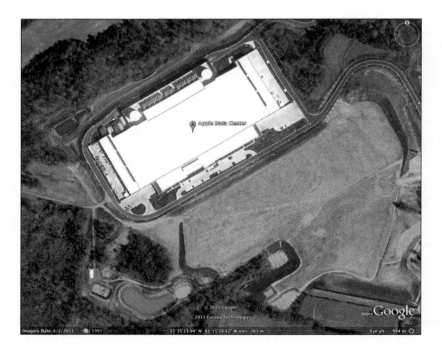

Figure 6-4 Apple Data Center in Maiden, NC

Source: Google Inc.

---

[1] Patrick Thibodeau, "Apple, Google, Facebook Turn N.C. into Data Center Hub," Computerworld, last modified June 3, 2011, *www.computerworld.com/s/article/9217259/Apple_Google_Facebook_turn_N.C._into_data_center_hub.*

[2] Description of Google's data centre is described at The Dalles, Oregon, *www.google.com/about/datacenters/inside/locations/the-dalles/* accessed July 15, 2017.

Over the Internet   Finally, with the cloud, resources are accessed **over the Internet**. "Big deal," you're saying. "I use the Internet all the time." Well, think about that for a minute. The car manufacturer in the previous example has contracted with the cloud vendor for an agreed on response time; the cloud vendor adds servers as needed to meet that requirement. As stated, the cloud vendor may be provisioning, nearly instantaneously, servers all over the world. How does it do that? And not for just one customer, like the car manufacturer, but for thousands?

In the past, for such interorganizational processing to occur, developers from the car manufacturer had to meet with developers from the cloud vendor and design an interface. "Our programs will do this, providing this data, and we want your programs to do that, in response, sending us this other data back." Such meetings took days and were expensive and error-prone. Given the design, the developers then returned home to write code to meet the agreed on interface design, which may not have been understood in the same way by all.

It was a long, slow, and expensive process prone to failure, and it had to be repeated for every pair of communicating companies. If organizations still had to do this, cloud provisioning would be unaffordable and infeasible.

Instead, the computer industry settled on a set of standard ways of requesting and receiving services over the Internet. **Service-oriented architecture (SOA)** is a way of designing computer programs so they can be flexibly combined, like Lego blocks, for cloud processing. Using SOA, programs formally define the services they perform, the data they expect, and the results they produce. **Web service standards** are worldwide standards that programs use to declare what they do, the structure of the data they process, and the ways they will communicate. SOA-designed programs that comply with Web service standards are called **Web services**. These standards enable computers that have never "met" before to organize a dizzying, worldwide dance to deliver and process content to users on PCs, iPads, smartphones, Xboxes, and even exercise equipment in a tenth of a second or less. It is an absolutely fascinating and gorgeous technology!

Why Is the Cloud Preferred to In-House Hosting?

Figure 6-5 compares and contrasts cloud-based and in-house hosting. As you can see, the positives are heavily tilted toward cloud-based computing. A cloud vendor, such as Rackspace will lease you one medium server for less than a penny per hour. You can obtain and access that server today, actually within a few minutes. Tomorrow, if you need thousands of servers, you can readily scale up to obtain them. Furthermore, you know the cost structure; although you might be surprised by how many customers want to access your website, you will not be surprised by the cost.

Another positive is that as long as you are dealing with large, reputable organizations, you will be receiving best-of-breed security and disaster recovery. In addition, you need not worry that you are investing in technology that will soon be obsolete; the cloud vendor is taking that risk. All of this is possible because the cloud vendor is gaining economies of scale by selling to an entire industry, not just to you.

The negatives of cloud computing involve loss of control. You are dependent on a vendor; changes in the vendor's management, policy, and prices are beyond your control. Further, you do not know where your data—which may be a large part of your organization's value—is located. Nor do you know how many copies of your data exist or even if they are located in the same place (or even the same country). Finally, you have no visibility into the security and disaster preparedness that is actually in place. You are unaware of how widely dispersed your data may be and who has access (your competition could be stealing your data).

The positives and negatives of in-house hosting are shown in the second column of Figure 6-5. For the most part, they are the opposite of those for cloud-based computing. You

Cloud-Based Hosting	In-House Hosting
Positive:	
Small capital requirements	Control of data location
Speedy development	In-depth visibility of security and disaster preparedness
Superior flexibility and adaptability to growing or fluctuating demand	
Known cost structure	
Possibly best-of-breed security/disaster preparedness	
No obsolescence	
Industry-wide economies of scale, hence cheaper	
Negative:	
Dependency on vendor	Significant capital required
Loss of control over data location	Significant development effort
Little visibility into true security and disaster preparedness capabilities	Annual maintenance costs
	Ongoing support costs
	Staff and train personnel
	Increased management requirements
	Difficult (impossible?) to accommodate fluctuating demand
	Cost uncertainties
	Obsolescence

Figure 6-5 Comparison of Cloud-Based Hosting and In-House Hosting

should note, however, the need for personnel and management. With in-house hosting, not only will you have to construct your own data centre, you will also need to acquire and train the personnel to run it and then manage those personnel and your facility.

Why Now?

A skeptic might respond to Figure 6-5 by saying, "If it's so great, why hasn't cloud hosting been used for years? Why now?"

In fact, cloud-based hosting (or a version of it under a different name) has been around since the 1960s. Long before the creation of the personal computer and networks, time-sharing vendors provided slices of computer time on a use-fee basis. However, the technology of that time, continuing up until the first decade of this century, did not favour the construction and use of enormous data centres, nor did the necessary standards exist.

Three factors have made cloud-based hosting advantageous today. First, processors, data communication, and data storage are nearly free. At the scale of a Web farm of hundreds of thousands of processors, providing a virtual machine for an hour costs essentially nothing, as suggested by the 1.5 cent-per-hour price. Because data communication is so cheap, getting the data to and from that processor is also nearly free.

Second, virtualization technology enables the near instantaneous creation of a new virtual machine. The customer provides (or creates in the cloud) a disk image of the data and programs of the machine it wants to provision. Virtualization software takes it from there. Finally, as stated, Internet-based standards enable cloud-hosting vendors to provide processing capabilities in flexible yet standardized ways.

When Does the Cloud Not Make Sense?

Cloud-based hosting makes sense for most organizations. The only organizations for which it may not make sense are those required by law or by industry standard practice to have physical control over their data. Such organizations might be forced to create and maintain their own hosting infrastructure. A financial institution, for example, might be legally required to maintain physical control over its data. Even in this circumstance, however, it is possible to gain many of the benefits of cloud computing using private clouds and virtual private clouds, possibilities we consider in Q6-4.

Q6-4 HOW DO ORGANIZATIONS USE THE CLOUD?

Organizations can use the cloud in several different ways. The first, and by far most popular, is to obtain cloud services from cloud service vendors.

Cloud Services from Cloud Vendors

In general, cloud-based service offerings can be organized into the three categories shown in Figure 6-6. An organization that provides **software as a service (SaaS)** provides not only hardware infrastructure, but also an operating system and application programs as well. For example, *Salesforce.com* provides hardware and programs for customer and sales tracking as a service. Similarly, Google provides Google Drive and Microsoft provides OneDrive as a service. With Office 365, Exchange, Skype for Business, and SharePoint applications are provided as services "in the cloud."

Cloud Category	Examples
SaaS (software as a service)	Salesforce.com Google Grid Microsoft OneDrive and Office 365 Apple iCloud
PaaS (platform as a service)	Microsoft Azure Oracle on Demand
IaaS (infrastructure as a service)	Amazon EC2 (Elastic Cloud 2) Amazon S3 (Simple Storage Service)

Figure 6-6 Three Fundamental Cloud Types

You have probably heard of, or used, Apple's iCloud. It is a cloud service that Apple uses to sync all of its customers' iOS devices. As of 2015, Apple provides 10 free applications in the iCloud. Calendar is a good example. When a customer enters an appointment in her iPhone, Apple automatically pushes that appointment into the calendars on all of that customer's iOS devices. Further, customers can share calendars with others that will be synchronized as well. Mail, pictures, applications, and other resources are also synched via iCloud.

An organization can move to SaaS simply by signing up and learning how to use it. In Apple's case, there's nothing to learn. To quote the late Steve Jobs, "It just works."

The second category of cloud hosting is **platform as a service (PaaS)**, whereby vendors provide hosted computers, an operating system, and possibly a DBMS. Microsoft Windows Azure, for example, provides servers installed with Windows Server. Customers of Windows Azure then add their own applications on top of the hosted platform. Microsoft SQL Azure provides a host with Windows Server and SQL Server. Oracle On Demand provides a hosted server with Oracle Database. Again, for PaaS, organizations add their own applications to the host. Amazon EC2 provides servers with Windows Server or Linux installed.

The most basic cloud offering is **infrastructure as a service (IaaS)**, which is the cloud hosting of a bare server computer or data storage. Rackspace provides hardware for customers to load whatever operating system they want and *Amazon.com* licenses S3 (Simple Storage Server), which provides unlimited, reliable data storage in the cloud.

Content Delivery Networks

A second major use of the cloud is to deliver content from servers placed around the world. A **content delivery network (CDN)** is an information system that stores user data in many different geographical locations and makes that data available on demand. A CDN provides a specialized type of PaaS but is usually considered in its own category, as it is here.

Consider CDN applications. A news organization could use a CDN to store copies of its news articles. The CDN vendor replicates articles on servers, possibly worldwide, so as to minimize latency. When a news reader accesses an article, her request is transmitted to a routing server that determines which CDN server is likely to deliver the article to her the fastest. Because traffic changes rapidly, especially for popular sites, such calculations are made in real time. A request for content could be served by a computer in San Diego, and a few moments later an identical request from the same user might be served by a computer in Salt Lake City.

In addition to news articles, CDNs are often used to store and deliver content that seldom changes. For example, the company banner on an organization's webpage might be stored on many CDN servers. Various pieces of the webpage could be obtained from different servers on the CDN; all such decisions are made in real time to provide the fastest content delivery possible.

Figure 6-7 summarizes CDN benefits. The first two are self-explanatory. Reliability is increased because data is stored on many servers. If one server fails, any of a potentially large number of other servers can deliver the content. You will learn about denial-of-service (DoS) attacks in Chapter 10. For now, just understand that such security threats send so much data to a given server that the server's performance for legitimate traffic becomes unacceptable. By having multiple servers, CDNs help to protect against such attacks.

Benefits of Content Delivery Networks
• Decreased, even guaranteed load time
• Reduced load on origin server
• Increased reliability
• Protection from DoS attacks
• Reduced delivery costs for mobile users
• Pay-as-you-go

Figure 6-7 Benefits of Content Delivery Networks

In some cases, CDNs reduce access costs for mobile users (particularly those who have a limited data account). By delivering the data faster, site connection charges can be reduced. Finally, many (but not all) CDN services are offered on a flexible, pay-as-you-go basis. Customers need not contract for fixed services and payments; they pay only for what they use, when they use it. Figure 6-8 shows an example of how CDN servers might be distributed. A number of vendors offer CDN.

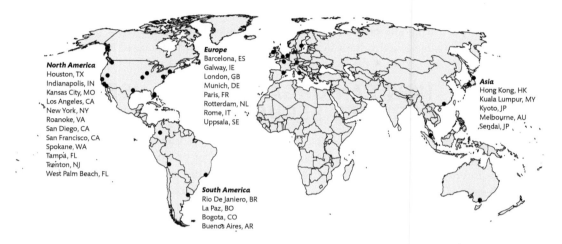

North America
Houston, TX
Indianapolis, IN
Kansas City, MO
Los Angeles, CA
New York, NY
Roanoke, VA
San Diego, CA
San Francisco, CA
Spokane, WA
Tampa, FL
Trenton, NJ
West Palm Beach, FL

Europe
Barcelona, ES
Galway, IE
London, GB
Munich, DE
Paris, FR
Rotterdam, NL
Rome, IT
Uppsala, SE

Asia
Hong Kong, HK
Kuala Lumpur, MY
Kyoto, JP
Melbourne, AU
Sendai, JP

South America
Rio De Janiero, BR
La Paz, BO
Bogota, CO
Buenos Aires, AR

Figure 6-8 Servers Used in a Typical CDN Service

Use Web Services Internally

The third way that organizations can use cloud technology is to build internal information systems using Web services. Strictly speaking, this is not using the cloud because it does not provide elasticity or the advantages of pooled resources. It does advantageously use cloud standards, however, so we include it here.

Figure 6-9 shows a Web services inventory application at a hypothetical online bicycle part retailer named Best Bikes. In this example, Best Bikes is running its own servers on its own infrastructure. To do so, Best Bikes sets up a private Internet within the company—an Internet that is generally not reachable from outside the company. Best Bikes writes the applications for processing inventory using Web services standards. Application users access the inventory Web services using JavaScript that is sent down to the users' browsers.

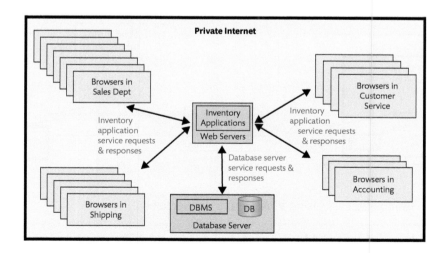

Figure 6-9 Web Services Principles Applied to Inventory Applications

Users of the inventory Web services include Sales, Shipping, Customer Service, Accounting, and other departments. Internal applications can use the inventory Web services like building blocks. They can use the services they need—and no more. Because the Web services are encapsulated, the inventory system can be altered without affecting other applications. In this way, systems development is more flexible, and it will be faster and hence less costly.

To learn more about Web services and encapsulation, read Knowledge Extension 9.

As stated, however, this is not a cloud. In this example, Best Bikes has a fixed number of servers; no attempt is made to make them elastic. Also, the servers are dedicated to inventory. During idle periods, they are not dynamically reused for other purposes. Some organizations remove this limit by creating a private cloud, as discussed in Q6-4.

Q6-5   HOW CAN ORGANIZATIONS USE CLOUD SERVICES SECURELY?

The Internet and cloud services based on Internet infrastructure provide powerful processing and storage services at a fraction of the cost of private data centres. However, the Internet is a jungle of threats to data and computing infrastructure, as discussed in Chapter 10. How can organizations realize the benefits of cloud technology without succumbing to those threats?

The answer involves a combination of technologies that we will address at a high level. As you read, realize that no security story is ever over; attackers constantly strive to find ways around security safeguards, and occasionally they succeed. Attackers become more innovative and cloud security continues to evolve. We begin with a discussion of **virtual private network (VPN)** a technology used to provide secure communication over the Internet.

Virtual Private Network (VPN)

A VPN uses the Internet to create the appearance of private, secure connections. In the IT world, the term *virtual* means something that appears to exist but in fact does not. Here a VPN uses the public Internet to create the appearance of a private connection on a secure network.

A Typical VPN   Figure 6-10 shows one way to create a VPN to connect a remote computer, perhaps an employee working at a hotel in Miami, to a LAN at a Chicago site. The remote user is the VPN client. That client first establishes a public connection to the Internet. The connection can be obtained by accessing a local ISP, as shown in Figure 6-10, or, in some cases, the hotel itself provides a direct Internet connection.

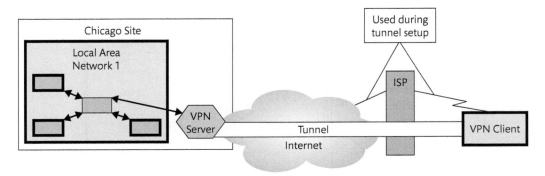

Figure 6-10   Remote Access Using VPN; Actual Connections

In either case, once the Internet connection is made, VPN software on the remote user's computer establishes a connection with the VPN server in Chicago. The VPN client and VPN server then have a secure connection. That connection, called a **tunnel**, is a virtual, private pathway over a public or shared network from the VPN client to the VPN server. Figure 6-11 illustrates the connection as it appears to the remote user.

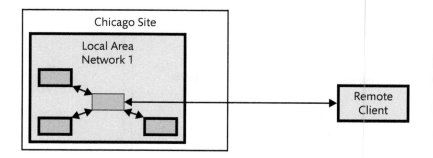

Figure 6-11 Remote Access Using VPN; Apparent Connection

To secure VPN communications over the public Internet, the VPN client software *encrypts*, or codes (see Chapter 10, page 332), messages so their contents are protected from snooping. Then the VPN client appends the Internet address of the VPN server to the message and sends that package over the Internet to the VPN server. When the VPN server receives the message, it strips its address off the front of the message, *decrypts* the coded message, and sends the plain text message to the original address inside the LAN. In this way, secure private messages are delivered over the public Internet.

Using a Private Cloud

A **private cloud** is a cloud owned and operated by an organization for its own benefit. To create a private cloud, the organization creates a *private* internet and designs applications using Web services standards as shown in Figure 6-9 (page 203). The organization then creates a farm of servers and manages those servers with elastic load balancing just as the cloud service vendors do. Because of the complexity of managing multiple database servers, most organizations choose not to replicate database servers. Figure 6-12 illustrates this possibility.

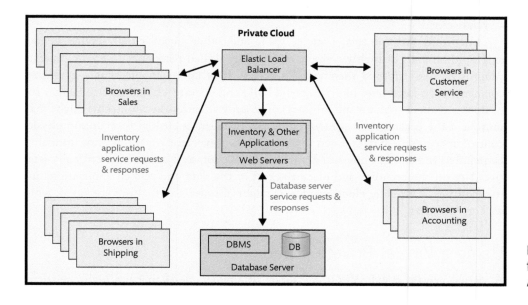

Figure 6-12 Private Cloud for Inventory and Other Applications

Private clouds provide security *within* the organizational infrastructure but do not provide secure access from outside that infrastructure. To provide such access, organizations set up a VPN and users employ it to securely access the private cloud as shown in Figure 6-13.

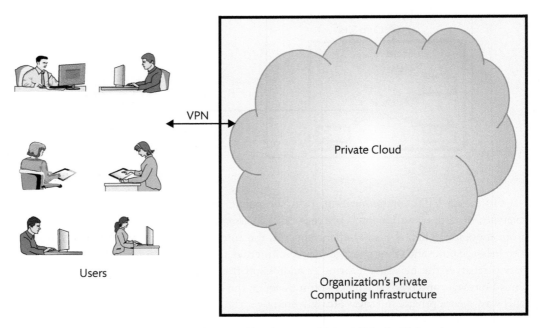

Figure 6-13 Accessing the Private Cloud over a Virtual Private Network

Private clouds provide the advantages of elasticity, but to questionable benefit. What can organizations do with their idle servers? They could realize some cost savings by shutting down idle servers. But unlike cloud vendors, they cannot repurpose them for use by other companies. Possibly a large conglomerate or major international company could balance processing loads across subsidiary business units and across different geographical regions. 3M, for example, might balance processing for its different product groups and on different continents, but it is difficult to imagine that, in doing so, it would save money or time. A company like Falcon Security is very unlikely to develop a private cloud.

Microsoft, *Amazon.com*, Oracle, IBM, and other major cloud service vendors employ thousands of highly trained, very highly skilled personnel to create, manage, administer, and improve their cloud services. It is unimaginable that a traditional company, even large ones like 3M, could build and operate a cloud service facility that competes (except perhaps the military). The only situation in which this might make sense is if the organization is required by law or business custom to maintain physical control over its stored data. Even in that case, however, the organization is unlikely to be required to maintain physical control over all data, so it might keep critically sensitive data on the premises and place the rest of the data and related applications into the facilities of a public cloud vendor. It might also use a virtual private cloud, which we consider next.

Using a Virtual Private Cloud

A **virtual private cloud (VPC)** is a subset of a public cloud that has highly restricted, secure access. An organization can build its own VPC on top of public cloud infrastructure like AWS or that provided by other cloud vendors. The means by which this is done are beyond the scope of this text, but think of it as VPN tunnelling on steroids.

Using a VPC, an organization can store its most sensitive data on its own infrastructure, and store the less sensitive data on the VPC. In this way, organizations that are required to have physical control over some of their data can place that data on their own

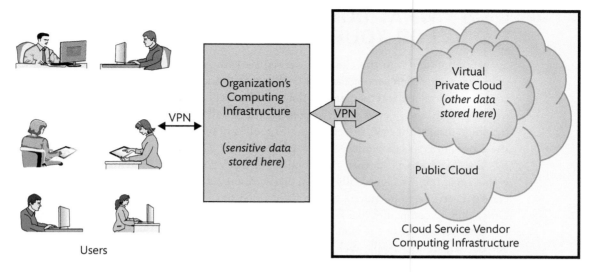

Figure 6-14 Using a Virtual Private Cloud (VPC)

servers and locate the rest of their data on the VPC as shown in Figure 6-14. By doing so, the organization gains the advantages of cloud storage and possibly cloud processing for the portion of its data that it need not physically control.

In some cases, organizations have obtained permission from regulating bodies to store even their very sensitive data on a VPC.

So What? | Net Neutrality Enabled

Have you ever wondered what it would have been like to live during the time of the Wild West? Outlaws were abundant, and early settlers were free to stake claim to land with minimal response or oversight from the government. If you stop and think about it, the spread of Internet-connected devices has, in many ways, created a similar environment—a digital Wild West.

The digital Wild West has many parallels to the old American frontier. Modern-day cyberspace bandits can commit deviant or criminal acts (e.g., cyberbullying, stealing data, denial-of-service attacks, cybervandalism, and cyberwarfare) and are rarely caught or prosecuted. This lack of legal response to criminal acts is often due to an absence of existing laws needed to convict such offenders. Cybercriminals are also difficult to physically track down.

In the frontier, land was "up for grabs" and people rushed to stake claim to valuable land. Similarly, today's digital resources are up for grabs. Companies are trying to stake claim to intellectual property, data streams, and bandwidth. Internet service providers (ISPs), for example, have little control over the amount, type, or origin of the content they deliver. Why is this a problem? Consider the fact that in roughly the past 5 years, Netflix's streaming services have grown so rapidly that 30 percent of all Internet traffic in the United States during peak hours is

Source: bakhtiarzein/Fotolia

associated with people watching movies and TV shows using Netflix.[3]

As an ISP, you may feel that Netflix should pay you a fee for clogging up your fiber lines with the release of a new season of a popular TV show. On the other hand, consumers and content providers want net neutrality. This would mean that all users and content providers would be treated equally. There would not be "fast" and "slow" lanes on the Internet. ISPs would not be allowed to block, or even slow, content associated with competing ISPs. They also could not charge heavy Internet users additional fees or taxes.

[3] M. Prince, "Thoughts on Network Neutrality, the FCC, and the Future of Internet Governance." February 27, 2015, accessed April 10, 2015, *https://blog.cloudflare.com/net-neutrality*.

Q6-6 WHAT DOES THE CLOUD MEAN FOR YOUR FUTURE?

So how important will the cloud be during the early years of your career? Absent some unknown factor such as a federal tax on Internet traffic or a consumer push-back on the government tracing Internet traffic, cloud services will become faster, more secure, easier to use, and cheaper. Fewer and fewer organizations will set up their own computing infrastructure; instead they will benefit from the pooling of servers across organizations and from the economies of scale produced by cloud vendors.

But, looking a bit deeper, the cloud brings both good and bad news. The good news is that organizations can readily obtain elastic resources at a very low cost. This trend will benefit everyone from individuals on the iCloud or Google Drive, to small groups using Office 365, to companies like Falcon Security.

The overall size of the cloud is getting bigger too. So what is the bad news? Recall the 500 000-square-foot Apple Web farm we mentioned earlier and note the size of the parking lot. According to Computerworld, that tiny lot accommodates the entire operations staff of 50 people (about eight people running the centre at any one time). Seems impossible, but is it? Again, look at the size of the parking lot.

And it is not just large companies like Apple. Every city of almost any size still supports small companies that install and maintain in-house email Exchange and other servers. If SaaS products like Google Drive or Office 365 replace those servers, what happens to those local jobs? They are gone! See Collaborative Exercises in this chapter, for more on this topic.

But, with computing infrastructure so much cheaper, new jobs should be available elsewhere. Where will they be? For one, there will be more tech-based startups. Cheap and elastic cloud services enable small startups like the football player evaluation company Hudl (www.hudl.com) to access CDN and other cloud services for next to nothing, a capability that would have taken years and thousands of dollars in the past. Go to the Hudl site and check the response time; it is fast!

An organization like Falcon Security can reduce its storage costs by 50 percent if it moves its data to the cloud. If the move is successful, Falcon Security can increase profitability, have a more reliable infrastructure, and scale its operations much more quickly. Large companies gain the same advantages but on a larger scale. So, the cloud lifts all boats and should enable organizations to develop more information systems at a faster rate and cheaper price, and thus (you knew it was coming!) increase the demand for employees who know how to use and manage information systems!

But what else? The cloud will foster new categories of work. During your career, everything will be connected to everything else, with most data stored in the cloud. Mobile systems will be the standard; desktops will be relegated to content creators. So what new opportunities might arise?

Consider remote action systems, IS that provide computer-based activity or action at a distance. By enabling action at a distance, remote action systems save time and travel expense and make the skills and abilities of an expert available in places where he or she is not physically located. They also enable experts to scale their expertise. Consider a few examples.

Telediagnosis is a remote action system that healthcare professionals use to diagnose illness for rural or remote areas. Telesurgery uses telecommunications to link surgeons to robotic equipment at distant locations. In 2001, Dr. Jacques Marescaux, located in New York City, performed the first trans-Atlantic surgery when he successfully operated on a patient in Strasbourg, France. Such examples, which are still rare, will become common during your lifetime.

Other uses for remote systems include telelaw enforcement, such as the RedFlex system that uses cameras and motion-sensing equipment to issue tickets for red light and speeding violations. The RedFlex Group, headquartered in South Melbourne, Victoria, Australia, earns 87 percent of its revenue from traffic violations in the United States. It offers a turn-key traffic citation information system that includes all five components.

Many remote systems are designed to provide services in dangerous locations, such as robots that clean nuclear reactors or biologically contaminated sites. Drones and other unoccupied military equipment are examples of remote systems used in war zones. Private security and law enforcement will increasingly take advantage of remotely controlled flying drones and robots. You may see an upgraded form of Knightscope's 300-pound robot, named K5, patrolling your neighbourhood in 10 years.

But, even with these exciting new opportunities, the news is not all good. New York's Metropolitan Opera is arguably the finest opera company in the world. To see a live perfor-mance, you can drive to Manhattan, park your car, taxi to Lincoln Center, and pay $300 per seat. Or you can watch the same opera, remotely broadcasted via Met Live, at a local movie theater, park your car for free, pay $12, and take a seat in the fourth row, where via the magic of digital broadcasting you can see details like the stitching on the singers' cos-tumes, details you are unable to see from the $300 seats at the Met. And the sound quality is better. Wonderful, but now, who will go to a local opera performance?

Teleaction reduces the value of local mediocrity. The claim "Well, I'm not the best, but at least I'm here" loses value in a teleaction world. In 1990, when former Secretary of Labor Robert Reich wrote The Work of Nations, he could sensibly claim that those who provide routine face-to-face services are exempt from the dangers of offshoring. That claim loses validity in the teleaction world.

In this era, the value of top-notch performers increases, possibly exponentially. Four million people watch the average Met Live broadcast; agents for the artists who perform at that venue will negotiate a sizable part of that $120 million gate. A famous surgeon or skating coach can reach a larger market more easily and efficiently, and might be much better paid. So, if you can be the world's best at something, do it!

But what about the rest of us? If you are not the world's expert at something, then find a way to be indispensable to someone who is. Own the theaters that broadcast Met Live. Own the skating rink for the remote figure skating coach. Be the food vendor at a teleac-tion event.

Or become essential to the development, use, and management of information systems that support these new opportunities. A business background with IS expertise will serve you very well. The next six chapters discuss many existing and new IS applications. Keep reading!

Q6-7 HOW IS MOBILE COMPUTING CHANGING THE WAY WE WORK AND LIVE?

The introduction of cloud services enables more mobile computing. How do you access the Internet? If you are like some people, you might use a personal computer. However, two trends have now become well established: (1) Your computer is more likely to be a portable laptop than a desktop; and (2) your smartphone is becoming your primary source for mobile computing. It is clear that cellular phones are no longer just phones but, rather, mobile computing devices that provide a wide variety of services. They are devices built for com-munication and collaboration and are, at the core of their designs, networking machines. These machines combine a powerful processor with sophisticated operating systems and cellular network technology to provide a host of applications, such as voice, text, email, Web browsing, camera, and much more, to their users. With these mobile devices, users can access email, instant message, respond via voice or text messaging, and browse the Internet anytime and anywhere. These devices are already changing the way that people work, and the changes are likely to continue for some time.

Figure 6-15 Touch Screen Smartphone

Source: Karlis Dambrans/ Shutterstock

Smartphones are also enabling new applications, which are often labelled **m-commerce (mobile commerce)**, to allow users to conduct new kinds of transactions. Mobile banking and mobile ticket purchases at movie theatres and sporting events are examples of m-commerce, although this really is just the beginning. There are applications that allow you to track the delivery of your pizza, deposit a cheque using just a photograph, or see if a cheaper price can be obtained while you are shopping in a mall. Mobile coupons are also a fast growing service in m-commerce. Mobile coupons are replacing paper coupons with electronic versions, which are delivered to your phone and can be context sensitive. Imagine getting a coupon for $2 off a meal at 11:30 a.m. as you pass by a fast food outlet. Beyond mobility, m-commerce can also include aspects of collaboration.

As a business student, you should consider how these changes will affect you. Traditionally, most people have thought about "work" as a place they go to, with an office, a phone, and a computer hooked into an organization's network. With the advent of mobile technology, workers are able to take their computing power with them when they leave the office. Now smartphones enable you to access your organization's network and all the data and services available on WANs, such as the Internet. And people are also storing their own personal information on these devices. With a smartphone, your office *is* your phone. The upside is that you now have access to all of the resources you need to work effectively. The downside is that now you have your office in your pocket, and so it can become very hard to leave the office behind (or deal with the consequences if it is stolen or lost). Organizations now often expect you to **bring your own device (BYOD)** to work. Balancing personal and professional lives is an increasingly important concern for business professionals.

MIS in Use, on page 211, outlines how some students have found business opportunities using networks. However, it is important to remember that although computer networks are important, human networks are even more important. Take some time to read the exercise "Human Networks Matter More" at the end of this chapter on pages 214–215 to gain insight into the importance of the human network you are building.

A Word of Caution

Have you ever misplaced your smartphone, even just for an hour or two? If so, you probably recall the wave of panic that sets in as you imagine it might be gone forever. Losing any digital device can be extremely troubling for a number of reasons. First, mobile devices and laptops are not cheap. The thought of spending hundreds (sometimes thousands) of dollars to replace the lost device is distressing. However, what often is often most disconcerting is the thought of the person now in possession of your device finding a way to access all of your data.

If you were to lose a digital device, what data would you be most concerned about—banking data, email archives, social media accounts, your collection of photos, or something else? There is no right or wrong answer to this question as responses will vary from person to person. However, there is a high probability that in the future someone could access your personal data. The frustrating part is that in most cases, the culprits will not even need physical access to your smartphone or laptop.

Despite the explosive growth in network technologies and the benefits of cloud computing, astute students are reminded that all change has both positive and negative consequences and the reality of technology can sometimes be a fraction of its promise. As the tragic cases of Amanda Todd and Rehtaeh Parsons illustrate, social networks can amplify bullying and enable criminal activity to take place over great distance. Furthermore, networks require expensive and hard to change infrastructure that tends to favour dense population over remote geography. This means that while bandwidth in urban centres is fuelled by the demands of Netflix and YouTube, significant gaps and intermittent connections can exist and that being always connected regardless of location remains much more of an idea than a reality. Network technology can create barriers between people with access and those without.

Students John Boxall and Igor Faletski have not added up how many hours they have spent waiting for the bus, nor have they counted the number of buses they have missed. But during their four years at Simon Fraser University's Burnaby campus, they spent a considerable amount of time commuting. They knew there had to be a better way. The problem was that to know when a bus was coming, you had to know the location of every bus stop and either have a copy of every bus schedule or be connected to the Internet—neither of which was very practical.

Not content to simply complain, John and Igor decided to take matters into their own hands. Although they realized that they could quickly assemble a Java-based application that would enable them to browse the transit website, they also knew that the number of students with a compatible unlocked handset and a low-cost data plan was below 1 percent. Instead, they realized that text messaging covered the majority of cellphone users and did not require any special configuration. More importantly, the population that sent the most number of text messages, teenagers and young adults, was also one of the biggest users of public transit.

Connecting with TransLink, the Greater Vancouver Transportation Authority's website, and using each bus stop's unique five-digit numerical ID, they built a system they named MyBus. Using the university's existing access to a text messaging application programming interface (API), MyBus parses text messages, retrieves bus information, and sends the results back in a properly formatted text message. Of course, this requires that riders first know the bus stop number, but even this was solved through the use of aliases created for the most popular stops and posted on the website.

The system worked well. With minimal advertising, it received more than 200 requests during the first three-week trial, and some students began to use it on a regular basis. MyBus received coverage in the local media, and John and Igor were soon invited to present it to the transit authority, which had been developing its own version.

Keeping in mind Alfred Sloan's admonishment that there is no resting place for competition, Igor and John continue to refine, improve, and extend the system. Working with Peter McLachlan, a Ph.D. student at the University of British Columbia, they have recently developed a Facebook version of the application, and with input from a few faculty members and advisers, they have formed a corporation to commercialize the technology.

QUESTIONS

1. What problem does MyBus solve?
2. How important was access to the Translink website and the text messaging API?
3. Does this system cooperate or compete with Translink?
4. What technological changes could affect John and Igor's efforts to commercialize MyBus?
5. What advice would you give John and Igor?

How Does the Knowledge in This Chapter Help You?

The cloud is the future of computing. Knowing what the cloud is, how organizations can benefit from it, and understanding the important security issues when using the cloud is advantageous to business professionals. Knowledge of the cloud will also help you anticipate new categories of jobs that you might find rewarding. Finally, cloud knowledge might also help you save your organization considerable amounts of money.

ACTIVE REVIEW

Use this Active Review to verify that you have understood the material in the chapter. You can read the entire chapter and then perform the tasks in this review, or you can read the material for just one question and perform the tasks for that question before moving on to the next one.

Q6-1 WHY SHOULD I CARE ABOUT NETWORKS?

Identify and think about all the computer networks you have used today. Did you buy gas? Withdraw money from an ATM? Search the Web? Consider how your day might have changed if you did not have access to these networks. Now, think about networks you used to collaborate. Did you check email? Text someone on your cellphone?

Instant message anyone? Does the ability to use these network technologies make you a more effective, and valuable, employee?

Q6-2 WHAT IS A COMPUTER NETWORK?

Define *computer network*. Explain the differences among LANs, WANs, internets, and the Internet. Describe the purpose of a protocol.

Q6-3 WHY IS THE CLOUD THE FUTURE FOR MOST ORGANIZATIONS?

Define *cloud* and explain the three key terms in your definition. Using Figure 6-5 as a guide, compare and contrast cloud-based and in-house hosting. Explain three factors that make cloud computing possible today. Explain the meaning of the terms *SOA, Web service standards,* and *Web services.* When does it not make sense to use a cloud-based infrastructure?

Q6-4 HOW DO ORGANIZATIONS USE THE CLOUD?

Define *SaaS, PaaS,* and *IaaS.* Provide an example of each. For each, describe the business situation in which it would be the most appropriate option. Define *CDN* and explain the purpose and advantages of a CDN. Explain how Web services can be used internally.

Q6-5 HOW CAN ORGANIZATIONS USE CLOUD SERVICES SECURELY?

Explain the purpose of a VPN and describe, in broad terms, how a VPN works. Define the term *virtual* and explain how it relates to VPN. Define *private cloud.* Summarize why the benefits of a private cloud are questionable. What kind of organization might benefit from such a cloud? Explain why it is unlikely that even very large organizations can create private clouds that compete with public cloud utilities. Under what circumstance might a private cloud make sense for an organization? Define *VPC* and explain how and why an organization might use one.

Q6-6 WHAT DOES THE CLOUD MEAN FOR YOUR FUTURE?

What is the likely future of the cloud? Summarize the good and bad news that the cloud brings. Explain why the photo in Figure 6-4 is disturbing. Explain the statement "The cloud lifts all boats." Describe three categories of remote action systems. Explain how remote systems will increase the value of super-experts but diminish local mediocrity. What can other-than-super-experts do?

Q6-7 HOW IS MOBILE COMPUTING CHANGING THE WAY WE WORK AND LIVE?

What are the important trends in computing and the three different types of devices? What is BYOD, and what organizational issues does it create?

MyLab MIS

MyLab MIS is an online learning and testing environment that features the perfect study tools to help you master the concepts covered in this chapter. Log in to MyLab to test your knowledge of key chapter concepts and explore additional practice tools, including videos, flashcards, and more!

KEY TERMS AND CONCEPTS

USING YOUR KNOWLEDGE

6-1. Define *cloud* and explain the three key terms in your definition. Compare and contrast cloud-based and in-house hosting using the comparison presented in Q6-1 as a guide. In your opinion, explain the three most important factors that make cloud-based hosting preferable to in-house hosting.

6-2. Apple invested more than $1B in a North Carolina data centre. For Apple to spend such a sum, it must perceive the iCloud as being a key component of its future. Using the principles discussed in Q3-2 of Chapter 3, explain all the ways that you believe the iCloud will give Apple a competitive advantage over other mobile device vendors.

6-3. Suppose you work at Falcon Security and Joni tells you she does not believe that cheap, elastic data storage is possible. "There has to be a catch somewhere," she says. Write a one-page memo to her explaining how the cloud works. In your memo, include the role of standards for cloud processing.

6-4. Changing technology has, for centuries, eliminated the need for certain products and services and created the need for new products and services. What is exciting is the rapid pace at which new technology is being created and adapted. Using cloud services as an example, create a statement about the posture that business professionals should take with regard to technology in order to thrive in this fast-changing environment. Notice the verb in this assignment is *thrive*, and not just *survive*.

COLLABORATIVE EXERCISES

Collaborate with a group of students on the following exercises. Have your team choose one of the hardware/software topics listed in question 2. Use the Internet and other resources to research the topic and do the following:

Collaborative Question

The cloud is causing monumental changes in the information systems services industry. In every city, you will still see the trucks of local independent software vendors (ISVs) driving to their clients to set up and maintain local area networks, servers, and software. You will know the trucks by the Microsoft, Oracle, and Cisco logos on their sides. For years, those small, local companies have survived, some very profitably, on their ability to set up and maintain LANs, connect user computers to the Internet, set up servers, sell Microsoft Exchange licenses, and install other software on both servers and user computers.

Once everything is installed, these companies continue to earn revenue by providing maintenance for problems that inevitably develop and support for new versions of software, connecting new user computers, and so forth. Their customers vary, but are generally smaller companies of 3 to 50 employees—companies that are large enough to need email, Internet connections, and possibly some entry-level software applications such as QuickBooks.

1. Using the knowledge of this chapter and the intuition of the members of your team, summarize the threats that cloud services present to such ISVs.

2. Suppose your team owns and manages one of these ISVs. You learn that more and more of your clients are choosing SaaS cloud services like Google for email, rather than setting up local email servers.

    a. What, if anything, can you do to prevent the encroachment of SaaS on your business?

    b. Given your answer to part a, identify three alternative ways you can respond.

MyLab MIS

Visit MyLab MIS to access the data files to complete these questions.

WHAT DO YOU THINK?

HUMAN NETWORKS MATTER MORE

Six Degrees of *Separation* is a play by John Guare that was made into a movie starring Stockard Channing, Donald Sutherland, and Will Smith. The title is related to the idea, originated by the Hungarian writer Frigyes Karinthy, that everyone on Earth is connected to everyone else by five (Karinthy) or six (Guare) people.[*] For example, according to this theory, you are connected to, say, Eminem by no more than five or six people because you know someone who knows someone, who knows someone . . . and so on. By the same theory, you are also connected to a Siberian seal hunter. With the Internet, the number may in fact be closer to three people than five or six, but in any case, the theory points out the importance of human networks.

Suppose you want to meet your university's president. The president has a secretary who acts as a gatekeeper. If you walk up to that secretary and say, "I'd like a half-hour with President Jones," you are likely to be palmed off on some other university administrator. What else can you do?

If you are connected to everyone on the planet by no more than six degrees, then surely you are connected to your president in fewer steps. Perhaps you play on the tennis team, and you know that the president plays tennis. In that case, it is likely that the tennis coach knows the president. So, arrange a tennis match with your coach and the president. Voilà! You have your meeting. It may even be better to have the meeting on the tennis court than in the president's office.

The problem with the six-degree theory, as Stockard Channing said so eloquently, is that even though those six people do exist, we do not know who they are. Even worse, we often do not know who the person is with whom we want to connect. For example, there is someone right now who knows someone who has a job for which you are perfectly suited. Unfortunately, you do not know the name of that person.

It does not stop when you get your job, either. When you have a problem at work, for example, setting up a blog within the corporate network, there is someone who knows exactly how to help you. You, however, do not know who that person is.

Accordingly, most successful professionals consistently build personal human networks. They keep building them because they know that somewhere there is someone whom they need to know or will need to know. They meet people in professional and social situations, collect and pass out cards, and engage in pleasant conversation (all part of a social protocol) to expand their networks.

You can apply some of the ideas about computer networks to make this process more efficient. Consider it as a type of network diagram. Assume that each line represents a relationship between two people. Note that the people in your department tend to know each other and that the people in the accounting department also tend to know each other. That is typical.

Now, suppose you are at the weekly employee afterhours party and you have an opportunity to introduce yourself either to Linda or Eileen. Setting aside personal considerations and thinking just about network building, which person should you meet?

If you introduce yourself to Linda, you shorten your pathway to her from two steps to one and your pathway to Shawna from three to two. You do not open up any new channels because you already have channels to the people on your floor.

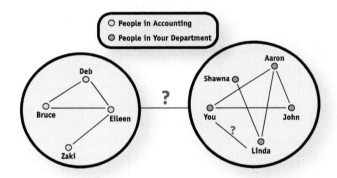

However, if you introduce yourself to Eileen, you open up an entirely new network of acquaintances. So, considering just network building, you use your time better by meeting Eileen and other people who are not part of your current circle. It opens up many more possibilities.

The connection from you to Eileen is called a *weak tie* in social network theory,[**] and such links are crucial in connecting you to everyone in six degrees. *In general, the people you know the least contribute the most to your network.*

This concept is simple, but you would be surprised how few people pay attention to it. At most company

---

[*] See "The third link" in Albert Laszlo Barabasi's book *Linked* (New York: Perseus Publishing, 2002), for background on this theory.

[**] See T. Granovetter, "The Strength of Weak Ties," *American Journal of Sociology*, May 1973, for more information.

events, everyone talks with the people they know—and if the purpose of the function is to have fun, then that behaviour makes sense. In truth, however, no business social function exists solely for having fun, regardless of what people say. Business functions exist for business reasons, and you can use them to create and expand networks. Given that time is always limited, you may as well use such functions efficiently.

Discussion Questions

1. Determine the shortest path from you to your university's president. How many links does it have?

2. Give an example of a network to which you belong and sketch a diagram of who knows whom for six or so members of that group.

3. Recall a recent social situation and identify two people, one of whom could have played the role of Linda (someone in your group whom you do not know) and one of whom could have played the role of Eileen (someone in a different group whom you do not know). How could you have introduced yourself to each person?

4. Does it seem too contrived and calculating to think about your social relationships in this way? Even if you do not approach relationships like this, are you surprised to think that others do? Under what circumstances does this kind of analysis seem appropriate, and when does it seem inappropriate? Are you using people?

5. Consider the phrase "It's not what you know, it's who you know that matters." Relate this phrase to a network diagram. Under what circumstances is this likely to be true? When is it false? When is it ethical?

6. Describe how you can apply the principle "the people you know the least contribute the most to your network" to the process of a job search. Are you abusing your relationships for personal advancement?

KNOWLEDGE EXTENSION 9

Chapter 6 provides the background for this extension.

Network and Cloud Technology

STUDY QUESTIONS

KE9-1   WHAT IS A COMPUTER NETWORK?

KE9-2   WHAT ARE THE COMPONENTS OF A LAN?

KE9-3   HOW DOES THE INTERNET WORK?

KE9-4   HOW DOES THE CLOUD WORK?

KE9-1 WHAT IS A COMPUTER NETWORK?

Before we can address how the cloud works, we need to discuss computer networks and the technology that underlies them. A computer **network** is a collection of computers that communicate with one another over transmission lines or wirelessly. As shown in Figure KE9-1, the four basic types of networks are personal area networks, local area networks, wide area networks, and internets.

A **personal area network (PAN)** connects devices located around a *single person*. Most PAN devices connect wirelessly to other devices located within 10 metres. A **local area network (LAN)** connects computers that reside in a single geographic location on the premises of the company that operates the LAN. The number of connected computers can range from two to several hundred. The distinguishing characteristic of a LAN is *a single location*. A **wide area network (WAN)** connects computers at different geographic locations. The computers in two separated company sites must be connected using a WAN. To illustrate, a smartwatch or fitness tracker will create a PAN by connecting to a student's smartphone. The computers for a college or university located on a single campus can be connected via a LAN. The computers for a college or university located on multiple campuses must be connected via a WAN.

The single- versus multiple-site distinction between LANs and WANs is important. With a LAN, an organization can place communications lines wherever it wants because all lines reside on its premises. The same is not true for a WAN. A company with offices in Chicago and Atlanta cannot run a wire down the freeway to connect computers in the two cities. Instead, the company contracts with a communications vendor that is licenced by the government and that already has lines or has the authority to run new lines between the two cities.

An **internet** is a network of networks. Internets connect LANs, WANs, and other internets. The most famous Internet is **"the Internet"** (with an uppercase letter *I*), the collection of networks that you use when you send email or access a website. In addition to the Internet, private networks of networks, called *internets*, also exist. A private internet that is used exclusively within an organization is sometimes called an **intranet**.

The networks that comprise an internet use a large variety of communication methods and conventions, and data must flow seamlessly across them. To provide seamless flow, an

Type	Characteristic
Personal Area Network (PAN)	Devices connected around a single person
Local area network (LAN)	Computers connected at a single physical site
Wide area network (WAN)	Computers connected between two or more separated sites
The Internet and internets	Networks of networks

Figure KE9-1 Basic Network Types

elaborate scheme called a *layered protocol* is used. The details of protocols are beyond the scope of this text. Just understand that a **protocol** is a set of rules that programs on two communicating devices follow.

Computers use protocols to exchange data. People use similar protocols to communicate. People, for example, follow a conversational protocol that says when one person talks, the other person listens. They switch back and forth until they are done communicating. Without a protocol for conversations people would continually talk over each other and nothing would be communicated.

There are many different protocols; some are used for PANs, some are used for LANs, some are used for WANs, some are used for internets and the Internet, and some are used for all of these. We will identify several common protocols in this Knowledge Extension.

KE9-2 WHAT ARE THE COMPONENTS OF A LAN?

As stated, a LAN is a group of computers connected together on a single site. Usually the computers are located within a half-mile or so of each other. The key distinction, however, is that all of the computers are located on property controlled by the organization that operates the LAN. This means that the organization can run cables wherever needed to connect the computers.

Figure KE9-2 shows a LANs typical of those in a **small office or a home office (SOHO)**. Typically, such LANs have fewer than a dozen or so computers and printers. Many businesses, of course, operate LANs much larger than this one. The principles are the same for a larger LAN, but the additional complexity is beyond the scope of this text.

The computers and printers in Figure KE9-2 communicate via a mixture of wired and wireless connections. Some devices use wired connections, and others use wireless connections. The devices and protocols used differ for wired and wireless connectivity.

The Institute for Electrical and Electronics Engineers (IEEE, pronounced "I triple E") sponsors committees that create and publish protocols and other standards. The committee that addresses LAN standards is called the *IEEE 802 Committee*. Thus, IEEE LAN protocols always start with the numbers 802.

The **IEEE 802.3 protocol** is used for wired LAN connections. This protocol standard, also called the **Ethernet**, specifies hardware characteristics, such as which wire carries which signals. It also describes how messages are to be packaged and processed for wired transmission over the LAN.

Most personal computers support what is called **10/100/1000 Ethernet**. These products conform to the 802.3 specification and allow for transmission at a rate of 10, 100, or 1000 Mbps (megabits per second). Switches detect the speed that a given device can handle and communicate with it at that speed. If you check computer listings at Dell, Lenovo, and other manufacturers, you will see PCs advertised as having 10/100/1000 Ethernet. Currently speeds of up to 1 Gbps are possible on wired LANs.

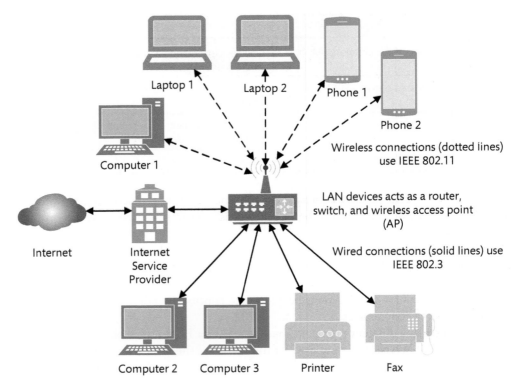

Figure KE9-2 Typical Small Office/Home Office

The abbreviations used for communications speeds differ from those used for computer memory. For communications equipment, *K* stands for 1000, not 1024 as it does for memory. Similarly, M stands for 1 000 000, not 1024 × 1024; G stands for 1 000 000 000, not 1024 × 1024 × 1024. Thus, 100 Mbps is 100 000 000 bits per second.

Also, communications speeds are expressed in *bits*, whereas memory sizes are expressed in *bytes*. These are different units of measurement. One byte consists of eight bits. This means a 1 MB file would consist of 8 388 608 bits. If you sent a 1 MB file over a 1 Mbps connection, it would take more than 8 seconds to send because your connection speed is measured in bits per second, not bytes per second.

Wireless LAN connections use the **IEEE 802.11 protocol**. Several versions of 802.11 exist, and as of 2015, the most current one is IEEE 802.11ac. The differences among these versions are beyond the scope of this discussion. Just note that the current standard, 802.11ac, allows speeds of up to 1.3Gps.

Bluetooth is another common wireless protocol used to make PAN connections. It is designed for transmitting data over short distances, replacing cables. Devices, such as wireless mice, keyboards, printers, and headphones, use Bluetooth to connect to desktop computers. Other devices like smartwatches and fitness trackers can use Bluetooth to connect to smartphones and send data over the Internet. More and more devices like clothing, automobiles, and sports equipment are becoming Bluetooth enabled.

Connecting your LAN to the Internet

Although you may not have realized it, when you connect your SOHO LAN, phone, iPad, or Kindle to the Internet, you are connecting to a WAN. You must do so because you are connecting to computers that are not physically located on your premises. You cannot start running wires down the street to plug in somewhere.

When you connect to the Internet, you are actually connecting to an **Internet service provider (ISP)**. An ISP has three important functions. First, it provides you with a legitimate Internet address. Second, it serves as your gateway to the Internet. The ISP receives the communications from your computer and passes them on to the Internet, and it receives communications from the Internet and passes them on to you. Finally, ISPs pay for the Internet. They collect money from their customers and pay access fees and other charges on your behalf.

Figure KE9-3 shows the three common alternatives for connecting to the Internet. Notice that we are discussing how your computer connects to the Internet via a WAN; we are not discussing the structure of the WAN itself. WAN architectures and their protocols are beyond the scope of this text. Search the Web for *leased lines* or *PSDN* if you want to learn more about WAN architectures.

Type	Topology	Transmission Line	Transmission Speed	Equipment Used	Protocol Commonly Used	Remarks
Local area network	Local area network	UTP or optical fiber	Common: 10/100/1000 Mbps Possible: 1 Gbps	Switch NIC UTP or optical	IEEE 802.3 (Ethernet)	Switches connect devices, multiple switches on all but small LANs.
	Local area network with wireless	UTP or optical for non-wireless connections	802.11n up to 600 Mbps, 802.11ac approx. 2–5 Gbps	Wireless access point Wireless NIC	IEEE 802.11n with 802.11ac becoming more popular	Access point transforms wired LAN (802.3) to wireless LAN (802.11).
Connections to the Internet	DSL modem to ISP	DSL telephone	Personal: Upstream to 1 Mbps, downstream to 40 Mbps (max 10 likely in most areas)	DSL modem DSL-capable telephone line	DSL	Can have computer and phone use simultaneously. Always connected.
	Cable modem to ISP	Cable TV lines to optical cable	Upstream to 1 Mbps Downstream 300 Kbps to 10 Mbps	Cable modem Cable TV cable	Cable	Capacity is shared with other sites; performance varies depending on other's use.
	WAN wireless	Wireless connection to WAN	500 Kbps to 1.7 Mbps	Wireless WAN modem	One of several wireless standards	Sophisticated protocol enables several devices to use the same wireless frequency.

Figure KE9-3   Office (SOHO) LAN

SOHO LANs (see Figure KE9-2) and individual home and office computers are commonly connected to an ISP in one of three ways: a special telephone line called a *DSL line*, a *cable TV line*, or a *wireless-phone-like connection*.

Digital Subscriber Line (DSL)   A **digital subscriber line (DSL)** operates on the same lines as voice telephones, but it operates so it does not interfere with voice telephone service. Because DSL signals do not interfere with telephone signals, DSL data transmission and telephone conversations can occur simultaneously. A device at the telephone company separates the phone signals from the computer signals and sends the latter signal to the ISP. Digital subscriber lines use their own protocols for data transmission.

Cable Line   A cable line is the second type of WAN connection. **Cable lines** provide high-speed data transmission using cable television lines. The cable company installs a fast, high-capacity optical fiber cable to a distribution centre in each neighborhood it serves. At the distribution centre, the optical fiber cable connects to regular cable-television cables that run to subscribers' homes or businesses. Cable signals do not interfere with TV signals.

Because up to 500 user sites can share these facilities, performance varies depending on how many other users are sending and receiving data. At the maximum, users can download data up to 50 Mbps and can upload data at 512 Kbps. Typically, performance is much lower than this. In most cases, the download speed of cable lines and DSL lines is about the same. Cable lines use their own protocols.

WAN Wireless Connection   A third way you can connect your computer, mobile device, or other communicating device is via a **WAN wireless** connection. *Amazon.com*'s Kindle, for example, uses a Sprint wireless network to provide wireless data connections. The iPhone uses a LAN-based wireless network if one is available and a WAN wireless network if not. The LAN-based network is preferred because performance is considerably higher. As of 2015, WAN wireless provides average performance of 1 Mbps, with peaks of up to 3.0 Mbps, as opposed to the typical 50 Mbps for LAN wireless.

KE9-3 HOW DOES THE INTERNET WORK?

The technology that underlies the Internet and the additional technology that enables the cloud to work are complicated. Here we will stay at a high level and help you learn overarching concepts and basic definitions. We begin with a simple example.

An Internet Example

Figure KE9-4 illustrates one use of the Internet. Suppose you are sitting in snowbound Minneapolis, and you want to communicate with a hotel in sunny, tropical northern New Zealand. Maybe you are making a reservation using the hotel's website, or maybe you are sending an email to a reservations clerk inquiring about facilities or services.

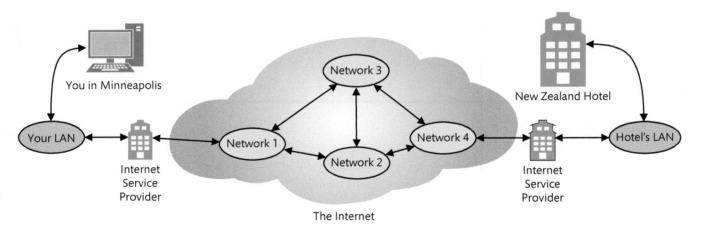

Figure KE9-4   Using the Internet for a Hotel Reservation

To begin, note that this example is an internet because it is a network of networks. It consists of two LANs (yours and the hotel's) and four networks. (In truth, the real Internet consists of tens of thousands of networks, but to conserve paper we do not show all of them.) A **hop** is the movement from one network to another. As shown, in Figure KE9-4, the shortest path from you to the hotel's LAN consists of four hops. By the way, this term is frequently used by CDN vendors when they discuss provisioning servers to minimize the number of hops.

Carriers and Net Neutrality

As your message, or **packet**, moves across the Internet, it passes through networks owned by large telecommunication providers known as **carriers**. Some of these large carriers include Sprint, AT&T, Verizon Business, and XO Communications. These large carriers exchange traffic freely via **peering** agreements without charging each other access fees. Carriers earn revenue by collecting subscription fees from end users, but not peers.

The problem with peering is that some people use more bandwidth than others. Netflix, for example, accounts for about 33 percent of all Internet traffic in North America between 9:00 P.M. and 12:00 A.M. Carriers argue that they should be able to charge varying rates based on content, application, or the user requesting the data.[1]

Netflix, eBay, Yahoo!, and *Amazon.com* say this could hurt consumers and innovation. They believe in the **net neutrality** principle where all data is treated equally. They argue that carriers should not be allowed to decide which sites load quickly, which apps are allowed on a network, and which content is acceptable.

In 2015, the Federal Communications Commission (FCC) "in the U.S." approved new net neutrality regulations ensuring ISPs cannot discriminate between different types of Internet traffic. This means all consumers have access to content on an equal basis. This ruling in many ways renders the Internet a utility like water or electricity that would be governed by comparable regulations. Several large carriers have already begun fighting these new regulations in court.

Internet Addressing

Just like regular surface mail, every location on the Internet needs an address. For reasons beyond this discussion, an Internet address is called an **IP address**, which is a number that identifies a particular device. **Public IP addresses** identify a particular device on the public Internet. In order to get on the Internet every device must have access to a public IP address. Because public IP addresses must be unique worldwide, their assignment is controlled by a public agency known as **ICANN (Internet Corporation for Assigned Names and Numbers)**.

Private IP addresses identify a particular device on a private network, usually on a LAN. Their assignment is controlled within the LAN, usually by the LAN device shown in Figure KE9-2. When you sign on to a LAN at a coffee shop, for example, the LAN device loans you a private IP address to use while you are connected to the LAN. When you leave the LAN, it reuses that address.

Use of Private IP Addresses   When your computer accesses a public site, say, *www. pearsonhighered.com*, from within a LAN at a coffee shop, your traffic uses your private IP address until it gets to the LAN device. At that point, the LAN device substitutes your private IP address with its public IP address and sends your traffic out onto the public Internet.

This private/public IP address arrangement has two major benefits. First, public IP addresses are conserved. All of the computers on the LAN use only one public IP address. Second, by using private IP addresses, you are protected from attackers directly attacking you because they cannot send attack packets to private IP addresses. They can only send packets to devices with public IP addresses.

Public IP Addresses and Domain Names   IP addresses have two formats. The most common form, called **IPv4**, has a four-decimal dotted notation such as 165.193.123.253; the second, called **IPv6**, has a longer format and will not concern us here. In your browser, if you enter *http://165.193.140.14*, your browser will connect with the device on the public Internet that has been assigned to this address.

---

[1] Don Reisinger, "Netflix Gobbles a Third of Peak Internet Traffic in North America," *CNET*, November 7, 2012, accessed June 6, 2014, *www.cnet.com/news/netflix-gobbles-a-third-of-peak-internet-traffic-in-north-america*.

Nobody wants to type IP addresses such as *http://165.193.140.14* to find a particular site. Instead, we want to enter names such as *www.pandora.com* or *www.woot.com* or *www.pearsonhighered.com*. To facilitate that desire, ICANN administers a system for assigning names to IP addresses. First, a **domain name** is a worldwide-unique name that is affiliated with a public IP address. When an organization or individual wants to register a domain name, it goes to a company that applies to an ICANN-approved agency to do so. GoDaddy (*www.godaddy.com*) is an example of such a company (Figure KE9-5).

Figure KE9-5 GoDaddy Screenshot

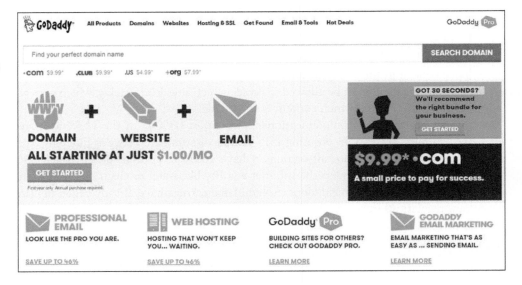

GoDaddy or a similar agency will first determine if the desired name is unique worldwide. If so, it will apply to register that name to the applicant. Once the registration is completed, the applicant can affiliate a public IP address with the domain name. From that point onward, traffic for the new domain name will be routed to the affiliated IP address.

Note two important points: First, several (or many) domain names can point to the same IP address. Second, the affiliation of domain names with IP addresses is dynamic. The owner of the domain name can change the affiliated IP addresses at its discretion.

In 2014, the U.S. Department of Commerce announced that it was giving up oversight over ICANN. Critics worry that countries might now try to force ICANN to disallow domain names for dissident groups, thereby kicking them off the Internet. It is still unclear how ICANN will be governed.

Before we leave addressing, you need to know one more term. A **URL (Uniform Resource Locator)** is an address on the Internet. Commonly, it consists of a protocol (such as http:// or ftp://) followed by a domain name or public IP address. A URL is actually quite a bit more complicated than this description, but that detailed knowledge is beyond the scope of this text. The preferred pronunciation of URL is to say the letters *U, R, L*.

Processing on a Web Server

At this point, you know basic networking terms and have a high-level view of how the Internet works. To understand the value of the cloud, how it works, and how your organization can use it, you need to know a bit about the processing that occurs on a Web server. For this discussion, we will use the example of a Web storefront, which is a server on the Web from which you can buy products.

Suppose you want to buy an item from zulily, a private buyer's site that sells clothing. To do so, you go to *www.zulily.com* and navigate to the product(s) you want to buy (see Figure KE9-6). When you find something you want, you add it to your shopping cart and

Figure KE9-6 Sample of Commerce Server Pages; Product Offer Pages

Source: Retrieved from *www.zulily.com*.

keep shopping. At some point, you check out by supplying payment data (credit card, Pay-Pal, etc.,). But what happens when your order data arrives at the server?

Three-Tier Architecture   Almost all Web applications use the **three-tier architecture**, which is a design of user computers and servers that consists of three categories, or tiers, as shown in Figure KE9-7. The **user tier** consists of computers, phones, and other mobile devices that have browsers that request and process webpages. The **server tier** consists of computers that run Web servers and process application programs. The **database tier** consists of computers that run a DBMS that processes requests to retrieve and store data.

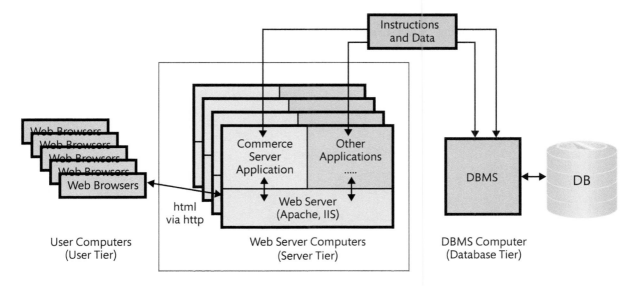

Figure KE9-7   Three-Tier Architecture

Figure KE9-7 shows only one computer at the database tier. Some sites have multicomputer database tiers as well.

When you enter *www.zulily.com* in your browser, the browser sends a request that travels over the Internet to a computer in the server tier at the zulily site. In response to your request, a server-tier computer sends back a **webpage**, which is a document coded in, usually, html (and, as discussed in Chapter 4, probably includes css, JavaScript, and other data).

Web servers are programs that run on a server-tier computer and manage traffic by sending and receiving webpages to and from clients. A **commerce server** is an application program that runs on a server-tier computer. Typical commerce server functions are to obtain product data from a database, manage the items in a shopping cart, and coordinate the checkout process. When a request comes to the server, the Web server examines it and sends it to the proper program for processing. Thus, the Web server passes e-commerce traffic to the commerce server. It passes requests for other applications to those applications. In Figure KE9-7, the server-tier computers are running a Web server program, a commerce server application, and other applications having an unspecified purpose.

KE9-4 HOW DOES THE CLOUD WORK?

In Chapter 6, Mateo and Joni are flabbergasted at the low cost of the cloud. They doubt that it is real. They would be less cautious if they understood how the cloud operates. This section will give you the basic understanding that they lack and enable you to be an effective consumer of cloud services.

Service-Oriented Architecture (SOA)

As stated in Chapter 6, the cloud would be impossible without a design philosophy called the **service-oriented architecture (SOA)**. According to this philosophy, all interactions among computing devices are defined as services in a formal, standardized way. This philosophy enables all the pieces of the cloud to fit together, as you will see. However, understanding SOA (pronounced "SO-ah") in depth requires you to learn more computer science than you need as a business professional. So, the best way for you to understand SOA is via a business analogy.

A SOA Analogy   Figure KE9-8 shows an arrangement of departments at a hypothetical online bicycle part retailer named Best Bikes. The Sales Department receives orders and follows a process to have them approved for shipping. On request, the Credit Department verifies customer credit as needed to approve orders, and the Inventory Department verifies the availability of the inventory needed to fulfill an order.

Figure KE9-8 Approval Request Interactions Among Three Departments

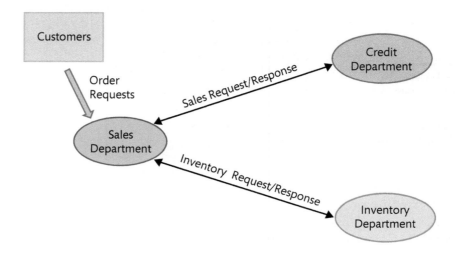

In an informal, non-SOA-type organization, one salesperson would contact someone he or she knows in Credit and ask something like "Can you approve an allocation of $10 000 of credit to the ABC Bicycle Company?" In response, the Credit person might say, "Sure," and the salesperson might note the name of the person who approved the amount. Some days, he or she might remember to record the date; other days, not so. Another salesperson might do something else, say, contact a different person whom he or she knows in Credit and ask something like, "I need $5000 in credit for Order 12345," and that other person in Credit might say, "I don't know, send the order over, and if I can, I'll write 'Approved' on it." Other irregular but similar interactions could occur between the Sales and the Inventory departments.

Such operations are definitely *not* service-oriented. People are asking for credit verification in different ways and receiving responses in different ways. The process for approving an order varies from salesperson to salesperson and possibly from day to day with the same salesperson. The records of approvals are inconsistent. Such an organization will have varying levels of process quality and inconsistent results, and should the company decide to open a facility in another city, these operations cannot be readily duplicated, nor should they be.

Using SOA principles, each department would formally define the services it provides. Examples are:

For the Credit Department:

- CheckCustomerCredit
- ApproveCustomerCredit

For the Inventory Department:

- VerifyInventoryAmount
- AllocateInventory
- ReleaseAllocatedInventory

Further, for each service, each department would formally state the data it expects to receive with the request and the data it promises to return in response. Every interaction is done exactly the same way. There is no personal contact between certain people in the departments; no salesperson need know who works in Credit or Inventory. Instead, requests are emailed to a generic email address in Credit or Inventory, and those departments decide who will process the request and how it will be processed. No department has or need have any knowledge of who works in another department, nor how the department accomplishes its work. Each department is free to change personnel task assignments and to change the way it performs its services, and no other department needs to know that a change occurred. In SOA terms, we would say the work of the department is **encapsulated** in the department.

With this organization, if Best Bikes wants to add another Inventory Department in another city, it can do so and no salesperson need change the way he or she sets up, submits, or receives responses to requests. Sales continues to send a VerifyInventoryAmount service request, formatted in the standard way, to the same email address.

With multiple sites, the Inventory function would change the way it implements service requests to first identify which of the several Inventory Departments should process the request. Sales would not know, nor need to know, this happened. Best Bikes could dynamically create 1000 Inventory Departments and the Sales Department need not change anything it does. Later, it could reduce those 1000 Inventory Departments to three and, again, Sales need not make any change.

SOA for Three-Tier Architecture   From this discussion, you can see how SOA is used to enable cloud processing. The description and advantages and disadvantages of this analogy for SOA are the same for the cloud. Consider Figure KE9-9, which shows the three-tier

Figure KE9-9 SOA Principles Applied to Three-Tier Architecture

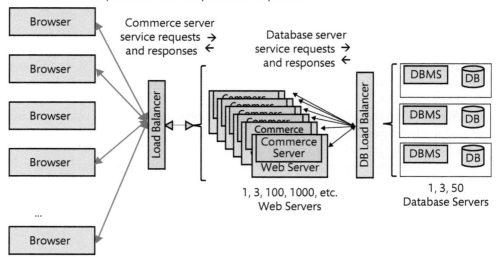

architecture with SOA drawn in. In this case, the commerce server application formally defines services that browsers can request, the data they must provide with the request, and the data that each will receive in response to the request. Sample services are:

- ObtainPartData
- ObtainPartImages
- ObtainPartQuantityOnHand
- OrderPart

Again each service also documents the data it expects and the data it will return.

Now, JavaScript (or another language) is written to invoke these services correctly. That JavaScript is included as part of the webpages the server sends to the browsers, and when users employ the browsers to purchase, the JavaScript behind the webpage invokes the services in the correct way.

The server tier can consist of three servers at 3 A.M., 3000 servers at 11 A.M., 6000 servers at 6 P.M., and 100 servers at 10 P.M. Furthermore, those servers can move around the world; at one time of day they can all be located in the United States, and at another time of day, they can all be located in Europe, and so on. Nothing, absolutely nothing, in the browsers need change as these servers are adjusted.

To take advantage of the multiple Web servers, a load balancing program receives requests and sends them to an available server. The load balancing program keeps data about the speed and health of all its assigned Web servers and allocates work to maximize throughput.

In addition, on the back end, SOA services are defined between the Web server and the database server. Accordingly, the database server need do nothing as the number and location of Web servers is adjusted. And that is a two-way street. Nothing in the Web servers need be changed if the number and location of database servers is adjusted. However, load balancing for database servers is considerably more complicated.

Do not infer from this discussion that SOA services and the cloud are only used for three-tier processing. Such services and the cloud are used for multitudes of applications across the Web. This three-tier application is just an example.

From this discussion, you can understand how cloud elasticity is possible. However, for many organizations to use the cloud and to be able to mix and match Web services, they need to agree on standard ways of formatting and processing service requests and data. That leads us to cloud standards and protocols. Again, we discuss these at a very high level.

Protocols Supporting Web Services

A protocol is a set of rules and data structures for organizing communication. Because the cloud's Web services use the Internet, the protocols that run the Internet also support cloud processing. We will start with them.

TCP/IP Protocol Architecture   The basic plumbing of the Internet is governed by protocols that are defined according to an arrangement called the **TCP/IP Protocol architecture**. This architecture has five layers; one or more protocols are defined at each layer. Data communications and software vendors write computer programs that implement the rules of a particular protocol. (For protocols at the bottom layer, the physical layer, they build hardware devices that implement the protocol.)

Internet Protocols: http, https, smtp, and ftp   The only Internet protocols that you as a business professional are likely to encounter are those at the top, or application, layer of the TCP/IP architecture, shown in Figure KE9-10. **Hypertext Transport Protocol (http)** is the protocol used between browsers and Web servers. When you use a browser such as Microsoft Edge, Safari, or Chrome, you are using a program that implements the http protocol. At the other end, at the New Zealand hotel mentioned earlier, for example, there is a server that also processes http. Even though your browser and the server at the hotel have never "met" before, they can communicate with one another because they both follow the rules of http. Similarly, in Figure KE9-9, the browsers send and receive service requests to and from the commerce server using http.

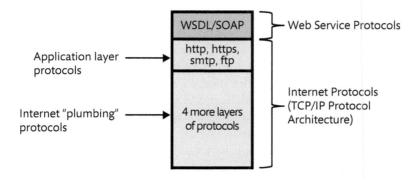

Figure KE9-10   Protocols That Support Web Services

As you will learn in Chapter 10, there is a secure version of http called **https**. Whenever you see *https* in your browser's address bar, you have a secure transmission, and you can safely send sensitive data like credit card numbers. When you are on the Internet, if you do not see *https*, then you should assume that all of your communication is open and could be published on the front page of your campus newspaper tomorrow morning. Hence, when you are using http, email, text messaging, chat, videoconferencing, or anything other than https, know that whatever you are typing or saying could be known by anyone else.

Two additional TCP/IP application-layer protocols are common. **Simple Mail Transfer Protocol, or smtp**, is used for email transmissions (along with other protocols). **File Transfer Protocol, or ftp**, is used to move files over the Internet. Google Drive and Microsoft OneDrive use ftp behind the scenes to transmit files to and from their cloud servers to your computer.

WSDL, SOAP, XML, and JSON   To wrap up the discussion, we will briefly consider four standards used extensively for Web services and the cloud. Those standards and their purpose are as follows:

WSDL (Web Services Description Language)	A standard for describing the services, inputs, outputs, and other data supported by a Web service. Documents coded according to this standard are machine readable and can be used by developer tools for creating programs to access the service.
SOAP (no longer an acronym)	A protocol for requesting Web services and for sending responses to Web service requests.
XML (eXtensible Markup Language)	A markup language used for transmitting documents. Contains much metadata that can be used to validate the format and completeness of the document, but includes considerable overhead (see Figure KE9-11a).
JSON (JavaScript Object Notation)	A markup language (such as html) used for transmitting documents. Contains little metadata and is preferred for transmitting volumes of data between servers and browsers. While the notation is the format of JavaScript objects, JSON documents can be processed by any language (see Figure KE9-11b).

Service authors (computer programmers) create WSDL documents to describe the services they provide and the inputs and outputs required. These WSDL documents are seldom read by humans; instead, developer tools like Microsoft Visual Studio read the WSDL and configure the programming environment so that the service will be properly used by developers who write programs to access that service.

As shown in Figure KE9-10, SOAP, which is not an acronym although it looks like one, is a protocol that sits on top of http and the lower-level Internet protocols. *Sits on top of* means that it uses http to send and receive SOAP messages. (SOAP can also use smtp.) Programs that use Web services issue SOAP messages to request services; the Web service uses SOAP messages to return responses to service requests.

Finally, XML and JSON are ways of marking up documents so that both the service requestor and the service provider know what data they are processing. Figure KE9-11 shows a simple example of both. As you can see, XML documents contain as much metadata as they do application data. These metadata are used to ensure the document is complete and properly formatted. XML is used when relatively few messages are being transmitted and when ensuring a complete and correct document is crucial. Both WSDLs and SOAP messages are coded in XML.

As its name indicates, JSON uses the notation that JavaScript uses to format object data. It has much less metadata and is preferred for the transmission of voluminous application data. Web servers use JSON as their primary way of sending application data to browsers.

Figure KE9-11a   Example
XML Document

```xml
<person>
    <firstName>Kelly</firstName>
    <lastName>Summers</lastName>
    <dob>12/28/1985</dob>
    <address>
        <streetAddress>309 Elm Avenue</streetAddress>
        <city>San Diego</city>
        <state>CA</state>
        <postalCode>98225</postalCode>
    </address>
    <phoneNumbers>
        <phoneNumber type="home">685 555-1234</phoneNumber>
        <phoneNumber type="cell">685 555-5678</phoneNumber>
    </phoneNumbers>
</person>
```

```
{
    "firstName": "Kelly",
    "lastName": "Summers",
    "dob": "12/28/1985",
    "address": {
        "streetAddress": "309 Elm Avenue",
        "city": "San Diego",
        "state": "CA",
        "postalCode": "98225"
    },
    "phoneNumber": [
        {
            "type": "home",
            "number": "685 555-1234"
        },
        {
            "type": "cell",
            "number": "685 555-5678"
        }
    ]
}
```

Figure KE9-11b Example JSON Document

With this technical background, you should no longer be skeptical that the benefits of the cloud are real. They are. However, this fact does not mean that every organization uses the cloud well. That is where you can define your career.

ACTIVE REVIEW

Use this Active Review to verify that you understand the ideas and concepts that answer this Knowledge Extension's study questions.

KE9-1 WHAT IS A COMPUTER NETWORK?

Define *computer network*. Explain the differences among PANs, LANs, WANs, internets, intranets, and the Internet.

KE9-2 WHAT ARE THE COMPONENTS OF A LAN?

Define *protocol* and explain the purpose of protocols. Explain the key distinction of a LAN. Describe the purpose of each component in Figure KE9-2. Define *IEEE 802.3* and *802.11* and explain how they differ. List three ways of connecting a LAN or computer to the Internet. Explain the nature of each.

KE9-3 HOW DOES THE INTERNET WORK?

Explain the statement "The Internet is an internet." Define *IP address* and explain the different ways that public and private IP addresses are used. Describe the purpose of a domain name and explain how such names are associated with public IP addresses. Explain the role of agencies like GoDaddy. Define *URL*. Define *three-tier architecture* and name and describe the role of each tier. Explain the role of each tier in Figure KE9-7 in the way that the page in Figure KE9-6 is processed.

KE9-4 HOW DOES THE CLOUD WORK?

Using the department analogy, define *SOA* and explain why departments are encapsulated. Summarize the advantages of using SOA in the three-tier architecture. Define *TCP/IP protocol architecture* and explain, in general terms, the purpose of http, https, smtp, and ftp. Define the purposes and roles of WSDL, SOAP, XML, and JSON. State a key difference between XML and JSON.

KEY TERMS AND CONCEPTS

10/100/1000 Ethernet 217
Bluetooth 218
Cable line 219
Carrier 221
Commerce server 224
Database tier 223
Digital subscriber line (DSL) 219
Domain name 222
Encapsulated 225
Ethernet 217
ftp (File Transfer Protocol) 227
Hop 220
http (Hypertext Transport Protocol) 227
https 227

ICANN (Internet Corporation for Assigned Names and Numbers) 221
IEEE 802.11 protocol 218
IEEE 802.3 protocol 217
Internet 216
Internet service provider (ISP) 219
Intranet 216
IP address 221
IPv4 221
IPv6 221
JSON (JavaScript Object Notation) 228
Local area network (LAN) 216

Net neutrality 221
Network 216
Packet 221
Personal area network (PAN) 216
Peering 221
Private IP address 221
Protocol 217
Public IP address 221
Server tier 223
Service-oriented architecture (SOA) 224
Small office/home office (SOHO) 217
smtp (Simple Mail Transfer Protocol) 227
SOAP 228

TCP/IP Protocol architecture 227
The Internet 216
Three-tier architecture 223
URL (Uniform Resource Locator) 222
User tier 223
WAN wireless 220
Webpage 224
Web servers 224
WSDL (Web Services Description Language) 228
Wide area network (WAN) 216
XML (eXtensible Markup Language) 228

USING YOUR KNOWLEDGE

KE9-1. Suppose you manage a group of seven employees in a small business. Each of your employees wants to be connected to the Internet. Consider two alternatives:

Alternative A: Each employee has his or her own device and connects individually to the Internet.

Alternative B: The employees' computers are connected using a LAN, and the network uses a single device to connect to the Internet.

a. Sketch the equipment and lines required for each alternative.

b. Explain the actions you need to take to create each alternative.

c. Which of these two alternatives do you recommend?

KE9-2. Suppose that you have a consulting practice implementing LANs for fraternities and sororities on your campus.

a. Consider a fraternity house. Explain how a LAN could be used to connect all of the computers in the house. Would you recommend an Ethernet LAN, an 802.11 LAN, or a combination? Justify your answer.

b. This Knowledge Extension did not provide enough information for you to determine how many switches the fraternity house might need. However, in general terms, describe how the fraternity could use a multiple-switch system.

c. Considering the connection to the Internet, would you recommend that the fraternity house use a DSL modem, a cable modem, or WAN wireless?

Although you can rule out at least one of these alternatives with the knowledge you already have, what additional information do you need in order to make a specific recommendation?

d. Should you develop a standard package solution for each of your customers? What advantages accrue from a standard solution? What are the disadvantages?

KE9-3. Suppose you own the business in question KE9-2 and you want to obtain a domain name. First, think of three suitable names for your business. Go to *GoDaddy.com* or another similar agency and determine if any of those names are still available. Choose other names if none of those are available and keep trying. Without buying anything, determine what is involved in obtaining that domain name. How much would it cost were you to do so?

MyLab MIS

Go to the Assignments section of your MyLab to complete these writing exercises.

KE9-1 Write a memo to Mateo and Joni at Falcon Security explaining SOA and the important Web service standards. In your memo, explain how the cloud would be impossible without SOA and the Web service standards. Describe a situation where Falcon Security could benefit from SOA.

KE9-2 Examine the documents at the end of KE9-4. Summarize differences in the ways that XML and JSON represent content. Which of these two standards would result in the most reliable processing? Which would be faster to transmit? Describe one good application for each standard.

PART 3

Using IS for Competitive Advantage

MIS in Action

In the previous six chapters, you gained a foundation of IS fundamentals. In Chapters 7–12, you will apply those fundamentals to learn how organizations use information systems to achieve their strategies. Part 3, Chapters 7–9, focuses on the application of IS; Part 4, Chapters 10–12, focuses on the management of IS.

Chapters 7–12 are introduced using a cloud-based, mobile application for the healthcare industry. To our knowledge, the system described here does not yet exist. However, it is entirely plausible, may be an excellent entrepreneurial opportunity, and features some of today's most exciting emerging technology in one of today's most important industries.

The figure on the next page shows the major actors involved in this system, which we will call Performance Recording, Integration, Delivery, and Evaluation (PRIDE). Using PRIDE, exercise workout data is collected from devices that conform to the ANT[1] protocol, which is a personal network communications protocol implemented by exercise equipment such as treadmills, stationary bikes, heart monitors, footpads, and the like. Using this protocol, data is transmitted from exercise devices to the Internet, either via a local area network or via a cell phone. That exercise data is then stored in a cloud database.

Once the data is stored in the cloud, individuals, healthcare professionals, health clubs, insurance companies, and employers can query and obtain exercise reports. Doctors can ensure that their patients are exercising neither too little nor too much;

[1] See *www.thisisant.com*.

health clubs can integrate exercise class data with personal exercise data; insurance companies can use the data to adjust policy rates for policy holders with healthy lifestyles; and employers can assess the effectiveness of investments they make into improving employee health.

A prototype of this system was developed by a cardiac surgeon, Dr. Romero Flores, for use in his practice. The system was popular and did help patients recover, at least as long as Flores was pushing it in his own practice. Flores had hoped to license this system to other doctors, but he had limited success.

Zev Friedman, one of Dr. Flores's patients, was one of the first to benefit from the PRIDE system. Friedman earned considerable wealth starting and selling small businesses over the past 30 years, and he liked what he experienced with PRIDE. So, during an office visit, Friedman asked how the system was being received. Knowing that Flores is a cardiologist and not a business professional, he was not surprised to learn that it was not getting very far. Friedman thought that with a refocus of its marketing and with experienced management, PRIDE could be a success. Accordingly, he bought the company for a small amount of cash and a royalty agreement with Flores. Using his business contacts, he then found and hired a new general manager, Jared Cooper, and a marketing professional, Nicki Jensen. He kept James Wu, who had been the technology manager under Flores. Jared subsequently hired Michele Russell as sales director.

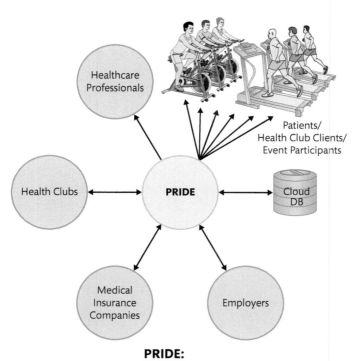

PRIDE:
Performance Recording, Integration, Display, and Evaluation

Organizations and Information Systems

MIS in Action

Zev Friedman, the owner of PRIDE Systems, Jared Cooper, general manager, Nicki Jensen, marketing professional, and James Wu, IS professional, are having an introductory meeting at Friedman's luxurious house on a Saturday morning.

After polite conversation, Zev gets down to business.

"Here's where Flores went wrong. Doctors don't care about exercise." Zev looks around the table as he speaks.

"They say they do." Nicki's not sure Zev will tolerate interruption, but it's not her style to sit back and listen.

"What people say and what they do are two different things. Doctors care about medicine, about operations. Some care most about *expensive* operations. If they cared about exercise, they'd own health clubs." Zev's tone is matter of fact; Nicki's interruption didn't bother him at all.

KE Chapter 7 optional knowledge extensions are

Knowledge Extension 10 Enterprise Resource Planning (ERP) Systems available in the MyLab MIS

Knowledge Extension 11 Supply Chain Management available in the MyLab MIS

"So we need to figure out who's got the pain and how much they'll pay." Jared, PRIDE Systems' new general manager, likes Zev's forthright manner.

"Right. Flores and his group demonstrated this thing works. You can use the cloud and all this exercise gear and mobile devices to collect, integrate, and report exercise data. So, who do we sell it to, and what do we tell 'em to induce them to buy?"

"I talked to a couple of insurance companies, and they're not promising." Jared looks at Zev.

"No? Why not?" Zev knows the answer, but he wants to see if Jared does.

"They don't like exercise. Exercise doesn't prevent disease. Well, maybe some cardiac diseases, and in the long term maybe some diabetes, but it doesn't do anything for cancer or Alzheimer's. The insurance companies think exercise just raises claims due to exercise-induced injury."

"You're kidding." Nicki can't believe what's she's hearing.

"Even worse, to them anyway, when you get in good shape you last longer when you do get cancer or whatever. So, you live longer on your way out the door, and their care expenses increase."

"I can't believe I'm hearing this!" Nicki says what she's been thinking.

"So, Zev, I'm wondering, you think there's any government money in this? Trudeau has a big push on both healthcare and innovation. Are there any Federal or Provincial funds we could tap?" Jared is looking right at Zev.

"Maybe. I'll ask some friends. That kind of money is slow to get, and the reporting requirements can be so painful it's not worth it. But I'll find out what I can learn. That won't help us immediately, though."

Q7-1 WHAT ARE THE FUNDAMENTAL WAYS OF ACHIEVING COMPETITIVE ADVANTAGE?

In Chapter 3, we looked at the ways in which organizations achieve a competitive advantage. We found that there are two basic ways to develop competitive advantage through systems. One way is to enhance the product or service through information systems. These changes enable organizations to differentiate themselves. An example of this kind of change is provided by Zipcar (www.zipcar.com), a car-sharing service available at more than 500 college and university campuses across North America and ten cities in Canada. Car sharing is a relatively new service that provides an alternative to buying or renting a car. Unlike traditional car rental agencies, Zipcar uses the Web and electronic card-reading technology to provide customers with access to short-term car rentals at a reasonable price.

Customers do not visit a Zipcar agency. Instead, they go to a parking garage, use their card to open the car, and then return the car to the garage. These services would not be reasonably priced without the information systems that support them. Zipcar, therefore, is a good example of a company that uses IS to introduce a new or enhanced service.

The second way of developing competitive advantage is through business processes. Organizations look to technology to help retain customers, reduce costs, and create entry barriers for competitors in the market. For example, Grand & Toy, Canada's largest commercial office-supply company (www.grandandtoy.com), has traditionally sold office supplies to organizations. In the last decade, however, the company has aggressively grown the list of services it offers through the Web. Website design and hosting, human resource management, and purchasing management are just a few of the professional services that Grand & Toy now offers. The information systems supporting these services help the company lock in their customers and create entry barriers for other office-supply companies.

The examples above demonstrate that information systems can affect competitive advantage by making the primary and support activities in an organization more productive than those of competitors. Increased productivity is realized when business processes within the organization become more effective, more efficient, or both. This is true for commercial companies as well as for nonprofit organizations and government. In this chapter, we look at the types of information systems that can be used to make organizations of all types more productive.

If you were to walk into any organization (say, your first employer), you would find a maze of different information systems. Some of the systems are designed to improve your personal productivity, such as Microsoft Office applications. Other systems, such as an accounts payable system, are designed to support business activities that relate to more than one person. The knowledge you derive from this chapter will help you to make sense out of that maze, to take a critical approach in identifying different kinds of information systems and what they do, and to understand how to help an organization achieve its competitive strategy.

Choosing the right information system may not be as easy as you think. Consider, for example, Bag Borrow or Steal Inc. (www.bagborroworsteal.com). This company uses Web systems to provide an online borrowing experience that gives its customers access to fashion accessories, such as handbags, jewellery, watches, and sunglasses, through rental agreements. To make a consistent profit, the company has to balance the resources it invests in marketing and customer relationship development, website applications, and online transaction processing, as well as purchasing, payroll, and operations. With a limited budget, which of these information systems would you invest more in, and which of these systems would contribute the most to the company's competitive advantage? These are the types of questions business professionals need to answer.

Q7-2 WHAT ARE BUSINESS FUNCTIONS AND FUNCTIONAL SYSTEMS?

We can use Porter's value chain model (introduced in Chapter 3) to explain the scope and purpose of different types of business functions within the organization. For our purposes, the value chain model will be more useful if we redraw it as shown in Figure 7-1. The value chain consists of two types of activities. **Primary activities** that, as the name implies, deal with the main or core parts of the good or service that the organization produces or provides and **support activities**, which are secondary or ancillary to the good or service that is produced. Determining whether an activity is primary or support will depend on the organization and what it produces. The value chain starts with marketing and sales activities, which are followed by inbound logistics, operations or manufacturing, outbound logistics, and, finally, service and support.

Organizational processes involve both primary and support activities, although for most organizations greater attention is paid to primary activities because these undertakings most often directly impact the customer. For example, a university may be more focused on its inbound logistics—how it manages student registration—than the human resource system used to manage the faculty and staff. The primary activities are facilitated by support activities: human resources, accounting and infrastructure, procurement, and technology. The primary activities of the value chain occur in the order shown in Figure 7-1. These primary and support activities are often referred to as *business functions*. These basic business functions (accounting, finance, human resources, marketing and sales, operations, procurement, etc.) are almost always present irrespective of the industry or organization.

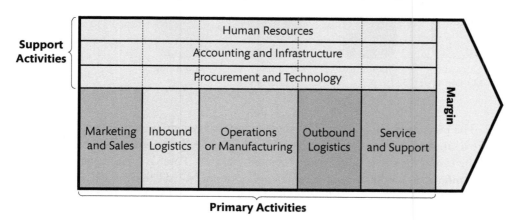

Figure 7-1 Reorganized Porter Value Chain Model

Source: Based on Michael E. Porter, *Competitive Advantage: Creating and Sustaining Superior Performance* (The Free Press, a Division of Simon & Schuster), Copyright © 1985, 1998.

These activities are often supported by what are called *functional systems*. **Functional systems** facilitate the work of a single department or business function. In each functional area, companies often add features and capabilities to information systems to support more functional-area activity. Figure 7-2 shows five functional systems and their relationship to the value chain. As you would expect, each functional system is closely allied with the activities it supports, and there is little crossover among activities.

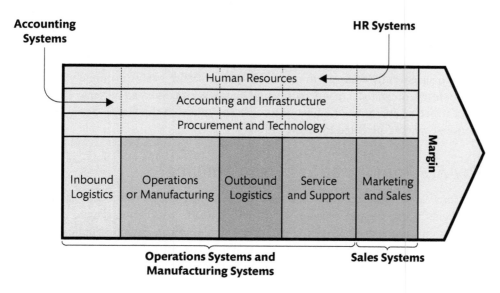

Figure 7-2 Reorganized Porter Value Chain Model and Its Relationship to Functional Systems

Source: Based on Michael E. Porter, *Competitive Advantage: Creating and Sustaining Superior Performance* (The Free Press, a Division of Simon & Schuster), Copyright © 1985, 1998.

Functional Silos and Cross-Functional Systems

The problem with functional applications is their isolation. In fact, these systems are sometimes called **functional silos** because they are designed to work independently. For example, the marketing department would do its work using the marketing and sales system.

The accounting department would use the general ledger and other accounting systems, and the operations department would work with a number of operational systems. The separation between systems makes it seem as if various departments in the same company could work separately, almost independently or in competition with each other. An example of functional silos is shown in Figure 7-3.

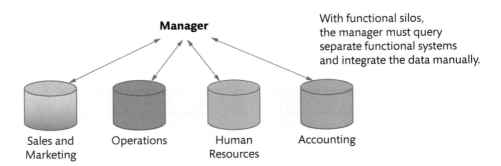

Manager

With functional silos, the manager must query separate functional systems and integrate the data manually.

Sales and Marketing   Operations   Human Resources   Accounting

Figure 7-3 Separate Functional Systems

The practical reality is that all of these functional systems are interrelated. When you make a sale to a customer, the rest of the company has to know what to deliver, the price, and the timing (point of sale, delivery of purchase, etc.). Purchasing influences inventory, which influences production, which influences customer satisfaction, which, in turn, influences future sales. All of these different functions are linked. Decisions that are appropriate when considering only a single business function, such as purchasing, may create inefficiencies when considering the entire business process. Business processes are cross-functional, that is, they are processes that cut across functional areas.

The isolation problems of functional systems led to the development of **cross-departmental** or **cross-functional systems**. These systems integrate data and business processes across different departments and systems. As cross-functional systems have become more sophisticated, some information systems have begun to cross not only functional boundaries but also organizational boundaries. These systems that are used by two or more related companies are referred to as **interorganizational systems**. The most common of these include supply chain management systems and some e-commerce applications. We will talk about supply chain management systems later in this chapter and in Chapter 8.

Most organizations today have a mixture of functional and integrated systems. In the future, to successfully compete internationally organizations must eventually achieve the efficiencies of integrated, cross-departmental, business process based systems. Thus, you can expect to see an increasing number of integrated systems in the future. Some examples of functional systems are listed in Figure 7-4.

Why Are Functional Systems Changing?

Functional systems provide tremendous benefits to the departments that use them, but these benefits are limited because the systems operate in isolation. Figure 7-5 lists the problems encountered with isolated functional systems. First, data are duplicated because each application has its own database. For example, customer data may be duplicated and possibly inconsistent when accounting and sales/marketing applications are separated. The principal problem of duplicated data is a potential lack of data integrity. Changes to product data made in one system may take days or weeks to reach the other systems. And during that period, inconsistent data will cause inconsistent application results.

Additionally, when systems are isolated, business processes become disjointed. There is no easy way for the sales/marketing system to integrate activity with the accounting system, for example. Just sending the data from one system to the other can be problematic.

Function	Examples of Information Systems
Marketing and sales	Product management Lead tracking Sales forecasting Customer management
Operations	Order entry Order management Inventory management Customer service
Manufacturing	Inventory Planning Scheduling Manufacturing operations
Human resources	Payroll and compensation Recruiting Assessment Development and training Human resources planning
Accounting and finance	General ledger Financial reporting Accounts receivable Accounts payable Cost accounting Budgeting Cash management Treasury management

Figure 7-4 Typical Functional Systems

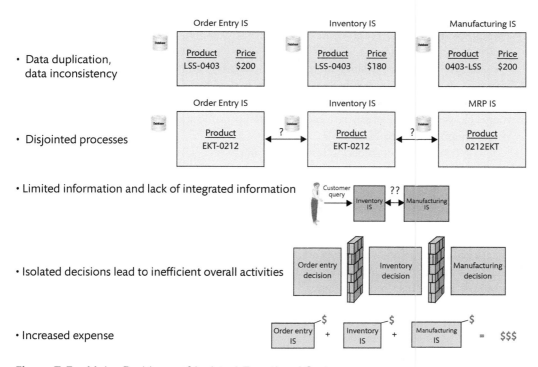

- Data duplication, data inconsistency
- Disjointed processes
- Limited information and lack of integrated information
- Isolated decisions lead to inefficient overall activities
- Increased expense

Figure 7-5 Major Problems of Isolated Functional Systems

- Order Entry System
  Product Number:
  Format: ccc-nnnn
  Example: COM-3344
- Manufacturing System
  Product Number:
  Format: nnnnccc
  Example: 3344COM

Figure 7-6 Example of System Integration Problem

Consider the example in Figure 7-6. Suppose the order entry and inventory systems define a product number as three characters, a dash, and four numeric digits. The manufacturing system in the same company, however, defines a product as four digits followed by three characters. Every time parts data are exported from order entry and imported into manufacturing (or vice versa), the data must be converted from one scheme to the other. Multiply this conversion process by several hundred data items, and possibly dozens of other systems, and you can see why processing is disjointed across functional applications.

A consequence of such disjointed systems is the lack of integrated enterprise information. When a customer asks about an order, several systems may need to be queried. For example, some order information is in the order entry system, some in the finished-goods inventory system, and some in the manufacturing system. Obtaining a consolidated statement about the customer's order will require processing each of these systems, with possibly inconsistent data.

Another consequence of isolated systems is inefficiency. When using isolated functional systems, a department can make decisions based only on the isolated data that it has. So, for example, raw materials inventory systems will make inventory replenishment decisions based only on costs and benefits in that single inventory. However, it may be that the overall efficiency of the sales, order entry, and manufacturing activities, considered together across the enterprise, will be improved by carrying a less-than-optimal number of products in raw materials inventory. Duplicated data, disjointed systems, limited information, and inefficiencies all mean higher costs. These kinds of inefficiencies led people to wonder if there were better ways to support business processes.

Q7-3 HOW CAN BUSINESS PROCESSES BE IMPROVED?

We learned in Chapter 2 that business processes are supported by information systems. In Chapter 3, we saw that IT often enables organizations to innovate and make significant change. In this chapter, we consider how IT can be used to improve processes that create value for organizations.

Before talking about technology, we should note that it is possible to improve business processes without technological change. For example, we can often get more done in a process by (1) adding resources (such as adding more workers); (2) adding increased specialization (such as adding more skilled workers); and/or (3) changing/eliminating unproductive activities. Adding resources, such as (1) and (2) above, often costs more money but enables more production. This approach might be called doing more with more. However, many organizations often attempt to do more with less—in which case, they very often turn to IT.

The first step in considering how IT can improve a business process is to understand where the improvements might take place. The key to process improvement is to consider the underlying activities and/or resources. If you can change the activities so that you get more done with the same resources or you can accomplish the same activities with less resource cost, then you have made a productive change. This is what business process management, which we introduced earlier in Chapter 2, is all about. When organizations have functional silos, the organization is not as productive as it could be. There are opportunities to improve processes by integrating activities and resources across the functional areas, but it often takes changes in technology to make these improvements possible.

For example, as advanced networks became prevalent in the 1990s, systems developers realized that these networks provided a way to do more than simply automate functional systems. Developers began to wonder how they could create systems that would integrate many different functional areas in an entire value chain. This thinking became the foundation of enterprise data architecture and resulted in the idea of **business process design** (or, sometimes, *business process redesign*). The central idea is that organizations should not simply automate or improve existing functional systems. The process of making efficient what already exists is sometimes referred to as paving the cowpath because, while it makes things easier, it does not fundamentally change the way things are done. Business process design was not about paving the cowpath. Instead, it was about making significant changes by integrating functional systems.

The basic approach would be to establish more efficient business processes that integrate the activities of many functional departments involved in a value chain. So, in the early 1990s, some organizations began to design new cross-functional business processes that integrated functional systems with the hopes of making data accessible to the entire enterprise (and not just one functional area). The goal was to take advantage of as many activity linkages as possible. For example, a cross-functional customer management process could integrate all interactions with the customer, from prospect through initial order through repeat orders, including customer support, outbound logistics, credit, and accounts receivable.

Integrating Functional Systems: EAI and ERP

Integrating functional systems can be very complex; it requires careful thinking and a consistent design approach. We will talk briefly about two approaches to integration.

Enterprise application integration (EAI) is an approach to combining functional systems, which uses layers of software as a bridge to connect different functional systems together. The main design principle for EAI is that it leaves the functional systems basically intact. The data for each functional system stay within the functional system. A customized EAI interface is then created for each functional system. These customized interfaces allow a central EAI server to pull whatever data are necessary from each of the functional systems. The EAI server, thus, acts to centrally integrate the necessary enterprise information from the functional system. Users of the system see only the data that are integrated on the EAI server. To them, it looks like one giant integrated database. Users are not aware of all the complex linkages within each of the EAI interfaces. EAI provides the integrated data that users are looking for while minimizing changes to the functional systems. Figure 7-7 demonstrates this EAI design principle.

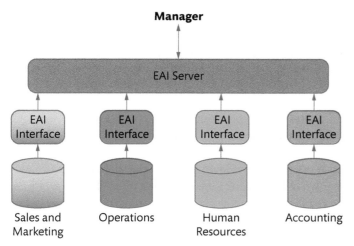

With enterprise application integration, the data stay in the functional system. The manager accesses the data through the EAI interface. The manager sees a single database.

The EAI interface sends data to the EAI Server.

The functional systems still exist separately and store actual data.

Figure 7-7 Enterprise Application Integration

A second approach to combining functional systems is through enterprise resource planning (ERP). We will learn more about ERP later in this chapter, but, for now, it is important to understand the main design principle behind it. One central database is combined with a set of standard business processes built on top of the database to ensure integration between functional areas. The standard processes ensure that the organization integrates data into a single database that can distribute accurate data throughout the organization. The ERP approach uses prebuilt software so that an organization adopting an ERP system must remove its existing functional systems before adopting the ERP system. This also means that the current business processes must be changed to fit into the structure of the ERP system. Figure 7-8 demonstrates the central importance of a single enterprise-level database in an ERP system.

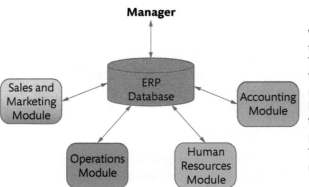

Manager

ERP Database

Sales and Marketing Module

Accounting Module

Operations Module

Human Resources Module

With enterprise resource planning, there is a single central database. The manager accesses data through this database.

People in the functional areas use ERP to send and receive data directly from the central database.

No functional systems exist. They were replaced by the ERP modules.

Figure 7-8 Enterprise Resource Planning

Q7-4 WHAT ARE THE CHALLENGES OF IMPLEMENTING BUSINESS PROCESS CHANGES?

Unfortunately, process design projects are expensive and difficult to implement. There are three reasons for this. The first is that departmental managers very often focus mainly on their aspects of the value chain and are willing to implement changes that may not integrate across the entire organization. A significant amount of detailed work is required to determine what to change, and many experts from different parts of the organization are needed to make an effective decision. Instead, managers may purchase point or individual solutions that simply address their specific problem rather than take the time and effort to provide a complete solution. Enterprise level systems by definition require that the entire organization adopt a common language and set of specifications and this is not a trivial undertaking. As we will see later in the text when we review project management the number of details can be staggering and there are serious consequences when implementing change at the enterprise or organizational level. For example, when Target expanded into Canada from the United States and implemented the U.S. based ERP approach Target Canada failed to consider the Canadian use of metric measurements (centimetres and metres) rather than the American use of imperial measurements (inches and feet). Furthermore, ensuring the correct orientation of merchandise on the shelves was extremely difficult because it was not clear what dimensions were being described (length, width, or height). These types of overlooked details were identified as contributing to Target failing in Canada and subsequently returning to the United States.[2]

Let us assume that the organization can work through this complexity. The next big challenge is to convince the organization that the changes are worth the effort. For some process changes, this can be easy. For other changes, the reasons are not as obvious. Understanding and estimating the business value that will emerge from business process changes

[2] http://www.canadianbusiness.com/the-last-days-of-target-canada/

is a risky endeavour. If you underestimate the benefits of the changes (i.e., you undersell the impact of the changes), the organization might not be convinced to undertake them. If you overestimate the benefits of the changes (i.e., you oversell the impact of the changes), then the organization may be disappointed in the outcome and could become reluctant to implement further changes.

Finally, once these first two challenges have been overcome and the new integrated processes are designed and approved, a new, even greater challenge arises. Many people like change but do not want to change. People often do not want to work in new ways, they do not want to see their department reorganized or abolished, and they do not want to work for someone new. Even if the process changes can be implemented in spite of this resistance, some workers will continue to resist the changes.

All these difficulties translate into more hours of labour, which translate into higher costs and increased risk of underperformance. Thus, business process design is very expensive, and the outcomes are often uncertain.

Q7-5 WHAT IS THE IMPORTANCE OF INDUSTRY STANDARD PROCESSES?

Many early business process design projects failed because they were tailor-made. They were customized to suit a particular organization, so just one company bore the cost of the design effort. In the mid-1990s, a number of successful software vendors began to market pre-made integrated applications, with built-in industry standard processes. Such processes saved hundreds of hours of design work.

When an organization acquires, for example, a business application from large system companies, such as Oracle, Salesforce.com, Microsoft, or SAP, the processes for using the software are built-in or **industry standard processes**. In most cases, the organization must conform its activities to these processes. If the software is designed well, the industry standard process will effectively integrate activities across departments. These pre-built processes can save the organization the substantial, sometimes staggering, costs of designing internal new processes.

Figure 7-9 shows an example of an industry standard process in a software product called **SAP R/3**, a product licensed by SAP (www.sap.com). When an organization licenses this product, SAP provides hundreds of diagrams just like this one. The diagram shows the business processes that must be followed to effectively use the software and the flow and logic of one set of processes. In the top lines, if the purchase requisition does not exist and if the request for quotation (RFQ) is to be created, then the purchasing department creates an RFQ and sends it to potential vendors. You can study the rest of this sample diagram to get the general idea of this process illustration.

To some people, when an organization licenses cross-functional software, the primary benefit is not the software but the inherent processes in the software. Licensing an integrated application not only saves the organization the time, expense, and agony of process design, but also enables the organization to benefit immediately from tried and tested cross-departmental processes.

There are, of course, disadvantages too. The industry standard processes may be very different from existing processes and, thus, require the organization to change substantially. Such change can be disruptive to ongoing operations and very disturbing to many employees. An example of this is provided in the "MIS in Use" on page 252. Similarly, using enterprise systems can make it difficult for organizations to differentiate themselves so that they can radically alter the basis for competition. The exercise "Available Only in Vanilla" at the end of this chapter on pages 256–257 discusses the effects of organizational change in more detail.

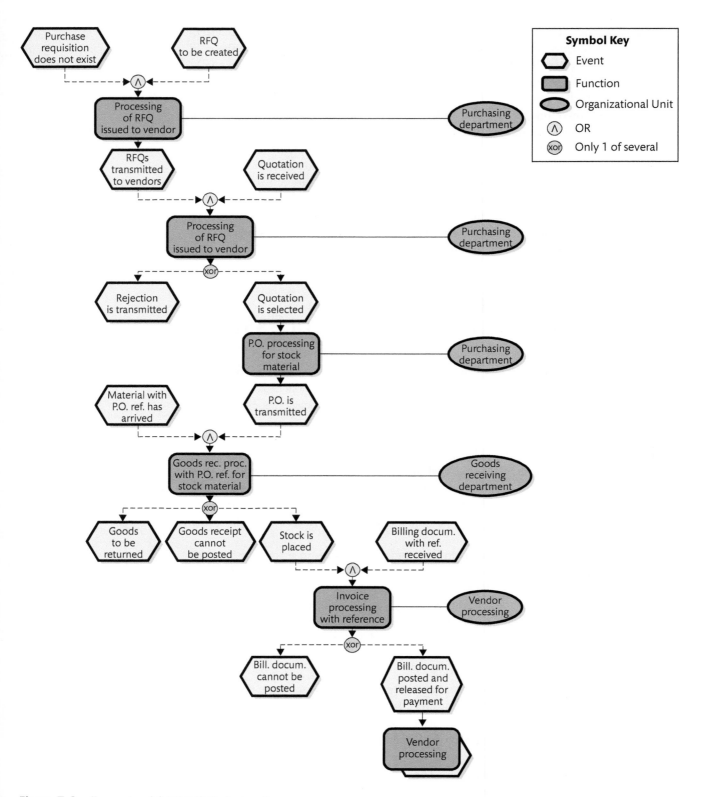

Figure 7-9 Example of SAP R/3 Ordering Process

Source: Thomas A. Curran, Andrew Ladd, Dennis Ladd, *SAP R/3 Reporting and e-Business Intelligence*, 1st ed., © 2000. Reprinted by permission of Pearson Education, Inc., Upper Saddle River, NJ.

Q7-6 WHAT ARE ERP SYSTEMS?

Enterprise resource planning (ERP) systems support many or all of the primary business processes as well as the human resources and accounting support processes. ERP is an outgrowth of materials resource planning (MRP), and the primary ERP users are manufacturing companies. One of the first vendors of ERP software for large organizations was a German company, SAP. Other large vendors include Oracle (www.oracle.com) and Infor (www.infor.com). For medium-sized businesses, Microsoft provides a number of solutions (NAV, AX, GP, and Solomon), and a large number of smaller vendors provide integrated enterprise solutions for smaller firms.

ERP represents the ultimate in cross-departmental process systems. The system can integrate sales, order, inventory, manufacturing, customer service, human resources, accounting, and other activities. ERP systems provide software, predesigned databases, industry standard procedures, and job descriptions for organization-wide process integration.

ERP Characteristics

Figure 7-10 lists the major ERP characteristics. First, as stated earlier, ERP takes a cross-functional, process view of the entire organization. With ERP, the entire organization is considered a collection of interrelated activities. There is a single central database for collecting enterprise information.

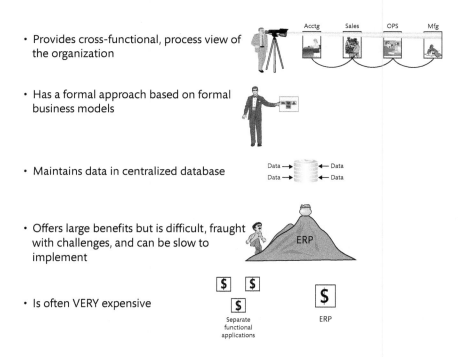

- Provides cross-functional, process view of the organization

- Has a formal approach based on formal business models

- Maintains data in centralized database

- Offers large benefits but is difficult, fraught with challenges, and can be slow to implement

- Is often VERY expensive

Figure 7-10
Characteristics of ERP

Second, true ERP is a formal approach that is based on documented, tested business models. ERP applications include a comprehensive set of inherent processes for all organizational activities. SAP defines this set as the **process blueprint**, and documents each process with diagrams that use a set of standardized symbols.

Because ERP is based on formally defined procedures, organizations must adapt their processing to the ERP blueprint. If they do not, the system cannot operate effectively, or even correctly. In some cases, it is possible to adapt ERP software to procedures that are different from the blueprint, but such adaptation is expensive and often problematic.

Once an organization has implemented an ERP system, it can achieve significant benefits. However, as shown in Figure 7-10, the process of moving from separated, functional applications to an ERP system can be slow and is often difficult and fraught with challenges. In particular, changing organizational procedures has proven to be a momentous challenge for many organizations and, in some cases, was even a pitfall that prevented successful ERP implementation. Finally, the switch to an ERP system is very costly (in some cases more than $50 000 000)—not only because of the need for new hardware and software but also because of the costs of developing new procedures, training employees, converting data, and other developmental expenses.

Benefits of ERP

Figure 7-11 summarizes the major benefits of ERP. First, the processes in the business blueprint have been tried and tested over hundreds of organizations. The processes are effective and often very efficient. Organizations that convert to ERP do not need to reinvent business processes. Rather, they gain the benefit of processes that have already been proved successful.

By taking an organization-wide view, many companies find that they can reduce their inventory, sometimes dramatically. With better planning, it is usually not necessary to maintain large buffer stocks. Additionally, items remain in inventory for shorter periods, sometimes no longer than a few hours or a day.

As discussed earlier, data inconsistency problems are not an issue because all ERP data are stored in an integrated database. Further, because all data about a customer, order, part, or other entity reside in one place, the data are readily accessible. This means that organizations can provide better information about orders, products, and customer status. All of this results in not only better customer service but also less costly customer service. Integrated databases also make company-wide data readily accessible and result in greater, real-time visibility, thus allowing a peek into the status of the organization.

Finally, ERP-based organizations often find that they can produce and sell the same products at lower costs because of smaller inventories, reduced lead times, and less expensive customer support. The bottom-line result is higher profitability. The trick, however, is getting there. Despite the clear benefits of inherent processes and ERP, there may be unintended consequences.

For example, it is reasonable to ask what the competitive advantage of ERP systems are if all competitors use the same "industry standard" processes. Although each firm might become more productive, the competitive advantage of ERP systems erodes as more and more competitors implement ERP products. This suggests that all companies within an industry that install ERP will receive the same benefits. We learned in Chapter 3 that this may not be the case, however. Software and hardware do not necessarily provide a sustained advantage. It is the combination of people, procedures, hardware, software, and data that creates sustainable advantage. Installing ERP, therefore, creates an initial hurdle for competitors. Learning to effectively use the information provided by the ERP will be the key source of advantage to those companies that are best able to use the system. Naturally, this is a finite process. Eventually a tipping point occurs where rather than obtain a benefit from adopting ERP technology, existing organizations that have not yet acquired ERP technology must adopt it just to keep up. For example, it is likely that the first students to use computers obtained advantages that were not available to other students. In 2018, however, it is much more likely that the few students that do not have good access to computers are disadvantaged compared to everyone else.

Q7-7 WHAT ARE CRM SYSTEMS?

Cross-functional systems were developed to overcome the problems of functional silos. Not all cross-functional systems go as far as ERP in integrating enterprise information. One type of cross-functional system currently in use is customer relationship management

---

- Efficient business processes
- Inventory reduction
- Lead-time reduction
- Improved customer service
- Greater, real-time insight into organization
- Higher profitability

Figure 7-11 Potential Benefits of ERP

(CRM). **Customer relationship management (CRM) systems** support the business processes of attracting, selling, managing, delivering, and supporting customers. CRM systems support all the direct value chain activities that involve the customer. There are many software vendors who provide a wide variety of CRM software. Maximizer Software (www.maximizer.com) is a Canadian company focused on contact management for small- and medium-sized businesses. Larger CRM vendors include Oracle/Siebel Systems, CDC/Pivotal Corp, and Salesforce.com.

The difference between CRM systems and traditional functional applications is that CRM systems address all activities and events that touch the customer and provide a single repository for data about all customer interactions. With functional systems, data about customers are sprinkled in databases all over the organization. Some customer data exist in customer management databases, some in order entry databases, some in customer service databases, and so forth. CRM systems store all customer data in one place and make it possible to easily access all data about the customer.

Figure 7-12 shows four phases of the **customer life cycle**: (1) marketing, (2) customer acquisition, (3) relationship management, and (4) loss/churn. Marketing sends messages to the target market to attract customer prospects. When prospects order, they become customers who need to be supported. Additionally, resell processes increase the value of existing customers. Inevitably, over time, the organization loses customers. When this occurs, win-back processes categorize customers according to value and attempt to win back high-value customers.

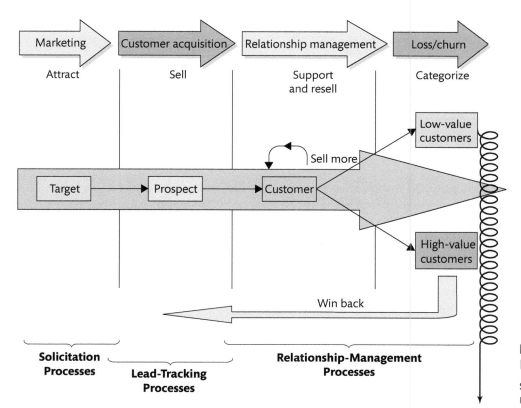

Figure 7-12 The Customer Life Cycle

Source: Douglas MacLachlan, University of Washington.

The organizational website is an increasingly important tool. Web addresses are easy to promote (and remember), and once a target prospect is on the site, product descriptions, use cases, success stories, and other solicitation materials can be easily provided. Further, the cost of distributing these materials via the Web is substantially lower than the cost of creating and distributing printed materials. Many websites require customer name and contact information before releasing high-value promotional materials. The compiled information then feeds lead-tracking applications.

The purpose of relationship management applications is to maximize the value of the existing customer base. As Figure 7-13 shows, two types of applications are used. *Sales management applications* support sales to existing customers. They have features that prioritize customers according to their purchase history. Salespeople can increase sales to existing customers by focusing on customers who have already made large purchases, by focusing on large organizations that have the potential to make large purchases, or both. The goal of such applications is to ensure that sales management has sufficient information to prioritize and allocate sales time and effort.

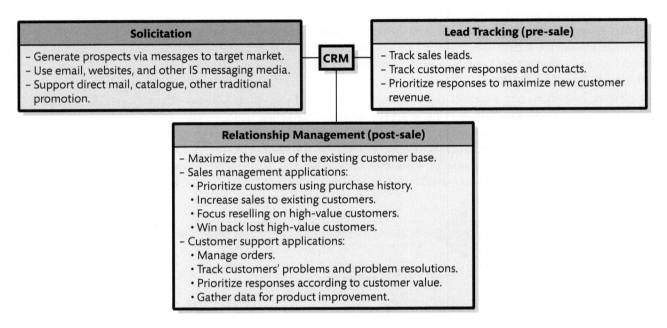

Solicitation		**Lead Tracking (pre-sale)**
– Generate prospects via messages to target market. – Use email, websites, and other IS messaging media. – Support direct mail, catalogue, other traditional promotion.	**CRM**	– Track sales leads. – Track customer responses and contacts. – Prioritize responses to maximize new customer revenue.

Relationship Management (post-sale)

– Maximize the value of the existing customer base.
– Sales management applications:
  • Prioritize customers using purchase history.
  • Increase sales to existing customers.
  • Focus reselling on high-value customers.
  • Win back lost high-value customers.
– Customer support applications:
  • Manage orders.
  • Track customers' problems and problem resolutions.
  • Prioritize responses according to customer value.
  • Gather data for product improvement.

Figure 7-13   CRM Components

Integrated CRM applications store data in a single database, as shown in Figure 7-14. Because all customer data reside in one location, CRM processes can be linked to one another. For example, customer service activities can be linked to customer purchase records. In this way, both sales and marketing know the status of customer satisfaction, both on an individual customer basis for future sales calls and also collectively for analyzing customers' overall satisfaction. As well, many customer support applications prioritize customers to avoid, for example, giving $10 000 worth of support to a customer who has a lifetime value to the company of $500. Finally, customer support has an important linkage to product marketing and development—it knows, more than any other group, what customers are doing with the product and what problems they are having with it.

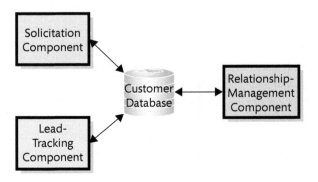

Figure 7-14   CRM Centred on Integrated Customer Database

Q7-8 WHAT ARE SCM SYSTEMS?

Supply chain management (SCM) systems are interorganizational systems that enable companies to efficiently handle the flow of goods from suppliers to customers. A **supply chain** is a network of organizations and facilities that transforms raw materials into products delivered to customers. Figure 7-15 shows a generic supply chain. Customers order from retailers, who, in turn, order from distributors, who, in turn, order from manufacturers, who, in turn, order from suppliers. In addition to the organizations shown here, the supply chain includes transportation companies, warehouses, inventories, and some means for transmitting messages and information among the organizations involved.

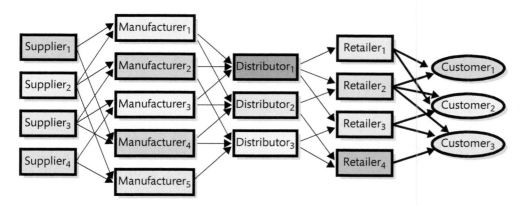

Figure 7-15 Supply Chain Relationships

Because of **disintermediation**, not every supply chain has all these organizations. Dell, for example, sells directly to the customer and seeks to begin manufacturing after the order is received (build to order) rather than before (build for the shelf). Both the distributor and retailer organizations are omitted from its supply chain. In other supply chains, manufacturers sell directly to retailers and omit the distribution level.

The term *chain* is misleading. *Chain* implies that each organization is connected to just one item up (toward the supplier) and down (toward the customer) the chain. However, this may not always be the case. Instead, at each level, an organization could work with many organizations both up and down the supply chain. Thus, a supply chain is most likely a supply network even though we used the term "chain."

To understand the operation of a supply chain, look at Figure 7-16. Suppose you decide to take up cross-country skiing. You go to REI.com (a company that sells outdoor sporting

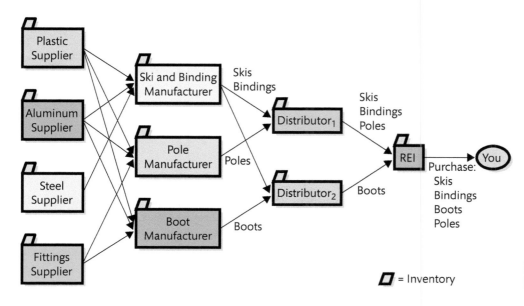

= Inventory

Figure 7-16 Supply Chain Example

equipment and supplies) and purchase skis, bindings, boots, and poles. After filling your order, REI removes those items from its inventory of goods.

Those goods have been purchased, in turn, from distributors. According to Figure 7-16, REI purchases skis, bindings, and poles from one distributor and boots from a second. The distributors, in turn, purchase the required items from the manufacturers, who, in turn, buy raw materials from their suppliers.

The only source of revenue in a supply chain is the customer. In the REI example, you spend your money on the ski equipment. From that point, all the way back up the supply chain to the raw material suppliers, there is no further injection of cash. The money you spend on the ski equipment is passed back up the supply chain as payment for goods or raw materials. Again, the customer is the only source of revenue.

Four major factors, or *drivers*, affect supply chain performance: facilities, inventory, transportation, and information.[3] We will focus our attention on the fourth factor, information. (You can learn in detail about the first three factors in operations management classes.)

Information influences supply chain performance by affecting the ways in which organizations in the supply chain request from, respond to, and inform one another. There are three factors of information: (1) purpose, (2) availability, and (3) means. The *purpose* of the information can be transactional, such as orders and order returns, or it can be informational, such as the sharing of inventory and customer order data. *Availability* refers to the ways in which organizations share their information—that is, which organizations have access to which information and when. Finally, *means* refers to the methods by which the information is transmitted.

Supplier Relationship Management

Figure 7-17 shows the three fundamental information systems involved in supply chain management: (1) supplier relationship management (SRM), (2) inventory, and (3) customer relationship management (CRM). We have discussed all these applications except supplier relationship management, which we will now discuss.

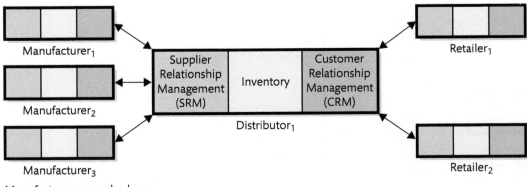

Figure 7-17 B2B in One Section of the Supply Chain

Supplier relationship management (SRM) is a business process for managing all contacts between an organization and its suppliers. The term *supplier* in *supplier relationship management* is broader than the use of the term *supplier* in Figures 7-15 and 7-16. In those figures, the term refers to the supplier of raw materials and assemblies to a manufacturer.

[3] S. Chopra and P. Meindl, *Supply Chain Management* (Upper Saddle River, NJ: Prentice Hall, 2004), pp. 51–53.

Supplier in SRM is used generically—it refers to *any organization* that sells something to the organization that has the SRM application. Thus, in this generic sense, a manufacturer is a supplier to a distributor.

SRM is an integrated system in the same way that CRM and MRP are. With regard to Porter's model, an SRM supports both the inbound logistics primary activity and the procurement support activity. Considering business processes, SRM applications support three basic processes: (1) source, (2) purchase, and (3) settle, as summarized in Figure 7-18.

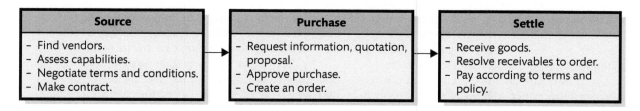

Source	Purchase	Settle
- Find vendors. - Assess capabilities. - Negotiate terms and conditions. - Make contract.	- Request information, quotation, proposal. - Approve purchase. - Create an order.	- Receive goods. - Resolve receivables to order. - Pay according to terms and policy.

Figure 7-18 Summary of SRM Processes

With regard to sourcing, the organization needs to find possible vendors of needed supplies, materials, or services; to assess the vendors that it does find; to negotiate terms and conditions; and to formalize those terms and conditions in a procurement contract. SRM software is especially relevant to finding and assessing vendors. Some SRM applications have features that let users search for product sources and find evaluations of vendors and products. You see something similar to this functionality when you search for electronics products on a website, such as www.cnet.com. There, you can readily determine which vendors provide which products, and you can also obtain evaluations of products and vendors. Similar capabilities are built into SRM packages.

Once the company has identified vendors and has the appropriate contracts in place, the next stage is to procure the goods. The SRM application requests information, quotations, and proposals from would-be suppliers. The company can then use the SRM to manage the approval workflow in order to approve the purchase and issue the order.

The third major SRM activity is settlement. Here, the accounting department reconciles the receipt of the goods or services against the purchase documents and schedules the vendor payment. The payment portion of the SRM typically connects to the cash management subsystem in the financial management application.

Information systems have had an exceedingly positive impact on supply chain performance (see Figure 7-19). CRM, SRM, and less integrated functional systems, such as e-commerce sales systems, have dramatically reduced the costs of buying and selling. Sourcing, buying, and settling have all become faster, easier, more effective, and less costly.

Furthermore, the presence of information systems has expanded supply chain speed (the dollar value of goods exchanged in a given period). Without information systems, Alibaba.com would not have been able to process more than a billion transactions (peaking at 120 000 transactions per second) and more than 657 million delivery orders for Singles Day (November 11, 2016).

As shown in Figure 7-19, a third factor is that information systems have also enabled both suppliers and customers to reduce the size of their inventories and thus reduce their inventory costs. These reductions have been possible because the speed and efficiency provided by information systems enable processing of small orders, quickly.

Information systems also improve delivery scheduling. Using these systems, suppliers can deliver materials and components at the time and in the sequence needed. Such delivery enables just-in-time inventory and allows manufacturers to reduce the size of raw materials inventory as well as the handling of raw materials.

- Reduce costs of buying and selling.
- Increase supply chain speed.
- Reduce size and cost of inventories.
- Improve delivery scheduling—enable just-in-time inventory.

Figure 7-19 Benefits of Information Systems on Supply Chain Performance

Implementing enterprise resource planning (ERP) software can be one of the most challenging projects for an organization of any size. "It takes a coordinated team effort," notes Eric Dang, systems administrator for Digital Payment Technologies in Burnaby, British Columbia, "and requires time upfront to understand what you want to accomplish before anything gets installed." Digital Payment Technologies (DPT) is a leader in the design, manufacture, and distribution of parking management technologies for the North American parking industry (www.digitalpaytech.com). DPT learned about implementing ERP the hard way, with an initial project that did not deliver expected results, but which eventually led to a second successful implementation.

In 2005, DPT was a medium-sized company that was growing quickly, averaging 29 percent annual growth, with 95 percent of its sales in the United States. With rapid growth came the challenge to quickly adjust to new sales and manufacturing targets. DPT felt the need for ERP software, but the core team at the company had little time and few resources to make it happen. The company was surviving on a combination of Excel spreadsheets and sales reports that were difficult, if not impossible, to integrate and share. So, after some investigation of ERP solutions and site visits with industry partners, DPT licensed Navision, a Microsoft product.

"Since our core people were busy just getting product out the door, we gave the task of installing the software to someone who had a little bit of time they could spare. We thought we could just install the program and run with it," noted Mark Gemino, VP of manufacturing. "But it didn't work the way we thought it would," he noted. "After a few months, nothing was working, and we couldn't balance our accounts or get simple BOM [bills of materials] working. We thought we had bought bad software. Later, we learned that it wasn't the software that was causing the problems. It was the way we had set the software up. We weren't aware that what seemed like small choices in the software setup could have really big implications on how the system as a whole operated. We also had to spend more time in getting our initial data correct. We hadn't invested enough time in understanding how we were going to really use the system."

Employees quickly lost faith in the information provided by Navision, and DPT was spending time trying to fix the errors the system was creating. The bad news for DPT was that Navision had not provided the expected benefits and had stalled their attempts to improve efficiency. The good news was that the challenge led the company to find someone who could get Navision working for DPT. "Everything changed quickly when we brought Eric on board,"

noted Gemino. "He was able to explain the system in a way we could understand."

Eric Dang was hired in 2006 and spent the first six months getting back to basics with the Navision product. It took a lot of effort, not only from Eric but also from a team of people from different departments at DPT, but eventually the Navision system was stabilized and started providing useful and accurate information. "People took this work seriously," noted Eric, "because they understood what would happen if we didn't get things right."

By 2007, the Navision ERP system was running smoothly—so smoothly, in fact, that people at DPT felt they were able to take on an additional task of implementing the warehouse module. "A consulting firm told us that they had seen several companies try to implement the warehouse module, but none of them had been successful," noted Eric, "but that didn't stop us. We thought, yes we can." DPT's previous experience provided the team with the confidence to do things right. They started the project with detailed process mapping, created a prototype, and involved important people in different departments in making the decisions about the new implementation before the system was rolled out. "When we rolled it out six months later, it went ahead with very few issues." DPT had learned an expensive and powerful lesson about teamwork, involving users, and detailed preplanning for project success. When asked about the secret to their success, Eric noted, "It is summed up in a book my two-year old daughter got out of the library, called *Yes We Can*. It is a simple picture book story about a group of animals with different strengths which, when they work together as a team, get things done. As far as I am concerned, it should be required reading for anyone doing ERP implementation."

QUESTIONS

1. Consider the five components of an information system provided in Figure 1-1 in Chapter 1. Which of these components was the reason for the lack of success in the first round of ERP implementation at DPT?

2. What do you think is the most important component in the success of DPT's ERP in the second implementation?

3. What role did Eric Dang play in the ERP implementation? What skills do you think were most important for Eric's success?

4. Do you think that DPT had to fail in its initial ERP implementation before it succeeded? That is, do you think it is necessary for companies to understand clearly what can go wrong before they fully commit to the project? Justify your answer.

How Does the Knowledge in This Chapter Help You?

The knowledge of this chapter will help you understand levels of information systems and the problems that each level can have. It will also help you to put information systems that you use into perspective and to understand how they may or may not be creating information silos. You also know the potential problems of silos and how to resolve them at both the workgroup and enterprise levels. Further, when you encounter CRM, ERP, and EAI applications in your future, you will know what such systems are, what they do, and some of the issues you will run into when using and implementing them. Finally, understanding how PRIDE uses the cloud to support an inter-enterprise system will give you the background for investigating the use of the cloud for other applications as well.

ACTIVE REVIEW

Use this Active Review to verify that you have understood the material in the chapter. You can read the entire chapter and then perform the tasks in this review, or you can read the material for just one question and perform the tasks for that question before moving on to the next one.

Q7-1 WHAT ARE THE FUNDAMENTAL WAYS OF ACHIEVING COMPETITIVE ADVANTAGE?

Define *competitive strategy*. Explain the relationships among competitive strategy, business processes, and information systems using technology.

Q7-2 WHAT ARE BUSINESS FUNCTIONS AND FUNCTIONAL SYSTEMS?

Name five categories of functional systems. Name three problems of functional silos, and describe each. Give an example of a data integration problem. Describe what is meant by a cross-functional system. What are the consequences of a lack of data integration?

Q7-3 HOW CAN BUSINESS PROCESSES BE IMPROVED?

Name three ways of improving processes without technology. What is business process design? Describe the differences between EAI and ERP.

Q7-4 WHAT ARE THE CHALLENGES OF IMPLEMENTING BUSINESS PROCESS CHANGES?

Why are process design projects expensive? Why are process design projects difficult to implement? "Many people like change but do not want to change." Explain.

Q7-5 WHAT IS THE IMPORTANCE OF INDUSTRY STANDARD PROCESSES?

Describe what is meant by the term *industry standard practices*. What are the advantages of standard processes? What are the disadvantages? Can an organization develop competitive advantage with industry standard processes? Explain your answer.

Q7-6 WHAT ARE ERP SYSTEMS?

What are ERP systems? Name three ERP vendors. Explain why ERP systems are difficult to implement. How does an ERP system help address the problems that arise from functional systems?

Q7-7 WHAT ARE CRM SYSTEMS?

Define the term *customer relationship management*. Describe the customer life cycle. How is it related to CRM? How can a CRM system create competitive advantage?

Q7-8 WHAT ARE SCM SYSTEMS?

Describe what is meant by SCM. Why can there be conflict between companies using SCM systems? What is supplier relationship management? How does this differ from CRM? Justify your answer.

KEY TERMS AND CONCEPTS

Business process design 240
Cross-departmental
    systems 238
Cross-functional
    systems 238
Customer life cycle 247
Customer relationship
    management (CRM)
    systems 247

Disintermediation 249
Enterprise application
    integration
    (EAI) 241
Enterprise resource
    planning (ERP)
    systems 245
Functional
    silos 237

Functional systems 237
Industry standard
    processes 243
Interorganizational
    systems 238
Primary
    activities 236
Process blueprint 245
SAP R/3 243

Supplier relationship
    management
    (SRM) 250
Supply chain 249
Supply chain management
    (SCM) systems 249
Support activities 236

USING YOUR KNOWLEDGE

7-1. Choose one of the following basic business processes: inventory management, operations, manufacturing, human resources management, or accounting/financial management. Use the Internet to identify three vendors that license a product to support that process. Compare offerings from the three vendors as follows:

a. Determine differences in terminology, especially differences in the ways vendors use the same terms.

b. Compare the features and functions of each product offering.

c. For each vendor, specify the characteristics of a company for which that vendor's offering would be ideal.

7-2. Consider a small retailer that uses one system to collect information about their customers, an Excel spreadsheet to collect information about their suppliers, a Word document to create invoices, and some accounting software to record revenues and expenses.

a. Give an example of some of the problems that could be faced by having these systems act as functional silos.

b. Then, provide some suggestions for how these systems could be combined to add value to the company.

7-3. Distance learning could be considered an application of interorganizational information systems.

a. Draw a process diagram of a regular, non-distance learning class. Label the activities and the flows among the activities.

b. Draw a second process diagram of a distance learning class. In what ways are the two diagrams similar? In what ways are they different?

c. What is the competitive strategy of your college or university? How do distance learning classes contribute to that competitive strategy?

d. Assuming that no face-to-face meeting is required to successfully teach a distance learning class, neither students nor professors need to live near campus. In fact, they do not even need to reside in the same continent. What opportunities does that fact present to your college or university? What new educational products might your college or university develop?

COLLABORATIVE EXERCISES

This chapter provides several examples of companies that use information systems to gain a competitive advantage. These include Zipcar, Grand & Toy, Bag Borrow or Steal, Amazon.com, Dell, REI, and DPT. In this collaborative exercise, your group has to take a more critical and in-depth look at the companies and their offerings. Using the Web as a resource, collaborate with your team to answer the following questions:

7-1. Create a maximum two-page information sheet that summarizes the company, the idea, and the system it uses. The summary should include the following:

a. Prepare an introduction to the company (example companies are listed above, but you are welcome to use another company).

b. Identify, as clearly as you can, the strategy of the company. (*Note:* You can use Porter's five forces to understand the company's industry.)

c. Outline how the company uses technology for competitive advantage.

d. Identify the information systems you think will be most critical to support the strategy.

e. Provide suggestions on how the company should consider investing in information systems to support its business. Justify your suggestions.

7-2. Choose one of the following companies (or ask your professor if you can choose a different company):

a. Zipcar (www.zipcar.com)

b. Bag Borrow or Steal (www.bagborroworsteal.com)

c. Grand & Toy (www.grandandtoy.com)

d. Dell (www.dell.ca)

e. My Virtual Model (www.MVM.com).

f. The Running Room (www.runningroom.com)

g. Ritchie Bros. Auctioneers (www.rbauction.com)

Create a presentation (using PowerPoint, Keynote, or another presentation software) on the topic to the students in your class. Be sure to include a title page.

CASE STUDY 7
MOVING LIKE A DEERE: DEERE'S INNOVATIVE REVOLUTION

Looking at cotton growing on a farm, one could be forgiven for thinking that other than fertilizers, pesticides, and the practical deployment of the modern cotton picker in the 1950s, the picture seems frozen in time. However, at Deere & Company (www.johndeere.com), a second revolution is brewing, and this one is definitely adding cutting-edge technology to an old-economy business.

Founded in 1837 as a one-man blacksmith operation, John Deere is currently a $US43.6-billion corporation that employs more than 56 750 people worldwide and is one of the oldest publicly traded industrial companies in the United States. But rather than the brutality and razor-thin margins that usually accompany price competition, market leader Deere has staked out a bold differentiation strategy that incorporates technology to compete on innovation.

John Deere's machines still pluck cotton fibres with hundreds of finger-like spindles and then vacuum the cotton into a huge bin, but this is where the similarities with its old machines end. The company has used advanced computer-aided design (CAD) to reshape the intake ducts, allowing the cotton to travel 20 percent faster and reducing horsepower requirements by 5 percent, thus saving on fuel consumption while maintaining speed. Inside the new cotton pickers is the computing power of eight personal computers and a communications system that beams wireless information to a base station, which can automatically monitor and signal when service is needed. At the same time, microwave sensors and the global positioning system (GPS) technology allow the farmer to map the field's exact yield while harvesting the cotton. And by overlaying this information with other enabled systems, fertilizers, pesticides, and water can be applied with precision instead of indiscriminately distributing them across the entire field. Finally, in an industry first, Deere's latest generation of picker spools the cotton into cylindrical bales that are wrapped and gently placed on the field without the machine having to stop every 10 to 15 minutes.

The cost of the new technology has not yet been determined, but the two-storey harvester has replaced four to six pieces of support equipment and has enabled a single operator to harvest nonstop until the 1100-litre fuel tank is depleted.

Questions

1. What are the advantages of the new technology used by Deere?
2. How does this technology allow Deere to compete against lower-cost manufacturers and producers?
3. Are there any other advantages to using this technology? What adaptation and extensions would increase the advantage? (*Hint*: Radio-frequency tags can be inserted into each bundle to track harvesting information and pinpoint where the cotton came from, identifying, for example, whether the cotton qualifies as organic.)

WHAT DO YOU THINK?

AVAILABLE ONLY IN VANILLA?

Designing business processes is difficult, time consuming, and very expensive. Highly trained experts conduct seemingly countless interviews with users and domain experts to determine business requirements. Then, even more experts join those people, and the team invests thousands of hours in designing, developing, and implementing effective business processes that meet those requirements. All of this amounts to a very high-risk activity that is prone to failure. And it must be done before information systems development can even begin.

ERP vendors, such as SAP, have invested millions of labour hours into the business blueprints that underlie their ERP solutions. These blueprints consist of hundreds or thousands of different business processes. Examples include processes for hiring employees, acquiring fixed assets, acquiring consumable goods, and developing custom one-off (a unique product with a unique design) manufacturing, to name just a few. Additionally, since ERP vendors implement their business processes in hundreds of organizations, they are forced to customize their standard blueprint for use in particular industries.

For example, SAP has a distribution business blueprint that is customized for the auto parts industry, the electronics industry, and the aircraft industry. Hundreds of other customized solutions exist as well. Even better, the ERP vendors have developed software solutions that fit their business process blueprints. In theory, no software development is required at all if the organization can adapt to the standard blueprint of the ERP vendor.

As described in this chapter, when an organization implements an ERP solution, it first determines any differences that exist between its business processes and the standard blueprint. Then the organization must remove that difference, which can be done in one of two ways: (1) It can change business processes to fit the standard blueprint, or (2) the ERP vendor or a consultant can modify the standard blueprint (and software solution that matches the blueprint) to fit the unique requirements. In practice, such variations from the standard blueprint are rare. They are difficult and expensive to implement, and they require the using organization to maintain the variations from the standard as new versions of the ERP software are developed.

Consequently, most organizations choose to modify their processes to match the blueprint, rather than the other way around. This is often referred to as installing the software *vanilla* (the basic software with no custom features). Although such process changes are also difficult to implement, once the organization has converted to the standard blueprint, it no longer needs to support a variation. So, from the standpoint of cost, effort, risk, and avoidance of future problems, there is a huge incentive for organizations to adapt to the standard ERP blueprint. Initially, SAP was the only true ERP vendor, but other companies have since developed and acquired ERP solutions as well. And given the competitive pressure across the software industry, these products are beginning to have the same sets of features and functions. ERP solutions are becoming a commodity.

This is all fine, as far as it goes, but it does introduce a nagging question: If, over time, every organization tends to implement the standard ERP blueprint and if, over time, every software company develops essentially the same ERP features and functions, then won't every business come to look just like every other business? How will organizations gain a competitive advantage if they all use the same business processes?

If every auto parts distributor uses the same business processes, based on the same software, are they not all merely clones of one another? How will a company distinguish itself? How will innovation occur? Even if one parts distributor does successfully innovate a business process that gives it a competitive advantage, will the ERP vendors be conduits to transfer that innovation to competitors? Does the use of commoditized standard blueprints mean that no company can sustain a competitive advantage?

Discussion Questions

1. In your own words, explain why an organization might choose to change its processes to fit the standard blueprint. What advantages does it accrue by doing so?

2. Explain how competitive pressure among software vendors will cause the ERP solutions to become commodities. What does this mean to the ERP software industry?

3. If two businesses use exactly the same processes and exactly the same software, can they be different in any way at all? Explain why or why not.

4. Explain the statement that an ERP software vendor can be a conduit to transfer innovation. What are the consequences to the innovating company? To the software company? To the industry? To the economy?

5. Such standardization might be possible in theory, but since worldwide there are so many different business models, cultures, people, values, and competitive pressures, can any two businesses ever be exactly alike?

CHAPTER 8
Decision Making and Business Intelligence

STUDY QUESTIONS

Q8-1 DO MANAGERS MAKE RATIONAL DECISIONS?

Q8-2 WHAT ARE OLTP AND OLAP AND HOW DO THEY SUPPORT DECISION MAKING?

Q8-3 WHAT ARE BUSINESS INTELLIGENCE SYSTEMS?

Q8-4 HOW DO ORGANIZATIONS USE DATA WAREHOUSES TO ACQUIRE DATA?

Q8-5 WHAT ARE THE DIFFERENCES BETWEEN DATA WAREHOUSES AND DATA MARTS?

Q8-6 WHAT ARE TYPICAL DATA MINING APPLICATIONS?

MIS in Action

"What'd you get for lunch, Nicki?" James asks as they walk back to the office together.

"That five-spice beef thing they do at Hong's. You?"

"Oh, pot stickers and stuff from New China."

"That place has good food; I should have gone there with you. Hey, James, I'm wondering if you can help me with something."

"I'll try. What's up?"

"Well, we're tracking winners and runners-up from each of our spinning events, and we're having unbelievable success selling products to them."

"Ah, competition. Participants want something to gain an advantage in the next heat?"

"Right. But I know there's more we can do if we can link in personal trainers somehow. Maybe go after the losers, the people who didn't win their heats. I'd like to send them to a trainer and earn a referral fee back to us . . . or maybe take a percent of the training fees."

"OK. Makes sense. So, where do you need my help?"

"Where do they live? The racers, I mean. Where are they? Are they clustered geographically? I mean, we don't want to send the name of a trainer in Vancouver to someone living in Montreal."

KE   Chapter 8 optional knowledge extensions are

Knowledge Extension 12 Database Marketing available in the MyLab MIS

Knowledge Extension 13 Reporting Systems and OLAP available in the MyLab MIS

"Well, we could ask racers to provide their addresses when they sign up for an event."

"Yeah, maybe, justify it by saying we need it for some sort of map we could display. They might like that. But I hate to ask them for anything that distracts them from the races."

"We could use their connection IP addresses. That would tell us where the bikes are that they're using . . . might not be where they live, though."

"I don't mean where they sleep; I mean where they work out. That would do."

"What if they're travelling?"

"I don't care . . . most people won't be. I'm not quite sure what I want, and I know that drives you crazy."

"It does for operational things; it's typical for BI."

"What's BI?"

"Business intelligence. Data analysis, where you don't know the second question to ask until you see the answer to the first one."

"Yeah. That's it exactly! That's where I am right now."

"Suppose we start with this. I'll sample a bunch of our data, maybe 5000 racers, and locate them with the connection IP. Then I'll give it to you in an Excel pivot table."

"Yeah, so what?"

"Well, then you can look at it by province, city, and postal code and see what we've got."

"How come you're not asking me for a budget?"

"I might, but this part is easy. We've got the data, and I can deliver it with Excel. And I've got just one user: *you*. So I don't have to make the UI easy, write documentation, develop procedures, et cetera. Besides, you're a pretty smart user."

"Thanks for the praise . . ."

"On the other hand, if you take off with this in some crazy way and you want to use it to build something for users or do some serious data mining, set up a data mart, then you'll need to come up with some money for my budget."

"You mean this Excel thing is sort of a taste teaser."

"Yeah, but you've got to like the taste."

"Hope it's better than that five-spice thing."

"See you later."

"When do I get my report?"

"Friday?"

"That soon?"

"It's just a teaser, Nicki."

Q8-1 DO MANAGERS MAKE RATIONAL DECISIONS?

For business managers, decision making or choosing from a range of alternatives is the essence of management. Indeed, decision making, in some cases, is such a natural act that we often seem to do it without thinking. As you read this chapter, for example, you have made a decision about how to allocate some of the 168 hours that exist in each week and decided how to prioritize the various things that you could be doing (of course, some students have decided NOT to read this part of the text, but, for now, we will ignore them).

For most people, decision making is a rational act in which individuals or groups consider the possible choices and the likely consequences and choose what they think is the best alternative. This process, however, is much more complicated than it may appear for three reasons. First, the concept of rationality can be frustratingly hard to define. In most cases, processes are considered rational if they result in outcomes that are deemed good or are likely to lead to good outcomes, a definition that is seems circular at best. Second, good outcomes may occasionally result from irrational processes, and bad outcomes can result from good processes. For example, it may not be rational to skip college or university and instead buy lottery tickets for three to four years, but try telling that to someone who has successfully used such a strategy. Finally, and most importantly for this chapter, as Nobel prize winning economist Herbert Simon pointed out, humans intend to be rational, but there are limits to our cognitive capabilities—a process that he identified as "bounded rationality." For a variety of reasons, we are simply not capable of thinking through all the various options and permutations that are available to us. Instead of seeking the optimal solution, Simon suggested that we *satisfice*, or choose the most reasonable and available solution rather than the perfect choice. As an example, imagine that you are shopping for a used car. Besides the practical considerations (how far are you willing to go to see a potential option), it is unlikely that you can keep track of more than five to seven options. Moreover, how do you make trade-offs for a car that is better mechanically but not quite the colour that you want?

Human beings are not what economists call "economic automatons" or "lightning-fast calculators" who can compute the "perfect choice"; instead, we tend to settle, or satisfice, with an alternative that is generally good enough across a range of criteria. In this chapter, our main focus is on data-driven decision making in such areas as data mining and analytical systems. These decisions are often supported by business intelligence systems. However, it is important to note that, on occasion, managers have been known to make decisions first and then construct evidence to support their positions[1] and that the processes used to make group decisions can be quite different from those used to make individual decisions. For now, it is enough to note that an important aspect of decision making is to consider as broad a range of choices as possible and consider the effects of each alternative.

Because computers deal with large amounts of information, it should be no surprise that applying computers to improve decision making has been popular for a long time. In fact, many of the early computer systems (such as the SAGE system in the 1950s) were originally designed to solve military calculation problems. As mainframe computers became more popular in the 1960s, Russell Ackoff, in his article titled "Management Misinformation Systems,"[2] suggested that designers of management information systems (MIS) make several erroneous assumptions about managerial decision making and that computers might not necessarily provide good solutions. Although written over 40 years ago, many of the points Ackoff made remain relevant today.

We will look at three of Ackoff's assumptions. The first assumption is that managers will have no problem making better decisions if they get the data they need. Ackoff countered that for most managers, too many possibilities exist. It is unlikely better decisions will be made even with perfect data. The uncertainty and complexity surrounding decisions make them challenging.

A second assumption is that poor decisions are made because managers lack relevant information. On the contrary, Ackoff argued, managers suffer more from an overabundance of irrelevant data. We refer to this overabundance as **information overload**.

[1] P. Tingling and M. Brydon, "Is Decision-Based Evidence Making Necessarily Bad?" *Sloan Management Review* 51, no. 4 (Summer 2010): 71–76.

[2] R. Ackoff, "Management Misinformation Systems," *Management Science* 14, no. 4 (December 1967): B147–156.

A third erroneous assumption is that managers know what data they need. Ackoff argued that in reality, managers are often not sure whether their requests are necessary or superfluous. And because they are unsure, the tendency is to ask for as much data as possible, thus promoting information overload.

Information Overload

It seems clear that managers are currently facing information overload. One interesting question to consider is just how much of an overload exists. According to a study done by the US multinational EMC, with analysis from International Data Corporation (IDC), the digital universe is doubling in size every two years, and by 2020 the data created and copied annually will reach 44 zettabytes, or 44 trillion gigabytes. Think about that number. How big is an **exabyte**? As shown in Figure 8-1, 200 **petabytes** is roughly the amount of all the printed material ever written. The study also found that data is growing at a rate of 40 percent a year, which suggests the challenge of information overload will continue to expand.[3]

Kilobyte (KB)	1000 bytes OR 10^3 bytes 2 Kilobytes: A typewritten page 100 Kilobytes: A low-resolution photograph
Megabyte (MB)	1 000 000 bytes OR 10^6 bytes 1 Megabyte: A small novel OR a 3.5-inch floppy disk 2 Megabytes: A high-resolution photograph 5 Megabytes: The complete works of Shakespeare 10 Megabytes: A minute of high-fidelity sound 100 Megabytes: 1 meter of shelved books 500 Megabytes: A CD-ROM
Gigabyte (GB)	1 000 000 000 bytes OR 10^9 bytes 1 Gigabyte: A pickup truck filled with paper 20 Gigabytes: A good collection of the works of Beethoven 100 Gigabytes: A library floor of academic journals
Terabyte (TB)	1 000 000 000 000 bytes OR 10^{12} bytes 1 Terabyte: 50 000 trees made into paper and printed 2 Terabytes: An academic research library 10 Terabytes: The printed collection of the U.S. Library of Congress 400 Terabytes: National Climactic Data Center (NOAA) database
Petabyte (PB)	1 000 000 000 000 000 bytes OR 10^{15} bytes 1 Petabyte: Three years of EOS data (2001) 2 Petabytes: All U.S. academic research libraries 20 Petabytes: Production of hard-disk drives in 1995 200 Petabytes: All printed material
Exabyte (EB)	1 000 000 000 000 000 000 bytes OR 10^{18} bytes 2 Exabytes: Total volume of information generated worldwide [in 1999] 5 Exabytes: All words ever spoken by human beings

Figure 8-1 How Big Is an Exabyte?

Source: www2.sims.berkeley.edu/research/projects/how-much-info/datapowers.html. Used with the permission of Peter Lyman and Hal R. Varian, University of California at Berkeley.

Why does this exponential growth in data matter? First, understand that growth is occurring both inside and outside of organizations. Every time Tesla builds another car, its information systems generate megabytes of data about designs, bills of materials, supplier performance, production costs, employee productivity, customer payment patterns, market and product trends, and so forth.

[3] "EMC Digital Universe Study with Research and Analysis by IDC", www.emc.com/leadership/digital-universe/index.htm.

Buried in all these data is information that, if found and made available to the right people at the right time, can improve the decisions Tesla makes. For example, when negotiating with a supplier, how flexible does the company want to be? The decision to reduce price must be based, in part, on past experience. What was the quality of the supplier's products compared with Tesla's requirements and the capabilities of its competitors? How many items were defective or late? How much service and support has the supplier provided?

The challenge for managers in a world overloaded with information is to find the appropriate data and incorporate them into their decision making processes. Information systems can both help and hinder this process.

Data Quality

A final challenge in decision making is the quality of data. Up to this point, we have assumed that the data stored in systems are clean and accurate. But this is the exception rather than the rule in most systems. It is hard enough to make decisions when you have good-quality data. But what if the data are of low quality? How would this affect your decisions?

Data from operational systems can be processed to create basic reports with few issues. If we want to know, for example, current sales and how those sales relate to sales projections, we simply process data in the order-entry database. However, raw operational data are seldom suitable for more sophisticated reporting or data mining. Figure 8-2 lists the major problem categories.

First, the data may be problematic or what is commonly termed **dirty data**. Examples include using values such as *B* for customer gender; *213* for customer age; 999-999-9999 for a phone number; *gren* for a part colour; and WhyMe@GuessWhoIAM.org for an email address. All these values can be problematic for data mining purposes.

Missing values are a second problem. A nonprofit organization can process a donation without knowing the donor's gender or age, but a data mining application can be impaired if these types of values are missing.

Inconsistent data, the third problem shown in Figure 8-2, are particularly common in data that have been gathered over time. When an area code changes, for example, the phone number for a given customer before the change will not match the customer's number after the change. Likewise, part codes can change, as can sales territories. Before such data can be used, they must be recoded for consistency over the period of the study.

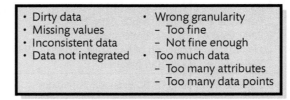

Figure 8-2 Problems with Using Operational Data for Business Intelligence Systems

Data not integrated, the fourth problem, can occur if the data reside in different sources or are incompatible with the intended purpose. Because data that are critical for successful operations must be complete and accurate, data that are only marginally necessary or were not designed and collected with the specific purpose in mind may not be. In the case of the National Hockey League, for example, information about where each player was on the ice when a goal was scored has only recently been collected and matching it up with the timing of each player's shift for analytic purposes is difficult.

Data can also be too fine or too coarse. Data **granularity** refers to the degree of summarization or detail. *Coarse data* are highly summarized; *fine data* express details that are too precise. For example, suppose we want to analyze the placement of graphics and controls on an order-entry webpage. It is possible to capture the customers' clicking behaviour in what is termed **clickstream data**. Those data are very fine; they include everything the customer does at the website. In the middle of the order stream are data for clicks on the news, email, instant chat, and a weather check. Although all those data are needed for the study of consumer computer behaviour, such data will be overwhelming if all we want to know is how customers respond to advertisement locations. Because the data are too fine, the data analysts often throw away millions and millions of clicks to avoid the problem of having too much data and too many attributes to work with.

Generally, it is better to have granularity that is too fine than too coarse. If the granularity is too fine, the data can be made coarser by summing and combining. Google Analytics (www.google.com/analytics) provides a good example of the power of summing and combining data. Only analysts' labour and computer processing are required. If the granularity is too coarse, however, there is no way to separate the data into constituent parts.

This section has suggested that a number of factors, including complexity, uncertainty, information overload, and data quality, make management decision making challenging. Information from information systems has the potential to meet some of these challenges. In this chapter, we outline categories of systems that support the decision making process.

Q8-2 WHAT ARE OLTP AND OLAP AND HOW DO THEY SUPPORT DECISION MAKING?

In Chapter 7, we noted that functional systems, such as general ledger systems, human resources systems, and operational systems, are used to capture details about business transactions and then create updated information by processing these transaction details. There are many types of business transactions. Purchasing a product or service, receiving a shipment from a supplier, creating a purchase order for a new printer, making a customer service call, and returning defective items to a store are all examples of transactions. Information systems are a critical component for capturing and processing the details about these transactions because they are very efficient and accurate.

Using computers to capture information electronically is often referred to as being online. When a bank's customer service representative accepts your deposit, he or she enters the transaction online so that he or she does not have to write down information on paper and then copy it into the system at a later time. Most Web-based applications are examples of online systems.

If you are collecting data electronically and processing the transactions online, then you are using an **online transaction processing (OLTP)** system. There are two basic ways that transactions can be processed. (1) If transactions are entered and processed immediately on entry, then the system is operating in real time because there is little or no delay in updating the system with new data. (2) The other option is to wait for many transactions to accumulate before you process them. For example, at a gas station, you might collect all the transactions that occurred during the day and then send them at the end of the day to the central office for processing. This is an example of batch processing because the system waits until it has a batch of transactions before the data are processed and the information is updated.

The choice of whether to use real-time processing or batch processing depends on the nature of the transactions, the cost of the system, and the needs of the organization. Real-time systems tend to be more complex and cost more to implement. However, real-time systems provide the most up-to-date information, and that is often important. For example, Ticketmaster (www.ticketmaster.ca), a company that sells concert and event tickets over the phone and online, would find it difficult to use a batch-processing system. Why? The most important thing for Ticketmaster is to make sure it does not sell more than one ticket for the same seat. A real-time system will ensure that only one ticket is sold per seat because the system is updated after every transaction. A batch-processing system, however, might register two tickets for one seat if the sales occur within a single batch.

OLTP systems are the backbone of all functional, cross-functional, and interorganizational systems in a company. They are designed to efficiently enter, process, and store data. OLTP systems combine large databases with efficient input devices, such as grocery store scanners, automated cash registers, and debit and credit card readers, to process transactions quickly and accurately. Large OLTP systems, such as airline reservation systems and banking systems, are capable of reliably processing thousands of transactions per second over a long period. Whether large or small, OLTPs support decision making by providing the raw information about transactions and status for an organization.

Using OLTP to collect data is important. Information is a competitive weapon and can be a source of competitive advantage for a company. But data alone are not enough. They do not create value if they are ignored or not used effectively. It is important to realize that the competitive advantage of information is often realized when organizations begin to *use* the data they have collected to make better decisions.

Systems that focus on making OLTP-collected data useful for decision making are often referred to as **decision support systems (DSSs)** or, more generally, as **online analytic processing (OLAP)** systems. OLAP provides the ability to sum, count, average, and perform other simple arithmetic operations on groups of data. The remarkable characteristic of OLAP reports is that their format is dynamic. The viewer of the report can change the report's structure—hence the term *online*.

An OLAP report has measures, or facts, and dimensions. A measure is the data item of interest. It is the item that is to be summed or averaged or otherwise processed in the OLAP report. Total sales, average sales, and average cost are examples of measures. A dimension is a characteristic of a measure. Purchase date, customer type, customer location, and sales region are all examples of dimensions.

Figure 8-3 shows a typical OLAP report. Here, the measure is Store Sales Net, and the dimensions are Product Family and Store Type. This report shows how net store sales vary by product family and store type. Stores of type Supermarket, for example, sold a net of $36 189 in nonconsumable goods.

	A	B	C	D	E	F	G
1							
2							
3	Store Sales Net	Store Type ▼					
4	Product Family ▼	Deluxe Supermarket	Gourmet Supermarket	Mid-Size Grocery	Small Grocery	Supermarket	Grand Total
5	Drink	$8 119.05	$2 392.83	$1 409.50	$685.89	$16 751.71	$29 358.98
6	Food	$70 276.11	$20 026.18	$10 392.19	$6 109.72	$138 960.67	$245 764.87
7	Nonconsumable	$18 884.24	$5 064.79	$2 813.73	$1 534.90	$36 189.40	$64 487.05
8	Grand Total	$97 279.40	$27 483.80	$14 615.42	$8 330.51	$191 901.77	$339 610.90

Figure 8-3 OLAP Product Family by Store Type

Source: Microsoft Excel

The presentation of a measure with associated dimensions, as in Figure 8-3, is often called an *OLAP cube*, or simply a *cube*. The reason for this term is that some products show these displays using three axes, like a cube in geometry. The origin of the term is unimportant here, however. You should just know that an OLAP cube and an OLAP report are the same thing.

The OLAP report in Figure 8-3 was generated by SQL Server Analysis Services and is displayed in an Excel pivot table. The data were taken from a sample instructional database, called *FoodMart*, which is provided with SQL Server. It is possible to display OLAP cubes in many ways other than Excel. Some third-party vendors provide more extensive graphical displays. Making data easier to understand through graphic displays is often referred to as data visualization.

For more information about data visualization software applications and products, check for OLAP vendors and products at the Data Warehousing Review website at www. dwreview.com/OLAP. Note, too, that OLAP reports can be delivered just like any of the other reports described for report management systems.

As stated earlier, the distinguishing characteristic of an OLAP report is that the user can alter the format of the report. Figure 8-4 shows such an alteration. Here, the user added another dimension, store country and state, to the horizontal display. Product Family sales are now dissected according to the location of the stores. Observe that the sample data include only stores in the United States and only in the western states of California, Oregon, and Washington. With an OLAP report, it is possible to **drill down** into the data. This term means to further divide the data into more detail.

	A	B	C	D	E	F	G	H	I
1									
2									
3	Store Sales Net			Store Type ▼					
4	Product Family ▼	Store ▼	Store State	Deluxe Supermarket	Gourmet Supermarket	Mid-Size Grocery	Small Grocery	Supermarket	Grand Total
5	Drink	USA	CA		$2 392.83		$227.38	$5 920.76	$8 540.97
6			OR	$4 438.49				$2 862.45	$7 300.94
7			WA	$3 680.56		$1 409.50	$458.51	$7 968.50	$13 517.07
8		USA Total		$8 119.05	$2 392.83	$1 409.50	$685.89	$16 751.71	$29 358.98
9	Drink Total			$8 119.05	$2 392.83	$1 409.50	$685.89	$16 751.71	$29 358.98
10	Food	USA	CA		$20 026.18		$1 960.53	$47 226.11	$69 212.82
11			OR	$37 778.35				$23 818.87	$61 597.22
12			WA	$32 497.76		$10 392.19	$4 149.19	$67 915.69	$114 954.83
13		USA Total		$70 276.11	$20 026.18	$10 392.19	$6 109.72	$138 960.67	$245 764.87
14	Food Total			$70 276.11	$20 026.18	$10 392.19	$6 109.72	$138 960.67	$245 764.87
15	Nonconsumable	USA	CA		$5 064.79		$474.35	$12 344.49	$17 883.63
16			OR	$10 177.89				$6 428.53	$16 606.41
17			WA	$8 706.36		$2 813.73	$1 060.54	$17 416.38	$29 997.01
18		USA Total		$18 884.24	$5 064.79	$2 813.73	$1 534.90	$36 189.40	$64 487.05
19	Nonconsumable Total			$18 884.24	$5 064.79	$2 813.73	$1 534.90	$36 189.40	$64 487.05
20	Grand Total			$97 279.40	$27 483.80	$14 615.42	$8 330.51	$191 901.77	$339 610.90

Figure 8-4 OLAP Product Family and Store Location by Store Type

Source: Microsoft Excel

In Figure 8-5, for example, the user has drilled down into the stores located in California; the OLAP report now shows sales data for the four cities in California that have stores.

Look at another difference between Figures 8-4 and 8-5. The user has not only drilled down but has also changed the order of the dimensions. Figure 8-4 shows Product Family and then store location within Product Family. Figure 8-5 shows store location and then Product Family within store location.

Both displays are valid and useful, depending on the user's perspective. A product manager might like to see product families first and then store location data. A sales manager might like to see store locations first and then product data. OLAP reports provide both perspectives, and the user can switch between them while viewing the report. Unfortunately, all this flexibility comes at a cost. If the database is large, doing the necessary calculating, grouping, and sorting of such dynamic displays will require substantial computing power. Although standard, commercial database management system (DBMS) products do have the features and functions required to create OLAP reports, they are not designed for such work. They are designed instead to provide rapid response to transaction-processing

Figure 8-5 OLAP Product Family and Store Location by Store Type

			Store Type	Deluxe Super	Gourmet Supermarket	Mid-Size Grocery	Small Grocery	Supermarket	Grand Total
Store Country	Store State	Store City	Product Family						
USA	CA	Beverly Hills	Drink		$2 392.83				$2 392.83
			Food		$20 026.18				$20 026.18
			Nonconsumable		$5 064.79				$5 064.79
		Beverly Hills Total			$27 483.80				$27 483.80
		Los Angeles	Drink					$2 870.33	$2 870.33
			Food					$23 598.28	$23 598.28
			Nonconsumable					$6 305.14	$6 305.14
		Los Angeles Total						$32 773.74	$32 773.74
		San Diego	Drink					$3 050.43	$3 050.43
			Food					$23 627.83	$23 627.83
			Nonconsumable					$6 039.34	$6 039.34
		San Diego Total						$32 717.61	$32 717.61
		San Francisco	Drink				$227.38		$227.38
			Food				$1 960.53		$1 960.53
			Nonconsumable				$474.35		$474.35
		San Francisco Total					$2 662.26		$2 662.26
	CA Total				$27 483.80		$2 662.26	$65 491.35	$95 637.41
	OR		Drink	$4 438.49				$2 862.45	$7 300.94
			Food	$37 778.35				$23 818.87	$61 597.22
			Nonconsumable	$10 177.89				$6 428.53	$16 606.41
	OR Total			$52 394.72				$33 109.85	$85 504.57
	WA		Drink	$3 680.56		$1 409.50	$458.51	$7 968.50	$13 517.07
			Food	$32 497.76		$10 392.19	$4 149.19	$67 915.69	$114 954.83
			Nonconsumable	$8 706.36		$2 813.73	$1 060.54	$17 416.38	$29 997.01
	WA Total			$44 884.68		$14 615.42	$5 668.24	$93 300.57	$158 468.91
USA Total				$97 279.40	$27 483.80	$14 615.42	$8 330.51	$191 901.77	$339 610.90
Grand Total				$97 279.40	$27 483.80	$14 615.42	$8 330.51	$191 901.77	$339 610.90

Source: Microsoft Excel

applications, such as order entry or manufacturing operations. Accordingly, special-purpose products called *OLAP servers* have been developed to perform OLAP analysis.

OLAP tools have become the primary tools used in the area of business intelligence (BI). "MIS in Use" (page 268) provides an example of how BI can be used to support decisions in pro-hockey. We will learn more about BI in the section that follows.

Not all organizations use their data effectively. For example, Thomas Davenport[4] noted that a major grocery chain used less than 2 percent of the scanner data it had collected over the years. So, although data may be collected in OLTP, they may not be used to improve decision making. We refer to this idea as the **data resource challenge**.

The quickest way to explain the data resource challenge is to consider whether a company views its data as an asset. An *asset* can be defined as a resource from which future economic benefits may be obtained. When you think about it in depth, data are particularly good assets. They do not take up much space, are easy to store, do not depreciate in the same way physical assets depreciate, and can provide input for improved decision making.

But here is the challenge. If data, as a whole, is an asset, like money and real estate, who in the company is in charge of managing the data? What are the generally accepted

[4] T. H. Davenport et al., "Data to Knowledge to Results: Building an Analytic Capability," *California Management Review* 43, no. 2 (2001): 117–38.

accounting principles associated with valuing data as an asset? Where do data show up on a balance sheet? Who is in charge of extracting as much value as possible out of the data? You will find that most companies have a hard time answering these questions. What this means is that although we like to think of data as an asset, we are not really treating data as an important resource. Treating data as a true resource begins with a focus on business intelligence.

Q8-3 WHAT ARE BUSINESS INTELLIGENCE SYSTEMS?

A **business intelligence (BI) system** is a system that provides information to improve decision making. BI systems vary in their characteristics and capabilities, and in the way they foster competitive advantage.

Figure 8-6 summarizes the characteristics and competitive advantage of five categories of BI systems. **Group decision support systems (GDSSs)** allow multiple parties to participate in decision making and improve outcomes by reducing often inherent biases. GDSSs, for example, allow participants across different geographical locations and times to provide anonymous input that is automatically summed or communicated to the group and contributes to a decision. **Reporting systems** integrate data from multiple sources and process those data by sorting, grouping, summing, averaging, and comparing. Such systems format the results into reports and deliver those reports to users. Reporting systems improve decision making by providing the right information to the right user at the right time.

Business Intelligence System	Characteristics	Competitive Advantage
Group Decision Support Systems (GDSS)	Allow multiple decision makers to collaborate, often anonymously and at different times and in different locations.	Improve decision outcomes by reducing many of the biases inherent in group discussion and option evaluation.
Reporting Systems	Integrate and process data by sorting, grouping, summing, and formatting. Produce, administer, and deliver reports.	Improve decisions by providing relevant, accurate, and timely information to the right person.
Data-Mining Systems	Use sophisticated statistical techniques to find patterns and relationships.	Improve decisions by discovering patterns and relationships in data to predict future outcomes.
Knowledge Management Systems	Share knowledge of products, product uses, best practices, etc., among employees, managers, customers, and others.	Improve decisions by publishing employee and others' knowledge. Create value from existing intellectual capital. Foster innovation, improve customer service, increase organizational responsiveness, and reduce costs.
Expert Systems	Encode human knowledge in the form of If/Then rules and process those rules to make a diagnosis or recommendation.	Improve decision making by non-experts by encoding, saving, and processing expert knowledge.

Figure 8-6 Characteristics and Competitive Advantage of BI Systems

How sports teams choose athletes has changed considerably in the past several decades. Although how fast an athlete can run or how many pushups he or she can do are still important, fewer and fewer general managers make multimillion-dollar decisions with regard to players on the basis of a scout's qualitative assessment. Instead of gut instinct and intuition, managers are increasingly turning to scientific and statistical techniques that capture more data and reduce biases.

First introduced in professional baseball, this approach is often credited to Oakland Athletics general manager Billy Beane, who used unconventional measures to select his athletes. Described in Michael Lewis's best-selling book *Moneyball* (and later in the movie starring Brad Pitt), decision making in professional sports now includes objective data that are often statistically analyzed to provide insight and reduce flaws. Although there has been some resistance from managers who claim that the *Moneyball* approach does not work in true team sports, technology, computation, and statistics are essential and accepted aspects of decision making, and adoption of the technique has been extended not only to basketball but to hockey as well.

The stakes are high, and mistakes can be expensive. The lowest National Hockey League rookie's salary in 2012 was $525 000, and yet research has found that less than 40 percent of drafted athletes will ever play in a single NHL game, and of those who do, 20 percent will play in fewer than 10 games. Even if a team can afford it, the salary cap (a fixed amount that a team can spend on its payroll) limits the ability of the team to buy up all the available talent.

Teams are reluctant, of course, to discuss the specifics of how they apply technology to decision making, but numerous sources have noted an increase in technology spending by professional teams. And the number of managers with advanced degrees in statistics or analytics is increasing as well.

Watch the MIT sports analytics video "Better off Guessing" available at http://video.mit.edu/watch/better-off-guessing-measuring-the-quality-of-draft-decisions-peter-tingling-7270/.

QUESTIONS

1. What process would you use to identify your choice of a first round athletic draft?

2. Is choosing athletes any different from hiring any other kind of employee?

3. Why do you think these techniques first appeared in baseball, rather than hockey or basketball?

4. Why would teams be reluctant to discuss how they use technology?

5. Is this increased sophistication in decision making inevitable? How do you make decisions, and how has this changed over time?

Data mining systems process data by using sophisticated statistical techniques, such as regression analysis and decision tree analysis. Data mining systems might find patterns and relationships that cannot be found by simpler reporting operations such as sorting, grouping, and averaging. Data mining systems improve decision making by using the discovered patterns and relationships to *anticipate* events or to *predict* future outcomes. An example of a data mining system is one that predicts the likelihood that a prospect will donate to a cause or political campaign on the basis of the prospect's characteristics, such as age, gender, and home postal code. **Market-basket analysis** is one of the data mining systems; it computes correlations of items on past orders to determine items that are frequently purchased together. We will discuss data mining in more detail later in this chapter.

Knowledge management (KM) systems create value from intellectual capital by collecting and sharing human knowledge—of products, product uses, best practices, and other critical information—with employees, managers, customers, suppliers, and others who need it. Knowledge management is a process supported by the five components of an information system. By sharing knowledge, KM systems foster innovation, improve customer service, increase organizational responsiveness by getting products and services to market faster, and reduce costs.

Expert systems are the fifth category of BI systems shown in Figure 8-6. Expert systems encapsulate the knowledge of human experts in the form of *If/Then* rules. In a medical diagnosis system, for example, an expert system might have a rule such as the following:

If Patient_Temperature > 103, *Then* Initiate High_Fever_Procedure

Operational expert systems can have hundreds or even thousands of such rules. Although few expert systems have demonstrated a capability equivalent to that of a human expert, some are good enough to considerably improve the diagnosis and decision making of non-experts.

As with all information systems, it is important to distinguish between BI *tools* and BI *systems*. SAP licenses the reporting tool Crystal Reports. SPSS licenses the data mining suite Clementine, and Microsoft offers SharePoint Server as, in part, a KM system. All these products are, however, just software tools. They represent only one of the five components.

To reap the benefits of improved decision making, organizations must incorporate data mining products into complete information systems. A reporting tool can generate a report showing that a customer has cancelled an important order. It takes a reporting *system*, however, to alert the customer's salesperson to this unwanted news in time for the salesperson to attempt to reverse the decision. Similarly, a data mining tool can create an equation that computes the probability that a customer will default on a loan. A data mining *system*, however, uses that equation to enable banking personnel to approve or reject a loan on the spot.

A relatively simple example of this is provided by RFM analysis. An **RFM analysis** is a way of analyzing and ranking customers according to their purchasing patterns.[5] It is a simple technique that considers how recently (R) a customer has ordered, how frequently (F) a customer orders, and how much money (M) the customer spends per order. We consider this technique here because it is a useful analysis that can be readily implemented.

To produce an RFM score, the application first sorts customer purchase records by the date of most recent (R) purchase. In a common form of this analysis, the program then divides the customers into five groups and gives customers in each group a score of 1 to 5. Thus, the 20 percent who have the most recent orders are given an R score of 1, the 20 percent who have the next most recent orders are given an R score of 2, and so on, down to the last 20 percent who are given an R score of 5.

The program then re-sorts the customers on the basis of how frequently they order. The 20 percent of customers who order most frequently are given an F score of 1, the next 20 percent are given a score of 2, and so on, down to the least frequently ordering customers, who are given an F score of 5.

Finally, the program sorts the customers again according to the amount spent on their orders. The 20 percent who have ordered the most expensive items are given an M score of 1, the next 20 percent are given an M score of 2, and so forth, down to the 20 percent who spend the least, who are given an M score of 5. A reporting system can generate the RFM data and deliver it in many ways. For example, a report with RFM scores for all customers can be given to the vice-president of sales; reports with scores for particular regions can be given to regional sales managers; and reports with scores for particular accounts can be given to the account salespeople. And all of this reporting can be automated.

Q8-4 HOW DO ORGANIZATIONS USE DATA WAREHOUSES TO ACQUIRE DATA?

Although it is possible to create basic reports and perform simple analyses from operational data, this course is not usually recommended. For reasons of security and control, IS professionals do not want data analysts processing operational data. If an analyst makes an error, that error could cause a serious disruption in the company's operations. Also, operational data is structured for fast and reliable transaction processing. It is seldom structured in a way that readily supports BI analysis. Finally, BI analyses can require considerable processing; placing BI applications on operational servers can dramatically reduce system performance.

[5] A. M. Hughes, "Boosting Response with RFM," *Marketing Tools*, May 1996. See also www.dbmarketing.com.

For these reasons, most organizations extract operational data for BI processing. For small organizations, the extraction may be as simple as an Access database. Larger organizations, however, typically create and staff a group of people who manage and run a **data warehouse**, which is a facility for managing an organization's BI data. The functions of a data warehouse are to:

- Obtain data
- Cleanse data
- Organize and relate data
- Catalog data

The purpose of a data warehouse is to extract and clean data from operational systems and other sources and to store and catalogue that data for processing by BI tools. Figure 8-7 shows the basic components of a data warehouse. Programs read operational data and extract, clean, and prepare that data for BI processing. The prepared data are stored in a data warehouse database using a data warehouse DBMS, which can be different from the organization's operational DBMS. For example, an organization might use Oracle for its operational processing, but SQL Server for its data warehouse. Other organizations use SQL Server for operational processing, but DBMSs from statistical package vendors, such as SAS or SPSS, in the data warehouse.

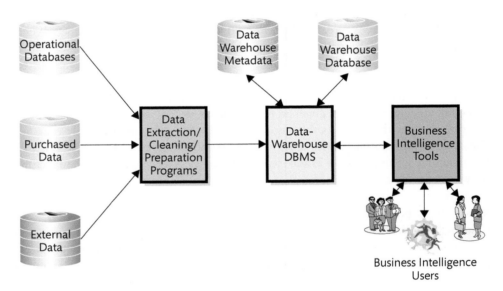

Figure 8-7 Components of a Data Warehouse

Data warehouses include data that are purchased from outside sources. A typical example is customer credit data. Figure 8-8 lists some of the consumer data that can be

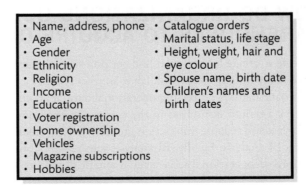

- Name, address, phone
- Age
- Gender
- Ethnicity
- Religion
- Income
- Education
- Voter registration
- Home ownership
- Vehicles
- Magazine subscriptions
- Hobbies
- Catalogue orders
- Marital status, life stage
- Height, weight, hair and eye colour
- Spouse name, birth date
- Children's names and birth dates

Figure 8-8 Consumer Data Available for Purchase from Data Vendors

purchased from commercial vendors. An amazing (and, from a privacy standpoint, frightening) amount of data is available.

Metadata are data about data. For example, a database might store not only data but also data about the source of the data, the format of the data, and other facts about the data. This type of data is stored as metadata in the data warehouse. The DBMS that runs the data warehouse can be used to extract information and provides data to BI tools, such as data mining programs.

By the way, do not interpret the term *warehouse* literally. It is a warehouse only in the sense that it is a facility for storing data for use by others. It is *not* a large building with shelves and forklifts buzzing through aisles loaded with pallets. Physically, a data warehouse consists of a few fast computers with very large storage devices. The data warehouse is usually staffed by a small department consisting of both technical personnel and business analysts. The technical personnel work to develop the best ways of storing and cataloguing the data warehouse's contents. The business analysts work to ensure that the contents are relevant and sufficient for the business needs of BI system users.

Q8-5 WHAT ARE THE DIFFERENCES BETWEEN DATA WAREHOUSES AND DATA MARTS?

A **data mart** is a data collection that is created to address the needs of a particular business function, problem, or opportunity. An electronic commerce (e-commerce) company, for example, might create a data mart storing clickstream data that are pre-sampled and summarized so as to enable the analysis of webpage design features.

That same company might have a second data mart for market-basket analysis. This second data mart would contain records of past sales data organized to facilitate the computation of item--purchase correlations. A third data mart could contain inventory data and may be organized to support a BI system used to plan the layout of inventory.

So, how is a data warehouse different from a data mart? In a way, you can think of a *data warehouse* as a distributor in a supply chain. The data warehouse takes data from the data manufacturers (operational systems and purchased data), cleans and processes the data, and locates the data on its shelves, so to speak—that is, on the disks of the data warehouse computers. The people who work with a data warehouse are experts at data management, data cleaning, data transformation, and the like. However, they are usually not experts in a given business function.

As stated, a *data mart* is a data collection, smaller than the data warehouse, which addresses a particular component or functional area of the business. If the data warehouse is the distributor in a supply chain, then a data mart is a retail store in a supply chain. Users in the data mart obtain data from the data warehouse that pertain to a particular business function. Such users do not have the data management expertise that data warehouse employees have, but they are knowledgeable analysts for a given business function. Figure 8-9 illustrates these relationships.

As you can imagine, it is expensive to create, staff, and operate data warehouses and data marts. Only large organizations with considerable resources can afford to operate a system like the one shown in Figure 8-9. Smaller organizations operate subsets of such a system; they may have just a simple data mart for analyzing promotion data, for example.

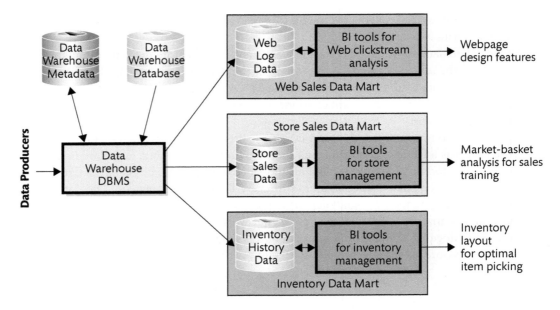

Figure 8-9 Data Mart Examples

Q8-6 WHAT ARE TYPICAL DATA MINING APPLICATIONS?

Now we can turn to the concept of data mining. **Data mining** is the application of statistical techniques to find patterns and relationships among data and to make classifications and predictions. As shown in Figure 8-10, data mining represents a convergence of disciplines. Data mining techniques emerged from statistics and mathematics and from artificial intelligence and machine-learning fields in computer science. As a result, data mining terminology is an odd blend of terms from these different disciplines.

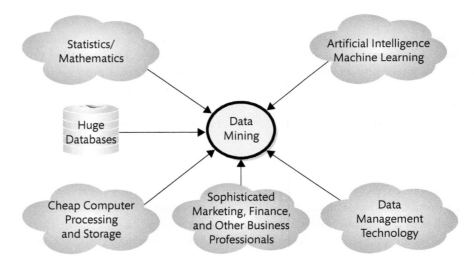

Figure 8-10 Convergence of Disciplines for Data Mining

Data mining techniques take advantage of developments in data management for processing the enormous databases that have emerged in the last several decades. Of course, these data would not have been generated were it not for fast and cheap computers and low-cost storage—and without these components, the new techniques would be impossible to compute.

Most data mining techniques are sophisticated, and many are difficult to use. Such techniques are valuable to organizations, however, and some business professionals, especially those in finance and marketing, have become expert in their use. In fact, there are many interesting and rewarding careers for business professionals who are knowledgeable about data mining techniques. It is important, however, to recognize that data mining has limitations, which we discuss in the collaborative exercise "Data Mining in the Real World" at the end of this chapter on pages 278–279.

Data mining techniques fall into two broad categories: *unsupervised* and *supervised*. We look at both types here.

Unsupervised Data Mining

With **unsupervised data mining**, analysts do not create a model or hypothesis before running the analysis. Instead, they apply the data mining technique to the data and observe the results. With this method, analysts create hypotheses after the analysis to explain the patterns found.

One common unsupervised technique is **cluster analysis**, in which statistical techniques identify groups of entities that have similar characteristics. A common use for cluster analysis is to find groups of similar customers from customer order and demographic data.

For example, suppose a cluster analysis finds two very different customer groups—one group has an average age of 33 years, and each member owns at least one laptop and at least one smartphone, drives an expensive sport utility vehicle (SUV), and tends to buy expensive children's toys. The second group has an average age of 64 years, and each member owns a vacation property, plays golf, and buys expensive wines. Suppose the analysis also finds that both groups buy designer children's clothing.

These findings are obtained solely by data analysis. There is no prior model of the patterns and relationships that exist. It is up to the analyst to form hypotheses, after the fact, to explain why two such different groups are both buying designer children's clothes.

Supervised Data Mining

With **supervised data mining**, data miners develop a model prior to the analysis and apply statistical techniques to data to estimate the parameters of the model. For example, suppose marketing experts in a communications company believe that cell phone usage on weekends is determined by the age of the customer and the number of months he or she has had the cell phone account. A data mining analyst would then run an analysis that estimates the impact of customer and account age. One such analysis, which measures the impact of a set of variables on another variable, is called a **regression analysis**. A sample result for the cell phone example is as follows:

CellPhoneWeekendMinutes =
12 + (17.5 × CustomerAge) + (23.7 × NumberMonthsOfAccount)

Using this equation, analysts can predict the number of minutes of weekend cell phone use by summing 12 plus 17.5 times the customer's age, plus 23.7 times the number of months of the account.

As you will learn in your statistics course, considerable skill is required to interpret the quality of such a model. The regression tool will create an equation such as the one above. Whether that equation is a good predictor of future cell phone usage depends on statistical factors, such as *t*-values, confidence intervals, and related statistical techniques.

Neural networks are another popular supervised data mining technique used to predict values and make classifications, such as good prospect or poor prospect customers. The term *neural networks* is deceiving, however, because it connotes a biological process similar to that in brains. In fact, although the original *idea* of neural networks may have come from the anatomy and physiology of neurons, a neural network is nothing more than a complex set of possibly nonlinear equations. Explaining the techniques used for neural networks is beyond the scope of this text. If you want to learn more, search www.kdnuggets.com for the term *neural network*.

Another technique is *market-basket analysis*. Suppose you run a dive shop, and one day you realize that one of your sales associates is much better than anyone else at upselling to your customers. Any of your sales associates can fill a customer's order, but this one person is especially good at upselling, that is, selling other items in addition to those customers ask for. One day, you ask her how she does it.

"It's simple," she says. "I just ask myself what the next product a customer would want to buy might be. If someone buys a dive computer, I don't try to sell her fins. If she's buying a dive computer, she's already a scuba diver and she already has fins. But dive computer displays are hard to read. So, a better mask makes it easier to read the display and get the computer's full benefit."

Without knowing it, your sales associate is using a market-basket analysis, which is a data mining technique for determining sales patterns. A market-basket analysis shows the products that customers tend to buy together. In marketing transactions, the fact that customers who buy product X also buy product Y creates a cross-selling opportunity. That is, "If they're buying X, sell them Y," or, "If they're buying Y, sell them X."

Figure 8-11 shows hypothetical sales data of 1000 items at a dive shop. The first row of numbers under each column is the total number of times an item was sold. For example, 270 in the first row of Mask means that 270 of the 1000 purchased items were masks. The number 120 under Dive Computer means that 120 of the 1000 purchased items were dive computers.

1000 Items	Mask	Tank	Fins	Weights	Dive Computer
	270	200	280	130	120
Mask	20	20	150	20	50
Tank	20	80	40	30	30
Fins	150	40	10	60	20
Weights	20	30	60	10	10
Dive computer	50	30	20	10	5
No additional product	10	—	—	—	5

Support = P (A & B)   Example: P (Fins & Mask) = 150/1000 = 0.15

Confidence = P (A | B)   Example: P (Fins | Mask) = 150/270 = 0.5556

Lift = P (A | B)/P (A)   Example: P (Fins | Mask)/P (Fins) = 0.5556/0.28 = 1.98

Note: P(Mask | Fins)/P(Mask) = (150/280)/0.27 = 1.98

Figure 8-11 Market-Basket Example

We can use the numbers in the first row to estimate the probability that a customer will purchase an item. Because 270 of the 1000 items were masks, we can estimate the probability that a customer will buy a mask to be 270/1000, or 0.27.

In market-basket terminology, *support* is the probability that two items will be purchased together. To estimate that probability, we examine sales transactions and count the number of times that two items occurred in the same transaction. For the data in Figure 8-11, fins and masks appeared together 150 times, and, thus, the support for fins and a mask is 150/1000, or 0.15. Similarly, the support for fins and weights is 60/1000, or 0.06, and the support for fins along with a second pair of fins is 10/1000, or 0.01.

The Market-Basket Example

These data are interesting in themselves, but we can refine the analysis by taking another step and considering additional probabilities. For example, what proportion of the customers who bought a mask also bought fins? Masks were purchased 270 times, and of those individuals who bought masks, 150 also bought fins. Thus, given that a customer bought a mask, we can estimate the probability that he or she will buy fins to be 150/270, or 0.5556. In market-basket terminology, such a conditional probability estimate is called *confidence*.

Reflect on the meaning of this confidence value. The likelihood of someone walking in the door and buying fins is 280/1000, or 0.28. But the likelihood of someone buying fins, given that he or she bought a mask, is 0.5556. Thus, if someone buys a mask, the likelihood that he or she will also buy fins almost doubles, from 0.28 to 0.5556. Thus, all sales personnel should be trained to try to sell fins to anyone buying a mask.

Now, consider dive computers and fins. Of the 1000 items sold, fins were sold 280 times, so the probability that someone walks into the store and buys fins is 0.28. But of the 120 purchases of dive computers, only 20 also bought fins. So, the likelihood of someone buying fins, given he or she bought a dive computer, is 20/120, or 0.1666. Thus, when someone buys a dive computer, the likelihood that he or she will also buy fins falls from 0.28 to 0.1666.

The ratio of confidence to the base probability of buying an item is called **lift**. Lift shows how much the base probability increases or decreases when other products are purchased. The lift of fins and a mask is the confidence of fins given a mask, divided by the base probability of fins. In Figure 8-11, the lift of fins and a mask is 0.5556/0.28, or 1.98. Thus, the likelihood that people buy fins when they buy a mask almost doubles. Surprisingly, it turns out that the lift of fins and a mask is the same as the lift of a mask and fins. Both are 1.98.

We need to be careful, however, because this analysis only shows shopping carts with two items. We cannot say from these data what the likelihood is that customers, given that they bought a mask, will buy both weights and fins. To assess that probability, we need to analyze shopping carts with three items. This statement illustrates, once again, that we need to know what problem we are solving before we start to build the information system to mine the data. The problem definition will help us decide whether we need to analyze three-item, four-item, or some other sized shopping carts.

Many organizations are benefiting from market-basket analysis today. You can expect that this technique will become a standard CRM analysis during your career.

Big Data

No MIS text today could ignore the relatively new but poorly defined term, **Big Data**. Although this term is poorly defined and its usage varies, almost all definitions and uses involve or reference the core concept that large amounts of varied data from a variety of sources over a period of time could be used to make better decisions. In 2008, for example, then-Senator Barack Obama's election project, Project Narwhal, used mail addresses, ZIP codes, and a variety of other data to customize email messages to appeal to voters most likely to support his election rather than send out a generic email message to everyone.

As might be expected, big data is controversial for a number of reasons. Beyond the lack of precision in its definition (when does data become big data), it is also criticized because it adds to excessive data collection, is expensive, and occasionally results in predictions that do not stand the test of time, are overly vague or general (left turns result in lower fuel economy), or confuse correlation with causality. While suntan lotion sales may go up in warm weather, no amount of suntan purchases will stop the rain. Nevertheless, while imprecise, big data is not likely to disappear soon.

How Does the Knowledge in This Chapter Help You?

As a future business professional, you will find that business intelligence is a critical skill. This chapter has given you the fundamentals of this increasingly important business decision making skills. You know characteristics and competitive advantages of business information systems, and you have learned common techniques for acquiring, processing, and publishing business intelligence. This knowledge will enable you to imagine innovative uses for data that your employer generates and also to know some of the constraints of such use.

ACTIVE REVIEW

Use this Active Review to verify that you have understood the material in the chapter. You can read the entire chapter and then perform the tasks in this review, or you can read the material for just one question and perform the tasks for that question before moving on to the next one.

Q8-1 DO MANAGERS MAKE RATIONAL DECISIONS?

Describe the factors, including information overload, uncertainty, and poor data quality, that make rational management decision making challenging. Explain how information systems have the potential to meet some of these challenges.

Q8-2 WHAT ARE OLTP AND OLAP AND HOW DO THEY SUPPORT DECISION MAKING?

Define the terms OLTP and OLAP. Explain why information systems are a critical component for capturing details about transactions. Explain how online transaction processing (OLTP) can be used to support decision making. Describe how OLAP differs from OLTP

Q8-3 WHAT ARE BUSINESS INTELLIGENCE SYSTEMS?

Define *business intelligence system*. Name five categories of BI systems, and describe the basic characteristics of each. Explain how systems in each category contribute to competitive advantage.

Q8-4 HOW DO ORGANIZATIONS USE DATA WAREHOUSES TO ACQUIRE DATA?

State the purpose of a data warehouse. Explain the role of each component in Figure 8-7. Of the many different types of data that can be purchased, name five that you think are the most problematic from a privacy standpoint. State several reasons why some businesses might want to purchase data. Explain why the term *warehouse* is misleading.

Q8-5 WHAT ARE THE DIFFERENCES BETWEEN DATA WAREHOUSES AND DATA MARTS?

Define *data mart*, and give an example of one that is not described in this chapter. Explain how data warehouses and data marts are like components of a supply chain. Under what conditions does an organization staff a data warehouse with several data marts?

Q8-6 WHAT ARE TYPICAL DATA MINING APPLICATIONS?

What is the purpose of data mining systems? Explain how data mining emerged from the convergence of different disciplines. Explain the characteristics and uses of unsupervised data mining. Explain the characteristics and uses of supervised data mining. Explain what is meant by market-basket analysis.

MyLab MIS

MyLab MIS is an online learning and testing environment that features the perfect study tools to help you master the concepts covered in this chapter. Log in to MyLab to test your knowledge of key chapter concepts and explore additional practice tools, including videos, flashcards, and more!

KEY TERMS AND CONCEPTS

Big Data 275
Business intelligence (BI) system 267
Clickstream data 263
Cluster analysis 273
Data mart 271
Data mining 272
Data mining systems 268
Data resource challenge 266
Data warehouse 270

Decision support systems (DSSs) 264
Dirty data 262
Drill down 265
Exabytes 261
Expert systems 268
Granularity 262
Group decision support systems (GDSSs) 267

Information overload 260
Knowledge management (KM) systems 268
Lift 275
Market-basket analysis 268
Metadata 271
Neural networks 273
Online analytic processing (OLAP) 264

Online transaction processing (OLTP) 263
Petabytes 261
Regression analysis 273
Reporting systems 267
RFM analysis 269
Supervised data mining 273
Unsupervised data mining 273

USING YOUR KNOWLEDGE

8-1. How does the data storage trend affect your college or university? What types of data are growing the fastest? Do students generate the most data? Compare data generated by students with data generated by classroom activities, administration, and research. Comment on similarities and differences.

8-2. OLTP systems are focused on providing three things: (a) efficient data input, (b) reliability, and (c) effective processing of a single transaction at a time. Use the knowledge you have gained to contrast these OLTP design principles with the design of OLAP systems. Do you see why the two types of systems require different designs?

8-3. Suppose you work for the university and have access to student, class, professor, department, and grade data. Now suppose you want to determine whether grade inflation exists, and, if so, where it seems to be the greatest. Describe a reporting system that would produce evidence of grade inflation. How would you structure the reports to determine where it is the greatest?

8-4. Suppose you work for the university and have access to student, class, professor, department, and grade data. Assume the student data include students' home address, high school, and prior post-secondary performance (if any). Describe an unsupervised data mining technique that could be used to predict which applicants are likely to succeed academically. Is it a responsible or irresponsible thing to use an unsupervised technique for such a problem?

8-5. Explain how a set of If/Then rules could be used to select a supplier. Give an example of five rules that would be pertinent to this problem. Given the nature of a dive shop's product, and the size and culture of the organization, do you think it is likely that the shop would embrace an expert system? What about a clothing business? Why or why not?

8-6. What do you think is the minimum size or the basic attributes that a company would need to consider a data warehouse? Figure 8-9 implies that data marts require the existence of a data warehouse, but this is not always the case. Some companies could construct a data mart containing inbound logistic and manufacturing data without a data warehouse. In this case, the data mart would need to clean and prep its own operational data. List seven decisions that such a data mart might support, and describe the BI system that would support each decision. Explain how such BI systems contribute to competitive strategy.

8-7. The list below shows a set of customers that a company has and their RFM scores. Answer the following questions using information from the list.

Customer	RFM Score
Ajax	1 1 5
Bistro	3 3 3
Carpenter	2 5 4
Dog Walker	1 5 1
Elephant Trainer	4 2 5

a. On which of the customers should the company focus its marketing efforts? Justify your answer.

b. Which customers bring in the most money to the organization? How can you tell?

c. If the organization had to drop one of the customers from the list, which customer would you choose to drop? Justify your answer.

COLLABORATIVE EXERCISES

Many grocery stores sponsor card programs, in which customers use special cards to receive purchase discounts. Shoppers Drug Mart, for example, sponsors the Optimum Card. The customer provides personal data, including his or her name, phone number, and address, and in return receives an identification card with a magnetic strip. When checking out, the customer gives the card to the cashier and points are added that can be redeemed for future purchases. The potential discount encourages people to use the card.

Card programs are popular; many grocery and retail chains have them, so they must provide value. The question is, what is that value?

8-1. Consider this question from a BI perspective:

a. What might Shoppers Drug Mart or a grocery chain do with data that can correlate a particular customer to that customer's purchases over time?

b. What information can such data provide? Assume that the data include not only the customer's identity, purchases, and purchase preferences, but the store location and the date and time of sale. The cards are valid at any store in the chain, so purchases at different stores can be associated with the same customer at a centralized data warehouse.

8-2. Describe market-basket analysis, and explain how a grocery store could perform such an analysis using its club card data. Suppose the lift of high-quality dog food and premium cheese is 3.4. Explain what this means. Describe four possible ways that Shoppers Drug Mart could use this information. As a team, rank the four possibilities from best to worst. Justify your ranking.

8-3. Mary Keeling owns and operates Carbon Creek Gardens, a retailer of trees and garden plants, including perennials, annuals, and bulbs. "The Gardens," as her customers call it, also sells bags of soil, fertilizer, small garden tools, and garden sculptures. Mary started the business 14 years ago, and it has grown steadily.

"The problem is, however," Mary says, "I have grown so large that I've lost track of my customers. The other day I ran into Tootsie Swan at the grocery store, and I realized I had not seen her in ages. I said hello and asked how she was doing, and that statement unleashed an angry torrent from her. It turns out she wanted to return a plant and one of my part-time employees apparently insulted her, and she has not been back since. She was one of my best customers, and I didn't even know she had decided not to shop at The Gardens."

Given this information, answer the following questions:

a. Describe the best possible application of an OLAP tool for Carbon Creek Gardens. Can it be used to solve the lost-customer problem? Why, or why not?

b. Describe the best possible application of market-basket analysis that could occur at Carbon Creek Gardens. Can it be used to solve the lost-customer problem? Why, or why not?

c. Which BI application would provide Mary with the best value? If you owned Carbon Creek Gardens, which application would you choose?

CASE STUDY 8
BUILDING DATA FOR DECISION MAKING AT HOME DEPOT

Home Depot is a major retail chain specializing in the sale of construction, home repair, and maintenance products. The company has more than 2240 retail stores in North America and employs over 340 000 people worldwide.

Suppose you are a buyer for the clothes washer and dryer product line at Home Depot. You work with seven different brands and numerous models within each brand. One of your goals is to turn your inventory as many times a year as you can, and to do so you want to identify poorly selling models (and even brands) as quickly as you can. This identification is not as easy as you might think because competition is intense among washer and dryer manufacturers, and a new model can quickly capture a substantial portion of another model's market share. Thus, a big seller this year can be a dog (a poor seller) next year.

Another problem is that while some sales trends are national, others pertain to specific regions. A strong seller on the East Coast may not sell as well on the West Coast. In other words, a brand can be a big seller in one region and a dog in another.

When answering the following questions, assume that you have total sales data for each brand and model, for each store, and for each month. Also assume that you know the store's city and province.

Questions

1. Explain how reporting systems could be helpful to you.

2. Show the structure of one or two reports you could use to identify poorly selling models. How would you structure the reports to identify different sales trends in different regions?

3. For one of these reports, write a description of your requirements that would be suitable for communication to an IT professional. Be as complete and thorough as you can in describing your needs.

4. Explain how data mining systems could be helpful to you.

5. How could cluster analysis help you identify poorly selling brands? How could it help you determine differences in sales for different geographical regions? Is the unsupervised nature of cluster analysis an advantage or a disadvantage for you?

6. Do you believe there is an application for a KM system for identifying poorly selling brands? Why, or why not?

7. Do you believe there is an application for an expert system for identifying poorly selling brands? Why, or why not?

WHAT DO YOU THINK?

UNSEEN CYBERAZZI

A **data broker** or **data aggregator** is a company that acquires and purchases consumer and other data from public records, retailers, Internet cookie vendors, social media trackers, and other sources and uses it to create business intelligence that it sells to companies and the government. Two prominent data brokers are Datalogix and Acxiom Corporation.

Data brokers gather vast amounts of data. According to *The New York Times*, as of June 2012, Acxiom Corporation had used 23 000 servers to process data of 50 trillion transactions on 500 million consumers. It stores more than 15 000 data points on some consumers.[6]

So, what do data brokers do with all this data? If you buy pizza online on Friday nights only when you receive a substantial discount, a data broker (or the broker's customer) knows to send you a discount pizza coupon Friday morning. If you use a customer loyalty card at your local grocery store and regularly buy, say, large bags of potato chips, the data broker or its customer will send you coupons for more potato chips or for a second snack product that is frequently purchased by potato chip consumers. Or, if you suddenly start buying certain lotions and vitamins, the data broker will surmise you might be pregnant.

Canadian federal law provides strict limits on gathering and using medical and credit data. For other data, however, the possibilities are less limited. In theory, data brokers enable you to view the data that is stored about you, but in practice it is difficult to learn how to request your data. Further, the process for doing so is torturous, and ultimately, the data that is released is limited to innocuous data such as your name, phone numbers, and current and former addresses.[7] Without an easy means for viewing all of your data, it is impossible to verify its accuracy.

Of even greater concern, however, is the unknown processing of such data. What BI techniques do these companies employ? Who verifies the accuracy and reliability of these techniques? If the data broker errs in predicting that you will buy a pizza on Friday night, who cares? But if the data broker errs in predicting that you are a terrorist, it matters. Data brokers are silent on these questions.

Discussion Questions

1. Using business intelligence on purchasing data for targeted marketing seems innocuous. Is it?

   a. Some people, whether from genetic factors, habit, lack of education, or other factors, are prone to overeating junk food. By focusing junk food sales offers at this market segment, are data brokers or their customers promoting obesity? Is their behavior ethical?

   b. Data brokers claim they can reliably infer ethnicity from consumer behavior data. Suppose they also determine that one ethnic group is more likely to attend college or university than others. Accordingly, they focus the marketing for college-prep/university-prep materials, scholarships, and college/university admissions applications on this ethnic group. Over time, that group will be guided into positive (assuming you believe college/university is positive) decisions that other groups will not. Is this behavior different from ethnic profiling? Is it ethical?

---

[6] Natasha Singer, "Mapping, and Sharing, the Consumer Genome," *The New York Times*, last modified June 16, 2012, *www.nytimes.com/2012/06/17/technology/acxiom-the-quiet-giant-of-consumer-database-marketing.html*.

[7] Lois Beckett, "What Data Brokers Know About You," *RealClearTechnology*, last modified March 8, 2013, *www.realcleartechnology.com/articles/2013/03/08/what_data_brokers_know_about_you_326.html*.

2. Suppose a data broker correctly identifies that your grandmother is addicted to playing online hearts. From its business intelligence, it knows that frequent hearts players are strong prospects for online gambling. Accordingly, the data broker refers your grandmother's data to an online gambling vendor. Grandma gets hooked and loses all of her savings, including money earmarked for your college/university tuition.

   a. Is the data broker's behavior ethical?

   b. Assume the data broker says, "Look, it's not us, it's our customer, the online gambling vendor, that's causing the problem." Does the broker's posture absolve it of ethical considerations for Grandma's losses?

   c. Assume the online gambling vendor says, "Look, it's not us; it's Grandma. We provide fair and honest games. If Grandma likes to play games where the odds of winning are low, talk to Grandma." Assume in your answer that the gaming company has gone to great lengths to provide the elderly with an emotionally rewarding user experience for games with low winning odds. Does the vendor's posture absolve it of any ethical considerations for Grandma's losses?

CHAPTER 9
Social Networking, Ecommerce, and the Web

MIS in Action

"It's all about eyeballs." Nicki Jensen is PRIDE Systems' new marketing director, and she's exploring ways to generate revenue from clicks on online ads. Zev Friedman, PRIDE Systems' new owner, told her to do this in their last meeting (page 235).

"What do you mean?" James Wu is PRIDE's manager of information systems. He was with the company when it was owned by Dr. Flores. When Friedman bought the company, he kept James on staff.

"I mean, the number of eyeballs we get to look at our ads," Nicki responds.

"Well, not quite. It's about clicks, too." Michele Wilson is PRIDE Systems' new sales director. Her job is to convince vendors to sign up for ads for display on PRIDE's competitions and events.

Nicki looks at James. "We get as many eyes to look at our ads as we can. Then we motivate them to click."

She continues, "So how many people can we get into a virtual race? When we have the cloud connecting the data, we can get people spinning from their homes, their health clubs, wherever, worldwide, to race against one another."

Michele jumps in, "It could be 10 000 at one time, no?" She's looking for some information to help make her case to vendors.

James shakes his head. "Maybe so, but we're getting way ahead of ourselves. PRIDE was designed to support eight to twelve people in an exercise class. People who

 KE Chapter 9 optional knowledge extension is
Knowledge Extension 14 Enterprise Social Networks and
Knowledge Management available in the MyLab MIS

were in treatment following a heart attack or something like that. Now you're saying, 'Let's have a class of 10 000.' Whoa. We're not there with our systems."

Nicki's heard this kind of talk in the past. "But we *could* support 10 000 in an event, no?"

"In theory, sure. But the devil's in the details . . . or in this case, in the requirements. What kind of a user experience do you want? You can't put 10 000 little dots on a cell phone to show people where they are in the race. Well, let me correct myself: Of course we can put 10 000 little dots in the middle of a cell phone screen. We do it all the time, in fact, but what possible meaning would that have to anyone? They would see a blur."

"Well, we can figure that out. Couldn't we just show users the five or so people in front of them?"

"Sure we could. We could do anything. It's just bits. We can build anything you want. How much money and time you got?" James is trying to sound positive.

He pauses to think, then continues, "And, like I said, the devil's in the details. Let's say the person in front of a user is only 0.00000005 seconds ahead. How do we display that? Scale it up so it appears the person is way ahead? Or what if the person in front is 10 minutes ahead, what then? And what if he or she is the leader? What do we show? A blank screen?"

"Ah, we can figure that out. That doesn't seem so hard."

"No, it's not. It's just bits. We can do it, just like we could build a 20-story building to replace this old relic of a warehouse we're in. But we can't do it tomorrow, and it won't be free."

"So, what do you want to tell Zev, James?" Nicki is frustrated.

"I don't want to tell him anything. But he bought a company that had software that supported 10 people in an exercise class, and now he has you two telling me that we should multiply that by 1000. All doable. Nothing wrong with the idea. But we are not there right now."

"Well," presses Nicki, "how long will it take? And what will it cost?"

"For goodness sake, Nicki! Let me try again. I want you to build a 20-story building to replace this one. How long will it take? How much will it cost?"

"I have no idea. I need an architect and a contractor, and I need to know how much it costs to tear this building down." Nicki smiles at James's analogy.

"OK. You've got it now."

As Michele listens to this, she wishes she hadn't left her last job. "Well, I'm telling you two: I can't sell anything with 10 people at an event. That's crazy."

"Well, what about 1000 events with 10 people? You'll still get your 20 000 eyes . . . assuming everyone has two eyes, of course. In reality, you'll probably get a few less than 20 000." James likes accuracy.

"Come on, James. No vendor's gonna ask me how many one-eyed racers we've got."

"Stop it, you two! Michele, James is on to something. Think about it. How many people are there in an online chess game?"

"Two, and let's assume that means four eyes, OK?" Michele is disgusted at James's comment.

"Let it go, Michele. But those online chess vendors make money. What if we did heats of races of 10 people each, then let the winner of each heat compete in the next round? We'd have continuing events, and we'd be able to sell between events . . ." Nicki trails off as she considers the possibilities.

Q9-1 WHAT IS A SOCIAL MEDIA INFORMATION SYSTEM (SMIS)?

Before we address this question, understand that this chapter will not discuss the latest features of Facebook, Twitter, LinkedIn, Instagram, Pinterest, Slack, or any other social type apps or media services. Most likely you know about these already, and further, they are changing so fast that whatever particulars you learn now will be old information when you graduate and possibly obsolete or superceded when you begin work. Instead, this chapter focuses on principles, conceptual frameworks, and models that will last rather than changes in social media services and technology. This way, the knowledge imparted will be useful when you address the opportunities and risks of social media systems in the early years of your professional career.

This awareness will also help you avoid costly mistakes. It is likely that you frequently hear businesspeople saying, "We're using Twitter" and "We've connected our Facebook page to our website." They often create ads and provide news releases that encourage clients and potential clients to, "Follow us on Twitter." Why are organizations engaging in this type of behaviour? To be modern? To be hip? Are these efforts cost effective? How do they advance the organization's strategy?

Social media (SM) is the use of information technology to support the sharing of content among networks of users. Social media enables people to form **communities of practice**, or **communities**, which are groups of people related by a common interest. A **social media information system (SMIS)** is an information system that supports the sharing of content among networks of users.

As illustrated in Figure 9-1, social media is a convergence of many disciplines. In this book, we will focus on the MIS portion of Figure 9-1 by discussing SMIS and how they contribute to organizational strategy. If you decide to work in the SM field as a professional, you will need some knowledge of all these disciplines.

Figure 9-1 Social Media Is a Convergence of Disciplines

Three SMIS Roles

Before discussing the components of a SMIS, we first need to clarify the roles played by the three organizational units of a SMIS:

- Social media providers
- Users
- Communities

Social Media Providers **Social media providers** such as Facebook, Google+, LinkedIn, Twitter, Instagram, and Pinterest provide platforms that enable the creation of **social networks**, or social relationships among people with common interests. The growth of SM providers over the past few years has been tremendous. Figure 9-2 shows the size of some well-known SM providers as of September 2017. Collectively, their number of active users is more than 10 times the total population of Canada. The growth of SM has drawn extraordinary interest from businesses, advertisers, and investors. Social media providers compete with one another for the attention of users—and the associated advertising dollars.

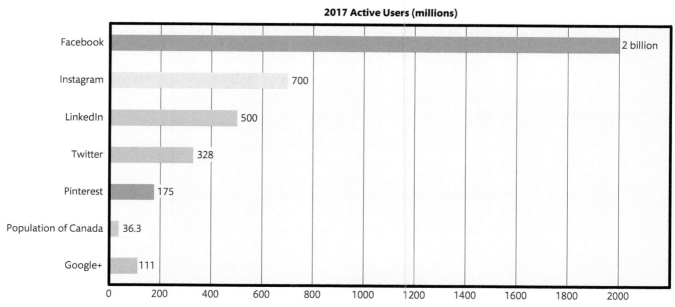

Figure 9-2   Number of Social Media Active Users

Users   **Users** include both individuals *and* organizations that use SM sites to build social relationships. As previously mentioned, hundreds of millions of individuals visit SM sites on a regular basis, and they do so in several ways. One report from early 2014 indicates that more than 73 percent of people with Internet access use SM, and at least 40 percent of them use SM via their mobile phones.[1] Social media providers frequently attract or target people from certain demographic groups. For example, about 70 percent of Pinterest users are female.[2] On LinkedIn, 80 percent of users are 35 or older.[3]

You may not think of organizations as typical SM users. However, organizations often create, use, and manage SM accounts. It is estimated that 77 percent of Fortune 500 companies maintain active Twitter accounts; 70 percent have Facebook pages, and 69 percent have YouTube accounts.[4] These companies hire staff to maintain their SM presence, promote their products, build relationships, and manage their images (interestingly though, few large company CEOs personally use SM or have active public profiles[5]).

[1] Pew Research Internet Project, "Social Networking Fact Sheet," Pew Research, February 27, 2014, accessed May 5, 2015, *www.pewinternet.org/fact-sheets/social-networking-fact-sheet/*.

[2] John McDermott, "Pinterest: The No-bro Zone," *Digiday.com*, February 20, 2014, accessed May 5, 2015, *http://digiday.com/platforms/why-pinterest-is-still-a-predominantly-female-platform/*.

[3] Quantcast, *LinkedIn.com* profile, accessed May 5, 2015, *www.quantcast.com/linkedin.com*.

[4] Amy Gesenhues, "Social Media Use Growing Among Fortune 500 List with 77% Tweeting & 70% on Facebook," Marketing Land, July 23, 2013, accessed May 5, 2015, *http://marketingland.com/fortune-500-companys-social-media-use-on-the-rise-52726*.

[5] https://globenewswire.com/news-release/2017/05/31/1004999/0/en/New-Report-Finds-that-Social-Media-Habits-of-Fortune-500-CEOs-are-Sputtering-Only-40-Have-a-Social-Media-Presence.html.

Depending on how organizations want to use SM, they can be users, providers, or both. For example, larger organizations are big enough to create and manage their own internal social media platforms such as wikis, blogs, and discussion boards. In this case, the organization would be a social media provider. (For more on how social media can be used within organizations please read Knowledge Extension 14.)

Communities   Forming communities is a natural human trait; anthropologists claim that the ability to form them is responsible for the progress of the human race. In the past, however, communities were based on family relationships or geographic location. In short, everyone who lived in a particular village formed a community. The key difference with SM communities is that they are formed based on mutual interests and transcend familial, geographic, and organizational boundaries.

Because of this transcendence, most people belong to a variety of different SM user communities (usually several or more). Google+ recognized this fact when it created circles that enable users to allocate their connections (*people*, using Google+ terminology) to one or more community groups. Facebook and other SM application providers are adapting in similar ways.

Figure 9-3 shows that, from the point of view of the SM site, Community A is a first-tier community. It consists of users that have a direct relationship to the site. User 1, in turn, belongs to three communities: A, B, and C (these could be, say, classmates, professional contacts, and friends). From the point of view of the SM site, Communities B–E are second-tier communities because the relationships in those communities are intermediated by first-tier users. The number of second- and third-tier community members grows exponentially. If each community had, for example, 100 members, then the SM site would have

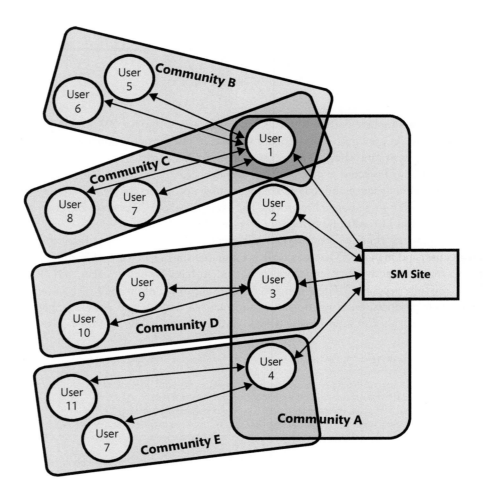

Figure 9-3   SM Communities

100 × 100, or 10 000, second-tier members and 100 × 100 × 100, or 1 million, third-tier members. However, this statement is not quite true because communities often overlap; in Figure 9-3, for example, User 7 belongs to Communities C and E. Thus, these calculations indicate the maximum—but not necessarily the actual—number of users.

How a SM site chooses to relate to these communities depends on its goals. If the site is interested in pure publicity, it will want to relate to as many tiers of communities as it can. If so, it will create a **viral hook**, which is a type of inducement, for passing communications along through the tiers, such as awarding a prize, providing some other enticing reward, or enthralling viewers with captivating content (recall the "blue dress' phenomenon of 2015 or the "Rebecca Black 'Friday'" video). If, however, the purpose of the SM site is to solve an embarrassing problem, say, to fix a product defect, then it would endeavour to constrain, as much as it can, communications between tiers (particularly to Community A).

The exponential nature of relationships via community tiers offers organizations both a blessing and a curse. For example, an employee who is a member of Community A can share her sincere and legitimate pride in her organization's latest product or service with hundreds or thousands of people in her communities. However, she can also blast her disappointment at some recent development to that same audience or, worse, inadvertently share private and proprietary organizational data with someone in that audience who works for the competition.

As this example illustrates, social media is a powerful tool. To use it well, organizations must know their goals and plan accordingly.

SMIS Components

Because they are information systems, SMIS have the same five components as all IS: hardware, software, data, procedures, and people. Keeping SMIS in mind, consider each component shown in Figure 9-4.

Component	Role	Description
Hardware	Social media providers	Elastic, cloud-based servers
	Users and communities	Any user computing device
Software	Social media providers	Application, NoSQL or other DBMS, Analytics
	Users and communities	Browser, iOS, Android, Windows 10, and other applications
Data	Social media providers	Content and connection data storage for rapid retrieval
	Users and communities	User-generated content, connection data
Procedures	Social media providers	Run and maintain application (beyond the scope of this text)
	Users and communities	Create and manage content, informal, copy each other
People	Social media providers	Staff to run and maintain application (beyond the scope of this text)
	Users and communities	Key users, adaptive, can be irrational

Figure 9-4 Five Components of SMIS

Hardware Both users and organizations process SM sites using desktops, laptops, and mobile devices. In most cases, social media providers host the SM presence using easily scalable servers in the cloud.

Software SM users employ browsers and client applications to communicate with other users, send and receive content, and add and remove connections to communities and other users. These include desktop and mobile applications for a variety of platforms, including iOS, Android, and Windows.

Social media providers develop and operate their own custom, proprietary, social networking application software. As you learned earlier, supporting custom software is expensive over the long term, but SM application vendors must do so because the features and functions of their applications are fundamental to their competitive strategy. They can afford to do so because they spread the development costs over the revenue generated by millions of users.

Many social networking vendors use a NoSQL database management system to process their data, though traditional relational DBMS products are used as well. Facebook began development of its own in-house DBMS (Cassandra), but later donated it to the open source community when it realized the expense and commitment of maintaining it. In addition to custom applications and databases, SM providers also invest in analytic software to understand how users interact with their site and with application software.

Data SM data falls into two categories: content and connections. **Content data** (sometimes also referred to as **User-generated content (UGC)**) consists of data and responses to data that are contributed by users. For example, you provide the source content data for your Facebook site, and your friends provide response content when they write on your wall, make comments, tag you, or otherwise publish on your site.

Connection data are data about relationships. On Facebook, for instance, the relationships to your friends are connection data. The fact that you were interested in a particular organization is also considered connection data. Connection data differentiates SMIS from website applications. Both websites and social networking sites present user and responder content, but only social networking applications store and process connection data.

SM providers store and retrieve SM data on behalf of users. They must do so in the presence of network and server failures, and they must do so rapidly. The problem is made somewhat easier, however, because SM content and connection data have a relatively simple structure.

Procedures For social networking users, procedures are informal, evolving, and socially oriented. You do what your friends do. When the members of your community learn how to do something new and interesting, you copy them. Software is designed to be intuitive and forgiving, easy to learn and use.

Such informality makes using SMIS easy; it also means that unintended consequences are common. The most troubling examples concern user privacy. Many people have learned not to post pictures of themselves in front of their house numbers on the same publicly accessible site on which they are describing their new high-definition television. Many others, alas, have not.

For organizations, social networking procedures are more formalized and aligned with the organization's strategy. Organizations develop procedures for creating content, managing user responses, removing obsolete or objectionable content, and extracting value from content. For example, setting up a SMIS to gather data on product problems is a wasted expense unless procedures exist to extract knowledge from that social networking data. Organizations also need to develop procedures to manage SM risk, as described in Q9-5.

Procedures for operating and maintaining a SM application are beyond the scope of this text.

People Users of social media do what they want to do depending on their goals and their personalities. They behave in certain ways and experience the consequences. They may or may not change their behavior. By the way, note that SM users are not necessarily rational, at least not in purely monetary ways. See, for example, the study by Vernon Smith in which people walked away from free money because they thought someone else was getting more![6]

[6] Vernon Smith, *Rationality in Economics: Constructivist and Ecological Forms* (Cambridge, UK: Cambridge University Press, 2007), pp. 247–250.

Organizations cannot be so casual. Anyone who uses his or her position in a company to speak for an organization needs to be trained on both SMIS user procedures and the organization's social networking policy. We will discuss such procedures and policies in Q9-5 but it is important to realize that even people who work in SM can make mistakes. One such example involved Hootsuite (a Canadian company that makes SM tools) when their CEO, Ryan Holmes, criticized an analyst who questioned some aspects of his company's performance[7].

Social media is creating new job titles, new responsibilities, and the need for new types of training. For example, what makes a good tweeter? What makes an effective wall writer? What type of people should be hired for such jobs? What education should they have? How does one evaluate candidates for such positions? How do you find these types of people? These types of questions are currently being asked and answered.

Q9-2 HOW DO SMIS ADVANCE ORGANIZATIONAL STRATEGY?

In Chapter 3, Figure 3-1 (page 57), you learned the relationship of information systems to organizational strategy. In brief, strategy determines value chains, which determine business processes, which determine information systems. Insofar as value chains determine *structured* business processes, such as those discussed in Chapter 7, this value chain is straightforward. However, social media is by its very nature *dynamic*; its flow cannot be designed or diagrammed, and, if it were, no sooner would the diagram be finished than the SM process would have changed.

Therefore, we need to back up a step and consider how value chains determine dynamic processes and thus set SMIS requirements. As you will see, social media fundamentally changes the balance of power among users, their communities, and organizations.

Figure 9-5 summarizes how social media contributes to the five primary value chain activities and to the human resources support activity. Consider each row of this table.

> You can learn more about knowledge management in Knowledge Extension 14.

Activity	Focus	Dynamic process	Risks
Sales and marketing	Outward to prospects	Social CRM; Peer-to-peer sales	Loss of credibility; Bad PR
Customer service	Outward to customers	Peer-to-peer support	Loss of control
Inbound logistics	Upstream supply chain providers	Problem solving	Privacy
Outbound logistics	Downstream supply chain shippers	Problem solving	Privacy
Manufacturing and operations	Outward for user design; Inward to operations and manufacturing	User-guided design; Industry relationships; Operational efficiencies	Efficiency/effectiveness
Human resources	Employment candidates; Employee communications	Employee prospecting, recruiting, and evaluation SharePoint for employee-to-employee communication	Error; Loss of credibility

Figure 9-5 SM in Value Chain Activities

[7] http://fortune.com/2017/03/02/hootsuite-ceo-sex-hotline/.

Social Media and the Sales and Marketing Activity

In the past, organizations controlled their relationships with customers using structured processes and related information systems. In fact, the primary purpose of traditional CRM was to manage customer touches. Traditional CRM ensured that the organization spoke to customers with one voice and that it controlled the messages, the offers, and even the support that customers received based on the value of each particular customer. For example, in 1990, if you wanted to know something about an IBM product, you would contact IBM's local sales office; that office would then classify you as a prospect and use that classification to control the literature and documentation you received and your access to IBM personnel.

As opposed to traditional CRM, **social CRM** is a dynamic, SM-based process. The relationships between organizations and customers emerge in an ever-changing process as both parties create and process content. In addition to the traditional forms of promotion, employees in the organization create wikis, blogs, discussion lists, frequently asked questions, sites for user reviews and commentary, and other dynamic content. Customers then search this content, contribute their own reviews and commentary, ask more questions, create user groups, and so forth. Thus, with social CRM, each customer crafts his or her own relationship with the company.

Social CRM flies in the face of the structured and controlled processes of traditional CRM. Because relationships emerge from joint activity, customers have as much control as companies. This characteristic is anathema to traditional sales managers who want structured processes for controlling what the customer reads, sees, and hears about the company and its products.

Further, traditional CRM is centred on lifetime value; customers that are likely to generate the most business get the most attention and have the most effect on the organization. However, with social CRM, the customer who spends 10 cents but who is an effective reviewer, commentator, or blogger can have more influence than the quiet customer who purchases $10 million a year. Such imbalance is incomprehensible to traditional sales managers.

Nonetheless, traditional sales managers *are* happy to have loyal customers sell their products using peer-to-peer recommendations. A quick look at products and their reviews on *Amazon.com* will show how frequently customers are willing to write long, thoughtful reviews of products they like or do not like. *Amazon.com* and other online retailers also allow readers to rate the helpfulness of reviews. In that way, substandard reviews are revealed for the wary.

Today, many organizations are struggling to make the transition from controlled, structured, traditional CRM processes to wide-open, adaptive, dynamic social CRM processes. This struggle represents a significant job opportunity for those interested in IS, sales, and social media.

Social Media and Customer Service

Product users are amazingly willing to help one another solve problems. Even more, they will do so without pay; in fact, payment can warp and ruin the support experience as customers fight with one another. SAP, for example, learned that it was better to reward its SAP Developer Network with donations to charitable organizations on their behalf than to give them personal rewards.

Not surprisingly, organizations whose business strategy involves selling to or through developer networks have been the earliest and most successful at SM-based customer support. In addition to SAP, Microsoft has long sold through its network of partners. Its MVP (Most Valuable Professional) program is a classic example of giving praise and glory in exchange for customer-provided customer assistance (*http://mvp.support.microsoft.com*).

Of course, the developers in Microsoft's networks have a business incentive to participate because that activity helps them sell their services to the communities in which they participate.

However, users with no financial incentive are also willing to help others. *Amazon.com* supports a program called *Vine* by which customers can be selected to give prerelease and new product reviews to the buyer community.[8] You will need your psychology course to explain what drives people to strive for such recognition. MIS just provides the platform!

The primary risk of peer-to-peer support is loss of control. Businesses may not be able to control peer-to-peer content, so negative comments about cherished products and recommendations for competitor's products are a real possibility. We address these risks in Q9-5.

Social Media and Inbound and Outbound Logistics

Companies whose profitability depends on the efficiency of their supply chain have long used information systems to improve both the effectiveness and the efficiency of structured supply chain processes. Because supply chains are tightly integrated into structured manufacturing processes, there is less tolerance for the unpredictability of dynamic, adaptive processes. Solving problems is an exception; social media can be used to provide numerous solution ideas and rapid evaluation thereof. For instance, hurricane Irma in the fall of 2017 created havoc in the numerous supply chains that passed through Florida and manufacturers lacked power and, in some cases, facilities to operate. Social media was thus used to dispense news, provide updates, and address ever-changing needs and problems.

As this example illustrates, SM communities may provide better and faster solutions to complex supply chain problems. Social media is designed to foster content creation and feedback among networks of users, and that characteristic facilitates the iteration and feedback needed for problem solving, as described in Chapter 2.

Loss of privacy is, however, a significant risk. Problem solving requires the open discussion of problem definitions, causes, and solution constraints. Because suppliers and shippers work with many companies, supply chain problem solving via social media may be problem solving in front of your competitors.

Social Media and Manufacturing and Operations

Operations and manufacturing activities are dominated by structured processes. The flexibility and adaptive nature of social media would result in chaos if applied to the manufacturing line or to the warehouse. However, social media does play a role in product design, developing supplier relationships, and improving operational efficiencies.

Crowdsourcing is the dynamic social media process of employing users to participate in product design or product redesign. For example, eBay often solicits customers to provide feedback on their eBay experience. As its site says, "There's no better group of advisors than our customers." Similarly, user-guided design has been used in the creation of video games, shoes, and many other products.

Since its inception, social media has been widely used in **business-to-consumer (B2C)** relationships to market products to end users. Now manufacturers are starting to use social media to become industry leaders, promote brand awareness, and generate new **business-to-business (B2B)** leads to retailers. For instance, a manufacturer might start a blog that discusses the latest industry-related news, posts interviews with experts, and comments on new product innovations. It could also create a YouTube channel and post videos of

---

[8] "About Customer Ratings," *Amazon.com*, accessed July 30, 2013, *www.amazon.com/gp/help/customer/display.html/ref=hp_200791020_vine?nodeId=200791020#vine*.

product reviews and testing and factory walk-throughs. Similarly, Facebook and Twitter accounts may be useful for promoting positive consumer stories, announcing new products, and following competitors. Retailers will view manufacturers who engage in these SM efforts as industry leaders.

Operations can use social media to improve communication channels within the organization as well as externally with consumers. For example, an enterprise social networking service like Yammer can be used to provide managers with real-time feedback about how to resolve internal operational inefficiencies. Externally, a retailer could monitor its corporate Twitter account and respond to product shortages or spikes in demand for new products around holidays.

Social Media and Human Resources

The last row in Figure 9-5 concerns the use of social media and human resources. As previously mentioned, social media is increasingly used for finding employee prospects, for recruiting candidates, and—in some organizations—for candidate evaluation.

Organizations use social media sites like LinkedIn to hire the best people more quickly and at a lower cost. For about $750 a month, recruiters can search through 450 million LinkedIn members to find the perfect candidate.[9] That $750 a month may sound like a considerable amount to you, but to corporate customers, it is very little. The cost of hiring just one new employee is often estimated at 1.2–1.4 times their base salary and if an independent recruiting company is involved, that cost can be as high as 30-50 percent of the new employee's salary. LinkedIn also gives employers access to *passive* candidates who might not be looking for a job but are a perfect fit for a particular position. Once hired, the employer can leverage that new employee's social network to hire more candidates just like him or her.

Repplier, a social networking image management company, reports that 93 percent of employers it surveyed used social media to screen candidates. Furthermore, 55 percent of survey respondents reported that they had reconsidered a candidate because of what he or she had on social media sites. The good news is that 39 percent of those were positive reconsiderations. The bad news is that 61 percent were negative reconsiderations based on finding profanity; spelling or grammar mistakes; and references to sex, drugs, alcohol, or guns.[10]

Social media is also used for employee communications, often via internal personnel sites such as MySite and MyProfile in SharePoint or other similar enterprise systems. SharePoint provides a place for employees to post their expertise in the form of "Ask me about" questions. When employees are looking for an internal expert, they can search SharePoint for people who have posted the desired expertise. SharePoint 2016 greatly extends support for social media beyond that in earlier SharePoint versions.

The risks of social media in human resources include the possibility of error when using sites such as Facebook to form conclusions about employees and job applicants. A second risk is that the SM site becomes too defensive or is obviously promulgating an unpopular management message. Again, study Figure 9-5 to understand the general framework by which organizations can accomplish their strategy via dynamic processes supported by SMIS. We will now turn to an economic perspective on the value and use of SMIS.

[9] LinkedIn Talent Solutions, "Recruiter," accessed May 5, 2015, *http://business.linkedin.com/talent-solutions/products/recruiter.html*.

[10] Jobvite Inc., "2014 Social Recruiting Survey," *Jobvite.com*, August 2014, accessed July 23, 2015, *https://www.jobvite.com/wp-content/uploads/2014/10/Jobvite_SocialRecruiting_Survey2014.pdf*.

Source: Tuomas Kujansuu/Getty Images

Social media is fun and entertaining for individuals, but what about for commerce?

For example, what would happen if you took Facebook functionality and created an enterprise social network? How would the organization change if everyone could talk with everyone? That is exactly what *Salesforce.com* did when it created Chatter.

Chatter can be used to connect employees and customers via social media. For example, retail salespeople can communicate directly with managers to give instant feedback about a new sales promotion. Chatter can also connect salespeople with presale support personnel or customer service personnel with customers.

With Chatter or its rival Yammer, organizational communities of practice identify and solve problems more quickly and more effectively than before. These communities readily find needed experts within the organization and recruit them to help solve problems. Organizations thus become more responsive because of faster project collaboration. Indeed, internal-facing communities of practice use all the things you like about your personal social media to make their organizations better.

Enterprise social media is taking off, and consumer social media is an established success. But what is next? Where will social media be applied next? Well, there is one important player that has been left out of this scenario so far: the machines.

For years, machines have helped facilitate communication, but they have not really been treated as communication partners. Recently, however, we have begun to see human-to-computer communication in applications like Apple's Siri and IBM's Watson, which allow humans to naturally interact with machines. The potential here is tremendous. But what about machine-to-machine communication?

A startling—and potentially groundbreaking—application is mentioned in a video featuring Beth Comstock, Chief Marketing Officer for General Electric, who says, "We want to use Chatter to connect our employees, our customers, and our machines." (Listen for yourself at www.youtube.com/watch?v=nHaBCcn-9BU.) Does Comstock mean that GE jet engines are going to be social media users? Will these engines share their flight data (weather, air speed, chop, pilot effectiveness, etc.) with other planes that fly their same routes? Will they be submitting reviews on mechanics, as in "Don't accept maintenance from Charlie Smith; he's too rough with his tools"? Will GE's jet engines chat with GE's servers about their performance and need for scheduled maintenance?

From a consumer perspective, social media among machines might have distinct advantages. For example, your car could communicate with each traffic light along your route to work to speed up your commute. No more sitting at red lights! Your car could also communicate with your phone, watch, tablet, and home (appliances, lights, doors, etc.) to solve problems you did not think were solvable. For instance, once self-driving cars become widely used, they will likely be able to interact with a host of different devices. Thus, your self-driving car might get information from your health monitor indicating that you have not eaten in 5 hours. Your car might also know, via your online calendar, that you have a meeting across town in an hour. Your car could then map out a route with a stop at your favorite bistro, pick up an electronic coupon, call in your order, and send the dietary information to your health monitor, all while getting you to your meeting on time.

Although this example may seem far-fetched, there is no doubt that social machines will change the way organizations operate as well as the way people live their lives. Embrace the change.

QUESTIONS

1. Visit www.salesforce.com/chatter to learn about Chatter's features and applications. How could Chatter affect value chain activities?

2. How might Chatter help Apple, Inc. create better products?

3. Why would employees, managers, and owners want to use Chatter? Consider each group individually.

4. One example of social media and machines involves having machines report operational status data (say, speed, temperature, fuel usage, and so on, depending on the type of machine) to a Chatter or other SM site. How can an organization use such reporting in the context of machine, customer, and employee social media?

5. How might machines use foursquare (location-based social networking)? Consider machine-to-machine interactions, as well as human-to-machine interactions.

6. Could machine-to-machine social interactions lead to security or privacy concerns? If so, how?

Q9-3 HOW DO SMIS INCREASE SOCIAL CAPITAL?

Business literature describes three types of capital: traditional, human, and social. Karl Marx defined **capital** as the investment of resources for future profit. This traditional definition refers to investments into resources such as factories, machines, manufacturing equipment, and the like. In comparison, **human capital** is the investment in human knowledge and skills for future profit. By taking this course, you are investing in your own human capital. In other words, you are investing your money and time to obtain knowledge that you hope will differentiate you from other workers and ultimately give you a wage premium in the workforce.

According to Nan Lin, **social capital** is investment in social relations with the expectation of returns in the marketplace.[11] You can see social capital at work in your personal life. You strengthen your social relationships when you help someone get a job, set a friend up on a date, or introduce a friend to someone famous. You weaken your social relationships by continually freeloading, declining requests for help, or failing to spend time with friends.

In your professional life, you are investing in your social capital when you attend a business function for the purpose of meeting people and reinforcing relationships. Similarly, you can use social media to increase your social capital by recommending or endorsing someone on LinkedIn, liking a picture on Facebook, retweeting a tweet, or commenting on an Instagram picture.

What Is the Value of Social Capital?

According to Nan Lin, people benefit from social capital in four ways:

- Information
- Influence
- Social credentials
- Personal reinforcement

First, relationships in social networks can provide *information* about opportunities, alternatives, problems, and other factors important to business professionals. On a personal level, this could come in the form of a friend telling you about a new job posting or recommending which teacher to choose for Business Law. As a business professional, this could involve a friend introducing you to a potential new supplier or letting you know about the opening of a new sales territory.

Second, social networks provide an opportunity to *influence* decision makers at one's employer or in other organizations that are critical to your success. For example, playing golf every Saturday with the CEO of the company you work for could increase your chances of being promoted. Such influence cuts across formal organizational structures, such as reporting relationships.

Third, being linked to a network of highly regarded contacts is a form of *social credential*. You can bask in the glory of those with whom you are connected. Others will be more inclined to work with you if they believe critical personnel are standing with you and may provide resources to support you.

Finally, being linked into social networks *reinforces* a professional's identity, image, and position in an organization or industry. It reinforces the way you define yourself to the world (and to yourself). For example, being friends with bankers, financial planners, and investors may reinforce your identity as a financial professional.

---

[11] Nan Lin, *Social Capital: The Theory of Social Structure and Action* (Cambridge, UK: Cambridge University Press, 2002), Kindle location 310.

As mentioned earlier, a social network is a network of social relationships among individuals with a common interest. Each social network differs in value. The social network you maintain with your high school friends probably has less value than the network you have with your business associates, but not necessarily so. According to Henk Flap, the **value of social capital** is determined by the number of relationships in a social network, by the strength of those relationships, and by the resources controlled by those related.[12] So, if your high school friend(s) happened to have been Mark Zuckerberg or Cameron and Tyler Winklevoss and if you still maintain strong relations via your high school network, then the value of that social network probably far exceeds the value of any network you will have at work. For most of us, however, our network of current professional contacts provides the most social capital.

So, when you use social networking professionally, consider these guidelines. You gain social capital by adding friends and by strengthening the relationships you have with existing friends. Further, you gain more social capital by strengthening relationships with people who control resources that are important to you. Such calculations may seem cold, impersonal, and possibly even phony. When applied to the recreational use of social networking, they may be. But when you use social networking for professional purposes, keep them in mind.

One way to measure the success of your social networking efforts is through an online service like *Klout.com*. *Klout.com* searches social media activity on Facebook, Twitter, and other sites and then creates what it calls a Klout score, which is a measure of an individual's social capital. Klout scores vary from 0 to 100; the more that others respond to your content, the higher your score. Also, responses from people who seldom respond are valued more than responses from those who respond frequently.[13] As a business professional, it is important to understand what social capital is, why it is valuable, and how you can benefit from it.

How Do Social Networks Add Value to Businesses?

Organizations have social capital just as humans do. Historically, organizations created social capital via salespeople, customer support, and public relations. Endorsements by high-profile people are a traditional way of increasing social capital.

Today, progressive organizations maintain a presence on Facebook, LinkedIn, Twitter, and possibly other sites. They include links to their social networking presence on their websites and make it easy for customers and interested parties to leave comments.

To understand how social networks add value to businesses, consider each of the elements of social capital: number of relationships, strength of relationships, and resources controlled by "friends."

Using Social Networking to Increase the Number of Relationships   In a traditional business relationship, a client (you) has some experience with a business, such as a restaurant or resort. Traditionally, you may express your opinions about that experience by word of mouth to your social network. If you are an **influencer** in your social network, your opinion may coax a change in others' behavior and beliefs.

However, such communication is unreliable and brief: You are more likely to say something to your friends if the experience was particularly good or bad—but even then, you are likely only to say something to those friends whom you encounter while the experience is still recent. And once you have said something, that's it; your words are usually forgotten or imperfectly remembered after a few days or weeks.

[12] Henk D. Flap, "Social Capital in the Reproduction of Inequality," *Comparative Sociology of Family, Health, and Education*, Vol. 20 (1991), pp. 6179–6202. Cited in Nan Lin, *Social Capital: The Theory of Social Structure and Action* (Cambridge, UK: Cambridge University Press, 2002), Kindle location 345.

[13] The Klout Score," *Klout*, accessed May 5, 2015, *http://klout.com/corp/score*.

However, consider what would happen if you used SM to instantly communicate your experience using text, pictures, and video to everyone in your social network. For example, suppose you are a wedding photographer who uses social media to promote your business by asking a recent client (user 1) to "like" your Facebook page as well as the wedding photos you took (Figure 9-6). You also tag people in the client's pictures on Facebook. You may even ask the client to tweet about her experience.

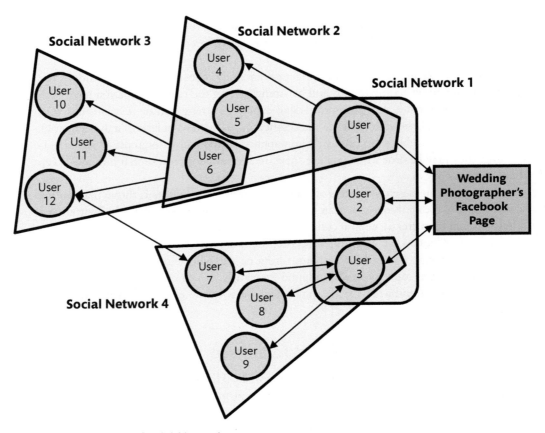

Figure 9-6 Growing Social Networks

All of the people in the client's social network (users 4–6) see the likes, tags, and tweets. If user 6 likes the pictures, they might be seen by users 10–12—and it is possible that one of those users may be looking for a wedding photographer. Using social media, you have grown your social network to reach potential clients who you would not have otherwise had access to. You also used SM to grow the number of relationships you have with clients. Depending on the number, strength, and value of those relationships, your social capital within those networks might increase substantially.

Such relationship sales have been going on by word of mouth for centuries; the difference here is that SMIS allow such sales to scale to levels not possible in the past. In fact, the photographer in our example (you) might even consider *paying* the client for the opportunity to take the wedding pictures if the client were a famous celebrity with hundreds of thousands of followers. In this way, social media may allow users to convert social capital into financial capital. In fact, some famous celebrities get paid more than $10 000 for a single 140-character tweet![14]

---

[14] *SponsoredTweets.com* maintains a list of celebrities, number of their followers, and their price for a sponsored tweet (*https://app.sponsoredtweets.com/tweeters*).

Using Social Networks to Increase the Strength of Relationships   To an organization, the **strength of a relationship** is the likelihood that the other entity (person or other organization) in the relationship will do something that benefits the organization. For example, an organization may have a strong relationship with you if you write positive reviews about it, post pictures of yourself using the organization's products or services, tweet about upcoming product releases, and so on.

In the previous scenario, the photographer asked a client to like her Facebook page and wedding photos. To the photographer, the number of friends the client has in her social network is important, but equally important is the strength of the relationships. Will the client's friends like the photographer's page and photos? Will they retweet the client's success story? If none of the client's friends like the photographer's page and photos, then the strength of the relationships is weak. If, however, all of the client's friends like the photographer's page and photos, then the strength of the relationships in the client's social network is strong.

In his autobiography, Benjamin Franklin provided a key insight.[15] He said that if you want to strengthen your relationship with someone in power, ask him to do you a favour. Before Franklin invented the public library system, he would ask powerful strangers to lend him their expensive books. In that same sense, organizations have learned that they can strengthen their relationships with you by asking you to do them a favour. When you provide that favour, it strengthens your relationship with the organization.

Of course, traditional capital depreciates. Machines wear out, factories get old, technology and computers become obsolete, and so forth. Does social capital also depreciate? Do relationships wear out from use? So far, the answer seems to be both yes and no.

Clearly, there are only so many favours you can ask of someone in power. Similarly, there are only so many times a company can ask you to review a product, post pictures, or provide connections to your friends. At some point, the relationship deteriorates due to overuse. So, yes, social capital can be spent.

However, frequent interactions strengthen relationships and hence increase social capital. The more you interact with a company, the stronger your commitment and allegiance—but continued frequent interactions occur only when both parties see value in continuing the relationship. Thus, at some point, the organization must provide an incentive for you to continue to do it favours.

So, social capital can be spent, but it can also be earned by adding something of value to the interaction. If an organization can induce the other parties in its relationships to provide more influence, information, social credentials, or personal reinforcement, it has strengthened those relationships. And continuing successful relationships over time substantially increases the strength of those relationships.

Using Social Networks to Connect to Those with More Resources   The third measure of the value of social capital is the value of the resources controlled by the parties in the relationships. An organization's social capital is thus partly a function of the social capital of those to whom it relates. The most visible measure is the number of relationships. Someone with 1000 loyal Twitter followers is usually more valuable than someone with 10—but the actual calculation is more subtle than that. For instance, if those 1000 followers are college students and the organization's product is adult diapers, then the value of the relationship to the followers is low. A relationship with 10 Twitter followers who are in retirement homes would be much more valuable.

---

[15] Founding father of the United States. Author of *Poor Richard's Almanac*. Successful businessman; owner of a chain of print shops. Discoverer of groundbreaking principles in the theory of electricity. Inventor of bifocals, the potbelly stove, the lightning rod, and much more. Founder of the public library system and the U.S. postal service. Darling of the French court and salons and, now, contributor to social network theory!

To illustrate this point, Figure 9-7 shows the top five most popular YouTube channels in the beauty and style category and the food and cooking category.[16] In general, the more views a channel gets, the more the content creator gets paid. However, notice that the food and cooking channels have higher earnings than the beauty and style channels. The number of views is not the only factor influencing earnings. The resources (money) controlled by the viewers of the food and cooking channels may be higher than the viewers of the beauty and style channels.

Top 5 Beauty and Style Channels	Monthy Views (millions)	Est. Monthly Earnings
Yuya	35.8	$41 476
grav3yardgirl	27.7	$32 292
Zoella	23.5	$27 375
Cute Girls Hairstyles	18.3	$21 078
Rclbeauty101	17.8	$20 960

Top 5 Food and Cooking Channels	Monthy Views (millions)	Est. Monthly Earnings
CharlisCraftyKitchen	29.1	$127 777
Mosogourmet	22.9	$100 031
CookiesCupcakesandCardio	17.1	$ 79 309
How To Cook That	16.4	$ 77 773
MyCupcakeAddiction	13.5	$ 64 268

Figure 9-7 Top YouTube Channels

Source: Based on Nat Ives, "What a YouTube Celeb Pulls In," Adage.com, April 15, 2015, accessed May 5, 2015, http://adage.com/article/news/a-youtube-celeb-pulls/298015.

There is no formula for computing social capital, but the three factors would seem to be more multiplicative than additive. Or, stated in other terms, the value of social capital is more in the form of

Social Capital = Number of Relationships × Relationship Strength × Entity Resources

than it is in the form of

Social Capital = Number of Relationships + Relationship Strength + Entity Resources

Again, do not take these equations literally; take them in the sense of the multiplicative interaction of the three factors. This multiplicative nature of social capital means that a huge network of relationships with people who have few resources may ultimately be of less value than a smaller network of relationships with people who have substantial resources. Furthermore, those resources must be relevant to the organization. Students with low incomes might be relevant to Pizza Hut; they are perhaps less relevant to a BMW dealership.

This discussion brings us to the brink of social networking practice. Most organizations often ignore the value of entity assets and simply try to connect to more people with stronger relationships. This area is ripe for innovation. Data aggregators such as ChoicePoint and Acxiom maintain detailed data about people worldwide. It would seem that such data could be used by information systems to calculate the potential value of a relationship to a particular individual. This possibility would enable organizations to better understand the value of their social networks as well as guide their behavior with regard to particular individuals.

[16] Nat Ives, "What a YouTube Celeb Pulls In," *Adage.com*, April 15, 2015, accessed May 5, 2015, *http://adage.com/article/news/a-youtube-celeb-pulls/298015*.

Stay tuned; many possibilities exist, and some ideas—maybe yours!—will be very successful.

Q9-4 HOW DO (SOME) COMPANIES EARN REVENUE FROM SOCIAL MEDIA?

Having a large social network with strong relationships may not be enough to guarantee profitability. Facebook, for example, has more than 1.4 billion active users that generate 4.5 billion likes each day.[17] YouTube has more than 1 billion active users that watch more than 6 billion hours of video each month.[18] Both companies have extremely large numbers of active users. The only problem is that they give their services away for free. Billions of anything multiplied by zero is, well, zero. Do all those users really matter if a company cannot make a single cent off of them?

As a business student, you know that nothing is free, even in the world of social media. Processing time, data communication, and data storage may be cheap, but they still cost something. Who pays for the hardware required by SMIS? Social media companies like Facebook, Twitter, and LinkedIn also need to pay people to develop, implement, and manage the SMIS. And where does Web content come from? *Fortune* pays authors for the content that it offers for free. Who is paying those authors? What is the revenue source?

You Are the Product

Social media has evolved in such a way that users expect to use SM applications without paying for them. SM companies want to establish a large network of users quickly, but they have to offer a free product in order to attract users. The dilemma then becomes how do the companies **monetize**, or make money from, their application, service, or content?

The answer is by making *users* the product. That may sound strange at first, and you probably do not want to think of yourself as a product. But try to look at the situation from the company's point of view. When a company runs an advertisement, it is essentially being paid to put the ad in front of its users. So, in a way, the company is renting your eyeballs to an advertiser for a short period of time. Google, for example, is paid to target users with ads based on their search terms, the sites they visit, and "scans" of their emails. In essence, then, users are the product being sold to advertisers. As the old saying goes, "If you're not paying, you're the product."

Revenue Models for Social Media

The two most common ways SM companies generate revenue are by advertising and by charging for premium services. On Facebook, for example, creating a company page is free, but Facebook charges a fee to advertise to communities that "like" that page.

Advertising   Most SM companies earn revenue through advertising. For example, Facebook made the majority of its Q3 2017 revenue of \$US10.142B from advertising.[19] About 85 percent of Twitter's \$US590M third quarter earnings came from advertising as well.[20]

[17] Dan Noyes, "The Top 20 Valuable Facebook Statistics," *Zephoria.com*, June 13, 2014, accessed July 7, 2014, *http://zephoria.com/social-media/top-15-valuable-facebook-statistics/*.

[18] "YouTube Press Statistics," *YouTube.com*, accessed May 5, 2015, *www.youtube.com/yt/press/statistics.html*.

[19] https://www.forbes.com/sites/greatspeculations/2017/11/13/how-much-revenue-can-instagram-drive-for-facebook-in-the-future/#6bff8b407b4f, accessed December 3, 2017, *http://techcrunch.com/2015/04/22/facebook-q1-2015-earnings*.

[20] "Twitter Expects Revenue Growth And Profitability in Q4" *https://www.forbes.com/sites/greatspeculations/2017/10/27/twitter-expects-revenue-growth-and-profitability-in-q4/#64f59d8467ec*, accessed December 3, 2017.

Advertising in SM can come in the form of paid search, display or banner ads, mobile ads, classifieds, or digital video ads.

Google led the way in making digital advertising revenue with paid search results, followed by Gmail and then YouTube. It does not seem like any great insight to realize that if someone is searching an Audi A5 Cabriolet, that person may be interested in ads from local Audi dealers and BMW and Mercedes dealers as well. Or if someone is watching a soccer game on YouTube, it seems sensible to assume that he or she may like soccer. Although not mind-boggling to imagine, Google was the first to realize substantial revenue streams from targeted ads based on user content. Other tech companies soon followed.

Advertisers like digital ads because, unlike traditional media such as newspapers, users can respond directly to these ads by clicking on them. Run an ad in the print version of *The Wall Street Journal*, and you are unsure of the strength and scope of the ad. But place an ad for the same product in the newspaper's online version, and you will soon know the percentage of viewers who clicked on the ad and what action they took next. The ability to track these statistics led to the development of the **pay-per-click** revenue model, in which advertisers display ads to potential customers for free and then get paid when the customer clicks on the ad.

Another way to grow ad revenue is to increase site value with user contributions. The phrase "*use increases value*" means that the more people use a site, the more value the site has, and the more people that visit it. Furthermore, the more value a site has, the more its existing users will return. This phenomenon led to the rise of user comments and reviews, blogging, and, within a few years, social media. Ad revenue, as a result, increased because more people were seeing, and clicking on, more ads on their favourite sites.

Freemium   The **freemium** revenue model offers users a basic service for free and then charges a premium for upgrades or advanced features. For example, LinkedIn earns part of its revenue by selling upgrades to its standard SaaS (software as a service) product. As of December 2017, regular users can access LinkedIn for free; individual upgrades range from $50 to $150 a month and offer advanced search capabilities, greater visibility of user profiles, and more direct email messages to LinkedIn users outside one's network. Similarly, businesses that want to use LinkedIn for recruiting can purchase a Recruiter Corporate account for $120 to $750 a month. About 19 percent of LinkedIn's revenue comes from premium subscriptions, 62 percent from online recruitment, and 19 percent from advertising.[21]

By diversifying its revenue streams, LinkedIn has reduced its dependence on fluctuating ad revenue and ad-blocking software. A recent report by PageFair indicated that 27.6 percent of Web surfers use **ad-blocking software** to filter out advertising content and rarely, if ever, see Internet ads.[22] The report also stated that use of ad-blocking software grew by 30 percent over the past year. SM companies that rely solely on ad revenue may therefore see their share prices plummet if the use of ad-blocking software becomes widespread.

Other ways of generating revenue on SM sites include the sale of apps and virtual goods; donations; affiliate commissions, or revenue paid as the result of referring paying customers. In 2012, Facebook generated more than $810M in revenue from virtual goods.[23] Wikipedia took in about $US91M in donations during 2017. Interestingly, some SM

[21] LinkedIn Corporation, "LinkedIn Announces First Quarter 2015 Results," *LinkedIn Investor Relations*, April 30, 2015, accessed May 5, 2015, *http://investors.linkedin.com*.

[22] Lara O'Reilly, " Ad blocker usage is up 30% — and a popular method publishers use to thwart it isn't working. Business Insider, January 31, 2017, accessed December 5, 2017, *http://www.businessinsider.com/pagefair-2017-ad-blocking-report-2017-1*.

[23] Brittany Darwell, "27M Users Bought Virtual Goods Using Facebook Payments in 2012; Zynga's Influence on Revenue Further Diminishes," *InsideSocialGames.com*, February 1, 2013, accessed July 7, 2014, *www.insidesocialgames.com/2013/02/01/27m-users-bought-virtual-goods-using-facebook-payments-in-2012-zyngas-influence-on-revenue-further-diminishes/*.

companies, like Pinterest, do not generate any revenue at all. They just focus on building a large network of users now and then figuring out how to make money later.

As these examples illustrate, social media is perhaps the ultimate expression of use increasing value. The more communities of practice a site connects with, the more people use the site, and the more incentive people will have to come back again and again. So, social media would seem to be the next great revenue generator, except, possibly, for the movement from PCs to mobile devices.

Does Mobility Reduce Online Ad Revenue?

The transition from PCs to mobile devices presents another interesting question related to social media. Specifically, the ad click revenue model described in the previous section emerged on PC devices where there is plenty of space for lots of ads. But now, as users increasingly move from PCs to mobile devices, particularly small-screen smartphones, there is much less ad space available. Does this mean a reduction in ad revenue?

On the surface, the answer is yes. According to Digiday, mobile based impressions and clicks are the primary growth drivers for digital advertising and mobile will remain a key driver beyond 2018. Ad spending is expected to grow by 31% through 2017 past the 2016 global $US81B spending and increase to $US215B by 2021.[24] By 2019, as shown in Figure 9-8, mobile ad spending should reach $195B and account for 70 percent of total digital ad spending. However, growth in the number of mobile devices far exceeds PC growth. Global mobile data traffic is increasing at a Compound Annual Growth Rate of 47 percent and the number of mobile devices worldwide exceeded 7 billion. By 2019, the number of mobile devices is expected to reach 10 billion, which will exceed the world's population.[25] Cisco predicts that by 2019, smartphones will account for 75 percent of total global mobile traffic.[26] So, even though the revenue per device may be lower for mobile devices than PCs, the sheer number of mobile devices in use may swamp the difference in revenue.

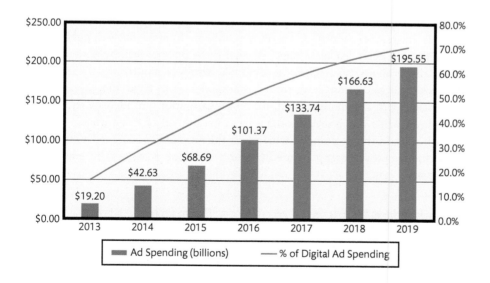

Figure 9-8 Mobile Ad Spending

[24] Digiday, "The state of mobile advertising *https://digiday.com/marketing/state-mobile-advertising/*, June 1 2017 accessed December 5, 2017, *www.emarketer.com/Article/Mobile-Ad-Spend-Top-100-Billion-Worldwide-2016-51-of-Digital-Market/ 1012299.*

[25] Cisco, "Cisco Visual Networking Index: Global Mobile Data Traffic Forecast Update, 2013–2018," *Cisco.com*, February 3, 2015, accessed May 6, 2015, *www.cisco.com/c/en/us/solutions/collateral/service-provider/visual-networking-index-vni/ white_paper_c11-520862.pdf.*

[26] Ibid.

Furthermore, the number of devices is not the whole story. According to Marin Software, the average click-through rate of smartphones is 3.75 percent, while that same rate on PCs is 2.29 percent.[27] So, mobile users click ads more often and hence generate more revenue. This is especially true in Facebook's case where 87 percent of their total ad revenue comes from mobile ads.[28]

However, clicks are not the final story. Because ads take up so much more space on mobile devices than they do on PCs, many of the mobile clicks could have been accidental. **Conversion rate** measures the frequency that someone who clicks on an ad makes a purchase, "likes" a site, or takes some other action desired by the advertiser. According to Monetate, conversion rates for PCs (3.41 percent) are higher than those for tablets (2.86 percent) or smartphones (0.92 percent). So, on average, PC ad clicks are more effective than mobile clicks.[29]

Clickstream data is easy to gather, and as we have seen, analyses of it are widespread. It is possible, for example, to measure click and conversion rates by type of mobile device. According to Moovweb, iOS users have higher conversion rates than Android users, 1.18 percent versus 1.04 percent.[30] But why? Is it the device? Is it the way the ads are integrated into the user experience? Is it the user? Are iOS users more curious than Android users? Or do they have more spendable income? We do not know for sure.

What we can conclude from this morass of confusing data, however, is that mobile devices are unlikely to spell the death of the Web/social media revenue model. The users are there, the interest is there, and what remains is a design problem: how best to configure the mobile experience to obtain legitimate clicks and conversions. The computer industry is superb at solving design problems; given the current dynamic evolution of mobile interfaces and USX, active, interesting, and compelling ways of presenting ads in iOS/Android/Windows 10 environments are just around the corner.

Q9-5 HOW CAN ORGANIZATIONS ADDRESS SMIS SECURITY CONCERNS?

Several decades ago, most organizations managed all public and internal messaging with the highest degree of control. Every press conference, press release, public interview, presentation, and even academic paper needed to be preapproved by both the legal and marketing departments. Such approval could take weeks or months.

Progressive organizations have turned that model on its head. Employees are encouraged to engage with communities and, in most organizations, to identify themselves with their employer while doing so. All of this participation, all of this engagement, however, comes with risks. In this section, we will discuss the need for a social media policy, consider risks from nonemployee user-generated content, and look at risks from employee use of social media.

Managing the Risk of Employee Communication

The first step that any organization should take is to develop and publicize a **social media policy**, which is a statement that delineates employees' rights and responsibilities. You can

[27] Marin Software, "Mobile Search Advertising Around the Globe: 2014 Annual Report," *MarinSoftware.com*, March 2014, accessed May 6, 2015, *www.marinsoftware.com/resources/whitepapers*.

[28] Josh Constine " Facebook beats in Q2 with $9.32B revenue despite slower user growth techcrunch.com, July 26, 2017 accessed December 5, 2017, *https://techcrunch.com/2017/07/26/facebook-earnings-q2-2017/*.

[29] Monetate, "Ecommerce Quarterly EQ4 2014: The Gift of Personalization," *Monetate.com*, February 2015, accessed May 6, 2015, *www.monetate.com/resources/research/#ufh-i-48179143-ecommerce-quarterly-q4-2014*.

[30] Moovweb, "Android vs iOS, Are iOS Shoppers More Valuable than Android Shoppers," *Moovweb.com*, December 9, 2014, accessed May 6, 2015, *www.moovweb.com/blog/android-vs-ios*.

find an index to over 100 different policies at the Social Media Today website.[31] In general, the more technical the organization, the more open and lenient the social media policies. The U.S. military has, perhaps surprisingly, endorsed social media with enthusiasm, tempered by the need to protect classified data.

Intel Corporation has pioneered open and employee-trusting SM policies, policies that continue to evolve as they gain more experience with employee-written social media. The three key pillars of its policy in 2015 are:

- Disclose
- Protect
- Use Common Sense[32]

Those policies are further developed as shown in Figure 9-9. Visit *www.intel.com/content/www/us/en/legal/intel-social-media-guidelines.html*. Comparing and contrasting these policies against those of your current employer may provide insight and provoke interesting questions.

Disclose	Be transparent—use your real name and employer Be truthful—point out if you have a vested interest Be yourself—stick to your expertise and write what you know
Protect	Don't tell secrets Don't slam the competition Don't overshare
Use Common Sense	Add value—make your contribution worthwhile Keep it cool—don't inflame or respond to every criticism Admit mistakes—be upfront and quick with corrections

Figure 9-9 Intel's Rules of Social Media Engagement

Source: Intel Social Media Guidelines, Intel, accessed May 7, 2015, www.intel.com/content/www/us/en/legal/intel-social-media-guidelines.html.

Two elements in this list are particularly noteworthy. The first is the call for transparency and truth. As an experienced and wise business professional once stated, "Nothing is more serviceable than the truth." It may not be convenient, but it is definitely serviceable, especially in the long term. Second, SM contributors and their employers should be open and candid. If you make a mistake, do not obfuscate; instead, correct it, apologize, and make amends. The SM world is too open, too broad, and too powerful to fool.

In 2013, Justine Sacco, a PR executive at IAC, was boarding a plane headed to South Africa and tweeted, "Going to Africa. Hope I don't get AIDS. Just kidding. I'm white." When she landed, she found out that she had been fired in flight and had elicited thousands of hostile posts.

The best way to avoid these types of missteps is to include a SM awareness module in users' annual security training. Social media is still new to many users. They may be honestly unaware a policy even exists. When cell phones first became popular they were constantly ringing in movie theaters. Over time, people learned to mute their phones before entering a crowded theater. It just takes time for society to catch up to technology. Training helps.

Managing the Risk of Inappropriate Content

As with any relationship, comments can be inappropriate in content, excessively negative in tone, or otherwise problematic. Organizations need to determine how they will deal with

---

[31] Ralph Paglia, "Social Media Employee Policy Examples from Over 100 Organizations," July 3, 2010, *Social Media Today*, accessed May 7, 2015, *http://socialmediatoday.com/ralphpaglia/141903/social-media-employee-policy-examples-over-100-companies-andorganizations*.

[32] Intel Social Media Guidelines," *Intel*, accessed May 7, 2015, *www.intel.com/content/www/us/en/legal/intel-social-media-guidelines.html*.

such issues before engaging in social media. This is done by designating a single individual to be responsible for official organizational SM interactions and by creating a process to monitor and manage SM interactions. This allows the organization to have a clear, coordinated, and consistent message.

User-generated content (UGC), which simply means content on your SM site that is contributed by users, is the essence of SM relationships. Below are a few examples of inappropriate UGC that can negatively affect organizations.

Problems from External Sources
The major sources of UGC problems are:

- Junk and eccentric contributions
- Inappropriate content
- Unfavorable reviews
- Mutinous movements

When a business participates in a social network or opens its site to UGC, it opens itself to misguided people who post junk unrelated to the site's purpose. Eccentrics may also use the network or UGC site as a way of expressing passionately held views about unrelated topics, such as UFOs, government cover-ups, fantastic conspiracy theories, and so forth. Because of the possibility of such content, organizations should regularly monitor the site and remove objectionable material immediately. Monitoring can be done by employees or companies such as Bazaarvoice that offer services not only to collect and manage ratings and reviews but also to monitor the site for irrelevant content.

Unfavorable reviews are another risk. Research indicates that customers are sophisticated enough to know that few, if any, products are perfect. Most customers want to know the disadvantages of a product before purchasing it so they can determine if those disadvantages are important for their application. However, if every review is bad, if the product is rated 1 star out of 5, then the company is using social media to publish its problems. In this case, some action must be taken, as described in the next section.

Mutinous movements are an extension of bad reviews. In January 2012, McDonald's opened a Twitter campaign to promote customer stories. Within a few hours, it was clear that disgruntled customers were hijacking the campaign. McDonald's pulled the Twitter hashtag, and within a few hours negative conversations stopped. To be able to respond promptly, McDonald's created a contingency plan for dealing with unwanted results in all of its social media marketing.[33]

Responding to Social Networking Problems
Part of managing social networking risk is to know the sources of potential problems and to monitor sites for problematic content. Once such content is found, however, organizations need to respond appropriately. Three possibilities are:

- Leave it
- Respond to it
- Delete it

If the problematic content represents reasonable criticism of the organization's products or services, the best response may be to leave it where it is. Such criticism indicates that the site is not just a shill for the organization but contains legitimate user content. Such criticism also serves as a free source of product reviews, which can be useful for product development. For the criticism to be useful, the development team needs to know about it, so, as stated, processes to ensure the criticism is found and communicated to the team are necessary.

---

[33] Marissa Brassfield, "McDonald's McDStories Twitter Promotion Sparks Huge Backlash," *Foodista*, last modified January 24, 2012, *www.foodista.com/blog/2012/01/24/mcdonalds-mcdstories-twitter-promotion-sparks-huge-backlash*.

A second alternative is to respond to the problematic content. However, this alternative is dangerous. If the response can be construed in any way as patronizing or insulting to the content contributor, it can enrage the community and generate a strong backlash. Also, if the response appears defensive, it can become a public relations negative.

In most cases, responses are best reserved for when the problematic content has caused the organization to do something positive as a result. For example, suppose a user publishes that he or she was required to hold for customer support for 45 minutes. If the organization has done something to reduce wait times, then an effective response to the criticism is to recognize it as valid and state, nondefensively, what has been done to reduce wait times.

If a reasoned, nondefensive response generates continued and unreasonable UGC from that same source, it is best for the organization to do nothing. Industry wisdom—never wrestle with a pig; you'll get dirty and the pig will enjoy it. Instead, allow the community to constrain the user. You might be surprised how often community fairness prevails.

Deleting content should be reserved for contributions that are inappropriate. Such content is usually published by eccentrics and often have nothing to do with the site, or the contributions may contain obscene or otherwise inappropriate content. However, deleting legitimate negative comments can result in a strong user backlash. In the early days of social media, NestlÉ created a PR nightmare on its Facebook account with its response to criticism it received about its use of palm oil. Someone altered the Nestlé logo, and in response Nestlé decided to delete all Facebook contributions that used that altered logo and did so in an arrogant, heavy-handed way. The result was a negative firestorm on Twitter.[34]

A sound principle in business is to never ask a question to which you do not want the answer. We can extend that principle to social networking; never set up a site that will generate content for which you have no effective response!

Internal Risks from Social Media

The increased adoption of social media has created new risks within organizations. These risks can be threats to information security, increased organizational liability, and decreased employee productivity.

First, the use of social media can directly affect the ability of the organization to secure their information resources. For example, suppose a senior-level employee tweets, "Married 20 years ago today in Dallas," or "Class of 1984 reunion at Central High School was awesome," or "remembering my honeymoon to Hawaii." These types of tweets provide attackers with the answers to password reset questions. Once attackers reset the user's passwords they could have full access to internal systems. Thus, seemingly innocuous comments can inadvertently leak information used to secure access to organizational resources. Unfortunately, it turns out that it is not a good idea to tell everyone it is your birthday because your date of birth (DOB) can be used to steal your identity.

Employees using social media can unintentionally (or intentionally) leak information about intellectual property, new marketing campaigns, future products, potential layoffs, budget woes, product flaws, or upcoming mergers. It is not just information leakage, either. Employees may install unauthorized apps that deliver content using SM that bypasses existing security measures. Or, worse, they may use their corporate password at less secure SM sites.

Second, employees may inadvertently increase corporate liability when they use social media. For example, suppose a coworker regularly looks at SM content with questionable sexual content on his or her own smartphone. The organization could be slapped with a sexual harassment lawsuit. Other organizations may face legal issues if employees leak information via social media. Schools, healthcare providers, and financial institutions must all

---

[34] Bernhard Warner, "Nestlé's 'No Logo' Policy Triggers Facebook Revolt," *Social Media Influence*, March 19, 2010, accessed August 27, 2014, *http://socialmediainfluence.com/2010/03/19/nestles-no-logo-policy-triggers-facebook-revolt/*.

follow specific guidelines to protect user data and avoid regulatory compliance violations. Tweeting about students, patients, or customer accounts could have legal consequences.

Finally, the increased use of social media can be a threat to employee productivity. Posts, tweets, pins, likes, comments, and endorsements all take time. This is often time employers are paying for, but not benefiting from. Forbes notes that 64 percent of employees visit non-work related websites each day and one study suggested that millennial employees waste about two hours a day of designated work time on non-productive activities[35]. Among the SM sites that are most detrimental to employee productivity include Tumblr (57 percent), Facebook (52 percent), Twitter (17 percent), Instagram (11 percent), and SnapChat (4 percent).[36]

From an employee's point of view, you might think a little lost productivity is okay. But if you are the employer or manager, which hopefully you will be soon, you might have objections to any reduced efficiency. Would you mind if your employees spend their days using SM to look for another job, chat with friends, or look at vacation pictures when pay cheques are tied to productivity? What if SM was being used for interoffice gossip that created HR problems, morale issues, and possible lawsuits? Smart managers understand that, like any technology, SM comes with both benefits and costs.

Q9-6 WHERE IS SOCIAL MEDIA TAKING US?

So much change is in the air: social media, **Web 2.0**, Enterprise 2.0. Is there an Enterprise 3.0 or 4.0 around the corner? Will social media become more unified on a single platform, or become more fragmented across many different platforms? We are not sure. However, new mobile devices with innovative mobile-device UX, coupled with dynamic and agile information systems based on cloud computing and dynamic virtualization, guarantee that monumental changes will continue to occur over the next several years.

Organizations like Harvard, Microsoft, and Starbucks are concerned enough with SM that they have hired Chief Digital Officers (CDOs), a position responsible for developing and managing innovative social media programs.[37]

Advance the clock 10 years. You are now the product marketing manager for an important new product series for your company . . . the latest in a line of, say, intelligent home appliances. How are you going to promote your products? Will your machines have SM interactions with family members? Will your refrigerators publish what kids are eating after school on the family's social media site? And what even more creative ideas will you need to have by then?

Think about your role as a manager in ten years. Your team has ten people, three of whom report to you; two report to other managers; and five work for different companies. Your company uses OpenGizmo 2025 with integrated mobile video, augmented by Google/Facebook's Whammo++ Star, all of which have many features that enable employees and teams to instantly publish their ideas in blogs, wikis, videos, and whatever other means have become available. Your employees no longer are assigned computers at work; a liberal, yet secure, BYOD policy enables them to use their own devices, often in their own unique way. Of course, your employees have their own accounts on whatever Facebook, Twitter, LinkedIn, foursquare, and other social networking sites have become popular, and they regularly contribute to them.

How do you manage this team? If "management" means to plan, organize, and control, how can you accomplish any of these functions in this emergent network of employees?

---

[35] Purelyhr I blog https://blog.purelyhr.com/banning-employees/ accessed December 5, 2017.

[36] Cheryl Conner, "Who Wastes the Most Time at Work," *Forbes*, September 7, 2014, accessed June 24, 2014, *www.forbes.com/sites/cherylsnappconner/2013/09/07/who-wastes-the-most-time-at-work/*.

[37] Jennifer Wolfe, "How Marketers Can Shape the Chief Digital Officer Role," *CMO.com*, March 21, 2013, accessed June 21, 2014, *www.cmo.com/articles/2013/3/20/how_marketers_can_shape.html*.

If you and your organization follow the lead of tech-savvy companies such as Intel, you will know you cannot close the door on your employees' SM lives, nor will you want to. Instead, you will harness the power of the social behavior of your employees and partners to advance your strategy.

In the context of CRM, the vendor might lose control of the customer relationship. Customers have the option of using all accessible vendor touch points to craft their own relationships. Emergence in the context of management means a considerable loss of control of employees. Employees can craft their own relationships with their employers, whatever that might mean in ten years. Certainly it means a loss of control, one that is readily made public to the world.

In the 1960s, when someone wanted to send a letter to Don Draper at Sterling Cooper, his or her secretary addressed the envelope to Sterling Cooper and down at the bottom added, "Attention: Don Draper." The letter was to Sterling Cooper and, oh, by the way, also to Don Draper.

Email changed that. Today, someone would send an email to *DonDraper@SterlingCooper.com* or even just to *Don@SterlingCooper.com*. That address is to a person and then to the company.

Social media changes addresses further. When Don Draper creates his own blog, people respond to Don's Blog and only incidentally do they notice in the "About Don" section of the blog that Don works for Sterling Cooper. In short, the focus has moved in over five decades from organizations covering employee names to employees covering organization names.

Does this mean that organizations go away? Hardly. They are needed to raise and conserve capital and to organize vast groups of people and projects. No group of loosely affiliated people can envision, design, develop, manufacture, market, sell, and support an iPad. Organizations are required.

So what, then? Maybe we can take a lesson from biology. Crabs have an external exoskeleton. Deer, much later in the evolutionary chain, have an internal endoskeleton. When crabs grow, they must endure the laborious and biologically expensive process of shedding a small shell and growing a larger one. They are also vulnerable during the transition. When deer grow, the skeleton is inside and it grows with the deer. No need for vulnerable molting. And, considering agility, would you take a crab over a deer?

In the 1960s, organizations were the exoskeleton around employees. In the coming years, organizations will be the endoskeleton, supporting the work of people on the exterior (in some companies this is already the case).

Mobility + cloud + social media mean fascinating opportunities for your nonroutine cognitive skills in the next few years!

Q9-7 WHAT IS ECOMMERCE, AND HOW IS IT USED?

An exact definition of *ecommerce* is harder than you might think. In this text, we define **ecommerce** as the buying and selling of goods and services over public and private computer networks. However, if you examine this definition closely, you may see that it is not as clear as it might appear. Note, for example, that this definition restricts ecommerce to buying and selling transactions. Checking the weather at yahoo.ca is not ecommerce, but buying a weather service subscription that is paid for and delivered over the Internet is. Similarly, researching and buying a good or service, such as a computer from Dell or OnStar from GM, qualifies as ecommerce, but researching a product over the Internet and purchasing it in a traditional retail store would not, even though these activities clearly contribute to the purchase decision. It is easier therefore to consider that ecommerce is a subset of the broader definition of electronic business. Electronic business is usually described as everything having to do with the application of information and communication technologies to the conduct of business.

This is an important distinction to keep in mind. The majority of commerce has historically been done in-person. Information was gathered directly from the sales person (e.g., the way that your parents may have purchased a new car). In ecommerce, this is not true. Modern consumers are less and less likely to use a single information channel to make buying decisions. A customer might search for the item online, look for prices in several stores offering the product, and read the manufacturer's website. A customer might also look at a few reviews and talk to people who have tried the product. All of this makes the customer quite knowledgeable. In fact, ecommerce customers can know more about a product or service than the salesperson who is actually facilitating the sale.

The emergence of ecommerce has provided much more information for consumers. Think about a recent large purchase that you may have made, for example, a new computer. It is possible that you simply walked into Future Shop or Best Buy to buy it or bought it online from Dell.ca, but it is much more likely that you first researched your options online and talked to your friends. You may even have gone into one store to familiarize yourself with the physical device, although you intended to buy it elsewhere. Depending on the specific purchase, it is also possible that you used a referral website, such as Yelp (or, when choosing classes, ratemyprofessor). Customers are now potentially more knowledgeable than ever before about products and services they purchase.

Ecommerce has other implications. From a technology perspective, additional infrastructure (more technology) for organizations will be required. Technological issues are sometimes not the most important consideration for organizations. Large organizations, such as Wal-Mart or Target, often provide and support many of these required technological capabilities. However, smaller organizations may have difficulty keeping up with technological change. So how might a smaller company keep up? One option is to purchase the technologies as business services. Goods or services offered by a smaller company may be listed on larger sites, such as eBay, Craigslist, Amazon.com, or the Apple store; payment processing may be handled by PayPal or a local bank; and hosting may be done by Internet service providers (ISPs), such as GoDaddy or Amazon.com.

A further implication of ecommerce is the increased coordination between organizations and systems. In the case of large companies, the linkages required by ecommerce could be extensive, especially when partners are involved. Inventory, for example, will need to be updated and require communications among the supply chain management (SCM) system, the customer relationship management (CRM) system, and the accounting system. In short, ecommerce may require interconnectedness of the entire enterprise resource planning (ERP) process.

Beyond the technology issues (which are significant), ecommerce has large implications for organizations and governments. Before the enterprise management systems are securely connected, organizations need to ensure that all aspects of the business operate smoothly and do not operate at cross purposes. Externally, companies need to ensure that end-to-end customer security is enabled and that the information is only shared appropriately and with customer permission.

Although the definition of *ecommerce* is not as broad as the definition of *ebusiness*, there are many varieties. These are listed in Figure 9-10.

Merchant Companies	Nonmerchant Companies
– Business-to-consumer (B2C) – Business-to-business (B2B) – Business-to-government (B2G)	– Auctions – Clearinghouses – Exchanges

Figure 9-10 Ecommerce Categories

Merchant companies are defined as those that take title to the goods they sell—they buy goods and resell them. **Nonmerchant companies** are those that arrange for the purchase and sale of goods without ever owning or taking title to those goods. Merchant companies sell services that they provide; nonmerchant companies sell services provided by others. We will consider merchants and nonmerchants separately in the following sections.

Ecommerce Merchant Companies

There are three main types of merchant companies: (1) those that sell directly to consumers, (2) those that sell to companies, and (3) those that sell to government. Each uses slightly different information systems in the course of doing business. **Business-to-consumer (B2C)** ecommerce concerns sales between a supplier and a retail customer (the consumer). A typical information system for B2C provides a Web-based application or **Web storefront** by which customers enter and manage their orders.

The term **business-to-business (B2B)** ecommerce refers to sales between companies. As Figure 9-11 shows, raw materials suppliers use B2B systems to sell to manufacturers, manufacturers use B2B systems to sell to distributors, and distributors use B2B systems to sell to retailers.

Business-to-government (B2G) ecommerce refers to sales between companies and governmental organizations. As Figure 9-11 shows, a manufacturer that uses an ecommerce site to sell computer hardware to a government ministry is engaging in B2G commerce. Suppliers, distributors, and retailers can sell to government as well.

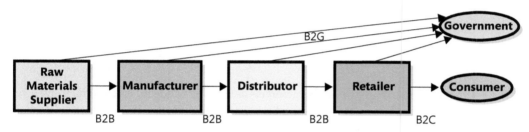

Figure 9-11   Examples of B2B, B2G, and B2C

B2C applications first captured the attention of mail order and related businesses. However, companies in all sectors of the economy soon realized the enormous potential of B2B and B2G ecommerce. The number of companies engaged in B2B and B2G commerce now far exceeds those engaging in B2C commerce. For example, consider Dell Computer. Although the basis for buying computers has changed and other competitors have replicated aspects, Dell has structured its website in such a way that almost anyone can configure and order a computer online. The site guides home users, novice business users, and expert users (from business and government) into different parts of the site that provide different experiences. Home users, for example, may be offered computer packages with easy-to-understand options. Business or government experts, who are more likely to be buying high-performance server computers, could be offered a larger and more complex array of options and choices. Dell's site offers extensive support, with definitions and explanations, all online. In this way, Dell has almost completely automated ordering and has dramatically reduced the cost of processing an order. The system is consistent with Dell's competitive strategy, which is to provide the computers to its customers at the lowest possible cost.

Today's B2B and B2G ecommerce applications implement just a small portion of their potential capabilities. Their full utilization is some years away. Although most experts agree that these applications involve some sort of integration of CRM and supplier relationship management (SRM) systems, the nature of that integration is not well understood, as it is still being developed. Consequently, you can expect further progress and development in B2B and B2G applications during your career.

Nonmerchant Ecommerce

The most common nonmerchant ecommerce companies are auctions (such as eBay) and clearinghouses. **Ecommerce auctions** match buyers and sellers by using an ecommerce version of a standard auction. This ecommerce application enables the auction company to offer goods for sale and to support a competitive-bidding process. The best-known auction company is eBay, but many other auction companies exist; many serve particular industries. One of the world's largest industrial auctioneers, Ritchie Bros. (www.rbauction.com), based in Richmond, B.C., uses the Web to hold virtual auctions that allow bidders from across the world to take part in industrial equipment auctions without having to physically attend an event.

Clearinghouses provide goods and services at a stated price and arrange for the delivery of the goods and services, but they never take title. One division of Amazon.ca, for example, operates as a nonmerchant clearinghouse and sells books owned by others. As a clearinghouse, Amazon.ca matches the seller and the buyer and then takes payment from the buyer and transfers the payment to the seller, minus a commission.

Other examples of clearinghouse businesses are **electronic exchanges** that match buyers and sellers; the business process is similar to that of a stock exchange. Sellers offer goods at a given price through the electronic exchange, and buyers make offers to purchase goods over the same exchange. Price matches result in transactions from which the exchange takes a commission. Priceline.com is an example of an electronic exchange used by consumers.

Benefits of Ecommerce

The debate continues among business observers as to whether ecommerce is something new or just a technology extension of existing business practice. During the dot-com heydays of 1999–2000, some claimed that ecommerce was ushering in a new era and a new economy. Although experts differ as to whether a new economy was created, all agree that ecommerce does lead to greater market efficiency.

One effect frequently associated with ecommerce is **disintermediation**—the removal of intermediaries between parties. As ecommerce first started to become popular, it was widely believed that some of the agents in the distribution process would be eliminated. This is illustrated by the hypothetical transactions on the left side of Figure 9-12. In this

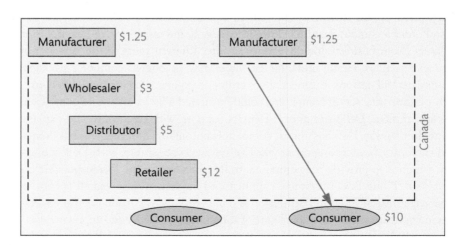

Figure 9-12 Disintermediation–Manufacturer to Consumer.

example, a manufacturer produces a good for $1.25, and it sells it to the wholesaler for $3. The wholesaler then sells it to the distributor for $5, who, in turn, sells it to the retailer for $12. The retailer is free to set the final price that is paid by the end consumer. The right side of Figure 9-12 shows the elimination of the intervening layers between manufacturers and end consumers facilitated by direct website sales.

The general results of disintermediation are higher revenues for manufacturers and lower consumer prices, but the broader implications are more significant. Canada is a very large country and much of the Canadian economy involves distribution. Some consultants estimate that 80% of the goods being sold are not actually in stores, but moving through the supply chain in transport or stored in warehouses and distribution centres. If Canadian consumers buy from Amazon.com rather than from local retailers, significant segments of the Canadian economy could be disrupted.

The good news is that consumers have generally benefited from ecommerce, and the net effect has not been quite as negative as initially imagined. In many cases, manufacturers have found it much more difficult to eliminate intermediaries, and although distribution channels have become more efficient, new players have inserted themselves into the sales and distribution processes (not surprisingly, this process is called *intermediation* or sometimes *re-intermediation*). Apple, for example, has become a significant actor in the retail of music and media. Often, rather than buying directly from airlines and hotels, many consumers prefer to use websites, such as Trivago.com, Travelocity. ca, Expedia.ca, Priceline.com, and AirBnB.com, to find low-cost airline tickets and accommodation.

Ecommerce also improves the flow of price information. As a consumer, you can go to any number of websites that offer product price comparisons. You can search for information on the high-definition television (HDTV) you want and sort the results by price and vendor reputation. You can find vendors that waive or reduce shipping charges. The improved distribution of information about price and terms enables you to pay the lowest possible price and serves ultimately to remove inefficient vendors. The market, as a whole, becomes more efficient.

From the seller's side, ecommerce produces information about price elasticity that has not been available before. **Price elasticity** measures how much demand rises or falls with changes in price. Using an auction as an example, a company can learn not only what the top price for an item is but also the second, third, and other prices of the losing bids. In this way, the company can understand more about various customers' willingness to pay a particular price, or what is often called the *shape of the price elasticity curve*.

Similarly, ecommerce companies can learn about price elasticity directly by conducting experiments with customers. For example, in one experiment, Amazon.com created three groups of similar books. It raised the price of one group by 10 percent, lowered the price of the second group by 10 percent, and left the price of the third group unchanged. Customers provided feedback on these changes by deciding whether to buy books at the offered prices. Amazon.com measured the total revenue (quantity times price) of each group and took the action (raise, lower, or maintain prices) on all books that maximized revenue. Amazon.com repeated the process until it reached the point at which the indicated action was to maintain current prices.

Managing prices by direct interaction with the customer yields better information compared with managing prices by watching competitors' pricing. By experimenting with customers, companies learn how customers have internalized competitors' pricing, advertising, and messaging. Customers may not know about a competitor's lower prices, in which case there is no need for a price reduction. Or the competitor may be using a price that, if lowered, would increase demand sufficiently to increase total revenue. Figure 9-13 summarizes ecommerce market consequences.

Figure 9-13 Ecommerce
Market Consequences

Greater Market Efficiency	Knowledge of Price Elasticity
- Disintermediation - Increased information on price and terms	- Losing-bidder auction prices - Price experimentation - More accurate information obtained directly from customer

The Challenges of Ecommerce

Although there are tremendous advantages and opportunities for many organizations to engage in ecommerce, the economics of some industries may disfavour ecommerce activity. Companies need to consider the following economic factors:

- Channel conflict
- Price conflict
- Logistics expense
- Customer service expense
- Showrooming
- Taxation

Figure 9-12 shows a manufacturer selling directly to a government agency. However, before engaging in this B2G ecommerce, the manufacturer should have considered each of the factors listed above. First, what channel conflict may develop if the manufacturer sells directly to the government employees of the agency but the employee had previously made their purchases through an intermediary, a local retailer? Likely the retailer will not appreciate the reduced sales and will resent what they believe to be a supplier now behaving like a competitor. If this happens the retailer could retaliate by dropping the manufacturer altogether or, if this is not possible, de-emphasizing or undermining the sales efforts. If the channel conflict results in a situation where the value of the lost sales exceeds the value of the B2G sales, ecommerce would not be a good solution, at least not on that basis.

Furthermore, when a business engages in ecommerce, it may also cause **price conflict** with its traditional channels. Because of disintermediation, the manufacturer may be able to offer a lower price and still make a profit. However, as soon as the manufacturer offers the lower price, existing channels may object. Even if the manufacturer and the retailer are not competing for the same customers, the retailer still will not want a lower price to be readily known via the Web.

Furthermore, the existing distribution and retailing partners do provide value; they are not just a cost. Without them, the manufacturer will have the increased **logistic expense** of entering and processing orders in small quantities. If the expense of processing a single-unit order is the same as that for processing a 12-unit order (which is possible), the average logistic expense per item will be much higher for goods sold via ecommerce.

Similarly, **customer service expenses** are likely to increase for manufacturers that use ecommerce to sell directly to consumers (B2C). The manufacturer will be required to provide service to less-sophisticated users and on a one-by-one basis. For example, instead of explaining to a single sales professional that the recent shipment of 100 Gizmo 3.0s requires a new bracket, the manufacturer will need to explain that 100 times to less knowledgeable and more frustrated customers. Such service requires additional training and expense.

A growing issue for merchants with traditional stores is that of showrooming. **Showrooming** occurs when a customer learns about or tries a product or service in the high cost bricks-and-mortar retail store while completing the sales transaction at the low-cost

Internet sales channel of another retailer. The ethics of showrooming and the impact on profitability have been widely debated, but there is little doubt that it occurs.

Shopping has been considered a social activity, and many people still want to see and touch goods before purchasing them. In May 2012, Target stopped selling Amazon.com's Kindle in their stores after realizing that consumers were using their stores to examine the Kindle but were actually buying the eReader from Amazon.com—a practice that they claimed Amazon.com encouraged by giving customers a 5 percent discount if they uploaded a copy of the UPC barcode (typically, this is only accessible in a traditional store). Online purchases are often (but not always) price sensitive, particularly when the product is interchangeable (or what economists refer to as fungible) and there are limited expectations for service. Some students, for example, may visit their college or university bookstore (the showroom) to identify the book needed for a particular course, inspect it, and decide if they are going to buy it (a practice that, as authors and professors, we highly recommend) before purchasing a copy at an online retailer (or photocopying one, a process we do not recommend). Of course, not all aspects of showrooming are unanticipated or counter-strategic. Future Shop, for example, considers its combination of both retail stores and ecommerce websites to be part of their strategic advantage, and customers are encouraged to browse the physical store and buy online or to browse online and then buy in the store.

For governments, a large problem is determining how to tax ecommerce. Normally, taxes are based on the location of the creation or consumption of the particular good or service, but this is complicated with regard to ecommerce. If, for example, Canadian consumers download an antivirus service from a website based in a U.S. state that does not have sales tax (as one of your authors has done), what taxes are due, and who is responsible for collecting and remitting them? This problem, of course, is not completely new. Consumers located near Alberta, which does not have a sales tax, have long been able to cross the provincial border for large (or small, depending on the distance) purchases. However, this is made worse through ecommerce and is a major concern for all levels of government. Online and predominantly service-based businesses that have more location flexibility compared with retail operations are often able to pay much lower taxes. Apple, for example, has an overall U.S. tax rate of 24.2 percent, whereas Wal-Mart's average U.S. tax rate is 32.5 percent.

Beyond these economic factors, another consideration for organizations that are contemplating ecommerce is reduced profitability and margin squeeze. Because information is so freely available to consumers, it is harder to raise prices. Customers often know more about competitive pricing than salespeople do, and prices can be driven below the point at which companies can earn a reasonable profit. This scenario, of course, is not just related to ecommerce. Even if a particular company does not participate in selling directly to consumers, more and more information is freely available on the Web and accessible via smartphones. This can increase consumers' ability to negotiate lower prices.

By the time that this book is published, we can be certain that more existing business models and ideas will have been disrupted. At the time of writing, for example, startups such as NowPublic (www.nowpublic.com) are changing the way news is collected and distributed by allowing anyone with a cell phone to gather and share videos (as we have seen from reports by local people in the Middle East), and services such as ShopSavvy (http://shopsavvy.mobi) are allowing anyone with a cell phone to scan a barcode to find the lowest price within the local area. Such services challenge the efficiency and effectiveness of retail supply chains. The fundamental drivers of ecommerce—low-cost computing and storage, ubiquitous networking, and collaborative services—are not likely to lose momentum any time soon.

You have just been hired as a marketing manager for a national clothing retailer. Your boss has made it crystal clear that your predecessor was fired because she could not get any traction with the company's social media campaign. He wants results—soon. This is your dream job, and you do not want to lose it.

You read an online news article about a person who bought an army of bots that would follow him on Instagram. This could immediately inflate your follower count and show your boss that you are making real progress. Of course, the bots would not be real followers, but if your follower count goes up, it might be easier to attract real human followers. People like popular people.

You do some searching and find online forums where users are bragging about how realistic their bots are. You even find websites (click farms) that advertise Facebook "likes" for sale. You decide to spend $100 and see what happens. You end up getting 15 000 followers that slowly trickle in over the next couple of weeks. Not bad. Not bad at all. Real progress that you can show your boss. Well, maybe not "real" progress. But at least it is progress.

You start looking at the profiles of your newly minted synthetic friends and find that they are pretty easy to identify. They only put one word in their name field. But the photos, names, and other content look very believable. You also noticed that you have started to attract annoying spammy accounts that leave URLs and discount codes in their comments. This is buggy, but it helps push up your follower count and that might mean more real followers.

Then comes the purge. Only a few months into your campaign, Instagram starts deleting bots! You lose about 2000 followers overnight. Ouch! But you still have loads of fictitious followers left. Justin Bieber had the worst hit—3.5 million followers deleted in one day.[38] Other celebrities lost millions of followers as well. You check the news, and it looks like nearly every company, actor, singer, politician, and popular user on Instagram lost followers. You immediately get a sinking feeling in the pit of your stomach. What if you are not the only one who bought followers?

DISCUSSION QUESTIONS

1. Consider your decision to use company funds to buy an army of bot followers.

   a. Is your action ethical according to the categorical imperative (that is, an unconditional moral obligation that is binding in all circumstances and is not dependent on a person's inclination or purpose)?

   b. Is your action ethical according to the utilitarian perspective (that is, the view that the best action is the one that maximizes utility)?

   c. What would your boss say if he found out that a good portion of the new corporate followers, Instagram followers, and Facebook likes are fake?

2. Consider Instagram's action to purge bot accounts.

   a. Is it ethical for Instagram to delete followers? Consider both the categorical imperative and utilitarian perspectives.

   b. Is it ethical for Instagram to allow any bots at all? Consider both the categorical imperative and utilitarian perspectives.

3. How hard should Instagram, or any other social media company, work to eliminate bots?

4. Suppose a social media startup decides to become a publicly traded company. It has not been profitable—yet. The number of average monthly users is one of the primary means of valuing the company.

   a. Does it have a legal obligation to find out how many of its users are bots?

Continued ➡

[38] Rex Santus, "Justin Bieber Dethroned as King of Instagram in Massive Follower Purge," *Mashable*, December 19, 2013, accessed April 2, 2015, *http://mashable.com/2014/12/19/instagram-purge*.

b. Does it have an ethical obligation to find out how many of its users are bots?

c. Is there any way for investors to determine how many users are bots? How?

5. Consider the position of an advertising agency, or social media company that sells your firm advertising.

a. Suppose your company is charged based on the number of ads shown to users and the number of clicks on those ads. Does the advertising agency have an ethical obligation to find out how many of the ads it sells are seen by actual humans—not bots?

b. The advertising agency offers to sell you "likes" for a new product line you are launching. It tells you that buying likes is just like hiring actors for a TV commercial. You are paying them to say they like your product. Is it ethical to buy or sell likes? Consider both the categorical imperative and utilitarian perspectives.

MIS in Use | Digital Is Forever

Have you ever told a friend something and asked him or her to keep it private? Most people have. Unfortunately, at some point, the person you confided in violated your trust. He or she shared that information with someone else. If so, you can probably recall the horrible feeling that accompanied the thought of other people knowing things you wanted kept private.

This is how several A-list celebrities felt when scores of their personal and highly sensitive photos stored in iCloud were hacked and subsequently plastered all over the Internet. You may be wondering how this could happen—how could cybercriminals access the private data of someone else stored on an iCloud account?

It turns out there was a security vulnerability associated with Apple's Find My iPhone application. Safeguards had not been implemented by Apple to limit the number of login attempts permitted before an account would be locked, a common security practice used to prevent hackers from entering endless combinations of usernames and passwords in an exhaustive attempt to guess the correct set of credentials (referred to as a brute-force attack).[39]

The celebrities affected by these attacks are still trying to remove their private data from the Web. The sad truth is that their private data will never completely be removed. Even more sobering is the fact that anyone who chooses to transmit any personal information using an Internet connection (i.e., send something via email, post something on a social media site, etc.) can become a victim too.

Privacy? What's That?

Once you click the button to send an email, post a photo, or share a video, you lose control over that data. It can be copied, shared, and copied again. Your data will travel through numerous servers until it is delivered to the intended recipient. It will also be stored on a data farm owned by the company whose app you are using. You can *never* withdraw this information—and once it is transmitted, it is nearly impossible (and in most cases, impossible) to delete.

Think about it this way. Have you ever heard the saying that "two can keep a secret if one of them is dead"? Well, from a technology perspective, "two *can't* keep a

Continued →

[39] Mohit Kumar, "Apple Patches 'Find My iPhone' Vulnerability Which May Caused Celebrities Photo Leak," *The Hacker News*, September 4, 2014, accessed April 24, 2015, *http://thehackernews.com/2014/09/apple-patches-find-my-iphone.html.*

→ **Continued**

secret if one of them is the Internet." Anything shared over the Internet morphs into a digital zombie, destined to wander the far reaches of cyberspace forever!

You may think that as long as you are sharing messages or photos with a trusted party you have nothing to worry about. Unfortunately, our digital world is rife with cybercriminals who spend countless hours trying to steal data from both companies and everyday citizens (just ask the Apple iCloud victims).

And cybercriminals are not the only ones trying to take advantage of your personal data. Companies also see value in accessing and running various analyses on everything you digitally say or do. Google, for example, scans the contents of your emails sent through Gmail so it can serve you targeted ads. In fact, Google looks at more than just your emails. Google also looks at your search queries, the sites you visit, and your Google profile in an effort to make its ads more relevant.[40]

Big Data = Big Money

Taking into account the actions of both cybercriminals and corporations, we can infer one thing—accessing the private data of Internet users equals big money as personal data can be (1) illegally accessed by criminals and sold on the black market to other nefarious actors or (2) legally accessed by companies and sold to other companies. The good news is that high-profile privacy breaches like the iCloud incident raise awareness for everyone concerning the risks of storing or sharing personal information online.

For example, a recent poll conducted by the Pew Research Center found that "86% of Internet users have taken steps online to remove or mask their digital footprints—ranging from clearing cookies to encrypting their email and from avoiding using their name to using virtual networks that mask their Internet protocol (IP) address."[41] This is encouraging, but they can do more. Rather than spending time trying to erase their digital footprint, users need to keep from making tracks in the first place. Think before you click, share, or post. Digital is forever.

DISCUSSION QUESTIONS

1. **Criminals and corporations both seek out the private data of Internet users for their own gains, but they are not the only ones trying to access your data. Why do you think employers might seek out data about applicants when making their hiring decisions?**

2. **You likely heard news reports about the iCloud and Sony breaches, both of which resulted in private photos and emails being shared with the masses on the Internet. But can you recall hearing about the perpetrators being brought to justice? If not, why do you think this is the case?**

3. **Stolen or compromised devices can also be used to access your private data. Even if that data has been deleted. Search the Web for information about software used to recover deleted files. Does normal deletion permanently remove a file from the memory of your device? Can it be recovered? How?**

4. **Take a few minutes to reflect on your online habits. Have you sent emails or posted messages or images that could be perceived as controversial in nature? Are there posts that you would not want a future employer to see? How might your emails or posts affect your career?**

How Does the Knowledge in This Chapter Help You?

You already know how to navigate Facebook, Twitter, and other social sites for your personal use. This chapter has shown you how to transition some of your knowledge to help organizations. You learned the components of a social media IS and the commitment that an organization makes when it places a Facebook or Twitter icon on its webpage. You also learned how organizations use SMIS to achieve their strategies across the five primary value chain activities and how SMIS can increase social capital. Finally, you learned how revenue can be earned from social media, how organizations need to manage the risks of social media, and how social media will challenge you in the future.

Stay tuned, however; the story is evolving. When you read about social media developments in the future, think about organizations and not just your own use.

---

[40] Google, "Ads in Gmail," *Gmail Help*, accessed April 26, 2015, *https://support.google.com/mail/answer/6603?hl=en.*

[41] Lee Rainie, Sara Kiesler, Ruogu Kang, and Mary Madden, "Anonymity, Privacy, and Security Online," September 5, 2013, *The Hacker News*, accessed April 26, 2015, *www.pewinternet.org/2013/09/05/anonymity-privacy-and-security-online.*

Use this Active Review to verify that you have understood the material in the chapter. You can read the entire chapter and then perform the tasks in this review, or you can read the material for just one question and perform the tasks for that question before moving on to the next one.

Q9-1 WHAT IS A SOCIAL MEDIA INFORMATION SYSTEM (SMIS)?

Define *social media, communities of practice, social media information systems, social media provider,* and *social networks.* Name and describe three SMIS organizational roles. Explain the elements of Figure 9-3. In your own words, explain the nature of the five components of SMIS for each of the three SMIS organizational roles.

Q9-2 HOW DO SMIS ADVANCE ORGANIZATIONAL STRATEGY?

Summarize how social media contributes to sales and marketing, customer support, inbound logistics, outbound logistics, manufacturing and operations, and human resources. Name SM risks for each activity. Define *social CRM* and *crowdsourcing.*

Q9-3 HOW DO SMIS INCREASE SOCIAL CAPITAL?

Define *capital, human capital,* and *social capital.* Explain four ways that social capital adds value. Name three factors that determine social capital and explain how "they are more multiplicative than additive." Define *influencer* and describe how you could use social media to increase the number and strength of your social relationships.

Q9-4 HOW DO (SOME) COMPANIES EARN REVENUE FROM SOCIAL MEDIA?

Define *monetize* and describe why it is difficult for social media companies to generate revenue. Give examples of how social media companies generate revenue from advertising and charging for premium services. Define *pay-per-click, conversion rate,* and *freemium.* Define *ad blocking* and explain how it hurts online companies' ability to generate revenue. Summarize how growth in mobile devices affected revenue streams. Explain why concerns about mobile devices limiting ad revenue are overreactions.

Q9-5 HOW CAN ORGANIZATIONS ADDRESS SMIS SECURITY CONCERNS?

Name and describe two sources of SM risk. Describe the purpose of a SM policy, and summarize Intel's guiding principles. Describe a SM mistake, other than one given in this text, and explain the wise response to it. Name four sources of problems of user-generated content; name three possible responses and give the advantages and disadvantages of each. Explain how internal use of social media can create risks to information security, organizational liability, and employee productivity.

Q9-6 WHERE IS SOCIAL MEDIA TAKING US?

Describe ways in which the use of social media is currently changing. Summarize possible management challenges when controlling employees ten years in the future. Describe the text's suggested response. How does the change in forms of address since the 1960s indicate a change in the relationship of employees and organizations to the business world? Discuss why it is hard to predict the impact of technological change. Explain Henry Ford's famous statement about "faster horses."

Q9-7 WHAT IS ECOMMERCE, AND HOW IS IT USED?

Define *ecommerce.* Explain the difference between ecommerce and ebusiness. Describe why the distinction is important. Differentiate each of the types of merchant sites and discuss the benefits and liabilities of ecommerce from the perspective of business, consumers, and society (government).

MyLab MIS

MyLab MIS is an online learning and testing environment that features the perfect study tools to help you master the concepts covered in this chapter. Log in to MyLab to test your knowledge of key chapter concepts and explore additional practice tools, including videos, flashcards, and more!

KEY TERMS AND CONCEPTS

Ad-blocking software 300
Business-to-business
    (B2B) 291
Business-to-consumer
    (B2C) 291
Business-to-government
    (B2G) 309
Capital 294
Channel conflict 312
Clearinghouses 310
Communities 284
Communities of
    practice 284

Connection data 288
Content data 288
Conversion rate 302
Crowdsourcing 291
Customer service
    expense 312
Disintermediation 310
Ecommerce 307
Ecommerce auctions 310
Electronic exchanges 310
Freemium 300
Human capital 294
Influencer 295

Logistic expense 312
Merchant companies 309
Monetize 299
Nonmerchant companies 309
Pay-per-click 300
Price conflict 312
Price elasticity 311
Showrooming 312
Social capital 294
Social CRM 290
Social media (SM) 284
Social media information
    system (SMIS) 284

Social media policy 302
Social media providers 285
Social networks 285
Strength of a
    relationship 297
User-generated content
    (UGC) 288
Users 285
Value of social capital 295
Viral hook 287
Web 2.0 306
Web storefront 309

USING YOUR KNOWLEDGE

9-1. Using the Facebook page of a company that you have "liked" (or would choose to like), fill out the five components of a SMIS. Strive to replace the phrases in the description column of that grid with specific statements that pertain to Facebook, the company you like, and you and users whom you know. For example, if you and your friends access Facebook using an Android phone, enter that specific device.

9-2. Name a company for which you would like to work. Describe, as specifically as you can, how that company could use social media in each of the areas from Q9-2 listed below. Include community type, specific focus, processes involved, risks, and any other observations.

   a. Sales and marketing

   b. Customer service

   c. Inbound logistics

   d. Outbound logistics

   e. Manufacturing and operations

   f. Human resources

9-3. Visit *www.lie-nielsen.com* or *www.sephora.com*. On the site you chose, find links to social networking sites. In what ways are those sites sharing their social capital with you? In what ways are they attempting to cause you to share your social capital with them? Describe the business value of social networking to the business you chose.

COLLABORATION EXERCISES

Read Knowledge Extensions 1 and 3 if you have not already done so. Meet with your team and build a collaboration IS that uses tools like Google Docs, SharePoint, or other collaboration tools. Do not forget the need for procedures and team training. Now, using that IS, answer the questions below.

Twitter's IPO on November 7, 2013, was one of the biggest tech IPOs in history. The social media giant's stock closed that day at $44.90 a share, making it worth an estimated $25B.[42]

---

[42] Olivia Oran and Gerry Shih, "Twitter Shares Soar in Frenzied NYSE Debut," November 7, 2013, *Reuters*, accessed May 28, 2014, *www.reuters.com/article/2013/11/07/us-twitter-ipo-idUSBRE99N1AE20131107*.

Not bad for a company that had never made a profit. In fact, Twitter posted a $70M loss the quarter before listing! How could a company be worth $25B and never have made any money?

Analysts argue that tech companies such as those shown in Figure 9-14 should be valued based on growth potential, user base, consumer engagement, and market size. It turns out that *Amazon.com*, Instagram, and Pinterest were not profitable when they went public, either.

Tech Companies	Market Cap ($)	P/E
Apple	721.63B	16.96
Google	368.92B	25.82
Facebook	219.51B	75.63
Amazon.com	198.24B	N/A
Netflix	34.20B	147.31
LinkedIn	25.35B	N/A
Twitter	24.68B	N/A

Traditional Companies	Market Cap ($)	P/E
General Electric	272.23B	N/A
Wal-Mart Stores	251.73B	15.45
Verizon Comm.	202.80B	20.88
Toyota	216.92B	12.91
BP	126.88B	34.17
Johnson & Johnson	277.11B	17.48
Ford	61.65B	19.44

Figure 9-14   Tech Company Valuations.

Source: Pearson Education

Traditional IPO valuations focus on measures of profitability. This means investors look at revenues, profits, assets, liabilities, and new products. Figure 9-14 shows price-to-earnings ratios (P/E) for several well-known companies. Using iteration and feedback, answer the following questions:

9-1. Compare the tech companies' P/E ratios in Figure 9-14 with the traditional companies' P/E ratios. Note that some of the tech companies have very high P/E ratios (a low P/E is good, a high P/E is bad). Some do not even have a P/E ratio because they did not turn a profit. As a group, list the reasons why the tech companies have such high P/E ratios. Are the prices of these stocks justified given the earnings? Why?

9-2. Identify public tech stocks you believe are undervalued (not limited to those shown in Figure 9-14). Design an investment portfolio consisting solely of tech stocks that you believe will be profitable. Justify your decision with regards to risk and return on those stocks.

9-3. Create a free online portfolio of these stocks (e.g., via Yahoo! Finance) and track its progress. Report on its performance.

9-4. Could overvalued tech stocks lead to a dot-com 2.0 crash like the original in 1999–2001? Discuss why this may or may not happen. Summarize your discussion in a couple of paragraphs.

MyLab MIS

1. According to Paul Greenberg, *Amazon.com* is the master of the 2-minute relationship, and Boeing is the master of the 10-year relationship.[43] Visit www.boeing.com and www.amazon.com. From Greenberg's statement and from the appearance of these websites, it appears that Boeing is committed to traditional CRM and *Amazon.com* to social CRM. Give evidence from each site that this might be true. Explain why the products and business environment of both companies cause this difference. Is there any justification for traditional CRM at *Amazon.com*? Why or why not? Is there any justification for social CRM at Boeing? Why or why not? Based on these companies, is it possible that a company might endorse Enterprise Social Networks but not endorse social CRM? Explain.

2. Suppose you are hired by the Visit California organization to develop a SMIS. The organization wants to promote travel to California, increase awareness about the fun things to do in California, increase traffic to its website, and direct visitors to its business partners. Which success metrics would indicate that Visit California has achieved its goals? Who would be the organization's target audience? What value would the SMIS provide to visitors? How could the organization make personal connections with its visitors? Which SM platform(s) would you recommend Visit California use? Justify your recommendation.

CASE STUDY 9

LET ME GET THAT: BUYATAB AND WHERE GOOD IDEAS COME FROM

Matias Marquez could be forgiven if his mind drifted off in his entrepreneurism class as the professor talked about the millions of people who must have pulled burrs off their clothes long before someone thought of Velcro. Matias was still in university, but working with fellow students he had already founded a customer-oriented company that continued to smash its revenue targets and had received national attention.

Buyatab (www.buyatab.com) first took shape when one of Matias's friends tried to give his father a surprise gift. Calling the Chicago restaurant where he knew his father was dining, he asked if he could "buy the tab" or pay the bill by putting it on his credit card. The problem, as he found out, was that although the restaurant had the policies and processes in place to sell him a physical gift card over the telephone (that they would later mail), the only way that he could pay the bill by telephone was if he faxed them a letter with a copy of the front and back of his credit card—something that would be very hard to do, since he was calling from his cellphone.

Matias' friend described the problem to Matias, and they tried to figure out how this could be solved. When they both realized that gift cards were really not about the tangible plastic but more about what they represented, their frustration only grew. The 16 to 24 digits that made up each gift card validated its authenticity and the restaurant could then trust that it was legitimate. There was no reason why this validation could not be done on the Internet, thought Matias. Customers should be able to go online, sign up at his website, and instantaneously be able to pick up the tab, or pay for meals at participating restaurants.

---

43 Paul Greenberg, *CRM at the Speed of Light*, 4th ed. (New York: McGraw-Hill, 2010), p. 105.

Of course, if things were really easy, very few of us would be sitting in this classroom. Getting the first restaurants signed up was immensely difficult, and Matias found that there were many technical and security problems to be addressed. Still, he was persistent, refined the process, and slowly managed to build his network. Parts of the business model evolved, and Matias soon realized that working with the gift card infrastructure was important; specifically, integrating the Buyatab technology with that of his customers' websites and working with credit card companies were crucial to his success.

The future for Buyatab is bright. Its customers include some of North America's most famous restaurant brands, and the company has added professional management, secured external financing, and won national innovation and entrepreneurial awards.

Questions

1. How hard would it be for Buyatab to sign its first customer?
2. Many others might have had this same problem, but why didn't they think of developing a solution?
3. Why wouldn't the credit card companies have solved this problem?
4. Could Buyatab have been formed in the 1980s? (*Hint:* What enabling technologies were required to form such a company?)

Visit MyLab to access the data files to complete these questions.

WHAT DO YOU THINK?

HIDING THE TRUTH?

No one is going to publish their least attractive picture on their Facebook page, but how far should you go to create a positive impression? If your hips and legs are not your best features, is it unethical to stand behind your sexy car in your photo? If you have been to one event with someone very popular in your crowd, is it unethical to publish photos that imply you meet on a daily basis? Surely, there is no obligation to publish pictures of yourself at boring events with unpopular people just to balance the scale after posting photos in which you appear unrealistically attractive and overly popular.

As long as all of this occurs on a Facebook or Twitter account that you use for personal relationships, it may not have any significant consequences. (Remember, though, that what goes around comes around.) However, consider social networking in the business arena.

a. Suppose a river-rafting company starts a group on a social networking site to promote rafting trips. Graham, a 15-year-old high school student who has no relationship with the company but wants to appear more grown up than he is, posts a picture of a handsome 22-year-old male as a picture of himself. He also writes witty and clever comments on the site photos and claims to play the guitar and be an accomplished masseur. Are his actions unethical? Suppose someone decided to go on the rafting trip, partly influenced by Graham's postings, and was disappointed when he learned the truth about Graham. Would the rafting company have any responsibility to refund that person's fees? Bonus question: Would it make a difference if Graham was related to one of the company owners?

b. Suppose you own and manage that same rafting company. Is it unethical for you to encourage your employees to write positive reviews about your company? Does your assessment change if you ask your employees to use an email address other than the one they have at work?

c. Again, suppose you own and manage the rafting company and that you pay your employees a bonus for every client they bring to a rafting trip. Without specifying any particular technique, you encourage your employees to be creative in how they obtain clients. One employee invites his Facebook friends to a party at which he shows photos of prior rafting trips. On the way back from the party, one of the friends is involved in an automobile accident and dies. His spouse sues your company. Should it be held accountable? Would it matter if you had known about the employee's party? Would it matter if you had not encouraged your employees to be creative?

d. Suppose your rafting company has a website for customer reviews. In spite of your best efforts at camp cleanliness, on one trip (out of dozens) one of your staff members accidentally serves contaminated food, and everyone becomes ill with food poisoning. One of those clients writes a poor review because of that experience. Is it ethical for you to delete that review from your site?

e. Assume that you have a professor who has written a popular textbook. You are upset with the grade you received in his class, so you write an extremely harsh review of that professor's book on Amazon.com. Are your actions ethical?

f. Suppose you were at one time employed by the previously mentioned river rafting company and you were, you think undeservedly, terminated by the company. To get even, you use Facebook to spread rumours among your friends (many of whom are river guides) about the safety of the company's trips. Are your actions unethical? Are they illegal? Do you see any ethical distinctions between this situation and that in item (d)?

g. Again, suppose that you were at one time employed by the previously mentioned rafting company and were undeservedly terminated. You notice that the company's owner does not have a Facebook account, so you create one for her. You have known her for many years and have dozens of photos of her, some of which were taken at parties and are unflattering and quite scandalous. You post those photos along with critical comments that she had made about clients or employees. Most of the comments were made when she was tired or frustrated, and they are hurtful, but they are also witty and humorous. You send friend invitations to people she knows including people mentioned in her biting and critical remarks. Are your actions unethical?

Discussion Questions

1. Read the situations in items (a) through (g), and answer the questions contained in each.

2. On the basis of your answers for Question 1, formulate ethical principles for creating or using social networks for business purposes.

3. On the basis of your answers for Question 1, formulate ethical principles for creating or using user-generated content for business purposes.

4. Summarize the risks that a business assumes when it chooses to sponsor user-generated content.

5. Summarize the risks that a business assumes when it uses social networks for business purposes.

PART 4

Information Systems Management

Part 4 addresses the management of information systems security, development, and resources. We begin with security because of its great importance today. With the Internet, the interconnectivity of systems, and the rise of interorganizational IS, security problems in one organization can lead to security problems in connected organizations as well. You will see how that affects PRIDE in the Chapter 10 opener.

While you can readily understand that IS security is important to you as a future manager, it may be more difficult for you to appreciate why you need to know about IS development. As a business professional, you will be the customer of development projects. You need basic knowledge of development processes to be able to assess the quality of the work being done on your behalf. As a manager, you may be required to allocate budget resources and release funds for IS development. You need knowledge that allows you to be informed, capable, and effective when contemplating choices, implementing decisions, and participating in projects.

Finally, you need to know how IS resources are managed so that you can better relate to your IS department. IS managers can sometimes seem rigid and overly protective of IS assets, but usually they have important reasons for their concerns. You need to understand the IS department's perspective and know your rights and responsibilities as a user of IS resources within your organization. Having such knowledge is key to success for any business professional.

MIS in Action

"Thanks for coming over on a Saturday morning. I just finished tennis, and the game went on longer than I expected. Anyway, forgive my appearance." Zev Friedman looks around the table.

"You must have won, Mr. Friedman. You look pleased." Michele is just getting to know PRIDE Systems' owner.

"Call me Zev. These other folks do. And yes, we won."

"Yes, sir." Michele is still a bit formal.

"OK, so, Jared, I understand you want to spend some real money. This morning you're going to tell me why, right?"

"That's why we're here, Zev. We've got a couple of options for you to consider. Here's a copy. I'm going to let James take you through it."

"I can hardly wait." Zev's mood is upbeat, but his demeanor and sleepy-eyed posture don't fool anyone. They know he's poised to detect errors or poor preparation.

"OK, Zev, you know that we were able to adjust our systems in order to support the new focus on multi-heat races." James is a little nervous as he starts.

"Yes, I do. And I understand that was your idea." Zev wants to make James comfortable with that compliment, and it works.

"It was a team discussion. Anyway, we were able to do that, and thanks to everyone's hard work, we're having success." James looks around the table as he speaks.

"It's a start, anyway." Zev knows they have a long way to go to establish a sustainable business.

"As you know, we only run on Apple and Android devices. We've done OK ignoring Surface and Windows phones."

"Yeah. I just don't understand Microsoft. They've blown every opportunity at mobile devices."

"Except, well, we think we can open the doors to an entirely new market if we start developing for the Xbox."

"The Xbox?"

"Yes, because these contests are very game-like. I'm spinning on my bike in my basement against 10 other players. They happen to be real people, but why don't we push the UI and use the Xbox to make it more visually exciting?"

"Interesting. Could be. So you want funds for Xbox development?"

"Yes, but take a look at the third page of the document we gave you. There are two ways to go. One is to develop using tools and technology specific to the Xbox. That would give us three separate code bases: Apple, Android, and Xbox."

"So?"

"We'll have essentially three different projects under way at the same time, with a lot of duplicated effort." From his voice and expression it's clear James hates the idea of duplicated effort.

CHAPTER 10
Acquiring Information Systems Through Projects

MIS in Action

"I've worked with him before, but not on an Android project." James Wu and Jared Cooper are discussing the pros and cons of outsourcing Amazon Fire phone development to India.

"But it was a phone application?" Jared trusts James to do his homework, but he wants to understand his risks in outsourcing.

"Right, and in native iOS. I'm not sure about his skills developing on Android."

"So tell me what you know about this guy."

"His name is Ajit Barid. At least that's the name of his company." James looks a little sheepish.

"That's not his name?"

"I don't know. Maybe. You know what Ajit Barid means?" He starts to smile . . .

"No. What?"

"Invincible cloud."

"Umm . . . probably not the name his mother gave him . . . or she was prophetic. James, this makes me nervous. I don't know anything about doing business in India. If the guy takes our money and runs, then what do we do?" Jared is down to business now.

"Well, we don't pay him until he delivers . . . or at least not much. But I've had a positive experience with him, and his references are good on a recent game development project."

"India is a long way away. What if he gives our code to somebody else? Or our ideas? What if we find some horrible bug in his code, and we can't find him to fix it? What if he just disappears? What if he gets two-thirds done and then loses interest . . . or goes to work on someone else's project?" Jared is on a roll.

"All are risks, I agree. But it will cost you four to six times as much to develop over here." James starts to list risks on the whiteboard.

"Well, it's been my experience that you get what you pay for in this life . . . "

"You want me to find some local developers we can outsource to?" James thinks local development is a poor choice but wants Jared to feel comfortable with the decision they reach.

"Yes, no, I mean no. I don't think so. How'd you meet him?"

"At a conference when he was working for Microsoft in its Hyderabad facility. He was programming SharePoint cloud features. When the iPad took off, he left Microsoft and started his own company. That's when I hired him to build the iOS app."

"That worked out OK?" Jared wants to be convinced.

"Yes, but it was one of his first jobs . . . he had to get it right for us."

"What do you think? What do you want to do?"

James ponders the questions. "Well, I think the biggest risk is his success. You know, the restaurant that gets the great reviews and then is buried in new customers and the kitchen falls apart."

"Doesn't he have more employees now?"

"Yes, he does, and I know he's a good developer, but I don't know whether he's a good manager."

"OK, what else?" Jared is all business.

"Well, Android development is different from iOS, which is what he used for the iPad. I guess I'd say inexperience with this development environment would be another risk factor."

"What about money?"

"Well, like I said, we structure the agreement so we don't pay much until we know it all works."

"So what else do you worry about?" Jared wants to get all of James's concerns on the table.

"Loss of time. Maybe he gets distracted, doesn't finish the app, or hires someone else to do it, and they can't. And September rolls around and we find that, while we're not out any real money, we've lost most of a year of time."

"I don't like the sound of that."

"Neither do I," James responds while he adds schedule risk to the list.

"You think maybe we should bite the bullet and hire our own programmers?"

"Good heavens, no! No way! That would be incredibly expensive, we couldn't keep them busy, not yet, anyway, and I don't have the time to manage a software project nor the money to hire someone who does." James is certain about this.

"But what about long term?"

"Long term, maybe. We'll have to see what we have for budget and what our long-term development needs are. That's a big step. We would need to build infrastructure we don't currently have like testing facilities, hire developers, QA personnel, and managers. If we make PRIDE Systems the success we hope, we'll do that. But not yet."

"So?" Jared's tone shows he wants to wrap up this conversation.

James summarizes, "Let me finish the requirements document and then get a proposal and bid from Ajit as well as a local, domestic developer. We'll look at the proposals and bids and then make a decision. One problem, though . . . "

"What's that?"

"The local developer may outsource it anyway."

"You mean we pay the local developer to hire Ajit or his cousin?" Jared shakes his head. "Something like that."

Jared gets up from the table to show James out of his office. "That's crazy."

"Maybe not. Let's see what we get."

Q10-1 HOW CAN INFORMATION SYSTEMS BE ACQUIRED?

In some ways, information systems are like any other product or service we want to acquire. For example, think about buying a car. Perhaps you are looking for a convertible with lots of horsepower and a great sound system. What options do you have? You could buy the car from a dealer. That would initially be expensive, but the car would be yours, and the dealer would usually offer you a warranty in case anything major went wrong with the car. You could see the car before you bought it and even take it for a test drive, which reduces the risk. Although the car may not be a perfect fit, it will likely serve its purpose and provide you with many of the benefits you desire.

What other options are there in acquiring the car? What if you bought it from the dealer but then made your own customizations? You could repaint it, change the wheels, upgrade the sound system, and make it fit you the way you like it. This is called *customizing*, and it is more expensive than just using the car the way it comes from the dealer. But it would be a closer fit with your needs.

You could also rent or lease the car. When you rent or lease a car, you do not actually own it. Instead, you own the right to use the car for a specific period. The car rental or dealer retains ownership, and you pay for the use of the car. Similarly, you can buy some software outright, but most applications are licenced, which is similar to renting. Some licences have a fixed term, while others have none.

Alternatively, if you were really good with your hands and had the proper tools, you might be able to build the car yourself. Of course, if you have never done this before, it is a risky undertaking, but if you (or your organization) know what you are doing, then this might be a realistic option. When you build a car yourself, you can make it fit your needs perfectly. You can choose the colour, the sound system, and every other feature. You custom-build it for yourself. And if you ever need to make changes or adapt it at some point in the future, you know exactly how to do it. Will it cost less? Will it work better than the dealer's car? That depends on how good you are at building cars. When an organization builds software, we call that software development (or application development).

There is one final method for acquisition. What if you do not have the expertise to build your customized car? You could hire another company to build it and maintain it for you. We might refer to this as outsourcing. When you outsource, you rely on another company to provide you with products or services that you are either unable or unwilling to develop yourself. For example, many companies outsource their office cleaning. Rather than hiring full-time cleaners, a company hires another company to do the cleaning for them. Many services, such as food services, building maintenance, and window washing, are outsourced.

Acquiring a new software application is similar to buying a car. And if we apply this logic to organizations, we can identify five basic ways to acquire a software application:

1. Buy it and use it as is.

2. Buy it and customize it.

3. Rent or lease it.

4. Build it yourself.

5. Outsource it.

Organizations use all of these methods; however, option 2, in which companies purchase prebuilt software and then customize it to some degree, is the most common method for acquiring software applications.

Before we end this section, it is important to reiterate a point made in Chapter 1: Acquiring *software applications* is *not* the same as acquiring *information systems*. If you read the advertisements in trade magazines, you might believe that substantial business process improvements are just around the corner, if only you could find a way to acquire the latest and greatest software applications.

The model of information systems we introduced in Chapter 1 suggested that systems combine hardware, software, data, procedures, and people. Acquiring an information system, therefore, involves more than just obtaining and installing software. It involves incorporating the software into the current technological infrastructure and integrating the software into the data and procedures people use to make things happen in an organization. This process is shown in Figure 10-1. Acquiring new software is *not* the same as acquiring new information systems, because there is much more to think about in systems than just software.

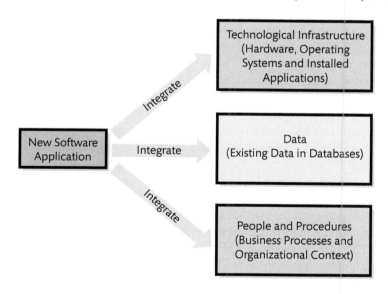

Figure 10-1 New Software Must Be Integrated Into Existing Systems

As a future business manager, it is important for you to realize that even if the software is free, or what is often referred to as *open source*, the organization will always face the cost of integrating the software with its current hardware, data, and procedures. These costs are often substantial—they can exceed the cost of the software itself. Organizations that understand these costs before acquiring applications are more likely to be successful in eventually integrating software compared with organizations that think software equals systems. Now you know better!

Q10-2 WHAT ARE IT PROJECTS, AND WHAT DOES PMBOK MEAN?

When an organization acquires an information system, it has embarked on a project. But what exactly is a project? To answer that question, we refer to the **project management body of knowledge (PMBOK)**, which was developed by the Project Management Institute (www.pmi.org). The guide to the PMBOK was first published in 1996, and the most recent sixth edition published in 2018. The guide to the PMBOK notes that a project "consists of a temporary endeavor undertaken to create a unique product, service or result."[1]

Projects often begin with a set of goals or objectives. From these, a scope for the project is developed, and project managers are given resources, such as people, money, and working space, to complete the project. Projects usually have a start date and an end date. Since the objective is to accomplish something new and unique, projects often represent change in an organization.

Projects that have a large IT component (in terms of budget or personnel) are often referred to as **IT projects**, and these include such things as the installation of a new email application, a CRM system, or an enterprise resource planning (ERP) system. Projects that require some fundamental changes to business processes are often also referred to as *IT projects* because the new IT supports the change in business processes. It is important to recognize that IT projects are rarely if ever exclusively about technology: They affect data, people, and processes.

Information technology project management (ITPM) is the collection of techniques and methods that project managers use to plan, coordinate, and complete IT projects. The tools of ITPM are basically the same tools used in any project management process. The tools include work breakdown structures; budgeting methods; graphical scheduling methods, such as PERT (Program Evaluation Review Technique) and Gantt charts; risk management techniques; communication planning; and high-tech team development. Knowledge Extension 16 Introduction to Microsoft Project provides introductory information about some of these tools.

A full description of project management techniques is beyond the scope of this book; however, project management skills are relevant to anyone considering a career in business. The guide to the PMBOK suggests that there are five process groups in any project: (1) initiating, (2) planning, (3) executing, (4) controlling and monitoring, and (5) closing. These process groups should not be viewed as independent entities but, rather, as a collection of activities that often overlap and occur throughout the project. Later in this chapter, you will see that these process groups are related to the notion of a systems development life cycle (SDLC), which is often used to describe IT projects. Each of these process groups can be related to one of the nine project knowledge areas: (1) integration management, (2) scope management, (3) time management, (4) cost management, (5) quality management, (6) human resources management, (7) communications management, (8) risk management, and (9) procurement management. Inside each of these knowledge areas are techniques that project managers use to manage their projects.

The increasing importance of projects, in particular IT projects, has led to a rapid increase in the number of people seeking certification of project management skills. For example, the PMI is a global institute that has certified over 620 000 **project management professionals (PMPs)**. The PMI also offers a Certified Associate in Project Management (CAPM) program, which includes an introduction to PM. It requires 36 hours of study in project management, after which one must pass a 150-question, three-hour examination.[2] Completing this program can be an effective way for you to differentiate yourself. The International Project Management Association (www.ipma.ch) also offers a Certified Project Manager certification, and the Project Management Association of Canada (www.pmac-ampc.ca) has recently joined the IPMA and offers a certification for Agile Project Managers.

---

[1] Project Management Institute, *A Guide to the Project Management Body of Knowledge (PMBOK Guide),* 4th ed. (Newtown Square, PA: Author, 2008).

[2] You can read more about CAPM at www.pmi.org/certification/~/media/pdf/certifications/pdc_capmhandbook.ashx.

These institutions indicate that a crucial skill for successful project managers, in IT and other industries, is communication. As the Canadian Coalition for Tomorrow's ICT Skills (www.ccict.ca) suggests, organizations are looking for *business professionals* who have the knowledge, skills, and personal qualities to lead and support the effective, competitive use of information technologies.[3] Although technical knowledge is an asset for an IT project manager, the ability to communicate with technical and business-oriented people about project objectives and challenges is a key requirement for successful managers.

The business environment continues to change rapidly. As a business student, you should realize that this rapid pace of change suggests that organizations must improve their ability to adapt to changing conditions. As we noted earlier and will discuss below, organizations adapt to change through projects. Project management skills are, therefore, likely to become even more important for managers in the future. Students should also recognize that most significant projects have some technological component. So, ITPM is central to the skills needed for organizations to adapt appropriately to an increasingly complex business environment.

Q10-3 WHAT SHOULD YOU KNOW ABOUT IT OPERATIONS AND IT PROJECTS?

The IT department is generally responsible for providing IT services to an organization. There are two basic activities required to provide these services. The first is maintaining the current IT infrastructure, while the second is renewing and adapting the infrastructure to keep IT working effectively in the future.

The delivery of service, maintenance, protection, and management of IT infrastructure are often accomplished as part of **IT Operations** or **IT Services**. These services demand a large portion of the IT department's operational budget. Industry professionals often refer to this as keeping the lights on, or KTLO.

The renewal and adaptation of IT infrastructure is normally accomplished through projects. IT projects come in all shapes and sizes. Large IT projects are often high profile, high-cost changes to the status quo of the organization and may be funded outside of the IT operations budget.

The distinction between operations and projects is important for several reasons. One, operational work and project work tend to attract two different types of IT professionals. IT people who prefer to work in operations often want to specialize in particular technologies. Networking specialists, operating systems specialists, database administrators, and hardware technicians are examples of these types of positions. These workers continually seek ways to improve the efficiency and security of the entire set of systems that support operations. These active systems are often referred to as **production systems**. *Stability, predictability, accountability, reliability,* and *security* are keywords in IT operations.

Other people in the IT department are responsible for changing the production systems, rather than maintaining them. These professionals work on IT projects. Because projects are temporary and often change existing infrastructure, they generally require broad skills, and they challenge project team members to learn new technologies. Since different projects often operate at the same time, team members may work on several projects simultaneously. This makes for an exciting (and, some would argue, hectic and chaotic) workday for many project team members. Since large IT projects are often funded from outside of the IT department, IT projects can provide more opportunities for contact with project stakeholders (such as users, managers, and sponsors) in other departments.

Beyond the people involved, there are also differences in the core practices of IT professionals. Within IT operations, the **Information Technology Infrastructure Library (ITIL)** is a well-recognized collection of books that provide a framework of best-practice

[3] See http://ccict.ca/challenge for more information.

approaches to IT operations. The ITIL offers a large set of management procedures that are designed to help businesses achieve value from IT operations. Developed during the 1980s, the ITIL has gone through several revisions; core books from the latest refresh (ITIL V4) were published in June 2011. As business students, it is not important for you to understand the details of the ITIL. What *is* important is that you recognize that a well-developed set of best practices that can support IT operations has been established.

It is important to note that while operations and IT projects are separate fields, they rely on each other for success. Projects come to an end and must be maintained, and infrastructure must eventually be replaced. So, there is always a natural balance between projects and operations within any IT department. This balance is shown in Figure 10-2.

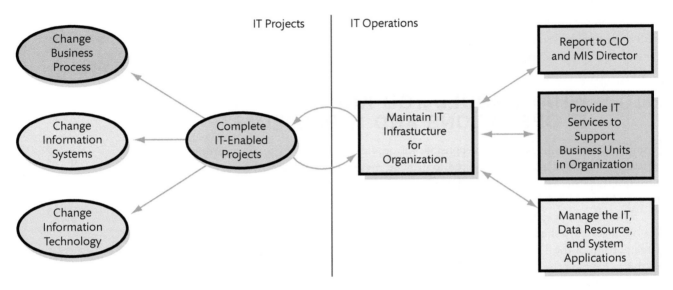

Figure 10-2   What the IT Department Does

What About the Web?

In Chapter 9, we discussed how the Web has become an important avenue for delivering IT services to both internal employees and external customers. Large and small IT departments use the Web as a first step in many internal service requests. For example, when a new employee joins a company, many IT services need to be provided. The new employee may require a computer, which needs to be set up with software the company uses. He or she will need network access, which requires an identification (ID) and password, as well as an email account. The employee may travel with a laptop computer, which requires a virtual private network (VPN) connection provided by the IT department. The IT department also determines where the employee can print documents and sometimes provides an access card so that the person can get into the building. Where can all these services be accessed?

In many companies, the IT department has developed an internal website with frequently asked questions (FAQ), Web-based forms for requesting services, and some Web-based applications that help support tasks, such as adding a new employee. Your school likely has a site like this. The people working at the IT help desk, which is normally the frontline of IT department services, often rely heavily on the Intranet site to help support customer issues and requests.

Support for external customers, such as FAQ, customer support information, and company contact information, are usually available on the company's website. The IT department is normally responsible for maintaining information about IT services on the site. In addition, the IT department supports the company website, making sure the servers and applications that maintain the website are up and running. The Web, therefore, plays a critical role in the delivery of IT services in many organizations.

Q10-4 WHY ARE IT PROJECTS SO RISKY?

Any project manager will tell you that all projects, no matter how small or how well defined, face risks. However, there is some dispute over the level of **IT project risk**. For example, the oft-quoted *CHAOS Report*, created by The Standish Group (www.standish-group.com), suggests that only 16 percent of IT projects were delivered on time, on budget, and on scope, whereas more than 30 percent of IT projects were cancelled before delivering any benefits. In a later study, Sauer, Gemino, and Horner-Reich (www.pmperspectives.org)[4] indicated that the success rate of IT projects was roughly two out of three, or 66 percent, with only 9 percent of projects cancelled. They also indicated, however, that IT projects underperformed at a rate of 25 percent, regardless of their size. Whatever the actual numbers are, it is clear that IT projects face significant risks.

So, what makes IT projects so risky? Consider a construction project, such as building a bridge. The project begins with an architect, who creates a model of the bridge. People involved in the project can look at the model and quickly understand what will be built.

Now, consider an IT project—for example, installing a new Web-based CRM. What does a model for an IT project look like? Have you ever seen one? What would the picture look like? How would you draw the hardware, software, data, procedures, and people? Most IT project definitions are not easy to represent graphically. This makes it difficult for people to understand what the system will "look like," and how it will behave when it is finished. The lack of a good model is, therefore, an important risk to recognize in IT projects.

What about estimating costs for a project? Besides labour, a bridge is built using steel, concrete, and other industrial products. These components are stable, well known, and have been used for hundreds of years. In an IT project, however, the tools for building the project are constantly changing. Computers get cheaper and faster; programming languages, operating systems, and databases get more complex; and the Web makes projects even more difficult to estimate. So, precise estimates for IT projects are difficult to develop because the technology is dynamic.

Assuming that you can make some relatively accurate estimates, the next step in the bridge-building project is to actually start building the bridge. How can you tell how far the project has gone? Well, you just look at the bridge—if it is halfway across the river, then the bridge is about half complete. But what about an IT project? What does a half complete IT project look like? It is hard to tell. It gets even more difficult to ascertain because systems development often means aiming at a moving target. System requirements change as the system is developed, and the bigger the system and the longer the project, the more those requirements alter. It is difficult to estimate how far an IT project has come and how far it needs to go. So, being able to monitor progress is another challenge for IT projects.

Clearly, there are some unavoidable risks inherent in IT projects. But how many risks should we consider, and what are the most important risks? First, recognize that the primary risks do not necessarily emerge from the technology. A comprehensive list of potential risks—52 in total—is provided in an article by Wallace and Keil.[5] These risks include lack of experience in the team, lack of support from top management, lack of participation from system users, unclear and uncertain project requirements, a high level of technical complexity, and changes in the project environment. Real IT projects are subject to many different effects.

---

[4] C. Sauer, A. Gemino, and B. Horner-Reich, "Managing Projects for Success: The Impact of Size and Volatility on IT Project Performance," *Communications of ACM* 50, no. 11 (November 2007): 79-84.

[5] L. Wallace and M. Keil, "Software Project Risks and Their Effect on Outcomes," *Communications of the ACM*, April 2004, 68-73.

Q10-5 WHAT IS A SDLC?

The **systems development life cycle (SDLC)** is the classic process used to acquire information systems. The IT industry developed the SDLC through the school of hard knocks—many early projects met with disaster, and companies and systems developers sifted through the ashes of those disasters to determine what went wrong. By the 1970s, many professionals began to recognize the basic tasks required to successfully acquire and maintain information systems. These basic tasks are combined into phases of **systems development**.

The number of phases in the SDLC varies by organization and author. To keep it simple, we will look at a five-phase process:

1. System definition
2. Requirements analysis
3. Component design
4. Implementation
5. System maintenance

Figure 10-3 shows how these phases are related. Acquisition begins when a business-planning process identifies a need for a new system. For now, suppose that management has determined in some way that the organization can best accomplish its goals and objectives by acquiring a new information system.

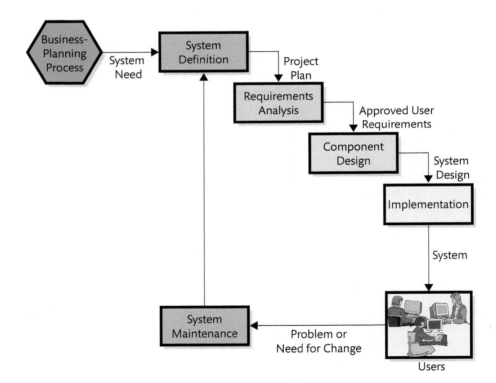

Figure 10-3 Phases in the SDLC

As a future business manager, you will likely play a key role in the SDLC at your organization. Employers are looking for individuals who have the knowledge and skills to innovate through IT. Although you might refer hardware, software, or data problems to the IT department, you cannot hand-off procedural or personnel problems: These are your problems. The single most important criterion for information systems success is for users to take ownership of their systems.

The IT industry has more than 50 years of experience acquiring and developing information systems, and, over those years, methodologies that successfully deal with many of these problems have emerged. In this section, we will consider SDLC, the classic process for systems development. Many other development methods exist, including rapid application development (RAD) and object-oriented systems development (OOD). In recent years, SCRUM has emerged from a movement toward **agile methods**. You can read about the principles underlying agile methods in the Manifesto for Agile Software Development (http://agilemanifesto.org).

You might be wondering why there are so many methodologies. There are several reasons. It is rare for any single process to work ideally for all organizational situations. Also, the scale of information systems varies widely. Personal systems support one person with a limited set of requirements. Workgroup systems support a group of people, normally with a single application. Enterprise systems support many workgroups with many different applications. Given the variety of possible systems, it is not surprising that there are different acquisition methodologies. Different methodologies are appropriate for different types of systems.

In this section, we will focus on the first two phases of the SDLC. These are the phases that you as a business manager will most likely be involved in. These phases are often called **systems analysis**.

Phase 1: Defining Systems

In response to the need for the new system, the organization will assign a few employees, possibly on a part-time basis, to define the requirements for the new system, assess its feasibility, and plan the project. Typically, someone from the IS department leads the initial team, but the members of that initial team are usually both users and IS professionals.

Define System Goals and Scope   As Figure 10-4 shows, the first step in the **system definition phase** is to define the goals and scope of the new information system. As you learned in Part 3, information systems exist to facilitate an organization's competitive strategy by supporting business processes or by improving decision making. At this step, the development team defines the goals and purposes of the new system in terms of these objectives.

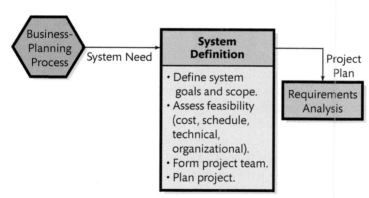

Figure 10-4   SDLC: System Definition Phase

A clear definition of project scope greatly simplifies requirements determination and other subsequent development work.

Assess Feasibility   Once the project's goals and scope have been defined, the next step is to assess feasibility. This step answers the question, "Does this project make sense?" The aim here is to eliminate obviously inappropriate projects before forming a project development team and investing significant resources. This step is sometimes referred to as *creating the business case for the project.*

Feasibility has four dimensions: **cost feasibility**, **schedule feasibility**, **technical feasibility**, and **organizational feasibility**. Because IS development projects are difficult to budget and schedule, *cost* and *schedule feasibility* might be only an approximate, back-of-the-envelope analysis. The purpose is to eliminate any obviously infeasible ideas as soon as possible. Cost and schedule feasibility are relatively straightforward, since they consider whether the organization has the money and time to complete the project. *Technical feasibility* refers to whether existing information technology is likely to be compatible with the needs of the new system. Finally, *organizational feasibility* concerns whether the new system fits within the organization's customs, culture, charter, or legal requirements.

Phase 2: Requirements Analysis

If the defined project is determined to be feasible, the next step is the **requirements analysis phase**, in which the project team is formed and requirements are developed. Developing requirements is a process that might be considered somewhat unique to the area of management information systems (MIS). This is why anyone interested in a career in MIS should take a course in systems analysis and design. The development of project requirements is essentially the management of scope in an IT project. The accounting department can teach us about maintaining budgets, and the operations research department can focus on minimizing project schedules, but only the MIS area focuses on how to define and manage project scope. This is why systems analysis and design is a core skill in MIS. The reason why MIS professionals are focused on defining requirements and scope centres around the difficulty of conceptualizing just what an information system looks like and what it should do.

When developing requirements, the team normally consists of both IT personnel and user representatives. The project manager and IT personnel can be internal personnel or outside contractors. Typical personnel on a development team are a manager (or managers, for larger projects), **systems analysts**, programmers, software testers, and users.

The work of analysis and design is often completed by **business analysts** and systems analysts. Business analysts tend to focus on the analysis of the current system and procedures, and they interact with the stakeholders of the system. Systems analysts tend to be more technically focused IT professionals who understand both business and technology. Both of these analysts are active throughout the systems development process and play a key role in moving the project through the process. Depending on the nature of the project, the team may also include hardware and communications specialists, database designers and administrators, and other IT specialists.

The team composition changes over time. During requirements definition, the team will mainly consist of business analysts and systems analysts. During design and implementation, the emphasis will shift to programmers, testers, and database designers. During integrated testing and conversion, the team will be augmented with testers and business users.

User involvement is critical throughout the system development process. Users are involved in many different ways. *The important point is for users to have active involvement and to take ownership of the project through the entire development process.*

If the new system involves a new database or substantial changes to an existing database, then the development team will create a data model. As you learned in Chapter 5, that model must reflect the users' perspective on their business and business activities. Thus, the data model is constructed on the basis of user interviews and must be validated by those users.

Once the requirements have been specified, the users must review and approve them before the project continues. The easiest and cheapest time to alter the information system is in the requirements phase. Changing a requirement at this stage is simply a matter of changing a description. Changing a requirement in the implementation phase may require weeks of reworking applications components and the database. Before going further, you might want to read about how estimates of budget and schedule are often created in the real world in the exercise "What Do You Think? The Real Estimation Process" at the end of this chapter on page 349. This exercise will help you understand how difficult it can be to develop accurate estimates for IT projects.

Q10-6 HOW ARE INFORMATION SYSTEMS DESIGNED, IMPLEMENTED, AND MAINTAINED?

While managers and system users are not often asked to implement and maintain systems, it is important to understand the choices made during these phases. Before we consider component design, we need to discuss the options we have for developing the system. Our previous discussion in this chapter suggested five ways to acquire an information system: (1) buy it, (2) buy it and customize it, (3) rent or lease it, (4) build it yourself, or (5) outsource it. For the first three of these methods, the information system is already built, so the organization does not have to do major development. This type of acquisition requires the organization to match its requirements with the capabilities of the software application that has already been built. Figure 10-5 summarizes this matching process.

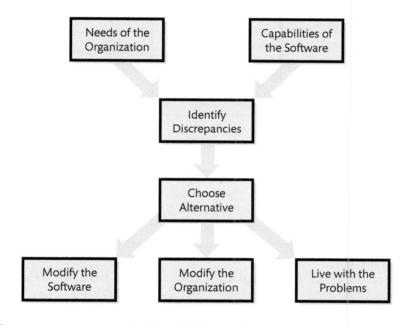

Figure 10-5 Matching Organizational Needs and COTS Software Capabilities

When an organization works through the matching process, it will almost always find discrepancies between the requirements of the business and the capabilities of the software application. The software application rarely fits perfectly. When these discrepancies are identified, the organization faces three choices, as shown in Figure 10-5. These choices are to (1) modify the software, (2) modify the organizational procedures and data, or (3) live with the problems. In reality, the final solution for the organization is likely a combination of these three options.

As a future business manager, it is important for you to realize that **commercial-off-the-shelf (COTS)** software will probably never fit your organizational requirements exactly. So, it is reasonable to expect and budget for some cost and some time before the software is successfully implemented in the organization. How long would that be? For a large implementation, like that of an ERP system, it is reasonable to consider a span of 18 months before things settle down. For smaller systems, a significantly shorter period should be expected.

In the rest of the chapter, we will discuss the steps in the SDLC, assuming that the organization will be building the system itself. What you should realize now is that regardless of whether you buy, rent/lease, or build the information system, the basic steps for acquiring it are the same. First, you have to understand your objectives and analyze your requirements. Next, you design the system using either COTS or a custom design. Then, you implement it and maintain it.

Phase 3: Component Design

Each of the five components of an information system must be designed. Typically, the team designs each component by developing alternatives, evaluating each of the options against the requirements, and then selecting among those alternatives. Accurate requirements are critical here; if they are incomplete or wrong, then they will be poor guides for evaluation. Figure 10-6 illustrates design tasks that pertain to each of the five IS components.

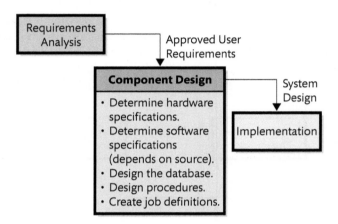

Figure 10-6 SDLC: Component Design Phase

For hardware, the team determines specifications for the hardware it wants to acquire. The team needs to specify the computers, operating systems, networks, and network connections that will process the data. The software design depends on the source of the programs. For off-the-shelf software, the team must determine candidate products and evaluate them against the requirements. For off-the-shelf-with-alterations software, the team identifies products to be acquired off the shelf and then determines the alterations required. For custom-developed programs, the team produces design documentation for writing program code.

If developers are constructing a database, then, during this phase, they need to convert the data model to a database design using techniques like those described in Chapter 5. If developers are using off-the-shelf programs, then little if any additional database design needs to be done—the programs usually handle their own database processing. For a business information system, the system developers and the organization must also design procedures for both users and operations personnel. Procedures need to be developed for normal processing, backup, and failure recovery operations, as summarized in Figure 10-7. Usually, teams of systems analysts and key users design the procedures.

Design also involves developing job descriptions for both users and operations personnel. Sometimes, new information systems require new jobs. If so, the duties and responsibilities for the new jobs need to be defined in accordance with the organization's human resources policies. More often, organizations add new duties and responsibilities to existing jobs. As with procedures, teams of systems analysts and users determine job descriptions and functions.

Phase 4: Implementation

Once the design is complete, the next phase is implementation. Tasks in this phase include building, testing, and converting the users to the new system (Figure 10-8). Developers construct each of the components independently. They obtain, install, and test hardware.

	Users	Operations Personnel
Normal processing	• Procedures for using the system to accomplish business tasks	• Procedures for starting, stopping, and operating the system
Backup	• User procedures for backing up data and other resources	• Operations procedures for backing up data and other resources
Failure recovery	• Procedures to continue operations when the system fails • Procedures to convert back to the system after recovery	• Procedures to identify the source of failure and get it fixed • Procedures to recover and restart the system

Figure 10-7 Procedures to Be Designed

They licence and install off-the-shelf programs and write adaptations and custom programs, as necessary. They construct a database and fill it with data. They document, review, and test procedures, and they create training programs. Finally, the organization hires and trains needed personnel.

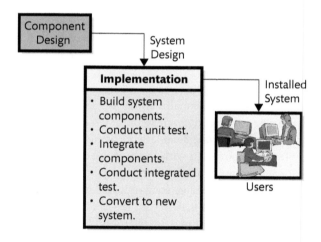

Figure 10-8 SDLC: Implementation Phase

System Testing   Once developers have constructed and tested all the components, they integrate the individual components and test the system. So far, we have glossed over testing, as if there was nothing to it. In fact, however, software and system testing are difficult, time-consuming, and complex tasks. Developers need to design and develop test plans and record the results of tests. They need to devise a system to assign fixes to people and to verify that fixes are correct and complete.

A **test plan** consists of sequences of actions that users take when using the new system. Test plans include not only the normal actions that users will take but also the incorrect actions. Today, many IT professionals work as testing specialists. Testing, or **product quality assurance (PQA)**, as it is often called, consists of constructing the test plan with the advice and assistance of users. PQA test engineers perform testing and supervise users' test activity.

Users can also be part of the test team. If you are invited to participate as a user tester, you should take the responsibility seriously. It will become much more difficult to fix problems after you have begun using the system in production.

Beta testing is the process of allowing future system users to try out the new system on their own. Software vendors, such as Microsoft, often release beta versions of their products for users to try and to test. These users then report problems back to the vendor. Beta testing is the last stage of testing. Usually, products in the beta test phase are complete and fully functioning; they typically have few serious errors.

System Conversion   Once the system has passed integrated testing, the organization will install it. The term **system conversion** is often used to refer to this activity because it implies the process of *converting* business activity from the old system to the new.

Organizations can implement a system conversion in one of four ways:

1. Pilot
2. Phased
3. Parallel
4. Plunge

IS professionals recommend any of the first three phases, depending on the circumstances. In all but the most extreme cases, companies generally avoid taking the plunge.

With **pilot installation**, the organization implements the entire system in a limited portion of the business. The advantage of pilot implementation is that if the system fails, the failure is contained within a limited boundary. This reduces the business's exposure and also protects the new system from developing a negative reputation throughout the organization.

As the name implies, with **phased installation**, the new system is installed in phases across the organization. Once a given piece works, the organization then installs and tests another piece of the system, until the entire system has been installed. Some systems are so tightly integrated that they cannot be installed in phased pieces. These must be installed using one of the other techniques.

With **parallel installation**, the new system runs in parallel with the old one until the new system is tested and fully operational. Parallel installation is expensive because the organization incurs the costs of running both systems. Users must work double time, if you will, to run both systems. Then, considerable work is needed to determine whether the results of the new system are consistent with those of the old system.

However, some organizations consider the cost of parallel installation a form of insurance. It is the slowest and most expensive style of installation, but it does provide an easy fallback position if the new system fails.

The final style of conversion is **plunge installation** (sometimes called *direct* or *cutover installation*). The organization shuts the old system down and starts the new system. If the new system fails, the organization is in trouble: Nothing can be done until either the new system is fixed or the old system is reinstalled. Because of this risk, organizations should avoid this conversion style, if possible. The one exception to this is when the new system is providing a service that is not vital to the day-to-day operation of the organization.

Figure 10-9 summarizes the tasks for each of the five components during the design and implementation phases. Use this figure to test your knowledge of the tasks in each phase.

Phase 5: Maintenance

The last phase of the SDLC is maintenance. The term *maintenance* is, however, somewhat of a misnomer: The work done during this phase is either to *fix* the system so that it works correctly or to *adapt* it to changes in requirements.

	Hardware	Software	Data	Procedures	People
Design	Determine hardware specifications.	Select off-the-shelf programs. Design alterations and custom programs, as necessary.	Design database and related structures.	Design user and operations procedures.	Develop user and operations job descriptions.
Implementation	Obtain, install, and test hardware.	License and install off-the-shelf programs. Write alterations and custom programs. Test programs.	Create database. Fill with data. Test data.	Document procedures. Create training programs. Review and test procedures.	Hire and train personnel.
	Integrated Test and Conversion				

Unit test each component

Figure 10-9 Design and Implementation for the Five Components

Figure 10-10 shows the tasks that must be completed during the **maintenance phase**. First, there needs to be a way to track both failures[6] and requests for enhancements to meet new requirements. For small systems, organizations can track failures and enhancements using word-processing documents. As systems become larger, however, and as the number of failure and enhancement requests increases, many organizations find it necessary to develop a failure tracking database. Such a database contains a description of each failure or enhancement.

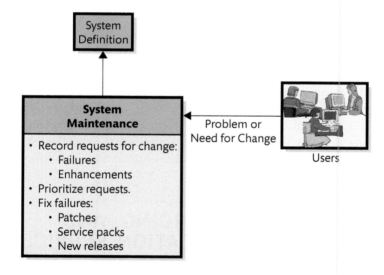

Figure 10-10 SDLC: System Maintenance Phase

Typically, IS personnel prioritize system problems according to their severity: They fix high-priority items as soon as possible, and they fix low-priority items as time and resources become available.

With regard to the software component, software developers group fixes for high-priority failures into a **patch** that can be applied to all copies of a given product.

---

[6] A *failure* is the difference between what the system actually does and what it is supposed to do. Sometimes, you will hear the term *bug* used instead of *failure*. As a future user, you should call failures *failures*, for that is what they are: Do not have a *bugs list*, have a *failures list*. Do not have an *unresolved bug*, have an *unresolved failure*. A few months of managing an organization that is coping with a serious failure will show you the importance of this difference in terms.

As described in Chapter 4, software vendors supply patches to fix security and other critical problems. They usually bundle fixes of low-priority problems into larger groups called **service packs**. Users apply service packs in much the same way that they apply patches, except that service packs typically involve fixes to hundreds or thousands of problems.

Keep in mind that although we usually think of failures and enhancements as applying to software, they can apply to the other components as well. There can be hardware or database failures or enhancements. There can also be failures and enhancements in procedures and people, though the latter is usually expressed in more humane terms, rather than as *failures* or *enhancements*. The underlying idea is the same, however.

Problems with the SDLC   Although the industry has experienced notable successes with the SDLC process, there have been many problems with it as well. One of the reasons for these problems is the **waterfall method** of the SDLC. Like a series of waterfalls, the process is often described as a sequence of non-repetitive phases. For example, the team completes the requirements phase and goes over the waterfall into the design phase, and on through the process (look again at Figure 10-3). Unfortunately, systems development seldom works so smoothly. Often, there is a need to crawl back up the waterfall, so to speak, and repeat the work done in a prior phase.

Agile methods have been suggested as a potential solution to some of these issues with waterfall methods. Agile methods use an iterative approach to design that includes user feedback. For example, teams using a SCRUM approach often work in two-week development "sprints" that are designed to deliver a working solution. After each sprint, the leaders analyze the requirements to see if changes can be made. Teams using agile methods expect that change will occur throughout the project and use methods that allow the team to adapt to these changes.

Another problem, especially with complicated systems, is the difficulty of documenting requirements in a usable way. One of the authors of this book once managed the database portion of a software project at Boeing, in which he and his team invested more than 70 labour-years into a requirements statement. The document comprised 20-some volumes that stood more than 2 metres tall when stacked. When the team entered the design phase, no one really knew all the requirements that concerned a particular feature. The team members would begin to design a feature only to find that they had not considered a requirement buried somewhere in the documentation. In short, the requirements were so unwieldy as to be nearly useless. Projects in which people spend so much time documenting requirements are sometimes said to be in **analysis paralysis**. These difficulties with the SDLC have led some companies to leave the job of designing, implementing, and maintaining systems to another organization. This option is explored in the next section.

Q10-7 WHAT IS OUTSOURCING, AND WHAT ARE APPLICATION SERVICE PROVIDERS?

Outsourcing is the process of hiring another organization to perform a service. Just about any business activity in the value chain can be outsourced, from marketing and sales to logistics, manufacturing, or customer service. The outsourced vendor can be domestic or international. When a vendor is overseas, outsourcing is referred to as *offshoring*. Offshoring has become an important consideration for IT services because of cost advantages. Offshoring experience has shown that establishing clear requirements is the key to providing success in an offshoring agreement.

Many companies have chosen to outsource portions of their information systems activities. Why? First, outsourcing can be an easy way to gain expertise. Suppose, for example, that an organization wants to upgrade its thousands of user computers on a cost-effective basis. To do so, the organization would need to develop expertise in automated software installation, unattended installations, remote support, and other measures that can be used to improve the efficiency of software management. Developing such expertise is expensive, and may not be part of the company's strategic direction. Consequently, the organization might choose to hire a specialist company to perform this service.

Other common reasons for choosing to outsource include cost reductions. Skilled programmers in other countries, such as China, India, and Russia, make as little as one-sixth the wage of an experienced programmer in North America. Even without this wage difference, organizations can obtain part-time services with outsourcing. An office of 25 lawyers does not need a full-time network administrator. It does need network administration, but only in small amounts. By outsourcing that function, the office can obtain network administration services only when it needs them.

Another reason for outsourcing might be to reduce development risk. Outsourcing can cap financial risk by setting specific prices on components of the system. In addition, outsourcing can reduce risk by ensuring a certain level of quality or avoiding the risk of having substandard quality. Organizations also choose to outsource IS activities to reduce implementation risk. Hiring an outside vendor can reduce the risk of picking the wrong hardware or the wrong software, using the wrong network protocol, or implementing incorrectly.

With so many advantages and with so many different outsourcing alternatives, you may wonder why any company has any in-house IS/IT functions. In fact, outsourcing presents significant risks, as listed in Figure 10-11.

Loss of control	Benefits outweighed by long-term costs	No easy exit
– Vendor in driver's seat. – Technology direction. – Potential loss of intellectual capital. – Product fixes, enhancements in wrong priority. – Vendor management, direction, or identity changes. – CIO superfluous?	– High unit cost, forever. – Paying for someone else's mismanagement. – In time, outsource vendor is de facto sole source. – May not get what you pay for but don't know it.	– Critical knowledge in minds of vendors, not employees. – Expensive and risky to change vendors.

Figure 10-11 Outsourcing Risks

The first risk of outsourcing is the ensuing loss of control over the service. Outsourcing puts the vendor in the driver's seat. Each outsource vendor has methods and procedures for its service, and an organization and its employees will have to conform to those procedures. For example, a hardware infrastructure vendor will have standard forms and procedures for requesting a computer, for recording and processing a computer problem, and for providing routine maintenance on computers. Once the vendor is in charge, the organization's employees must conform to the vendor's procedures.

In addition, the outsource vendor may change its pricing strategy over time. Initially, an organization obtains a competitive bid from several outsource vendors. However, as the winning vendor learns more about the business and as relationships develop between the organization's employees and those of the vendor, it becomes difficult for other firms to compete for subsequent contracts. The vendor becomes the de facto sole source and, with little competitive pressure, may increase its prices.

Another problem is that an organization can find itself paying for another organization's mismanagement, with little recourse. Over time, if the outsource vendor is mismanaged or suffers setbacks in other areas, costs may increase to compensate for these difficulties.

The final category of outsourcing risk concerns ending the agreement. There is no easy exit. For example, the outsource vendor's employees have gained significant knowledge of the company. Only they may know the server requirements in customer support, the patterns of usage, and the best procedures for downloading operational data into the data warehouse. Consequently, lack of knowledge within the company may make it difficult to bring the outsourced service back in-house.

Application Service Providers

Application service providers (ASPs) are a particular form of outsourcing. In an ASP agreement, an organization contracts with a vendor to "rent" applications from the vendor company on a fee-for-service basis. In traditional outsourcing, the vendor often maintains the systems at the organization's location. But that is not the case for an ASP. In an ASP,

---

MIS in Use   From Lemons to Lemonade

"Why would you want to leave our company? You have such a promising career here in research."

That was the last thing that Chantelle Jones[7] remembered her boss telling her as she resigned from her position at the local office of a national market research firm. For Chantelle, the question was certainly difficult and one that she had pondered for a long time.

At her first job since graduating with a business degree and a MIS concentration, Chantelle was the sole employee on the company help desk, and, by any definition, it was not what she had expected. Working from 6:00 A.M. to 2:00 P.M. (the early start allowed her to support offices in the Eastern Time zone) at a peanut-shaped desk, she was frequently alone, and her day was spent almost entirely on the telephone talking to people throughout the company. She felt underutilized and unmotivated. She remembered thinking, "Is this MIS? I thought I was going to be a liaison between business and technology, a part of great system builds, and at the very forefront of communication!"

Fortunately, despair did not set in. Realizing that all of the support calls had given her extensive knowledge of the entire organization and what each system could do, Chantelle began to track and analyze the calls. Quickly realizing that she was often being asked the same questions over and over, she knew that if she could automate that part of her job she would be well positioned to move somewhere else in the company. So, using the knowledge gained from the MIS classes at university, she wrote a

knowledge base that allowed people to solve many of their own problems. This improved productivity brought her to the attention of senior managers, who allowed her to focus on more interesting things. Her initiative and the knowledge of what the systems could do resulted in her becoming very valued within the company, and she was frequently asked to participate in new and more interesting assignments.

Now, one year later, Chantelle reflected on her boss's question and admitted that she was nervous. Her most recent project had brought her to the attention of a new company, and she had been offered a much more senior position with a 50 percent increase in salary. After she had accepted the new position, she said, "I felt uneasy about that at first, and then realized I'm not in just one position, I'm in MIS. I fit into EVERY business model. I have skills that I can mould and make relevant for all businesses, if I so choose—MIS has opened a lot of doors for me."

QUESTIONS

1. **What do you think is Chantelle's biggest asset for an employer?**

2. **How would you decide how and when to change jobs?**

3. **How have jobs and careers changed in the past 20 years?** (*Hint:* How many employers have your parents worked for? How many do you anticipate working for?)

4. **Do you think Chantelle's job allowed her to see more of the company compared with jobs in other functional areas?**

5. **Would Chantelle's situation have been any different if she worked for a much larger company?**

[7] The subject of this "MIS in Use" (a former student of one of the authors), asked that we not use her real name, but this case reflects her actual experience.

---

the vendor maintains the system at its own Web location, and the client organization accesses the application on the vendor's website. The application software, therefore, does not have to be located with the client. The vendor can then offer standardized software to many companies while maintaining only a single site (where the actual application resides). This reduces the costs of supporting the application and theoretically reduces the costs associated with outsourcing. The payments are made either monthly or yearly and are often based on the number of employees or on the number of users of the software.

The ASP model has some significant risks. The client company loses physical control over some corporate data that are stored in the vendor's machines. In addition, any failure of the Internet means that the client company cannot operate, even internally. Finally, there is the potential for lock in of the ASP, which may not allow corporate data to be easily ported to competing vendor's sites. Ownership of the data has to be very clearly stated in the ASP contract. The potential benefits of an ASP must be weighed against these significant risks.

ASPs are just one type of outsourcing alternative. There are many other alternatives, and each type carries with it benefits and risks. Business managers need to be aware of the alternatives and be able to balance the benefits and risks associated with them. What is clear is that what works for one company may not work for another. It is very important to consider the fit between the client and the vendor and to carefully develop the relationship between the two companies. Outsourcing deals are very similar to partnership agreements. Companies that are successful with outsourcing have recognized the importance of establishing the relationship first before engaging in significant outsourcing arrangements.

How Does the Knowledge in This Chapter Help You?

You now know the primary responsibilities of the IS department and can understand why that department may implement the standards and policies that it does. You know the planning functions of IS and how they relate to the rest of your organization. You also know the reasons for outsourcing IS services, the most common and popular outsource alternatives, and the outsourcing risks. Finally, you know your rights and responsibilities with regard to services provided by your IS department.

All of this knowledge will help you be a better consumer of the services of your IS department. If you work in a small company, with little or no IS support, you know the kinds of work that must be done and the advantages, disadvantages, and choices for outsourcing that work. If you find yourself in James's position, you know the advantages and disadvantages of outsourcing software development. Finally, knowledge of your rights and responsibilities will enable you to be a more effective business professional by setting reasonable expectations as to what you can expect from the IS department while at the same time knowing what the IS department expects of you.

 ACTIVE REVIEW

Use this Active Review to verify that you have understood the material in the chapter. You can read the entire chapter and then perform the tasks in this review, or you can read the material for just one question and perform the tasks for that question before moving on to the next one.

Q10-1 HOW CAN INFORMATION SYSTEMS BE ACQUIRED?

Explain the four ways that systems can be acquired. What is the most popular method for acquiring systems? Explain why buying software is different from acquiring information systems.

Q10-2 WHAT ARE IT PROJECTS, AND WHAT DOES PMBOK MEAN?

What is a project? What does PMBOK mean? What is an IT project? What is ITPM? What are the five process groups in project management? What is the most important skill in IT project management? Why?

Q10-3 WHAT SHOULD YOU KNOW ABOUT IT OPERATIONS AND IT PROJECTS?

What is the difference between IT operations and IT projects? What is ITIL? How is it related to the PMBOK? What are some of the ways the Web has altered IT operations?

Q10-4 WHY ARE IT PROJECTS SO RISKY?

Explain why IT projects tend to be risky. List some of the major risks associated with IT projects.

Q10-5 WHAT IS A SDLC?

What are the five phases of the SDLC? Explain each of these phases. Why are systems analysis and design unique to management information systems? Explain why requirements development is not just for technical experts. What activities can a nontechnical business manager be expected to do in an IT project? Explain why developing a clear list of requirements is important for IT project success.

Q10-6 HOW ARE INFORMATION SYSTEMS DESIGNED, IMPLEMENTED, AND MAINTAINED?

Summarize design activities for each of the five components of an information system. Name the two major tasks in systems implementation. Summarize the system testing process. Describe the difference between system testing and software testing. Name four ways to implement system conversion. Describe each way, and give an example of when each way would be effective.

Q10-7 WHAT IS OUTSOURCING, AND WHAT ARE APPLICATION SERVICE PROVIDERS?

Define *outsourcing*. Explain why some companies choose to outsource their projects. Explain what risks can be associated with outsourcing. Define what an application service provider is. Explain the benefits and risks of the ASP model.

MyLab MIS

MyLab MIS is an online learning and testing environment that features the perfect study tools to help you master the concepts covered in this chapter. Log in to MyLab to test your knowledge of key chapter concepts and explore additional practice tools, including videos, flashcards, and more!

KEY TERMS AND CONCEPTS

Agile methods 335
Analysis paralysis 342
Application service provider (ASP) 344
Beta testing 340
Business analysts 336
Commercial-off-the-shelf (COTS) 337
Cost feasibility 335
Information Technology Infrastructure Library (ITIL) 331
Information technology project management (ITPM) 330

IT operations 331
IT project risk 333
IT projects 330
IT services 331
Maintenance phase 341
Organizational feasibility 335
Outsourcing 342
Parallel installation 340
Patch 341
Phased installation 340
Pilot installation 340
Plunge installation 340
Product quality assurance (PQA) 339

Production systems 331
Project management body of knowledge (PMBOK) 330
Project management professionals (PMPs) 330
Requirements analysis phase 336
Schedule feasibility 335
Service packs 342
System conversion 340
System definition phase 335

Systems analysis 335
Systems analysts 336
Systems development 334
Systems development life cycle (SDLC) 334
Technical feasibility 335
Test plan 339
Waterfall method 342

USING YOUR KNOWLEDGE

10-1. Using the knowledge you have gained from this chapter, summarize the roles that you think users should take during an information systems development project. What responsibilities do users have? How closely should they work with the IS team? Who is responsible for stating requirements and constraints? Who is responsible for managing requirements?

10-2. When you ask users why they did not participate in requirements specification, some of the common responses include the following:

a. "I wasn't asked."

b. "I didn't have time."

c. "They were talking about a system that would be here in 18 months, and I'm just worried about getting the order out the door today."

d. "I didn't know what they wanted. I was not trained in requirements specification."

e. "I didn't know what they were talking about."

f. "I didn't work here when they started the project."

g. "The whole situation has changed since they were here; that was 18 months ago!"

Comment on each of these statements. What strategies do they suggest to you as a future user and as a future manager of users?

10-3. Consider outsourcing the following business functions:

- Employee cafeteria
- General ledger accounting
- Corporate IT infrastructure (networks, servers, and infrastructure applications such as email)

a. Compare the benefits of outsourcing for each business function.

b. Compare the risks of outsourcing for each business function.

c. Do you believe that the decision to outsource is easier for some of these functions than for others? Why, or why not?

10-4. Assume that you are a project manager charged with developing the implementation plan to switch an entire country from driving on the right side of the road to the left. Which conversion approach would you use and why?

COLLABORATIVE EXERCISES

10-1. Take a look at the Labour Market Outlook 2015–2019 available at www.digcompass. ca/labour-market-outlook-2015-2019. The report suggests that changes in the demands for skills have created new opportunities for students, companies, and educators in the ICT sector. Discuss the findings in this report, and answer the following questions:

a. What skills are employers looking for in 2019? How do these skills differ from the skills required in previous years?

b. What will the anticipated changes in the information and communication technology industry (ICT) as outlined in this report mean to the members of your group? How will traditional business jobs change? Create a list of at least five ways that you, as a business professional, can take advantage of the changes that are coming to the industry.

c. Where could a student best begin to develop the skills that are noted in the report? Develop a list of opportunities that people who are interested in developing these skills can be a part of.

10-2. Visit sites that offer certification for project managers and business analysts (for example, www.pmi.org, www.iiba.org, www.businessanalystworld.com, and www. pmac-ampc.ca). Use the information you find to answer the following questions:

a. Compare and contrast the roles of a project manager and a business analyst. Identify the most important skills for each of these roles. Are there skills that are common to both roles?

b. Identify five different types of certification that a person could collect in project management and/or business analysis. Provide at least three reasons why certification is important for those who are interested in project management or business analysis.

c. Provide three reasons why the roles of project manager and business analysis are getting so much attention in the workplace.

CASE STUDY 10
EMAIL OR FREEMAIL?

Everybody knows that email is important, but should each company develop, own, support, and maintain its own email infrastructure, or should it instead use lower-cost or free services? That is the question that Michael Jagger, CEO of Provident Security, faced as he contemplated a costly upgrade of the company's internal email infrastructure.

Founded in 1996 by Michael Jagger as a way to pay his undergraduate tuition, Provident (www.providentsecurity.ca) started out as a company that provided special event security. Today, it has grown to become a full-service security company with more than 4500 customers and 200 employees. Offering a wide range of services for residential, commercial, and industrial clients, Provident is organized into three divisions: guard services, alarm services, and special event/personal protection. Guard services offers uniformed security guards and specializes in high-tech and pharmaceutical markets; it also offers community and mobile patrol services that guarantee a five-minute response to burglar alarms and client emergencies. The alarm services division installs, services, and monitors alarm systems for residential and industrial clients, including sophisticated closed circuit television (CCTV) and access control systems for the high-risk buildings of clients such as the federal government. The special event/personal protection division provides security for many important public figures, including elected officials and business leaders.

The company's email system was based on Microsoft Exchange/Outlook and completely managed by the company's small but effective internal information systems staff. After an increase in volume, however, the system was beginning to show signs of strain. In addition, recent analysis indicated that to cope with projected growth, Provident would have to invest a further $60 000 in a combination of hardware and software upgrades and operating expenses.

To combat this expense, one employee suggested that Provident convert its internal email to Google's $50-per-user corporate Gmail service (www.google.com/apps/intl/en/business/messaging.html#mail). This service was very similar to Google's popular consumer email system and could be accessed from any Web browser, which meant that it required no hardware or software and was available anywhere. And not only was the service comparatively inexpensive, but it allowed Provident to maintain its existing email IDs and it integrated easily into other popular and useful Google applications, such as Google Docs and Google Calendar.

A few other organizations had already converted to Gmail, and as he considered whether to authorize the increased expenditure or not, Michael wondered whether it was time for Provident to get out of the email business.

Questions

1. What are the benefits and risks that Provident faces when considering maintaining its own email system or moving to another service, such as Gmail? (*Hint:* How much control do *you* have when you use free Web services, and how are those services funded?)

2. How is email different, if at all, from other technology or nontechnology services, such as telephone systems or regular mail? (*Hint:* How differentiated are these services, and are there various levels of service?)

3. How should a company decide which functions should be provided internally and which ones should be obtained externally? Is there a difference between the cafeteria or health services and an information system?

4. How does the industry in which a firm operates or the actions of its competitors affect your recommendation? (*Hint:* Would your recommendation differ if Provident was a health services organization?)

5. Are there any other options that Provident should consider? (*Hint:* Is there a midpoint between self-service options and using free services?)

Source: Data from Michael Jagger, Provident Security Corp.

WHAT DO YOU THINK?

THE REAL ESTIMATION PROCESS

Estimating the development costs of systems is a difficult task. With changes in technologies and organizations, it can be difficult to know how much a working system will cost or how long it will take to implement it. The statements below come from a software developer with a fair amount of system development experience. If you spend time working in the IT industry, you will hear people with opinions like this. Some of the things stated below are factual, some are convenient "memories" and others are just one person's opinion. It is important for you to develop your own opinion about this topic. The questions at the end of the statement below are designed to help you develop your own opinion about the real estimation process.

A Software Developer's Statement

I'm a software developer. I write programs in an object-oriented language called C++. I'm a skilled object-oriented designer, too. I should be—I've been at it for 12 years and have worked on major projects for several software companies. For the last four years I've been a team leader. I lived through the heyday of the dot-com era and now work in the IT department of a giant pharmaceutical company.

All this estimating theory is just that—theory. It's not really the way things work. Sure, I've been on projects in which we tried different estimation techniques. But here's what really happens: You develop an estimate using whatever technique you want. Your estimate goes in with the estimates of all the other team leaders. The project manager sums all those estimates together and produces an overall estimate for the project.

By the way, in my projects, time has been a much bigger factor than money. At one software company I worked for, you could be 300 percent over your dollar budget and get no more than a slap on the wrist. Be two weeks late, however, and you were finished.

Anyway, the project managers take the project schedule to senior management for approval, and what happens? Senior management thinks they are negotiating.

'Oh, no,' they say, 'that's way too long. You can surely take a month off that schedule. We'll approve the project, but we want it done by February 1 instead of March 1.

Now, what's their justification? They think that tight schedules make for efficient work. You know that everyone will work extra hard to meet the tighter time frame. They know Parkinson's Law—'The time required to perform a task expands to the time available to do it.'

So, fearing the possibility of wasting time because of too-lenient schedules, they lop a month off our estimate.

Estimates are what they are; you can't knock off a month or two without some problem, somewhere. What does happen is that projects get behind, and then management expects us to work longer and longer hours. Like they said in the early years at Microsoft, 'We have flexible working hours. You can work any 65 hours per week you want.'

Not that our estimation techniques are all that great, either. Most software developers are optimists. They schedule things as if everything will go as planned, but things seldom do. Also, schedulers usually don't allow for vacations, sick days, trips to the dentist, training on new technology, peer reviews, and all the other things we do in addition to writing software.

So, we start with optimistic schedules on our end, then management negotiates a month or two off, and, voilà, we have a late project. After a while, management has been burned by late projects so often that they mentally add a month or even more back to the official schedule. Then both sides work in a fantasy world, where no one believes the schedule, but everyone pretends they do.

I like my job. I like software development. Management here is no better or worse than in other places. As long as I have interesting work to do, I'll stay here. But I'm not working myself silly to meet these fantasy deadlines.

Discussion Questions

1. What do you think of this developer's attitude? Do you think he is unduly pessimistic, or do you think there is merit in what he says?

2. What do you think of his idea that management thinks they are negotiating? Should management negotiate schedules? Why, or why not?

3. Suppose a project actually requires 12 months to complete. Which do you think is likely to cost more: (a) having an official schedule of 11 months with at least a 1-month overrun, or (b) having an official schedule of 13 months and, following Parkinson's Law, having the project take 13 months?

4. Suppose you are a business manager and an information system is being developed for your use. You review the scheduling documents and see that little time has been allowed for vacations, sick leave, miscellaneous other work, and so forth. What do you do?

5. Describe the intangible costs of having an organizational belief that schedules are always unreasonable.

6. If this developer worked for you, how would you deal with his attitude about scheduling?

7. Do you think there is a difference between scheduling information systems development projects and scheduling other types of projects? What characteristics might make such projects unique? In what ways are they the same as other projects?

8. What do you think managers should do in light of your answer to Question 7?

KNOWLEDGE EXTENSION 16
Introduction to Microsoft Project

STUDY QUESTIONS

KE16-1   WHAT IS PROJECT MANAGEMENT SOFTWARE?

KE16-2   HOW DO I CREATE AND MANAGE TASKS?

KE16-3   HOW DO I MANAGE RESOURCES?

This Knowledge Extension teaches basic skills with Microsoft Project 2016, a product designed to help organize and manage projects. If you already know how to use MS Project, use this Knowledge Extension as a review. Otherwise, use it to gain essential knowledge that every business manager needs.

KE16-1 WHAT IS PROJECT MANAGEMENT SOFTWARE?

There are many types of project management software. Some software focuses on organizing tasks. Other software helps you manage resources or schedules. Still other software tracks employee work hours on different projects, or provides repositories for storing and providing access to project documentation. What is important to understand is that no one piece of project management software does it all. So, the choice as to which software to use in an organization is something that takes careful analysis.

Although no one product does it all, there are many products that provide strong support for the project management process. MS Project is an example of this type of full-service product. The program has the largest number of installed users in project management software and provides an excellent entry point into how project management software differs from other applications, such as spreadsheets and databases.

Though MS Project often looks like a spreadsheet, it is best described as a database product. Underlying MS Project is a sophisticated relational database that stores information about tasks, resources, schedules, baselines, and budgets. MS Project allows you to enter information into the database through specifically designed forms and then presents the project data through specially designed views that often focus on one or two aspects of the project. Since projects are often complex, it is difficult to present all of the information about them on one screen. So, MS Project provides a variety of screens to capture the full picture of the project. The interface for MS Project is illustrated in Figure KE16-1.

The default view for MS Project is the Gantt Chart view. In the Gantt Chart view, all of the tasks (or work packages) associated with the project are listed on the left side of the screen. On the right side, a bar indicates when the activity is estimated to begin and how long that activity is expected to last. A **Gantt chart** is a quick way to see which activities are happening and how much further the project has to go before completion. Note that the Gantt Chart view shown in Figure KE16-1 also lists the people who are working on

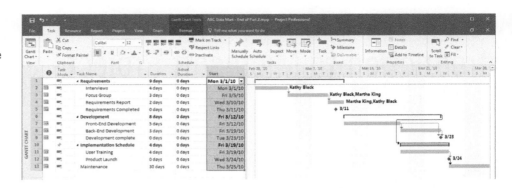

the project. The arrows that point towards bars indicate a dependency between two activities, which means that one activity must be completed before the other one can begin. These **dependencies** are important when scheduling a project.

The Gantt Chart is one view provided by MS Project. **Resource Sheet view** is another, as shown in Figure KE16-2. In this view, we see the people who are available to work as well as their available work hours. Resource Sheet view provides a place to enter project team member roles, chargeout rates, expected hours of work, and other items.

A related view is the Resource Usage view, as shown in Figure KE16-3. This view shows the date and number of hours that each employee is expected to work on a project. This view lets you quickly see whether an employee is over-allocated (has too many hours) and whether to expect overtime or to find someone who can fill in for the employee.

There are a number of other views in MS Project, including Tracking Gantt (where project progress is measured against a baseline), Network Diagram, Calendar, and Resource Graph views. We will not look at these views in detail in this introduction.

Now that you have been introduced to what MS Project can do, you can start adding tasks to a project.

KE16-2 HOW DO I CREATE AND MANAGE TASKS?

In this Knowledge Extension, we will use the example of a systems development project where requirements are created, some development is undertaken, and then the system is implemented. Regardless of what project you may be working on, all project management begins with an understanding of the tasks that need to be accomplished. Let us begin with a brand-new file. To do this, open MS Project, select New File, and create a blank project. Then, save this project as "Intro to MSProject." If you are successful, your screen should look like the screen in Figure KE16-4.

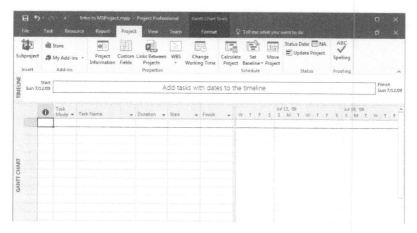

Figure KE16-4 Blank Project in MS Project

Source: Microsoft Project Software

You are now ready to add a task. Start at the top of the Task Name column and complete the following:

1. Click in the first row of Task Name column.
2. Type "Requirements."
3. Press Enter.

You will see the word "Requirements" at the top of the list, followed by some information about duration, and start and end dates. Do not worry about adding the duration right now. This is shown in Figure KE16-5. Note how a one-day-long task has been added on the Gantt Chart on the right of the screen.

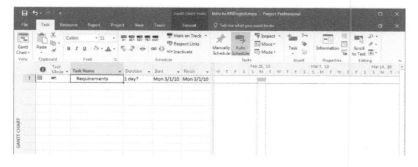

Figure KE16-5 Adding a Task to a New Project

Source: Microsoft Project Software

Let us add more tasks. Take a minute or two and add the tasks provided below in Table 1 (in the same order) and their durations into your project. Note that the tasks Requirements, Development, Implementation Schedule, and Product Launch are examples of high-level tasks. We will calculate the duration of these tasks based on the time needed for subtasks.

Table 1 Tasks and Durations

Task Name	Duration
Requirements	1 day
Interviews	3 days
Focus Group	4 days
Requirements Report	2 days
Development	1 day
Front-End Development	5 days
Back-End Development	3 days
Implementation Schedule	1 day
User Training	4 days
Product Launch	0 days

Creating Subtasks

We are now going to organize our tasks a little more, by creating tasks and **subtasks**. To create a subtask, select one or more tasks and then click the right tab button, as shown in Figure KE16-6. The three selected tasks then become subtasks. The opposite happens when you select a task and click on the left tab button. Note as well what happens to the Gantt Chart, where tasks and subtasks are created. The higher-level tasks are given a different icon, which envelops all the subtasks within it. You will also notice that the duration time for the tasks is now also equal to the largest subtask duration. This happens automatically when you create tasks and subtasks. Figure KE16-7 shows the arrangement of tasks and

Figure KE16-6 Preparing to Create Subtasks

Source: Microsoft Project Software

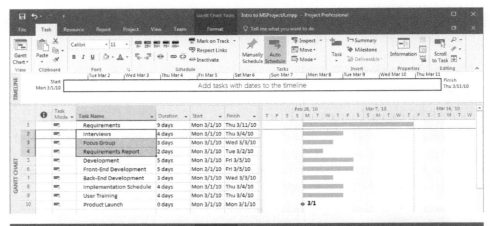

Figure KE16-7 Project Tasks and Subtasks Created

Source: Microsoft Project Software

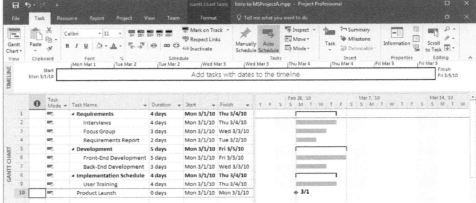

subtasks we will use in our project. Spend a little time creating the appropriate tasks and subtasks as shown in Figure KE16-7.

Creating Dependencies

We noted earlier that some tasks cannot be completed until other tasks are completed. When this is the case, we say that there is a dependency between the two tasks. One task therefore becomes the **predecessor** (must happen before) and the other task is the successor (occurs after the predecessor is completed). These dependencies are crucial for creating a meaningful schedule.

To assign predecessors, we use the task window in MS Project. In this example, we will make Task 2, Interviews, the predecessor of Task 3, Focus Group. To get to the task window, double-click on the Focus Group tasks (which has Task ID 3). The task window will pop up. Next, look at the top of the screen, and find the Predecessors tab. Click on the tab, and you will be taken to the Predecessors window. Now type "2" in the list of predecessors, as shown in Figure KE16-8, and hit Enter. This will set Task 2, Interviews, as a predecessor to Task 3. Look at how the Gantt Chart has changed to reflect the dependency.

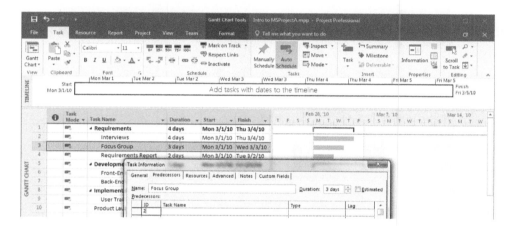

Figure KE16-8 Assigning a Predecessor to Task 3—Focus Group

Source: Microsoft Project Software

Now use Table 2 to set predecessors for your project tasks. If you set the predecessor correctly, your project Gantt Chart should now look like the chart in Figure KE16-9. There is more we can do with tasks, but what we have learned is enough for this introduction. Our next question will look at resources.

Table 2 Tasks and Predecessors

Task Name	Predecessors
1. Requirements	
2. Interviews	
3. Focus Group	2
4. Requirements Report	3
5. Development	
6. Front-End Development	4
7. Back-End Development	4
8. Implementation Schedule	
9. User Training	7
10. Product Launch	8

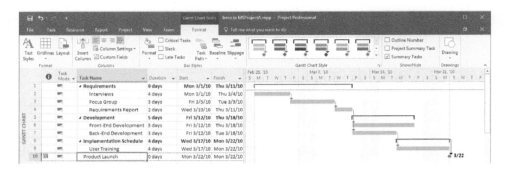

KE16-3 HOW DO I MANAGE RESOURCES?

Let us now turn our attention to resources. We will work with the Resource Sheet view in MS Project. The view can be selected by clicking on the View menu and highlighting the Resource Sheet view, as shown in Figure KE16-10. You can also select the Resource Sheet icon that is provided on the quick navigator, located on the far left side of the screen.

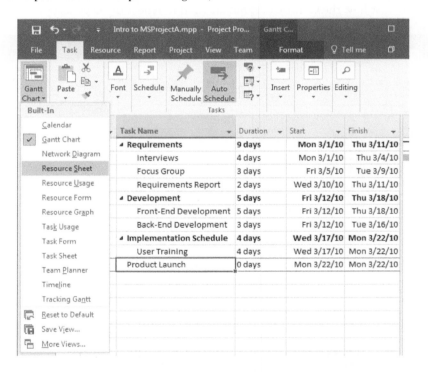

Once Resource Sheet is selected, a blank Resource Sheet pops up. The Resource Sheet is empty because no one has filled in the information about the people who may be working on your project. Table 3 provides you with some information about the people working on this project. Enter this information into the Resource Sheet. The data entry in the Resource Sheet is the same as that for the Gantt Chart. Click in the appropriate cell, and type the information in.

If you are successful, your Resource Sheet should look like the one in Figure KE16-11.

We are now ready to use the Resource Sheet and assign people to the tasks that need to be accomplished. To do this, let us return to the Gantt Chart view.

Adding Resources to Tasks

Next, we will assign people on our Resource Sheet to the tasks we defined earlier. Let us start in the Gantt Chart view. This view can be selected by clicking on the View menu

Resource Name	Initial	Group	Max Units	Std Rate	Ovr Rate
Martha King	M	BA	100%	$30.00/hr	$50.00/hr
Kathy Black	K	BA	100%	$40.00/hr	$60.00/hr
Tim Pape	T	PM	100%	$100 000.00/yr	$0.00/hr
Jack Booth	J	FD	100%	$50.00/hr	$75.00/hr
Edward Healy	E	FD	100%	$50.00/hr	$75.00/hr
Peter Draude	P	BD	100%	$50.00/hr	$75.00/hr
Harry Dion	H	BD	100%	$50.00/hr	$75.00/hr
Kim Trent	K	UT	100%	$90.00/hr	$115.00/hr

Table 3 Resource Information for a Sample Project

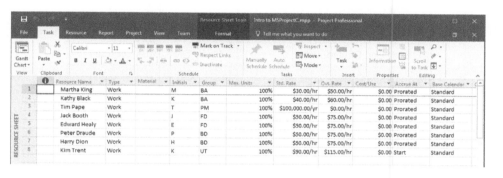

Figure KE16-11 Completed Resource Sheet

Source: Microsoft Project Software

and highlighting the Gantt Chart view, or by selecting the Gantt Chart view icon that is provided on the quick navigator on the far left-hand side of the screen.

Start by assigning resources to Task 2, Interviews. To add a resource, double-click on the Task 2, Interviews row. This will bring up the Task Window. Look to the top of that window, and you will find the Resources tab. Click on this tab, and you will get a form that allows you to add resources to this task. Click in the top box in the resource table, and you will see a drop-down box appear. This is a list of all of the resources that can work on this task. Select Kathy Black as a resource for this task, as shown in Figure KE16-12.

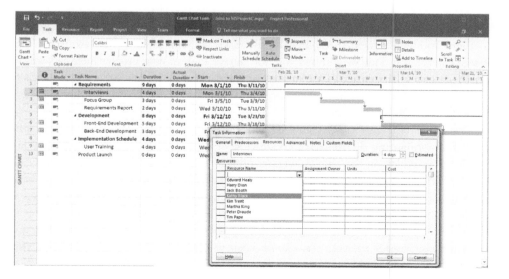

Figure KE16-12 Assigning a Resource to a Task

Source: Microsoft Project Software

To add more than one resource to a task, use another row in the resource form. Now that you are able to add resources, use Table 4 as a guide to adding the appropriate resources to each of the subtasks in your project. If you are successful, your Gantt Chart should resemble Figure KE16-13.

Table 4 Resource Allocations for Tasks

Task Name	Predecessors
1. Requirements	
2. Interviews	Kathy Black
3. Focus Group	Kathy Black, Martha King
4. Requirements Report	Kathy Black, Martha King
5. Development	
6. Front-End Development	Jack Booth, Edward Healy
7. Back-End Development	Harry Dion, Peter Draude
8. Implementation Schedule	
9. User Training	Kim Trent
10. Product Launch	

Figure KE16-13 Resources Allocated to Tasks

Source: Microsoft Project Software

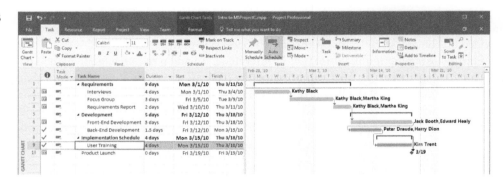

Once you have allocated resources to the tasks, you can look at the **Resource Usage view** of the project. This view shows you how active each of your project members will be over the course of the project. One important thing you are looking for as a manager is to make sure that people are not working overtime (unless it is necessary) and that no one is overburdened with work.

The Resource Usage view (Figure KE16-14) can be selected by clicking on the View menu and highlighting the Resource Usage view or by selecting the Resource Usage view icon that is provided on the quick navigator on the far left side of the screen.

This Knowledge Extension has introduced you to MS Project and some of its basic features. You have learned how to create and manage tasks, define predecessors, enter resources, and assign those resources to tasks. Although there are many other features in MS Project, the features we have described in this extension are critical to planning and executing a successful project. You should keep using MS Project and developing your project management skills.

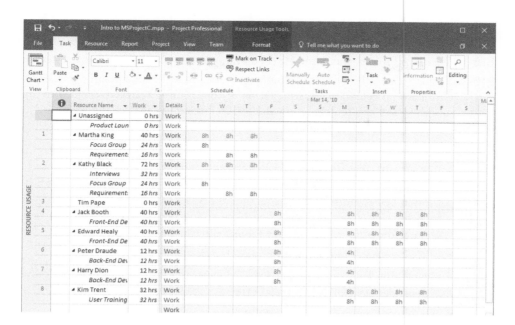

Figure KE16-14 The Resource Usage View of the Project

Source: Microsoft Project Software

Use this Active Review to verify that you have understood the material in the Knowledge Extension. You can read the entire extension and then perform the tasks in this review, or you can read the material for just one question and perform the tasks for that question before moving on to the next one.

KE16-1 WHAT IS PROJECT MANAGEMENT SOFTWARE?

Is MS Project more like a spreadsheet or a database? What is a Gantt chart? What are dependencies? What is the Resource Sheet view of a project? How does the Resource Sheet view differ from the Resource Usage view? Can you show a Network Diagram for a project?

KE16-2 HOW DO I CREATE AND MANAGE TASKS?

Can you open a new MS Project file? Can you add tasks to a new project? Can you create subtasks within a task list? Can you create a dependency between two tasks? Can you enter resources into the resource page?

KE16-3 HOW DO I MANAGE RESOURCES?

Can you select the Resource Sheet view? Can you add information about resources (std. rate, ovt. rate, etc.)? Can you add resources to tasks? How does adding resources change the Gantt Chart? Can you select the Resource Usage view?

MyLab MIS

MyLab MIS is an online learning and testing environment that features the perfect study tools to help you master the concepts covered in this chapter. Log in to MyLab to test your knowledge of key chapter concepts and explore additional practice tools, including videos, flashcards, and more!

KEY TERMS AND CONCEPTS

USING YOUR KNOWLEDGE

KE16-1. Open MS Project, and duplicate each of the actions in this Knowledge Extension.

KE16-2. This exercise is best done as a group exercise. Your group is planning an end-of-term party to celebrate the completion of your course. You have decided to organize the party as a project. You will use MS Project to organize the party.

    a. Name and save a new MS Project file.

    b. Brainstorm a set of tasks that you will need to accomplish to successfully hold your party (e.g., finding a venue, writing invitations, booking entertainment, deciding on food and beverages, organizing setup and take down, etc.). It is often best to think of the end of the process—holding a successful party—and then think about the tasks you have to accomplish to achieve this result. Enter these tasks into the MS Project file you created.

    c. Add estimates of the duration of each task.

    d. Find the dependencies that exist between the different tasks. Create these dependencies in the MS Project file.

    e. Add your group members as resources in the Resource Sheet view.

    f. Assign resources to each task. You can add more than one resource to each task.

    g. Print the Gantt Chart for the party project that you have designed.

KE16-3. This exercise is best done as a group exercise. Your group is planning a project that will send extremely rich tourists on trips to the International Space Station. You have decided to organize this project using MS Project.

    a. Name and save a new MS Project file.

    b. Brainstorm a set of tasks that you will need to accomplish to successfully offer your tour (for example, finding/negotiating space on the shuttle for the trip, marketing, insurance, transportation logistics, etc.). If you are having trouble, think of the end of the process—successfully returning the tourists to Earth—and then think about the tasks you have to accomplish to get them back. Enter these tasks into the MS Project file you created.

    c. Add estimates of the duration of each task.

    d. Find the dependencies that exist between the different tasks. Create these dependencies in the MS Project file. Identify any subtasks.

    e. Add your group members as resources in the Resource Sheet view.

    f. Assign resources to each task. You can add more than one resource to each task.

    g. Print the Gantt Chart for the International Space Station tour that you have designed.

CHAPTER 11
Structure, Governance, and Ethics

STUDY QUESTIONS

Q11-1 HOW IS THE IT DEPARTMENT ORGANIZED?

Q11-2 WHAT JOBS EXIST IN IT SERVICES?

Q11-3 WHAT IS IT ARCHITECTURE?

Q11-4 WHAT IS ALIGNMENT, WHY IS IT IMPORTANT, AND WHY IS IT DIFFICULT?

Q11-5 WHAT IS INFORMATION SYSTEMS GOVERNANCE?

Q11-6 WHAT IS AN INFORMATION SYSTEMS AUDIT, AND WHY SHOULD YOU CARE ABOUT IT?

Q11-7 WHAT IS INFORMATION SYSTEMS ETHICS?

Q11-8 WHAT IS GREEN IT, AND WHY SHOULD YOU CARE ABOUT IT?

MIS in Action

"OK, we have 15 minutes – let's get started." Zev Friedman, as was his custom, stood in the boardroom gazing out at the mountains.

"OK, so, Jared, I understand you want to spend some real money. This morning you're going to tell me why, right?"

"That's why we're here, Zev. I know that you normally like to hear the bad news first but in this case the good news creates the bad news so I will start with that. You know how you encouraged us to apply to BCIP, the Built in Canada Innovation Program that helps entrepreneurs break into government by providing funding? – Well we just got the notification that we were successful. OHIP, the Ontario Hospital Insurance Plan wants to consider a pilot with us but since it is the government there are a bunch of hoops for us to jump through and we need to think carefully. Here's a copy of the proposal but I'm going to let James take you through it."

"I can hardly wait." Zev's mood is upbeat, but his demeanor and sleepy-eyed posture don't fool anyone. They know he's poised to detect errors or poor preparation.

"OK, as you know the government, especially under Trudeau, is really innovation focused. They are tired of hearing how much easier it is to start up companies in the Silicon Valley and they want more Canadian success stories" James is a little nervous as he starts.

"Yes, I do. The opposition is really hammering them on the innovation agenda – saying that actions speak louder than words and that we need more home grown companies that could be the next Google or Facebook. I know that BCIP is supposed to

reduce the risk of implementation within the government by funding the innovation implementation costs. When you first raised this idea I remember thinking that it was a good initiative and I understand that was your idea." Zev wants to make James comfortable with that compliment, and it works.

"It was a team discussion. Anyway, we were able to do that, and thanks to everyone's hard work, we won the competitive process and we can proceed to the next stage." James looks around the table as he speaks.

"It's validating to even make it this far but getting OHIP as a client would not only be a good chunk of revenue it would also open other doors and give us a lot of legitimacy." Zev knows getting marquee clients is a major step in establishing a sustainable business.

"The issue is that the government and OHIP have huge amounts of bureaucracy. BCIP is designed to spur adoption and innovation by reducing the financial risks by underwriting the costs but given what has been happening with the Phoenix payroll systems and other big failures we have to prove that we have good processes and cover all the details. They want to see our process and procedure documentation, risk matrix, organization structure, everything. We are going to have to hire at least five new people and clearly define their roles and responsibilities and that is before we get to the technical and language issues."

"Language issues?"

"Yes. Even though our systems are intuitive we are mainly English only. That will not fly in Ottawa"

"That will be one of the easier pieces. On the documentation side we can hire a translator. I think the going rate is $0.12 a word so we can get an estimate fairly quickly. The good thing is that we architected the software with translation tables so the programming changes and development side should not be too difficult. The government and OHIP though are huge. I think we can open the doors to an entirely new market if we start in Hospital health. The problem though is organizational."

"Organizational?"

"Yes, the government has a big push on transparency and accountability. They also have some fairly strict security requirements. We could have a lot of different types of data and we need to demonstrate that we know what we are doing. For starters, while we have already thought about PIPEDA this takes it to a whole other level. We have to have security checks on all of our people, explain who has access to what data, we even need to have a security officer to sign off on these types of things. We need to show them our organizational chart and they expect us to have people doing things that we just don't have in place yet."

"I am all for process but some of this sounds like bureaucracy to me. The market and legitimacy are good but does that mean that we will not make money on this project?"

"The government wants us to make money but we have to detail every little thing. There are really three phases or issues. 1) Getting the bureaucratic, as you call them, issues out of the way. These are process and procedural things – making sure that we have our 'ducks in a row'. 2) Detailing the fit between the opportunity and our systems – the project plan. And 3) Executing the agreement with 'no surprises'. If an item is not in the project plan we cannot bill for it"

"So what do we do next?"

"I have a list of what they need. I put forward an initial proposal when I submitted the application but that was somewhat high level. We now need to break it down, price it out, and then you have to decide if we should go ahead. This will likely mean hiring people that most startups do not hire until they are a fair bit older. There is an easy out if you don't think it is worth it and I am pretty excited by the opportunity – but a small business working with government has been compared to a mouse going on a date with an elephant." From his voice and expression it's clear James is concerned.

"Hmph."

"But—and I'll spare you the details—if we can make this work we can use this to move into an entirely new market with a client that can open a lot of doors and get paid for work that we might have to do anyway. OHIP is a big name."

"I guess most big companies started out small and the process issues might be good. Spare me some of the details. I'll let Jared be my guide there. Do you have a cost and revenue estimate on this and a list of the big rocks?"

"As shown on the third page, for the first pilot we have a funding envelope of between $675 and $900 000."

"Big range." Zev sounds dubious.

"And, as shown on the fourth page, there are a potential series of phases. The first one is somewhere between $225K and $300K." James sits back to watch Zev's reaction.

"Jared, what do you think?" Zev looks at Jared.

"It's a question of how much we want to spend to position ourselves for the future, Zev." Jared knows its Zev's money and his decision.

"That it is, that it is," Zev ponders.

"Nicki, what's your thinking?" Zev moves in his seat to get a better look at her face.

"Healthcare is a big market. No doubt about it. And we'd be the first of our type to really get into that market space."

"Can you sell this, Michele?"

"Without a doubt. It would be huge. It has to be incredibly exciting, though. This would be something that would get us in the news."

Zev sits silently for a minute or two. Then he looks back at the group, each person at a time, as he speaks.

"I want to do this. We're not really ready for it. But if we wait till we are the opportunity will have passed and someone else will have done it. We can focus on what they are asking for and work backwards to our organization. We might have been small and casual before but there is a reason why processes, job descriptions, roles and responsibilities, and all of the other stuff exists. We just have to make sure that it adds value rather than just slowing us down and bulking us up. We need to figure out how to get there in the fastest way possible. Then I want to try it out … not with all the overhead and bells and whistles, but with enough that we can see how structure makes us better. Jared, bring me back a plan to do that. James, I want you there too. Questions?"

Silence prevails until Jared speaks, "Thanks, Zev, we'll do just that."

Q11-1 HOW IS THE IT DEPARTMENT ORGANIZED?

Most organizations rely on information technology (IT) services. All of the email systems, accounting applications, desktop computers, and mobile devices used in an organization require some form of technical support. The department of people who provide this support is often referred to as *IT Services* or *Information Systems Services*. This group needs to be organized and managed like any other business department. Figure 11-1 shows typical top-level reporting relationships in an organization that has IT services. As you will learn in your future management classes, organizational structure varies, depending on the organization's size, culture, competitive environment, industry, and other factors. Larger organizations with independent departments will have a group of senior executives, such as those shown here, for each department. Smaller companies may combine some of these departments under a single executive.

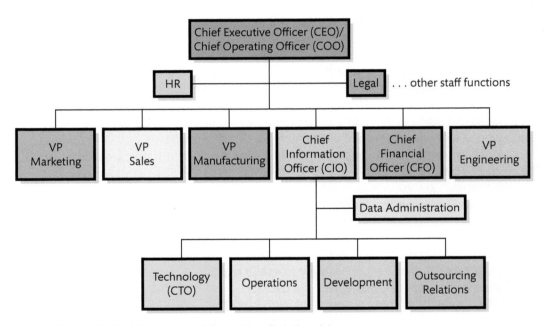

Figure 11-1   Typical Senior-Level Reporting Relationships

The title of the principal manager of the IT department varies from organization to organization. A common title is **chief information officer (CIO)**. Other common titles are vice-president of information services, director of information services, and, less commonly, director of computer services.

In Figure 11-1, the CIO, like other senior executives, reports to the chief executive officer (CEO), though sometimes these executives report to the chief operating officer (COO), who, in turn, reports to the CEO. In some companies, the CIO reports to the chief financial officer (CFO). That reporting arrangement may make sense if the primary information systems support accounting and finance activities. In some organizations, such as manufacturers, which operate significant non-accounting information systems, the arrangement shown in Figure 11-1 is more common and effective. It shows a typical IT department with four subgroups and a data administration staff function.

Most IT departments include a *technology office* that investigates new information systems technologies and determines how the organization can benefit from them. For example, many organizations are using Web services technology and planning how they can best use that technology to accomplish their goals and objectives. A **chief technology officer (CTO)** often heads the technology group. The CTO sorts through new ideas and products to identify those that are most relevant to the organization. The CTO's job requires deep knowledge of information technology and the ability to envision how new IT will affect the organization over time.

The next group in Figure 11-1, *operations*, manages the computing infrastructure, including individual computers, computer centres, networks, and communications media. This group includes system and network administrators. An important function of this group is to monitor user experience and respond to user concerns or problems.

The third group in the IT department in Figure 11-1 is *development*. This group manages projects that acquire new information systems and maintains existing information systems. The size and structure of the development group depends on whether programs are developed in-house. If they are not, this department will be staffed primarily by **business analysts** and/or **systems analysts** who work with users, operations, and vendors to acquire and install licensed software and to set up the system components around that software. Business analysts are normally involved in developing the business case for a newly proposed system (which includes assessing the impact of financial and technical risks) as well as the requirements for that system. Systems analysts are normally involved in designing and implementing the new system. If the organization develops programs in-house, then this department will also include programmers, project managers, test engineers, technical writers, and other development personnel.

The last IT department group shown in Figure 11-1 is *outsourcing relations*. This group exists in organizations that have negotiated outsourcing agreements with other companies to provide equipment, applications, or other services (this continues to be a growing area since information systems can be quite complex, are often expensive, may require specialized skills, and could have large elements of risk). These relationships require constant attention, so this department monitors service levels and focuses on developing good relations with outsourcing vendors. Figure 11-1 also includes a *data administration* staff function. The purpose of this group is to protect data and information assets by establishing data standards and data management practices and policies.

There are many variations on the structure of the IT department shown in Figure 11-1. In larger organizations, the operations group may itself consist of several different departments. In smaller organizations, one person might serve as an entire department. Sometimes, there is a separate group for data warehousing and data marts.

What About the Web?

The Web has had a significant impact on the organization of IT departments. In its early years, the responsibility for supporting the Web, as well as for the content and design of a company's website, was exclusively within the IT services department. But as companies recognized the impact that the Web could have on its brand and its customers, control of the content and the look and feel of the website were moved to marketing departments, while IT maintained the technical responsibilities.

Of course, creating a well-designed company website requires knowledge of branding and marketing. It also requires knowledge of such things as TCP/IP (Transmission Control Protocol/Internet Protocol) networks, HTML (Hypertext Markup Language), XML (eXtensible Markup Language), content management systems, and Web design applications, such as Adobe Flash. Recognition of the importance of website design created a whole new set of related jobs. These jobs combine traditional business skills (like branding and marketing) with technical skills.

Many companies have faced difficulties attracting and retaining employees who have the combination of Web design skills and business skills necessary to create excellent websites. (Perhaps this is a competitive advantage you could use when you graduate. It is certainly a good reason to include some IS courses, or even an IS major, in your marketing degree.)

As a result, a whole new industry, the Web design consulting industry, was born. There are many small and large Web design firms. Two large Canadian firms are: Blast Radius (www.blastradius.com) which was created in 1997 and has grown to more than 300 employees while serving international clients, such as Nike, BMW, Converse, Nintendo, and Virgin and Traction on Demand (www.tractionondemand.com), which was founded in 2006 and with more than 3000 CRM projects and is Saleforce.com's largest dedicated implementation partner.

One important point you should learn in this chapter is that it can take a considerable amount of people to make a great website because a number of skills are involved. For example, a Web design project of any size will require the following people:

- *Project manager:* Responsible for interacting with the client and moving the project successfully towards completion.
- *Lead designer/analyst:* Responsible for understanding client needs and developing the overall look and feel of the site and all the design elements (colours, navigation, graphics, buttons, animation, etc.).
- *Developer:* Responsible for taking the design and creating the functioning site; usually specializes in static content (i.e., information that is not automatically updated).
- *Technical architect:* Responsible for making decisions about technical issues related to the site, including server/browser support, database integration, administrator access, and any scripting issues.

There is a misperception among many business people that putting together a website is relatively easy. Actually, it is harder than most people think. While it might be easy to get a site on the Web, ensuring that the site is properly designed, easy to maintain, and provides an enjoyable customer experience is work for professionals. This has made the job of the IT department not only more important but also more challenging. Web design has changed the skill set of many IT workers and created both challenges and opportunities for employees who can combine the right types of business design and technical skills.

Q11-2 WHAT JOBS EXIST IN IT SERVICES?

We noted in Chapter 1 that the Information and Communications Technology sector has a wide range of interesting and well-paying jobs. Many students enter an introductory MIS class thinking that the industry consists only of programmers and computer technicians who have great technical skills. If you reflect on the five components (hardware, software, data, procedures, and people) of an information system, you can understand why this cannot be true. The *data, procedures,* and *people* components of an information system require professionals with highly developed interpersonal communication skills. The reality is that most jobs that are in the highest demand in the ICT sector require a mix of interpersonal and technical skills. The most effective MIS personnel are often people who are thoughtful communicators, have basic technology skills, and are comfortable leading significant projects that change business practices. The entire sector is looking for people who can bridge the knowledge gap between computer technicians and business system users. Your training in business is an excellent foundation for doing this type of work.

Figure 11-2 lists the major job positions in the IS industry. With the exception of computer technicians and possibly professional quality assurance (PQA) test engineers, almost all of these positions require a four-year degree. Furthermore, with the exception of programmers and PQA test engineers, all of these positions require business knowledge. In most cases, successful professionals have a degree in business. Note, too, that most positions

Title	Responsibilities	Knowledge, Skills, and Characteristics Requirements	2006 Cdn. Salary Range ($CDN)
Computer technician	Install software, repair computer equipment and networks	Associate degree, diagnostic skills	$30 000–$60 000
Quality Assurance (QA) test engineer	Develop test plans, design and write automated test scripts, perform testing	Logical thinking, basic programming, superb organizational skills, detail oriented	$40 000–$75 000
User support representative	Help users solve problems, provide training	Communications and people skills, product knowledge, patience	$35 000–$60 000
Technical writer	Write program documentation, help-text, procedures, job descriptions, training materials	Quick learner, clear writing skills, high verbal and communications skills	$35 000–$60 000
Programmer/ Developer	Design and write computer programs	Logical thinking and development, skills, programming	$45 000–$110 000
Website Designer	Work with clients to develop designs for websites, work with developers to finalize designs	Excellent interpersonal skills, design skills, detail oriented, good technical skills, flexible business/marketing skills	$45 000–$110 000
Network administrator	Monitor, maintain, fix, and tune computer networks	Diagnostic skills, in-depth knowledge of communications, technologies, and products	$65 000–$120 000+
Database administrator	Manage and protect database (see Chapter 12)	Diplomatic skills, database technology knowledge	$65 000–$120 000
Systems analyst, Business analyst	Work with users to determine system requirements, design procedure	Strong interpersonal and communications skills, business and technology knowledge	$50 000–$110 000
Consultant	Wide range of activities: programming, testing, database design, communications and networks, project management, strategic planning	Quick learner, entrepreneurial attitude, communications and people skills, respond well to pressure, particular knowledge depends on work	From $35 per hour for a contract tester to more than $400 per hour for strategic consulting to executive group
Salesperson	Sell software, network, communications, and consulting services	Quick learner, knowledge of product, superb professional sales skills	$65 000–$200 000+
Project manager (PM)	Initiate, plan, manage, monitor, and close down projects	Management and people skills, technology knowledge, highly organized	$75 000–$150 000
Enterprise Architect (EA)	Manage and document the technological infrastructure of the firm	Diplomatic skills, database technology knowledge, strategic planning	$100 000–$200 000
Chief technology officer (CTO)	Advise CIO, executive group, and project managers on emerging technologies	Quick learner, good communications skills, deep knowledge of IT	$100 000–$250 000+
Chief information officer (CIO)	Manage IT department, communicate with executive staff on IT- and IS-related matters, member of the executive group	Superb management skills, deep knowledge of business, and good business judgment; good communicator, balanced and unflappable	$150 000–$300 000, plus executive benefits and privileges

Figure 11-2 Job Positions in the Information Systems Industry

require excellent verbal and written communication skills. Business, including information systems, is a social activity.

Many of the positions in Figure 11-2 have a wide salary range. Lower salaries are paid to professionals with limited experience or to those who work in smaller companies or on small projects. Larger salaries are paid to those with deep knowledge and experience who work for large companies on large projects. Do not expect to begin your career at the high end of these ranges.

The authors of this book, who have more than 80 years of combined experience, have worked as systems analysts, programmers, small- and large-scale project managers, consultants, business unit managers, and chief technology officers (CTO). They have enjoyed their experience in the field, as the industry becomes more and more interesting each year. Give these IT careers some thought while you are in school. Keep in mind that the changing nature of technology—and of business generally—will demand that you incorporate technology into the way you work.

For most technical positions, knowledge of a business specialty can really add to marketability. Note that the high-paying jobs towards the bottom of the list all require communication, leadership, and business skills. If you have the time, a dual major can be an excellent choice that can open up opportunities for you. Popular and successful dual majors include accounting and information systems, marketing and information systems, and management strategy and information systems.

So What? Jumping Aboard the Bulldozer

A recent popular theme in the media is how overseas outsourcing is destroying the North American labour market: "Jobless recovery" is how it is headlined. However, a closer look reveals that overseas outsourcing is not the culprit. The culprit—if *culprit* is the right word—is productivity. Because of information technology (IT), Moore's Law, and all of the information systems that you have learned about in this book, worker productivity continues to increase, and it is possible to have an economic recovery without a binge of new hiring.

Austrian economist Joseph Schumpeter called processes such as outsourcing and technological innovation "creative destruction" and said that these processes are the cleansers of the free market.[1] Economic processes operate to remove unneeded jobs, companies, and even industries, thereby keeping the economy growing and prospering. In fact, the lack of such processes hindered the growth of Japan and some European nations in the 1990s.

So, what should you do? How do you respond to the dynamics of shifting work and job movements? As you

have learned, management information systems (MIS) are about the development and use of information systems that enable organizations to achieve their goals and objectives. When you work with information systems, you are more than a professional in any one particular system of technology; rather, you are a developer or user of systems that help your organization achieve its goals and objectives.

From this perspective, lessons from this course can help you pursue a wide range of opportunities in your career. If information systems based productivity is the bulldozer that is mowing down traditional jobs, then use what you have learned here to jump aboard that bulldozer—not as a technologist, but as a business professional who can determine how best to use that bulldozer to enhance your career. Your long-term success depends not on your knowledge of specific technologies but, rather, on your ability to think, communicate, solve problems, and use technology and information systems to help your organization achieve its goals and objectives.

Q11-3 WHAT IS IT ARCHITECTURE?

We learned in Chapter 3 that an organization's goals and objectives help determine its competitive strategy. We used Porter's five forces model to consider the structure of the industry under which a company operates. Given that structure, we could develop a

[1] J. Schumpeter, *Capitalism, Socialism, and Democracy* (New York: Harper, 1975), pp. 82–85.

competitive strategy for the organization. This strategy is supported by activities in the value chain, which consist of a collection of business processes supported by information systems. This idea is illustrated in Figure 11-3.

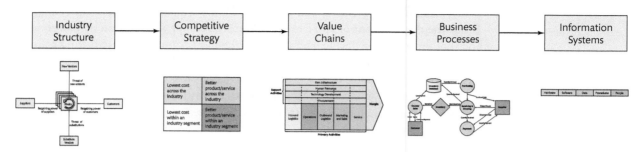

Figure 11-3 Organizational Strategy and Information Systems

In Chapter 2, we learned that information systems exist to help organizations achieve their goals and objectives. Thus, in an ideal world, the information systems that a company chooses to use should support the company's competitive strategy.

We will learn in this section that effectively managing information systems so that they support business objectives is a difficult process. The challenge in developing these plans is that it requires an understanding of both organizational strategy and the technological architecture underlying information systems. And because it is so challenging, organizations sometimes get it wrong, resulting in a misalignment between information systems and business strategy.

Take a moment and think about what it means to understand the technology that supports an organization. How many computers are there in the company? Are they all the same brand? When were they bought? What operating system are they using? What applications are being run? What software, official and unofficial, is installed on the computing devices? Who purchased the software? What company is supporting the software if there are bugs or other problems? What networks are the computers connected to? Does the company limit Internet addresses to and from computers within the company? If so, who is monitoring this? Which email package is the company using? What is the company's policy regarding spam? What are its privacy and security policies? When is the company upgrading machines, software licences, network protocols, etc.? Does the company support wireless access? If so, what levels of access and where? The questions can go on and on.

An **IT architecture** is like a city plan that lays out the street network, water system, sewer system, emergency services, and power grids. An IT architecture is the basic framework for all the computers, systems, and information management that support organizational services. Like a city plan, an IT architecture is complex, and that complexity is increasing as more services are supported and different technologies are used.

In response to this complexity, some organizations have created a new job description—the **enterprise architect**—to describe the person who does this work. One organization that supports enterprise architects is Enterprise-Wide IT Architecture (EWITA; www.ewita.com); there are others as well. The enterprise architect's job is to create a blueprint of an organization's information systems and the management of these systems. The blueprint should provide an overview that helps people in the organization better understand current investments in technology and plan for changes. In developing the architecture, the enterprise architect usually considers organizational objectives, business processes, databases, information flows, operating systems, applications and software, and supporting technology.

So, what does an IT architecture look like?[2] The first thing to note is that there are few standards because companies and systems are so diverse that it is hard to develop an IT architecture. An IT architecture is usually a long document with many sections that include quite complicated diagrams (see footnote 2) as well as management policies (such as privacy, sourcing, and security) and discussion of future changes to the architecture.

Since the development of an IT architecture is so complex, it is often helpful to use a method that organizes the development. One of the most popular of these is the **Zachman framework**, conceived by John Zachman at IBM in the 1980s. The framework divides systems into two dimensions: One is based on six reasons for communication (*what*—data, *how*—function, *where*—network, *who*—people, *when*—time, *why*—motivation), and the other is based on stakeholder groups (planner, owner, designer, builder, implementer, and worker). The intersection of these two dimensions helps provide a relatively holistic view of the enterprise. An example from Zachman International (zachmaninternational.com) is provided in Figure 11-4.

Layer	What? Data	How? Function	Where? Network	Who? People	When? Time	Why? Motivation
Planner	List of important things for business	List of business processes	List of where enterprise operates	List of business functional units	List of business events and cycle	List of business goals and strategies
Owner	Entity relationship model	Moving down provides higher levels of detail	Moving across shows different perspectives on systems			
Builder	Normalized data model					
Implementer	Relational data model					
Worker	Input screens					

Figure 11-4   A Framework of Enterprise Architecture

While it may sound boring to some people, the development of an enterprise architecture can be critically important when organizations are considering significant changes, such as mergers, acquisitions, divestiture, or rapid growth. Like a city, information systems are continually in use and often involved in change. Having a single planning office where all of the different systems are viewed from the big perspective can often have advantages.

Defining the architecture is the first step in understanding how information systems support business objectives. You should carefully consider getting involved in discussions about enterprise architecture at your company. These discussions are a great opportunity to better understand how the company currently works and how it will have to change to work more effectively. This knowledge is often very valuable regardless of where you work, so try not to run too fast when you hear the architects coming your way.

[2] A number of graphic models of enterprise architectures can be viewed on the Web. Examples include an enterprise modelling process (www.enterpriseunifiedprocess.com/essays/enterpriseArchitecture.html), an enterprise model for a laboratory (commons.lbl.gov/display/cio/Architecture); and an architecture developed using the Zachman framework (zachmaninternational.com).

Q11-4 WHAT IS ALIGNMENT, WHY IS IT IMPORTANT, AND WHY IS IT DIFFICULT?

The process of matching organizational objectives with IT architecture is often referred to as **alignment**, but the term has been somewhat difficult to define. MIS researchers have suggested that alignment should be viewed as an ongoing process—that fitting IT architecture to business objectives is continually evolving. The alignment process takes advantage of IT capabilities as they develop, at the same time maintaining a balance between business objectives and IT architecture. What works for one organization as a balance may not work for another, since alignment depends on business goals, the organizational context, and the state of IT architecture in an organization.

Matching investments in IT with organizational strategy is not as straightforward as it may seem. Take the example of Wal-Mart, the largest retailer in the world. Customers know that when they shop at Wal-Mart they are getting the goods they buy at low prices. Wal-Mart has been very successful in maintaining a competitive strategy based on being a low-price retailer, which means maintaining costs that are lower than the industry average. So, if Wal-Mart is focused on maintaining low costs, one might think that aligning IT objectives with this strategy would see Wal-Mart spending less on IT than the industry average.

In fact, just the opposite is true. Wal-Mart spends more than the industry average on IT. Why? Because, over several decades, the company has developed a sophisticated network of IT applications that allows it to collect and share vast amounts of enterprise information throughout the organization. Access to these data allows Wal-Mart employees and suppliers to make more effective decisions and to operate more efficiently. Wal-Mart is very much a high-technology company that has found success as a low-cost retailer.

It is clear that supporting business objectives with appropriate IT investments remains a critical part of IT management. In their study of IS alignment, Chan, Sabherwal, and Thatcher[3] considered both the factors affecting alignment and the impact of alignment on perceived business performance. Results showed improvements in perceived performance when technology was aligned with some strategic objectives.

If alignment is recognized as important, then what makes it so difficult to achieve? Canadian researchers Reich and Benbasat[4] first measured alignment as the degree to which the IT department's missions, objectives, and plans overlapped with the overall business missions, objectives, and plans. In a later paper, the authors[5] recognized the importance of the social dimension of alignment. Effective alignment occurred in organizations that had developed a climate supporting the sharing of domain knowledge and common business practices. The importance of the social dimension was further confirmed by Chan.[6]

Communication between business and IT executives is the most important indicator of alignment. Successful companies find ways to help share knowledge and frustrations between the IT department and the business functions. This shared knowledge can become a source of competitive advantage for firms because the firms are better able to align their IT investments with the overall business objectives.

Alignment remains a difficult issue for many firms, but it can help provide competitive advantage for those who are willing to make the investment in developing communication and sharing knowledge.

[3] Y. Chan, R. Sabherwal, and J.B. Thatcher, "Antecedents and Outcomes of Strategic IS Alignment: An Empirical Investigation," *IEEE Transactions on Engineering Management* 53, no. 1 (February 2006): 27–47.

[4] B. H. Reich and I. Benbasat, "Measuring the Linkage between Business and Information Technology Objectives," *MIS Quarterly* 20, no. 1 (March 1996): 55–81.

[5] B. H. Reich and I. Benbasat, "Factors That Influence the Social Dimension of Alignment between Business and Information Technology Objectives," *MIS Quarterly* 24, no. 1 (March 2000): 81–111.

[6] Chan, Y.E., "Why haven't we mastered alignment? The importance of the informal organization structure," *MIS Quarterly Executive* 1, no. 2 (June 2002): 97–112.

Q11-5 WHAT IS INFORMATION SYSTEMS GOVERNANCE?

Governance has become a popular word in the field of information systems. The term suggests that some committee or group has the ability to govern or decide on expectations for performance, to authorize appropriate resources, and perhaps eventually to verify whether expectations have been met. In publicly traded organizations, one purpose of governance is to ensure that an organization is working on behalf of its shareholders to produce positive results and avoid negative ones.

For business organizations, **governance** is the development of consistent, cohesive management policies and verifiable internal processes for information technology and related services. Managing at a corporate level often involves establishing the way in which governing boards oversee a corporation and developing the rules that apply to such issues as sourcing, privacy, security, and internal investments. The goal of information systems governance is to improve the benefits of an organization's IT investment over time. Figure 11-5 shows how stakeholder value can be increased, for example, by better aligning with business objectives, improving service quality, and controlling IT risks. Reporting structures and review processes can be established and can work over a period to improve quality, reduce service costs and delivery time, reduce IT risks, and better support business processes. It is the responsibility of those charged with information systems governance to make sure that these benefits are realized over time.

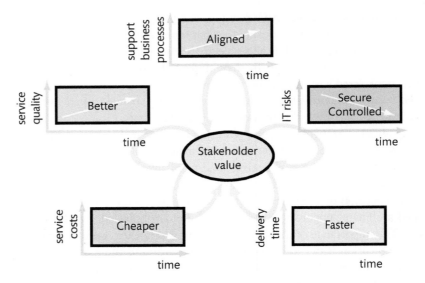

Figure 11-5 Creating Benefits from IT Governance

Information systems governance is a piece of organizational governance that is associated with IT architecture. The increasing interest in information systems governance is the result of laws, such as the **Sarbanes-Oxley Act (SOX)** in the United States and the **Budget Measures Act (Bill 198)** in Ontario. These laws force companies to comply with governance standards for collecting, reporting, and disclosing information.

The Sarbanes-Oxley Act (SOX) and the Budget Measures Act (Bill 198)

In recent years, the Sarbanes-Oxley Act (SOX) in the United States and the Budget Measures Act (Bill 198) in Ontario have affected many information systems, particularly accounting information systems. The SOX of 2002 governs the reporting requirements of publicly held companies. SOX was enacted to prevent corporate frauds, such as those perpetrated by WorldCom, Enron, and others. In 2003 Ontario introduced similar legislation in the form of Bill 198. Its regulations increase the level of responsibility and accountability of executive management of publicly held Canadian companies traded on the Toronto Stock Exchange in a fashion similar to that described in SOX.

Both pieces of legislation require management to create internal controls sufficient to produce reliable financial statements and to protect the organization's assets. As well, management is required to issue a statement indicating it has done so. The organization's external auditor must also issue an opinion on the quality of the internal controls and the credibility of management's statement. Bill 198 and SOX expose both management and the external auditor to financial and potential criminal liability if subsequent events show that internal controls were defective.

One example of an internal control is the separation of duties and authorities. In an accounts payable system, for example, three separate individuals are required: one to authorize the expense, one to issue the cheque, and a third to account for the transaction. No one person should perform two or more of these actions. You will learn about other such controls in your accounting courses.

If management is relying on computer-based accounting information systems for the preparation of financial statements—and all large organizations do—then those computer-based systems must have appropriate controls, and management must assert that those controls are reliable. This places a greater burden on the development and use of information systems than was prevalent prior to Bill 198 and SOX.

Additionally, information systems can produce valuable assets that are subject to liability. For example, the database of an order-processing information system that stores customer identities and credit card data represents an organizational asset. If the design of the information systems is ineffective in preventing unauthorized persons from accessing data, then a contingent (possible) liability exists. Without effective controls, someone could steal a customer's name and credit card data and cause harm to the customer. The customer could then sue the organization. Even if no one has yet sued, if the results could be considered significant, management is required to report the liability in its financial statements and to take action to remedy the situation by eliminating the contingent liability.

Summary

A consistent message surrounding information systems governance is that the IT department can no longer appear as a black box or an unknown process to the organization or to external stakeholders. In years past, corporate boards have tended to leave key IT decisions to IT professionals. This often occurred because board members lacked expertise in the IT area. Information systems governance in the future will require that all stakeholders, including corporate board members, have input into important information systems decisions. This may be a silver lining for some IT departments, since they may no longer be blamed exclusively for poor decisions, and users will have fewer grounds to complain that systems did not perform as predicted.

Q11-6 WHAT IS AN INFORMATION SYSTEMS AUDIT, AND WHY SHOULD YOU CARE ABOUT IT?

A financial audit can be defined as an examination and verification of a company's financial and accounting records and supporting documents by an accredited professional. In Canada, that is a Chartered Professional Accountant (CPA). A financial audit is closely related to the processes involved in financial governance of an organization.

The concept of an **information systems audit** is analogous to a financial audit. However, instead of financial and accounting records, the focus is placed on information resources that are used to collect, store, process, and retrieve information. Standards for information systems audits were first developed in the early 1970s and have been evolving with changes in technology. The recent increase in attention on information systems governance has meant a greater focus on the information systems audit and the establishment of methods for examining and verifying organizations' information systems policies and procedures.

Many firms offer information systems audit services. The **Information Systems Audit and Control Association (ISACA)** is an organization that was formed in 1969 by a group of individuals who were in charge of auditing controls for newly developed computer systems (www.isaca.org). The group has grown to more than 140 000 members in more than 180 countries (in 2017) and has become a leader in developing knowledge and standards relating to IT audit and IT governance. The **Certified Information Systems Auditor (CISA)** certification is recognized globally and has been earned by more than 100 000 professionals. Members have job titles such as information systems auditor, consultant, information systems security professional, regulator, chief information officer, and internal auditor.[7]

In Canada, the Canadian Institute of Chartered Accountants (CICA) has an agreement with ISACA that recognizes the Certified Information Systems Auditor (CISA) designation developed by ISACA as the only designation that leads to recognition as a CA-designated specialist in information systems audit, control, and security. One of the developments provided by ISACA along with the IT Governance Institute (ITGI) is the **Control Objectives for Information and Related Technology (COBIT)**. COBIT is a framework of best practices designed for IT management.[8] This framework provides board members, managers, auditors, and IT users with a set of generally accepted measures, indicators, processes, and best practices to assist them in getting the best from their organizational IT investments.

The latest edition, COBIT 5, was released in June 2012 and provides a set of tools and guidelines for establishing IT management practices. The COBIT control framework establishes links between strategic objectives and business requirements, organizes IT activities into a generally accepted process model, identifies the major IT resources in the organization, and defines the management control objectives to be considered. In establishing these foundations, COBIT can help link business goals to IT goals, providing metrics and maturity models to measure their achievement and identifying the associated responsibilities of business and IT process owners.

The simple translation is that COBIT provides a process through which alignment between IT and business objectives is developed. As noted earlier, processes such as COBIT are not likely to guarantee alignment on their own; researchers have found that the ability to communicate and share knowledge across organizational boundaries remains an important determinant for successful alignment. IT auditing frameworks such as COBIT enable the organization to move in the right direction.

Why Should You Care About Information Systems Governance and Information Systems Audits?

Our discussion of information systems governance and information systems audits has demonstrated the growing importance of information systems issues and operations across all business functions. The increased need to report and disclose information systems

---

[7] If you are interested, ISACA offers an inexpensive ($25 annual fee) student membership. You can find more details at the ISACA site (www.isaca.org) under the Membership > Student Membership.

[8] For those interested in understanding more about COBIT, an executive summary can be found at the ISACA site (www.isaca.org).

operational information will require employees at all levels of an organization to become more familiar with the issues facing IT management. Although this familiarity comes at a cost, the increased exposure to IT issues should improve the ability of organizations to use IT more effectively and efficiently. An argument can be made that the result of increased reporting compliance should be improved alignment between organizational strategy and business objectives. Since compliance issues will remain for the foreseeable future, business students across all functions will gain from increased knowledge of IT issues.

This chapter's Case Study, "Governance at Pacific Blue Cross" on pages 381–382, provides a glimpse of the importance of information systems governance. If you are not yet convinced that you, as a general business major, need the knowledge that this MIS course will give, the advent of legislation such as Bill 198 and SOX should convince you. As a senior manager, you will be required to make assertions about the controls on your information systems that will expose you to both financial and criminal penalties. When that day arrives, it will be well worth knowing the fundamentals of information systems. For a more critical review of SOX, see this chapter's "MIS in Use" on page 376.

Q11-7 WHAT IS INFORMATION SYSTEMS ETHICS?

In Part 3 of this book, we discussed how organizations gain a competitive advantage by achieving objectives with the effective use of IT. We understand that cross-functional systems help realize advantages by more efficiently or effectively handling business processes. We learned in Chapter 8 that the information we collect in business intelligence systems can be used to improve decision making and, ultimately, performance. In Chapter 9, we have shown that utilizing social media and Web 2.0 can create new opportunities for developing competitive advantage.

It may seem as though there are few limits to the use of IT and information systems in developing competitive advantage—but there are. For example, some use of IT may be against the law, and illegal behaviour has legal consequences. Another important limit for business students to recognize is that of ethical behaviour. Actions may not be illegal, but they could be unethical. It is important to understand the difference. The questions provided at the end of What Do You Think? in Chapters 1, 8, 9, and this chapter help make this difference clear.

In previous chapters, some of our exercises have focused on specific ethical issues. These exercises help you establish the ethical boundaries that are comfortable for you. In this section, we address the issue of **information systems ethics** more generally.

It is important to note that information systems ethics is not about hardware or software but, rather, about the people involved in the system. Computers do not threaten our privacy; it is the people who will use our private information who create threats. Computers are great at manipulating logic, but a machine does not understand what it is doing. Machines are not people, so they have no sense of decency or established character, which is an important part of being human.

Advances in IT bring new opportunities as well as new risks to individuals and organizations. As humans, we can choose to take advantage of technological innovation; however, we should be sensitive to the risk of abusing these advances. Our concern should be placed on the people whose lives can be affected by our actions and not on the computers that complete the actions.

Information systems ethics is not about detailing appropriate rules for our behaviour. The legal system develops rules of law and their enforcement. If we could put ethics into rule-based behaviour, then computers could control ethics. Instead, information systems ethics is about understanding our own behaviour—the way we think and act in situations in which our choices affect others. We face choices in situations, and these choices should be guided by principles. There are many examples of ethical principles: the United Nations Declaration of Human Rights, the Canadian Charter of Rights and Freedoms, and the Association for Computing Machinery's code of ethics (www.acm.org/about/code-of-ethics) are three good examples.

MIS in Use | Sarbanes-Oxley: Boon or Bane?

In 2002, in response to the corporate crimes committed by Enron, WorldCom, and others, the U.S. Congress passed the Sarbanes-Oxley Act (SOX). The goal of this act was to strengthen and upgrade financial reporting and, thus, maintain and improve trust in public companies' financial reports. Such trust is crucial; without it, the investment community and the entire U.S. economy would come to a standstill.

CIO Magazine publishes articles of interest and importance to chief information officers (CIOs). If you search for topics on SOX at www.cio.com, you will find a series of revealing articles. The initial articles reported confusion and concern among CIOs. Subsequent articles explain how to comply.

Most recently, *CIO Magazine*'s editor, Gary Beach, published an editorial entitled "Repeal Sarbanes-Oxley." What happened? Surely no one is opposed to accurate financial reporting. Mr. Beach stated, "While foreign companies are free to grab market share, U.S. executives are instead grabbing their Sarbanes-Oxley manuals" to learn how to comply with the Act.

According to a poll conducted by *CIO Magazine*, large companies expect to divert more than 15 percent of their information systems budgets to compliance with SOX. That represents a huge investment, but, given the importance of a favourable audit report, it is an expense that organizations view as mandatory, whether or not it is sensible.

Part of the problem is that no one knows exactly what is necessary to comply with SOX. The Act requires external auditors to become even more independent than they have been in the past, and, thus, many will not issue opinions on the specific controls that information systems need. The attitude seems to be, "Show us what you have, and we'll tell you if it's enough." IT managers are understandably frustrated. Further, the wording of the Act is so vague that auditors have taken the broadest possible interpretation to protect themselves. Consider, for example, Section 409, which requires disclosure of significant financial events within 48 hours. But what characterizes an event as significant? If a customer cancels a large order, is that significant? If so, how large must an order be before it is considered large? If a supplier is devastated by a hurricane, is that significant? Many CIOs ask, "How can we determine from our information systems that a significant event has occurred within 48 hours? Are we supposed to reprogram our applications to include alerts on all such events? What other events should we look for? And who's paying for all this?"

One thing is certain—SOX will provide abundant employment for internal auditors in general and for IT auditors in particular. Organizations will have to sponsor a flurry of activity, however uneconomical, to show that they are doing something to comply. No company can afford to ignore the Act.

Senators Sarbanes and Oxley are both attorneys, neither of whom has ever worked in a publicly traded company. In light of the financial disasters at Enron and WorldCom, their law was highly praised by the public. But is it worth the cost?

QUESTIONS

1. In your opinion, are the millions, perhaps billions, of dollars spent on compliance with SOX and Bill 198 an unnecessary waste?

2. In the long run, will these Acts hamper North American corporations in their competition with international corporations that are not burdened by them? Will they ultimately work to reduce investor choices?

3. Given the requirements of SOX, do you believe that a privately owned company still has an incentive to choose to become a public company?

It is not our intention in this chapter to establish any set of principles for ethical behaviour relating to information systems. Rather, our intention is to raise your awareness of the need to understand your own principles related to your use of information systems. When your actions can cause harm to others, you need to be aware of that potential harm and to understand the principles you are working under in making your choice.

Whistleblowers have shown us that it is no longer acceptable to do what your boss says or do what the system tells you when it comes to ethical situations. It is up to you to establish the boundaries within which you are comfortable working. Understanding your own personal principles is an important part of establishing your ethical behaviour.

A good way to understand your ethical principles is to envision yourself in ethical situations and to think about what you would do. The exercise at the end of this chapter on page 380 provides an opportunity to try this. We invite you to test your principles using this exercise or similar exercises at the end of Chapters 3, 8, 9, and 10.

Q11-8 WHAT IS GREEN IT, AND WHY SHOULD YOU CARE ABOUT IT?

So far, we have talked about aligning organizational objectives with IT architecture. We have explored the concepts of information systems governance and information systems audits and considered what is meant by information systems ethics. The concepts of IT architecture, information systems governance, information systems audits, and information systems ethics all surround the idea of choices. In making choices about the systems we build and use, we are often guided by ethics, audit and control principles, or alignment principles. Green IT provides a good example of the importance of understanding the choices an organization makes and the impact of those choices.

Green IT, or green computing, means using IT resources to better support the **triple bottom line** for organizations. The triple bottom line includes measures of traditional profit along with ecological and social performance. There are many elements of Green IT, but its primary goals are to improve energy efficiency, promote recyclability, and reduce the use of materials that are hazardous to the environment. Green IT, therefore, represents a choice to consider not only the financial implications of adopting and using IT but also the effects of those choices on people and the environment.

In many cases, Green IT is simply a common-sense approach to computing. An example of this approach is the **ENERGY STAR** program, which is an international government–industry partnership that is intended to produce equipment that meets high-energy efficiency specifications or promotes the use of such equipment. For example, simple ideas, such as using the sleep mode on your computer, can provide energy savings with little impact on performance. Laptops also use less power (maximum of 15 watts) compared with desktop computers (80 to 160 watts). As well, laptops often automatically power down after several minutes of inactivity. The U.S. Environmental Protection Agency (EPA) notes that if all computers sold in the United States met ENERGY STAR requirements, the savings in energy costs would be more than $2 billion every year. This is the equivalent of removing nearly 3 million vehicles and their greenhouse gas emitting engines from the road every year.[9]

Many agencies promote and support Green IT. For example, the Green Computing Impact Organization—now the Object Management Group (OMG)—is a nonprofit organization that suggests ways in which end-users can be more environmentally responsible (www.omg.org). You will find some helpful ideas here to make your own computing more green.

One of the most important issues in Green IT is **e-cycling**, or the recycling of electronic computing devices. The **e-waste** industry has only recently developed and is expanding quickly. An example of a company in this industry is Electronics Product Recycling Association (EPRA). Insightful information is provided on their website (www.recyclemyelectronics.ca). Companies in this industry benefit from stricter government controls on e-waste by helping other companies comply with e-waste guidelines.

The fact that the e-waste industry faces significant regulatory restrictions suggests that e-cycling will be an important consideration for any significant user of IT. It will affect information systems governance and information systems audit procedures. You may or may

[9] See www.energystar.gov/index.cfm?fuseaction=find_a_product.showProductGroup&pgw_code=CO.

not agree with the focus of Green IT, but it is clear that any business professional will need to understand how he or she can support its development. We started this section with the idea that we need to understand the choices that we make and the impact of these choices. Understanding more about green IT gives us more information about the choices we are making in responsibly using IT.

How Does the Knowledge in This Chapter Help You?

If you are like most undergraduate students when you first started this course your view of MIS was one that was predominantly technological. Perhaps framed by issues dealing with your personal computer, using Excel, or setting up your new phone, you saw the Information Technology (IT) aspects of MIS but were less aware of the Information Systems (IS) aspects. In fact MIS is like many other departments in that it has multiple responsibilities and it is important to make sure that the right roles are staffed with the right people. Planning and design of a MIS system is done through a process of architecture and while it is usually not perfect (just like the architecture in any major city), the extent to which this is consistent with the business requirements is called *alignment*. If an organization is to achieve or maximize the benefits of its MIS, then it is essential that there be a high level of architectural alignment. Other essential concepts in this chapter include governance, the processes by which decisions regarding MIS are made, the need to audit MIS processes to ensure that they conform and comply with regulations and objectives, and the importance of ethics and the environment.

There are no simple answers. This is a challenge and at the same time it is an opportunity for you to excel. You can differentiate yourself from the others in your chosen field and make a significant difference in this new interconnected global network economy.

ACTIVE REVIEW

Use this Active Review to verify that you have understood the material in the chapter. You can read the entire chapter and then perform the tasks in this review, or you can read the material for just one question and perform the tasks for that question before moving on to the next one.

Q11-1 HOW IS THE IT DEPARTMENT ORGANIZED?

Draw an organization chart for a typical IT department. Explain the functions of the CIO and the CTO. Describe typical reporting relationships of the IT department and the CIO. What positions require mostly technical skills? What positions require mostly business skills?

Q11-2 WHAT JOBS EXIST IN IT SERVICES?

Identify the different types of IS and IT positions available in mid-sized organizations and contrast the education and skill requirements. Which appeal most to you? How can you prepare yourself for these positions? Explain why a joint major of IS and another functional discipline may make sense.

Q11-3 WHAT IS IT ARCHITECTURE?

Why do organizations need an IT architecture? What is an enterprise architect? What does an IT architectural document look like? How can a method such as the Zachman framework support the development of an IT architecture?

Q11-4 WHAT IS ALIGNMENT, WHY IS IT IMPORTANT, AND WHY IS IT DIFFICULT?

Why do organizations have a difficult time aligning IT planning and organizational objectives? In what ways can you measure alignment? What factors make for improved alignment? When should organizations care about alignment, and what can they do to improve it?

Q11-5 WHAT IS INFORMATION SYSTEMS GOVERNANCE?

What is governance? Why do organizations need governance? How does information systems governance differ from financial governance? Why has information systems governance increased in prominence only recently?

Q11-6 WHAT IS AN INFORMATION SYSTEMS AUDIT, AND WHY SHOULD YOU CARE ABOUT IT?

Why do companies need auditors? What do information systems auditors do? What organization supports information systems auditors? What is the designation for an information systems auditor in Canada? What is the relationship between information systems audits and information systems governance? Do you believe that information systems governance is an issue that will affect many business people? Justify your answer.

Q11-7 WHAT IS INFORMATION SYSTEMS ETHICS?

Do you believe ethics is an important consideration in information systems? Can computers act unethically? Explain your answer. What is the difference between illegal behaviour and unethical behaviour? Why is it important to understand your own ethical behaviour?

Q11-8 WHAT IS GREEN IT, AND WHY SHOULD YOU CARE ABOUT IT?

What is Green IT? What is meant by the triple bottom line? Provide two examples of agencies that are focused on supporting efforts in Green IT. What is e-cycling, and why should you, as a business professional, care about e-waste?

MyLab MIS

MyLab MIS is an online learning and testing environment that features the perfect study tools to help you master the concepts covered in this chapter. Log in to MyLab to test your knowledge of key chapter concepts and explore additional practice tools, including videos, flashcards, and more!

KEY TERMS AND CONCEPTS

Alignment 371
Budget Measures Act (Bill 198) 372
Business analysts 365
Certified Information Systems Auditor (CISA) 374
Chief information officer (CIO) 364

Chief technology officer (CTO) 365
Competitive strategy 369
Control Objectives for Information and Related Technology (COBIT) 374
E-cycling 377
ENERGY STAR 377

Enterprise architect 369
E-waste 377
Governance 372
Green IT 377
Information systems audit 374
Information Systems Audit and Control Association (ISACA) 374

Information systems ethics 375
IT architecture 369
Sarbanes-Oxley Act (SOX) 372
Systems analysts 365
Triple bottom line 377
Zachman framework 370

USING YOUR KNOWLEDGE

11-1. Figure 11-3 illustrates the links between industry structure, competitive strategy, value chains, business processes, and information systems. As we have learned in this chapter, there can be misalignment between strategy and information systems. In your opinion, where do things go wrong, and how does misalignment occur? How do organizations get out of alignment?

11-2. Research the IT architecture at your university or college. Is an IT architecture available, and do you have enterprise architects? What IT architectural issues can you see developing, and how would you manage them?

11-3. Consider two car repair shops. One is newly renovated and has a bright, clean reception/office area at the front of the shop and standard company overalls for all employees. It has just invested in a new computer application that integrates its parts ordering, repair, and service cost estimates and accounting. Next door, the other repair shop has a small, dimly lit office at the rear of the shop, crammed with notes and papers. The office looks as though it was last painted in the early 1960s. It has no computer and still runs on a paper-based system. When you ask the owners of the two repair shops, they both state that their company's strategic objectives are well aligned with their IT planning and that each maintains a competitive advantage. How can this be true?

11-4. The goal of information systems governance is to improve the benefits of an organization's IT investment over time. However, people who are accountable for governance usually do not manage directly but sit on a corporate board that oversees the company's operations. What mechanisms can the board use to improve the benefits a company realizes from its IT investment? Use the Web or other resources to provide some specific examples of board techniques to improve IT performance.

11-5. Explain how information systems governance and information systems audits are related. Can a firm complete an information systems audit without having information systems governance in place? Can information systems governance exist without an information systems audit?

11-6. The Zachman framework is explained in detail at www.zachmaninternational.com. Use this information and the Zachman framework to develop a diagram of your personal IT architecture. Remember to include all the technical support you would use (including resources and school as well as mobile devices).

11-7. COBIT is just one method for developing a document to support information systems governance. Identify reasons why companies would choose not to use COBIT for an information systems audit. Search the Web for at least one other method, and develop a comparison between this method and COBIT. What are the benefits of using the new method? Can you suggest ways to improve COBIT?

COLLABORATIVE EXERCISES

11-1. This chapter introduced the concept of Green IT. Do some research into methods that will help make your personal computing more green. To complete the assignment, your team should do the following:

    a. Identify at least three things that you can do to reduce the energy consumption of your everyday computing resources.

    b. Estimate the savings that your group could achieve from the above recommendations.

    c. Combine what you have learned in parts (a) and (b) and create a one-page description of your proposal to reduce energy consumption. Your description should be aimed at people who are not familiar with green computing. Be prepared to share your document.

11-2. Read the "What Do You Think?" titled "The Ethics of Misdirected Information" on pages 382–383.

    a. Discuss your answers to the questions, and talk about any differences you may have. Try to form a consensus, and come up with a set of group answers to the questions. Did your group find this to be a difficult task? Why, or why not?

    b. What did you learn about ethics from this exercise? Be prepared to share your thoughts.

CASE STUDY 11
GOVERNANCE AT PACIFIC BLUE CROSS

The data on information systems projects almost speaks for itself. Although better than its 1994 survey results, the 2015 Standish Group (www.standishgroup.com) survey on IT projects found that only 29 percent of these projects could be considered successes (on time, on budget, and delivering the desired benefits), 52 percent were challenged (delivered late, exceeded their budget, or lacked critical features and requirements), and a full 19 percent were out-and-out failures.

For Dr. Catherine Boivie, a large part of the solution begins with governance. Before joining Pacific Blue Cross (PBC)—British Columbia's leading provider of extended health and dental benefits—as chief information officer and senior vice-president, her impression of IT projects was that although all of them were important to some aspect of the business, most IT departments were kept busy constantly putting out fires.

Governance, says Dr. Boivie, simply deals with who makes which decisions and does not have to be complex; it consists of four iterative steps:

1. Identify the areas that require formal decision making processes.

2. Document how decisions are currently made, the people involved, and their respective roles (i.e., do they recommend, approve, or concur with decisions, or do they provide input or need to be notified?).

3. Use this information as input into a discussion of how decision processes could be improved.

4. Develop a plan for implementing the new processes—including communication and buy-in with all affected parties.

Dr. Boivie's first action at PBC was to build on these ideas and to make certain her two foundational principles were shared by the chief executive officer. Principle 1: Technology has no value by itself. Principle 2: The technology management department must switch its focus from operations to business enablement. Once this was established and after working through the governance stages, PBC implemented a process to ensure that all projects under consideration were evaluated using the same mechanism and criteria. Using the Balanced Scorecard approach,[10] the strategic alignment, architecture, business process impact, direct payback, and risk of each project were measured against qualitative and quantitative perspectives and infrastructure, clients, people, and community-related goals.

The project approval process consists of five decision stages or gates. The first gate, sometimes called the *"Thumbs Up/Down"* stage, requires sponsorship by a vice-president who presents the idea to the executive committee. If approved, the project proceeds to gate two, which requires a business case outlining the costs and benefits. Gates three and four are similar, but have minimum price floors of $500 000 and $1 000 000 or include projects that are considered much more organizationally or technologically complex. Projects at these gates require comprehensive definition and analysis. Gate five is the post implementation review, which verifies and validates the costs and attainment of the benefits previously described in the business case.

Ongoing project reports are provided to the executive committee and board of directors using an aptly named "Traffic-Light Report." This report visually identifies, with red, yellow, or green symbols, whether a project is on time, on budget, and on scope.

Dr. Boivie anticipates further enhancements, but so far, the process seems to be working. Business leaders have welcomed the new process and noted that it gives them enhanced visibility, a much better view of all projects, and greater control and accountability.

[10] R. S. Kaplan and D. P. Norton, *The Balanced Scorecard: Translating Strategy into Action* (Boston, MA: Harvard Business School Press, 1996).

Questions

1. What are the various roles of decision making participants at PBC?

2. How important is communication to implementing the new system? How important is buy-in?

3. Can you think of reasons why an organization would resist governance processes?

4. What challenges may exist in the system?

5. Are the foundational principles valid or reasonable? Why did Dr. Boivie decide these principles needed to be shared by the CEO?

WHAT DO YOU THINK?

THE ETHICS OF MISDIRECTED INFORMATION

Consider the following situations:

Situation A: Suppose you are buying a condominium and you know that at least one other party is bidding against you. While agonizing over your best strategy, you stop at a local Starbucks. As you sip your latte, you overhear a conversation at the table next to yours. Three people are talking so loudly that it is difficult to ignore them, and you soon realize that they are the real estate agent and the couple who is competing for the condo you want to buy. They are preparing their offer. Should you listen to their conversation? If you do, do you use the information you hear to your advantage?

Situation B: Consider the same situation from a different perspective—instead of overhearing the conversation, suppose you receive that same information in an email. Perhaps an administrative assistant at the agent's office confuses you and the other customer and mistakenly sends you the terms of the other party's offer. Do you read the email? If so, do you use the information you now have to your advantage?

Situation C: Suppose you sell computer software. In the midst of a sensitive price negotiation, your customer accidentally sends you an internal email that contains the maximum amount the customer can pay for your software. Do you read that email? Do you use the information it contains to guide your negotiating strategy? What do you do if your customer discovers that the email may have reached you and asks, "Did you read my email?" How do you answer?

Situation D: Suppose a friend mistakenly sends you an email that contains sensitive personal medical data. You read the email before you realize what you were reading, and you are embarrassed to learn something very personal about your friend that truly is none of your business.

Your friend asks, "Did you read that email?" How do you respond?

Situation E: Suppose you work as a network administrator and that your position allows you unrestricted access to your company's mailing lists. Assume that you have the skill to insert your email address into any company mailing list without anyone knowing about it. You insert your address into several lists and, consequently, begin to receive confidential email that no one intended for you to see. One of those emails indicates that your best friend's department is about to be eliminated and all of its personnel fired. Do you warn your friend?

Discussion Questions

1. Do your answers to the questions in situations A and B differ? Does the medium through which the information is obtained make a difference? Is it easier to avoid reading an email than it is to avoid overhearing a conversation? If so, does that difference matter? How responsible are the parties involved? Is information obtained in a public setting fair game?

2. Do your answers to the questions in situations B and C differ? In situation B, the information is for your personal gain; in C, the information is for both your personal gain and your organization's gain. Does this difference matter? How do you respond when asked if you have read the email?

3. Do your answers to the questions in situations C and D differ? Would you lie in one case and not in the other? Why, or why not?

4. Answer the question in situation E. What is the essential difference between situations A through D

and situation E? Suppose you had to justify your behaviour in situation E. How would you argue? Do you believe your own argument?

5. In situations A through D, if you access the information, you have done nothing illegal. You were the passive recipient. Even in situation E, although you undoubtedly violated your company's employment policies, you most likely did not break the law. So, for this discussion, assume that all of these actions are legal.

   a. What is the difference between *legal* and *ethical*? Look up both terms in a dictionary, and explain how they differ.

   b. Make the argument that business is inherently competitive, and that if something is legal, then it is acceptable to do it if it helps to further your goals.

   c. How responsible are the parties involved? Make the argument that it is never appropriate to do something unethical.

6. Summarize your beliefs about proper conduct when you receive misdirected information.

CHAPTER 12
Managing Information Security and Privacy

STUDY QUESTIONS

Q12-1   **WHAT IS IDENTITY THEFT?**

Q12-2   **WHAT IS PIPEDA?**

Q12-3   **WHAT TYPES OF SECURITY THREATS DO ORGANIZATIONS FACE?**

Q12-4   **HOW CAN TECHNICAL SAFEGUARDS PROTECT AGAINST SECURITY THREATS?**

Q12-5   **HOW CAN DATA SAFEGUARDS PROTECT AGAINST SECURITY THREATS?**

Q12-6   **HOW CAN HUMAN SAFEGUARDS PROTECT AGAINST SECURITY THREATS?**

Q12-7   **WHAT IS DISASTER PREPAREDNESS?**

Q12-8   **HOW SHOULD ORGANIZATIONS RESPOND TO SECURITY INCIDENTS?**

MIS in Action

James and Michele are videoconferencing with Sam Ide, the manager of security for San Diego Sports, a large sports equipment vendor that Michele wants to involve in race events. Mr. Ide's job is to determine if PRIDE Systems provides an acceptable level of security. Michele has gone over this several times with San Diego Sports personnel, and they asked to speak with someone outside of sales who has direct knowledge of PRIDE Systems' security. Michele asked James to participate in the videoconference with Mr. Ide.

"Sam, I have James Wu, our IS manager here, on our videoconference line. Why don't I let you explain your concerns and I'll ask James to respond?"

"Sure. James, thanks for taking the time to speak with me."

"Happy to do it."

"OK, we at SDS . . . that's how we refer to ourselves . . . we at SDS have always been concerned with security. But, given the recent troubles at Equifax and Target, our

KE   Chapter 12 optional knowledge extensions are
Knowledge Extension 19 Data Breaches available in the MyLab MIS
Knowledge Extension 20 Business Process Management available in the
MyLab MIS

senior management team has asked us to be even more careful. It appears that criminals have begun to focus attacks on inter-organizational systems, and so we address security with all of our partners."

"I understand, Sam. Although in this case, we're not talking about any connection between your systems and ours. As I understand it, we just want to feature San Diego Sports in a major way in our advertising and promotion of events." James is careful as he gains a sense of his interests.

"Thanks, James, that's my understanding as well. All the same, we don't want to become affiliated in the mind of our market with any company that has a major security problem, and that's the reason for this call."

"Got it. Do you have specific matters you'd like me to address?"

"Actually, I do. Michele has explained to me the basics of your security program, and she said that, given the fact that your systems were originally designed to store medical data, you have designed security deep into your systems." Sam sounds like he's reading from notes.

"Correct." James nods at Michele as he says this.

"I wonder if you could explain that to me with some specifics."

"Sure, but first, may I ask if you have a technical background?" James isn't sure how much detail to provide him.

"I'm not a developer, not by a long shot, but I was closely involved as a systems analyst in the development of many of our systems." Sam's actually quite a bit more technical than he reveals.

"Great. Let me dive in then, and if the dive is too deep, just let me know." There's not the least bit of condescension in James's voice as he speaks. "Each user is in charge of the distribution of his or her data. Initially, users' data is not shared at all. But we provide a simple-to-use UI that allows users to change their security settings."

"OK. Michele told me that. But how do you implement that security?" Sam wants to dive deeper.

"Because we have thousands and thousands of users, we store all privacy settings in a database and we have elaborate security on that database that I can go into later, if you want." James wants to focus on specific PRIDE features.

"Maybe. Just keep explaining."

"It turns out that event participants have a many-to-many relationship with all of our major players. Thus, for example, a participant may belong to several health clubs, and of course a health club has a relationship to many of our participants. Similarly, a participant has a relationship to potentially many insurance companies, and each company can have a relationship to many of our participants. Are you with me?"

"Yes, keep going." Sam sounds curious.

"So, as you know, to represent a many-to-many relationship we create an intersection or bridge table. And we store the security preferences for each person and his or her relationship to the external agent in that intersection table."

Michele jumps in at this point. "Sam, let me see if I can bring up an illustration onto your screen. Do you see the table diagram?"

"Just a second. Something's loading. Ah, yes, there it is."

James continues, "OK, the data for each participant is stored in the Person table in the centre. Actually, we store quite a bit more data than shown here, but this will give you an idea of what we do. The security allowed is stored in attributes called *PolicyStatements* in the intersection tables. By default, the value is 'None.' However, if someone decides to share his or her data with, say, a health club, then he or she uses a form to specify what he or she wants, and we store the result of that decision in the PolicyStatement attribute. All of our code uses the value of that attribute to limit data access."

"That makes sense; it's a clean design. But what about SQL injection?"

"Good question. There are four types of access allowed: None, which is the default; Non-identifying; Summary; and Full Access. The last two include the person's identity. In the form, those four are presented with radio buttons and the user picks. There's no place for SQL injection to occur."

The meeting continues in this vein for another 15 minutes. Sam seems satisfied with James's responses. Afterward, James and Michele walk back to their offices together.

"James, that was the best meeting I've had with him. He is impatient with me, but he related to you really well."

"Michele, I'm glad you're happy with it. I couldn't tell what he thought, but his questions were good and ones that we've thought about a lot."

"Well, James, you're good at explaining things. Ever think about going into sales?"

"Heavens, no, Michele. But I'll take that as a compliment."

"Thanks again."

Q12-1 WHAT IS IDENTITY THEFT?

We begin this chapter by considering your personal security and one of the fastest growing threats to it—identity theft. It is very important to be aware of security issues. Once you are aware of threats to your own security, it is often easier to consider security threats to the organizations you work for. The focus of this chapter is on understanding and managing security threats to organizations, but understanding threats to your own privacy will help make you more sensitive to the importance of security and privacy.

Consider all of the things you do in a day and how many of those things revolve around electronic information. If someone else had your personal information, what could they do with it? In **identity theft**, vital information, such as a person's name, address, date of birth, social insurance number, and mother's maiden name, are often all that is needed to facilitate impersonation. With this information, the identity thief can take over a victim's financial accounts; open new bank accounts; transfer bank balances; apply for loans, credit cards, and other services; purchase vehicles; take luxury vacations; and so on.

Identity theft is one of the fastest-growing crimes in Canada because it is relatively easy to do. Take for example Equifax, which is a global technology company specializing in providing credit scores and personal privacy protection. The company announced in September 2017 that a cybersecurity incident occurred that potentially impacted personal information relating to 143 million consumers including approximately 100 000 Canadian customers. Compromised personal information included names, social insurance numbers, birth dates, addresses and, in some instances, driver's licence numbers. This kind of theft potentially involves stealing, misrepresenting, or hijacking the identity of another person or business and provides an effective way to commit other crimes. The Public Safety Canada website (https://www.getcybersafe.gc.ca/index-en.aspx) provides useful information about what identify theft is and who to contact if it happens to you. You can read about protecting yourself from identify theft in the box on page 387.

Q12-2 WHAT IS PIPEDA?

We all do business with many companies. Every time we buy or ask for something, we create a transaction. When you interact with organizations, you often leave behind personal information about yourself. Your name, address, debit card number, and other behaviours are information, and they can be of great value to an organization. The **Personal Information Protection and Electronic Documents Act (PIPEDA)** is intended to balance an individual's right to the privacy of his or her personal information with an organization's need to collect, use, and share that personal information for business purposes. To oversee this Act, the Privacy Commissioner of Canada was created as the ombudsperson for privacy complaints in Canada.

Every Canadian business professional needs to be aware of PIPEDA because it governs how data are collected and used. One of the most critical elements in PIPEDA is the principle that individuals have the right to know what type of information an organization collects about them and also how that information is going to be used. PIPEDA suggests that organizations should not use the information collected for any purpose other than what the organization agreed to use it for. For example, if an organization collects information about a customer, it cannot sell or move that information to another company unless it initially told the customer that the organization might share personal information with others. PIPEDA, therefore, creates some protection of personal privacy.

A second responsibility that an organization takes on when it collects personal information is securing that information. PIPEDA suggests that it is the duty of an organization to protect the information it collects. To ensure this, PIPEDA provides an individual with the right to know who in the organization is responsible for securing the information. PIPEDA also requires that this information be complete, up to date, and accurate.

When organizations collect information, PIPEDA ensures that they do so only by fair means and that their terms and policies are clearly expressed so that people understand them before using the services of the organizations. PIPEDA does not,

---

So What? Protecting Yourself from Identity Theft

According to the Royal Canadian Mounted Police (www.rcmp-grc.gc.ca/scams-fraudes/id-theft-vol-eng.htm), you can do many simple things to lower your risk of identity theft:

- Be wary of unsolicited emails, telephone calls, or mail asking for personal or financial information. Do not fill in forms for contests, rebates, or draws that ask for more information than you are prepared to give.

- Remove identity documents from your purse or wallet if you do not need them and store them in a secure place.

- Periodically check your credit reports, banking information, and credit card statements and report any irregularities.

- It is safer to swipe your card than it is to allow a cashier to do it for you. If you must hand over your card, never lose sight of it.

- Shield your personal identification number when using an ATM or a PIN pad.

- Trash bins are a goldmine for identity thieves. Make sure you shred personal and financial documents before disposing of them.

- Cut up expired and unused credit cards. The numbers on these cards could still be used by an identity thief.

- Do not give personal information to anyone who phones or emails you unless you know who they are. Identity thieves may pose as representatives of financial institutions, Internet service providers, or government agencies to get you to reveal identifying information.

Be very careful with the identification you provide, especially if it is one of the main identity documents, such as a birth certificate, driver's licence, or social insurance number (SIN). These source documents can be used to produce other identification (ID) and gain access to more of your personal and financial information.

Source: Data from Royal Canadian Mounted Police (www.rcmp-grc.gc.ca/scams-fraudes/id-theft-vol-eng.htm).

however, facilitate individuals suing organizations. If issues arise that cannot be resolved between an individual and an organization, they should file a complaint with the Office of the Privacy Commissioner of Canada. The Privacy Commissioner then reviews the case and produces a report stating its conclusions. This report cannot be used directly to obtain compensation but can be used in a federal court when and if a lawsuit is filed.

PIPEDA has helped establish some confidence in the collection of digital information to support e-commerce. It does not completely establish personal privacy and cannot eliminate the problems of information theft. PIPEDA has, however, been used to reduce risk and safeguard the rights of individuals. PIPEDA has also helped assure other countries, such as those of the European Union, that Canadian laws on personal information privacy are sufficient to protect the rights of their citizens.

Q12-3 WHAT TYPES OF SECURITY THREATS DO ORGANIZATIONS FACE?

It is not just individuals who face threats to their security. Organizations face similar threats. There are three sources of **security threats**: (1) human error and mistakes, (2) malicious human activity, and (3) natural events and disasters.

Human errors and mistakes include accidental problems caused by both employees and others outside the organization. An example is an employee who misunderstands operating procedures and accidentally deletes customer records. Another example is a physical accident, such as an employee driving a forklift through the wall of a computer room.

The second source is *malicious human activity*. This category includes employees and others who intentionally destroy data or other system components. It also includes hackers who break into a system, virus and worm writers who infect computer systems, and people who send millions of unwanted emails (referred to as **spam**).

Natural events and disasters are the third source of security problems. This category includes fires, floods, hurricanes, earthquakes, tsunamis, avalanches, and other acts of nature or accidents. Problems in this category include not only the initial loss of capability and service but also losses stemming from actions to recover from the initial problem.

Figure 12-1 summarizes threats by type of problem and source. Five types of security problems are listed: (1) *unauthorized data disclosure*, (2) *incorrect data modification*, (3) *faulty service*, (4) *denial of service*, and (5) *loss of infrastructure*. We will consider each type below.

Unauthorized Data Disclosure

Unauthorized data disclosure can occur by human error when someone inadvertently releases data in violation of policy. An example at a college or university would be a new department administrator who posts student names, numbers, and grades in a public place (incorrect public releasing of names and grades could violate provincial law). In Canada, this type of disclosure is covered by PIPEDA. Personal information is defined under this Act as information about an identifiable individual that includes the name, title, address, or telephone number of an employee of an organization. The Act gives individuals the right to know why an organization collects, uses, or discloses personal information. So, organizations are required to identify why they are collecting information and how they will use it. As we noted earlier, PIPEDA also requires organizations to identify anyone in the organization responsible for keeping personal information private and secure and who allows other individuals to have access to this information, as necessary, to check its accuracy.[1]

[1] You can learn more about PIPEDA at www.priv.gc.ca/leg_c/leg_c_p_e.asp.

		Source		
		Human Error	**Malicious Human Activity**	**Natural Events and Disasters**
Problem	**Unauthorized data disclosure**	Procedural mistakes	Pretexting Phishing Spoofing Sniffing Computer crime	Disclosure during recovery
	Incorrect data modification	Procedural mistakes Incorrect procedures Ineffective accounting controls System errors	Hacking Computer crime	Incorrect data recovery
	Faulty service	Procedural mistakes Development and installation errors	Computer crime Usurpation	Service improperly restored
	Denial of service	Accidents	DOS attacks	Service interruption
	Loss of infrastructure	Accidents	Theft Terrorist activity	Property loss

Figure 12-1 Security Threats

The popularity and efficacy of search engines have created another source of inadvertent disclosure. Employees who place restricted data on websites that can be uncovered by search engines may mistakenly publish proprietary or restricted data over the Web.

Of course, proprietary and personal data can also be released maliciously. **Pretexting** occurs when someone deceives by pretending to be someone else. A common scam involves a telephone caller who pretends to be from a credit card company and claims to be checking the validity of credit card numbers: "I'm checking your MasterCard number; it begins with 5181. Can you verify the rest of the number?" The first four digits of most credit cards can be easily identified from the Internet (Wikipedia, for example) and it is likely that the caller is attempting to obtain a complete and valid number.

Phishing is a similar technique for obtaining unauthorized data, and it uses pretexting via email. The *phisher* pretends to be a legitimate company and sends an email requesting confidential data, such as account numbers, social insurance numbers, account passwords, and so on. Phishing compromises legitimate brands and trademarks. Case Study 12, on pages 405–406, looks in more detail at some examples of phishing.

Spoofing is another term for someone pretending to be someone or somewhere else. If you pretend to be your professor, you are spoofing your professor. **IP spoofing** occurs when an intruder uses another site's IP (Internet Protocol) address as if it were that other site. An example of this is using an American IP address in place of a Canadian IP address in order to access the U.S. version of Netflix. **Email spoofing** is a synonym for phishing.

Sniffing is a technique for intercepting computer communications. With wired networks, sniffing requires a physical connection to the network. With wireless networks, no such connection is required—**drive-by sniffers** simply access computers with wireless connections through an area and search for unprotected wireless networks. They can monitor and intercept wireless traffic at will. Even protected wireless networks are vulnerable, as you will learn. Spyware and adware are two other sniffing techniques discussed later in this chapter.

Ransomware is an example of malicious software that encrypts a computer user's data (including pictures, documents, contacts, etc.) resulting in unreadable files. The Wanna-Cry and Petya ransomware attacks are examples of this type of software. The culprit then requests a payment (i.e., "ransom") be made before agreeing to decrypt the files and allow access. It is important to note that paying the ransom does not guarantee the return of a user's data. Experts advise against paying a ransom as people report not getting their data back after payment. Successful attacks and high revenues from this malicious software will likely encourage more of these campaigns.

Incorrect Data Modification

The second problem category in Figure 12-1 is *incorrect data modification*. Incorrectly increasing a customer's discount or incorrectly modifying an employee's salary, earned days of vacation, or annual bonus are actions that might fall under this category. Other examples include placing incorrect information, such as erroneous price changes, on the company's website or portal or accidently giving students in a course the wrong grades. This happened to one of the authors of this textbook and interestingly enough only students who got lower grades advised the author. The students who got higher grades kept mysteriously quiet.

Incorrect data modification can occur through human error when employees follow procedures incorrectly or when procedures have been incorrectly designed. For proper internal control on systems that process financial data or that control inventories of assets, such as products and equipment, companies should ensure separation of duties and authorities and have multiple checks and balances in place.

A final type of incorrect data modification caused by human error is *system errors*. An example is the lost-update problem discussed in Chapter 5.

Hacking occurs when a person gains unauthorized access to a computer system. Although some people hack for the sheer joy of doing it, other hackers invade systems for the malicious purpose of stealing or modifying data. One major difference between computer crime and other types of crime is that when data are stolen the original data are still there and there may be no trace of the crime. Computer criminals often invade computer networks to obtain critical data or to manipulate the system for financial gain. Examples include reducing (or increasing) account balances or directing a shipment of goods to unauthorized locations and customers.

Faulty Service

The third problem category, *faulty service*, includes problems due to incorrect system operations. Faulty service encompasses incorrect data modification (as described above), as well as systems that incorrectly send the wrong order to customers, programs that incorrectly bill customers, and software that sends erroneous information to employees. Humans can also inadvertently cause faulty service by making procedural mistakes. System developers can write programs incorrectly or make errors during the installation of hardware, software programs, and data.

Denial of Service

Human error in following procedures or a lack of protocols can result in **denial of service (DOS)**. For example, employees can inadvertently shut down a Web server or corporate gateway router by starting a computationally intensive application. An online analytic processing (OLAP) application that uses the operational database management system (DBMS) might consume so many DBMS resources that order-entry transactions are unable to get through.

Denial-of-service attacks are often launched maliciously. A malicious hacker can flood a Web server, for example, with millions of bogus or fraudulent service requests to hinder the server from processing legitimate requests. Computer worms can infiltrate a network with so much artificial traffic that legitimate traffic cannot get through. Finally, natural disasters may cause systems to fail, resulting in denial of service.

Loss of Infrastructure

Human accidents can cause *loss of infrastructure*. Examples are a bulldozer cutting fibre-optic cables, or the maintenance staff unplugging an important device in order to plug in a vacuum cleaner.

Theft and terrorist events may cause loss of infrastructure. A disgruntled former employee or contractor (such as Eric Snowden) can walk off with corporate data servers, routers, or other crucial equipment. Terrorist events can also cause the loss of physical plants and equipment. Natural disasters present a large risk for infrastructure loss. A fire, flood, earthquake, or similar event can destroy data centres and all they contain. You may be wondering why Figure 12-1 does not include viruses, worms, and zombies. The answer is that viruses, worms, and zombies are *techniques* for causing some of the problems in the figure. They can cause a denial-of-service attack, or they can be used to cause malicious, unauthorized data access or data loss.

Elements of a Security Program

The problems listed in Figure 12-1 are as real and as serious as they sound. Accordingly, organizations must address security in a systematic way. A security program[2] has three components: (1) senior management involvement, (2) safeguards of various kinds, and (3) incident response.

The first component, senior management involvement, has two critical security functions. First, senior management must establish the security policy. This policy sets the stage for the organization's response to security threats. However, because no security program is perfect, there is always risk. Senior management's second function, therefore, is to manage risk by balancing the costs and benefits of the security program.

Safeguards are protections against security threats. An effective way to view safeguards is in terms of the five components of an information system, as shown in Figure 12-2. Some of the safeguards involve computer hardware and software; some involve data; and others involve procedures and people. In addition to these safeguards, organizations must also consider disaster-recovery safeguards.

Hardware	Software	Data	Procedures	People

Technical Safeguards	Data Safeguards	Human Safeguards
Identification and authentication	Data rights and responsibilities	Hiring
Encryption	Passwords	Training
Firewalls	Encryption	Education
Malware protection	Backup and recovery	Procedure design
Application design	Physical security	Administration
		Assessment
		Compliance
		Accountability

Effective security requires balanced attention to all five components!

Figure 12-2 Security Safeguards as They Relate to the Five Components

---

[2] Note that the word *program* is used here in the sense of a management program that includes objectives, policies, procedures, directives, and so forth. Do not confuse this term with *computer program*.

The final component of a security program consists of the organization's planned response to security incidents. Clearly, the time to think about what to do is not when computers are crashing throughout the organization. We will discuss incident response in the last section of this chapter.

Q12-4 HOW CAN TECHNICAL SAFEGUARDS PROTECT AGAINST SECURITY THREATS?

Technical safeguards involve the hardware and software components of an information system. Figure 12-3 lists primary technical safeguards. We have discussed all of these safeguards in prior chapters. In this chapter, we will supplement those prior discussions.

- Identification and authentication
- Encryption
- Firewalls
- Malware protection
- Design for secure applications

Figure 12-3 Technical Safeguards

Identification and Authentication

Every non-trivial information system should require some form of authentication. Users should sign on with a user name and password, for example. The user name *identifies* the user (the process of **identification**), and the password *authenticates* that user (the process of **authentication**). See the box "How Can You Create a Strong Password?" on page 399 for more on this topic. Note that authentication methods fall into three categories: (1) what you know (password or PIN), (2) what you have (smart card), and (3) what you are (biometric).

Passwords   Passwords have many weaknesses. First, users tend to be careless in their use. Despite repeated warnings to the contrary, yellow sticky notes holding written passwords adorn many computers. In addition, users tend to be free in sharing their passwords with others. Finally, many users choose ineffective, simple passwords or use the same password for many systems. Intrusion systems can very effectively guess these easy passwords.

These deficiencies can be reduced by using smart cards and biometric authentication.

Smart Cards   A **smart card** is a plastic card that is similar to a credit card. Unlike credit, debit, and ATM (automatic teller machine) cards, which have a magnetic strip, smart cards have a microchip. The microchip holds far more data than a magnetic strip and has identifying data or algorithms. Users of smart cards are required to enter a **personal identification number (PIN)** to be authenticated. Alternatively, smart cards can enable **challenge-response** authentication, in which a new password is generated at each login by an algorithm accessed by or stored on the chip. In a simple example (the real algorithms are highly sophisticated), the chip uses a 'multiply by 2 and subtract 1' formula to validate the correct user. When challenged with '8', the correct response would be '15', and, since the challenge varies each time, responding '15' (rather than '5') to a challenge of '3' would be invalid.

Biometric Authentication   **Biometric authentication** uses personal physical characteristics, such as fingerprints, facial features, and retinal scans, to authenticate users. Biometric authentication can provide strong authentication, but the required equipment is expensive. Often, too, users resist biometric identification because they feel it is invasive. Also, sometimes simple work-arounds, such as using a photograph to bypass facial recognition, are quickly discovered and publicized.

Single Sign-On for Multiple Systems

Information systems often require multiple sources of authentication. For example, when you sign on to your personal computer, you need to be authenticated. When you access the LAN (local area network) in your department, you need to be authenticated again. When you traverse your organization's WAN (wide area network), you will need to be authenticated to even more networks. Also, if your request requires database data, the DBMS server that manages that database will authenticate you yet again. It would be annoying to enter a name and password for every one of these resources.

Today's operating systems can authenticate you to networks and other servers. You sign on to your local computer and provide authentication data; from that point on, your operating system authenticates you to another network or server, which can authenticate you to yet another network and server, and so on.

Encryption and Firewalls

The next two categories of technical safeguards, as shown in Figure 12-3, are encryption and firewalls. In Chapter 6, firewalls were discussed briefly and encryption was noted in the discussion of VPNs (virtual private networks). We will not repeat that discussion here. You should just understand that they are very important technical safeguards.

Malware Protection

The next technical safeguard in our list in Figure 12-3 is malware. The term **malware** has several definitions. Here we use the broadest one: *malware* includes viruses, worms, Trojan horses, spyware, and adware. We discussed viruses, worms, and zombies in Chapter 4; you should review that material now if you have forgotten the definitions.

Spyware and Adware   **Spyware** programs are installed on the user's computer without the user's knowledge or permission. Spyware resides in the background and, without the user's knowledge, observes the user's actions and keystrokes, monitors computer activity, and reports that activity to sponsoring organizations. Some malicious spyware captures keystrokes to obtain user names, passwords, account numbers, and other sensitive information. Other spyware supports marketing analyses, observing what users do, the websites they visit, the products they examine and purchase, and so on.

Adware is similar to spyware in that it is installed without the user's permission and resides in the background to observe user behaviour. Most adware is benign in that it does not perform malicious acts or steal data. It does, however, watch user activity and produce pop-up ads. Adware can also change the user's default window or modify search results and switch the user's search engine. For the most part, it is simply annoying, but users should be concerned any time they discover unknown programs on their computers that perform unrequested functions.

Figure 12-4 lists some of the symptoms of adware and spyware. Sometimes, these symptoms develop slowly over time as more malware components are installed. Should these symptoms occur on your computer, you can remove the spyware or adware using anti-malware programs.

Malware Safeguards

Unfortunately, viruses and malware are a growing problem. Most safeguards require that the virus first be identified, so antivirus systems are predominantly reactive rather than proactive. However, many of the existing or known problems can be avoided by adhering to the following safeguards:

1. *Install antivirus and anti-spyware programs.* Your IT department will have a list of recommended (perhaps required) programs for this purpose. If you choose a program yourself, make sure it is from a reputable vendor. Check reviews of anti-malware software on the Web before purchasing.

- Slow system start-up
- Sluggish system performance
- Many pop-up advertisements
- Suspicious browser homepage changes
- Suspicious changes to the taskbar and other system interfaces
- Unusual hard-disk activity

Figure 12-4   Spyware and Adware Symptoms

2. *Set up your anti-malware programs to scan your computer frequently.* You should scan your computer at least once a week, possibly more often. When you detect malware code, use the anti-malware software to remove it. If the code cannot be removed, contact your IT department or anti-malware vendor.

3. *Update malware definitions.* **Malware definitions**—patterns that exist in malware code—should be downloaded frequently. Anti-malware vendors update these definitions continually, and you should install these updates as they become available.

4. *Open email attachments only from known sources.* As well, even when opening attachments from known sources, do so with great care. According to professor and security expert Ray Panko, about 90 percent of all viruses are spread through email attachments.[3] This statistic is not surprising because most organizations are protected by firewalls. With a properly configured firewall, email is the only outside-initiated traffic that can reach user computers.

   Most anti-malware programs check email attachments for malware code. However, all users should form the habit of *never* opening an email attachment from an unknown source. Also, if you receive an unexpected email from a known source or an email from a known source that has a suspicious subject, odd spelling, or poor grammar, do not open the attachment without first verifying with the source that the attachment is legitimate.

5. *Promptly install software updates from legitimate sources.* Unfortunately, all programs are chock full of security holes; vendors are fixing them as rapidly as they are discovered, but the practice is inexact. Install patches to the operating system and application programs promptly.

6. *Browse only in reputable Internet neighbourhoods.* It is possible for some malware to install itself when you do nothing more than open a webpage. Do not go there!

Q12-5 HOW CAN DATA SAFEGUARDS PROTECT AGAINST SECURITY THREATS?

Data safeguards protect databases and other organizational data. Two organizational units are responsible for data safeguards. **Data administration** refers to an organization-wide function that is in charge of developing data policies and enforcing data standards. As discussed in Chapter 11, data administration is typically a staff function reporting to the chief information officer (CIO).

Database administration refers to a function that pertains to a particular database. The enterprise resource planning (ERP), customer relationship management (CRM), and supply chain management (SCM) databases each have a database administration function. Database administration ensures that procedures exist to facilitate orderly multiuser processing of the database, to control changes to the database structure, and to protect the database.

Both data and database administration are involved in establishing the data safeguards shown in Figure 12-5. First, data administration should define data policies that govern how customer data will be used and shared—for example, "We will not share identifying customer data with any other organization." Then, data administration and database administration(s) work together to specify user data rights and responsibilities. Third, those rights should be enforced by user accounts that are authenticated by, at a minimum, passwords.

An organization should protect sensitive data by storing them in encrypted form. Such encryption uses one or more keys in ways similar to that described for data communication

- Defined data policies
- Data rights and responsibilities
- Rights enforced by user accounts authenticated by passwords
- Data encryption
- Backup and recovery procedures
- Physical security

Figure 12-5 Data Safeguards

[3] R. Panko, *Corporate Computer and Network Security* (Upper Saddle River, NJ: Prentice Hall, 2004), p. 165.

encryption. One potential problem with stored data, however, is that the key might be lost or that disgruntled or terminated employees might destroy it. Because of this possibility, when data are encrypted, a trusted party should have a copy of the encryption key. This safety procedure is sometimes called **key escrow**.

Another data safeguard is to periodically create backup copies of database contents. The organization should store at least some of these backups off the premises, possibly in a remote location. Additionally, IT personnel should periodically practise recovery, to ensure that the backups are valid and that effective recovery procedures exist. Do not assume that just because a backup is made, the database is protected.

Physical security is another data safeguard. The computers that run the DBMS and all devices that store database data should reside in secure, controlled-access facilities. If not, they are subject not only to theft but also to damage. For better security, the organization should keep a log showing who entered the facility, when, and for what purpose.

In some cases, organizations contract with other companies to manage their databases. If so, all the safeguards in Figure 12-5 should be part of the service contract. As well, the contract should give the owners of the data permission to inspect the premises of the database operator and to interview its personnel on a reasonable schedule.

Q12-6 HOW CAN HUMAN SAFEGUARDS PROTECT AGAINST SECURITY THREATS?

Human safeguards involve the people and procedures components of information systems. In general, human safeguards result when authorized users follow appropriate procedures for system use and recovery. Restricting access to authorized users requires effective authentication methods and careful user account management. In addition, appropriate security procedures must be designed as part of every information system, and users should be trained in the importance and use of those procedures. In this section, we will consider the development of human safeguards, first for employees and then for non-employees.

Human Safeguards for Employees

Figure 12-6 lists security considerations for employees. We discuss these considerations below.

Position Definitions Effective human safeguards begin with creating definitions of job tasks and responsibilities. In general, job descriptions should provide a separation of duties and authorities. For example, no single individual should be allowed both to approve expenses and to write cheques. Instead, one person should approve expenses, another should pay them, and a third should account for the payment. Similarly, in inventory, no single person should be allowed to authorize an inventory withdrawal and also to remove the items from inventory.

Given appropriate job descriptions, user accounts should be defined to give users the *least possible privilege* needed to perform their jobs. For example, users whose job description does not include modifying data should be given accounts with read-only privileges. Similarly, user accounts should prohibit users from accessing data that their job description does not require. Because of the problem of security, even access to seemingly innocuous data may need to be limited.

Finally, the security sensitivity should be documented for each position. Some jobs involve highly sensitive data (e.g., employee compensation, salesperson quotas, and proprietary marketing or technical data). Other positions involve no sensitive data. Documenting *position sensitivity* enables security personnel to prioritize their activities in accordance

- Position definition
  - Separate duties and authorities.
  - Determine least privilege.
  - Document position sensitivity.

"OK to pay this"

- Hiring and screening

"Where did you last work?"

- Dissemination and enforcement (responsibility, accountability, compliance)

"Lets talk security..."

- Termination
  - Friendly

"Congratulations on your new job."

  - Unfriendly

"We've closed your accounts. Goodbye."

Figure 12-6 Security Policy for In-House Staff

with the possible risk and loss. "MIS in Use" on page 397 provides an example of the need for position sensitivity.

Hiring and Screening Security considerations should be part of the hiring process. Of course, if a position involves no sensitive data and no access to information systems, then screening for information systems security purposes will be minimal. When hiring for high-sensitivity positions, however, extensive interviews, references, and background investigations are appropriate. Note, too, that security screening applies not only to new employees but also to employees who are promoted to sensitive positions.

Dissemination and Enforcement Employees cannot be expected to follow security policies and procedures that they are not aware of. Therefore, employees need to be made aware of the security policies and procedures and of their responsibilities. Employee security training begins during new-employee orientation. This general training must increase in accordance with the position's sensitivity and responsibilities. When employees are promoted, they should receive the security training that their new position requires. As well, the company should not provide user accounts and passwords until employees have completed required security training.

Enforcement consists of three interdependent factors: (1) responsibility, (2) account-ability, and (3) compliance. First, the company should clearly define the security *responsibilities* of each position. The design of the security program should be such that employees can be held *accountable* for security violations. Second, procedures should exist so that when critical data are lost, it is possible to determine how the loss occurred and who is accountable. Finally, the security program should encourage security *compliance*. Employee

Howard Roark, a professor at a large Canadian university, would often log on to the websites of various textbook publishers to review or order copies of textbooks he was considering for his courses or to obtain access to restricted instructor materials, such as test banks and sample examinations.

Registering with a publisher was usually a relatively simple process of completing an online request form on the website with information, such as name, university, and contact details. Once verified by the publisher (usually by email or telephone), log-in information (an ID and password) would then be emailed back to the professor.

One day, as he was reading an email message from a publisher, Roark wondered whether the existing processes were adequate.

The publisher had noticed that the email address used in a recent request for access did not match the email address on file for Roark, and so the publisher asked him to confirm that it was valid. Rather than the standard university address of Howard.Roark@universitydomain. com, a new account had been set up at a generic email service (such as Yahoo! or Hotmail) with the same name (i.e., Howard.Roark@emailservice.com). All other details in the request, such as address, title, and so on, were correct.

Roark was alarmed—was someone trying to impersonate him? What could he do about it?

QUESTIONS

1. Why do you think this situation has occurred? (*Hint:* Who could benefit from this?)
2. Who has been harmed (if anyone), or is this a victimless situation?
3. Are the registration procedures adequate? What changes, if any, would you recommend?
4. What action should be taken by Roark, the university, or the publisher? Does it matter where the request came from (e.g., what if it was a student at Roark's university)?
5. Is this a case of identity theft?
6. Assuming that the individual is identified, what would be an appropriate penalty?

activities should be regularly monitored for compliance, and management should specify action to be taken in the event of noncompliance.

Management attitude is crucial: If managers write passwords on staff bulletin boards, shout passwords down hallways, or ignore physical security procedures, then employee security attitudes and employee security compliance will suffer.

Termination Companies also must establish security policies and procedures for the termination of employees. Most employee terminations are friendly and occur as the result of promotion, retirement, or when the employee resigns to take another position. Standard human resources policies should ensure that system administrators receive notification in advance of the employee's last day so that they can remove accounts and passwords. The need to recover keys for encrypted data and any other special security requirements should be part of the employee's out-processing.

Unfriendly termination is more difficult because employees may be tempted to take malicious or harmful actions in retaliation for the termination. If such a possibility exists, system administrators may need to remove user accounts and passwords prior to notifying the employee of his or her termination. Other actions may also be needed to protect the company's information assets. A terminated sales employee, for example, may attempt to take the company's confidential customer and sales-prospect data for future use at another company.

As the line between personal and professional time becomes more blurred and more companies employ a "Bring Your Own Device" (BYOD) strategy, data protection has become more complicated. In one case, for example, an employee found that their personal telephone was reset back to the original condition (erasing many personal photographs) within hours of resigning from their position.

The human resources department should be aware of the importance of giving information systems administrators early notification of employee termination. Often no blanket policy exists and the information systems department must assess each case on an individual basis.

Human Safeguards for Non-employees

Business requirements may necessitate opening information systems to non-employees—temporary personnel, vendors, partner personnel (employees of business partners), volunteers, and the public. Although temporary personnel can be screened, to minimize costs the screening process is often reduced compared with that for employees. In most cases, companies cannot screen vendor or partner personnel and public users cannot be screened at all. Similar limitations apply to security training and compliance testing.

In the case of temporary, vendor, and partner personnel, the contracts that govern the activity should call for security measures appropriate to the sensitivity of the data and the information systems resources involved. The situation differs for public users of websites. In general, the best safeguard from threats from public users is to *harden* the website or other facility against attacks as much as possible. **Hardening** a site means to take extraordinary measures to reduce a system's vulnerability. Hardened sites use special versions of the operating system and lock down or eliminate operating system features and functions that are not required by the application. Hardening is actually a technical safeguard, but we mention it here as the most important safeguard against public users.

Finally, note that the business relationship with the public, and with some partners, differs from that with temporary personnel and vendors. The public and some partners use the information system to receive a benefit. Consequently, safeguards need to protect such users from internal company security problems. A disgruntled employee who maliciously changes prices on a website potentially damages both public users and business partners. As one experienced IT manager put it, "Rather than protecting ourselves from them, we need to protect them from us."

Account Administration

The third human safeguard is account administration. The administration of user accounts, passwords, and help-desk policies and procedures is an important component of the security system.

Account Management   Account management concerns the creation of new user accounts, the modification of existing account permissions, and the removal of unneeded accounts. Information system administrators perform all these tasks, but account users are responsible for notifying the administrators of the need for these actions. The IT department should create standard procedures for this purpose. As a future user, you can improve your relationship with information systems personnel by providing early and timely notification of the need for account changes.

The existence of accounts that are no longer required or in use is a serious security threat. It can be difficult for information systems administrators to know if an account should be removed; so it is up to users and managers to provide this notification.

Password Management   Passwords are the primary means of authentication. They are important not just for access to the user's computer, but also for authentication to other networks and servers. Because of the importance of passwords, the National Institute of Standards and Technology (NIST) recommends that employees be required to sign statements similar to the one shown in Figure 12-7.

When an account is created, users should immediately change the password they are given to a password of their own. In fact, well-constructed systems require the user to change the password on first use.

Additionally, users should change passwords frequently thereafter. Some systems require a password change every three months or even more frequently. Users grumble at the nuisance of making such changes, but frequent password changes reduce not only the risk of password loss but also the extent of damage if an existing password is compromised.

> I hereby acknowledge personal receipt of the system password(s) associated with the user IDs listed below. I understand that I am responsible for protecting the password(s), will comply with all applicable system security standards, and will not divulge my password(s) to any person. I further understand that I must report to the Information Systems Security Officer any problem I encounter in the use of the password(s) or when I have reason to believe that the private nature of my password(s) has been compromised.

Figure 12-7 Sample Account Acknowledgment Form

Source: From National Institute of Standards and Technology, Introduction to Computer Security: The NIST Handbook, Special Publication 800–812, p. 112. Copyright © 1995 by National Institute of Standards and Technology. Used by permission of National Institute of Standards and Technology.

Some users create two passwords and switch back and forth between them. This strategy results in poor security, and some password systems do not allow the user to reuse recently used passwords. Again, users may view this policy as a nuisance, but it is important.

Help-Desk Policies   In the past, help desks have been a serious security risk. A user who had forgotten his or her password would call the help desk and plead with the

How Can You Create a Strong Password?

Whatever opportunities you find for using information systems in your career—and your life—one issue that will remain constant is the security of those systems. Security is vitally important. As a user of information systems in a business organization, you will be given a user name and password. You will be instructed to create a strong password, and it is vitally important for you to do so. (In fact, you should now be using such passwords at your college or university.) So, what is a strong password, and how do you create one?

STRONG PASSWORDS

Microsoft, a company that has many reasons to promote effective security, defines a strong password as one that has the following characteristics:

- Contains seven or more characters
- Does not contain your user name, real name, or company name
- Does not contain a complete dictionary word in any language
- Is different from previous passwords you have used
- Contains both uppercase and lowercase letters, numbers, and special characters (such as ~ ! @; # $ % ^ &; * () _ +; − =; { } | [ ] \ : "; ' <; >; ?,. /)

Examples of good passwords are the following:

- Qw37^T1bb?at
- 3B47qq<3>5!7b

The problem with such passwords is that they are nearly impossible to remember. And the last thing you want to do is write your password on a piece of paper and keep it near your workstation. Never do that!

One technique for creating memorable, strong passwords is to base them on the first letter of the words in a phrase. The phrase could be the title of a song or the first line of a poem, or one based on some fact about your life. For example, you might take the phrase, "I was born in Calgary, Alberta, before 1990." Using the first letters from that phrase and substituting the character < for the word before, you create the password IwbiC,AB<1990. This is an acceptable password, but it would be better if all the numbers were not placed at the end. So, you might try the phrase, "I was born at 3:00 A.M. in Calgary, Alberta." That phrase yields the password Iwba3:00AMiC, AB—a strong password that is easily remembered.

PASSWORD ETIQUETTE

Once you have created a strong password, you need to protect it. Proper password etiquette is one of the marks of a business professional. Never write down your password, and do not share it with others. Never ask others for their passwords, and never give your password to anyone else.

But what if you need someone else's password? Suppose, for example, you ask someone to help you with a problem on your computer. You sign on to an information system, and for some reason, you need to enter that other person's password. In this case, say to the other person, "We need your password," and then get out of your chair, offer your keyboard to the other person, and look away while he or she enters the password. Among professionals working in organizations that take security seriously, this little do-si-do move—one person getting out of the way so that another person can enter a password—is common and accepted.

If someone asks for your password, do not give it out. Instead, get up, go over to that person's machine, and enter your own password yourself. Be around while your password is in use, and ensure that your account is logged out at the end of the activity. No one should mind or be offended in any way when you do this. It is the mark of a professional.

help-desk representative to reveal the password or to reset the password to something else. "I can't get this report out without it!" was (and is) a common lament.

The problem for help-desk representatives is, of course, that they have no way of determining that they are talking to the true user. But they are in a difficult situation: If they do not help in some way, the help desk is perceived to be the unhelpful desk.

To resolve such problems, many systems give the help-desk representative a way of authenticating the user. Typically, the help-desk information system has answers to questions that only the true user would know, such as the user's birthplace, mother's maiden name, or last four digits of an important account number. Usually, when a password is changed, notification of that change is sent to the user in an email. Email, as you learned, is sent as plain text, however, so the new password itself ought not to be emailed. If you ever receive notification that your password was reset when you did not request it, immediately contact IT security. Someone has likely compromised your account.

System Procedures   Figure 12-8 shows a grid of procedure types—normal operation, backup, and recovery. Procedures of each type should exist for each information system. For example, the order-entry system will have procedures of each of these types, as will the Web storefront, the inventory system, and so forth. The definition and use of standardized procedures reduces the likelihood of computer crime and other malicious activity by insiders. It also ensures that the system's security policy is enforced.

	System Users	**Operations Personnel**
Normal Operation	Use the system to perform job tasks, with security appropriate to sensitivity.	Operate data centre equipment, manage networks, run web servers, and do related operational tasks
Backup	Prepare for loss of system functionality.	Back up website resources, databases, administrative data, account and password data, and other data.
Recovery	Accomplish job tasks during failure. Know tasks to do during system recovery.	Recover systems from backed-up data. Perform role of help desk during recovery.

Figure 12-8 System Procedures

Procedures exist for both users and operations personnel. For each type of user, the company should develop procedures for normal, backup, and recovery operations. As a future user, you will be primarily concerned with user procedures. Normal-use procedures should provide safeguards appropriate to the sensitivity of the information system.

Backup procedures concern the creation of backup data to be used in the event of failure. Whereas operations personnel have the responsibility for backing up system databases and other systems data, departmental personnel need to back up data on their own computers. Good questions to ponder are, "What would happen if I lost my computer (tablet or phone) tomorrow?" "What would happen if someone dropped my device during an airport security inspection?" "What would happen if it was stolen?" Employees should ensure that they back up critical data on their computers. The IT department may help in this effort by designing backup procedures and making backup facilities available.

Finally, systems analysts should develop procedures for system recovery. First, how will the department manage its affairs when a critical system is unavailable? Customers will want to order, and manufacturing will want to remove items from inventory even though a critical information system is unavailable. How will the department respond? Once the system is returned to service, how will records of business activities during the outage be entered into the system? How will service be resumed? The system developers should ask and answer these questions and others like them and develop procedures accordingly.

Security Monitoring

Security monitoring is the last of the human safeguards we will consider. Important monitoring functions are analysis of activity logs, security testing, and investigating and learning from security incidents.

Many information system programs produce *activity logs*. Firewalls produce logs of their activities, including lists of all dropped packets, infiltration attempts, and unauthorized access attempts from within the firewall. DBMS products produce logs of successful and failed log-ins. Web servers produce voluminous logs of Web activities. The operating systems in personal computers can produce logs of log-ins and firewall activities.

MIS in Use | Privacy and the Federal Government

Social networking sites, such as Facebook, LinkedIn, Pinterest, and Twitter, are cultural phenomena that have attracted billions of people. These sites let users easily communicate with existing friends, gather new ones, and re-establish contact with others who may have moved away or become temporarily forgotten. However, while there is no doubt of their popularity, some serious concerns have been raised about their impact on productivity and personal privacy.

Acting on a complaint from the Canadian Internet Policy and Public Interest Clinic (CIPPIC), the Office of the Privacy Commissioner of Canada (www.priv.gc.ca) filed a multifaceted complaint against Facebook Inc. in 12 areas, ranging from the collection of members' birthdates during registration to the sharing of users' personal information with third-party application developers. After a series of meetings with Facebook and a cooperative investigation in June 2009, the Privacy Commissioner found that four of the concerns were unfounded and could be dismissed and that four others, although reasonable, had been addressed by Facebook or could be controlled by the individual settings made by each user (e.g., changing the default privacy options).

On the remaining subjects of third-party applications, account deactivation and deletion, accounts of deceased users, and nonusers' personal information, the Privacy Commissioner found Facebook to be in contravention of the Privacy Act. Most notably, regarding third-party applications, the Privacy Commissioner determined that Facebook did not have adequate safeguards in place to prevent unauthorized access to users' personal information and was not doing enough to ensure that meaningful consent had been obtained.

QUESTIONS

1. How important are such agencies as the Office of the Privacy Commissioner of Canada?

2. What tools does the Privacy Commissioner have, and how can they be used? (*Hint:* Does it matter if the organization in question resides outside of Canada?)

3. How might Facebook respond to the Privacy Commissioner?

4. How does an organization respond to conflicting privacy issues (e.g., PIPEDA and the U.S. Patriot Act)?

None of these logs adds any value to an organization unless they are used. Accordingly, an important security function is to analyze these logs for threat patterns, successful and unsuccessful attacks, and evidence of security vulnerabilities.

Additionally, companies should test their security programs. Both in-house personnel and outside security consultants should conduct such testing.

Another important monitoring function is to investigate security incidents. How did the problem occur? Have safeguards been created to prevent a recurrence of such problems? Does the incident indicate vulnerabilities in other portions of the security system? What else can be learned from the incident?

Security systems reside in a dynamic environment. Organizational structures change: Companies are acquired or sold; mergers occur. New systems require new security measures. New technology changes the security landscape, and new threats arise. Security personnel must constantly monitor the situation and determine whether the existing security policy and safeguards are adequate. If changes are needed, security personnel need to take appropriate action.

Security, like quality, is an ongoing process. There is no final state that represents a secure system or company. Instead, companies must monitor security on a continuing basis.

Q12-7 WHAT IS DISASTER PREPAREDNESS?

A substantial loss of computing infrastructure caused by acts of nature, crime, or terrorist activity can be disastrous for an organization. Of course, the best way to solve a problem is to prevent it. The best safeguard against a disaster is appropriate location. If possible, place computing centres, Web farms, and other computer facilities in locations not prone to floods, earthquakes, hurricanes, tornados, or avalanches. Even in those locations, place infrastructure in unobtrusive buildings, basements, back rooms, and similar locations well within the physical perimeter of the organization. As well, locate computing infrastructure in fire-resistant buildings designed to house expensive and critical equipment.

Sometimes, however, business requirements necessitate locating the computing infrastructure in undesirable locations. And, even at seemingly ideal locations, disasters do occur. Therefore, some businesses prepare backup processing centres in locations geographically removed from the primary processing site.

Figure 12-9 lists major disaster preparedness tasks. After choosing a safe location for the computing infrastructure, the organization should identify all mission-critical systems. These are systems without which the organization cannot carry on and which, if lost for any period, could cause the organization's failure. The next step is to identify all resources necessary to run those systems. Such resources include computers, operating systems, application programs, databases, administrative data, procedure documentation, and trained personnel.

Next, the organization creates backups for the critical resources at the remote processing centre. So-called **hot sites** are remote processing centres and may be run by commercial disaster-recovery services. For a monthly fee, they provide all the equipment needed to continue operations following a disaster and there may be minimal downtime or unavailability following a disaster. **Cold sites**, in contrast, provide space and limited technology and customers provide and install the equipment needed to continue operations following a disaster. Recovery time is considerably longer. **Warm sites** are somewhere in the middle of the two extremes.

Once the organization has backups in place, it must train and rehearse cutover of operations from the primary centre to the backup. Periodic refresher rehearsals are mandatory.

Preparing a backup facility is very expensive; however, the costs of establishing and maintaining that facility are a form of insurance. Senior management must decide whether to prepare such a facility by balancing the risks, benefits, and costs. In some cases where the service is considered essential, for example banking, backup sites and disaster plans are required by law.

- Locate infrastructure in safe location.
- Identify mission-critical systems.
- Identify resources needed to run those systems.
- Prepare remote backup facilities.
- Train and rehearse.

Figure 12-9 Disaster Preparedness Guidelines

Q12-8 HOW SHOULD ORGANIZATIONS RESPOND TO SECURITY INCIDENTS?

The last component of a security plan we will consider is incident response. Figure 12-10 lists its major factors. Every organization should have an incident-response plan as part of the security program. No organization should wait until some asset has been lost or compromised before deciding what to do. The plan should include how employees are to respond to security problems, who they should contact, the reports they should prepare, and steps they can take to reduce further loss.

Consider, for example, a virus. An incident-response plan will stipulate what action is to be taken in the event of a virus. It should specify who to contact and what to do. It may

- Have plan in place
- Centralized reporting
- Specific responses
  - Speed
  - Preparation pays
  - Don't make problem worse
- Practise!

Figure 12-10 Factors in Incident Response

stipulate that the employee should turn off his or her computer and physically disconnect from the network or shut down the server. The plan should also indicate what users with wireless computers should do.

The plan should provide centralized reporting of all security incidents. Such reporting will enable an organization to determine whether it is under systemic attack or whether an incident is isolated. Centralized reporting also allows the organization to learn about security threats, take consistent actions in response, and apply specialized expertise to all security problems.

When an incident does occur, speed is of the essence. Viruses and worms can spread very quickly across an organization's networks, and a fast response will help mitigate the consequences. Because of the need for speed, preparation pays. The incident-response plan should identify critical personnel and their off-hours contact information. These personnel should be trained in where to go and what to do when they get there. Without adequate preparation, there is substantial risk that the actions of well-meaning people will make the problem worse. Also, there may be many rumours and incorrect or inappropriate ideas about what to do. A team of well-informed, trained personnel will serve to dampen such rumours.

Finally, organizations should periodically practise incident response. Without such practise, personnel will be poorly informed on the response plan, and the plan itself may have flaws that become apparent only during a drill.

How Does the Knowledge in This Chapter Help You?

The knowledge in this chapter helps you by making you aware of the threats to personal privacy and computer security both for you as an individual and business professional as well as for any organization in which you work. You know that both you and your organization must trade off the risk of loss against the cost of safeguards. You have learned techniques that you can and should employ to protect your own computing devices and your data. Also, you know how organizations should optimally respond to security threats (before, during, and after). You are equipped with knowledge about technical, data, and human safeguards and you know how organizations should respond to security incidents. This information is personally and professionally invaluable. Understanding potential threats and anticipating appropriate strategies is vital to protecting yourself and your organization in the current digital economy.

ACTIVE REVIEW

Use this Active Review to verify that you have understood the material in the chapter. You can read the entire chapter and then perform the tasks in this review, or you can read the material for just one question and perform the tasks for that question before moving on to the next one.

Q12-1 WHAT IS IDENTITY THEFT?

What is identity theft? List five ways you can protect yourself from identity theft.

Q12-2 WHAT IS PIPEDA?

What is PIPEDA? How does PIPEDA restrict the use of personal information by organizations? Can an individual sue an organization because of PIPEDA? What role does the privacy commissioner have with PIPEDA?

Q12-3 WHAT TYPES OF SECURITY THREATS DO ORGANIZATIONS FACE?

Explain the differences among security threats, threat sources, and threat types. Give one example of a security threat for each cell in the grid in Figure 12-1. Describe a phishing attack. Explain the threat of phishing to individuals. Explain the threat of phishing to company and product brands.

Q12-4 HOW CAN TECHNICAL SAFEGUARDS PROTECT AGAINST SECURITY THREATS?

List five technical safeguards. Define *identification* and *authentication*. Describe three types of authentication. Define *malware*, and name five types of malware. Describe six ways to protect against malware. Summarize why malware is a serious problem.

Q12-5 HOW CAN DATA SAFEGUARDS PROTECT AGAINST SECURITY THREATS?

Define *data administration* and *database administration*, and explain their differences. List data safeguards.

Q12-6 HOW CAN HUMAN SAFEGUARDS PROTECT AGAINST SECURITY THREATS?

How do you create a strong password? Summarize human safeguards for each activity in Figure 12-6. Summarize safeguards that pertain to non-employees. Describe three dimensions of safeguards for account administration. Explain how system procedures can serve as human safeguards. Describe security monitoring techniques.

Q12-7 WHAT IS DISASTER PREPAREDNESS?

Define *disaster*. List major considerations for disaster preparedness. Explain the difference between a hot site and a cold site.

Q12-8 HOW SHOULD ORGANIZATIONS RESPOND TO SECURITY INCIDENTS?

Summarize the actions that an organization should take when dealing with a security incident.

MyLab MIS

MyLab is an online learning and testing environment that features the perfect study tools to help you master the concepts covered in this chapter. Log in to MyLab to test your knowledge of key chapter concepts and explore additional practice tools, including videos, flashcards, and more!

KEY TERMS AND CONCEPTS

Adware 393
Authentication 392
Biometric
    authentication 392
Cold sites 402
Data administration 394
Data safeguards 394
Database
    administration 394
Denial of service
    (DOS) 390

Drive-by sniffers 389
Email spoofing 389
Hacking 390
Hardening 398
Hot sites 402
Human safeguards 395
Identification 392
Identity theft 386
IP spoofing 389
Key escrow 395
Malware 393

Malware definitions 394
Personal identification
    number (PIN) 392
Personal Information
    Protection and
    Electronic Documents
    Act (PIPEDA) 387
Phishing 389
Pretexting 389
Security threats 388
Smart card 392

Sniffing 389
Spam 388
Spoofing 389
Spyware 393
Technical
    safeguards 392
Unauthorized data
    disclosure 388
Warm sites 402

USING YOUR KNOWLEDGE

12-1. Find the cheapest way possible to purchase your own credit report. Two sources to check are www.equifax.com and www.transunion.com.

   a. Search for guidance on how best to review your credit records. Summarize what you learn.

   b. What actions should you take if you find errors in your credit report?

   c. Define *identity theft*. Search the Web, and determine the best course of action for someone who has been the victim of identity theft.

12-2. Suppose you lose your company laptop at an airport. What is more valuable, the laptop or the data? Under what circumstances should you now focus on updating your résumé?

12-3. Suppose a company is located in a hurricane zone and that it has been given 36 hours' warning that a serious, category 4 hurricane is headed its way.

    a. List all the information systems assets that might be in danger.

    b. For each asset in your list in (a), describe an appropriate safeguard.

    c. Suppose the company has done some disaster preparedness planning. Summarize what should be done in that 36-hour period.

    d. Suppose the company does not have a disaster preparedness plan. Summarize what you think the company should do in that 36-hour period.

    e. Compare your answers to (c) and (d). In your own words, state the advantages of having a disaster preparedness plan.

COLLABORATIVE EXERCISES

12-1. Your group has been given the task of finding ways to enjoy a free pancake breakfast at a restaurant. Do not feel limited by any ethical or legal issues related to getting the breakfast. In a brainstorming session, come up with as many ideas as you can for getting a free breakfast.

    a. List and prioritize the ideas most likely to succeed suggested by your group.

    b. Try the exercise again, but this time, ask your group to come up with as many ideas as they can for gathering someone else's personal information so that it could be used for identity theft. Suggest whatever mechanisms you think might be successful. Again, do not consider only ethical or legal means.

    c. Recognize that there are groups of people, with lots of resources, thinking about exactly what your group has just thought about. Using your list, create a list of things that can be done to protect your personal information. Be ready to share your insights.

CASE STUDY 12
PHISHING FOR CREDIT CARD ACCOUNTS

Before you read further, you need to know that the graphics in this case are fake. They were not produced by a legitimate business but were generated by a phisher. A *phisher* is an operation that spoofs legitimate companies in an attempt to illegally capture credit card numbers, email accounts, driver's licence numbers, and other data. Some phishers even install malicious program code on users' computers.

Phishing is usually initiated via an email. Go to www.fraudwatchinternational.com/phishing to view several examples that appear to be email messages from legitimate senders but that are, in fact, fake. The most common phishing attack is initiated with a bogus email. For example, you might receive the email shown in Figure 12-11.

This bogus email is designed to cause you to click on the "See more details here" link. When you do so, you will be connected to a site that will ask you for personal data, such as credit card numbers, card expiration dates, your driver's licence number, your social insurance number, or other data. In this particular case, you will be taken to a screen that asks for your credit card number.

This webpage is produced by a non-existent company and is entirely fake, including the link "Inform us about fraud." The only purpose of this site is to illegally capture your credit

Your Order ID: "17152492"
Order Date: "09/07/12"
Product Purchased: "Two First Class Tickets to Cozumel"
Your card type: "CREDIT"
Total Price: "$349.00"

Hello, when you purchased your tickets, you provided an incorrect mailing address.
See more details here
Please follow the link and modify your mailing address or cancel your order. If you have questions, feel free to cortact with us account@usefulbill.com

Figure 12-11 Phishing Email

card number. It might also install spyware, adware, or other malware on your computer. If you were to get this far, you should immediately close your browser and restart your computer. You should also run anti-malware scans on your computer to determine if the phisher has installed program code on your computer. If so, use the anti-malware software to remove that code.

How can you defend yourself from such attacks? First, you know you did not purchase two first-class tickets to Cozumel. (If, by some odd coincidence, you *have* just purchased airline tickets to Cozumel, you should contact the legitimate vendor's site *directly* to determine whether there has been some mix-up.) Given you have not purchased such tickets, suspect a phisher.

Second, note the implausibility of the email. It is exceedingly unlikely that you can buy two first-class tickets to any foreign country for $349. Additionally, note the misspelled words and the poor grammar ("cortact with us"). All these facts should alert you to the bogus nature of this email. However, be aware that these types of email are becoming more sophisticated.

Third, do not be misled by legitimate-looking graphics. Phishers are criminals; they do not bother to respect international agreements on the legitimate use of trademarks. The phisher might use names of legitimate companies, such as Visa, MasterCard, Discover, and American Express, on the webpage, and the presence of those names might lull you into thinking this is legitimate. However, it is likely the phisher is illegally using those names. In some instances, the phisher may copy the entire look and feel of a legitimate company's website.

Phishing is a serious problem. To protect yourself, be wary of unsolicited email, even if the email appears to be from a legitimate business. If you have questions about an email, contact the company directly (*not* using the addresses provided by the phisher!) and ask about the email. And above all, never give confidential data, such as account numbers, social insurance numbers, driver's licence numbers, or credit card numbers, in response to *any* unsolicited email.

WHAT DO YOU THINK?

THE FINAL, FINAL WORD

Congratulations! You have made it through the entire book. With the knowledge gained from your studies, you are well prepared to be an effective user of information systems. And with hard work and imagination, you can be much more than that. Many interesting opportunities are available to those who can apply information in innovative ways. Your professor has done what she or he can do, and the rest, as they say, is up to you.

Thoughts and Predictions

We believe that today, computer communications and data storage are free—or so close to free that the cost is not worth mentioning. What are the consequences? Our experience in the IT business makes us wary of predictions that extend beyond next year. But we know that free communication and data storage will cause fundamental changes in the business environment. When a company, such as Getty Images, can create its products at zero marginal cost, something is fundamentally different. Further, Getty Images is not the only such business; consider YouTube.

We suspect that the rate of technology development will slow in the next five years. Businesses are still digesting the technology that already exists. According to Harry Dent, technology waves always occur in pairs.* The first phase is wild exuberance, in which new technology is invented, its capabilities flushed out, and its characteristics understood. That first phase always results in overbuilding, but it sets the stage for the second phase, in which surviving companies and entrepreneurs purchase the overbuilt infrastructure for pennies on the dollar and use it for new business purposes.

The automotive industry, for example, proceeded in two stages. The irrational exuberance phase culminated in a technology crash; General Motors' stock fell 75 percent from 1919 to 1921. However, that exuberance led to the development of the highway system, the development of the petroleum industry, and a complete change in the conduct of commerce in the United States. Every one of those consequences created opportunities for business people alert to the changing business environment. We believe that we are poised today to see a similar second stage in the adoption of information technology. Businesses are configuring themselves to take advantage of the new opportunities. Dell builds computers to order and pays for the components days after the customer has paid Dell for

* H. Dent, *The Next Great Bubble Boom* (New York: The Free Press, 2004).

the equipment. A customer begins using his or her new computer before Dell pays the supplier for the monitor.

Fibre-optic cable has come to many homes and created new services previously unavailable. Companies such as Netflix have taken advantage of this new bandwidth, and this has signalled an end to the traditional video store rental. This is another example of how technological changes can drive changes in industries.

Bloggers and social media sites, such as YouTube, Twitter, and Facebook, have changed mainstream media with their commentary and access to real-time information. A new age has emerged as media, journalism, and mass communication have been altered by social media. The readership of newspapers has fallen consistently for more than a decade; newsprint cannot last in an era of free data communications.

So, as you finish your business degree, stay alert for new technology-based opportunities. Watch for the second wave and catch it. If you found this course interesting, take more information systems (IS) courses. Think about becoming an IS major. Even if you do not want to be an IS major, consider enrolling in courses such as database applications, project management, or systems analysis and design. If you are technically oriented, try a data communications course or a security course. You might want to explore computer programming. There are tremendous opportunities for programmers and nonprogrammers in the information systems industry. Look for novel applications of information systems technology to the emerging business environment. Hundreds of them abound! Find them, and have fun!

Discussion Question

1. How will you further your career with what you have learned in this course? Give this question serious thought, and write a memo to yourself to read from time to time as your career progresses.

GLOSSARY

10/100/1000 Ethernet A type of *Ethernet* that conforms to the IEEE 802.3 protocol and allows for transmission at a rate of 10, 100, or 1000 Mbps (megabits per second).

Access A popular personal and small workgroup DBMS product from Microsoft.

Access control list (ACL) A list that encodes the rules stating which packets are to be allowed through a firewall and which are to be prohibited.

Access points (APs) Points in a wireless network that facilitate communication among wireless devices and serve as points of interconnection between wireless and wired networks. APs must be able to process messages according to both the 802.3 and 802.11 standards because they send and receive wireless traffic using the 802.11 protocol and communicate with wired networks using the 802.3 protocol.

Accurate information Information that is factual and verifiable.

ACID An acronym standing for *atomic, consistent, isolated,* and *durable.* Used to describe the processing of transactions such that all of the transaction is processed or none of it is (atomic), transactions are processed in the same manner (consistent) whether processed alone or in the presence of millions of other transactions (isolated), and that once a transaction is stored, it never goes away—even in the presence of failure (durable).

Activities Parts of a business process that transform resources and information of one type into resources and information of another type; can be manual or automated.

Actor In a business process, a person, group, department, organization, or information system.

Ad-blocking software Software that filters out advertising content.

Advanced Research Projects Agency Network (ARPANET) The world's first operational packet switching network, which provided access to many research investigators who were geographically separated from the small number of large, powerful research computers available at the time.

Adware Programs installed on the user's computer without the user's knowledge or permission that reside in the background and, unknown to the user, observe the user's actions and keystrokes, modify computer activity, and report the user's activities to sponsoring organizations. Most adware is benign in that it does not perform malicious acts or steal data. It does, however, watch user activity and produce pop-up ads.

Agile methods Development methods, such as rapid application development (RAD), object-oriented systems development (OOD), and extreme programming (XP).

Alignment The ongoing, continually evolving challenge of fitting IT architecture to business objectives.

Alternatives formulation A step in the decision-making process in which decision makers lay out various alternatives.

Analog A continuously variable electronic signal.

Analysis paralysis When too much time is spent documenting project requirements.

Android A mobile operating system that is a version of Linux. Android runs on the Google Nexus 7 and the Amazon Kindle Fire as well as many other mobile devices.

Antivirus program Software that detects and possibly eliminates viruses.

Application service provider (ASP) A special form of outsourcing, in which an organization contracts with a vendor to rent applications from the vendor company on a fee-for-service basis.

Application software Programs that perform a business function. Some application programs are general purpose, such as Excel or Word. Other application programs are specific to a business function, such as accounts payable.

Applications Computer programs.

Asymmetric digital subscriber line (ADSL) ADSL line that has different upload and download speeds.

Attribute (1) A variable that provides a property for an HTML tag. Each attribute has a standard name. For example, the attribute for a hyperlink is *href,* and its value indicates which webpage is to be displayed when the user clicks the link. (2) Characteristic of an entity. Examples of attributes of *Order* would be *OrderNumber, OrderDate, SubTotal, Tax, Total,* and so forth. Examples of attributes of *Salesperson* would be *SalespersonName, Email, Phone,* and so forth.

Authentication The process whereby an information system approves (authenticates) a user by checking the user's password.

Automated system An information system in which the hardware and software components do most of the work.

Basic Input/Output System (BIOS) An important piece of firmware used when a computer is initially booted up. The first thing a computer does is to load BIOS from ROM and run through the commands provided by the firmware. BIOS checks to make sure the memory and input devices are functional. Once these are working, the operating system will be loaded.

Beta testing The process of allowing future system users to try out the new system on their own. Used to locate program failures just prior to program shipment.

Big Data An imprecise term that generally refers to large volumes of a variety of data over a long period of time that are used to draw general and specific inferences and analysis—for example the spread of disease, customer preferences, or individual behaviors.

Bigtable A nonrelational data store developed by Google.

Bill 198 or Budget Measures Act Law enforcing compliance with standards for collecting, reporting, and disclosing information.

Binary digits The means by which computers represent data; also called *bits.* A binary digit is either a zero or a one.

Biometric authentication The use of personal physical characteristics, such as fingerprints, facial features, and retinal scans, to authenticate users.

Bit The means by which computers represent data; also called *binary digit.* A bit is either a zero or a one.

Bluetooth A common wireless protocol designed for transmitting data over short distances, replacing cables.

Botnet A set of computers or applications that are coordinated through a network and used to perform malicious tasks.

Bring Your Own Device (BYOD) A policy in which employees are encouraged to simply use their own devices for work rather than being provided with additional company-issued devices.

Browser A program that processes the HTTP protocol; receives, displays, and processes HTML documents; and transmits responses.

Bus Means by which the CPU reads instructions and data from main memory and writes data to main memory.

Business analysts Analysts who develop the business case for a newly proposed system and develop the requirements for the system.

Business intelligence (BI) system A system that provides the right information, to the right user, at the right time. A tool produces the information, but the system ensures that the right information is delivered to the right user at the right time.

Business process A network of activities, resources, facilities, and information that interact to achieve some business function; sometimes called a *business system.*

Business process design The creation of new, usually cross-departmental business practices during information systems development. With process design, organizations do not create new information systems to automate existing business practices. Rather, they use technology to enable new, more efficient business processes.

Business process management (BPM) The process of generating information that will be useful for management and strategy decisions.

Business Process Modelling Notation (BPMN) A standard set of terms and graphical notations for documenting business processes.

Business system Another term for *business process.*

Business Technology Management (BTM) A category of skills focused on the ability to effectively innovate using information technology in organizations.

Business value Tangible benefits for organizations through either more efficient use of resources or more effective delivery of their services to customers.

Business-to-business (B2B) Ecommerce sales between companies.

Business-to-consumer (B2C) Ecommerce sales between a supplier and a retail customer (the consumer).

Business-to-government (B2G) Ecommerce sales between companies and governmental organizations.

Byte (1) A character of data. (2) An 8-bit chunk.

Cable line Cable television lines that provide high-speed data transmission.

Cable modem A type of modem that provides high-speed data transmission using cable television lines. The cable company installs a fast, high-capacity optical fibre cable to a distribution centre in each neighbourhood that it serves. At the distribution centre, the optical fibre cable connects to regular cable-television cables that run to subscribers' homes or businesses. Cable modems modulate in such a way that their signals do not interfere with TV signals. Like DSL lines, they are always on.

Cache A file on a domain name resolver that stores domain names and IP addresses that have been resolved. Then, when someone else needs to resolve that same domain name, there is no need to go through the entire resolution process. Instead, the resolver can supply the IP address from the local file.

Canadian Coalition for Tomorrow's ICT Skills (CCICT) A nonprofit organization created to support the development of skills for the information and computing technology industry.

Capital Resources that are invested with the expectation of future gain.

Carriers A telecommunications company that provides voice and data transportation services.

Cassandra A durable, nonrelational data store that operates over hundreds or thousands of servers. Originally developed by Facebook but later turned over to the open source community; has become an Apache Top-Level Project (TLP).

Cell The intersection of a column and row in a Microsoft Excel spreadsheet.

Central processing unit (CPU) The CPU selects instructions, processes them, performs arithmetic and logical comparisons, and stores results of operations in memory.

Certified Information Systems Auditor (CISA) A globally recognized certification earned by more than 50 000 professionals; members have job titles like information systems auditor, consultant, information systems security professional, regulator, chief information officer, and internal auditor.

Challenge/Response A form of authentication that uses a varying form of numeric question and algorithmic response (usually involving sophisticated computerized tokens) to validate users.

Channel Conflict Differences in the way that products or services are delivered or supported by different sales channels. For example, if products sold online are priced lower than those sold in traditional stores or if they have a different level of after sales support. See also *Showrooming* and *Price Conflict*.

Chief information officer (CIO) The title of the principal manager of the IT department. Other common titles are *vice-president of information services*, *director of information services*, and, less commonly, *director of computer services*.

Chief technology officer (CTO) The head of the technology group. The CTO sorts through new ideas and products to identify those that are most relevant to the organization. The CTO's job requires deep knowledge of information technology and the ability to envision how new IT will affect the organization over time.

Choice A step in the decision-making process in which decision makers analyze their alternatives and select one.

Clearinghouses Entities that provide goods and services at a stated price and arrange for the delivery of the goods, but never take title to the goods.

Clickstream data E-commerce data that describe a customer's clicking behaviour. Such data include everything the customer does at the website.

Client A computer that provides word processing, spreadsheets, database access, and usually a network connection.

Closed source Source code that is highly protected and only available to trusted employees and carefully vetted contractors.

Cloud A term that refers to elastic leasing of pooled computer resources over the Internet.

Cloud computing Customers do not necessarily own the computer they use. Instead, hardware, software, and applications are provided as a service, usually through a web browser. The cloud is a metaphor for the internet, which makes software and data services available from any location at any time.

Cluster analysis An unsupervised data-mining technique whereby statistical techniques are used to identify groups of entities that have similar characteristics. A common use for cluster analysis is to find groups of similar customers in data about customer orders and customer demographics.

Cold sites Remote processing centres that provide office space and limited computer equipment for use by companies that need to continue operations after a loss of their primary computing site (see *Warm* and *Hot sites*).

Collaboration Occurs when two or more people work together to achieve a common goal, result, or product.

Columns Also called *fields*, or groups of bytes. A database table has multiple columns that are used to represent the attributes of an entity. Examples are *PartNumber*, *EmployeeName*, and *SalesDate*.

Commerce server An application program that runs on a server tier computer. A typical commerce server obtains product data from a database, manages items in users' shopping carts, and coordinates the checkout process.

Commercial-off-the-shelf (COTS) Software that is purchased as-is and is not customized.

Communication systems Email, virtual private networks, instant messaging, and more sophisticated communications systems, dependent on the network technology available in an organization.

Communities See *communities of practice*

Communities of practice Groups of people related by a common interest. Also called communities.

Competitive strategy The strategy an organization chooses as the way it will succeed in its industry. According to Michael Porter, there are four fundamental competitive strategies: cost leadership across an industry or within a particular industry segment, and product differentiation across an industry or within a particular industry segment.

Computer hardware One of the five fundamental components of an information system.

Connection data In social media systems, data about relationships.

Content data In social media systems, data and responses to data that are contributed by users and SM sponsors.

Content delivery network (CDN) An information system that serves content to Web pages over the Internet. To reduce wait time, data is typically stored and served from many geographic locations.

Content management systems (CMSs) An information system that tracks organizational documents, webpages, graphics, and related materials.

Control Objectives for Information and Related Technology (COBIT) A framework of best practices designed for IT management; provides board members, managers, auditors, and IT users with a set of generally accepted measures, indicators, processes, and best practices to assist in getting the best from organizational IT investments.

Conversion rate Measures the frequency with which someone who clicks on an ad makes a purchase, "likes" a site, or takes some other action desired by the advertiser.

Cost feasibility One of four dimensions of feasibility.

Cross-departmental systems The third type of computing systems. In this type, systems are designed not to facilitate the work of a single department or function but, rather, to integrate the activities of a complete business process.

Cross-functional systems Synonym for *cross-departmental systems*.

Crow's foot A line on an entity-relationship diagram that indicates a 1:N relationship between two entities.

Crow's-foot diagram A type of entity-relationship diagram that uses a crow's foot symbol to designate a 1:N relationship.

Crowdsourcing A process through which users can provide customer support to one another or even participate in the creation of product specifications, designs, and complete products.

Custom-developed software Software that is tailor-made for a company or organization.

Customer life cycle Taken as a whole, the processes of marketing, customer acquisition, relationship management, and loss/churn that must be managed by CRM systems.

Customer relationship management (CRM) system An information system that maintains data about customers and all their interactions with the organization.

Customer service expense The costs involved in supporting a customer's purchase or use of a product or service.

Data Recorded facts or figures. One of the five fundamental components of an information system.

Data administration A staff function that pertains to *all* of an organization's data assets. Typical data administration tasks are setting data standards, developing data policies, and providing for data security.

Data channel Means by which the CPU reads instructions and data from main memory and writes data to main memory.

Data flows An element in a data flow diagram that depicts the movement of data.

Data flow diagram (DFD) A diagram focused on information processes that is composed of four basic elements (data flow, data store, external entity, and process).

Data integrity problem In a database, the situation that exists when data items disagree with one another. An example is two different names for the same customer.

Data mart A database that prepares, stores, and manages data for reporting and data mining for specific business functions.

Data mining The application of statistical techniques to find patterns and relationships among data and to classify and predict.

Data model A logical representation of the data in a database that describes the data and relationships that will be stored in the database. Similar to a blueprint.

Data resource challenge Occurs when data are collected in OLTP but are not used to improve decision making.

Data safeguards Steps taken to protect databases and other organizational data by means of data administration and database administration.

Data store A diagram element in a data flow diagram depicting a database.

Data warehouse A facility that prepares, stores, and manages data specifically for reporting and data mining.

Database A self-describing collection of integrated records.

Database administration The management, development, operation, and maintenance of the database so as to achieve the organization's objectives. This staff function requires balancing conflicting goals—protecting the database while maximizing its availability for authorized use. In smaller organizations, this function is usually served by a single person. Larger organizations assign several people to an office of database administration.

Database application A collection of forms, reports, queries, and application programs that process a database.

Database application system Applications with the standard five components that make database data more accessible and useful. Users employ a database application that consists of forms, formatted reports, queries, and application programs. Each of these, in turn, calls on the database management system (DBMS) to process the database tables.

Database management system (DBMS) A program used to create, process, and administer a database.

Database tier In the three-tier architecture, the tier that runs the DBMS and receives and processes requests to retrieve and store data.

Data-mining system Information system that processes data using sophisticated statistical techniques, such as regression analysis and decision-tree analysis, to find patterns and relationships that cannot be found by simpler operations, such as sorting, grouping, and averaging.

DB2 A popular, enterprise-class DBMS product from IBM.

Decision support systems (DSSs) Systems that focus on making data collected in OLTP useful for decision making.

Denial of service (DOS) Security problem in which users are not able to access an information system; can be caused by human errors, natural disaster, or malicious activity.

Dependencies When one activity must be completed before the other one can begin.

Desktop virtualization Also called client virtualization and PC virtualization. The process of storing a user's desktop on a remote server. It enables users to run their desktop from many different client computers.

Dial-up modem A modem that performs the conversion between analog and digital in such a way that the signal can be carried on a regular telephone line.

Diffusion of innovation The process by which an innovation is communicated through certain channels over time among the members of a social system.

Digital subscriber line (DSL) modem A special telephone line that connects home and small-business computers to an ISP.

Dirty data Problematic data. Examples are a value of *B* for customer gender and a value of *213* for customer age. Other examples are a value of *999-999-9999* for a North American phone number, a part colour of *green*, and an email address of *WhyMe@GuessWhoIAM.org*. All these values are problematic when data mining.

Disintermediation Elimination of one or more middle layers in the supply chain.

Disruptive technology A product that introduces a very new package of attributes from the accepted mainstream products.

Domain name system (DNS) A system that converts user-friendly names into their IP addresses. Any registered, valid name is called a *domain name.*

Drill down With an OLAP report, to further divide the data into more detail.

Drive-by sniffers People who take computers with wireless connections through an area and search for unprotected wireless networks in an attempt to gain free internet access or to gather unauthorized data.

Dual processor A computer with two CPUs.

Dynamo A nonrelational data store developed by Amazon.com.

Ecommerce The buying and selling of goods and services over public and private computer networks.

Ecommerce auctions Applications that match buyers and sellers by using an ecommerce version of a standard auction. This ecommerce application enables the auction company to offer goods for sale and to support a competitive bidding process.

E-cycling The recycling of electronic materials.

Effective business process A business process that enables the organization to accomplish its strategy.

Effectiveness Doing the right things.

Efficiency A measure of productiveness also refers to accomplishing a business process either more quickly with the same resources or as quickly with fewer resources.

Elastic In cloud computing, the situation that exists when the amount of resource leased can be dynamically increased or decreased, programmatically, in a short span of time, and organizations pay for just the resources that they use. This term was first used in this way by Amazon.com.

Electronic exchanges Sites that facilitate the matching of buyers and sellers; the business process is similar to that of a stock exchange. Sellers offer goods at a given price through the electronic exchange, and buyers make offers to purchase over the same exchange. Price matches result in transactions from which the exchange takes a commission.

Email spoofing A synonym for *phishing.* A technique for obtaining unauthorized data that uses pretexting via email. The *phisher* pretends to be a legitimate company and sends email requests for confidential data, such as account numbers, social insurance numbers, account passwords, and so forth. Phishers direct traffic to their sites under the guise of a legitimate business.

Encapsulated A characteristic of systems design in which the details of a process are hidden from users of that process. A formal interface is defined for the process that specifies how the process is to be accessed, what data it requires, and the data that it will produce. The means by which that process creates those results are never exposed, nor do they need to be.

Encryption The process of transforming clear text into coded, unintelligible text for secure storage or communication.

ENERGY STAR An international government–industry partnership that is intended to produce equipment that meets high-energy efficiency specifications or promotes the use of such equipment.

Enterprise application integration (EAI) An approach to combining functional systems that uses layers of software as a bridge to connect different functional systems together.

Enterprise architect Manages the company's complex information systems.

Enterprise DBMS A product that processes large organizational and workgroup databases. These products support many users, perhaps thousands, and many different database applications. Such DBMS products support 24/7 operations and can manage databases that span dozens of different magnetic disks with hundreds of gigabytes or more of data. IBM's DB2, Microsoft's SQL Server, and Oracle's Oracle are examples of enterprise DBMS products.

Enterprise resource planning (ERP) system The integration of all the organization's principal processes. ERP is an outgrowth of MRP II manufacturing systems, and most ERP users are manufacturing companies.

Entity In the E-R data model, a representation of something that users want to track. Some entities represent a physical object; others represent a logical construct or transaction.

Entity-relationship (E-R) data model Popular technique for creating a data model, in which developers define the things that will be stored and the relationships among them.

Entity-relationship (E-R) diagram A type of diagram used by database designers to document entities and their relationships to one another.

Ethernet Another name for the IEEE 802.3 protocol, Ethernet is a network protocol that operates at Layers 1 and 2 of the TCP/IP–OSI architecture. Ethernet, the world's most popular LAN protocol, is used on WANs as well.

E-waste Electronic garbage.

Exabytes 10^{18} bytes.

Expert systems Knowledge-sharing systems that are created by interviewing experts in a given business domain and codifying the rules used by those experts.

External entity (Interface) An element in a data flow diagram that signifies a component that is outside of the internal system being considered.

Facilities Structures used within a business process.

Fields Also called *columns*, groups of bytes in a database table. A database table has multiple columns that are used to represent the attributes of an entity. Examples are *PartNumber, EmployeeName,* and *SalesDate.*

File A group of similar rows or records. In a database, sometimes called a *table.*

File Transfer Protocol, or ftp A Layer-5 TCP/IP protocol used to copy files from one computer to another. In interorganizational transaction processing, ftp enables users to easily exchange large files.

Firewall A computing device located between a firm's internal and external networks that prevents unauthorized access to or from the internal network. A firewall can be a special-purpose computer or it can be a program on a general-purpose computer or a router.

Firmware Computer software that is installed on devices, such as printers, print services, and various types of communication devices. The software is coded just like other software, but it is installed on special, programmable memory of the printer or other device.

Five forces model A model proposed by Michael Porter that assesses industry characteristics and profitability by means of five competitive forces—bargaining power of suppliers, threat of substitutions, bargaining power of customers, rivalry among firms, and threat of new entrants.

Five-component framework The five fundamental components of an information system—computer hardware, software, data, procedures, and people—that are present in every information system, from the simplest to the most complex.

Foreign keys A column or group of columns used to represent relationships. Values of the foreign key match values of the primary key in a different (foreign) table.

Form Data entry forms are used to read, insert, modify, and delete database data.

Freemium A revenue model offering a basic service for free and then charging a premium for upgrades or advanced features.

Functional silos An organizational area (such as marketing or finance) that operates without considering other organizational areas.

Functional systems The second era of information systems. The goal of such systems was to facilitate the work of a single department or function. Over time, in each functional area, companies added features and functions to encompass more activities and to provide more value and assistance.

Gantt chart A project management diagram that depicts a project schedule and task relationships.

Gigabyte (GB) 1024 megabytes.

Global Positioning System (GPS) A collection of dozens of satellites orbiting the earth that transmit precise microwave signals. A GPS receiver can calculate its position by measuring the distance between itself and several of the satellites.

Governance Using a committee to decide on expectations for performance, to authorize appropriate resources and power to meet expectations, and perhaps eventually to verify whether expectations have been met.

Granularity The level of detail in data. Customer name and account balance are large granularity data. Customer name, balance, and the order details and payment history of every customer order are smaller granularity.

Green IT Using information technology resources to better support the triple bottom line for organizations.

Group decision support systems (GDSSs) An application that enables more than one individual to undertake a decision. Often includes voting and brainstorming functions.

GNU A set of tools for creating and managing open source software. Originally created to develop an open source Unix-like operating system.

GNU general public license (GPL) agreement One of the standard license agreements for open source software.

Hacking Occurs when a person gains unauthorized access to a computer system. Although some people hack for the sheer joy of doing it, other hackers invade systems for the malicious purpose of stealing or modifying data.

Hardening The process of taking extraordinary measures to reduce a system's vulnerability. Hardened sites use special versions of the operating system, and they lock down or eliminate operating systems features and functions that are not required by the application. Hardening is a technical safeguard.

Hardware Electronic components and related gadgetry that input, process, output, store, and communicate data according to instructions encoded in computer programs or software.

Hertz Cycles of CPU speed.

Hop In an internet, the movement from one network to another.

Horizontal-market application Software that provides capabilities common across all organizations and industries; examples include word processors, graphics programs, spreadsheets, and presentation programs.

Host operating system In virtualization, the operating system that hosts the virtual operating systems.

Hot sites Remote processing centres in an advanced state of readiness that have equipment companies need to continue operations in the event of a loss of their main computing sites (see *Cold* and *Warm sites*).

https An indication that a Web browser is using the SSL/TLS protocol to provide secure communications.

Human capital The investment in human knowledge and skills with the expectation of future gain.

Human safeguard Steps taken to protect against security threats by establishing appropriate procedures for users to follow for system use.

Hypertext transfer protocol (HTTP) A Layer-5 protocol used to process webpages.

ICANN (Internet Corporation for Assigned Names and Numbers) The organization responsible for managing the assignment of public IP addresses and domain names for use on the Internet. Each public IP address is unique across all computers on the Internet.

Identification The process whereby an information system identifies a user by requiring the user to sign on with a user name and password.

Identifier An attribute (or group of attributes) whose value is associated with one and only one entity instance.

Identity theft Stealing, misrepresenting, or hijacking the identity of another person or business.

IEEE 802.11 protocol A standard for packaging and managing traffic on wireless local area networks.

IEEE 802.3 protocol This standard, also called *Ethernet*, is a network protocol that operates at Layers 1 and 2 of the TCP/IP–OSI architecture. Ethernet, the world's most popular LAN protocol, is used on WANs as well.

Implementation A step in the decision-making process in which decision makers implement the alternative they have selected.

Industry standard processes Processes built into business applications from companies such as Oracle or SAP.

Influencer An individual in a social network whose opinion can force a change in others' behaviour and beliefs.

Information (1) Knowledge derived from data, where the term *data* is defined as recorded facts or figures. (2) Data presented in a meaningful context. (3) Data processed by summing, ordering, averaging, grouping, comparing, or other similar operations. (4) A difference that makes a difference.

Information and Communications Technology (ICT) Sector Provides products and services that other industries rely on to get their work done.

Information overload An overabundance of irrelevant data.

Information system (IS) A group of components that interact to produce information.

Information systems audit An audit focusing on information resources that are used to collect, store, process, and retrieve information.

Information Systems Audit and Control Association (ISACA) A key organization in developing knowledge and standards relating to information systems audits and information systems governance.

Information systems ethics Concern for the people whose lives can be affected by our actions.

Information technology (IT) The products, methods, inventions, and standards that are used for the purpose of producing information.

Information Technology Infrastructure Library (ITIL) A well-recognized collection of books providing a framework of best practice approaches to IT operations. ITIL provides a large set of management procedures that are designed to support businesses in achieving value from IT operations.

Information technology project management (ITPM) The collection of techniques and methods that project managers use to plan, coordinate, and complete IT projects.

Infrastructure as a service (IaaS) The cloud hosting of a bare server computer or data storage.

Innovation Rogers' five characteristics: relative advantage, compatibility, complexity, trialability, and observability.

Input devices Hardware devices that attach to a computer; for example, keyboards, mouse, document scanners, and barcode (Universal Product Code) scanners.

Instruction set The collection of instructions that a computer can process.

Intellectual property A form of creative endeavour that can be protected through a trademark, patent, copyright, industrial design, or integrated circuit topography.

Intelligence gathering The first step in the decision-making process in which decision makers determine what is to be decided, what the criteria for selection will be, and what data are available.

Internet Either a private network of networks or, more commonly, the public network known as the internet.

Internet of Things (IoT) The idea that objects are becoming connected to the Internet so they can interact with other devices, applications, or services.

Internet service provider (ISP) An ISP provides a user with a legitimate internet address, it serves as the user's gateway to the internet, and it passes communications back and forth between the user and the internet. ISPs also pay for the internet. They collect money from their customers and pay access fees and other charges on the users' behalf.

Interorganizational systems Information systems processing of routine transactions between two or more organizations.

Intranet An intranet is a private network created, accessed and supported by technologies typically used and supported by the public internet (i.e. browsers, HTML etc).

iOS The operating system used on the iPhone, iPod Touch, and iPad.

IP address A series of dotted decimals in a format, such as 192.168.2.28, which identifies a unique device on a network or internet. With the IPv4 standard, IP addresses have 32 bits. With the IPv6 standard, IP addresses have 128 bits. Today, IPv4 is more common but will likely be supplanted by IPv6 in the future. With IPv4, the decimal between the dots can never exceed 255.

IP spoofing A type of spoofing whereby an intruder uses another site's IP address as if it were that other site.

IPv4 The most commonly used Internet layer protocol; has a four-decimal dotted notation, such as 165.193.123.253.

IPv6 An Internet layer protocol that uses 128-bit addresses and is gradually replacing IPv4.

IT architecture The basic framework for all the computers, systems, and information management that support organizational services.

IT operations Service, maintenance, protection, and management of IT infrastructure.

IT project risk Structural risk, volatility risk, and project process; performance, knowledge resources, organizational support, project management practices, and both process and product performance.

IT projects Projects of all shapes and sizes that renew and adapt IT infrastructure.

IT Services Commonly used name for service area within organizations focused on providing basic computing infrastructure, networking and security, standard business applications, and end user support.

JSON (JavaScript Object Notation) A markup language (such as html) used for transmitting documents. Contains little metadata and is preferred for transmitting volumes of data between servers and browsers. While the notation is the format of JavaScript objects, JSON documents can be processed by any language.

Just barely so (information) Information that meets the purpose for which it is generated, but just barely so.

Key (1) A column or group of columns that identifies a unique row in a table. (2) A number used to encrypt data. The encryption algorithm applies the key to the original message to produce the coded message. Decoding (decrypting) a message is similar; a key is applied to the coded message to recover the original text.

Key escrow A control procedure whereby a trusted party is given a copy of a key used to encrypt database data.

Kilobyte (KB) 1024 bytes.

Knowledge management (KM) systems Information systems for storing and retrieving organizational knowledge, whether that knowledge is in the form of data, documents, or employee know-how.

Lean production A manufacturing method focused on using resources as efficiently as possible.

Level-0 diagram The most basic level of data flow diagram.

Level-1 diagram A data flow diagram that shows basic processes contained within a system.

Levelling Creating a series of data flow diagrams that incrementally show more levels of detail within a system.

License An agreement that stipulates how a program can be used. Most specify the number of computers on which the program can be installed and sometimes the number of users that can connect to and use the program remotely. Such agreements also stipulate limitations on the liability of the software vendor for the consequences of errors in the software.

Lift In market-basket terminology, the ratio of confidence to the base probability of buying an item. Lift shows how much the base probability changes when other products are purchased. If the lift is greater than 1, the change is positive; if it is less than 1, the change is negative.

Linux A version of Unix that was developed by the open-source community. The open-source community owns Linux, and there is no fee to use it. Linux is a popular operating system for web servers.

Local area network (LAN) A network that connects computers that reside in a single geographical location on the premises of the company that operates the LAN. The number of connected computers can range from two to several hundred.

Logistic expense The costs associated with the coordination or movement, transportation, and storage of goods or services, particularly if the supply chain involves multiple parties or remote locations.

Lost-update problem An issue in multiuser database processing, in which two or more users try to make changes to the data but the database cannot make all the changes because it was not designed to process changes from multiple users.

MAC (media access control) address Also called *physical address*. A permanent address given to each network interface card (NIC) at the factory. This address enables the device to access the network via a Level-2 protocol. By agreement among computer manufacturers, MAC addresses are assigned in such a way that no two NIC devices will ever have the same MAC address.

Mac OS An operating system developed by Apple Computer, Inc., for the Macintosh. The current version is Mac OS X. Mac OS was developed for the PowerPC but, as of 2006, runs on Intel processors as well.

Machine code Code compiled from source code and ready to be processed by a computer. Cannot be understood by humans.

Macro-viruses Viruses that attach themselves to Word, Excel, PowerPoint, or other types of documents. When the infected document is opened, the virus places itself in the startup files of the application. After that, the virus infects every file that the application creates or processes.

Main memory A set of cells in which each cell holds a byte of data or instruction; each cell has an address, and the CPU uses the addresses to identify particular data items.

Mainframe The first digital computing machine used in business and government.

Maintenance phase Last part of the SDLC, which starts the process all over again.

Malware Viruses, worms, spyware, and adware.

Malware definitions Patterns that exist in malware code. Anti-malware vendors update these definitions continuously and incorporate them in their products in order to better fight against malware.

Management information systems (MIS) Information systems that help businesses achieve their goals and objectives.

Managerial decisions Decisions that concern the allocation and use of resources.

Manual system An information system in which the activity of processing information is done by people, without the use of automated processing.

Many-to-many (N:M) relationship A relationship involving two entity types in which an instance of one type can relate to many instances of the second type, and an instance of the second type can relate to many instances of the first. For example, the relationship between Student and Class is N:M. One student may enroll in many classes and one class may have many students. Contrast with *one-to-many (1:N) relationship*.

Margin The difference between value and cost.

Market-basket analysis A data-mining technique for determining sales patterns. A market-basket analysis shows the products that customers tend to buy together.

Maximum cardinality The maximum number of entities that can be involved in a relationship. Common examples of maximum cardinality are 1:N, N:M, and 1:1.

M-commerce Short for *mobile commerce*, its applications allow mobile phones to conduct certain kinds of transactions, such as mobile banking and mobile ticket purchases at movie theatres and sporting events.

Megabyte (MB) 1024 kilobytes.

Memory swapping The movement of programs and data into and out of memory. If a computer has insufficient memory for its workload, such swapping will degrade system performance.

Merchant companies In ecommerce, companies that take title to the goods they sell. They buy goods and resell them.

Metadata Data that describe data.

Microcomputer Smaller than mainframes, the precursor to personal computers.

Microsoft Windows The most popular nonmobile client operating system. Also refers to Windows Server, a popular server operating system that competes with Linux.

Minimum cardinality The minimum number of entities that must be involved in a relationship.

Modem Short for *modulator/demodulator*, a modem converts the computer's digital data into signals that can be transmitted over telephone or cable lines.

Modern-style applications Windows applications that are touch-screen oriented and provide context-sensitive, pop-up menus.

Monetize A social media company's ability to make money from its application, service, or content.

Moore's Law A law, created by Gordon Moore, stating that the number of transistors per square inch on an integrated chip doubles every 18 months. Moore's prediction has proved generally accurate in the 40 years since it was made. Sometimes, this law is stated as the speed of a computer chip doubles every 18 months. While not strictly true, this version gives the gist of the idea.

Multiuser processing When multiple users process the database at the same time.

MySQL A popular open-source DBMS product that is licence-free for most applications.

Native applications A software application that requires programs other than just the browser on a user's computer; that is, that requires code on both client and server computers. See also *thick-client application*.

Net neutrality The idea that all data should be treated equally as it passes between networks regardless of its type, source, or quantity.

Network A collection of computers that communicate with one another over transmission lines.

Network externality The larger the number of people using a network, the more valuable that network becomes.

Network interface card (NIC) A hardware component on each device on a network (computer, printer, etc.) that connects the device's circuitry to the communications line. The NIC works together with programs in each device to implement Layers 1 and 2 of the TCP/IP–OSI hybrid protocol.

Neural networks A popular supervised data-mining technique used to predict values and make classifications, such as good prospect or poor prospect.

Nonmerchant companies Ecommerce companies that arrange for the purchase and sale of goods without ever owning or taking title to those goods.

Nonvolatile (memory) Memory that preserves data contents even when not powered (e.g., magnetic and optical disks). With such devices, you can turn the computer off and back on, and the contents will be unchanged.

Normal form A classification of tables according to their characteristics and the kinds of problems they have.

Normalization The process of converting poorly structured tables into two or more well-structured tables.

Off-the-shelf software Commercial software.

Off-the-shelf with alterations software Commercial software that has been modified for a particular organization.

Onboard NIC A built-in NIC.

One-of-a-kind application Software that is developed for a specific, unique need, usually for a particular company's operations.

One-to-many (1:N) relationship A relationship involving two entity types in which an instance of one type can relate to many instances of the second type, but an instance of the second type can relate to at most one instance of the first. For example, the relationship between Department and Employee is 1:N. A department may relate to many employees, but an employee relates to at most one department.

Online analytic processing (OLAP) A dynamic type of reporting system that provides the ability to sum, count, average, and perform other simple arithmetic operations on groups of data. Such reports are dynamic because users can change the format of the reports while viewing them.

Online transaction processing (OLTP) Collecting data electronically and processing transactions online.

Open-source community A loosely coupled group of programmers who mostly volunteer their time to contribute code to develop and maintain common software. Linux and MySQL are two prominent products developed by such a community.

Operating system (OS) A computer program that controls the computer's resources: It manages the contents of main memory, processes keystrokes and mouse movements, sends signals to the display monitor, reads and writes disk files, and controls the processing of other programs.

Operational decisions Decisions that concern the day-to-day activities of an organization.

Optical fibre cable A type of cable used to connect the computers, printers, switches, and other devices on a LAN. The signals on such cables are light rays, and they are reflected inside the glass core of the optical fibre cable. The core is surrounded by a *cladding* to contain the light signals, and the cladding, in turn, is wrapped with an outer layer to protect it.

Oracle Software company focused on large scale database systems providing enterprise global cloud computing.

Organizational feasibility One of four dimensions of feasibility.

Output hardware Hardware that displays the results of the computer's processing. It consists of video displays, printers, audio speakers, overhead projectors, and other special-purpose devices, such as large flatbed plotters.

Outsourcing The process of hiring another organization to perform a service. Outsourcing is done to save costs, to gain expertise, and to free up management time.

Over the Internet When applied to cloud computing, the provisioning of worldwide servers over the Internet.

Packet A formatted message that passes through networks.

Packet switching network A system in which messages are first disassembled into small packets, then sent through the network and reassembled at the destination.

Packet-filtering firewall A firewall that examines each packet and determines whether to let the packet pass. To make this decision, it examines the source address, the destination addresses, and other data.

Parallel installation A type of system conversion in which the new system runs in parallel with the old one for a while. Parallel installation is expensive because the organization incurs the costs of running both systems.

Patches A group of fixes for high-priority failures that can be applied to existing copies of a particular product. Software vendors supply patches to fix security and other critical problems.

Payload The program code of a virus that causes unwanted or hurtful actions, such as deleting programs or data or, even worse, modifying data in ways that are undetected by the user.

Pay-per-click Revenue model in which advertisers display ads to potential customers for free and pay only when the customer clicks.

PC virtualization Synonym for desktop virtualization.

Peering Exchanging information between telecommunication providers without charging an access fee.

People As part of the five-component framework, one of the five fundamental components of an information system; this component includes those who operate and service the computers, those who maintain the data, those who support the networks, and those who use the system.

Personal area network (PAN) A computer network used for moving data across personal devices such as computers, tablets, and phones.

Personal computers (PCs) Classic computing devices that are used by individuals. Examples of PCs include laptop or desktop computers.

Personal DBMS DBMS products designed for smaller, simpler database applications. Such products are used for personal or small workgroup applications that involve fewer than 100 users and normally fewer than 15. Today, Microsoft Access is the only prominent personal DBMS.

Personal identification number (PIN) A form of authentication whereby the user supplies a number that only he or she knows.

Personal Information Protection and Electronic Documents Act (PIPEDA) In Canada, PIPEDA gives individuals the right to know why an organization collects, uses, or discloses their personal information.

Petabytes 10^{15} bytes.

Phased installation A type of system conversion in which the new system is installed in pieces across the organization(s). Once a given piece works, then the organization installs and tests another piece of the system, until the entire system has been installed.

Phishing A technique for obtaining unauthorized data that uses pretexting via email. The *phisher* pretends to be a legitimate company and sends an email requesting confidential data, such as account numbers, social insurance numbers, account passwords, and so forth.

Pilot installation A type of system conversion in which the organization implements the entire system on a limited portion of the business. The advantage of pilot implementation is that if the system fails, the failure is contained within a limited boundary. This reduces exposure of the business and also protects the new system from developing a negative reputation throughout the organization(s).

Pivot Tables Application provided in Microsoft Excel that defines a 2 dimensional data table and provides a interactive visual querying/summarization capability that allows users to pivot through various views of a defined data set.

PixelSense The Microsoft product formerly known as Surface. It allows many users to process the same tabletop touch interface. Primarily used in hotels and entertainment centres.

Platform as a service (PaaS) Vendors provide hosted computers, an operating system, and possibly a DBMS.

Plunge installation Sometimes called *direct installation*, a type of system conversion in which the organization shuts off the old system and starts the new system. If the new system fails, the organization is in trouble: Nothing can be done until either the new system is fixed or the old system is reinstalled. Because of the risk, organizations should avoid this conversion style if possible.

Pooled The situation in which many different organizations use the same physical hardware.

Port A number used to uniquely identify a transaction over a network.

Predecessor In project management, it is a work package that must come before another work package can be completed.

Pretexting A technique for gathering unauthorized information in which someone pretends to be someone else. A common scam involves a telephone caller who pretends to be from a credit card company and claims to be checking the validity of credit card numbers. *Phishing* is also a form of pretexting.

Price conflict Differences in the price of a good or service based on the way that it is obtained or delivered. For example, U.S. prices may be lower than Canadian prices even after adjusting for currency exchange rate, or online products may cost less than those sold in traditional stores. 286 See also *Channel conflict* and *Showrooming*.

Price elasticity A measure of the sensitivity in demand to changes in price. It is the ratio of the percentage change in quantity divided by the percentage change in price.

Primary activities In Michael Porter's value chain model, the fundamental activities that create value—inbound logistics, operations, outbound logistics, marketing/sales, and service.

Private cloud In-house hosting, delivered via Web service standards, which can be dynamically configured.

Private IP address A private IP address is a non-internet facing IP address on a private or internal network. Private IP addresses need not be unique beyond their specific domain.

Procedures Instructions for humans. One of the five fundamental components of an information system.

Process Symbolizes a set of related activities.

Process aware When people view their actions in the light of the larger business process and think about ways to improve the processes they are involved in.

Process blueprint In an ERP product, a comprehensive set of inherent processes for organizational activities.

Process modelling applications Computer programs that enable the drawing of models of business processes.

Process modelling techniques Collections of diagrams and instructions for creating process models of information systems.

Processing devices Computing technology that allow for the modification, storage, or deletion of data.

Product quality assurance (PQA) The testing of a system. PQA personnel usually construct a test plan with the advice and assistance of users. PQA test engineers perform testing, and they also supervise user-test activity. Many PQA professionals are programmers who write automated test programs.

Production systems The entire set of systems that support operations.

Productivity The creation of business value.

Productivity paradox The lack of evidence of an increase in worker productivity associated with the massive increase in investment in information technology.

Project management body of knowledge (PMBOK) Provides project managers, sponsors, and team leaders with a large array of accepted project management techniques and practices.

Product management professionals (PMPs) Individuals certified by the Product Management Institute as having product management skills.

Protocol A standardized means for coordinating an activity between two or more entities.

Public IP address A public IP address is a unique address that conforms to the global internet addressing schema and publicly identifies a particular IP location.

Quad processor A computer with four CPUs.

Query A request for data from a database.

Random access memory (RAM) Memory that is external to the processing unit that is used for primary working memory in a computing system.

Records Also called *rows*, groups of columns in a database table.

Regression analysis A type of supervised data mining that estimates the values of parameters in a linear equation. Used to determine the relative influence of variables on an outcome and also to predict future values of that outcome.

Relation The more formal name for a database table.

Relational databases Databases that carry their data in the form of tables and that represent relationships using foreign keys.

Relationship Association among entities or entity instances in an E-R model or an association among rows of a table in a relational database.

Relevant (information) Information that is appropriate to both the context and the subject.

Report A presentation of data in a structured, or meaningful, context.

Reporting systems Systems that create information from disparate data sources and deliver that information to the proper users on a timely basis.

Repository In a business process model, a collection of something; for example, a database is a repository of data.

Requirements analysis phase The second phase in the SDLC, in which developers conduct user interviews, evaluate existing systems, determine new forms/reports/queries, identify new features and functions, including security, and create the data model.

Resource Sheet view The view of employees available to work on a project in Microsoft Project.

Resource Usage view The view of how much a particular employee is being used on a project in Microsoft Project.

Resources Items of value, such as inventory or funds, that are part of a business process.

Review The final step in the decision-making process, in which decision makers evaluate results of their decision and, if necessary, repeat the process to correct or adapt the decision.

RFM analysis A way of analyzing and ranking customers according to their purchasing patterns.

Ribbon The wide bar of tools and selections that appears just under the tabs in Microsoft Office programs.

Role In a business process, a collection of activities.

Router A special-purpose computer that moves network traffic from one node on a network to another.

Rows Also called *records*, groups of columns in a database table.

SAP R/3 A software product licensed by German company SAP that integrates business activities into *inherent processes* across an organization.

Sarbanes-Oxley Act (SOX) Law passed by the U.S. Congress in 2002 that governs the reporting requirements of publicly held companies. Among other things, it strengthened requirements for internal controls and management's responsibility for accurate financial reporting.

Schedule feasibility One of four dimensions of feasibility.

Security threats A problem with the security of information or the data therein, caused by human error, malicious activity, or natural disasters.

Self-driving car An autonomous, or driverless, car that uses a variety of sensors to navigate like a traditional car but without human intervention.

Sequence Flow Diagram element used to show the order in which activities in a business process are performed.

Server farm A large collection of server computers that coordinates the activities of the servers, usually for commercial purposes.

Servers Computers that provide certain types of service, such as hosting a database, running a blog, publishing a website, or selling goods. Server computers are faster, larger, and more powerful than client computers.

Server tier In the three-tier architecture, the tier that consists of computers that run Web servers for generating Web pages and responding to requests from browsers. Web servers also process application programs.

Server virtualization The process of running two or more operating system instances on the same server. The host operating system runs virtual operating system instances as applications.

Service-oriented architecture (SOA) A design philosophy that dictates that all interactions among computing devices are defined as services in a formal, standardized way. SOA makes the cloud possible.

Service packs A large group of fixes that solve low-priority software problems. Users apply service packs in much the same way that they apply patches, except that service packs typically involve fixes to hundreds or thousands of problems.

Showrooming A customer visits a store to examine or gain information about a product but then purchases the product online.

Simple Mail Transfer Protocol, or smtp A TCP/IP protocol used for email transmission.

Site License A type of software license that allows the installation of a software application in several computers simultaneously, usually a particular site or multiple sites.

Six sigma A business process improvement method developed by Motorola that focuses on developing quality.

Skills Framework for the Information Age (SFIA) A set of skills thought to be useful for those employees focused on developing and maintaining information technology.

Small office/home office (SOHO) A business office with usually fewer than 10 employees, often located in the business professional's home.

Smart card A plastic card similar to a credit card that has a microchip. The microchip, which holds much more data than a magnetic strip, is loaded with identifying data. Normally, it requires a PIN.

Smart device A device that has processing power, memory, network connectivity, and the ability to interconnect with other devices and applications.

Smartphone Phones that combine a powerful processor with sophisticated operating systems and cellular network technology to provide a host of applications to their users including voice, text, email, web browsing, and much more.

Sniffing A technique for intercepting computer communications. With wired networks, sniffing requires a physical connection to the network. With wireless networks, no such connection is required.

SOAP A protocol for requesting Web services and for sending responses to Web service requests.

Social capital The investment in social relations with expectation of future returns in the marketplace.

Social CRM CRM that includes social networking elements and gives the customer much more power and control in the customer/vendor relationship.

Social media (SM) The use of information technology to support the sharing of content among networks of users.

Social media information system (SMIS) An information system that supports the sharing of content among networks of users.

Social media policy A statement that delineates employees' rights and responsibilities when generating social media content.

Social media providers Companies that provide platforms that enable the creation of social networks. Facebook, Twitter, LinkedIn, and Google are all social media providers.

Social networking (SN)/Social networks: The social relationships among people with common interests.

Software Instructions for computers. One of the five fundamental components of an information system.

Software as a service (SaaS) Leasing hardware infrastructure, operating systems, and application programs to another organization.

Solver Application provided in the Analysis Pak add-in within Microsoft Excel that provides capability for goal programming and linear programming.

Source code Computer code written by humans and understandable by humans. Source code must be translated into machine code before it can be processed.

Spam Unwanted email messages.

Special function devices Devices that can be added to the computer to augment the computer's basic capabilities.

Spoofing When someone pretends to be someone else with the intent of obtaining unauthorized data. If you pretend to be your professor, you are spoofing your professor.

Spreadsheet A table of data having rows and columns.

Spyware Programs installed on the user's computer without the user's knowledge or permission that reside in the background and, unknown to the user, observe the user's actions and keystrokes, modify computer activity, and report the user's activities to sponsoring organizations. Malicious spyware captures keystrokes to obtain user names, passwords, account numbers, and other sensitive information. Other spyware is used for marketing analyses, observing what users do, websites visited, products examined and purchased, and so forth.

SQL Server A popular enterprise-class DBMS product from Microsoft.

Storage hardware Hardware that saves data and programs. Magnetic disk is by far the most common storage device, although optical disks, such as CDs and DVDs, also are popular, and semiconductor-based storage (also called solid-state drives) are gaining marketshare.

Strategic decisions Decisions that concern broader-scope, organizational issues.

Strength of a relationship In social media, the likelihood that a person or other organization in a relationship will do something that will benefit the organization.

Structured decision A type of decision for which there is a formalized and accepted method for making the decision.

Structured Query Language (SQL) An international standard language for processing database data.

Subtask The hierarchy of tasks within a project in Microsoft Project.

Sufficient (information) Adequate information to perform the task.

SUM A shorthand way of summing the values in a set of Excel cells using a function built in to the program.

Supervised data mining A form of data mining in which data miners develop a model prior to the analysis and apply statistical techniques to data to estimate values of the parameters of the model.

Supplier relationship management (SRM) A business process for managing all contacts between an organization and its suppliers.

Supply chain A network of organizations and facilities that transforms raw materials into products delivered to customers.

Supply chain management An information system that integrates the primary inbound logistics business activity.

Support activities In Michael Porter's value chain model, the activities that contribute indirectly to value creation—procurement, technology, human resources, and the firm's infrastructure.

Sustained competitive advantage The development of people and procedures that are well supported by the underlying technology.

Sustaining technologies Changes in technology that maintain the rate of improvement in customer value.

Swimlane format A type of business process diagram. Like swim lanes in a swimming pool, each role is shown in its own horizontal rectangle. Swimlane format can be used to simplify process diagrams and to draw attention to interactions among components of the diagram.

Switch A special-purpose computer that receives and transmits data across a network.

Switching costs The process of locking in customers by making it difficult or expensive for them to switch to another product.

Symbian A now defunct mobile operating systems designed for early smartphones.

Symmetric digital subscriber lines (SDSL) DSL lines that have the same upload and download speeds.

System conversion The process of *converting* a business activity from the old system to the new.

System definition phase The first phase in the SDLC, in which developers, with the help of eventual users, define the new system's goals and scope, assess its feasibility, form a project team, and plan the project.

Systems analysis The process of creating and maintaining information systems, sometimes called *systems development*.

Systems analysts Information systems professionals who understand both business and technology. They are active throughout the systems development process and play a key role in moving the project from conception to conversion and, ultimately, maintenance. Systems analysts integrate the work of the programmers, testers, and users.

Systems development The process of creating and maintaining information systems. It is sometimes called *systems analysis and design*.

Systems development life cycle (SDLC) The classic process used to develop information systems. These basic tasks of systems development are combined into the following phases: system definition, requirements analysis, component design, implementation, and system maintenance (fix or enhance).

Table Also called a *file*, a group of similar rows or records in a database.

Tablets Computing device that allows interaction through a flat touch screen.

Tailor made (software) Software adapted to a particular organization's needs.

TCP/IP protocol architecture A protocol architecture having five layers and one or more protocols defined at each layer. Programs are written to implement the rules of a particular protocol.

Technical feasibility One of four dimensions of feasibility.

Technical safeguards Safeguards that involve the hardware and software components of an information system.

Terabyte (TB) 1024 gigabytes.

Test plan Groups of sequences of actions that users will take when using the new system.

Thick-client applications A software application that requires programs other than just the browser on a user's computer—that is, that requires code on both a client and server computers.

Thin-client applications A software application that requires nothing more than a browser and can be run on only the user's computer.

Three-tier architecture Architecture used by most e-commerce server applications. The tiers refer to three different classes of computers. The user tier consists of users' computers that have browsers that request and process Web pages. The server tier consists of computers that run Web servers and in the process generate Web pages and other data in response to requests from browsers. Web servers also process application programs. The third tier is the database tier, which runs the DBMS that processes the database.

Timely information Information that is produced in time for its intended use.

Total quality management (TQM) A business process improvement method focused on improving quality.

Transaction processing system (TPS) An information system that supports operational decision making.

Transmission control program/Internet protocol (TCP/IP) Provides definition and specification of the network layers.

Transmission media Physical media, such as copper cable and optical fibre (glass fibre) cable, or wireless media transmitting light or radio frequencies (including cellular and satellite systems) which transmit electronic signals.

Triple bottom line A concept that expands the notion of traditional financial reports, which are based solely on financial performance, to take into account ecological and social performance.

Tunnel A virtual, private pathway over a public or shared network from the VPN client to the VPN server.

Unauthorized data disclosure Can occur because of human error when someone inadvertently releases data in violation of policy, or when employees unknowingly or carelessly release proprietary data to competitors or the media.

Unified Modelling Language (UML) A series of diagramming techniques that facilitates OOP development. UML has dozens of different diagrams for all phases of system development. UML does not require or promote any particular development process.

Uniform resource locator (URL) A document's address on the web. URLs begin on the right with a top-level domain, and, moving left, include a domain name and then are followed by optional data that locates a document within that domain.

Unix An operating system developed at Bell Labs in the 1970s. It has been the workhorse of the scientific and engineering communities since then.

Unshielded twisted pair (UTP) cable A type of cable used to connect the computers, printers, switches, and other devices on a LAN. A UTP cable has four pairs of twisted wire. A device called an *RJ-45 connector* is used to connect the UTP cable into NIC devices.

Unstructured decision A type of decision for which there is no agreed-on decision-making method.

Unsupervised data mining A form of data mining whereby the analysts do not create a model or hypothesis before running the analysis. Instead, they apply the data-mining technique to the data and observe the results. With this method, analysts create hypotheses after the analysis to explain the patterns found.

User tier In the three-tier architecture, the tier that consists of computers, phones, and other mobile devices that have browsers and request or process Web pages and other services.

User-generated content (UGC) Content on an organization's social media presence contributed by nonemployee users.

Users Individuals and organizations that use social media sites to build social relationships.

Value chain A network of value-creating activities.

Value of social capital Value of social network that is determined by the number of relationships in a social network, the strength of those relationships, and the resources controlled by those related.

Vertical market application Software that serves the needs of a specific industry. Examples of such programs are those used by dental offices to schedule appointments and bill patients, those used by auto mechanics to keep track of customer data and customers' automobile repairs, and those used by parts warehouses to track inventory, purchases, and sales.

Viral hook An inducement that causes someone to share an ad, link, file, picture, movie, or other resource with friends and associates over the Internet.

Virtual machines (vm) Computer programs that present the appearance of an independent operating system within a second host operating system. The host can support multiple virtual machines, possibly running different operating system programs (Windows, Linux), each of which is assigned assets such as disk space, devices, and network connections over which it has control.

Virtual private cloud (VPC) A subset of a public cloud that has highly restricted, secure access.

Virtual private network (VPN) A WAN connection alternative that uses the internet or a private internet to create the appearance of private point-to-point connections. In the IT world, the term *virtual* means something that appears to exist that does not exist in fact. A VPN usually uses the public internet to create the appearance of a private connection.

Virtualization The process whereby multiple operating systems run as clients on a single host operating system. Gives the appearance of many computers running on a single computer.

Virus A computer program that replicates itself; unchecked replication is like computer cancer, by which ultimately the virus consumes the computer's resources. Many viruses also take unwanted and harmful actions.

Volatile (memory) Data that will be lost when the computer or device is not powered.

WAN wireless A communications system that provides wireless connectivity to a wide area network.

Warm sites Remote processing centres that have some equipment that may be used in the event that an organization loses its primary computing facility. Readiness is somewhere between a *Cold site* and a *Hot site*.

Waterfall method A sequence of nonrepetitive phases.

Web 2.0 The term used to describe applications and platforms on the web.

Web crawler A software program that browses the web in a very methodical way.

Web page Document encoded in html that is created, transmitted, and consumed using the World Wide Web.

Web servers Programs that run on a server-tier computer and that manage http traffic by sending and receiving Web pages to and from clients and by processing client requests.

Web service standards Worldwide standards that programs use to declare what they do, the structure of the data they process, and the ways they will communicate.

Web services SOA-designed programs that comply with Web service standards.

Web storefront In ecommerce, a web-based application that enables customers to enter and manage their orders.

Wide area network (WAN) A network that connects computers located at different geographical locations.

Windows An operating system designed and sold by Microsoft. It is the most widely used operating system.

Windows 10 (mobile) A Windows operating system designed for mobile devices.

Wireless NIC (WNIC) Devices that enable wireless networks by communicating with wireless *access points*. Such devices can be cards that slide into the PCMA slot or they can be built-in, onboard devices. WNICs operate according to the 802.11 protocol.

Workbook A collection of worksheets in Microsoft Excel.

Workflow A process or procedure by which content is created, edited, used, and disposed.

Worksheet The basic structure of a spreadsheet in Microsoft Excel.

Worm A virus that propagates itself using the internet or some other computer network. Worm code is written specifically to infect another computer as quickly as possible.

Worth its cost (information) When an appropriate relationship exists between the cost of information and its value.

WSDL (Web Services Description Language) A standard for describing the services, inputs, outputs, and other data supported by a Web service. Documents coded according to this standard are machine readable and can be used by developer tools for creating programs to access the service.

XML (eXtensible Markup Language) A markup language used for transmitting documents. Contains much metadata that can be used to validate the format and completeness of the document, but includes considerable overhead.

Zachman framework Conceived by John Zachman at IBM in the 1980s, it divides systems into two dimensions, one based on six reasons for communication (*what*—data, *how*—function, *where*—network, *who*—people, *when*—time, *why*—motivation), and the other based on stakeholder groups (planner, owner, designer, builder, implementer, and worker). The intersection of these two dimensions helps to provide a relatively holistic view of the enterprise.

Zettabyte A unit of digital information that equates to one sextillion (10 exponent 21) bytes.

Zombies Subsequent computers infected with the worm or virus that infected an initial computer.

INDEX

Numbers

3D printing, 3, 13, 112–113, 113*f*
3D Systems, 113
3M, 206
5G mobile, 13
10/100/1000 Ethernet, 217

A

account acknowledgment form, 399*f*
account administration, 398–400
account management, 398
accurate information, 29
ACID (atomic, consistent, isolated, durable) transactions, 146–147
Ackoff, Russell, 260
activities
    automating, 31–32
    defined, 26, 45
activity logs, 401
actors, 45
Acxiom Corporation, 280, 298
ad-blocking software, 300
advertising, 299–302, 301*f*
adware, 393, 393*f*
agile methods, 335
Agile Project Managers, 330
Airbus, 127
alignment, 371
alternatives formulation, 36, 36*f*
Amazon, 62, 70–73, 71*f*
Amazon EC2 (Elastic Cloud 2), 201*f*
Amazon Marketplace Web Service (MWS), 73
Amazon S3 (Simple Storage Service), 201*f*
Amazon.com, 147, 197, 202, 291, 311, 313
analysis paralysis, 342
Android operating system, 116, 122
anti-spyware programs, 393
antivirus programs, 393
Apache, 121, 147
APIS Cor, 113
Apple, 62, 64, 109, 116, 117, 198*f*, 208, 311, 313, 315
Apple iCloud, 201, 201*f*
application service providers (ASPs), 344–345
application software
    custom-developed, 120, 121*f*
    defined, 119
    firmware, 121
    horizontal, 119–120, 121*f*
    modern-style applications, 115
    off-the-shelf, 120, 121*f*

off-the-shelf with alterations, 120, 121*f*
one-of-a-kind, 120, 121*f*
open source, 121–123
selecting, 120–121
terminology, 7
types of, 114, 114*f*, 119–121, 121*f*
vertical, 120, 121*f*
Arab Spring, 9
artificial intelligence, 13
assets, 266–267
Association for Computing Machinery's code of ethics, 376
attributes, 159
audits, 373–375
augmented reality, 13
authentication, 392
AutoCAD, 127
Autodesk, 127
automated systems, 31–32, 32*f*
autonomous vehicles, 110–112

B

backups, 395, 400, 400*f*, 402
Bag Borrow or Steal Inc., 236
Balanced Scorecard approach, 381
barriers, entry, 64
batch processing, 263–264
Bateson, Gregory, 28, 30
Bazaarvoice, 304
Beach, Gary, 376
Beane, Billy, 268
Bell Labs, 116
Benbasat, I., 371
beta testing, 340
"Better off Guessing" (MIT), 268
Bezos, Jeff, 72
Bieber, Justin, 314
Big Data, 275–276, 316
Bigtable, 147
binary digits, 106
biometric authentication, 392
bits, 106, 106*f*
Blackberry, 62, 64
Blast Radius, 366
blockchain, 13
Bluetooth, 218
Boeing, 342
Boivie, Catherine, 381
bounded rationality, 260
Bower, J., 61
Box, George, 30
Boxall, John, 211
bring your own device (BYOD), 210
Budget Measures Act (Bill 198), 372–373
bugs, 341*n*
bus tracking, 211

business analysts, 336, 365, 367*f*
business functions, 237
business intelligence (BI) systems
    categories of, 267*f*
    characteristics of, 267*f*
    compared to tools, 269
    competitive advantage of, 267*f*
    data mining systems, 267*f*
    expert systems, 267*f*, 268–269
    group decision support systems, 267, 267*f*
    knowledge management systems, 267*f*, 268
    reporting systems, 267, 267*f*
business process design
    challenges of, 242–243
    explained, 240–241
business process management (BPM), 30–31
business process modelling, 44–46, 45*f*
Business Process Modelling Notation (BPMN), 27, 44, 45*f*, 46*f*, 47*f*
business process redesign, 241
business processes
    change, challenges of, 242–243
    competitive advantage and, 64
    components of, 26–27
    counter sales, 32, 32*f*
    defined, 25, 44
    examples of, 25
    improvement of, 240–242
    industry standard processes, 243, 244*f*
    information, role in, 30–31
    information systems (IS) and, 31–34
    information technology (IT) and, 240–242
    interaction of, 25
    inventory management, 25*f*
    payment, 33, 33*f*
    process quality and, 47–49
    productivity and, 56–59
    purchasing, 33–34, 34*f*
    with single vendor repository, 48*f*
    supplier relationship management (SRM) and, 251
    value chains and, 57–59, 57*f*
business systems, 25
business technology management (BTM), 55–56
business value, 54–55
business-planning process, 334*f*
business-to-business (B2B), 291, 309, 309*f*
business-to-consumer (B2C), 291, 309, 309*f*
business-to-government (B2G), 309, 309*f*
Buyatab, 320–321
bytes, 107, 107*f*, 136

human-to-computer communication, 293
Hypertext Transport Protocol (http), 227

I

IAC, 303
IBM, 117, 140
ICANN (Internet Corporation for Assigned Names and Numbers), 221
iCloud, 201, 201*f*
"ICTS Jobs 2.0," 17
identification, 392
identifiers, 159
identity theft, 386, 387
IEEE 802 Committee, 217
IEEE 802.11 protocol, 218
IEEE 802.3 protocol, 217
if/then rules, 268–269
implementation, 36, 36*f*
implementation phase (of systems development), 334*f*, 338–340, 339*f*, 341*f*
implementation stage of diffusion, 63
inappropriate content, 303–305
inbound logistics, 291
incident response, 402–403, 402*f*
inconsistent data, 262, 262*f*
incorrect data modification, 389*f*, 390
Industrial Internet, 109–110
industry standard processes, 243, 244*f*
industry structure
    innovation and, 61
    organizational strategy and, 59–61
influencers, 295
information
    accuracy characteristic of, 29
    in business processes, 27, 30–31
    characteristics of, 29–30, 29*f*
    defined, 27–28, 143
    flows of, 30
    just barely sufficient characteristic of, 29–30
    location of, 28
    relevance characteristic of, 29
    timely characteristic of, 29
    worth its cost characteristic of, 30
Information and Communications Technology Council (ICTC) of Canada, 13
Information and Communications Technology (ICT)
    business value and, 54–55
    in Canada, 11
    employment in, 12, 12*f*, 14
    future trends in, 14–17
    innovation and, 56
    productivity and, 54, 55–56
information overload, 260, 261–262
Information Systems Audit and Control Association (ISACA), 374
information systems audits, 373–375

information systems (IS), 12*f*
    acquisition of, 328–329, 334–335, 337
    alignment in, 371
    audits of, 373–375
    business processes and, 31–34, 240–242
    compared to information technology (IT), 10
    competitive advantage and, 63–65, 235–236
    components of, 6*f*, 7, 31, 32*f*, 49*f*
    counter sales and, 32, 32*f*
    decision making and, 34–37
    defined, 6
    development and use of, 8
    as element of MIS, 7
    employment in, 11, 11*f*
    estimation process, 349–350
    ethics of, 375–377
    functional systems, 236–240
    governance of, 372–373, 372*f*, 381
    healthcare and, 232–233
    importance of to economy, 11–12, 11*f*
    importance of to organizations, 13
    IT architecture and, 369–370
    job positions in, 366–368, 367*f*
    organizational strategy and, 368–370, 369*f*
    outsourcing and, 342–345, 343*f*
    payment and, 33, 33*f*
    people, role in, 37
    process quality and, 47–50
    productivity and, 56–59
    purchasing and, 33–34, 34*f*
    subsectors of, 11*f*
    supplier relationship management (SRM), 250–251, 251*f*
    supply chain performance and, 251, 251*f*
    systems development life cycle and, 334–342
    transaction processing and, 263
    use of by professionals, 12–14
    vendor data storage and, 49–50, 50*f*
information systems services. *See* IT services
Information Technology Infrastructure Library (ITIL), 331–332
information technology (IT). *See also* IT entries
    business processes and, 240–242
    characteristics of, 15
    compared to information systems (IS), 10
    competitive advantage and, 62
    defined, 10
    future predictions in, 15–17
    innovation and, 61–63
    networks and, 104
    organization of department, 364–366
    price and performance, 103
    size of, 104
information technology project management (ITPM), 330

infrastructure, loss of, 389*f*, 391
infrastructure as a service (IaaS), 201*f*, 202
in-house hosting, 199–200, 200*f*
in-memory DBMS, 147
innovation
    at Amazon, 71*f*
    diffusion of innovation, 62–63, 62*f*
    disruptive technologies and, 61
    importance of, 53–55
    Information and Communications Technology (ICT) sector and, 56
    information technology (IT) and, 61–63
    sustaining technologies and, 61
Instagram, 306
Institute for Electrical and Electronics Engineers (IEEE), 217
integrated chips, 14–15
integrated CRM applications, 248, 248*f*
integrated systems
    enterprise application integration (EAI), 241, 241*f*
    enterprise resource planning (ERP), 241–242, 242*f*
    importance of, 238
    problems with, 240*f*
    software applications and, 329*f*
Intel Corporation, 62, 303, 303*f*
intellectual property, 134
intellectual wealth, 73–74
intelligence gathering, 36, 36*f*
intermediation, 311
International Project Management Association, 330
Internet
    access to, 73–74
    addresses, 221–222
    carriers and net neutrality, 221
    cloud computing and, 199
    connecting LAN to, 218–220
    defined, 216, 217*f*
    example of, 220, 220*f*
    how it works, 220–224
    as network type, 196, 196*f*
    three-tier architecture, 223–224, 223*f*
Internet of Things (IoT)
    explained, 108–109
    impact of, 109–110
Internet protocols, 227–228
Internet service provider (ISP), 219
internets, 196, 196*f*, 216, 217*f*
interorganizational systems, 238
inventory, 250
inventory database, 26
inventory management business process, 25–26, 25*f*
iOS operating system, 116
IP addresses, 221
IP spoofing, 389
iPhone, 12, 109, 109*f*, 220
IPv4, 221
IPv6, 221